Unparalleled, time-saving teaching and learning tools are yours when you adopt Constance Staley's new text.

These outstanding resources save you time and help your students FOCUS on College Success:

THE NEW *FOCUS ON COLLEGE SUCCESS* RESOURCE CENTER
pages 2–3

THE COLLEGE SUCCESS FACTORS INDEX
page 3

POWERLECTURE CD-ROM
page 4

LOOK INSIDE!

The College Success Factors Index (CSFI)

Developed by Edmond Hallberg, Kaylene Hallberg, and Loren Sauer

The perfect tool to help your students assess their college success needs— and validate your college success program. Easy to take in or outside class.

How much of a difference does your college success course make in your students' academic success? The **College Success Factors Index** (CSFI) is an online survey that will give you the answers you're looking for. At the start of the course, it helps you assess incoming students and tailor your course topics to meet their needs. As a post-test, it allows you and your students to measure their progress.

When students finish, they can immediately see their score, based on how they compare with a norm group comprised of more than 10,000 students nationwide in two- and four-year public and private institutions. The **CSFI** site also presents intervention techniques related to the eight factors to help students improve their chances for success in college. A special section for instructors offers information and advice on how to administer, interpret, and report the data.

The **CSFI** tool is accessed online through the ***FOCUS on College Success Resource Center***, so students can take the assessment in a lab, their home, or anywhere they have access to a computer with an Internet connection. It includes 80 statements on eight areas that have been proven to correlate with college success:

* Responsibility and control
* Competition
* Task precision
* Expectations
* Wellness
* Time management
* College involvement
* Family involvement

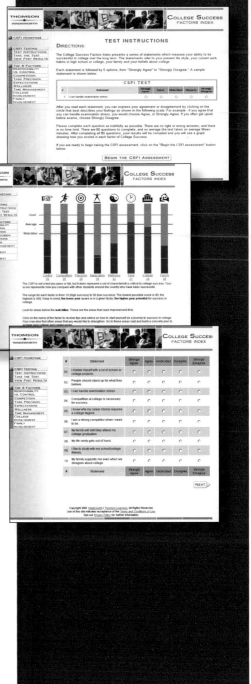

Get started in seconds

If you order an access code for the **Resource Center** to be packaged with each new student text, students also have access to the **CSFI**. For a product tour, go to **academic-cengage.com/login**.

An access code card can be packaged with new copies of ***FOCUS on College Success,*** giving students instant access to these resources—with just one password! Students use the code on the card to create an account at **academic-cengage.com/login** and they're in—with full access to the ***FOCUS on College Success*** Resource Center and the **CSFI**.

Contact your local Wadsworth Cengage Learning sales representative to order new copies of the text packaged with the access code card.

The new
FOCUS on College Success
Resource Center

Interactive learning for students—and time-saving tools for you.

The *FOCUS on College Success* **Resource Center** is a gateway to experiences for your students as they learn new skills and build confidence. Since students have more fun when they learn by doing, this **Resource Center** is the perfect vehicle for sparking in them a lifelong appreciation of learning—in so many areas. Students can explore and study in ways not possible in lecture or with a textbook alone, and will experience the fun of learning with dynamic exercises that help them prepare for exams and conduct research for papers. Once they log on, students are presented with a variety of study tools:

Book-specific Videos show realistic scenarios specific to the first-year experience, and include follow-up questions and activities.

Audio Study Products provide audio reinforcement of key concepts your students can listen to from their personal computer or MP3 player. **Audio Study Products** provide upbeat audio content, giving your students a quick and convenient way to master key concepts and see their applied nature. These downloadable audio files allow students to test their knowledge with chapter summaries that provide brief overviews reflecting the major themes of each chapter.

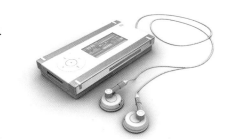

Rich learning resources and online test-prep resources include **Team Career** exercises (integrated with the text's *Focus on Careers* feature), and **Challenge Yourself** online quizzes that help students understand more about themselves and their attitudes toward life and learning.

Plus:

* Learning Objectives
* Book for Children about Parents Going Back to School (in PDF)
* Access to the College Success Factors Index (see next page)

For Instructors (Password Protected)

* Entrance/Exit Interviews (in PDF)
* Instructor's Manual
* PowerPoint lecture slides
* Messaging Center that allows registered users (instructors and students) to manage communication and send messages to one another

Access to the *FOCUS on College Success* Resource Center is available via an access code that can be packaged with Staley's text—at no additional cost to your students. Contact your Wadsworth Cengage Learning representative for ordering information.

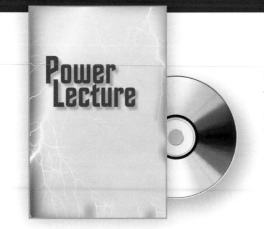

PowerLecture™
A 1-Stop Microsoft® PowerPoint® Tool

The fastest, easiest way to build powerful, customized, media-rich lectures, PowerLecture™ includes preloaded PowerPoint® lecture images, bullet points, and links for every chapter.

Organized around 14 common college success topics, this easy-to-use CD helps you assemble, edit, and present tailored multimedia lectures.

* Pre-assembled college success Microsoft® PowerPoint® lecture slides with graphics and other powerful images

* Book-specific videos with thorough descriptions, suggestions on how to integrate them into the course, and follow-up questions

* Book-specific, video-based polling and quiz questions that can be used with the **JoinIn™ Student Response System**

* Helpful links to college success websites

* **ExamView® Computerized Testing**, featuring automatic grading, allows you to create, deliver, and customize tests and study guides (both print and online) in minutes

* An electronic version of the **Instructor's Manual with Test Bank**

* Built-in Entrance and Exit instruments that evaluate the impact of the college success course on student performance and retention

ANNOTATED INSTRUCTOR'S EDITION

FOCUS
ON COLLEGE SUCCESS

Constance Staley

University of Colorado, Colorado Springs

WADSWORTH
CENGAGE Learning™

Australia • Brazil • Japan • Korea • Mexico • Singapore • Spain • United Kingdom • United States

WADSWORTH
CENGAGE Learning™

FOCUS on College Success, First Edition
Annotated Instructor's Edition
Constance Staley

Editor in Chief: PJ Boardman

Publisher: Lyn Uhl

Director of College Success: Annie Todd

Development Editor: Marita Sermolins

Editorial Assistant: Dan DeBonis

Technology Project Manager: Stephanie Gregoire

Marketing Manager: Kirsten Stoller

Marketing Communications Manager: Darlene Amidon-Brent

Content Project Manager: Jennifer Kostka

Creative Director: Rob Hugel

Art Director: Linda Helcher

Print Buyer: Marcia Locke

Permissions Manager, Images: Sheri Blaney

Permissions Manager, Text: Tim Sisler

Production Service/Compositor: Lachina Publishing Services

Text Designer: Anne Carter

Cover Designer: George Restrepo

For product information and technology assistance, contact us at
Cengage Learning Academic Resource Center, 1-800-423-0563
For permission to use material from this text or product,
submit all requests online at **www.cengage.com/permissions**
Further permissions questions can be emailed to
permissionrequest@cengage.com

Library of Congress Control Number: 2007942011

ISBN-13: 978-0-534-63866-5

ISBN-10: 0-534-63866-X

Wadsworth Cengage Learning
25 Thomson Place
Boston, MA 02210
USA

Cengage Learning products are represented in Canada by Nelson Education, Ltd.

For your course and learning solutions, visit **academic.cengage.com**

Purchase any of our products at your local college store or at our preferred online store **www.ichapters.com**

Constance Staley

Thirty-how-many-years? she thought.

What a long time to work at one job in one place. But she had learned so much over that time, especially about students and about teaching, about learning and about knowing.

When she first began, the campus consisted of a few buildings and a dirt parking lot. Now it was a thriving community with thousands of students and buildings going up everywhere. *Of course, you can enhance your career by moving from one school to another,* she thought to herself, *but you can also learn a lot by sticking with a good thing over a long period of time.* So that's what she'd done. There had been brief excursions, working in private industry and teaching students in the former Soviet Union as a Fulbright Scholar. But for the most part, Constance Staley had spent her entire career as a professor on one campus, University of Colorado, Colorado Springs. As the campus had "grown up," so had she as a teacher. It wasn't unusual for her to run into her students everywhere—in restaurants, at the movies, or in stores. "Remember me?" they'd say. "You were my professor twenty-five years ago." She'd smile politely and nod. But the truth was she couldn't always exactly remember. Her brain was very full of students after all this time.

Connie had always been a student herself. As a kid, her favorite game was "playing school" with friends. Growing up in a military family, she'd gone to plenty of different schools herself—ten in twelve years. By the time she started kindergarten, she'd already seen much of the world and was bilingual. Some people might have called her a nerd or a geek or a teacher's pet, or remarked about how she always worked for extra credit and lingered over her homework. But the truth was, she loved to learn.

Over her years as a professor, she'd worked with thousands of students. She concentrated on being the kind of teacher who listened and cared, who sent encouraging e-mails to students when they needed them, or congratulatory ones when they made brilliant contributions in class, or sometimes "reality check" e-mails when they needed an academic pep talk because they weren't doing so well. She loved the give and take, walking up the aisles of her classroom as she worked to engage everyone, trying to be dramatic or funny, convincing students that this class wasn't about how much *she* knew. It was about how much *they* could learn.

About halfway through her career, Connie decided to focus on first-year students by directing the Freshman Seminar Program on her campus. She saw that many students eased into college as if they were finally in their element. But then there were students like Ethan Cole in this book, who lost his focus and considered dropping out of college, and Gloria Gonzales, who wasn't sure college would be worth it or whether her first-year seminar class could really teach her anything new. And there were students like Katie Alexander, a kinesthetic learner who found it hard to engage in material that wasn't naturally interesting to her, or Anthony Lopez, who partied too much and studied too little.

But it was challenges like the ones presented by these students—and all the others in this book—that motivated Constance Staley to write *FOCUS on College Success*. She knew that getting a college degree was their key to a better life, a more fulfilling career, and most importantly, achieving their potential. She knew it was her job to help them through the rough patches and find the motivation within themselves to accomplish something they'd always be proud of. She knew that whether they were 18 or 48, college would introduce them to new worlds where they, too, could "grow up" as students and become learners for life. The Roman poet Manlius said it well centuries ago: "The end depends on the beginning."

Since her early days of teaching, Constance Staley has seen substantial change. Today's students are busy, impatient multi-taskers who want *efficient* learning. Nearly one-third of them admit on national studies that they do just enough academic work to get by, despite their desire for fast-track, high-paying careers. They want to learn what *they* see as valuable, *their* way, with *results*. Overwhelmingly, they work at jobs in order to finance college, crowd their days with too many obligations, and don't slow down long enough to hone their metacognitive skills. They see a college education as a *product*, rather than a *process*. Returning students are stretched, often nearly to the breaking point, in multiple directions. No matter their age, many beginning students today simply don't have the time, the motivation, or the skills they need to focus. And on top of these formidable challenges, today's students often come to college with emotional issues that add another layer of complexity for instructors. Simply put, many require considerable support: academically, psychologically, and emotionally.

In her work with institutions across the country, Connie has seen the credibility of first-year seminars challenged by results-oriented administrators, skeptical faculty, and students who assume they "already know this stuff." Yet she has witnessed their power to effect change in thousands of students, firsthand, because she has developed engaging teaching strategies that work.

Her goal was to build much of what she has learned into a single tool: a book that would almost teach itself, freeing instructors to do what they need to do with their students, collectively and individually. According to nearly 100 reviewers, some of the strengths of *FOCUS on College Success* are its ability to build rapport with students, engage them, unlock intrinsic motivation, demonstrate that learning is taking place, and help them learn how to focus. The visual display on the following pages will walk you through *FOCUS on College Success*, feature by feature.

It's been said that teaching is the ultimate act of optimism. When a Gloria Gonzales, an Ethan Cole, or a Kia Washington is engaged and succeeds, we know why we do what we do as instructors. And we continually challenge ourselves to do it better.

FOCUS is for all the first-year students who sit in your classrooms, and for you in your own personal and professional journey as their teacher.

ASK THE AUTHOR: CONSTANCE STALEY

1. Many first-year students today are NOT AVID READERS. How have you addressed this instructor challenge in *FOCUS on College Success*?

I call today's students "Generation Why." *Why is this course important? Why should I learn how to study when I've already been doing it for years?* Why? Why? Why? First-year students need a college success textbook that not only tells them *what* to do, but also *why* doing these things is important. As one scholar noted, the watchword for today's students is "*convince,*" rather than "*command.*" No matter their age, they are savvy, busy, and pragmatic. They want to learn what *they* see as valuable in their own way. They want a college success text to meet them where they are, understand the complexity of their lives, and give them tools to learn better and faster. That's the philosophy behind *FOCUS*.

2. How will *FOCUS* help GET STUDENTS MORE ENGAGED in a course that they often don't feel they need to take?

For real learning to take place, students must find personal meaning in what they read. Abstract information is less engaging than practical coaching that gets results. As much as it is about metacognition—thinking about thinking and learning about learning—*FOCUS* is about students. It stars a cast of twelve of my own students (and one colleague), like a stage play. One student "actor" is featured in each chapter's opening "*FOCUS* Challenge Case." All thirteen cast members reappear throughout the book, so that readers feel they're getting to know the cast as they read. Students are naturally interested in other students (witness the popularity of social networking), and the case studies provide a non-threatening way to discuss problems that readers themselves may be facing. Woven through the entire text is a learning system that makes a distinction between insight and action. While students may know (or think they know) how to use particular academic tools, *knowing* and *doing* are two different things. *FOCUS* emphasizes doing.

3. Many colleges and universities seem to be STRUGGLING WITH RETENTION and are trying to understand why many students don't return after their first year. How can *FOCUS* help with this?

As an introductory activity in *FOCUS*, students complete an Entrance Interview (on paper or online) that will help instructors flag potential risk factors for individual students and profile the class as a whole. Similarly, at the end of the term, students will complete an Exit Interview that will inform them and their instructors about how they've progressed. These two tools measure the gap between initial *expectations* and actual *experience*. Instructors can design interventions based on issues that surface, and then measure their degree of success in implementing them. No other textbook employs this type of pre- and post-test tool for instructors to use, but it's something I've done with my students for years. This type of *very* "early alert" system can make all the difference when it comes to retention.

4. **CREDIBILITY** seems to be an issue with first-year seminar courses; students and administrators sometimes question the value of the college success course. How will your book help address the credibility issue?

Each chapter of *FOCUS* starts with a "*FOCUS* Challenge Case" to which students respond in a non-threatening way, giving suggestions to resolve the real-life conflict before having read the chapter. Then, throughout each chapter, readers are prompted to identify what they already know about particular topics *before* they read about them with the Challenge → Reaction questions. After they read, they are asked to apply the information to themselves as learners through the Insight → Action questions. The Challenge → Reaction → Insight → Action system in *FOCUS* demonstrates to students that learning is taking place, and the extensive research base (invisible to students) assures faculty readers that *FOCUS* is grounded in the scholarship of teaching and learning. Research indicates that the majority of entering students say they would welcome advice about how to tackle challenging academic tasks, but that advice must be real, relevant, and results-driven in order to be valued by today's students.

5. Today's **INCOMING STUDENTS HAVE VARIED LEARNING STYLES**: many are kinesthetic, some are visual, and few are aural and read/write. How do you ensure that students identify their learning style and gain the skills necessary to improve their learning throughout their college career?

FOCUS informs students about their own learning styles right away so that they can streamline their efforts and translate between the teaching "language" spoken by their instructors and learning "language" they themselves prefer. My suspicion is that many students who drop out of college are kinesthetic learners who don't know how to navigate an academic world that is predominantly aural and read/write. *FOCUS* encourages students to realize that learning is a *process*, and helps them customize their learning, just as they customize *products* in their lives—everything from MP3 players and cell phones to specialty coffee drinks! We live in a culture with a previously unfathomable amount of choice. Throughout the text, students are encouraged to become responsible learners, apply *FOCUS* material to their toughest course, and tailor their learning to the level of challenge that is right for them. When students become more successful academically and when they build a support network within a community of learners, they are more likely to stay in college and succeed.

6. Because they lack focus, many first-year students become discouraged, find college to be less exciting than they expected, or recognize that they are not well prepared for the sustained investment college requires over time. How will *FOCUS* help solve this **PROBLEM OF MOTIVATION**?

FOCUS asks students at the beginning of every chapter to assess their level of motivation, interest, and readiness to begin (via Readiness Checks). At the end of every chapter, readers are asked to respond to a similar set of questions retrospectively (by use of Reality Checks). In addition to helping students develop realistic expectations of what it takes to learn, they are reminded that they are central to the learning process and that they must be fully invested. *FOCUS* also uses research on emotional intelligence and intrinsic motivation to get at underlying affective issues that influence college success. Many students today go to college because their par-

ents want them to, because their friends are going, or because it's the expected "next step." They don't realize how much their own motivation to propel themselves toward a degree is at the heart of their success. Adult students with myriad responsibilities often must make day-by-day and minute-by-minute decisions about their priorities. Students may not realize that EQ can be as important as—or even more important than—IQ in achieving their goals. Recent reports indicate that while 95 percent of entering students are strongly motivated at the outset, only half of them will finish what they start. *FOCUS* has these critical non-cognitive concepts interwoven with cognitive applications throughout the text.

7. Most instructors have multiple course preps per semester, and though they want to make the college success course as engaging and interactive as possible, they just don't have time to write or research a plethora of **CLASSROOM ACTIVITIES**. How will your book help?

FOCUS is designed as a learning system with built-in motivational tools, built-in activities (many from my resource book, *50 Ways to Leave Your Lectern*), and built-in journal/discussion prompts. My goal was to build much of what I have learned over the years into a single tool: a book that would encourage instructors to stress high expectations, while also providing a high level of support. Teaching a first-year seminar is challenging, and instructors need support, too. Before I began writing, and continuously along the way, I asked myself, "What would I, as an instructor, want in a first-year seminar textbook?" Having worked with so many students over so many years, I know first-hand the range of challenges instructors face and what would give them what they need—conveniently and comprehensively—to do the best job they can. As a first-year seminar course should be, the book has been "VARKed," by including, for example:

- Visual: memorable, unusual photographs with powerful, famous quotations as captions, and bold colors to interest
- Aural: content-rich and compelling chapter summary podcasts with a humorous twist to capture student interest
- Read/Write: research-based, comprehensive chapters on timely topics with new subtopics written for today's students
- Kinesthetic: real-life students as cast members and provocative, innovative web content, including mock television shows to reinforce chapter points

8. How do you spice up **LECTURES AND DISCUSSIONS** in your classroom and keep yourself engaged?

Many college success instructors have great passion for what they do. They teach a first-year seminar as an overload or extra duty, they find great fulfillment in witnessing student transformations during the first year of college, and they draw support from other instructors. My advice? Share information with your colleagues. Exchange ideas about what works and what doesn't. Energize each other! I have found that my work with faculty across the country has been a powerful way for me to learn. *FOCUS* gave me an opportunity to give back what I've learned from my students and from other instructors. My goal is to continue that learning process through *FOCUS*.

Now that I've had the opportunity to talk about how *FOCUS* addresses the issues of engagement, credibility, motivation, retention, and varied learning styles, let's address specifically how all those problem areas are tackled in *FOCUS*.

How does *FOCUS* address the issue of ENGAGEMENT?

Voice: *FOCUS* offers a conversational tone that is accessible, non-condescending, and treats readers as adults. It builds rapport with student readers, and works to convince them of key concepts rather than simply telling them.

Picture this: You sit down to work on a challenging homework assignment. After a few minutes, you think, *Man, I'm thirsty*, so you get up and get a soda. Then you sit back down to continue your work. A few minutes later, you decide that some chips would go nicely with your soda and you head to the kitchen. Again, you sit down to face the task before you, as you concentrate more on eating than on working. Ten minutes go by and a nagging thought starts taking over: *Must do laundry*. Up you go again and throw a load of clothes in the washer. Before long you're wondering where all the time went. Since you only have an hour left before your next class, you think, *Why bother getting started now? Doing this project will take much more time than that, so I'll just start it tomorrow*. Despite good intentions at the beginning of your work session, you've just succeeded in accomplishing zip, nadda, nothing.

What you told us... "The writing is real; students will know this author is telling them the straight truth of what they need to do to succeed in college and beyond."
— *Marty Marty, Missouri State University*

"Connie Staley's 'voice' comes through so clearly! Having been to many of her workshops, I can hear her saying these words as she directs this exercise! Like many, many other people who learn from her, I listen to her 'voice'!"
— *Sally Firmin, Baylor University*

FOCUS Challenge Cases: Readers have the opportunity to read and react to a challenge in each case study and revisit it at the end of the chapter to see if/how their perceptions about the case have changed. These provide an applied, real-life, kinesthetic approach to learning, and allow students a "safe" way to discuss problems they may be facing themselves.

Gloria Gonzales

Teaching tip: Use these cases (and the accompanying follow-up questions) to spur discussion in the classroom or as brief writing assignments.

What you told us... "The case studies are fantastic. It is rare to read case studies that don't feel/sound contrived. These case studies are the most realistic that I have come across."
— *Peg Adams, Northern Kentucky University*

Activities and Self-Assessments: *FOCUS* provides dozens of classroom-ready exercises, so you'll no longer have to locate or create them on your own.

Teaching tip: To get students into the book (and your course), assign the exercises and self-assessments. The Annotated Instructor's Edition provides ideas for using all the activities in the classroom, as well as suggesting additional activities.

Exercise 5.1 And Just Why Is Critical Thinking Important?
Here is a list of reasons why it's important to improve your critical thinking skills. Beside each entry, mark the degree to which you'd like to concentrate your efforts as a college student, soon ready to enter a new career path. On a scale from 1 to 10 with 10 representing the highest degree, would you like to:

1. _____ **Become a more successful college student?** Most college courses require you to think critically (in answering essay questions, for example). In one study of over 1,100 college students, higher scores on critical thinking skills tests correlated highly with better grades.[9] There's even evidence that interaction with other students in

What you told us... "The chapters are very interactive and require a lot more effort than just reading them. If well taught, the likelihood of engagement seems high."
— *David Campagne, University of South Florida*

How does *FOCUS* address the issue of CREDIBILITY?

Challenge → Reaction → Insight → Action (CRIA) Learning System: In this learning system,
1. a challenge is presented
2. initial reactions, perceptions, and misperceptions are uncovered
3. content/resources/new knowledge is presented, leading to new insights
4. final thoughts and discoveries lead to action/change.

This system demonstrates that learning is taking place. Students may assume they "know all this stuff" when they actually don't. The CRIA system will also help students realize the value of the College Success course.

CHALLENGE ⊖ REACTION
What are your core values? Review the following list and check off the items that you value. Don't spend too much time thinking about each one; just go with your initial gut reaction. For each item, ask yourself "Is this something that's important to me?"

_____ Health	_____ Wealth	_____ Financial wealth
_____ Fitness/Physical strength	_____ Independence	_____ Commitment
_____ Loyalty	_____ Honesty	_____ Compassion
_____ Academic achievement	_____ Children	_____ Leisure time
_____ Success	_____ Leadership	_____ Balance
_____ Happiness	_____ Family	_____ Friendship
_____ Social life	_____ Marriage/Partnership	_____ Recognition
_____ Athletics	_____ Spirituality	_____ Status

Teaching tip: Making use of this system will show students their existing level of understanding and what remains to be learned.

What you told us... "I like these activities a great deal. I think students respond particularly well to scales that they can take and get feedback on that tell them a little about themselves."
— *Kimberly Cummings, University of Tampa*

Heavily Research-Based: Instructors will appreciate that the text is built on a solid foundation of research and that the advice to students is current and relevant.

Every chapter of *FOCUS* is research rich, although hidden from students via endnotes.

Teaching tip: Knowing that the advice and methods are backed by evidence helps support the credibility of the course as well as give students (if they are interested) proof that these skills lead to success.

What you told us... "The author uses respected research among several disciplines more broadly and more effectively than other current books on this subject matter."

— *Marty Marty, Missouri State University*

How does *FOCUS* address the issue of MOTIVATION?

Readiness Checks and Reality Checks: Students learn to *FOCUS* on the material before them and narrow the gap between initial expectations and the reality of what's required to study successfully. These checks help students develop a more realistic approach to learning.

Teaching tip: Open and close a course topic with these checks to see where students stand before and after learning a topic. Eventually, assessing their readiness to learn may become ingrained and considered as they begin their academic work in any class.

What you told us... "Based on the students I've had the pleasure of working with in the past, they would approach this as a game...wanting to "win" by knowing it all at the conclusion of the lesson. This section also helps students to actually prepare for the chapter BEFORE the teacher goes over it (imagine that!)."

— *Phebe Simmons, Blinn College*

Emotional Intelligence (EI) Coverage: Because they lack *FOCUS*, many first-year students become discouraged, find college to be less exciting than they expected, or recognize that they are not well prepared for the sustained investment college requires over time. Retaining first-year students is a serious concern on many campuses, and many students give up due to EI factors like discouragement or disillusionment.

Emotional Intelligence (EI) Research In 1988, Olympic swimmer Matt Biondi lost his first race only to win the gold in the next five. Martin Seligman, a psychologist from the University of Pennsylvania, had tested Biondi earlier that year and discovered that even when given negative feedback, Biondi went on to perform well. Seligman defines optimism by the way people describe their successes and failures.

Teaching tip: *FOCUS* includes considerable information on emotional intelligence since students' EQs, can be as important as their IQs to their college success.

What you told us... "I thought that the emotional intelligence section could be particularly useful to students in understanding the ways in which emotions can impact academics."

— *Carrie L. Cokely, Meredith*

AIMS (Academic Intrinsic Motivation Scale): Features throughout the book trigger intrinsic motivation (four C-Factors):

1. the level of **challenge** in coursework (Challenge Yourself Online Quizzes)
2. the level of **control** over outcomes (Control Your Learning: Your Toughest Class)
3. the degree of **curiosity** prompted by coursework (Cultivate Your Curiosity)
4. the extent of *FOCUS* on graduation and **careers** (Create a Career Outlook)

The themes of motivation and personal responsibility (self-regulation) are in line with current research on today's students.

C CULTIVATE Your Curiosity

C CONTROL Your Learning

C CREATE A Career Outlook

C CHALLENGE Yourself Quizzes

Teaching tip: Assign the "Challenge Yourself Online Quizzes" as homework and ask students to hand in their results; use the "Control Your Learning" feature to schedule an office hours visit with each student to talk about applying course content to their toughest class.

What you told us... "The C boxes allow another way for students to engage. I like how they are used to provide deeper insight into the concepts...I really think these C boxes emphasize the value of learning—and help illustrate why this is important!"

— *Allison Cumming-McCann, Springfield College*

How does *FOCUS* address the issue of RETENTION?

Entrance and Exit Interviews: Data gathering instruments provide administrators and faculty with valuable data, evidence of students' *expectations* of college early in the term and their *experience* of college at the end of the course. No other text contains these tools to be used at the beginning and end of the First-Year Seminar course.

FOCUS ENTRANCE INTERVIEW

Although you may not have experienced life as a new college student for long, we're interested in how you expect to spend your time, what challenges you think you'll face, and your general views of what you think college will be like. Please answer thoughtfully.

INFORMATION ABOUT YOU

Name _____

Student Number _____ Course/Section _____

Instructor _____

Gender _____ Age _____

1. Ethnic identification:
   ___ Native American/American Indian   ___ Hispanic
   ___ Caucasian   ___ African American
   ___ Asian or Pacific Islander   ___ Prefer not to answer

Teaching tip: Included in the front and back of every book, the data of these surveys can be used for one-on-one interviews at the beginning and end of the course, to identify risk factors for individual students, or shared with the class to foster discussion. Online versions are available from the companion web site.

What you told us... "The Entrance/Exit Interviews I think will be very effective in assisting students to truly evaluate themselves. Additional information gathered...will give instructors a better understanding of their students and their needs."

—*Mercy Azeke, Norfolk State University*

Career Integration: The "*FOCUS* on Careers" feature shares an interview with a real professional working in a particular field, and it demonstrates how the content of the chapter has practical applications in that particular profession. These role models provide examples of healthy life management choices, which reinforce to students that today's choices create tomorrow's opportunities. Students value the content of their college success course more by seeing its practical use in the workplace.

FOCUS ON CAREERS: JOHN M. HEARN JR., IT Systems Analyst

Teaching tip: Ask students to complete "Create a Career Outlook" questions in each chapter, which will help them *FOCUS* on where their career interests lie and how their own personality type and skills apply to the featured career.

What you told us... "Reading true stories of real people in different careers will be extremely useful as students try to maneuver through their career choices. They will think back to these examples long after this textbook is not in their daily use; they will likely attempt to meet career standards as high as the professionals that they've read about."

—*Rebecca Reed, Johnson & Wales University*

How does *FOCUS* address the issue of VARIED LEARNING STYLES?

VARK: Following the VARK assessment in Chapter 2, VARK activities at the end of each chapter will *FOCUS* on the four sensory modalities and learning. If students are multimodal, they will be encouraged to select activities from several modalities. Over the course of the term, these activities will provide students with an array of techniques to improve their learning in all their classes.

EXERCISE 2.3 VARK Activity

Complete the recommended activity for your preferred VARK learning modality. If you are multimodal, select more than one activity. Your instructor may ask you to (a) give an oral report on your results in class, (b) send your results to him or her via e-mail, (c) post them online, or (d) contribute to a class chat.

Visual: Think about a particular course or exam you studied for in the past. Create a personal chart that compares the learning strategies for each of the four VARK modalities you used and the degree of success you had using each one.

Aural: Interview another student who is a member of a campus honor society. Which VARK strategies does this student use and why? Determine whether these strategies would work for you.

Read/Write: Write a one-page summary of what you have learned about yourself as a result of reading this chapter.

Kinesthetic: If your campus has a Learning Center, visit it to gather additional information about your learning style. Apply what you have learned to create a plan to prepare for your next exam.

Teaching tip: Complete the VARK assessment in Chapter 2 either in the classroom or as a homework assignment to help students assess their learning style(s).

What you told us... "This is an excellent tool for self examination... I have had a number of students be quite surprised at the results of the VARK and how simple strategies (according to the results) enhance their learning."

—*Janet Breaker, Milwaukee Area Technical College*

YoUR TYpE iS ShOwing

What's the relationship between personality type and managing money? What would you predict? Here's what some experts say:

FINANCIAL PLANNERS. Picture an accountant in a prestigious Wall Street firm, sitting behind a desk, calculating your investment portfolio. There's a good chance he's an SJ (sensor and judger). Why? SJ's are detail-oriented, realistic, and organized. They work within clients' financial parameters and monitor saving and investing—just what you want in an accountant, right? In their personal lives, SJ's are often careful about spending money, too. They calculate, plan, spend, invest, and save. A student with a strong SJ preference might think twice about an exotic spring break vacation if she knew it would seriously blow her already-tight budget.

FUN-LOVING SPENDERS. Picture someone on a shopping spree, finding incredible bargains, and loving every minute of it. That's most likely an SP (sensor and perceiver). SP's are detail-oriented and practical just like SJ's, but they are also on a perpetual serendipity quest. They enjoy unplanned discoveries, and saving a dollar or two just makes it that much more fun. But they find everyday spending that must be done—like paying the rent—to be much less satisfying.

BIG-HEARTED PHILANTHROPISTS. Picture a generous, wealthy community leader who donates millions to a good cause. NF's (iNtuitive and feeler) are visionaries, people who don't just see things as they are, but who are able to envision how things could be. In particular, they build connections with others to help them accomplish their goals. An NF student might join with other campus leaders, solicit broad-based donations, and begin a scholarship fund for needy students.

GRAND SCHEMERS. Picture someone at the helm of a giant Fortune 500 corporation who has a big-picture view of the future. She's intuitive—she trusts her instincts—but she also thinks things through very carefully. On a personal level, NT's (iNtuitive and thinker) think about how they spend and save money, and they can work toward long-term financial goals. An NT student, for example, who might be planning to move to an off-campus apartment next year, might buy ahead—a bedspread on sale or a set of towels, for example.

Teaching tip: Encourage students to take the full MBTI.

What you told us... "Helps in helping students realize the type of learning style that works best for them and to utilize it."

—*Miriam Chiza, North Hennepin Community College*

Resources & Ancillaries

Annotated Instructor's Edition

Written by Catherine Andersen of Gallaudet University, the Annotated Instructor's Edition of *FOCUS* helps instructors at any stage of their teaching careers succeed and provides the guidance needed with any new text. Among other notable strengths, Catherine is particular recognized for her work in emotional intelligence in higher education. Annotations are categorized into five groups for easy recognition, allowing instructors to pay attention to annotations they are most interested in:

- **Teachable Moments.** These annotations note places where instructors can pause to capitalize on chapter content by making particular points that enrich the learning environment.
- **Sensitive Situations.** These annotations point out places where an in-class discussion could generate potential discomfort in the learning environment. These annotations keep instructors from being caught off guard by these triggers and provide suggestions for how to handle these provocative teaching challenges.
- **Activity Options.** If instructors wish to pursue further active learning strategies in class, these annotations provide other ideas for a variety of ways to do this.
- **Chapter Crossover.** These annotations link material to that found in previous or upcoming chapters so that students tie together related content and understand the connectedness of knowledge.
- **Emotional Intelligence (EI) Research.** Many first-year instructors are interested in learning more about emotional intelligence, but aren't sure about exactly how it relates to the content of college success courses. These annotations make the connections and provide short summaries of related EI research.

Instructor's Manual and Test Bank

Also written by Catherine Andersen of Gallaudet University, the Instructor's Manual serves as a quick guide to every chapter, providing all the frequently asked questions about how to teach the course, from what the main focus of every chapter should be to yet more activity options. The online quizzes allow students to adjust the challenge level of the course by selecting easy, medium, and challenging questions to answer (following Bloom's taxonomy from simple to more cognitively complex questions).

Power Lecture

Organized around the topics covered in the book, this easy-to-use tool helps you assemble, edit, and present tailored multimedia lectures. You can create a lecture from scratch, customize the provided templates, or use the ready-made PowerPoint® slides as they are.

Resource Center

In addition to rich resources, additional in-class activities, and downloadable podcasts (pithy chapter summaries with a humorous twist), the website will include short "YouTube"-type vignettes, "Inside the *FOCUS* Studio," a mock television show, featuring the author and *FOCUS* cast members. These "What's the Big Idea?" streaming videos focus on five chapters and how the chapter content can be made real and memorable to today's students.

MEET THE CAST

Chapter 1

Gloria Gonzalez / Debbie

Hometown: Saguache, Colorado

Major: Business with a minor in Communication

Expected Graduation Date: 2010

Lessons Learned: Debbie learned through her first-year seminar course that it takes time and effort to establish great relationships. She got involved in intramural sports, which helped her meet new people and make friends. Although she's doing well now, she wishes she'd studied more her first term.

Toughest First-Year Class: Microeconomics because it was an entirely new subject for her.

Advice to New Students: "Get your priorities straight; college is a great place to be, so get a great start by setting good study habits, and I HIGHLY recommend a planner because you will be surprised at how fast your time can become occupied."

Chapter 2

Tammy Ko / Jessica

Hometown: Manitou Springs, Colorado

Major: Marketing

Expected Graduation Date: 2009

Lessons Learned: Juggling a part-time job while in school, Jessica loved living on campus her first term and meeting new people, but she regretted not talking to other students about which professors and courses to take towards her marketing major. In order to succeed, she says, you've "gotta give it all you've got!"

Toughest First-Year Class: Microeconomics because it wasn't like high school courses that just required memorizing a lot of facts.

Advice to New Students: "Talk to other students to learn about the best professors, and make sure you are studying something that you are interested in."

Chapter 3
Jessica Taylor / Tarren

Background: Like her *FOCUS* Challenge Case character, Tarren also graduated from a private high school and found the transition from high school to college a bit overwhelming. Having lived overseas most of her life, Tarren now calls Colorado Springs home.

Major: English

Expected Graduation Date: 2011

Lessons Learned: "Stay on top of your studies and understand how important teachers are in college and how they can positively influence students."

Toughest First-Year Class: Biology because of heavy reading assignments

Advice to New Students: "Get involved on campus and definitely choose to take a first-year seminar course!"

Free Time: horseback riding, playing tennis, and skiing

Chapter 4
Derek Johnson / Derrick

Hometown: Colorado Springs, Colorado

Major: Communications/Recording Arts

Graduation Date: 2007

Lessons Learned: Even though he's not married and has no children, Derrick and his case study character have much in common—too much to do and too little time! Derrick felt his biggest mistake his first year was not asking enough questions in class. He knows now he should have asked for clarity on content or assignments he didn't understand.

Toughest First-Year Class: English because he and his instructor had differing opinions, but he communicated through the tough spots and earned an "A".

Advice to New Students: "Surround yourself with positive people. As the saying goes, 'you are the company you keep.' I've seen many of my friends drop out because the people they called friends were holding them back from their full potential. Now that I have graduated, I look back at all the people I hold close and know that I wouldn't have made it without them."

Free Time: composing music and producing films

Chapter 5

Annie Miller / Meagan

Hometown: Albuquerque, New Mexico

Major: Nursing

Expected Graduation Date: 2011

Lessons Learned: Megan admits that her biggest mistake her first term was not asking anyone for help with anything. But she enjoyed moving away from home and being more independent, meeting new people, and having a more laid-back academic schedule than her high school schedule had been.

Toughest First-Year Course: Calculus because she was overconfident and didn't study for exams.

Advice to New Students: "Don't give up! College is amazing! Oh, and don't spend all of your money on food."

Free Time: biking, hiking, playing Ultimate Frisbee, and giving campus tours

Chapter 6

Lindsey Collier / Heather

Hometown: Her parents just moved to another state—so where *is* home?

Major: Nursing

Expected Graduation Date: 2010

Lessons Learned: Heather made the mistake of not making academics her first priority, but she learned from her first-year seminar course that she needed to be willing to sacrifice social time for study time.

Advice to New Students: "College isn't like high school—you do actually have to study three times as much for any course. No matter what course it is, study for it. You'll feel much better about receiving high marks than about partying with friends. And get involved on your campus. It's your home away from home, so why not make the most of it?"

Free Time: college Step and Dance Team

Chapter 7

Kevin Baxter / Dave

Hometown: St. Paul, Minnesota

Background: Portraying a student returning to school after fifteen-plus years in the working world, Dave is currently a professor of chemistry at University of Colorado at Colorado Springs.

College Memories: Dave remembers how much he liked the different social environment college provided after graduating from high school.

Toughest First-Year Course: English Composition since writing wasn't exactly his forte.

Advice to New Students: "Study hard, and use your time wisely."

Free Time: woodworking, hiking, and climbing

Chapter 8

Katie Alexander / Christina

Hometown: Colorado Springs, Colorado. Since she went to college in her hometown, Christina really enjoyed the opportunity college provided to meet new people.

Major: Nursing

Expected Graduation Date: 2009

Lessons Learned: Spending her free time with her friends watching movies, going bowling or dancing, and just hanging out, Christina found that like her *FOCUS* Challenge Case character, she, too, would make up excuses to get out of studying and doing her homework. She quickly learned the importance of reading and taking notes. "As weird as it may sound, reading cuts your end study time by more than half. Reading the material ahead of time helps you understand everything so much better."

Advice to New Students: "Stay motivated. College is going to FLY by! If you stay motivated and get good grades, it really will be over before you know it."

Chapter 9

Joe Cloud / Alvin

Hometown: Ganado, Arizona (Navajo Nation)

Major: Business

Expected Graduation Date: 2010

Toughest First-Year Course: Spanish because he came from a place where no other languages are ever spoken.

Lessons Learned: President of the American Indian Science and Engineering Society on campus, Alvin identifies closely with his *FOCUS* Challenge Case character. He, too, is one of a minority of Native Americans in higher education, so a lot of people in his hometown are carefully watching his academic success. Alvin admits his biggest mistake in his first term was not opening up to people—he came to school for class and left without trying to meet new people. But he learned from his mistakes and eventually came to value meeting all sorts of different people through activities on campus.

Advice to New Students: "Learn from *my* mistakes: Be open to try new things, get out of your comfort zone, and be free to be silly—everyone is at some point. You meet a lot of new people that way and it makes your first year the experience of a lifetime."

Chapter 10

Darnell Williams / Calil

Hometown: Colorado Springs, Colorado

Major: History with a secondary education emphasis

Expected Graduation Date: 2009

Lessons Learned: Calil noticed many similarities between himself and the *FOCUS* Challenge Case character he portrayed, besides playing football and watching movies. Calil, too, had problems with the transition from high school to college. He admits he was a student who "coasted" through his senior year of high school, which made his first year of college more difficult. He didn't study as hard as he should have as a first-year student.

Toughest First-Year Class: English, like Darnell, because he wasn't fully aware of the instructor's expectations.

Advice to New Students: "Determination is the key to success. If you are determined, there is nothing in the world that can stop you."

Chapter 11

Kia Washington / Charmaine

Hometown: Colorado Springs, Colorado

Major: Psychology and Sociology

Graduation Date: 2006 (Charmaine is now working towards a graduate degree in Student Affairs in Higher Education.)

Toughest First-Year Course: General psychology because there was so much to learn in such a short period of time.

Lessons Learned: In her first-year seminar, Charmaine learned how to manage her time more effectively, as well as the necessity of keeping yourself healthy in mind, body, and spirit, something she felt her *FOCUS* Challenge Case character could have benefited from.

Advice to New Students: "Remember to have fun in everything that you do, both academically and otherwise. Take care of yourself first and don't feel as though you have to do everything all the time; sometimes the best parts of life come during moments of down time. This is where you are able to truly reflect on what it is you're doing and remember why you're doing it in the first place!"

Chapter 12

Ethan Cole / Josh

Hometown: Fort Morgan, Colorado

Major: Sociology

Expected Graduation Date: 2008

Lessons Learned: Like his *FOCUS* Challenge Case character, Josh noticed that he, too, didn't always push himself to reach his potential. But he learned through his first-year seminar course that he is responsible for himself and that professors aren't like high school teachers. They will let you fail a class if you don't do what you need to. It's up to you.

Advice to New Students: "Not only did getting involved on campus help me have more fun in school, but it has also helped me academically. It has taught me how to manage my time and has made it so much easier for me to participate with confidence in class. Just make sure you get what you need to do done, and you will enjoy your college experience so much more."

Free Time: "Free time? What's that?! I'm too busy to have free time!" (But he secretly admits he snowboards, plays guitar, draws, and spends time with friends.)

Chapter 13

Anthony Lopez / Luis

Hometown: Aguascalientes, Mexico

Major: Spanish with an emphasis in secondary education

Expected Graduation Date: 2009

Lessons Learned: Luis is extremely involved on campus and within his community—he is President of the Association of Future Teachers, sings with his church choir, plays intramural soccer, and works for the Air Force on weekends—and as a first-year student, in order to cope with stress on a few occasions, he found himself doing the same things his *FOCUS* case study character did—partying too much. Luis thinks one mistake he made in his first term was that he procrastinated with homework because his new freedom let him think he could have fun first and study later, but he quickly learned he was wrong.

Advice to New Students: "Be smart and be involved, but always do your homework first. If you are involved on campus, you will meet people that will help make your college experience easier and more fun."

MEET THE AUTHOR

Constance Staley

Hometown: Pittsburgh, Pennsylvania (although she never actually lived there. Instead, she lived all over the world and went to ten schools in twelve years.)

Background: Connie has taught at the University of Colorado at Colorado Springs for more than 30 years after getting a bachelor's degree in education, a master's degree in linguistics, and a Ph.D. in communication.

College Memories: Connie remembers loving her public speaking class as a first-year student and having tons of friends, but being extremely homesick for her family.

Advice to New Students: "Earning a college degree is hard work, takes a long time, and requires a substantial investment of your time, energy, and resources. But it's the best investment you can make in your own future—one you'll never regret."

Free Time: Spending time with her husband, her two daughters, and her boy-girl grandtwins; relaxing at her cabin in the mountains; and traveling around the country to speak to other professors who also care about their first-year students and their success.

ACKNOWLEDGEMENTS

It's been said that "Achievement is a *we* thing, not a *me* thing, always the product of many heads and hands." Certainly that's true of the monumental effort involved in writing a first edition textbook. There are so many people to thank that this acknowledgements section could be as long as a chapter of *FOCUS on College Success*! However, here I'll at least mention those who have contributed the most, including all the students over the last 30-plus years who have taught me more than I've ever taught them.

Family   Let me start at the center of my life. My deepest thanks go to Steve, my Sean-Connery-look-alike husband (How do I put up with it?), who almost forgot what *I* looked like over the last few years. As I *FOCUS*ed away in my attic office day after day and night after night, he brought me too many cups of tea to count. I cherish his devotion. My daughters Shannon and Stephanie helped bring some much-needed balance to my life, and aside from being the most adorable children on the planet, my grandtwins Aidan and Ailie have been a living learning laboratory for me. As little children mastering one new thing after another, they truly have taught me about of the pure joy of learning. And to my beautiful 80-something Mom, who lovingly alternated between urging me to "slow down and relax" and "hurry up and finish," thanks for all your motherly love.

Reviewers   The list of reviewers who have contributed their insights and expertise to *FOCUS on College Success* is long. Starting any new edition from scratch requires substantial input. My heartfelt thanks to all of them: Peg Adams, Northern Kentucky University; Josie Adamo, Buffalo State College; Barbara Anderson, Midlands Technical College; Jon Aoki, University of Houston-Downtown; Mercy Azeke, Norfolk State University; Michael Becraft, Austin Peay State University; Lynda Bennett, Blue Mountain Community College; Janet Breaker, Milwaukee Area Technical College; Beverly Brucks, Illinois Central College; Toi Buchanan, Fayetteville Technical Community College; Castell Burton, Valencia Community College; David Campaigne, University of South Florida; Lea Campbell, North Harris Montgomery Community College; Barbara Chavis, Cleveland Community College; Miriam Chiza, North Hennepin Community College; G. Jay Christensen, California State University, Northridge; Regina Vincent Clark, Tennessee State University; Karen Clay, Miami Dade College; Geoff Cohen, University of California, Riverside; Carrie Cokely, Meredith College; Della Colantone, Alderson-Broaddus College; Therese Crary, Highland Community College; Kimberly Cummings, University of Tampa; Allison Cumming-McCann, Springfield College; Janice A. Daly, Florida State University; Vrita H. Delaine, The University of Southern Mississippi; Mark Demark, Alvin Community College; Gigi Derballa, Asheville-Buncombe Technical Community College; Anne Dickens, Lee College; Michael Discello, Pittsburgh Technical Institute; Carmen Etienne, Oakland University; Sally Firmin, Baylor University; Becky Garlick, Blinn College; Sharol Gauthier, University of South Carolina Upstate; Jayne Geissler, East Carolina University; Dee Allen Goedeke, High Point University; Laura Goppold, Central Piedmont Community College; Marie Gore, University of Maryland, Baltimore County; Laurie Grimes, Lorain County Community College; Valerie Hewitt, Remington College; Joseph Jumpeter, Pennsylvania State University, Wilkes-Barre Page Keller, College of Charleston; Lois Lawson-Briddell, Gloucester County College; Kelly Lee, Orange Coast College; Janet Lindner, Midlands Technical College; Brenda Marina, The University of Akron; Marty Marty, Missouri State University; Claudia McDade, Jacksonville State University; Michelle McDaniel, Middle Tennessee State University; Bridgett McGowen, Prairie View A&M University; Aiesha Miller, The University of Akron; Brian Mitchell, Gibbs College of Boston; Karen Mitchell, Northern Essex Community College; Kelly Morales, University of Texas-Pan American; Gail Muse, Holmes Community College; Bonnie Porter Pajka, Luzerne County; Community College; Kate Pandolpho, Ocean County College; Stan Parker, Charleston Southern University; James Penven, Virginia Polytechnic Institute and State University; Joni Webb Petschauer, Appalachian State University; Amy Poland, Buena Vista University; Margaret Puckett, North Central State College; Terry Rafter-Carles, Valencia Community College; Melanie Rago, Indiana University; Margaret Rapp, Tyler Junior College; Rebecca Reed, Johnson & Wales University; Virginia Reilly, Ocean County College; Saundra Richardson,

University of North Carolina at Pembroke; Chuck Rhodes, Sonoma State University; Jennifer Rockwood, The University of Toledo; Lawrence Rodriguez, Palo Alto College; Bea Rogers, Monmouth University; Keri Rogers, Sam Houston State University; Tara Ross, Keiser College; Patty Santoianni, Sinclair Community College; Sarah Shutt, J. Sargeant Reynolds Community College; Phebe Simmons, Blinn College; Brenda A. Smith, Norfolk State University; Kim Smokowski, Bergen Community College; Marilyn Starkes, Thomas Nelson Community College; Angie Walston, Barton College; Janice Waltz, Harrisburg Area Community College; Jodi Webb, Bowling Green State University; Jill Wilks, Southern Utah University.

Focus Group Participants   The same may be said of all the people who helped react to various versions of the design and responded to my ideas for some new features in a college success textbook: Lea Campbell, North Harris Montgomery Community College; Brenda Marina, The University of Akron; Marty Marty, Missouri State University; Claudia McDade, Jacksonville State University; Brian Mitchell, Gibbs College of Boston; Margaret Puckett, North Central State College; Rebecca Reed, Johnson & Wales University; Bea Rogers, Monmouth University; and Angie Walston, Barton College.

The Wadsworth Team   No book, of course, gets very far without a publisher, and *FOCUS* has had the best publishing team imaginable: the dynamic, highly people-skilled Annie Todd, Director of College Success; the meticulous, multi-talented Marita Sermolins, Associate Development Editor; the energetic, industrious Kirsten Stoller, Marketing Manager; true professionals who combed the first pages and probably did more than I'll ever know, Jennifer Kostka, Content Project Manager and Annette Plemmons, Director of Content and Media; the ultimate on-the-ball Editorial Assistant, Dan DeBonis; the obviously talented and conscientious Art Director, Cate Barr; the artistic voice who came all the way to Colorado for the photo shoot, Sheri Blaney, Senior Permissions Account Manager; and lots of folks I never met, other than on e-mail: Tim Sisler, Text Permissions Researcher; Darren Wright, Photo Permissions Researcher; and Annie Beck, Project Manager at Lachina Publishing Services. I'd like to especially thank Larry Harwood, the master photographer who spent a long, hard weekend clicking photos of the *FOCUS* cast on the University of Colorado at Colorado Springs campus. And heartfelt thanks to Wadsworth's Annie Mitchell and Sean Wakely, who believed in this project from the very start; Sylvia Shepherd, whose creative vision shaped much of this book, and Lauren Larsen, whose wit and wisdom formed the basis for several of the early chapters.

Other Contributors   I'd also particularly like to thank the "*FOCUS* All-Stars," as I call them, my students (and one colleague) who modeled for the photo shoots and starred in the "Inside the *FOCUS* Studio" videos. They followed artistic direction like pros, and they make this book unique. I'd also like to thank my colleagues at UCCS who have helped me develop many of the ideas in this book, whether they know it or not—all the Freshman Seminar faculty past and present, and three key colleagues and friends: Kathy Andrus, Nina Ellis, and Barb Gaddis. I also can't go without thanking the many authors who granted me permission to use their work and four essential scholars who allowed me to use, apply, and extend their instruments throughout the book: Neil Fleming, Brian French, John Bransford, and John Pelley. And thanks to my expert student research assistants, Phil Wilburn and Sarah Snyder, and my best buddy Liz for all her encouraging words. And finally, I'd like to thank Matt McClain, the comedy writer who brought his innovative humor to the learning process through podcast summaries of the chapters and television scripts for the website TV shows. He took the "big ideas" from *FOCUS* chapters and made them memorable to students by using their own best-loved media.

Above all, *FOCUS* has taught me truly to focus. Writing a book takes the same kind of endurance and determination that it takes to get a college degree. My empathy level for my students has, if anything, increased—and I am thankful for all I've learned while writing. It has been a cathartic experience to see what has filled each computer screen as I've tapped, tapped, tapped away. Ultimately, what I have chosen to put into each chapter has told me a great deal about who I am, what I know (and don't), and what I value. There's no doubt: I am a better teacher for having written this book. May all my readers grow through their *FOCUS* experience, too.

This descriptive data gathering instrument can be used at the beginning and similarly at the end of the *FOCUS* experience to compare incoming students' *expectations* of college (Entrance Interview) with their actual *experience* of college (Exit Interview) at the end of the term. It can be filled out online or on paper and tabulated. The Entrance Interview is intended to act as a (very) "early alert" system by providing instructors with information that could take weeks to uncover otherwise. It can help instructors, peer mentors, first-year seminar program directors, and institutions by generating individual/student, class/section, or combined classes/institutional data. It can help instructors decide if specific risk factors warrant intervention. The instrument provides valuable information for working with individual students during the course.

1. Does your campus have an Office of Student Multicultural Affairs (or an office with a similar title)? Students from underrepresented populations can often benefit by connecting with this office and with other students in their particular ethnic group.

2. Do non-native speakers of English have ESL test scores that are sufficient for successful academic achievement? Could they benefit from additional ESL coursework? With ever increasing numbers of international students, these questions could be worth pursuing.

3. Some research indicates that residential students have a higher likelihood of being retained, although this varies by institution, environment, and situation. Living on campus can also be costly, which can lead to students working more hours to pay for room and board. Instructors should also note that students living on their own, perhaps for the first time, may feel isolated and have difficulty integrating into the campus community.

4. Research indicates that first-generation students often experience more challenges, partly because they lack role models who are able to help them transition smoothly.

5. Students who are taking too many credit hours may be at risk, academically. They may have skirted academic advising somehow, or assume they can handle more than they actually can, subjecting themselves to serious stress.

6. Students who are on a second or third try at college may be experiencing academic or non-academic problems that resurface.

FOCUS ENTRANCE INTERVIEW

Although you may not have experienced life as a new college student for long, we're interested in how you expect to spend your time, what challenges you think you'll face, and your general views of what you think college will be like. Please answer thoughtfully.

INFORMATION ABOUT YOU

Name _____

Student Number _____   **Course/Section** _____

Instructor _____

Gender _____   **Age** _____

1. **Ethnic identification:**
   ____ Native American/American Indian   ____ Hispanic
   ____ Caucasian   ____ African American
   ____ Asian or Pacific Islander   ____ Prefer not to answer

2. **Is English your first (native) language?**
   ____ yes   ____ no

3. **Where are you living this term?**
   ____ in campus housing   ____ on my own
   ____ with my immediate family   ____ other (please explain)
   ____ with a relative other than my immediate family

4. **Did your parents graduate from college?**
   ____ yes, both   ____ neither
   ____ yes, father only   ____ not sure
   ____ yes, mother only

5. **How many credit hours are you taking this term?**
   ____ 6 or fewer   ____ 15–16
   ____ 7–11   ____ 17 or more
   ____ 12–14

6. **Did you start college elsewhere before attending this school?**
   ____ yes   ____ no

7. **In addition to going to college, do you expect to work for pay at a job (or jobs) this term?**
   ____ yes   ____ no

8. **If so, how many hours per week do you expect to work?**
   ____ 1–10   ____ 31–40
   ____ 11–20   ____ 40+
   ____ 21–30

9. **Which of the following describes why you are working for pay this term? (Mark all that apply.)**
   ____ to pay for college tuition   ____ to pay for child care
   ____ to pay for basic expenses that I need (rent, housing, food, etc.)   ____ to pay for textbooks
   ____ to pay for extra expenses that I want (clothes, entertainment, etc.)   ____ to save money for the future
   ____ to buy a car   ____ to see how much I can make
   ____ to support a family   ____ other (please explain)

10. **How will you pay for your college expenses? (Check all that apply.)**

____ my own earnings   ____ scholarships and grants

____ my parents' contributions   ____ loans

____ my spouse or partner's contributions   ____ other (please explain)

____ my employer's contributions

7–10. Students who are working more than 35 hours per week at a job for pay may be putting themselves at risk, academically. Although many students work for legitimate reasons relating to college and living expenses, some students work more hours to pay for expensive lifestyle choices. Working can help students learn to manage their time; however, both traditional and nontraditional students must find the right balance between work, school, family, and perhaps other responsibilities.

11. **If you plan to work for pay, where will you work?**

____ on campus   ____ off campus   ____ at more than one job

11. There is some evidence that indicates that working on campus actually increases the likelihood of retention. Naturally, working multiple jobs subtracts hours available for academic work.

12. **If you are entering college soon after completing high school, on average, how many total hours per week did you spend studying outside of class in high school?**

____ 0–5   ____ 26–30

____ 6–10   ____ 31–35

____ 11–15   ____ 36–40

____ 16–20   ____ 40+

____ 21–25   ____ I am a returning student and attended high school some time ago.

13. **What was your high school grade point average?**

____ A+   ____ C+

____ A   ____ C

____ A–   ____ C–

____ B+   ____ D or lower

____ B   ____ I don't remember.

____ B–

12–13. Many students enter college thinking that their high school academic efforts, perhaps ratcheted up a notch or two, will suffice. Some are caught off guard by the more rigorous demands of college classes.

INFORMATION ABOUT YOUR COLLEGE EXPECTATIONS

14. **How do you expect to learn best in college? (Check all that apply.)**

____ by looking at charts, maps, graphs   ____ by reading books

____ by looking at color-coded information   ____ by writing papers

____ by looking at symbols and graphics   ____ by taking notes

____ by listening to instructors' lectures   ____ by going on field trips

____ by listening to other students during an in-class discussion   ____ by engaging in activities

____ by talking about course content with friends or roommates   ____ by actually doing things

14. This question previews the VARK Learning Styles Questionnaire in Chapter 2.

15. **For each of the following pairs of descriptors, which set sounds most like you? (Please choose between the two options on each line and place a checkmark by your choice.)**

____ Extraverted and outgoing   or   ____ Introverted and quiet

____ Detail-oriented and practical   or   ____ Big-picture and future-oriented

____ Rational and truthful   or   ____ People-oriented and tactful

____ Organized and self-disciplined   or   ____ Spontaneous and flexible

15. This question previews the SuccessTypes Learning Styles Type Indicator in Chapter 2.

16. **FOCUS is about 13 different aspects of college life. Which are you most interested in? Which may contain information you expect to find most challenging to apply in your own life? (Check all that apply.)**

Most interested in	Most challenging to apply to myself		Most interested in	Most challenging to apply to myself
____	____ Building dreams, setting goals		____	____ Developing your memory
____	____ Learning to learn		____	____ Reading and studying
____	____ Using resources: finances, technology, and campus support		____	____ Taking tests
____	____ Managing time and energy		____	____ Writing and speaking
____	____ Thinking critically and creatively		____	____ Building relationships, valuing diversity
____	____ Engaging, listening, and note-taking in class		____	____ Choosing a major and career
			____	____ Working toward wellness

16. This question previews all the topics included in FOCUS and asks students to think about which ones interest them and which ones will be most challenging to apply themselves.

17. **Which one of your current classes do you expect to find most challenging this term and why?**

Which class? (course title *or* department and course number) _____

Why? _____

Do you expect to succeed in this course? ____ yes ____ no

Perhaps (please explain): _____

17. This question previews the feature, "Control Your Learning: Your Toughest Class," by asking students to identify which of their current classes this is likely to be. Throughout FOCUS, readers are asked to apply content from the text to their most challenging course—a general education or discipline-based course.

18–22. The following questions relate to students' motivation, engagement, and predicted challenges. Note the level of response, and initiate conversations around numbers that are unrealistic or unusual responses.

18. How many total hours per week do you expect to spend outside of class studying for your college courses this term?

___ 0–5	___ 26–30
___ 6–10	___ 31–35
___ 11–15	___ 36–40
___ 16–20	___ 40+
___ 21–25	

19. Which of the following on-campus resources do you plan to use once or more this term? (Please check all that apply.)

___ library

___ campus learning centers (whatever is available on your campus, such as a Writing Center, Math Learning Center, etc.)

___ computer labs

___ the Student Success Center or New Student Center, if one is available

___ the Counseling Center, if one is available

___ professors' office hours for individual meetings/conferences/help

___ student clubs or organizations

___ none

20. For the following sets of opposite descriptive phrases, put a checkmark on the line between the two that best represent your response.

I expect my first term of college to:

challenge me academically	___ ___ ___ ___ ___	be easy
be very different from high school	___ ___ ___ ___ ___	be a lot like high school
be exciting	___ ___ ___ ___ ___	be dull
be interesting	___ ___ ___ ___ ___	be uninteresting
motivate me to continue	___ ___ ___ ___ ___	discourage me
be fun	___ ___ ___ ___ ___	be boring
help me feel a part of this campus	___ ___ ___ ___ ___	make me feel alienated

21. Please mark your *top three areas of concern* relating to your first term of college by placing 1, 2, and 3 next to the items you choose.

___ I might not fit in.

___ I might have difficulty making friends.

___ I might not be academically successful.

___ My performance might disappoint my family.

___ My personal life might interfere with my studies.

___ My studies might interfere with my personal life.

___ I might have financial difficulties.

___ My job might interfere with my studies.

___ My studies might interfere with my job.

___ My social life might interfere with my studies.

___ My studies might interfere with my social life.

___ My professors might not care about me as an individual.

___ I might not finish my degree.

___ I might miss the company of my friends.

___ I might miss the company of my family.

___ I might not manage my time well.

___ I might be bored in my classes.

___ I might feel intimidated by my professors.

___ I might feel overwhelmed by all I have to do.

___ other (please explain)

22. Broadly speaking, which area do you expect to major in?

___ Arts & Sciences	___ Nursing/Health Sciences
___ Education	___ Business
___ Engineering	___ other, please explain

23–28. The next few questions relate to intentions in terms of choice of major and likely persistence both in college and at your institution. Generate a conversation with individual students based on these responses.

23. How certain are you now of a chosen major? (1 = totally sure, 5 = totally unsure) ___

24. How certain are you now that you will complete your degree? (1 = totally sure, 5 = totally unsure) ___

25. How certain are you now that you will complete your degree at this school? (1 = totally sure, 5 = totally unsure) ___

26. How certain are you now of your intended career choice? (1 = totally sure, 5 = totally unsure) ___

27. How certain are you now about whether you'll obtain an advanced degree after you finish college? (1 = totally sure, 5 = totally unsure) ___

28. What do you expect your grade point average to be at the end of your first term of college?

___ A+	___ B	___ C
___ A	___ B–	___ C–
___ A–	___ C+	___ D or lower
___ B+		

29. **All college students develop expectations of what college will be like from various sources. How did you develop your expectations of what college might be like? (Mark your top three information sources with 1, 2, and 3.)**

   ____ TV and movies   ____ talks with my parents

   ____ friends/siblings who have already gone to college   ____ talks with my friends who are also now freshmen

   ____ discussions with teachers/counselors in high school   ____ the Internet

   ____ information I received from colleges in the mail   ____ other (please explain)

29. Students develop their expectations of college from a variety sources from relatively accurate to not-so-accurate ones. If the latter, they may have "glamorized," inflated expectations that are difficult, if not impossible, to realize.

30. **How confident are you in yourself in each of the following areas? (1 = very confident, 5 = not at all confident)**

   ____ overall academic ability   ____ technology skills

   ____ mathematical skills   ____ physical well being

   ____ leadership ability   ____ writing skills

   ____ reading skills   ____ social skills

   ____ public speaking skills   ____ emotional well being

   ____ study skills   ____ teamwork skills

30. According to one major study, the majority of entering first-year students see themselves as above average or in the top ten percent academically. They are more likely to be successful if their self knowledge is realistic.

31. **Why did you take the course for which you are using this textbook? (Mark your top three reasons with 1, 2, and 3.)**

   ____ It was required.   ____ My advisor recommended it.

   ____ It sounded interesting.   ____ A high school teacher/counselor recommended it.

   ____ I thought it would help make my transition to college easier.   ____ The information I received in campus mailings convinced me.

   ____ I thought it would help me learn about the campus.   ____ The materials I received at freshman orientation convinced me.

   ____ I thought it would help me make friends.   ____ A friend/sibling who'd taken this course recommended it.

   ____ I thought it would help me academically.   ____ Other (please explain)

   ____ My parent(s) or other family member(s) thought it was a good idea.

31. Even if students are required to enroll in the course for which *FOCUS* is used, it may be helpful for you to know their other motivations.

32. **What is the most important reason you decided to attend this school? (Check one)**

   ____ Recommendation of friend(s) who attended here   ____ Financial aid I was offered

   ____ Reasonable cost   ____ Recommendation of high school teachers/counselors

   ____ Reputation of the school   ____ Campus website

   ____ Location of the school   ____ other (please explain)

   ____ Availability of academic programs I'm interested in

32–38. The following questions relate to students' decision to attend college and your institution, specifically.

33. **Was this school your first choice among the colleges you considered?** ____ yes ____ no

34. **Why did you decide to go to college? (Check all that apply)**

   ____ because I want to build a better life for myself.   ____ because it was expected of me.

   ____ because I want to build a better life for my family.   ____ because I was recruited for athletics.

   ____ because I want to be very well off financially in the future.   ____ because I want to continue learning.

   ____ because I need a college education to achieve my dreams.   ____ because the career I am pursuing requires a degree.

   ____ because my friends were going to college.   ____ because I was unsure of what I might do instead.

   ____ because my family encouraged me to go.   ____ other (please explain)

35. **Looking ahead, how satisfied do you expect to be with your decision to attend this school?**

   ____ very satisfied   ____ somewhat dissatisfied

   ____ satisfied   ____ very dissatisfied

   ____ not sure

36. **What are you most looking forward to in college?** _____

_____

37. **How would you describe the best outcomes you hope for at the end of this term? Why are they important to you?** _____

_____

38. **Do you expect to achieve these outcomes? Why or why not?** _____

_____

CONTENTS

CHAPTER 7: DEVELOPING YOUR MEMORY   199

1 Building Dreams, Setting Goals

YOU'RE ABOUT TO DISCOVER...

> How this book will help you learn

> What motivates you

> How your attitude can sabotage you

> How your beliefs about your intelligence can affect your college success

> What separates *performers* and *learners*

> What your core values say about you

> Why you should distinguish between dreams and goals

> How to develop goals that work

> What it takes to succeed in college

"The best way to predict the future is to create it."

Peter Drucker, management expert (1909–2005)

Gloria Gonzales

It was her first day of college. As Gloria Gonzales walked to her first class, "College Success," she had mixed feelings: excitement, anticipation, anxiety, and apprehension. She wondered if she'd meet any interesting people, if she'd like her instructor, and if she'd learn anything important in this class. After all, she'd gotten good grades in high school without even trying hard. If she just put in some effort, she thought, she'd be successful in college, too. How can you study something like "College Success" for a whole term? she asked herself.

To be honest, Gloria thought she probably already knew most of what there was to learn in this course, and if she didn't, so what? She knew what she had to do to get good grades—everyone does—but she didn't always choose to do it, that's all. School was part of her life, but it wasn't always her top priority. At least this course would probably be easier than her math course or her composition course with all that writing.

Gloria wasn't the first person in her family to go to college. Her sister had attempted it, but she'd dropped out after her first term and gotten a job. "College, who needs it?" she'd exclaimed. "I want to start earning good money right away, not years from now!" There were times when Gloria thought her sister might be right. Her sister certainly seemed able to afford some of the things Gloria had always wanted herself. Was college really going to be worth all the time, effort, and expense? But everyone she knew was going to college; it was the right thing to do after high school, and everyone expected it of her.

Gloria's family didn't have much money. They were sacrificing to help finance her college education. She'd better perform, they'd said. They'd told her point-blank that her sister had set a bad example, and that her first-term grades had better not include anything lower than a B. Frankly, Gloria was beginning to feel a twinge of performance pressure. Of all the children in her family, her sister had always been considered the smartest, and she'd given up after only one term. If her sister couldn't do it, how could Gloria? If she were to succeed, exactly what would it take?

Despite her worries as she walked down the hallway toward the classroom, Gloria was sure of one thing: She looked good today—really good. Her sister's skirt fit perfectly, the new red shirt was definitely her color, and thankfully it was a good hair day. Gloria had always been able to make heads turn.

Beneath it all, Gloria knew what she wanted, anyway. She was going into the fashion industry. She'd dreamed of that since she was ten years old. She wasn't sure exactly what she'd need to do to make

it, but she'd worked in a clothing store at the mall all through high school, and she was good at it. In fact, the store kept trying to give her more hours because she had such exceptional customer service skills. She thought she'd probably just work her college courses around her thirty-five hours a week there.

Gloria's parents wanted her to major in engineering because they thought it would be a lucrative and stable profession. They were always clipping articles about engineering jobs from the newspaper and giving them to her, but she kept telling them she had no interest. "There'll always be good jobs for engineers," they said. She'd heard it so many times that her usual response now was "Yeah, whatever. . . ." While they talked engineering, she dreamed of becoming a famous fashion designer with her own line of clothing. She was going to call it "Gloria." Her parents had named her after their favorite rock-and-roll song of all time, "G-L-O-R-I-A." Imagine—her own clothing label with her name on it!

As she reached for the classroom doorknob, Gloria couldn't help wondering about the two questions at the forefront of her mind: "What will college really be like?" and "Will I be successful?" She took a deep breath as she opened the classroom door. *This is it*, she thought. Somehow, she felt as if she were outside herself, watching on the big screen—replete with Panavision and DTS sound. *This is real; this is me, starring in my own movie*, she said to herself. And even though it felt good, Gloria had to wonder about the ending. All she could do was hope for the best.

WHAT DO YOU THINK?

Now that you've read about Gloria Gonzales, answer the following questions. You may not know all the answers yet, but you'll find out what you know and what you stand to gain by reading this chapter.

1. Describe Gloria's motivation to succeed in college. Is she sufficiently motivated to succeed?
2. Describe Gloria's beliefs about her intelligence. Does she think college is mostly about effort or about ability? Is Gloria a *learner* or a *performer*?
3. Is Gloria's vision of becoming a famous fashion designer a goal or a dream? Why?
4. Identify three things (attitudes, beliefs, fears, and so on) that do not show focus and might cause Gloria to make poor life management choices.
5. Identify three things that do show focus and might help Gloria make good life management choices.
6. What elements of Gloria's situation are similar to your own college experience thus far?
7. Gloria's parents' definition of success in school meant getting good grades. Do you agree with this definition? Why or why not? Could equating good grades with success actually hinder Gloria's ability to succeed? If so, how?

Before beginning to read this chapter, take two minutes to answer the following questions on a scale of 1 to 10. Your answers will help you assess how ready you are to focus.

1 = not very/not much/very little/low   10 = very/a lot/very much/high

Based on reading the "You're about to discover..." list and skimming this chapter, how much do you think you probably already know about the subject matter?

1   2   3   4   5   6   7   8   9   10

How much do you think this information might affect your college success?

1   2   3   4   5   6   7   8   9   10

How much do you think this information might affect your career success after college?

1   2   3   4   5   6   7   8   9   10

In general, how motivated are you to learn the material in this chapter?

1   2   3   4   5   6   7   8   9   10

This book describes four key factors related to intrinsic, or internal, motivation: curiosity, control, career outlook, and challenge. The next four questions relate to these **C-Factors:**

How *curious* are you about the content you expect to read in this chapter?

1   2   3   4   5   6   7   8   9   10

How much *control* do you expect to have over mastering the material in this chapter?

1   2   3   4   5   6   7   8   9   10

How much do you think this chapter might help you develop your *career outlook*?

1   2   3   4   5   6   7   8   9   10

How *challenging* do you think the material in this chapter will be for you?

1   2   3   4   5   6   7   8   9   10

Before beginning any task, including studying, it's important to check in with yourself to ensure that you're physically, intellectually, and emotionally ready to focus. How ready are you, physically, to focus on this chapter? (Are you rested, feeling well, and so on?)

1   2   3   4   5   6   7   8   9   10

How ready are you, intellectually, to focus on this chapter? (Are you thinking clearly, focused on this course, interested in this subject?)

1   2   3   4   5   6   7   8   9   10

How ready are you, emotionally, to focus on this chapter? (Are you calm, confident, composed?)

1   2   3   4   5   6   7   8   9   10

If your answer to any of the last three questions is below a 5 on the scale, you may need to address the issue you're facing prior to beginning this chapter. For example, if you're hungry, get a quick bite to eat. If you're feeling scattered, take a few moments to settle down and focus.

Finally, how long do you think it will take you to complete this chapter? _____ Hour(s) _____ Minutes

> **"It's always smart to learn from your mistakes. It's smarter to learn from the mistakes of others."**
>
> **Hillel Segal and Jesse Berst, computer experts**

Sensitive Situation A key to students developing self-insight is to do the "Readiness Check" in each chapter. Don't skip this section. Also, keep in mind that some students may not want to be completely honest about how they feel about taking this course. Students may feel that they don't need it and may not be ready to focus. Consider a brief discussion about why it is important to be honest when they fill out this "Readiness Check," and that the results are only for themselves and not for the instructor.

Who Are You?
And What Do You Want?

Imagine this voicemail greeting: "Hi. At the tone, please answer two of life's most important questions. Who are you? And what do you want?" Beep. Very clever, don't you think? Can you answer these questions right now? Have you thought much about them? How much do you really know about yourself and what you want from this life of yours?

Don't worry. These aren't trick questions and there are no wrong answers. But there are some answers that are more right for you than others. College is a great time to think about who you are and what you want. In addition to learning about biology or history or business—whatever you choose for a major—college will be a time to learn about yourself: your motivation, values, dreams, and goals. College is a time when you'll make some of the most important choices of your life. Which major will you choose? Which career will you aim for? How many lifelong friends will you make? From this point on, it's up to you. Have you ever heard this phrase with ten two-letter words: "If it is to be, it is up to me"? It's true.

Think about it: a college education is one of the best investments you can make. Once you've earned a college degree, it's yours forever. Someone can steal your car, walk away with your cell phone, or carry off your laptop, but once you've earned a college degree, no one can ever take it from you. Your choice to be a college graduate will pay off in many ways. So even if you aren't sure exactly how you want to spend the rest of your life right now, you can't go wrong by investing in your future.

This book starts with the big picture: your life. It's about managing your life, being fully invested in what you're doing, and using your abilities to their utmost. Notice the phrase "managing your life"—not *controlling* your life. Let's face it: many things in life are beyond our control. We can't control international politics, set tuition rates, or advise characters in our favorite movies about what to do next. But you can manage your life by making smart choices, setting realistic goals, monitoring your time and energy, motivating yourself, and ultimately creating your own future. As the title of this book states boldly, it's about focus.

For many of us, focusing is a challenge. We work too many hours, crowd our lives with obligations, and rush from one thing to the next. We're good at multitasking. We can surf the Internet, listen to a new CD, watch a DVD, and read this chapter—all at the same time! But think about Gandhi's wise words applied to today's lifestyle, "There is more to life than increasing its speed." In short, while we've become skilled at multitasking, we may have sacrificed some of the self-discipline required for in-depth study. Multitasking may be a great skill to have when you're a corporate CEO, running many divisions of a large company, but learning to focus is what most college students need. In fact, recent research indicates that multitasking hurts your brain's ability to learn, and that what you learn while you're distracted by other things is harder to use and recall.[1]

Ours is a fast-paced society. We expect results quickly. We've become accustomed to instant gratification, as it's called. We want what we want, and we want it right now! In our society, if you don't want to wait until you can afford something, what do you do? Charge it! But earning a college degree takes time, commitment, and determination. It won't happen overnight and it won't happen automatically. Unlike almost anything else you can buy, you must invest more than money to become truly educated.

Of course, some people achieve success without a college degree, but by and large, they're the exception. Even Steven Spielberg, self-made billionaire in the film industry and winner of Academy Awards for *Schindler's List* and

> **"What is important is to keep learning, to enjoy challenge, and to tolerate ambiguity. In the end there are no certain answers."**
>
> Martina Horner, former President of Radcliffe College

Activity Option Take some time here for students to briefly get to know each other. Later in the chapter there will be a getting-to-know-you activity, but it's important to set the tone of the class early on. One simple activity is for students to write their name, where they are from, and possible major on an index card or piece of paper. Collect and redistribute the index cards. Have students read the card they received and guess who in the class they are describing.

Teachable Moment Have you ever been asked if your students knew more about something than you did? How might you respond? Share with your students that there are probably people in the class who know more about some things than you and how you look forward to learning from them. Set the tone in the classroom that you too are a learner—we are all lifelong learners. Share something that you have learned from your students (i.e., Facebook, MySpace).

Activity Option Before class, write on index cards something that might cause a student to lose focus in school (i.e., your roommate blasts music all day, your grandmother is ill, your books cost more money than you thought, your babysitter's last day is Friday). Make as many cards as you need for the size and composition of your class. Pass out the cards, one per student, and as each student holds up his or her card, ask the class whether it's possible to exert some control over the situation, and if so, how.

> ❝**Furious activity is no substitute for understanding.**❞
>
> H. H. Williams, British poet and playwright

Saving Private Ryan, felt the need to finish the college degree he had started more than thirty years before. "I wanted to accomplish this for many years as a 'thank you' to my parents for giving me the opportunity for an education and a career, and as a personal note for my own family—and young people everywhere—about the importance of achieving their college education goals," he said. "But I hope they get there quicker than I did. Completing the requirements for my degree 33 years after finishing my principal education marks my longest post-production schedule."[2]

If you read this book carefully and follow its advice, it will help you become the best student you can possibly be. It will give you practical tools to help you manage your life. It will take you beyond college into your career. And most of all, it will encourage you to become a true scholar. That is this book's challenge to you as you begin your college career.

Sensitive Situation The backgrounds and challenges students face have changed dramatically over the years. Not everyone has an iPod or a DVD player. Some students may be working two jobs to pay for college, while others' expenses are fully funded by scholarships or parents. Some students are supporting families. Some students may have learning disabilities while others are academically talented. Keep in mind that the challenges may be greater for some students than others. Open the door for students to let you know if they are facing any unusual challenges. Now is a good time to give them your e-mail address, office hours, and any other ways that they might contact you.

Activity Option Be sure that *you* do Exercise 1.1 along with your students. Remember that they want to get to know you, too. Pair up students and have them share their information with a partner. Have the partner introduce the student to the class and report on two or three items that were really interesting. Another activity you can do is called "You would never guess." Ask students to write something on an index card that no one would guess about them. Collect the cards and read them aloud. Have students guess who it might be.

EXERCISE 1.1 We'd Like to Get to Know You...

Take a few minutes to finish the following statements. Think about what each sentence says about you. Use your responses to introduce yourself to the class or form pairs, talk over your responses together, and use your partner's answers to introduce him or her to the class.

1. I'm happiest when _____.

2. I'm disappointed when _____.

3. If I had an extra $100, I'd _____.

4. The thing I'm most proud of is _____.

5. Once people get to know me, they're probably surprised to find I'm _____.

6. My family wants me to _____.

7. I'd really like to become _____.

8. My friends enjoy me because _____.

9. I've been known to consume large quantities of _____.

10. I'd rather be _____ than _____.

11. When I'm under pressure, _____.

12. My best quality is _____.

13. My worst quality is _____.

14. The academic skill I'd most like to develop is _____.

15. One thing I'd like to figure out about myself is _____.

Spending Time "in the System"

Spending time "in the system"? No, being in college isn't like being in jail—far from it. Many people reflect back on their college days as one of the most enjoyable, active, and interesting times of their lives. Get involved on campus, make lifelong friends, and gain as much as you can from your college experience.

"The system" is the approach used in this book to structure productive learning: the Challenge → Reaction → Insight → Action system. It is based on the work of Dr. John Bransford and his colleagues, who together wrote an influential book called *How People Learn* (2000).

Figure 1.1 summarizes how learning requires focus, and focus involves the four steps in this system. Ideally, it would be interesting to hear the conversation going on in your head as you learn—what's called metacognition, or knowing how you come to know something. But since that's impossible, this book asks you to write and discuss things along the way: your reactions, your insights, and the actions you plan to take. You'll come to realize things about yourself. This book's goal for you is *transformative learning*: "a process of examining, questioning, validating, and revising [your] perceptions."[3] What you'll learn by reading it has the potential to *transform*, or *change* you, so that you're ready to meet the many challenges that await you in college and in life. Here's a step-by-step explanation of the learning system used in this book.

Sensitive Situation Keep in mind that for some students the idea of getting involved and making friends is not a priority. College is an endurance test and they "just want to get out of here." Remind students that those who are the most successful make academic progress *and* connections to the campus. Working with others and learning from and with them, getting involved—if only minimally—will enrich their college experience. For those who do see "time in the system" as jail time, getting involved and meeting others will make this time in their lives more enjoyable. As an instructor, think of ways you can get your students working together. Your job is to convince students that education is a *process* and not a *product*.

> "Surround yourself with people who take their work seriously, but not themselves, those who work hard and play hard."
>
> **Colin Powell, former U.S. Secretary of State**

Figure 1.1
How People Learn

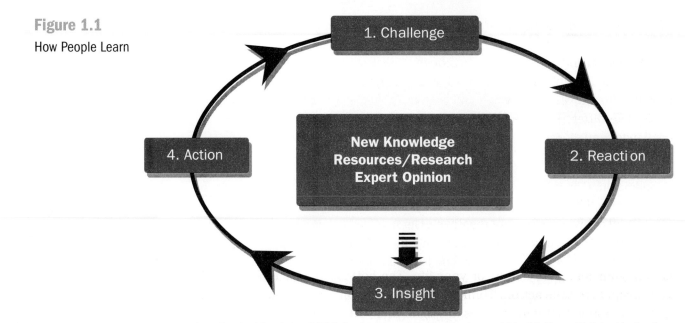

Source: Based on J. Bransford, et al. (2000). *How People Learn: Brain, Mind, Experience, and School.* Washington, DC: National Academy Press.

Activity Option Have students add up the cost of their tuition, room, board, books, and any other expenses related to school and divide that total by the number of hours they are in school (number of weeks multiplied by the number of hours they are supposed to be in class). Students will then see how much money each class costs them—and the cost of missing class! (See Staley, 2003, "Spending Time," p. 54.)

Teachable Moment The Challenge → Reaction → Insight → Action system is a very important feature of this text. The cycle is to react to a presented challenge, find out how much you already know, use the new knowledge provided to gain insight, and then turn that insight into action. Keep reminding students about this chain reaction.

STEP 1: Accept the *FOCUS* challenge. Every time you study a new subject or take a new course, you are challenged, right? Within each chapter of this book, you'll be presented with challenges, beginning with a case study about a college student—perhaps someone like you or a friend—who is experiencing something new and difficult. Research shows that people can learn more from examples of things going wrong than they can from examples of things going perfectly smoothly. As you continue to read, you'll be presented with additional challenges related to the chapter's content to pique your curiosity, motivate you to keep reading, and start a learning chain reaction. Don't skip over this step; it's an important part of the learning process. Challenge yourself!

STEP 2: React to the challenge. Whenever you're learning something new, the best place to start is by identifying what you think you already know—your gut reaction. You're a novice to any new field you're studying, not an expert, but you bring with you to the learning process a set of preconceptions, assumptions, sometimes biases or misperceptions, and of course, all your previous experiences. Your reaction to each challenge will tell you what you think you already know. If you come across an unfamiliar term, look it up in the dictionary. Of course, you won't know everything there is to know in reacting to the challenge yet. But you'll find out what you do know and what you don't, and by the end of the chapter, you'll know more about all the challenges you've encountered throughout your reading. The goal of this book is to help you become a deep learner, as opposed to skimming the surface and simply rushing on to the next assignment and the next course—as many college students do. It will ask you to pause, take stock, focus, and think.

STEP 3: Use new knowledge to gain insights. After your initial reaction, you must pay attention to your inner voice—insights you've gained from new knowledge. "Insight → Action" activities will help you keep track of them. Your instructor may ask you to record your answers online or in a notebook, or you may discuss these questions in class. Let's say, for example, that you read later in this chapter about goal setting. When you first thought about it, the whole idea of setting goals seemed simple, but after reading about it, you decide you really hadn't thought about it very deeply and had only vague notions about setting your own goals. The difference between step 2 (whatever reaction you provided to the challenge) and step 3 (the insights you've gained) demonstrates that learning is taking place.

STEP 4: Use your insights to propel you toward action. Insights have no impact unless they become integrated into your life, unless they lead to change. Decide how an insight affects your existing beliefs, how it changes them, and therefore, what you've learned. Your insights may lead you to change your behavior, develop an informed opinion, or make choices about your education, your job, your family, or your life. The bottom line is: You must use your insights to take action. Think of this comparison. One day you feel sluggish, you notice that your clothes are tight, and you are suddenly aware that you're out of shape. You realize that you must make healthier food choices and exercise more. But if you don't take action, it won't happen. You've just gained an insight. You can do nothing about it, or you can use your insight to take action. To become real, new knowledge must lead to personal insights that result in action.

Each step in this four-part system is important. For example, if you skip step 2, *react to the challenge*, by identifying what you *think* you know, you may assume you already know all the new information you're reading or hearing. You may think, "Sure, of course, that makes sense. I already knew that," when you really didn't. In truth, the French philosopher Voltaire was right: "Common sense is not so common." Realizing there's a gap between steps 2 and 3—what you thought you knew and the insights you've gained from new knowledge—is important. And actually putting the insights you gain into real, live, honest-to-goodness action is vital.

As you work through this book, the Challenge → Reaction → Insight → Action system will continue cycling back to step 1, presenting you with new challenges. If you follow the system built into this book and integrate it into your other academic pursuits, you can become a lifelong learner. Thinking in terms of the learning cycle will become ingrained. Someone once said that change is accelerating in such mind-boggling ways today that "Learning is what most adults will do for a living in the 21st century." Life management is about knowing how to learn.

Chapter Crossover Look ahead to Chapter 11 on emotional intelligence (EI). Strong emotional intelligence enables individuals to take control over their lives as opposed to letting emotions and reactions to situations take over.

Teachable Moment Another important part of helping students understand the Challenge → Reaction → Insight → Action system is to stress the importance of reflection (thinking about a situation—what happened?) and self-assessment (what did I do? why and how might I do it differently?). Insight that leads to new action or changed action is key to college success.

Activity Option Have students respond to the following challenge: It's Friday, and a student has a ten-page paper due on Monday. His roommate has invited him home for the weekend and the student wants to go. What are the possible reactions, insights, and actions related to this situation?

Emotional Intelligence (EI) Research In relation to the "Activity Option," what strong EI skills would the student who chooses to stay home and get the paper done demonstrate? What about the student who chooses to do it at the last minute? This is a good time to discuss impulse control. In the famous marshmallow challenge done by Walter Mischel in the 1960s, four-year-olds were given marshmallows and told to wait 15 to 20 minutes before they could eat them. The same students were followed 12–14 years later. Those who couldn't wait and grabbed the marshmallows were the same people years later that had a somewhat troubled life and were still unable to put off gratification.

INSIGHT ⊖ ACTION

1. What do you think about the Challenge → Reaction → Insight → Action system? Does it make sense? Do you understand how it works? Write a few paragraphs describing it in your own words.

2. Are you committed to using it throughout this book to validate its effectiveness? If so, write down exactly what will be required of you.

How Motivated *Are* You and *How* Are You Motivated?

CHALLENGE ⊖ REACTION

How intrinsically motivated are you? Read each of the following statements and circle the number beside each statement that most accurately represents your views about yourself.

	Completely Not True	Somewhat Not True	Neutral	Somewhat True	Completely True
1. I have academic goals.	1	2	3	4	5
2. I am confident I can complete my degree.	1	2	3	4	5
3. I determine my career goals.	1	2	3	4	5
4. I enjoy solving challenging, difficult problems.	1	2	3	4	5
5. I work on an assignment until I understand it.	1	2	3	4	5
6. I am confident I will graduate from college.	1	2	3	4	5
7. I determine the quality of my academic work.	1	2	3	4	5
8. I am pursuing a college degree because I value education.	1	2	3	4	5
9. I feel good knowing that I determine how my academic career develops.	1	2	3	4	5
10. I have high standards for academic work.	1	2	3	4	5
11. Staying in college is my decision.	1	2	3	4	5
12. I study because I like to learn new things.	1	2	3	4	5
13. I enjoy doing outside readings in connection to my future coursework.	1	2	3	4	5
14. I am intrigued by the different topics introduced in my courses.	1	2	3	4	5
15. I study because I am curious.	1	2	3	4	5
16. I look forward to going to class.	1	2	3	4	5
17. I am excited to take more courses within my major.	1	2	3	4	5

	Completely Not True	Somewhat Not True	Neutral	Somewhat True	Completely True
18. I enjoy learning more within my field of study.	1	2	3	4	5
19. I like to find answers to questions about material I am learning.	1	2	3	4	5
20. I enjoy studying.	1	2	3	4	5
21. I have pictured myself in a profession after college.	1	2	3	4	5
22. I am excited about the job opportunities I will have when I graduate.	1	2	3	4	5
23. I have pictured myself being successful in my chosen profession.	1	2	3	4	5
24. I believe I will make a substantial contribution to my chosen profession.	1	2	3	4	5
25. I feel good knowing I will be a member of the professional community in my area of study.	1	2	3	4	5

Total each column, then add your scores across. _____ + _____ + _____ + _____ + _____ =

_____ OVERALL SCORE

Continue reading to find out what your overall score means.

Let's get serious. When it comes to getting a college education, where does motivation come into the picture? In general, motivation is your desire to engage and put forth effort, even when the going gets rough. The word *motivation* comes from Medieval Latin, *motivus*, meaning "moving or impelling." What moves you to learn? There are many ways to define motivation, and different people are motivated by different things.

How motivated would you be to learn something difficult, such as a new language, one you'd never studied before? Let's say that you were offered a chance to learn Finnish, a challenging language that is not related to English. For example, in Finnish *Kiitoksia oikein paljon* means "thank you very much." Finnish would be a challenge to learn. To determine your level of motivation, it would help to know your attitude toward Finland and Finnish people, whether you needed to learn Finnish for some reason, how you felt about learning it, if you thought you could learn it successfully, if you were reinforced in some way for learning it, and just how stimulating you found the learning process to be.[4] In other words, your motivation level depends on many factors, right?

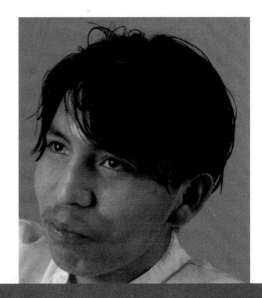

"You are never given a wish without the power to make it come true. You may have to work for it, however."

Richard Bach, from *Illusions*

Teachable Moment: Motivation and optimism are connected. If you are not very optimistic about the outcome of something and have an "I can't" attitude, motivation will be minimized. Why do something if you think you will fail? Make sure students understand this relationship, and focus on their control of their own learning.

You'd probably be more motivated to learn Finnish if these sorts of things were part of the picture: (a) you were going to visit relatives in Finland and were excited about it, (b) you'd always excelled at learning foreign languages and you expected to learn this one easily, (c) your boss was planning to transfer you to Helsinki as part of a big promotion, or (d) you enjoyed your Finnish language class, thought the instructor was a gifted teacher, and found the other students to be as motivated as you were. So, whose job is it to motivate you? Your instructor's? Your parents'? This book's? Yours? *Can* anyone else besides you motivate you? This book will ask you: how motivated *are* you to succeed in college? And *how* are you motivated?

To assess your own motivation, it's important to understand the difference between *extrinsic* and *intrinsic* motivation. People who are *extrinsically,* or externally, motivated learn in order to get a grade, earn credits, or complete a requirement, for example. They are motivated by things outside themselves. You could be motivated to learn Finnish to earn three credits, or to get an A, or to avoid getting an F, or to meet a foreign language requirement. People who are *intrinsically,* or internally, motivated learn because they're curious, fascinated, challenged, or because they truly want to master a subject. They are motivated from within. You could be motivated to learn Finnish for the challenge, because you're curious about it, or because you find it fascinating. Let's be realistic, however. Extrinsic motivation is real and important. You need a particular number of credit hours to graduate. You'd rather get A's than F's. But how intrinsically motivated you are in college will have a great deal to do with just how successful you are. The motivation to become truly educated must come from within you.

You completed the Academic Intrinsic Motivation Scale (AIMS) in the previous "Challenge → Reaction," which is designed to measure your intrinsic, or internal, motivation to succeed in college in terms of these four C-Factors:

1. **Curiosity.** Do you want to acquire new knowledge? Are you truly interested in what you're learning? Do you ask questions? Do you allow your curiosity to propel your learning?

2. **Control.** Do you think the academic investment you make will lead to successful outcomes? Do you believe you can control how successful you'll be?

3. **Career outlook.** Are you goal oriented? Are you future oriented? Can you imagine yourself graduating and getting a job you want?

4. **Challenge.** Does your college coursework challenge you appropriately? Too much challenge can cause you to become frustrated and give up. Not enough challenge can cause you to lose interest.[5]

Sensitive Situation Some students in your class may have low AIMS scores. Debriefing this activity is important because these students may be losing hope. Consider having students write a journal entry to you, a private conversation, in which they reflect on their scores and speculate on why they are low. Ask students to consider if they would like their scores to be different than what they are, and whether they have any ideas about what they will do to improve their scores.

If your overall score on the AIMS was 100–125, you're intrinsically motivated at a high level. If you scored between 75 and 99, you're intrinsically motivated at a moderate level, but increasing your intrinsic motivation may help you achieve more. If you scored below 75, a lack of intrinsic motivation could interfere with your college success. If you're intrinsically motivated, you'll accept challenges, react to them by identifying what you already know, seek insights from new knowledge, and take action based on what you've learned.

Like the Challenge → Reaction → Insight → Action system, the Academic Intrinsic Motivation Scale's C-Factors reappear throughout the book to boost your intrinsic motivation:

CULTIVATE Your Curiosity   Each chapter includes a short article based on current research, a *New York Times* bestseller, a workplace application, or a new way of looking at what is required for college success. You'll read cutting-edge information that may pique your curiosity and lead you to consider exploring the original source or related material on your own.

CONTROL Your Learning   You are encouraged throughout this book to apply the content covered to your most challenging class this term and to take charge of your own learning. The challenge in your chosen class may be the level—either too high-level because the material is extremely difficult (a killer course) or too low-level (a no-brainer, boring course). This book will help you succeed in your chosen class by prompting you to work with your instructor through an office hours visit or e-mail, for example. Taking charge of your own learning is vital to college success.

CREATE A Career Outlook   Each chapter includes a "Focus on Careers" interview with a professional who specializes in the skills described in the chapter. As you read these interviews, think about the interviewees' stories, their success, and ask yourself whether you have the interest and motivation required to get where they are. Following the interview, you'll read some quick facts in a section called "Create a Career Outlook" to see how this career might fit you.

CHALLENGE Yourself Quizzes   In general, if a course is too challenging, you may be tempted to give up. If it's too easy, you may lose interest. Adjusting the level of challenge to one that's right for you is key to keeping yourself motivated to learn. Online quizzes for each chapter will challenge you so that you can work at your best.

For more practice online, go to http://www.academic.cengage.com/collegesuccess/staley to take the Challenge Yourself online quizzes.

INSIGHT ⟶ ACTION

1. Describe a time when you succeeded in learning something. Perhaps you wanted to learn to work on your own car, play the flute, or cook an exotic meal. What was the learning experience like? Were you extrinsically or intrinsically motivated? Why?

2. Now describe a situation in which you failed to learn something. What were you trying to learn, and what was the experience like? Were you extrinsically or intrinsically motivated? Why?

3. What types of things fascinate you and fire up your intrinsic motivation?

4. What actions can you take to help you think more deliberately about your motivation and how it affects your learning?

EXERCISE 1.2 The Ideal Student

Create your own personal top-ten list of the characteristics of an ideal student. Bring your completed list to your next class session where everyone can read their lists, and begin to add, delete, merge, and create a master list to which everyone can subscribe. Put your initials next to each of the ten items on the master list that you promise to do throughout the term. Your personal top-ten list, which your instructor may discuss with you individually at a later time, will become your learning contract for the course.

Activity Option Give each student ten sticky notes. Ask students to write one word on each note to fill in the blank: Successful students _____. Repeat this phrase ten times, each time giving the students only seconds to fill in the blank. On the board, write "Student has control" on one side and "Student has no control" on the other. Have students put each sticky note under the heading they believe is true of their statement. Some students believe that they have no control on issues that they really do. Let students lead the discussion.

Give Yourself an Attitude Adjustment

There's a difference of opinion on the subject of attitude. Some people say attitude is not all that important. Atttude-schmattitude, they say. Others say that *attitude* is more important than *aptitude*. What do you think?

In research studies conducted by Rick Snyder at the University of Kansas, students who scored high on a measure of hope got higher grades. Snyder explained that students with high hopes set themselves higher goals and know how to work hard to attain them.

Quick quiz. How many times in the past week did you catch yourself saying "Whatever...," rolling your eyes when someone—perhaps a teacher, parent, or friend—offered you feedback or suggestions that you didn't want to hear? Be honest now. Think of all of those moments. Whatever-ness—an attitude of cynicism, apathy, disdain, or impatience—takes a lot less effort than optimism, respect, kindness, or any other positive response. Whether you realize it or not, whatevers chip away at your motivation, and they can contribute to self-sabotaging your opportunities to succeed in life. When it comes to your college education, one good thing you can do for yourself is to purge the word *whatever* from your vocabulary. Your education is much too important for whatevers—and so are you.

> **"A positive attitude is your most priceless possession, one of your most valuable assets. To a great extent, it determines the overall quality of your life."**
>
> **Keith Harrell, from**
> *Attitude Is Everything*

FOCUS ON CAREERS: ERIC SWEEN, Psychologist

Courtesy of Eric Sween

Q1: What do you do in your work?
My specialization is in the psychological field known as narrative therapy—in other words, how people make meaning of the events in their lives. In my private practice I see both individuals and couples. People come into therapy for a wide variety of reasons, for example, when they feel stuck with something in their lives—some with unemployment, or relationships, or divorce. Others come to therapy because they feel too anxious, or because someone close to them has died. My responsibilities include listening, understanding people's perspectives, and helping them set and reach their goals. I especially value working with people who are at some sort of turning point in their lives.

Q2: What are the three most important skills you need to do well in this career?
First, a therapist needs to be able to listen really well and appreciate another person's perspective. Second, a therapist must be genuinely curious about people and try to understand what is most meaningful to them. And finally, it's important to be flexible and tailor what you do with each person you are working with. Some people need problem solving and concrete steps. Some need to be really heard and empathized with. And some need information and a connection to

additional resources. The key is to know the difference in what clients need in order to reach their goals.

Q3: What is the most challenging aspect of your work? How do you deal with it?
I care about the people I work with and what happens to them. Sometimes I take that home with me. Over time, I've gotten better at drawing a line between my work life and my home life. But I don't want to lose my compassion. It's difficult when people are going through hard things. What helps me is to make sure my own life stays in balance—getting enough time for exercise, friends, and creative projects.

Q4: How important is goal setting in your work?
Setting goals is crucial. How are we going to know we've arrived at "the destination," unless we are specific about what the destination is? Many people don't realize it is the small steps that get you to the big dreams. When someone is feeling depressed or dealing with a lot of stress, they can forget about how important it is to break goals down into manageable chunks.

Q5: How important is motivation in your work—for both you and your clients?
Motivation gets me out of bed in the morning. I think motivation is essential for everyone. But it comes in more than one flavor. There are

Eight Ways to Adjust Your Attitude

The good thing about attitude is that you can change it yourself. In fact, you can give yourself an overall attitude adjustment, which can lead to better control over your learning and deeper investment in your own education. As you think about benefits of fine-tuning your attitude, keep these eight recommendations in mind:

1. **Know that you always have choices.** Regardless of circumstances—your income, your background, or your prior academic record—you always have a choice, even if it's limited to how you choose to perceive your current situation.

2. **Take responsibility for your own outcomes.** Coach Vince Lombardi used to have his players look in a mirror before every game and ask themselves, "Am I looking at the person who is helping me win or the one who is holding me back?" Blaming others simply diminishes your own power to work toward constructive responses to challenges.

3. **Convert turning points into learning points.** Instead of beating yourself up when things don't go well, figure out why. See what you can learn from the experience and then move on. As Henry Ford once said, "Failure is the opportunity to begin again, more intelligently."

4. **Choose your words carefully.** "Can't" and "won't" are two of the biggest inhibitors to a healthy attitude. Also pay attention to how you describe things. Is the cup half empty or half full? State things in the positive rather than the negative (for example, "stay healthy" rather than "don't get sick"). Language is a reflection of attitude.

Chapter Crossover Chapter 2 includes information on learning styles. Since students may not yet have taken the instruments included there, give them a quick introduction to how certain personality tendencies fit certain careers better than others.

Activity Option Ask students to work in groups to decide what a student might do in this situation described by Daniel Goleman in his book *Emotional Intelligence: Why It Can Matter More Than IQ* (1994): Although you set yourself a goal of getting a B, when your first exam worth 30 percent of your final grade is returned, you received a D.

Teachable Moment Pose the following question to your students: Is psychology a good career choice for everyone? Why or why not? Consider this activity for every career that is described throughout the book to get students thinking about skills and career choices.

things we do because we *love* to and things we do because we *have* to. But the critical element to anything is how much meaning it holds for us. I see many people who lack motivation because they aren't doing what is meaningful to them. I also find that people are motivated by different things at different times in their lives. That's completely natural.

Q6: How important is it to understand personal values in your work?
Critical. If I don't explore and understand my clients' personal values, I tend to impose my own. That never works out well because people are so different. When people are stuck in their lives, it is often because they have lost touch with their personal values and goals, so I ask a lot of questions to try and help them clarify these things.

Q7: What advice would you give college students who are interested in exploring a career in psychology or psychotherapy?
Earn that degree, and beyond that, continue your schooling. If you are interested in any career that involves psychology, spend time with people. People are endlessly interesting. Talk to people who are different than you. See if you can understand another person's worldview so that it really makes sense to you. If you enjoy doing these things, then you might enjoy a career similar to the one I've chosen.

C CREATE a Career Outlook

PSYCHOLOGIST

Have you ever considered a career as a psychologist or counselor? Here are some facts about this career to consider and some questions about yourself to ponder.

Facts to Consider

Academic preparation required: a master's or doctoral degree

Future workforce demand: growth projected at a faster rate than the average job category through 2014, particularly for highly trained specialists

Work environment: Four of ten psychologists are self-employed; the rest work in clinics, hospitals, schools, nonprofit agencies, or industrial settings

Most common psychological type preferences: extraverted (and to a lesser extent, introverted), intuitive, feeling, perceiving[6]

Essential skills: listening, communicating, analyzing, rapport building (for clinical psychologists), and research and statistical skills (for experimental psychologists)

Questions to Ponder

1. Do you have (or could you acquire) the skills this career requires?
2. What would you find most satisfying about this type of career?
3. What would you find most challenging about this type of career?
4. Are you interested in a career like this? Why or why not?

For more information, see U.S. Department of Labor, Bureau of Labor Statistics, *Occupational Outlook Handbook, 2006–2007 Edition.*[7]

For more career activities online, go to http://www.academic.cengage.com/collegesuccess/staley to do the Team Career exercises.

5. **Fill your mind with messages about the attitude you want to have.** The old adage, "garbage in, garbage out," applies to attitudes as well. There are numerous books, CDs, and films that offer positive, motivating messages. Paying attention to role models whose traits you admire is also a great way to bolster your outlook.

6. **Remember that negative experiences can be great teachers.** Have you ever watched someone do something so badly that you've said to yourself, "I'm never going to do that! I'm going to do it differently!"? You can also choose to learn from your own mistakes and setbacks. They all offer some sort of lesson—be it greater clarity, personal growth, or a new vision—even if it takes a bit of distance from the event to see what you can learn. It's hard to believe, but Michael Jordan was cut from his high school basketball team. He once observed, "I've failed over and over again in my life. That is why I succeed."

7. **Offer help without expecting something in return.** Give freely of yourself, with no expectations of *quid pro quo*, and life will reward you in unexpected ways— not the least of which is a positive outlook. Offer to help someone study for a test or suggest that a classmate practice a presentation for class in front of you, for example. Engage in random acts of kindness; it'll do amazing things for your attitude.

8. **Acknowledge your blessings.** Taking time at the end of each day to recognize and feel gratitude for the blessings in your life—no matter how large or small—is a great way to amplify a positive attitude.

Activity Option Divide students up so that at least two students are assigned to each of the eight ways to adjust attitude. Ask students to describe a real-life example related to the numbered point they have been assigned.

Statements That Ought to Be Outlawed in College ... and Why

Since words reflect attitudes (and help shape them), listen for statements like these escaping from your mouth. They can negatively affect your attitude and therefore your learning:

> ➤ **"I thought college classes would be more interesting than they are."** Some students, especially those who didn't find high school classes particularly interesting, expect something different in college. *Interesting* is in the mind of the beholder. You may not, but your professors think chemistry, calculus, and psychology are the most interesting things on the planet. It's up to *you* to generate your own enthusiasm for learning, rather than expecting your instructors to do it for you. Not all college classes will be naturally interesting to you; you'll have your favorites. But you'll be much more successful if you decide to learn all you can, regardless of the wow factor.

> ➤ **"I didn't learn a thing in that class."** This statement may say more about you than it does about the quality of the instructor, teaching assistant, or course content. Actively search for what you can take away from a class, even if it didn't quite meet your expectations. When you play the blame game, you lose.

> ➤ **"The textbook is really dull. Why bother reading it?"** This question is about personal responsibility, too. Hey, it's your college experience. If you choose

not to learn because the written material doesn't meet your entertainment criteria, how sad is that?

> "The professor is soooo-o-o boring." Again—it's your choice. Life isn't all Comedy Central. In your career, you'll be interacting with an array of personalities, so it's good to begin now to appreciate that different people communicate differently. Get beneath the surface and you'll be amazed at how much you can learn.

> "Why do I have to take this required course? What's the point?" The point is to broaden your horizons, expand your skills as a critical thinker, and become a lifelong scholar. Care enough to give yourself every opportunity to do your best. And, yes, every class, every situation in life, is an opportunity. You're worth it.[8]

EXERCISE 1.3 Your Academic Autobiography

Write a three-page academic autobiography describing your preparation for college. Describe the quality of your primary, middle, and high school learning experiences. Did they prepare you for what you're experiencing now in college? What do you think will be your strengths and weaknesses as a college student? Look back at your academic self throughout your schooling and look ahead to the kind of student you're planning to be in college, then write your academic autobiography. Or as an alternative, create a presentation answering these questions for your classmates.

Teachable Moment Choosing an alternative to writing can also indicate the student's preferred way of communicating. Early in the semester it is good to give students choices. Students who choose to write their academic autobiography are probably somewhat comfortable with writing. Other students might be more comfortable presenting. One way to tap into another learning strength is to allow students to draw or use clip art to describe their learning paths. Students can present this to the class, or simply turn it in.

Ability versus Effort: What's More Important?

Successful people have several things in common: they love learning, seek challenges, value effort, and persevere even when things become difficult.[9] They demonstrate both ability and effort. These two things are the basic requirements for success. College is about both.

We could focus on ability, but almost all of your classmates have considerable ability, right? That's why they're in college. In one recent study, 47 percent of college freshmen reported that they graduated from high school with an A average.[10] Nearly half!

That said, think about some of the possible combinations of ability and effort. If you have high ability and exert great effort, you'll most likely succeed. If you have high ability and exert little effort, and still succeed, you've just proved how smart you must be! But if you have high ability and exert little

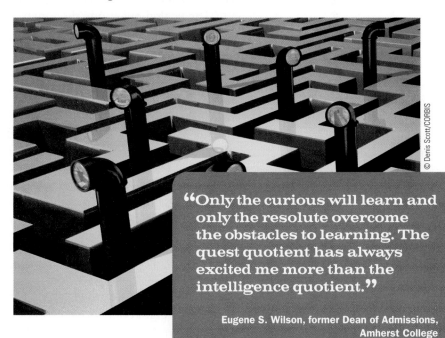

© Denis Scott/CORBIS

"Only the curious will learn and only the resolute overcome the obstacles to learning. The quest quotient has always excited me more than the intelligence quotient."

Eugene S. Wilson, former Dean of Admissions, Amherst College

Emotional Intelligence (EI) Research In a study by James Flynn in *Asian-American Achievement Beyond I.Q.* (1991), Flynn reports that Asian-American students with similar IQs to their Caucasian counterparts do better in school. He attributes this to higher motivation and persistence. In part, effort may be a culturally derived variable.

effort and fail, you can always claim you didn't have the time to invest or you didn't care, right? You can always maintain that you could have done well if you'd tried harder. "I could have been another J. K. Rowling; I'm a great writer." If you had really tried for that kind of success, you wouldn't have been able to say that. That's a dangerous strategy, one that's called "self-handicapping."[11] Some college students actually consciously or unconsciously apply this strategy. They exert little effort, perhaps because they have no confidence in themselves or because they fear failure, and then they rationalize when they don't do well.

CHALLENGE → REACTION

What is intelligence? Are people born with a certain amount? Or can it be cultivated through learning? Using the following scale, indicate the extent to which you agree or disagree with each of the following statements by writing the number that corresponds to your opinion in the space next to each statement. There are no right or wrong answers.

Theories of Intelligence Scale

1	2	3	4	5	6
Strongly Agree	Mostly Agree	Agree	Disagree	Mostly Disagree	Strongly Disagree

_____ 1. You have a certain amount of intelligence, and you can't really do much to change it.

_____ 2. You can learn new things, but you can't really change your basic intelligence.

_____ 3. You can always substantially change how intelligent you are.

_____ 4. No matter how much intelligence you have, you can always change it quite a bit.

Research shows that what you *believe* about your own intelligence—your *mindset*—can make a difference in how successful you'll be in college. At first glance this statement seems absurd. After all, you're either smart or you're not, right? Wrong.

The scaled questions demonstrate that there are two basic ways to define intelligence. Some of us are *performers*, who agree with statements 1 and 2, while others of us are *learners*, who agree more with statements 3 and 4. *Performers* believe that intelligence is a fixed trait that cannot be changed. From the moment you're born, you have a certain amount of intelligence that's been allotted to you, and that's that. *Learners*, on the other hand, believe you can grow your intelligence if you capitalize on opportunities to learn. Whenever you tackle a tough challenge, you learn from it. The more you learn, the more intelligent you can become. Understanding which view of intelligence you endorse will make a difference in how you approach your college classes, as well as the outcomes—both positive and negative—that you'll achieve.

These two contrasting views of intelligence have been revealed through the research of Dr. Carol Dweck of Stanford University, her graduate students, and other social psychologists. Some of their original work began with children, who were first asked to agree or disagree with questions similar to those you just answered to determine which view of intelligence they held. Afterward, they were given eight conceptual problems to solve, problems that were appropriate for their grade level. As they worked on the problems, the researchers asked them to talk aloud about whatever was on their minds, even if it was unrelated to the actual problems. After they had solved the first eight problems success-fully, they were given four additional problems that were far too difficult for them to solve. This is where their views about the nature of intelligence made a difference.

As they tried to tackle the problems that were too difficult for them, the *performers* talked about feeling helpless. They became discouraged and anxious, forgot that they had solved the first eight problems successfully, and told themselves they weren't very smart. The *learners*, on the other hand, coached themselves on how to do better, remained optimistic, and actually improved their problem-solving strategies. They wanted to master what they were working on. To *learners*, academic challenges were opportunities for growth; to *performers* academic challenges were threats that might reveal their deficiencies. Performance is about measuring ability, "trying to convince your-self and others that you have a royal flush when you're secretly worried it's a pair of tens."[12] Learning is about investing the effort required to master new things: "Why waste time proving over and over how great you are, when you could be getting better?"[13]

Sometimes students who are highly confident are *performers*. They've always been told they're smart, and they have an image to protect. They become focused on the possibility of failure, which they need to avoid at all costs, instead of develop-ing strategies to help them succeed. If you believe you only have a certain amount of intelligence, whether you realize it or not, your goal in college may be to prove you have enough. When you come to a tough course, you think, "If I have to work hard at this, I must not be very good at it." But if you believe you can develop your intelligence through learning, your goal will be to increase your ability: "If I have to work hard at this, eventually I'll become *very* good at it." Note that the research is not claiming that everyone is equally intelligent. That's not true, but what is true is that for any given individual, intellectual capacity can be increased with effort and guidance. Think of college as your opportunity to do that. According to Dweck, just learning about the importance of mindset can make a difference.

Let's admit it: We live in a performance-based society. Getting good grades is what it's all about, we're told. We all want to do well, look good, appear smart, and impress others. Did your previous schooling emphasize the performance mindset? Do you come from a family that overemphasizes grades (like Gloria's in the opening "FOCUS Challenge Case")? Are you from an underrepresented population on campus and because of this you feel performance pressure to succeed? That's normal, but your view of intelligence can be changed, and changing it may be your key to academic success.

There is evidence that students who are taught the value of a learning mindset over a performance mindset can actually achieve more than students who don't.[14] In one study, college students' views of intelligence predicted the goals students valued in college. *Performers* were more likely to want to give up in challenging situations; learners wanted to try harder. Over their years at the university, *perform-ers*, who had originally entered with higher SAT scores, did not perform better than *learners*, and they had lower self-esteem.[15] In one new study that measured the elec-trical activity in college students' brains as they performed a difficult task, brain activity showed that *performers* cared most about whether their answers were right or wrong, while *learners* were interested in follow-up information they could learn from.[16] Yet another new study showed that *learners* are more likely to buckle down

Teachable Moment Consider that parents may play a role in the development of performers versus learners; however, instructors can, too. Ask students to describe what they want from professors to help them become learners versus performers. What if professors can't change? What can the students do? This discussion should lead to the fact that despite how the professor may teach, it is still ultimately up to the student to be a learner.

Emotional Intelligence (EI) Research Daniel Goleman tells us in *Emotional Intelligence* that "whether it be in controlling impulse and putting off gratification, regulating our moods so that they facilitate rather than impede thinking, motivating ourselves to persist and try, try again in the face of setbacks, or finding ways to enter flow and so perform more effectively—all speak to the power of emotion to guide effective effort" (95).

academically, even when they feel depressed.[17] It's clear: believing you're a *learner* provides advantages in motivation, achievement, enjoyment, and commitment.

Regardless of what you believe about your precise intelligence level, the fact is this: *intelligence can be cultivated through learning.* And people's theories about their intelligence levels can be shifted.

Sensitive Situation Many of the "Insight → Action" examples will be personal. See if there are a few students in the class willing to share one of their examples. Keep in mind that not all students want to share, as some will use this as self-assessment and create an action plan that is private. Consider using "Insight → Action" boxes as journal prompts so that students could keep this private, just between the two of you.

Activity Option Ask students to call out loud the names of their most challenging courses. Make a list of the top five most challenging courses in the group. Ask for suggestions on how the C-Factors and intrinsic motivation apply. Have students share what they plan to do to be motivated in these challenge courses. Remind students that *plan* and *follow-through* are the key words. Success (all A's) doesn't just happen.

INSIGHT → ACTION

1. Think of a time in your past when you faced a challenge in school—either with academics or co-curricular activities—that overwhelmed you to the point where you chose not to see the challenge through. Describe the challenge and how you avoided it. How might that experience have ended differently for you if you had adopted a learning perspective toward it? What would you have gained by mastering the challenge?

2. Think of a time in your past when you faced a challenge in school that you saw through to completion. Describe the challenge and how it made you feel to master the task at hand. What temptations to quit did you face along the way? How would you have felt if you hadn't conquered that particular challenge?

3. What actions can you take to become more of a *learner* and less of a *performer*, particularly in your most challenging class this term?

C CONTROL Your Learning

YOUR TOUGHEST CLASS

Think about all the courses you're enrolled in this term. Use the following matrix to analyze your C-Factors for these courses. Describe each course in terms of its *challenge* level, your *curiosity* about the subject, how much *control* you believe you have to succeed, and the way each class impacts your *career outlook*. (Keep in mind that many first-year introductory courses are broad-based. They may seem less directly related to your career than later classes in your major, but it's still important to consider what skills you can gain that will lead to a more successful career.) Once you've determined the levels of challenge, curiosity, control, and career outlook you perceive in your courses, remember that it's *your* responsibility to adjust them. Instructors can't always meet the differing requirements of each student in a class. But *you* can make your own adjustments to gain as much as possible from each of your courses. Take a look at the following example, assess your C-Factors in each of your classes, and consider the adjustments you need to make.

Course Title	Challenge	Curiosity	Control	Career Outlook	Adjustments Required
Composition	Very High: never been good at writing	Very Low: had a discouraging teacher in H.S.	Moderate: probably higher than it feels to me	Will need to know how to write in any job	Need to spend more time pre-writing and going to the campus Writing Center for help

Which of the classes you listed will be your most challenging this term? What is the relationship between the four C-Factors and your intrinsic motivation to learn in each one of these courses? What can you do to increase your intrinsic motivation and become more successful?

What Drives You?
Values, Dreams, and Goals

CHALLENGE → REACTION

What are your core values? Review the following list and check off the items that you value. Don't spend too much time thinking about each one; just go with your initial gut reaction. For each item, ask yourself "Is this something that's important to me?"

_____ Health	_____ Wealth	_____ Financial wealth
_____ Fitness/Physical strength	_____ Independence	_____ Commitment
_____ Loyalty	_____ Honesty	_____ Compassion
_____ Academic achievement	_____ Children	_____ Leisure time
_____ Success	_____ Leadership	_____ Balance
_____ Happiness	_____ Family	_____ Friendship
_____ Social life	_____ Marriage/Partnership	_____ Recognition
_____ Athletics	_____ Spirituality	_____ Status
_____ Creativity	_____ Variety	_____ Wisdom
_____ Meaningful work	_____ Challenge	_____ Time spent alone
_____ Adventure	_____ Personal growth	_____ Other (list here)

Now review all of the items you checked off and circle the five that are most important to you at this point in your life. Then rank them by putting a number next to each of the five circled values with number one as your top priority. Finally, take stock. Is this the person you want to be? Is there anything about your values that you would like to change? If so, what's keeping you from making this change?

Teachable moment Students need to understand that individuals have different values. However, if you ask members of the class to list their top five values, you should find some similarities. Research shows that attaining great wealth is important to today's students. Students should discuss why they think this is important to them. What might they be missing?

Before tackling the big questions about what you want to create with your life, it's important to first take a close look in the mirror. Who are you? What makes you tick? What do you value? What are your goals? Where will your dreams take you?

Values at the Core

One way to gain some insights about who you are is to look at your core values. So what do you value in life? By taking time to examine your personal values, managing your life will become easier and make more sense. Values can be intangible concepts such as love or respect, or tangible things such as family or money, and understanding how they motivate you isn't as simple as it might seem. Values can change as you go through life. For example, if you're single now, you may value the freedom to meet a variety of potential romantic partners. Just get to know people and have fun, that's all. Later, however, you may want a committed relationship because you value companionship and stability more than you used to. For this reason, it's important to reassess your values from time to time and reprioritize them.

> **"Knowing others is intelligence; knowing yourself is true wisdom. Mastering others is strength; mastering yourself is true power."**
>
> Lao Tzu, Taoist philosopher

Another complicating factor is that values can conflict with one another. Suppose that you value honesty and kindness, and you are at a party and a friend asks you what you think of her new hair color. You honestly think it's hideous, but telling her so would hurt her feelings, thus violating your value of being kind. How do you respond? That would depend on which value is a higher priority for you. You have to make an on-the-spot decision about which value to tap. Once you define your values, however, they can serve as guideposts in helping you make choices every day—everything from the insignificant day-to-day choices to more significant ones such as which major to pursue in college.

In the Challenge → Reaction → Insight → Action system, knowing your values in life is key to understanding your reaction. Once you've defined your values, you can use them in your daily life to guide your actions. For example, if academic achievement is one of your top values, the next time you have the urge to cut class, consider the impact that choice would have on your value system. There is a great inner satisfaction that comes from living a life tied to core values.

Dreams versus Goals

Do you agree or disagree with this statement: "I can be anything I want to be"? If you are like most students, people have probably told you this frequently. Your parents and teachers all want you to have positive self-esteem, and certainly there are many career options available today. But is it true? Can you be *anything* you want to be? What's the difference between a dream and a goal?

As a college student, you may dream of being a famous doctor or a famous athlete or just plain famous. That's the beauty of dreams—you can imagine yourself in any career, any circumstances. When you're dreaming, you don't even have to play by the rules of reality. Dreams are fantasy-based—*you* in a perfect world. But when it's time to come back to reality, you discover that there are, in fact, rules. You may have dreamed of becoming a top-earning NBA player or a top fashion model when you were a child, but you have grown up to be the same height as Uncle Al or Aunt Sue—and that's not tall enough.

Activity Option Ask students to answer the following question: "If I could spend one day with someone who has died, who would it be?" Have students share their choice and explain why. This activity demonstrates what values really seem to be important to that individual. Suggest reading Mitch Albom's book *For One More Day* (2006).

Chapter Crossover Students often hear the term *reality check*. Reality testing is an important EI skill (Chapter 11), and Gloria's lack of realism was evident in the FOCUS Challenge Case when she described how much she could work while going to school. Ask students to take a quick reality check. Ask them, "Can you be anything you want to be?"

© Patrick Giardino/CORBIS

"Self-knowledge is far more important than self-confidence."

Simon Cowell, *American Idol* judge, from *I Don't Mean to Be Rude, But . . .*

Dreams alone are not enough when it comes to "creating the future." As professional life coach Diana Robinson says, "A dream is a goal without legs." And without legs, that goal is going nowhere. Dreaming is the first step to creating the future you want, but making dreams come true requires planning and hard work. Gloria Gonzales wanted to become a fashion designer because she liked clothes and people always told her she looked good. As she continues through college, however, she will come to understand the nuts and bolts of the fashion design business. Perhaps she'll learn that famous fashion designer Yves Saint Laurent got his first fashion designer job with Christian Dior after winning an International Wool Secretariat design competition. The fashion industry might be challenging to break into, but that doesn't mean she should abandon her dream. Instead, she must realize that dreams and goals are not the same thing. She must find a reality-based path to help her turn her dreams into goals. Just dreaming isn't enough.

Dreams are exciting; you can let your imagination run wild. Goals are real; you must work out how to actually achieve your dreams. Goal setting is an important part of the life management skills this book will help you develop. Your goals may not seem at all clear to you right now, but the important thing is to learn that there's a right way and a wrong way to go about goal setting. The best way to ensure that the goals you set will serve you well is to make sure you *FOCUS*. Here's a brief overview of what that means.

F Fit. Your goal must fit your values, your character, and who you are as a person. Goals that conflict with any of these things will not only be difficult to accomplish, but they just won't work. If your goal is to become a writer for a travel magazine because you love adventure, but you have a fear of flying, you're in trouble.

O Ownership. You must own your goals. In other words, you've got to see it, taste it, want it! It must be your goal, not someone else's goal for you. Ask yourself: Does the thought of achieving this goal get me fired up? Do I genuinely own this goal or do I feel I ought to have this goal because it sounds good or pleases someone else?

C Concreteness. For any goal to be effective, it must be real. In other words, you must be able to describe your goal—and it's ultimate outcome—in complete and specific detail, including your deadline for accomplishing it. "To run a mile in less than six minutes by March 4th" is much more concrete than "to eventually run faster." The more concrete, the better.

U Usefulness. Goals must have utility, or usefulness. They must serve a purpose, and that purpose should be tied to your long-term vision of the person you want to become. For example, if you want to work for an international corporation some day, it would be useful to begin studying a foreign language now.

S Stretch. In the business world, people talk about stretch goals. These are goals that require employees to stretch beyond their predictable limits to achieve something more challenging. The key to stretching is to find a good balance between being realistic and being challenged. Realistic goals are those whose outcomes are within your control. (Winning the lottery, for example, is beyond your control, and therefore not a very realistic goal.) Goals must be based in reality, but also offer you a chance to grow beyond the person you currently are.

Goals should be set for different time frames in your life to include both short- and long-term goals. Once your long-term goals are set (though they may shift over time as *you* shift over time), you will then want to set some short-term goals, which act as intermediate steps to achieving your long-term goals.

Long-Term Goals	Short-Term Goals
What do I want to accomplish…	What do I want to accomplish…
In my lifetime?	This year?
In the next twenty years?	This month?
In the next ten years?	This week?
In the next three to five years?	Today?

Activity Option Put students in groups of three or four and assign each group two letters of the word *FOCUS*. Ask students to think of successful student behaviors that begin with the letters they are assigned. Ask them how these behaviors connect to goal-setting.

Activity Option Have students write a letter to themselves, their parents, loved ones, or a friend listing their goals for the semester and what they will do to meet them. Provide envelopes for students and seal their letters and return these to your students at the end of the term to see if they met their goals. Have them write a paragraph about why they did or did not meet their goals upon return of the envelopes.

INSIGHT ⟶ ACTION

1. Briefly describe one of your dreams for the future.

2. Now list several goals that, when accomplished, would help you create the dream you listed in question 1. First think of long-term goals, followed by short-term goals. Next to each goal, write the time frame (that is, 10 years, 3–5 years, within 1 year, within a month, and so on).

3. Select one of your goals listed. Run it through a quick check to ensure that it's a FOCUS goal. Circle the appropriate answer:

   - Does this goal **fit** me?   Yes   No

   - Do I really want this goal?
     Do I **own** it?   Yes   No

   - Does my goal have **concrete** details and deadlines?   Yes   No

   - Is this goal **useful** to me?
     Does it serve a purpose?   Yes   No

   - Does this goal **stretch** me?
     Is it challenging, yet achievable?   Yes   No

   If you answered "no" to any of the previous questions, your goal needs to be more *FOCUS*ed.

4. Pick one of the short-term goals from your list in question 2. What could you do today to work toward accomplishing that goal? List one to three to-do items.

5. Pick one of the items on your to-do list from question 4 and do it now. It may be something seemingly insignificant, or you may be tempted to tell yourself that you could easily do it tomorrow. But doing it today—*now*—will not only put you one step closer to your dream, but it will help you accomplish something concrete.

Digital Vision/Getty Images

"What you get by achieving your goals is not as important as what you become by achieving your goals."

Zig Ziglar, Motivational speaker, writer, and trainer

KNOW THYSELF!
HOW HARD CAN THAT BE?

Knowing yourself doesn't sound like much of a challenge, does it? After all, you've lived with yourself for a long time. You know every freckle, every dimple, every quirk. Or do you?

Socrates advised many centuries ago, "Know thyself." But David Dunning, professor of psychology at Cornell University and author of *Self-Insight: Roadblocks and Detours on the Path to Knowing Thyself* (2005), says that most of us really don't know ourselves as well as we think we do. In fact, when we're asked to predict how well we'll do at something, and that prediction is compared to our actual performance afterward, most of us are off base. In one study, college students were given a pop quiz to test their logical reasoning skills. After they finished, they were asked to compare their performance with that of their peers, and to predict the number of items they got right.

Dunning and his research colleague, Justin Kruger, split the test-takers into four quarters: students who performed in the bottom quarter, the second, third, and top quarter. Then they compared how students actually performed with how well they thought they'd done.

In general, students who thought they did best often performed in the bottom quarter, and students with the highest scores sometimes underestimated their performance. Take a look at Figure 1.2, which summarizes the typical pattern uncovered in Dunning's research to date. In particular, compare participants in the bottom quarter with those in the top one, and you'll see that the participants who did the worst were the ones who were the most optimistic!

To be fair, when it comes to overestimating abilities, college students aren't the only culprits. Elderly people see themselves as better drivers than others their age. Grocery store cashiers see themselves as better than other cashiers at spotting underage alcohol purchasers. Bungee jumpers think they're less likely to plummet than the average bungee jumper.

If Dunning's research is right, why is this so? Why aren't we all right on the mark? Specifically, why can't people tell when they're not doing a good job? One

hypothesis Dunning offers is that people can't be expected to recognize when they're not performing adequately. Because they *don't* know how to do what they're doing (and therefore they aren't doing it well), they're simply not in a position to know. The skills they need in order to *do* a good job are the exact same skills they need to *recognize* whether they are doing a good job. So they hope for the best. And while optimism isn't a bad thing—in fact, it's generally a good thing—realism is critical, too, in college and in life.

That's why it's important to seek input from your instructors about the quality of your work. Assessing it is their job! Work with other students so that you can observe their skill levels compared with your own. Learn from self-assessment instruments. Use your classes as an opportunity to gather all the self-knowledge you can. Rather than simply hoping for the best, do all you can to get to know yourself better and give college your best shot.

Figure 1.2

Typical Relationship Found Between Perceived and Actual Performance

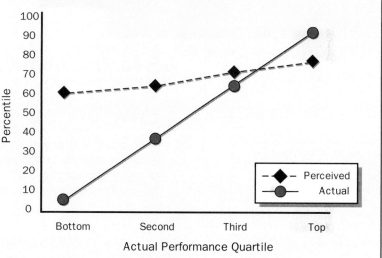

Source: D. Dunning. (2005). *Self-Insight: Roadblocks and Detours on the Path to Knowing Thyself.* New York: Psychology Press, p. 18.

College Success: You Make the Call

What does it mean to succeed? Actually, success is difficult to define, and different people define success differently. Right now in college, you may think of success in terms of your future income. But is success simply about material wealth? Is it about fame? Status?

According to motivational author Robert Collier, "Success is the sum of small efforts, repeated day in and day out." Perhaps to you, success is somewhere off in the distant future, and it happens more or less suddenly, like winning the lottery. Actually, success begins right now. You should be the one to define what success will look like in your life, but generally, success is *setting out to do something that's personally meaningful, and then being fully engaged while*

Emotional Intelligence (EI) Research In 1988, Olympic swimmer Matt Biondi lost his first race only to win the gold in the next five. Martin Seligman, a psychologist from the University of Pennsylvania, had tested Biondi earlier that year and discovered that even when given negative feedback, Biondi went on to perform well. Seligman defines optimism by the way people describe their successes and failures.

© Grace/zefa/CORBIS

> **"We are what we repeatedly do. Excellence, then, is not an act, but a habit."**
>
> **Aristotle, Greek philosopher (384–322 B.C.)**

doing it. It's that simple. And it applies to your college experience as well. It starts now.

In order to understand your own definition of success in college, first you need to ask yourself why you're here. Why *did* you come—or return—to college, anyway? Do you want to develop into a more interesting, well-rounded, educated human being? Are you working toward a degree that leads to a specific career? Do you have children and want an education in order give them a better life? Did your mom or dad tell you that college wasn't optional?

We will assume that part of your definition of succeeding in college includes *graduating* from college. This book will provide you with an honest look at what that takes, including numerous opportunities to assess yourself in these areas. It will also offer an array of tools you can use throughout your college career and in your life beyond college.

Graduating from College: What It Takes

Teachable Moment Students should take a moment to reflect and honestly answer the question "why did I come to college?" Remind students that there is a strong connection between reasons for coming to college and success. If the reason for coming to college is to have fun and meet people, then that reason alone is not enough. The most successful students are those who enjoy college *and* are academically motivated.

CHALLENGE ⊖ REACTION

Many factors (besides past grades and entrance test scores) impact your success in college. Read down this list and ask yourself how you measure up in each of these areas. Mark an honest response from 1 to 7. If you're just beginning college and you're unsure about how you'll do, use your habits in the past to gauge your responses.

1	2	3	4	5	6	7
NO!	NO	No	Maybe/Sometimes	Yes	YES	YES!

_____ **Ability to adapt.** Are you the type of person who thrives in new environments? Do you enjoy meeting new classmates, new professors, and new counselors? In general, do you like—and do well—with change?

_____ **Attitude.** Do you have a positive attitude toward your education? Do you want to be here? Are you motivated to learn and grow? Are you confident that you can learn and do well in school? Are you willing to do the hard work involved in earning a college degree? Are you respectful of your instructors, your fellow students, and yourself?

_____ **Maturity.** Are you emotionally mature? Are you willing to display the level of maturity required to manage your college education over time and earn a degree?

_____ **Class attendance.** Do you have a good track record of attending class in the past? Are you willing to commit to attending each of your college classes regularly, regardless of whether or not you actually *feel* like attending on a particular day? Did you know that class attendance is a major predictor of college success?

_____ **Study Habits.** Do you spend enough time studying? Do you study until you understand the material or do you simply study until you're out of time or need to move on to the next thing? Are you willing to make the necessary commitment to time spent studying?

_____ **Note-taking skills.** Note-taking is not an ability we're born with. It's a skill that must be learned and can be taught to just about anyone. Regardless of the fact that you may not be an auditory learner, many of your professors will expect you to learn through lectures. How complete and comprehensive are your notes? Do you work with them *after* class (color-coding, retyping, and so on)? Do you work with your notes so that they're useful aids at exam time?

_____ **Academic support services.** Do you know what resources are available on campus to help you with academic issues? Have you visited any offices that provide support services on your campus to familiarize yourself with them? Are you willing to use a tutor to help with a particular course that overwhelms you?

_____ **Personal support system.** How strong is your personal support system? Who cares about your success in college? Do you have parents, siblings, and friends who support you, encourage you, and ask how you're doing? How often do you see or e-mail these people? How willing are you to make friends on campus who also value academic success?

_____ **Faculty connections.** Do you plan to interact with your instructors? Are you interested in knowing more about your instructors, their backgrounds, and their academic interests beyond the particular class you're taking with them? Are you willing to visit your instructors during their office hours if you are having difficulty with a class? Would you consider finding a mentor among your instructors?

_____ **Campus connection.** Are you connected to people and events on your campus? Are you involved in any co-curricular activities in which you interact with others? Do you plan to participate in or attend on-campus events? Sometimes students unknowingly fall prey to the PCP (parking lot, class, parking lot) syndrome. They're only on campus for their classes, and as soon as they get out of class, they're outta there. Believe it or not, connecting to your campus, other students, and your instructors is critical to your success.

_____ **Time management skills.** Are you capable of managing your time effectively so that the important things—not necessarily just the urgent or exciting, fun things—get completed? Have you ever purposefully learned a system of time management? Are you willing to learn these skills? Do you understand that *time* management is really about *energy* management?

_____ **Money management skills.** How good are you at managing your money? Are you currently debt-free aside from any student loans required to attend college? Some students fall into the trap of using their school loans or grants to pay off credit card debt. Or they work far too many hours, which takes time away from their studies and makes academic success difficult to achieve. While managing your money isn't an academic skill, per se, not knowing how to do it can substantially impact your college career.

Now add up your scores on each item for a final tally. While this list isn't exhaustive, these factors are vital to college success. If your score was 60 or higher, you're in good shape. If not, take a close look at the areas that could affect your college success, read more about them in this book, and develop insights that lead to more effective action.

Some students think obtaining a college degree is merely a financial transaction. Think about this analogy: If you want to buy a gallon of milk, you go to the supermarket, select the kind of milk you want—whole milk, two percent, or nonfat—take it to the cashier, slide your debit card, and the milk is yours. Some students think a college education should work the same way. They think if they select the kind of degree they want—sociology, English, or geography— and pay tuition, the degree is theirs. Not so. There's much more to it than that.

Photodisc/Getty Images

"Students' expectations must match reality, they must be challenged, and they must make connections with their teachers and their peers."

Dr. Vincent Tinto, expert on higher education

A college education requires more than a financial commitment. It requires you to invest your ability, your intellect, your drive, your effort—and yourself.

Many people falsely assume that the best indicator of whether or not you will graduate from college has to do with the brain matter found between your ears. Wrong! Brains alone—especially brains measured by your high school grade point average or even your SAT or ACT scores—are no guarantees that you'll earn a college degree. What does it take?

Did you notice that none of the things listed in the "Challenge → Reaction" are innate talents that you're simply born with? That's the good news. All of these factors that support your goal of graduating from college are things you can become better at if you are committed to doing so. And in making commitments to improving these factors *now*, you are making a commitment to graduate from college *later*.

INSIGHT → ACTION

1. Why did you choose to attend college? Be as specific as you can in listing the reason(s). Review your list and put an asterisk next to the positive, goal-oriented reasons to attend college.

2. Imagine that you are at the end of your college career and you are successful. What does that look like? Describe in detail what you have accomplished, the person you are, and the journey you're about to embark on as you leave college. What specific actions were required to get where you now are?

The Bad News: Obstacles along the Way

Getting accepted to college is a good thing! You should feel proud. But a major national report indicates that "college attendance in the United States has grown so rapidly over the past four decades that now 75 percent of high school graduates get some postsecondary education within two years of receiving their diplomas. Student aspirations are even loftier, with nearly 90 percent saying they hope to attend college. Older adults, too, have recognized the benefits of college study and account for more than one-third of matriculants [new students].... Possession of a college degree today ... is the passport to most careers, and without it, people can find themselves trapped in unrewarding jobs."[18] While everybody's doing it, or so it seems, not everyone is doing it successfully. Only 28 percent of American adults have college degrees, and nearly one of three Americans in their mid-twenties drops out of college.[19] Gloria Gonzales in the "FOCUS Challenge Case" was going on to college because all her friends were, and everyone expected her to. While these are common reasons, they may not motivate her enough to continue and fulfill her dreams.

Realistically, the distance between getting accepted to college and graduating from college is considerable, and the journey can be both exhilarating and discouraging at times. Of all the college students who began as first-year students in 1992, only two-thirds had graduated eight years later.[20]

Risk factors include working more than thirty hours per week, going to school part-time, being a single parent or having children at home, and being a first-generation college student.[21] The important thing to keep in mind as you think about risk factors is that they alone cannot determine your ultimate level of success. Don't throw in the towel now if you had a child at age sixteen or are working thirty-five hours per week off campus. These factors are presented merely as information to assist you on your journey. They are simply *predictors*—not *determiners*. Only you can determine your outcomes in life, and that includes college.

It's worth taking a close look at these success inhibitors now, rather than becoming a statistic yourself later. Your effort, attitude, and willingness to get any help you need to succeed are all vital. Henry Ford was right: "Whether you think you can or you can't, you're right."

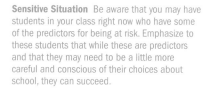

Sensitive Situation Be aware that you may have students in your class right now who have some of the predictors for being at risk. Emphasize to these students that while these are predictors and that they may need to be a little more careful and conscious of their choices about school, they can succeed.

© Mika/zefa/CORBIS

"It's never too late—in fiction or life—to revise."

Nancy Thayer, novelist

The Good News: Benefits at the End of the Road

Regardless of how you choose to define success as it pertains to your college experience, it's a fact that there are plenty of benefits to graduating from a college or university. Here's a quick look at some of them:

1. **Higher Earning Potential.** On average, college graduates earn twice as much income as their peers with only a high school diploma (see Figure 1.3).[22]

2. **Lower Unemployment Rates.** College graduates are more employable than their non-degreed peers. This is especially helpful during cyclic downturns in the economy, when many people—even talented and committed employees—find themselves out of work.

3. **Wisdom.** College students have the opportunity to gain understanding about a broad array of topics—politics, sociology, and current affairs to name a few. A well-educated person knows Sigmund Freud's contribution to psychological theory, Charles Darwin's contribution to evolutionary theory, and Adam Smith's contribution to economic theory. But beyond theories, facts, and dates, a well-educated person knows how to think critically, contribute to society, and manage his or her life.

4. **Insight.** College students have the opportunity to understand themselves better as they participate in the academic, social, and co-curricular opportunities of higher education.

5. **True Scholarship.** College students have the opportunity to become life-long learners. True scholarship is not about making the grade. It's about becoming the best student-learner you can be—inside or outside of the classroom. The value of this benefit is beyond measure and will serve you throughout your life.

Chapter Crossover In Chapter 12 students will have the opportunity to take an in-depth look at majors and careers. They will begin to piece together their values, interests, and skills and see how they might connect to a career they will enjoy.

Figure 1.3

Education, Earnings, and Employment: The Quantifiable Value of a College Degree

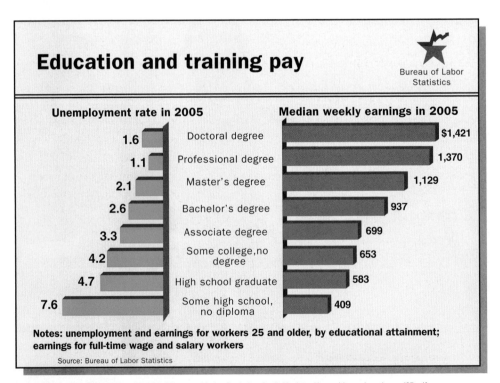

Source: Education and Training Pay. (2005) U.S Bureau of Labor Statistics. Available: http://www.bls.gov/emp/emped05.pdf

6. **Lifelong Friendships.** Many college graduates report that some of their strongest lifelong relationships were formed during their time at college. Choosing to attend college and choosing a specific major puts you in touch with a network of people who share your specific interests.

This Course Has a Proven Track Record

If you're reading this book, there's a good chance you're enrolled in a first-year seminar course. It may be called "Freshman Seminar," "First-Year Forum," "University 101," "First-Year Experience," "College Success," "A Learning Community," or any of a host of other names. These courses are designed to introduce you to college life, familiarize you with your own campus, and help you refine your academic skills. Do they work? According to experts, "In short, the weight of evidence indicates that FYS [first-year seminar] participation has statistically significant and substantial, positive effects on a student's successful transition to college. . . . And on a considerable array of other college experiences known to be related directly and indirectly to bachelor's degree completion."[23] Of course, you have to keep your part of the bargain, but in general, students who participate in first-year seminars complete more credit hours, adjust to college more quickly, become more involved in campus life, view themselves and their skills more accurately, enjoy and appreciate their college experience, and ultimately, graduate. That's what this course is about. Your instructor and your classmates are rooting for you. Now it's up to you!

For more practice online, go to http://www.academic.cengage.com/collegesuccess/staley to take the Challenge Yourself online quizzes.

> "Ability is what you're capable of doing. Motivation determines what you do. Attitude determines how well you do it."
>
> Lou Holtz, former college football coach and ESPN sports analyst

 NOW WHAT DO YOU THINK?

At the beginning of this chapter, Gloria Gonzales, an excited but anxious student, was about to begin her college career. Now after reading this chapter, would you respond differently to any of the questions you answered about the "FOCUS Challenge Case"?

REALITY CHECK

On a scale of 1 to 10, answer the following questions now that you've completed this chapter.

1 = not very/not much/very little/low   10 = very/a lot/very much/high

In hindsight, how much did you *really* know about this subject matter before reading the chapter?

1   2   3   4   5   6   7   8   9   10

How much do you think this information might affect your college success?

1   2   3   4   5   6   7   8   9   10

How much do you think this information might affect your career success after college?

1   2   3   4   5   6   7   8   9   10

How long did it actually take you to complete this chapter (both the reading and writing tasks)? _____ Hour(s) _____ Minutes

Take a minute to compare these answers to your answers from the "Readiness Check" at the beginning of this chapter. What gaps exist between the similar questions? How might these gaps between what you thought before starting the chapter and what you now think after completing the chapter affect how you approach the next chapter in this book?

To download mp3 format audio summaries of this chapter, go to http://www .academic.cengage.com/collegesuccess/staley.

2 Learning about Learning

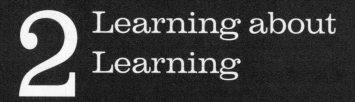

YOU'RE ABOUT TO DISCOVER...

> How learning changes your brain

> How people are intelligent in different ways

> How you learn through your senses

> How your personality affects your learning style

> How to become a more efficient and effective learner

"They know enough who know how to learn."

John Adams, second President of the United States

Tammy Ko

"How depressing!" Tammy Ko whispered under her breath as she walked out of her "Introduction to Criminology" class on a dark, rainy Thursday afternoon. *What's with him, anyway?* she asked herself pointedly about the professor.

Tammy was a first-semester student at a large state campus several hours from her tiny hometown, where she'd been a popular student. If you leafed through her high school yearbook, you'd see Tammy's picture on nearly every page. There Tammy had been a big fish in a small pond, but now it was the other way around.

Even though she found college life at the large state university overwhelming, Tammy was excited about her major, forensic chemistry. The crime shows on TV were her favorites. She watched them all each week. She rationalized how much time it took by thinking of it as career development. The fun was picturing herself as an investigator solving headline cases: "Man Slain, Found in City Park" or "Modern Day 'Jack the Ripper' Terrorizes Las Vegas." She could envision herself hunched over laboratory equipment, testing intently for fibers or DNA, and actually breaking the case.

When she registered for classes, her academic advisor had told her that taking an "Introduction to Criminology" course from the sociology department would be a good idea. "It'll teach you how to think," he'd said, "and it'll give you the background you need to understand the criminal mind. At the end of this class," he said, "you'll know if you really want to pursue a career in forensics." *Maybe it would teach me how to think*, Tammy thought to herself now that the term was underway, *if only I could understand the professor. Forget understanding the criminal mind—I'd just like a glimpse into his!*

Professor Caldwell was quiet and reserved, and he seemed a bit out of touch. He dressed as if he hadn't bought a new article of clothing in as many years as he'd been at the university. In class, he was very articulate, knowledgeable, and organized with his handouts neatly piled on the desk, and he covered each day's material methodically, point by point. Tammy wished he'd venture from his notes occasionally to explore fascinating, related tangents. Tammy had always preferred teachers who created exciting things to do in class over teachers who went completely by the book.

Tammy's biggest complaint about Professor Caldwell was that he only talked about *theories* of criminology. When was he ever going to get to the hands-on part of the course? She couldn't help thinking, *When will we stop talking about theories and start working on real cases—like the ones on all those TV shows?*

To make matters worse, learning from lectures was not Tammy's strong suit. She hadn't done well on the first exam because she'd had to resort to memorizing things that didn't make much sense to her, and her D grade showed it. The exam consisted of one question: "Compare and contrast two theories of criminology discussed in class thus far." Tammy hated essay tests. She was at her best on tests with right or wrong answers, like true-false or multiple-choice questions. Making sense out of spoken words that go by very quickly during a lecture and trying to psych out professors' preferred answers on essay tests were challenges to her.

But her "Introduction to Criminology" class was far from hands-on. In fact, Tammy had noticed that many of her teachers preferred talking about things to doing things. They seemed to take more interest in theories than in the real world. *Too bad*, she thought, *the real world is where exciting things happen.* Although she hated to admit it, sometimes Tammy couldn't wait for college to be over so that she could begin her career in the real world. A few of Tammy's friends had taken Professor Caldwell's classes. "Just try and memorize the stuff; that's all you can do," they'd advised her. Regardless of what they happened to be talking about, somehow the conversation always came around to Professor Caldwell and how impossible it was to learn in his classes.

Sensitive Situation Take advantage of this case study to discuss student behaviors and attitudes in a safe situation. However, keep in mind that some students in the class were exactly like Tammy—a big fish in a small pond. Be sensitive to the Tammy types in the class but, if students are willing, discuss the effects of being in a reversed situation now.

Teachable Moment This is an important time to share how you learn and something about some of the instructors you had in college. There was not always a perfect match, was there? Students need to think about and discuss how they learn and how that might not be a good fit with how some instructors teach. While the same professor may be a great fit for their friend, they may struggle. Remind students that there may not be a choice in instructors and it will be their job to figure out how to adapt to any teaching situation.

WHAT DO **YOU** THINK?

Now that you've read about Tammy Ko, answer the following questions. You may not know all the answers yet, but you'll find out what you know and what you stand to gain by reading this chapter.

1. Why is Tammy having difficulty learning in her "Introduction to Criminology" class?

2. Is Tammy smart? If so, in what ways? What is she particularly good at?

3. What sensory modality does Tammy prefer for taking in information?

4. What do you think Tammy's personality type is? How does her personality type relate to her learning style?

5. How would you describe Professor Caldwell's teaching style? His personality type? How does his personality type relate to his teaching style?

6. What are the differences between Professor Caldwell's teaching style and Tammy's learning style? How do these differences impact Tammy's learning?

7. What should Tammy do to become a better learner in Professor Caldwell's class?

> **"O! this learning, what a thing it is."**
>
> **William Shakespeare**

Before beginning to read this chapter, take two minutes to answer the following questions on a scale of 1 to 10. Your answers will help you assess how ready you are to focus.

1 = not very/not much/very little/low   10 = very/a lot/very much/high

Based on reading the "You're about to discover…" list and skimming this chapter, how much do you think you probably already know about the subject matter?

1   2   3   4   5   6   7   8   9   10

How much do you think this information might affect your college success?

1   2   3   4   5   6   7   8   9   10

How much do you think this information might affect your career success after college?

1   2   3   4   5   6   7   8   9   10

In general, how motivated are you to learn the material in this chapter?

1   2   3   4   5   6   7   8   9   10

This book describes four key factors related to intrinsic, or internal, motivation: curiosity, control, career outlook, and challenge The next four questions relate to these **C-Factors:**

How *curious* are you about the content you expect to read in this chapter?

1   2   3   4   5   6   7   8   9   10

How much *control* do you expect to have over mastering the material in this chapter?

1   2   3   4   5   6   7   8   9   10

How much do you think this chapter might help you develop your *career outlook*?

1   2   3   4   5   6   7   8   9   10

How *challenging* do you expect the material in this chapter to be for you?

1   2   3   4   5   6   7   8   9   10

Before beginning any task, including studying, it's important to check in with yourself to ensure that you're physically, intellectually, and emotionally ready to focus. How ready are you, physically, to focus on this chapter? (Are you rested, feeling well, and so on?)

1   2   3   4   5   6   7   8   9   10

How ready are you, intellectually, to focus on this chapter? (Are you thinking clearly, focused on this course, interested in this subject?)

1   2   3   4   5   6   7   8   9   10

How ready are you, emotionally, to focus on this chapter? (Are you calm, confident, composed?)

1   2   3   4   5   6   7   8   9   10

If your answer to any of the last three questions is below a 5 on the scale, you may need to address the issue you're facing prior to beginning this chapter. For example, if you're hungry, get a quick bite to eat. If you're feeling scattered, take a few moments to settle down and focus.

Finally, how long do you think it will take you to complete this chapter? _____ Hour(s) _____ Minutes

Activity Option Divide the class into two groups: those who consider themselves spontaneous and those who do not, those who like predictability. Ask the two groups to describe the ideal teacher. In addition, ask students to rate Professor Caldwell's teaching on a scale of 1 to 10. After five minutes, ask the groups to read aloud their responses. Generate a list and see if there are differences in their responses and the number they assigned to Professor Caldwell's teaching. There should be differences. Those who like predictability may think that professor Caldwell is okay and describe ideal teachers as organized. The spontaneous students will most likely describe their ideal teacher and Professor Caldwell differently.

Go to the HEAD of the Class: Learning and the Brain

CHALLENGE ⟶ REACTION

Challenge: What is learning?

Reaction: The following statements represent common student views on learning. Think about each statement, and mark it **true** or **false** based on your honest opinion.

_____ 1. Learning is often hard work and really not all that enjoyable.

_____ 2. Memorization and learning are basically the same thing.

_____ 3. The learning done in school is often gone in a few weeks or months.

_____ 4. In college, most learning takes place in class.

_____ 5. Learning is usually the result of listening to an instructor lecture or reading a textbook.

Let's start our exploration of the learning process close to home—in our own heads. What's going on up there, anyway? While your hands are busy manipulating test tubes in chemistry lab, or your eyes are watching your psychology professor's PowerPoint presentation, or your ears are taking in a lecture on American politics, what's your brain up to? The answer? Plenty.

Use It or Lose It

The human brain consists of a complex web of connections between neurons. This web grows in complexity as it incorporates new knowledge. But if the connections are not reinforced frequently, they degenerate. As you learn new things, you work to hardwire these connections, making them less susceptible to degeneration. When your professors repeat portions of the previous week's lecture or assign follow-up homework to practice material covered in class, they're helping you to form connections between neurons through repeated use—or, in other words, to learn. Repetition is vital to learning. You must use and reuse information in order to hardwire it.

American humorist Will Rogers once said, "You know, you've got to exercise your *brain* just like your muscles." He was right. Giving your brain the exercise it needs—now and in your years after college—will help you form connections between neurons that, if you keep using them, will last a lifetime. From a biological point of view, that's what being a lifelong learner means. The age-old advice "use it or lose it" is true when it comes to learning.

Ask Questions and Hardwire Your Connections

Your professors have been studying their disciplines for years, perhaps decades. They have developed extensive hardwired connections between their brain neurons. They are *experts*. Woodrow Wilson once said, "I not only use all the brains I have, but all that I can borrow." Think of college as an ideal time to borrow some excellent brains—your professors'!

By contrast, you are a *novice* to whatever discipline you're studying. You've not yet developed the brain circuitry that your

> **"Learning is not so much an additive process, with new learning simply piling up on top of existing knowledge, as it is an active, dynamic process in which the connections are constantly changing and the structure reformatted."**
>
> K. Patricia Cross, Professor Emerita of Higher Education, University of California, Berkeley

© Darren Winter/CORBIS

❝The art and science of asking questions is the source of all knowledge.❞

Thomas Berger, American novelist

professors have developed. This realization points to a potential problem. Sometimes professors are so familiar with what they already know from years of traveling the same neuron paths that what you're learning for the first time seems obvious to them. Without even realizing it, they can expect what is familiar to them to be obvious to you. Sometimes, it isn't obvious at all. One learning expert says this: "The best learners . . . often make the worst teachers. They are, in a very real sense, perceptually challenged. They cannot imagine what it must be like to struggle to learn something that comes so naturally to them."[1] Think of how challenging it is when you try to teach something that you understand thoroughly to another person who doesn't, like teaching someone who has never used a computer before how to upload an assignment.

Since you're a novice, you may not understand everything your professors say. Ask questions, check, clarify, probe, and persist until you do understand. Sometimes your confusion is not due to a lack of knowledge, but a lack of the *correct* knowledge. You may be getting interference from misinformation or unproductive habits of thinking and learning that have become hardwired in your brain. For example, you may study for a test by doing only one thing—reading and re-reading the textbook. Actually, it's important to be familiar with an array of study tools and choose the ones that work best for you.

Think of it this way. Some of the neural connections you brought with you to college are positive and useful, and some are counterproductive. When you learn, you not only add new connections, but you rewire some old connections. While you're in college, you're under construction![2]

Take Charge and Create the Best Conditions for Learning

Throughout this discussion, we've been talking about internal processes in your brain. *Your* brain, not anyone else's. The bottom line is this: Learning must be *internally initiated*—by you. It can only be *externally encouraged*—by someone else. You're in charge of your own learning. Learning changes your brain.

Let's look at food as an analogy: If learning is a process that is as biological as digestion, then no one can learn for you, in the same way that no one can eat for you. The food in the refrigerator doesn't do you a bit of good unless you walk over, open the door, remove the object of your desire, and devour it. It's there for the taking, but you must make that happen. To carry the analogy further, you eat on a daily basis, right? "No thanks, I ate last week" is a senseless statement. Learning does for your brain what food does for your body. Nourish yourself!

CAN YOU BUILD A BETTER BRAIN?

Don't look now, but you're a very busy person! If you were watching a movie of your life at this moment, what would the scene look like? A cell phone in your hand, a website open on your computer screen, your iPod plugged in, the TV lit up, and this book propped in your lap? So much to do, so little time! There's no way to squeeze more than twenty-four hours into a day. All we can hope for is that some scientist somewhere will develop a way to get a bigger, better brain! But let's face it: brain enhancement surgery won't be available any time soon.

Even so, scientists have been busy recently learning more about this heady organ of ours. Now in new and fascinating ways, the sciences of biology and psychology are joining hands to study the human brain.[3]

A healthy adult brain weighs about two pounds—about the size and weight of a cauliflower—and the more we use this *pliable* organ, the more efficient it gets. A sample the size of a rice kernel contains a million neurons, twenty miles of axons, and ten billion synapses. It's crowded up there—sounds like a headache waiting to happen!

From birth to adolescence, we lay the brain's basic circuitry. Stimulation is critical. When children grow up in isolated, sterile environments, their brains suffer. But when they grow up in fertile, rich environments, their brains thrive. The more our Moms and Dads read to us and play learning games with us, the better. By the time we're eighteen or so, we have an individual "brain-print." Our basic circuitry is hardwired for life. Once that occurs, certain opportunities are lost—forever. It's unlikely that learning a new language now at this time in your life, for example, will ever come as naturally to you as learning your native tongue did.

What's the secret to a healthy brain? When we think of fitness, most of us think from the neck down—strong abs, bulging pecs, and tight glutes. But brain health tops them all. New evidence shows that physical exercise helps our brains shrug off damage, reinforce old neural networks, and forge new ones. Denser neural networks help us process information better, store it, and ultimately result in a smarter brain!

Current research focuses on a protein called BDNF, for brain-derived neurotrophic factor. BDNF, which helps nerve cells in our brains grow and connect, is important for development in the womb, but it's also important in adult brains. Simply put: it helps us learn. According to researchers, rats that eat a high-calorie, fast-food diet and have a couch-potato lifestyle have less BDNF in their brains. Omega-3 fatty acids found in fish normalize BDNF levels and counteract learning disabilities in rats with brain injuries. Scientists are working to see if the same thing may be true for humans.[4]

"Exercise your brain. Nourish it well. And the earlier you start the better," scientists tell us.[5] New research indicates that the goal should be to store up a cognitive reserve. And just how do we do that? Education! People who are less educated have twice the risk of getting Alzheimer's disease in later life, and people who are less educated and have ho-hum, nonchallenging jobs have three to four times the risk. According to researchers, "College seems to pay off well into retirement."[6] It *can* help you build a better brain!

Brain researchers tell us the best state for learning has ten conditions. Read each one, along with some suggestions about how to get there.

1. You're intrinsically motivated (from within yourself) to learn material that is appropriately challenging.

> *Examine where your motivation to learn comes from.* Are you *internally* motivated because you're curious about the subject and want to learn about it or externally motivated to get an A or avoid an F? Can you generate your own internal motivation, rather than relying on external "carrots" and "sticks"? This book has built-in reminders to boost your intrinsic motivation. Use them to your advantage as a learner.

> *Adjust the level of challenge yourself.* If you're too challenged in a class, you become anxious. Make sure you're keeping up with the workload and that you've completed the prerequisites. In many disciplines, you must know the fundamentals before tackling more advanced concepts. If you're not challenged enough, you can become bored and disengaged. Your professor will provide the baseline challenge for everyone in the class. But it's up to you to fine-tune that challenge for yourself. Get extra help if you aren't quite up to the task or bump up the challenge a notch or two if you're ahead of the game so that you're continually motivated to learn.

© Collin Anderson/Blend Images/CORBIS

"When we come to know something, we have performed an act that is as biological as when we digest something."

Henry Plotkin, *Darwin Machines and the Nature of Knowledge* (1994)

2. You're appropriately stressed, but generally relaxed.

> *Assess your stress.* According to researchers, you learn best in a state of *relaxed alertness*, a state of high challenge and low threat.[7] While relaxed alertness may sound like an oxymoron, it can be achieved. No stress at all is what you'd find in a no-brainer course. Some stress is useful; it helps engage you in learning. How stressed are you—and why—when you get to class? Are you overstressed because you've rushed from your last class, cruised the parking lot for half an hour to find a good spot, or because you haven't done the reading and hope you won't be called on? Prepare for class so that you're ready to jump in. Or instead of too much stress, are you understressed because you don't value the course material? Consider how the information can be useful to you—perhaps in ways you've never even thought of. Here's the vital question to ask yourself: How much stress do I need in order to trigger my best effort?

> *Attend to your overall physical state.* Are you taking care of your physical needs so that you can stay alert, keep up with the lecture, and participate in the discussion?

3. You enter into a state researchers call "flow" when you're so totally absorbed in what you're doing that you lose track of everything else.[8]

> *Identify the kinds of learning situations that help you "flow."* Do you get fully engaged by hands-on activities? Do you find that certain courses naturally capture your attention such that you're surprised when it's time for class to end? Understanding your own preferences and style as a learner are key here.

> *Think about what you can do as a learner to get yourself there.* Not all classes or subjects will naturally induce a flow state in you. Nevertheless, ask yourself what *you* can do to focus on learning and exclude distractions. How can you become more engrossed in what you're learning?

4. You're curious about what you're learning, and you look forward to learning it.

> *Get ready to learn by looking back and by looking ahead.* When you're about to cross the street, you must look both ways, right? Keep that image in mind because that's what you should do before each class. What did class consist of last time? Can you predict what it will consist of next time? Considering the big picture can help you fit your learning into a larger whole.

> *Focus on substance, not style.* Part of Tammy's bias against Professor Caldwell focused on his appearance. Despite society's obsession with attractiveness, grooming, and fashion, a student's job is to ask: What can I learn from this person? Passing judgment on physical appearance just encourages you to play the blame game and derails your learning.

5. You're slightly confused, but only for a short time.[9]

> *Use confusion as a motivator.* You may not be getting the lecture's main points because you don't understand new terms used along the way. Look them up early on in the learning process. Ask yourself what background information would help things click—and find out the answers to those questions.

> *Ask questions!* To your professor, questions indicate *interest*, not *idiocy*. Don't be afraid to probe more deeply into the material. As they say, "The only stupid question is the one you don't ask."

6. You search for personal meaning and patterns.

> *Ask yourself: What's in it for me?* Why is knowing this important? How can I use this information in the future? Instead of dismissing material that appears unrelated to your life, try figuring out how it *could* relate. You may be surprised!

> *Think about how courses relate to one another.* How does this new knowledge align with other things you're learning in other courses? Does sociology have anything to do with history? Psychology with economics?

Chapter Crossover Chapter 12 has a good discussion on how courses relate to each other.

7. Your emotions are involved, not just your mind.

> *Evaluate your attitudes and feelings.* Do you like the subject matter? Do you admire the teacher? Remember your high school teacher, Mr. Brown (let's call him), whose class you just couldn't stand? Studying for Mr. Brown's tests was absolute torture. Not every class will be your favorite. That's natural. But if a class turns you off as a learner, instead of allowing your emotions to take over, ask why and whether your feelings are in your best interest.

> *Make a deliberate decision to change negative feelings.* Fortunately, feelings can be changed. Hating a course or disliking a professor can only build resentment and threaten your success. It's possible to do a one-eighty and transform your negative emotions into positive energy.

Emotional Intelligence (EI) Research Emotional self-awareness is the foundation of change. Sometimes it's simply taking a few moments to think about "why am I feeling this way?" A school program for adolescents in New Haven, Connecticut, had posters in the classroom with red, yellow, and green stoplights. A red light encouraged students to calm down, think things through; the yellow light included processing, thinking, and setting goals; and the green light meant to proceed with the best plan.

8. You realize that as a learner you use what you already know in constructing new knowledge.[10]

> *Remember that passive learning is an oxymoron.* When it comes to learning, you are the construction foreman, building on what you already know to construct new knowledge. You're not just memorizing facts someone else wants you to learn. You're a full partner in the learning process!

> *Remind yourself that constructing knowledge takes work.* No one ever built a house by simply sitting back or just hanging out. Builders work hard, but in the end, they have something to show for their efforts. In your college courses, you must identify what you already know and blend new knowledge into the framework you've built in your mind. By constructing new knowledge, you are building yourself into a more sophisticated, more polished, and most certainly, a more educated person.

"Personal participation is the universal principle of knowing."

Michael Polanyi, Hungarian-British scholar (1891–1976)

Activity Option Ask students to work in teams to build a learning tower. Draw a tower consisting of four blocks on the bottom row, three on the third, two on the second, and one at the top. The top block should be labeled "successful student." Students are to fill in what they need to know first before they are successful students. Each row should be a prerequisite to the next row.

Teachable Moment Remind students that they do have choices. They have the choice to focus or allow distractions, to come to class or not, to do the homework or skip it, and to do their best work or not. It's their choice, and choices have consequences.

9. You understand that learning is both conscious and unconscious.

➤ *Watch where your mind goes when it's off duty.* Does learning take place when you're not deliberately trying to learn? Some of what you learn will be immediately obvious to you, and some will dawn on you after class is over, while you're in the shower, or eating lunch, or falling asleep at night, for example. Pay attention to your indirect learning and move it into your line of vision.

➤ *Remember that both kinds of learning are important.* Both conscious learning and unconscious learning count. There are no rules about when and where learning can occur. Capitalize on both.

10. You're given a degree of choice in terms of what you learn, how you do it, and feedback on how you're doing.

➤ *Make the most of the choices you're given.* As Yogi Berra said, "When you come to a fork in the road, take it." College isn't a free-for-all in which you can take any classes you like toward earning a degree. However, which electives you choose will be up to you. Or in a particular course, if your instructor allows you to write a paper or shoot a video, choose the option that will be more motivating for you. When you receive an assignment, select a topic that fires you up. It's easier to generate energy to put toward choices you've made yourself.

➤ *Use feedback to improve, and if feedback is not given, ask for it.* It's possible to get really good at doing something the wrong way. Take

> **"It is what we think we know already that often prevents us from learning."**
>
> **Claude Bernard, French physiologist (1813–1878)**

a golf swing or a swimming stroke, for example. Without someone intervening to give you feedback, it may be difficult to know how to improve. Your instructors will most likely write comments on your assignments to explain their grades. Assessing your work is their job; it's what they must do to help you improve. Take their suggestions to heart and try them out.

All of us are already good learners in some situations. Let's say you're drawn to technology, for example. You're totally engrossed in computers and eagerly learn everything you can from books, classes, and online sources—and you sometimes totally lose yourself in a flow state as you're learning. No one has to force you to practice your technology skills or pick up an issue of *Wired* or *PC World*. You do it because you want to. In this case, you're self-motivated and therefore learning is easy. This chapter provides several different tools to help you understand your own personal profile as a learner so that you can try to learn at your best in *all* situations.

Sensitive Situation Giving or getting feedback can be a very sensitive situation. Instructors have to be aware that some students see feedback as negative and never get beyond that. Always say something positive to students about their work whenever possible, while still providing the constructive criticism they need to improve. Remind students that not every instructor will have positive things to say and that they have to look for what they can learn from the feedback and not concentrate on what is negative. Share experiences that writers have. Writers have many editors, who give plenty of feedback before the final product is complete.

Activity Option Determine whether there are any commonalities among the students' responses to this "Control Your Learning" exercise. Which courses do most students find the easiest? Which are the most difficult? Which are the least interesting? Have students share their responses so they can learn from their peers.

C CONTROL Your Learning

YOUR TOP-TEN LIST

Reflect on yourself as a learner in each of the classes you're enrolled in this term. How optimal are the conditions for learning? How can you adjust the learning environment *yourself* to optimize it? Label the classes you're taking this term, and put checkmarks next to the conditions that are present in each class. Reflect on why you chose to mark these items (or didn't) in each class.

Ten Conditions for Optimal Learning

COURSE NAMES	Class 1:	Class 2:	Class 3:	Class 4:	Class 5:
1. You're intrinsically motivated to learn material that is appropriately challenging.	☐	☐	☐	☐	☐
2. You're appropriately stressed, but generally relaxed.	☐	☐	☐	☐	☐
3. You enter into a state researchers call flow.	☐	☐	☐	☐	☐
4. You're curious about what you're learning, and you look forward to learning it.	☐	☐	☐	☐	☐
5. You're slightly confused, but only for a short time.	☐	☐	☐	☐	☐
6. You search for personal meaning and patterns.	☐	☐	☐	☐	☐
7. Your emotions are involved, not just your mind.	☐	☐	☐	☐	☐
8. You realize that as a learner you use what you already know in constructing new knowledge.	☐	☐	☐	☐	☐
9. You understand that learning is both conscious and unconscious.	☐	☐	☐	☐	☐
10. You're given a degree of choice in terms of what you learn, how you do it, and feedback on how you're doing.	☐	☐	☐	☐	☐

Which course has the most checkmarks? Is this the course that you find easiest? The most engaging? Which course has the least number of checkmarks? Is this the course that you find the most difficult? The least interesting? Considering these ten optimal conditions for learning, what specific actions can you take to enhance your learning in your most challenging class?

PhotoAlto/Getty Images

> **"It is of the utmost importance that we recognize and nurture all of the varied human intelligences, and all of the combinations of intelligences. We are all so different largely because we all have different combinations of intelligences. If we recognize this, I think we will have at least a better chance of dealing appropriately with the many problems that we face in the world."**
>
> **Howard Gardner, Harvard Professor of Psychology**

Multiple Intelligences: *How* Are You Smart?

CHALLENGE ⊖ REACTION

Challenge: Are people smart in different ways? How so?

Reaction: On each line, put checkmarks next to all the statements that best describe you.

Linguistic Intelligence: **The capacity to use language to express what's on your mind and understand others ("word smart")**

_____ I'm a good storyteller.

_____ I enjoy word games, puns, and tongue twisters.

_____ I'd rather listen to the radio than watch TV.

_____ I've recently written something I'm proud of.

_____ I can hear words in my head before I say or write them.

_____ When riding in the car, I sometimes pay more attention to words on billboards than I do to the scenery.

_____ In high school, I did better in English, history, or social studies than I did in math and science.

_____ I enjoy reading.

Logical-Mathematical Intelligence: The capacity to understand cause/effect relationships and to manipulate numbers ("number/reasoning smart")

_____ I can easily do math in my head.

_____ I enjoy brainteasers or puzzles.

_____ I like it when things can be counted or analyzed.

_____ I can easily find logical flaws in what others do or say.

_____ I think most things have rational explanations.

_____ Math and science were my favorite subjects in high school.

_____ I like to put things into categories.

_____ I'm interested in new scientific advances.

Spatial Intelligence: The capacity to represent the world visually or graphically ("picture smart")

_____ I like to take pictures of what I see around me.

_____ I'm sensitive to colors.

_____ My dreams at night are vivid.

_____ I like to doodle or draw.

_____ I'm good at navigating with a map.

_____ I can picture what something will look like before it's finished.

_____ In school, I preferred geometry to algebra.

_____ I often make my point by drawing a picture or diagram.

Bodily-Kinesthetic Intelligence: The capacity to use your whole body or parts of it to solve a problem, make something, or put on a production ("body smart")

_____ I regularly engage in sports or physical activities.

_____ I get fidgety when asked to sit for long periods of time.

_____ I get some of my best ideas while I'm engaged in a physical activity.

_____ I need to practice a skill in order to learn it, rather than just reading or watching a video about it.

_____ I enjoy being a daredevil.

_____ I'm a well-coordinated person.

_____ I like to think through things while I'm doing something else like running or walking.

_____ I like to spend my free time outdoors.

Musical Intelligence: The capacity to think in music, hear patterns and recognize, remember, and perhaps manipulate them ("music smart")

_____ I can tell when a musical note is flat or sharp.

_____ I play a musical instrument.

_____ I often hear music playing in my head.

_____ I can listen to a piece of music once or twice, and then sing it back accurately.

_____ I often sing or hum while working.

_____ I like music playing while I'm doing things.

_____ I'm good at keeping time to a piece of music.

_____ I consider music an important part of my life.

Interpersonal Intelligence: The capacity to understand other people ("people smart")

_____ I prefer group activities to solo activities.

_____ Others think of me as a leader.

_____ I enjoy the challenge of teaching others something I like to do.

_____ I like to get involved in social activities at school, church, or work.

_____ If I have a problem, I'm more likely to get help than tough it out alone.

_____ I feel comfortable in a crowd of people.

_____ I have several close friends.

_____ I'm the sort of person others come to for advice about their problems.

Intrapersonal Intelligence: **The capacity to understand yourself, who you are, and what you can do ("self-smart")**

_____ I like to spend time alone thinking about important questions in life.

_____ I have invested time in learning more about myself.

_____ I consider myself to be independent minded.

_____ I keep a journal of my inner thoughts.

_____ I'd rather spend a weekend alone than at a place with a lot of other people around.

_____ I've thought seriously about starting a business of my own.

_____ I'm realistic about my own strengths and weaknesses.

_____ I have goals for my life that I'm working on.

Naturalistic Intelligence: **The capacity to discriminate between living things and show sensitivity toward the natural world ("nature smart")**

_____ Environmental problems bother me.

_____ In school, I always enjoyed field trips to places in nature or away from class.

_____ I enjoy studying nature, plants, or animals.

_____ I've always done well on projects involving living systems.

_____ I enjoy pets.

_____ I notice signs of wildlife when I'm on a walk or hike.

_____ I can recognize types of plants, trees, rocks, birds, and so on.

_____ I enjoy learning about environmental issues.

Which intelligences have the most checkmarks? Although this is an informal instrument, it can help you think about the concept of multiple intelligences, or MI. _How_ are you smart?

Based on Armstrong, T. (1994). _Multiple intelligences in the classroom._ Alexandria, VA: Association for Supervision and Curriculum Development, pp. 18–20.

Emotional Intelligence (EI) Research In 1986, Daniel Goleman interviewed Howard Gardner about his work on multiple intelligences. Gardner reinforced the notion that emotional and relationship abilities are critical and that "many people with IQs of 160 work for people with IQs of 100. The former have poor intrapersonal (awareness of self) and the latter have a high one."

Activity Option Have students add up the number of checks they had in each category. Then group students according to their highest numbers. Give each group five minutes to share with each other their favorite classes (present or past). Ask students to find common threads in the classes they identified. Have the groups report to the class and discuss what they do to succeed in classes that they don't enjoy as much.

Have you ever noticed that people are smart in different ways? Consider the musical genius of Mozart, who published his first piano pieces at the age of five. Or think about Tiger Woods, who watched his father hit golf balls and mimicked his dad's swing while still in his crib. When he was two, Tiger played golf with comedian and golfer Bob Hope on national television, and he was featured in _Golf Digest_ at the age of five. Not many of us are as musically gifted as Mozart or as physically gifted as Tiger Woods, but we all have strengths. We're all smart in different ways. You may earn top grades in math, and not-so-top grades in English, and your best friend's grades may be just the opposite.

According to Harvard psychologist Howard Gardner, people can be smart in at least eight different ways. Most schools focus on particular types of intelligence, linguistic and logical-mathematical intelligence, reflecting the three R's: reading, writing, and 'rithmetic. But Gardner claims intelligence is actually multifaceted. It can't be measured by traditional one-dimensional standardized IQ tests and represented by a three-digit number: 100 (average), 130+ (gifted), or 150+ (genius). Gardner defines intelligence as "the ability to find and solve problems and create products of value in one or more cultural setting."[11]

So instead of asking the traditional question "How smart are you?" a better question is "How are you smart?" The idea is to find out *how*, and then apply this understanding of yourself to your academic work in order to achieve your best results.

Translate Content into Your Own Intelligences

Do you sometimes wonder why you can't remember things for exams? Some learning experts believe that memory is intelligence-specific. You may have a good memory for people's faces but a bad memory for their names. You may be able to remember the words of a country-western hit but not the dance steps that go with it. The Theory of Multiple Intelligences may explain why.[12]

Examine your own behaviors in class. If your instructors use their linguistic intelligence to teach, as many do, and your intelligences lie elsewhere, can you observe telltale signs of your frustration? Instead of zeroing in on the lecture, do you fidget (bodily-kinesthetic), doodle (spatial), or socialize (interpersonal)? You may need to translate the information into your own personal intelligences, just as you would if your professor speaks French and you speak English. This strategy might have worked for Tammy Ko from the "FOCUS Challenge Case." Professor Caldwell's most developed intelligence is linguistic, whereas Tammy's are bodily-kinesthetic (manipulating test tubes) and interpersonal (interacting with people). Tammy's learning problems are partially due to a case of mismatched intelligences between Professor Caldwell and herself.

Let's say one of your courses this term is "Introduction to Economics," and the current course topic is the Law of Supply and Demand. Basically, "the theory of supply and demand describes how prices vary as a result of a balance between product availability at each price (supply) and the desires of those with purchasing power at each price (demand)."[13] To understand this law, you could read the textbook (linguistic); study mathematical formulas (logical-mathematical); examine charts and graphs (spatial); observe the Law of Supply and Demand in the natural world, through the fluctuating price of gasoline, for example (naturalist); look at the way the Law of Supply and Demand is expressed in your own body, using food as a metaphor (bodily-kinesthetic); reflect on how and when you might be able to afford something you desperately want, like a certain model of car (intrapersonal); or write (or find) a song that helps you understand the law (musical). How about the 1964 Beatles' hit, "[Money] Can't Buy Me Love"?[14] You needn't try all eight ways, but it's intriguing to speculate about various ways to learn that may work for you, rather than assuming you're doomed because your intelligences don't match your instructor's.

Emotional Intelligence (EI) Research There are strong relationships between the kinds of skills people have and success on the job. Research reported by Reuven Bar-On and Richard Handley indicates that the most successful salespeople, for example, are those who have a strong sense of self, are able to assert their ideas, have good empathy, and can relate well with others.

Teachable Moment Think about how you best learn—don't forget to do the "Challenge → Reaction" yourself and share your responses with the class. You might be surprised to realize that you've never thought about this much either. Share your thinking with the class. Tell them what you do as an instructor. You might get a good conversation going about what kind of discussion students should have with instructors about learning, particularly if they have a different style than the instructor.

Use Intelligence-Oriented Study Techniques

What if your strongest intelligence is different from the one through which course material is presented? What can you do about it? Take a look at the following techniques for studying using different intelligences. Tweaking the *way* you study may make a world of difference.

Linguistic --→	1. Rewrite your class notes. 2. Record yourself reading through your class notes and play it as you study. 3. Read the textbook chapter aloud.
Logical Mathematical --→	1. Create hypothetical conceptual problems to solve. 2. Organize chapter or lecture notes into logical flow. 3. Analyze how the textbook chapter is organized and why.
Spatial --→	1. Draw a map that demonstrates your thinking on course material. 2. Illustrate your notes by drawing diagrams and charts. 3. Mark up your textbook to show relationships between concepts.
Bodily–Kinesthetic --→	1. Study course material while engaged in physical activity. 2. Practice skills introduced in class or in the text. 3. Act out a scene based on chapter content.
Musical --→	1. Create musical memory devices by putting words into well-known melodies. 2. Listen to music while you're studying. 3. Sing or hum as you work.
Interpersonal --→	1. Discuss course material with your classmates in class. 2. Organize a study group that meets regularly. 3. Meet a classmate before or after class for coffee and course conversation.
Intrapersonal --→	1. Keep a journal to track your personal reactions to course material. 2. Study alone and engage in internal dialogue about course content. 3. Coach yourself on how to best study for a challenging class.
Naturalistic --→	1. Search for applications of course content in the natural world. 2. Study outside (if weather permits and you can resist distractions). 3. Go to a physical location that exemplifies course material (for example, a park for your geology course).

Activity Option Group students again according to their multiple intelligences (responses from the "Challenge → Reaction" about Multiple Intelligences) and create a sign that indicates the strength of the group (i.e., the intrapersonal group). Assign the groups the task of coming up with careers that a group different from theirs would enjoy and report to the class. Have the group to which the job relates respond to why they would or would not enjoy the job.

Choose a Major and Career That Fit Your Intelligences

If linguistic intelligence isn't your most developed type, but spatial intelligence is, architecture would probably be a much better major for you than English. If you're an adult student returning to school in order to change careers, perhaps the Theory of Multiple Intelligences can help you understand why. For example, perhaps you've always enjoyed working outdoors. But you may have disliked working a construction job that required heavy physical labor (bodily-kinesthetic, a lesser intelligence for you) and returned to school to pursue a degree in geology (naturalist, your most developed intelligence). Take a look at Figure 2.1 for ideas about careers that emphasize particular intelligences and famous achievers in each category.

Intelligence Type	Careers in Intelligences	Well-Known Examples
Linguistic	journalist	Diane Sawyer
	teacher	Your instructor
	lawyer	Lin Wood
	talkshow host	Oprah Winfrey
Logical-Mathematical	accountant	Henry W. Bloch (H&R Block)
	engineer	Dean Kamen, inventor
	computer programmer	Bill Gates, entrepreneur
Spatial	architect	Norma Merrick Sklarek, first African American woman architect, designed the Los Angeles International Airport Terminal
	artist	Christo, environmental artist
	artistic director	Grant Major, Academy Award Winner, *Lord of the Rings: The Return of the King,* 2003
Bodily-Kinesthetic	professional athlete	Venus Williams, tennis player
	coach	Mike Shanahan, Denver Broncos
	actor	Brad Pitt
Musical	musician	Faith Hill, country singer
	composer	John Williams, composer/conductor
Interpersonal	salesperson	Sam Walton, Wal-Mart Founder
	teacher	Your instructor
	counselor	Carl Rogers (1902–1987)
Intrapersonal	theorist	Ilya Prigogine (1917–2003), Nobel prize winner, chemistry, 1977
	researcher	John Wheeler, physicist
	philosopher	W. V. Quine, American philosopher
Naturalistic	landscape architect	Frederick Law Olmsted
	anthropologist	Jane Goodall
	botanist	Peter Raven

Figure 2.1

Choosing an Intelligence-Based Career

Chapter Crossover Let students know that they will spend a lot of time exploring careers later in Chapter 12.

Develop Your Weaker Intelligences

It's important to cultivate your weaker intelligences. Why? Because life isn't geared to one kind of intelligence. It's complex. Even in the particular career fields listed for each intelligence in the preceding chart, more than one intelligence may be required. A photo journalist for *National Geographic*, for example, might need linguistic intelligence, spatial intelligence, interpersonal intelligence, and naturalist intelligence. Being well-rounded, as the expression goes, is truly a good thing. Artist Pablo Picasso once said, "I am always doing that which I cannot do, in order that I may learn how to do it."

Use your multiple intelligences to multiply your success. Remember that no one is naturally intelligent in all eight areas. Each individual is a unique blend of intelligences. But the Theory of Multiple Intelligences claims that we all have the capacity to develop all of our eight intelligences further. That's good news! Howard Gardner puts it this way: "We can all get better at each of the intelligences, although some people will improve in an intelligence area more readily than others, either because biology gave them a better brain for that intelligence or because their culture gave them a better teacher."[15]

Emotional Intelligence (EI) Research While IQ cannot really be increased dramatically, there are areas of multiple intelligences that can, and research indicates that you can develop your EI. Once you focus on just one area of EI, let's say impulse control, EI improves in other areas, too—for example, stress management and overall happiness increase when someone is less impulsive.

INSIGHT → ACTION

1. What are your most developed intelligences? Describe a situation in which you excelled as a learner and how the Theory of Multiple Intelligences helps explain your success.

2. Now do the opposite. Describe a situation in which you did not excel as a learner and how the Theory of Multiple Intelligences helps explain your difficulty.

3. Identify a career field you are interested in. Which intelligences would be important?

4. Which of your intelligences would you like to develop further? Why? What actions can you take to do so?

How Do You Perceive and Process Information?

Activity Option Ask students to have someone who knows them well fill out the same "Challenge → Reaction" about them. Does their roommate or spouse know that they must have music on to study, for example? Encourage students to share their needs with roommates and family members who may have a different style. The responses will help students see how others perceive them as well.

CHALLENGE → REACTION

Challenge: You've lived with yourself for many years now, but how well do you know yourself as a learner?

Reaction: List as many descriptive phrases about your learning preferences as you can. For example, you might write, "I learn best when I listen to an instructor lecture" or "I learn best when I make color-coded binders for each class." Use this activity to discover some specifics about your learning style.

Style—we all have it, right? What's yours? Baggy jeans and a T-shirt? Sandals, even in the middle of winter? A signature hairdo that defies gravity? A stocking cap that translates into I-just-rolled-out-of-bed-before-class? When it comes to appearance, you have your own style. You know it, and so does everyone who knows you.

Think about how your mind works. For example, how do you decide what to wear in the morning? Do you turn on the radio or TV for the weather forecast? Jump on the Internet? Stick your head out the front door? Ask someone else's opinion? Try on your new jeans to see how they feel? Throw on whatever happens to be clean? We all have different styles, don't we?

So what's a learning style? A learning style is defined as your "characteristic and preferred way of gathering, interpreting, organizing, and thinking about information."[16]

Here's one way of looking at things. The way you perceive information and the way you process it—your perceiving/processing preferences—are based in part on your senses. Which sensory modalities do you prefer to use to take in information—your eyes (visual-graphic or visual-words), your ears (aural), or all your senses using your whole body (kinesthetic)? Which type of information sinks in best? Which type of information do you most trust to be accurate? Do you prefer teachers who lecture? Teachers who use visuals such as charts, web pages, and diagrams to explain things? Or teachers who plan field trips, use role-plays, and create simulations?

To further understand your preferred sensory channel, let's take this hypothetical example. Assume a rich relative you didn't even know you had leaves you some money, and you decide to use it to buy a new car. You must first answer many questions: What kind of car do you want to buy—an SUV, a sedan, a sports car, a van, or a truck? What are the differences between various makes and models? How do prices, comfort, and safety compare? Who provides the best warranty? Which car do consumers rate highest? How would you go about learning the answers to all these questions?

> **"Learning how to learn is life's most important skill."**
>
> **Tony Buzan, memory expert**

Visual. Some of us would **look**. We'd study charts and graphs comparing cars, mileage, fuel tank capacity, maintenance costs, and customer satisfaction. We learn through symbolic representations that explain what could have been said in normal text format.

Aural. Some of us would **listen**. We'd ask all our friends what kind of cars they drive and what they've heard about cars from other people. We'd pay attention as showroom salespeople describe the features of various cars. We learn through sounds by listening.

Read/Write. Some of us would **read** or **write**. We'd buy a copy of *Consumer Reports* annual edition on automobiles, or copies of magazines such as *Car and Driver* or *Road and Track*, and write lists of each car's pros and cons. We learn through words by reading and writing.

Kinesthetic. Some of us would want to **do it**. We'd go to the showroom and test drive a few cars to physically try them out. We learn through experience when all our sensory modalities are activated.

Sensitive Situation Keep in mind that you may have some students in your class with either disclosed or undisclosed disabilities. Open up the door for this kind of discussion and encourage students to learn more about themselves, and share their needs with their instructors, especially if they have a learning disability, a hearing loss, low vision, ADHD, or any other unique need.

Teachable Moment As students move from one assessment to the other, it's important that they see how these instruments and results taken together will give them a clearer picture of themselves as learners. Remind students to connect instruments; tell them that the areas they were strong in the multiple intelligence questionnaire will most likely connect with their VARK results.

What would you do? Eventually, as you're deciding which vehicle to buy, you might do all these things, and do them more than once. But learning style theory says we all have preferences in terms of how we perceive and process information.

After reading the car-buying description, you probably have a gut feeling about your own style. However, take a few minutes to answer the questions about yourself in Exercise 2.1—for confirmation or revelation—to verify your hunches or to learn something new about yourself.

You can take the VARK online at http://www.vark-learn.com/english/page .asp?p=questionnaire and your results will be tabulated for you.

EXERCISE 2.1 VARK Learning Styles Assessment

Choose the answer which best explains your preference and circle the letter. Please select more than one response if a single answer does not match your perception. Leave blank any question that does not apply.

1. You are helping someone who wants to go downtown, find your airport or locate the bus station. You would:
   a) draw or give her a map.
   b) tell her the directions.
   c) write down the directions (without a map).
   d) go with her.

2. You are not sure whether a word should be spelled "dependent" or "dependant." You would:
   a) see the word in your mind and choose by the way different versions look.
   b) think about how each word sounds and choose one.
   c) find it in a dictionary.
   d) write both words on paper and choose one.

3. You are planning a group vacation. You want some feedback from your friends about your plans. You would:
   a) use a map or website to show them the places.
   b) phone, text or email them.
   c) give them a copy of the printed itinerary.
   d) describe some of the highlights.

4. You are going to cook something as a special treat for your family. You would:
   a) look through the cookbook for ideas from the pictures.
   b) ask friends for suggestions.
   c) use a cookbook where you know there is a good recipe.
   d) cook something you know without the need for instructions.

5. A group of tourists want to learn about the parks or wildlife reserves in your area. You would:
   a) show them internet pictures, photographs or picture books.
   b) talk about, or arrange a talk for them, about parks or wildlife reserves.
   c) give them a book or pamphlets about the parks or wildlife reserves.
   d) take them to a park or wildlife reserve and walk with them.

6. You are about to purchase a digital camera or cell phone. Other than price, what would most influence your decision?
   a) Its attractive design that looks good.
   b) The salesperson telling me about its features.

c) Reading the details about its features.

d) Trying or testing it.

7. Remember a time when you learned how to do something new. Try to avoid choosing a physical skill, like riding a bike. You learned best by:

a) diagrams and charts—visual clues.

b) listening to somebody explaining it and asking questions.

c) written instructions—e.g. a manual or textbook.

d) watching a demonstration.

8. You have a problem with your knee. You would prefer that the doctor:

a) showed you a diagram of what was wrong.

b) described what was wrong.

c) gave you a pamphlet to read about it.

d) used a plastic model of a knee to show what was wrong.

9. You want to learn a new software program, skill or game on a computer. You would:

a) follow the diagrams in the book that came with it.

b) talk with people who know about the program.

c) read the written instructions that came with the program.

d) use the controls or keyboard and try things out.

10. I like websites that have:

a) interesting design and visual features.

b) audio channels where I can hear music, radio programs or interviews.

c) interesting written descriptions, lists and explanations.

d) things I can click on or try out.

11. Other than price, what would most influence your decision to buy a new non-fiction book?

a) The cover looks appealing.

b) A friend talks about it and recommends it.

c) You'd quickly read parts of it.

d) It contains real-life stories, experiences and examples.

12. You are using a book, CD or website to learn how to take photos with your new digital camera. You would like to have:

a) diagrams showing the camera and what each part does.

b) a chance to ask questions and talk about the camera and its features.

c) clear written instructions with lists and bullet points about what to do.

d) many examples of good and poor photos and how to improve them.

13. Do you prefer a teacher or a presenter who uses:

a) diagrams, charts or graphs?

b) question and answer, talk, group discussion or guest speakers?

c) handouts, books or readings?

d) demonstrations, models, fieldtrips, role plays or practical exercises?

14. You have finished a competition or test and would like some feedback. You would like to have feedback:

a) using graphs showing what you had achieved.

b) from somebody who talks it through with you.

(continued)

c) in a written format, describing your results.

d) using examples from what you have done.

15. You are going to choose food at a restaurant or cafe. You would:

a) look at what others are eating or look at pictures of each dish.

b) ask the server or friends to recommend choices.

c) choose from the written descriptions in the menu.

d) choose something that you have had there before.

16. You have to give an important speech at a conference or special occasion. You would:

a) make diagrams or create graphs to help explain things.

b) write a few key words and practice your speech over and over.

c) write out your speech and learn from reading it over several times.

d) gather many examples and stories to make the talk real and practical.

Source: N. Fleming. (2001–2007). *VARK, a Guide to Learning Styles.* Version 7.0. Available at http://www
.vark-learn.com/english/page.asp?p=questionnaire. Adapted and used with permission from Neil Fleming.

Scoring the VARK

The VARK learning style assessment was created by two professors, Neil Fleming and Colleen Mills, working with students at Lincoln University in Canterbury, New Zealand. They began with three traditional sensory modalities: visual, aural, and kinesthetic. Later, based on student input, they divided the visual mode (in which we use our eyes) into two categories: Visual (pictures, graphs, colors, symbols, and so on) and Read/Write (printed information). Let's tabulate your results.

Count your choices in each of the four VARK categories.	(a)	(b)	(c)	(d)
	Visual	Aural	Read/Write	Kinesthetic

Activity Option On the board or on a large piece of poster board, list the four modalities (Visual, Aural, Read/Write, and Kinesthetic) and have students write their name and score of their top two modalities. For example, a student might put her name and a 10 under Visual and her name and an 8 under Aural. Are there similarities in the class? Do these students enjoy the same classes? Now ask students to put their dominant multiple intelligence next to their name. Are they beginning to see any patterns? Ask each student to describe one way in which they can use their dominant learning style and strong intelligence to help them in college (if there is not enough time in class, they can e-mail the class with their answer, or bring their response to the next class).

Now that you've calculated your scores, do they match your perceptions of yourself as a learner? Could you have predicted them? The VARK's creators believe that *you* are best qualified to verify and interpret your own results.[17]

Using Your Sensory Preferences

Knowing your preferences can help you in your academic coursework. If your highest score (by 4 or 5 points) is in one of the four VARK modalities, that particular learning modality is your preferred one.[18] If your scores are more or less even between several or all four modalities, these scores mean that you don't have a strong preference for any single modality. It's estimated that 55 to 65 percent of the population is multimodal, which gives most of us flexibility in the way we learn.[19] A lower score in a preference simply means that you are more comfortable using other styles. If your VARK results contain a zero in a particular learning modality, you may realize that you do indeed dislike this mode or find it unhelpful. "Why would anyone want to use *that* mode?" you may have asked yourself in the past. It may be helpful to reflect on why you omit this learning modality. To learn more about your results and suggestions for applying them, see Figure 2.2 for your preferred modality.

Figure 2.2

Visual, Aural, Read/Write, and Kinesthetic Learning Strategies

READ/WRITE

General Strategies

Make lists.
Take lecture notes (almost verbatim).
Journal about what you're learning.
Pay attention to headings.
Read textbooks thoroughly.
Compile/read glossaries.
Write out definitions.
Read/find quotations.
Look up words in the dictionary.
Pay attention to printed handouts.
Read outside library materials.
Read websites and web pages.
Read manuals (for computers or labs).
Listen to teachers and students who are articulate.

Study Strategies

Write out your lecture notes again and again.
Read your notes (silently) again and again.
Put ideas and principles into different words.
Translate diagrams, graphs, etc. into text.
Rearrange words and "play" with wording.
Turn diagrams and charts into words.

Exam Strategies

Write out potential exam answers.
Practice creating and taking exams.
Type out your answers to potential test questions.
Organize your notes into lists or bullets.
Write practice paragraphs, particularly beginnings and endings.

KINESTHETIC

General Strategies

Go on field trips.
Find real examples of abstract concepts.
Apply information.
View exhibits, samples, and photos.
Use hands-on approaches—computers, for example.
Take advantage of labs.
Engage in service-learning related to the course.
Listen to teachers who give real-life examples.
Don't forget that you need to do things in order to remember them.
Use all your senses.

Study Strategies

Recall experiments, field trips, etc.
Remember the real things that happened.
Talk over your notes with another "K" person.
Use photos and pictures that make ideas come to life.
Go back to the lab, your manual, or your notes that include real examples.
Remember that your lecture notes will have gaps if topics weren't concrete or relevant for you.
Use case studies to help you learn abstract principles.

Exam Strategies

Role-play the exam situation in your room (or the actual classroom).
Put plenty of examples into your answers.
Write practice answers and sample paragraphs.
Give yourself practice tests.

VISUAL

General Strategies

Draw maps.
Create charts.
Develop graphs.
Use symbols.
Draw diagrams.
Underline text.
Make flowcharts.
Use highlighters.
Write with different colors.
Draw pictures.
Use word imagery.
Use spatial arrangements.
Pay attention to teachers who are dramatic and dynamic.

Study Strategies

Convert your lecture notes to a visual format.
Study the placement of items, colors, and shapes in your textbook.
Put complex concepts into flowcharts or graphs.
Redraw ideas you create from memory.

Exam Strategies

Practice turning your visuals back into words.
Practice writing out exam answers.
Recall the pictures you made of the pages you studied.
Use diagrams to answer exam questions, if your instructor will allow it.

AURAL

General Strategies

Discuss topics with other students.
Use a tape recorder so you can listen more than once.
Attend as many class lectures as you can.
Leave space in your lecture notes for later recall and filling in.
Join a study group.
Find ways to talk about and listen to conversations about the material.
Describe the material to a student who wasn't there.
Make a point of remembering examples, stories, and jokes—things people use to explain things.
Tune in to your teacher's voice.

Study Strategies

Read your notes aloud.
Explain your notes to another auditory learner.
Ask others to "hear" your understanding of the material.
Talk about your learning to others or to yourself.
Record your notes onto tapes or CDs or listen to your instructors' Podcasts.
Realize that your lecture notes may be incomplete. You may have become so involved in listening that you stopped writing. Fill your notes in later by talking with other students or getting material from the textbook.

Exam Strategies

Practice by speaking your answers aloud.
Listen to your own voice as you answer questions.
Opt for an oral exam if allowed.
Imagine you are talking with the teacher as you answer questions.

Your highest score represents your preferred learning style; your lowest score, your least preferred. Most college classes emphasize reading and writing; however, if your lowest score is in the Read/Write modality, don't assume you're academically doomed. VARK can help you discover alternative, more productive ways to learn the same course material.

Learning style descriptions aren't meant to put you into a cubbyhole or stereotype you. And they certainly aren't meant to give you an excuse when you don't like a particular assignment. It might work in a restaurant to send back your entrée if it's not cooked to your liking, but most of the time in life, we don't get to choose how information is served. (Imagine saying to your professor: "I'm afraid this won't do. Can you bring me information I can digest in my own learning style?") You may learn to adapt naturally to a particular instructor or discipline's preferences, using a visual modality in your economics class to interpret graphs and a kinesthetic modality in your chemistry lab to conduct experiments.

However, you may also find that you need to deliberately and strategically re-route your learning methods in some of your classes, and knowing your VARK preferences can help you do that. Learning to capitalize on your preferences and translate challenging course material into your preferred modality

may serve you well. Remember these suggestions about the VARK, and try them out to see if they improve your academic results.

1. VARK preferences are not necessarily strengths. However VARK is an excellent vehicle to help you reflect on how you learn and begin to reinforce the productive strategies you're already using or select ones that might work better.

2. If you have a strong preference for a particular modality, practice multiple suggestions listed in Figure 2.2 for that particular modality. Reinforce your learning through redundancy.

3. Remember that an estimated 55 to 65 percent of people are multimodal. In a typical classroom of 30 students (based on VARK data):

   > 17 students would be multimodal,

   > 1 student would be Visual,

   > 1 student would be Aural,

   > 5 students would be Read/Write,

   > 6 students would be Kinesthetic,

   and the teacher would most likely have a strong Read/Write preference![20]

Teachable Moment Ask students to describe the differences between teaching elementary or secondary students and college students. Given that the most common psychological type is introverted, sensing (or intuitive), thinking, and judging, do they see where there might be differences in instructors' teaching and students' learning styles?

Chapter Crossover As students begin to think about careers again, remind them that they will be exploring this more in Chapter 12.

C CREATE a Career Outlook

COLLEGE PROFESSOR

Have you ever considered a career as a college professor? Here are some facts about this career to consider and some questions about yourself to ponder.

Facts to Consider

Academic preparation required: A master's degree, or more often, a doctoral degree is required, although in some fields highly cultivated expertise or practical experience is sufficient. (A former politician without a Ph.D. may be hired to teach a course in political science, for example.)

Future workforce demand: Prospects for new jobs will be good in the future, although many openings will be for part-time teachers.

Work environment: College professors have flexible schedules, teach a wide variety of subjects (usually related within one field) to sixteen million full- and part-time college students nationwide, and conduct research.

Most common psychological type preferences: introverted, sensing, (and to a lesser extent, intuitive), thinking, judging[21]

Essential skills: reading, writing, communicating with individual students, to a classroom of students, or in work-related committees, collecting and analyzing data, using technology (to teach distance-learning courses, communicate with students, and present information)

Questions to Ponder

1. Do you have (or could you acquire) the skills this career requires?
2. What would you find most satisfying about this type of career?
3. What would you find most challenging about this type of career?
4. Are you interested in a career like this? Why or why not?

For more information, see U.S. Department of Labor, Bureau of Labor Statistics, *Occupational Outlook Handbook, 2006–2007 Edition*.[22]

For more career activities online, go to http://www.academic .cengage.com/collegesuccess/staley to do the Team Career exercises.

that every year in my classrooms, and I try not to forget it. But I think we must use the word *intelligence* cautiously, because it sounds like a "thing" that some have and others don't.

Q6: How do students sabotage their own learning?
Students often fail themselves by using methods of learning that are not suited to them. In the past, the students that saddened me were those who were trying to copy the learning methods of their sister or friend or the student who got high grades in their class. Learning requires a lot of hard work, and if there is less than a major effort, in the end, little will be learned.

Q7: In your opinion, are most students today visual, aural, read/write, or kinesthetic learners? Have learning styles shifted over the course of your teaching career? Why do you think this is? How do you teach to different learning styles in the classroom?
The VARK data I've collected indicate that the most common preference for students is kinesthetic, that is, they want to experience the learning or have the teacher relate the learning to things that they know, have, seen, or can do. The plain truth is that the teacher who can provide links to the reality of students is going to reach more students. Despite popular conceptions, this is not a very "visual" world as defined by VARK, and unfortunately the "Read/Write" world is made for teachers rather than students. The power of VARK is in the practical strategies that students can use to learn efficiently, effectively, and personally.

Q8: How can students who want to go into the teaching profession best prepare themselves?
If students want to become teachers at any level, they must understand how people learn, and they must devote themselves to helping people do it. In my view, it's the best profession in the world. If students want a fulfilling career, a career in which they have the potential to bring forth lasting, and sometimes life-altering, change, they should consider teaching.

4. If you are multimodal, as most of us are, it may be necessary to use all your modalities to boost your confidence in your learning. Practice the suggestions for all of your preferred modalities.

5. While in an ideal world, it would be good to try to strengthen lesser preferences, you may wish to save that goal for later in life. Fleming's students eventually convinced him that college isn't the place to experiment. Academic results are important, and often scholarships and graduate school acceptance hang in the balance. You, too, may decide it's better to try to strengthen existing preferences now and work on expanding your repertoire later. This book will give you an opportunity to practice your VARK learning preferences—whatever they are—in each chapter.

INSIGHT ⊖ ACTION

Go back to the earliest days of your schooling and identify three peak learning experiences—times when you were most engaged as a learner. Perhaps during these learning peaks you were operating in "flow" mode. You were so engrossed in what you were learning that you lost track of everything around you and how long you had been working. After you've identified these experiences, list the primary VARK modality or modalities that you were using at the time. Does your list match your results on the VARK instrument? Were you using your most preferred modality? List some specific ways you can translate tasks in your most challenging classes into your VARK preferences.

What Role Does Your Personality Play?

CHALLENGE ⊖ REACTION

Challenge: How does your personality affect your learning style?

Reaction: _____

One of the best things about college, no matter which one you've chosen to attend, is meeting so many different kinds of people. At times you may find these differences intriguing. At other times, they may baffle you. Look around and listen to other students, and you'll start to notice. Have you heard students voicing totally opposite opinions about college life by saying things like this?

"There's no way I can study in the dorm. It's way too noisy."

"There's no way I can study in the library. It's way too quiet."

"My roommate is terrific! We're getting along great."

"My roommate is unbearable! I can hardly stand being around him."

"Each person is an exception to the rule."

Carl Jung, Swiss psychiatrist (1875–1961)

"I'm so glad I've already decided on a major. Now I can go full steam ahead."

"My sociology prof is great. She talks about all kinds of things in class, and her essay tests are actually fun!"

"I have no idea what to major in. I can think of six different majors I'd like to choose."

"My sociology prof is so confusing. She talks about so many different things in class. How am I supposed to know what to study for her tests?"[23]

You're likely to run into all kinds of viewpoints and all kinds of people, but as you're bound to discover in college, differences make life much more interesting! We're each unique. You've seen it on sappy greeting cards, "There's only one you." But it's true. Perhaps your friends comment on your personality by saying, "She's really quiet," or "He's the class clown," or "He's incredibly logical," or "She trusts her gut feelings." What you may not know is how big a role your personality plays in how you prefer to learn.

The Myers-Briggs Type Indicator® (MBTI) is the most well known personality assessment instrument in the world. Each year, approximately four million people worldwide obtain significant insights about their personalities, their career choices, their interaction with others, and their learning styles by completing it.

This chapter will introduce you to a shorter instrument based on the MBTI, the SuccessTypes Learning Style Type Indicator. Created by Dr. John Pelley at Texas Tech University, this instrument focuses specifically on how you prefer to learn. If you are able to complete the full Myers-Briggs Type Indicator in the class for which you're using this textbook, or through your college counseling center or learning center, do so. You'll learn even more about yourself.

Here's an important point: Both the SuccessTypes Learning Style Type Indicator and the Myers-Briggs Type Indicator show you your preferences. These instruments are not about what you *can* do. They're about what you

Activity Option Before students fill out the SuccessTypes Learning Style Type Indicator, have them guess their type. Let them know that an "E" learns from doing, an "I" prefers studying in quiet, an "S" likes to memorize, "N's" like to think about the big picture, "F's" relate information to people, while "T's" are logical, "J's" love organized classrooms and clear syllabi, and "P's" don't mind change and going with the flow. After the assessment, see if they were correct on any of the indicators.

prefer to do. That's an important distinction. Here's an illustration. Try writing your name on the line below.

_____

Now put the pen in your other hand, and try writing your name again.

_____

What was different the second time around? For most people, the second try takes longer, is less legible, probably feels odd, and requires more concentration. But could you do it? Yes. It's just that you prefer doing it the first way. The first way is easier and more natural; the second way makes a simple task seem like hard work! It's possible that you might have to try "writing with your other hand" in college—doing things that don't come naturally. Practice, rehearsal, and focus might be extra important, but you can do it!

Throughout this book, you will find "Your Type Is Showing" features. These articles will summarize MBTI research that investigates the chapter's topic. They are intended to pique your interest and invite you to go beyond what you see in the chapter. Chances are you'll be fascinated by what you can learn about yourself through the MBTI. But in the meantime, let's zero in on how your personality affects your learning style, specifically.

EXERCISE 2.2 The SuccessTypes Learning Style Type Indicator

Each of the following statements represents opposites in your thinking when you are learning. Choose the one that describes the way you really are. It is common to want to choose the one that represents what you want to be or what others think you ought to be. Try to imagine that you are learning for yourself and not for a teacher and that there is no grade involved. For example, you are learning about something that interests you like a new hobby or outside interest. Just choose the description that best fits you, and write the letter associated with that sentence in the box to the left, and you will total them when you are done.

1. ☐   E   I study best with other people.

       I   I study best by myself.

2. ☐   E   When I study with other people, I get the most out of expressing my thoughts.

       I   When I study with other people, I get the most out of listening to what others have to say.

3. ☐   E   When I study with other people, I get the most out of quick, trial-and-error thinking.

       I   When I study with other people, I get the most out of thinking things through before I say them.

4. ☐   E   I prefer to start my learning by doing something active and then considering the results later.

       I   I prefer to start my learning by considering something thoroughly and then doing something active with it later.

5. ☐   E   I need frequent breaks when I study and interruptions don't bother me.

       I   I can study for very long stretches and interruptions are *not* welcome.

6. ☐   E   I prefer to demonstrate what I know.

           I   I prefer to describe what I know.

7. ☐   E   I like to know what other people expect of me.

           I   I like to set my own standards for my learning.

8. ☐   S   I am more patient with routine or details in my study.

          N   I am more patient with abstract or complex material.

9. ☐   S   I am very uncomfortable with errors of fact.

          N   I consider errors of fact to be another useful way to learn.

10. ☐   S   I am very uncomfortable when part of my learning is left to my imagination.

          N   I am bored when everything I am supposed to learn is presented explicitly.

11. ☐   S   I prefer to learn fewer skills and get really good at them.

          N   I prefer to keep learning new skills and I'll get good at them when I have to.

12. ☐   S   I learn much better in a hands-on situation to see what-is.

          N   I learn much better when I'm thinking about the possibilities to imagine what might be.

13. ☐   S   I prefer to learn things that are useful and based on established principles.

          N   I prefer to learn things that are original and stimulate my imagination.

14. ☐   S   I always re-examine my answers on test questions just to be sure.

          N   I usually trust my first hunches about test questions.

15. ☐   S   I emphasize observation over imagination.

          N   I emphasize imagination over observation.

16. ☐   S   I'm more comfortable when the professor sticks closely to the handout.

          N   I'm likely to get bored if the professor sticks closely to the handout.

17. ☐   T   I prefer to have a logical reason for what I learn.

          F   I prefer to see the human consequences of what I learn.

18. ☐   T   I prefer a logically organized teacher to a personable teacher.

          F   I prefer a personable teacher to a logically organized teacher.

19. ☐   T   I prefer group study as a way to give and receive critical analysis.

          F   I prefer group study to be harmonious.

20. ☐   T   I prefer to study first what should be learned first.

          F   I prefer to study first what appeals to me the most.

21. ☐   T   The best way to correct a study partner is to be blunt and direct.

          F   The best way to correct a study partner is to be tactful and understanding.

22. ☐   J   I prefer to study in a steady, orderly fashion.

          P   I prefer to study in a flexible, even impulsive, way.

(continued)

23. ☐ J I stay on schedule when I study regardless of how interesting the assignment is.

P I tend to postpone uninteresting or unpleasant assignments.

24. ☐ J I tend to be an overachiever in my learning.

P I tend to be an underachiever in my learning.

25. ☐ J I prefer to structure my study now to avoid emergencies later.

P I prefer to stay flexible in my study and deal with emergencies when they arise.

26. ☐ J I prefer to give answers based on the information I already have.

P I prefer to seek more information before deciding on an answer.

27. ☐ J I prefer to finish one assignment before starting another one.

P I prefer to have several assignments going at once.

28. ☐ J I like well defined learning assignments.

P I like learning from open-ended problem solving.

Let's boil it down to four letters:

E or I ☐ Record the letter which occurred the most for questions 1–7.

S or N ☐ Record the letter which occurred the most for questions 8–16.

T or F ☐ Record the letter which occurred the most for questions 17–21.

J or P ☐ Record the letter which occurred the most for questions 22–28.

Adapted from Table 5.1 in SuccessTypes for Medical Students, J. W. Pelley and B. K. Dalley (Texas Tech Univ. Extended Learning, 1997). Used by permission of John W. Pelley.

Activity Option Have students develop a six-slide PowerPoint presentation for the class describing something they do and explaining why they do it that way based on their type. For example, if they were to describe plans for fall break, would they go with a few people or a group, would it be spontaneous or planned, would they be the leader or prefer someone else to take charge?

You can take the SuccessTypes Learning Style Type Indicator online at http://www.ttuhsc.edu/SOM/Success/LSTI.htm.

Interpreting Your SuccessTypes Learning Style Type Profile

Look at your four-letter profile. Are you an ESFP? An ESTP? An INTJ? What do those four letters say about you? There are many sources of information about the sixteen possible combinations of letters, or type, in books and online resources.[24] However, here are some things you need to know about measuring psychological type.

First, most abbreviated type indicators—even this one—are not scientifically reliable. They are designed to illustrate type, not prove it. As the instrument's creator asserts, "Your type is the starting line, not the finish line. . . . Type is more than the sum of its parts."[25]

Second, the SuccessTypes Learning Style Type Indicator forces you to make a choice between two opposites. That's because, theoretically, you can't simultaneously prefer two opposite things at once. That doesn't mean you'd never under any circumstances choose the other one. It just means that most of the time the one you chose would be your preference.

Third, any Myers-Briggs type instrument answers four questions about you (see Figure 2.3 for further explanations of typical characteristics of the preferences):

Figure 2.3

Learning Style Preferences

Extravert (E)

"How do you recharge your batteries"? Students who prefer extraversion pay attention to people and things around them. That's also where they get their energy. As learners, they:

- Learn best when actively involved
- Like to study with others
- Like background noise while studying
- Don't particularly enjoy writing papers
- Want teachers to encourage discussion in class

Introvert (I)

Students who prefer introversion focus on the world inside their heads. They pay attention to their own thoughts, feelings, and ideas, and draw energy from their inner experience. As learners, they:

- Learn best by pausing to think
- Like to study alone
- Say they aren't good public speakers
- Need to study in quiet
- Want teachers to give clear lectures

Sensing (S)

What kind of information do you rely on? Students who are sensors become aware of things that are real through their senses: sound, touch, taste, feel, and smell. They focus on what is happening in the here and now. As learners, they:

- Look for specific information
- Memorize facts
- Follow instructions
- Like hands-on experiences
- Want teachers to give clear assignments

Intuition (N)

Students who trust their intuition, or sixth sense, look for patterns, possibilities, and the big picture. As learners, they:

- Look for quick insights
- Like theories and abstract thinking
- Read between the lines
- Create their own directions
- Want teachers to encourage independent thinking

Thinking (T)

Students who are thinkers like to make decisions objectively using logic, principles, and analysis. They weigh evidence in a detached manner. As learners, they:

- Use their logic to guide their learning
- Like to critique ideas
- Learn through challenge and debate
- Can find flaws in an argument
- Want teachers to present logically

Feeling (F)

Students who are feelers value harmony and focus on what is important to them or to others when they make decisions. As learners, they:

- Want information to apply to them personally
- Like to please their teachers
- Find value or good in things
- Learn when they are supported or appreciated
- Want teachers to establish rapport with students

Judging (J)

Students who are judgers like to make quick decisions, settle things, and structure and organize their worlds. As learners, they:

- Like more formal class structures
- Plan their work in advance
- Work steadily toward their goals
- Like to be in charge
- Want teachers to be organized

Perceiving (P)

Students who are perceivers want to adapt to the world around them. They don't like to close off options; instead they'd rather experience whatever comes up. As learners, they:

- Like informal learning situations
- Enjoy spontaneity
- Stay open to new information
- Work in energy bursts
- Want teachers to entertain and inspire

Source: Based on J. K. DiTiberio & A. L. Hammer. (1993). *Introduction to Type in College.* Palo Alto, CA: Consulting Psychologists Press.

1. What energizes you and where do you direct energy? E or I

2. How do you gather information and what kind of information do you trust? S or N

3. How do you make decisions, arrive at conclusions, and make judgments? T or F

4. How do you relate to the outer world? J or P

Using Your SuccessTypes Learning Style Type Profile

What does it all mean? Now that you know some important things about yourself as a learner, there are several other points about learning styles you should know.

First, look at your first and second letters (ES, IS, EN, or IN). Statistically, twice as many instructors as students are Introverted Intuitives (IN). By and large, students are Extraverted Sensors (ES), preferring concrete, practical learning, while instructors often prefer theories and learning for its own sake.[26]

In the "FOCUS Challenge Case," Tammy's extraverted sensing (ES) learning style clashed with Professor Caldwell's introverted intuitive (IN) learning style. It's unlikely that Professor Caldwell will change his teaching style, and even if he did, students in his class have a variety of learning styles. Whose style would he try to match? Both Tammy's personality and Professor Caldwell's are representative of the most common types found in college classrooms.

Now look at your second and last letters (SP, SJ, NP, or NJ). Three times as many college students prefer sensing and perceiving (SP) as their professors, who are likely to be intuitive and judging (NJ). Generally, students want a more concrete, flexible approach to learning while instructors like to teach abstract, structured theories.[27]

While simply knowing about these mismatches is good, it's important to go further and act on that knowledge. As a single learner in a larger class, you will need to adjust to the teaching style of your instructor in ways such as the following:

> **Translate for maximum comfort.** The way to maximize your comfort as a learner is to find ways to translate from your instructor's preferences to yours. If you know that you prefer feeling over thinking, and your instructor's style is based on thinking, make the course material come alive by personalizing it. How does the topic relate to you, your lifestyle, your family, and your future choices?

> **Make strategic choices.** While learning preferences can help explain your academic successes, it's also important not to use them to rationalize your nonsuccesses. An introvert could say, "I could have aced that assignment if the professor had let me work on an individual project instead of a group one! I really dislike group projects." Become the best learner you can be at what you're naturally good at. But also realize that you'll need to become more versatile over time. In the

workforce, you won't always be able to choose what you do and how you do it. Actively choose your learning strategies, rather than simply hoping for the best. Remember: no one can learn for you, just as no one can eat for you.

> **Take full advantage.** College will present you with an extensive menu of learning opportunities. You will also build on your learning as you move beyond your general, introductory classes into courses in your chosen major—and across and between disciplines. Don't fall victim to the temptation to rationalize and victimize as some students do ("I could have been more successful in college if . . . I hadn't had to work so many hours . . . I hadn't had a family to support . . . my friends had been more studious . . . my roommate had been easier to live with . . . my professors had been more supportive. . . ." If, if, if. College may well be the most concentrated and potentially powerful learning opportunity you'll ever have.

Ultimately, learning at your best is up to you. Each chapter of this book will remind you of your VARK preferences with special activities to reinforce your sensory modalities. And you'll have a chance to re-explore your SuccessType Learning Style preferences in short sections called "Your Type Is Showing," in which you'll get a short flash of current research findings on the Myers-Briggs Type Indicator and the chapter's particular focus.

Gaining the insights provided in this chapter and acting on them have the potential to greatly affect your college success. Understand yourself, capitalize on your preferences, build on them, focus, and learn!

EXERCISE 2.3 VARK Activity

Complete the recommended activity for your preferred VARK learning modality. If you are multimodal, select more than one activity. Your instructor may ask you to (a) give an oral report on your results in class, (b) send your results to him or her via e-mail, (c) post them online, or (d) contribute to a class chat.

 Visual: Think about a particular course or exam you studied for in the past. Create a personal chart that compares the learning strategies for each of the four VARK modalities you used and the degree of success you had using each one.

 Aural: Interview another student who is a member of a campus honor society. Which VARK strategies does this student use and why? Determine whether these strategies would work for you.

Read/Write: Write a one-page summary of what you have learned about yourself as a result of reading this chapter.

 Kinesthetic: If your campus has a Learning Center, visit it to gather additional information about your learning style. Apply what you have learned to create a plan to prepare for your next exam.

For more practice online, go to http://www.academic.cengage.com/collegesuccess/staley to take the Challenge Yourself online quizzes.

NOW WHAT DO YOU THINK?

At the beginning of this chapter, Tammy Ko, a frustrated and disgruntled student, faced a challenge. Now after reading this chapter, would you respond differently to any of the questions you answered about the "FOCUS Challenge Case"?

REALITY CHECK

> > > >> > REALITY CHECK < << <<<

On a scale of 1 to 10, answer the following questions now that you've completed this chapter.

1 = not very/not much/very little/low   10 = very/a lot/very much/high

In hindsight, how much did you *really* know about this subject matter before reading the chapter?

1   2   3   4   5   6   7   8   9   10

How much do you think this information might affect your college success?

1   2   3   4   5   6   7   8   9   10

How much do you think this information might affect your career success after college?

1   2   3   4   5   6   7   8   9   10

How long did it actually take you to complete this chapter (both the reading and writing tasks)? _____ Hour(s) _____ Minutes

Take a minute to compare these answers to your answers from the "Readiness Check" at the beginning of this chapter. What gaps exist between the similar questions? How might these gaps between what you thought before starting the chapter and what you now think after completing the chapter affect how you approach the next chapter in this book?

To download mp3 format audio summaries of this chapter, go to http://www.academic.cengage.com/collegesuccess/staley.

3 Making Use of Resources: Finances, Technology, and Campus Support

YOU'RE ABOUT TO DISCOVER...

Teachable Moment Sometimes students who on paper appear as though they should sail through college leave for reasons that we could not have predicted. Knowledge of campus resources and stressing the message that it is okay to ask for help is critical to student success.

> What resources exist to help you through college

> Why managing your finances is so important

> Why plastic is perilous

> How to get "fiscally fit"

> How your Net life relates to your college success

> How the Internet can become addictive

> What information literacy is and why it's important

> Why HELP is not a four-letter word

> How to manage a learning disability

"Money is better than poverty, if only for financial reasons."

Woody Allen

Jessica Taylor

Jessica Taylor could still remember

the day she'd gotten her college acceptance letter. It began, "It is my distinct pleasure to tell you that you have been accepted …. " Accepted by her first choice school! How fortunate could she be?

Before she left for college everything was going Jessica's way. She'd felt ready to leave her family, her small private high school, the suburbs, and ready to be on her own.

Even though she didn't think about it much, Jessica had led a relatively privileged life. She'd gone to a select, private college prep high school, called The Oaks, in the suburbs where the teachers always reminded the students that they were being groomed for college.

Jessica had struggled with an eating disorder in high school, but thanks to her parents, her teachers, and a wonderful counselor, she'd managed to get a handle on it. Her counselor had told her that the actual percentage of people with diagnosed eating disorders is low, but she also knew that lots of girls have symptoms at one time or another. In fact, she wondered if her new college roommate, Angela, who skipped most meals in the dining hall and whose size 2 jeans bagged on her, might be one of them. Anyway, Jessica was doing well now, and she had things in perspective. But she was going to find the Counseling Center on campus, just in case she needed it. She didn't know exactly where it was. In fact, she didn't know where a lot of things were. The campus seemed huge to her.

The best thing that had happened to Jessica in college was her new circle of friends. She met them in her First-Year Seminar class, and then she noticed many of them in her other Learning Community classes and even in her residence hall. They'd all go to "The Village" close to campus, browse through the boutiques, get manicures, and have lunch. It was a good thing she'd applied for four credit cards during the campus promos. Sometimes she had to put her purchases on more than one card so that she wouldn't exceed her limit. Her male friends spent a lot of money, too, on computer games, and they stayed up half the night playing them. She'd heard that college was supposed to be fun, and she could see why.

But, Jessica's spending was getting out of control. Over time there were gas for trips to see her boyfriend, Collin, groceries she kept in her room since she didn't like the residence hall

food, cell phone bills—you name it. She and her parents had never talked about budgeting and spending money before she'd left home. Her family wasn't independently wealthy, but they were comfortable. They'd opened a bank account for her, put a fairly generous amount in it, and told her to ration it out for the term.

But when her first credit card statement arrived, she was flabbergasted. This one bill alone would wipe her out! *Should I ask my parents for more?* she thought. *Or should I just make the minimum payment for now and plan to cut down on my spending?* Her parents had advised her not to get a job in college. "Just concentrate on your studies, Jessica," they'd said.

Also, she'd received a worrisome instant message that morning from collin which hinted that he'd met somebody at his school he wanted to get to know better. They'd had an agreement to keep their long-distance relationship going while they were in college, but now it seemed that he was going back on his word. She hadn't met anyone at college who came close to Collin in looks or personality. The thought that they might not be together was devastating.

Besides the worry about her finances and Collin, Jessica found out she'd earned a C- on her first history test. Everything had gotten off to such a good start, but now it all seemed beyond her control. Depressed and anxious for the first time since she'd left home, Jessica skipped not only breakfast, but lunch and dinner, too. At least eating was one thing she *could* control. She didn't know where to turn. Maybe college would be more overwhelming than she'd first thought. Maybe her worst fears would come true after all. Maybe she couldn't fool everyone into thinking she was the totally together person she wasn't sure she really was.

WHAT DO **YOU** THINK?

Now that you've read about Jessica Taylor, answer the following questions. You may not know all the answers yet, but you'll find out what you know and what you stand to gain by reading this chapter.

1. What potential problems could affect Jessica's success in college? List all the problems you can identify and their possible impact.

2. What, in particular, is Jessica doing wrong with her finances?

3. Identify three money management techniques that Jessica should begin to use immediately.

4. What specific campus resources that might help Jessica are available at your school?

Before beginning to read this chapter, take two minutes to answer the following questions on a scale of 1 to 10. Your answers will help you assess how ready you are to focus.

1 = not very/not much/very little/low   10 = very/a lot/very much/high

Based on reading the "You're about to discover . . ." list and skimming this chapter, how much do you think you probably already know about the subject matter?

1   2   3   4   5   6   7   8   9   10

How much do you think this information might affect your college success?

1   2   3   4   5   6   7   8   9   10

How much do you think this information might affect your career success after college?

1   2   3   4   5   6   7   8   9   10

In general, how motivated are you to learn the material in this chapter?

1   2   3   4   5   6   7   8   9   10

This book describes four key factors related to intrinsic, or internal, motivation: curiosity, control, career outlook, and challenge. The next four questions relate to these **C-Factors**:

How *curious* are you about the content you expect to read in this chapter?

1   2   3   4   5   6   7   8   9   10

How much *control* do you expect to have over mastering the material in this chapter?

1   2   3   4   5   6   7   8   9   10

How much do you think this chapter might help you develop your *career outlook*?

1   2   3   4   5   6   7   8   9   10

How *challenging* do you think the material in this chapter will be for you?

1   2   3   4   5   6   7   8   9   10

Before beginning any task, including studying, it's important to check in with yourself to ensure that you're physically, intellectually, and emotionally ready to focus. How ready are you, physically, to focus on this chapter? (Are you rested, feeling well, and so on?)

1   2   3   4   5   6   7   8   9   10

How ready are you, intellectually, to focus on this chapter? (Are you thinking clearly, focused on this course, interested in this subject?)

1   2   3   4   5   6   7   8   9   10

How ready are you, emotionally, to focus on this chapter? (Are you calm, confident, composed?)

1   2   3   4   5   6   7   8   9   10

If your answer to any of the last three questions is below a 5 on the scale, you may need to address the issue you're facing prior to beginning this chapter. For example, if you're hungry, get a quick bite to eat. If you're feeling scattered, take a few moments to settle down and focus.

Finally, how long do you think it will take you to complete this chapter?
_____ Hour(s) _____ Minutes

Teachable Moment By now students should be getting used to the "Readiness Checks" for each chapter. Ask students if they would share anything that they are doing differently now than in the beginning of the course. Have they changed any habits, or do they find themselves better able to focus?

College Success: Resources That Can Help

CHALLENGE ⟶ REACTION

Challenge: What types of campus resources can help college students become academically successful?

Reaction: _____

Activity Option Make up index cards with a typical first-year student challenge, hand one out to each student, or groups of students, and ask them to describe a campus resource that would help students deal with this challenge. How would this resource help? If they were facing this challenge, would they be willing to use the resource they've identified?

Do you know this student? After his first year of college, James got a summer job in the brutally hot warehouse for the new superstore in his town. He moved huge boxes of paper towels, giant bags of dog food, and everything else you could think of across the floor. Actually, he discovered it felt good to take home a fairly substantial paycheck. He didn't mind the hard work, and it wasn't long until the bonuses gave him more earning power than his parents. Secretly, he enjoyed his job more than he'd enjoyed college, and he didn't want the summer to end. So instead of quitting his job, he quit college. James joined one of the fastest growing groups in America, along with one in three other Americans in their mid-twenties today. He became a college dropout. Ten years and three kids later, he still hopes to return, but it just never seems to work out. It's the only decision he's made in his life that he regrets.[1]

Could James have been successful in college? Most likely he could have been, but he didn't take to college right away, for whatever reasons, so he went for short-term *gains* over long-term *goals*. If he's ever laid off and seeking new employment, he may find himself unable to get hired into a job he really wants.

If you run into roadblocks, remember that many different support systems are in place for you in college. You just need to know what they are and take advantage of them. If you need financial help, there's an Office of Financial Aid or an Office of Campus Employment—perhaps known by another title, but a unit performing the same functions. If you need technology assistance, visit the Campus Technology Helpdesk online, call their hotline, or just walk in and ask your question. And the Campus Counseling Center is there to help with adjustment issues, self-esteem problems, eating disorders, or whatever you need. Most campuses today go to great lengths to help you succeed because they don't want you to become another "James." They want you to stay in college and succeed.

Unfortunately, many first-year students allow their coursework to slip a bit, miss a class here or there, get behind on assignments, and gradually begin to slack off. Once that happens, they never catch up. They never have time to use the campus learning center or writing center or counseling center, when all those helping hands are there for the taking. Is the answer to quit college as James did? If *you* ran into difficulties and dropped out as he did, is that something you'd eventually regret, too?

This chapter will explore three types of resources—finances, technology, and campus support—in some detail so that you can make smart decisions during your time in college.

Hot Ideas/IndexOpen

"**Fame is a vapor, popularity is an accident, money takes wings, those who cheer you today may curse you tomorrow. The only thing that endures is character.**"

Horace Greeley, American newspaper editor and politician (1811–1872)

Sensitive Situation There is a student in your class, male or female, that is just like James. Keep in mind that sometimes students like James leave college for reasons that are beyond their control. When we ask "could James have been successful in college," the "James" sitting in your class may think "yes . . . if only I had parents who could afford to help me" or some other reason out of his or her control. You want to emphasize that those like James who return to college are brave and can be very successful. Remind students also that in most situations, they *can* exert some kind of control.

INSIGHT ⊖ ACTION

1. Are there any potential reasons why you'd consider dropping out of college?

2. Why would these factors influence you? Do you expect them to? What hangs in the balance?

3. What actions can you take *now* to help prevent these issues from overtaking your college education?

4. How might a clear understanding of your goals help to keep you focused?

Exercise 3.1 *Picture* Success!

As a group of two to four students, purchase a disposable camera. (Or your instructor may provide you with a digital camera, checked out from your campus media center.) Go on a scouting expedition and take pictures of all the things you'll need in order to be successful in college. Your pictures may be of campus support centers, people, other students—whatever you find that will contribute directly to your academic success. Bring your pictures to class and present them to your classmates, explaining the reasons why you chose to include each picture. If your pictures are digital, put them into a PowerPoint presentation to show your classmates.

Financial Resources: Managing Your Money

CHALLENGE → REACTION

Challenge: How good are you at managing your finances?

Reaction: Fill out this ten-question survey to get an indication of how financially savvy you are.

	Always true of me	Sometimes true of me	Never true of me
1. At any given moment in time, I know the balance in my checkbook.			
2. I use my credit card for particular types of purchases only, such as gas or food.			
3. I pay off my credit card bills in full every month.			
4. I know the interest rate on my credit card.			
5. I resist impulse buying and only spend when I need things.			
6. I have a budget and I follow it.			
7. I put money aside to save each month.			
8. When I get a pay raise, I increase the proportion of money I save.			
9. I keep track of my spending on a daily or weekly basis.			
10. I don't allow myself to get pressured by others into buying things I don't really need.			

> "I'd say it's been my biggest problem all my life ... it's money. It takes a lot of money to make these dreams come true."
>
> **Walt Disney, American animator, entrepreneur, and philanthropist (1901–1966)**

Look over your responses. If you have more checks in the "Never true of me" column than you do in either of the two others, you may be able to put the information you're about to read in this chapter to good use!

Let's face it: money is important. Even though they say money can't buy happiness, plenty of folks would like to test the hypothesis! In one recent national study, nearly three-quarters of first-year students said they think it's essential or very important to be "very well-off financially," and in another study, 80 percent of 18- to 25-year-olds in America cited getting rich as a top goal for this generation of students.[2] How do you feel about that? Can money buy happiness? So what does financial management in college have to do with financial success in life? Studies show that working too many hours for pay increases your chances of dropping out of college, the route to life success.[3] Many students find themselves working more to pay off major credit card debt, which in turn takes time away from their studies, or taking a semester off from college to work to pay off their credit cards and never coming back: "Finances are the most common reason college students give for dropping out."[4] While there's evidence that working a moderate amount can help you polish your time and energy management skills, the real secret to financial success in college can be reduced to one word: *budget*. Unpleasant as the word *budget* is to many of us, you can't count on winning the lottery or falling into money from a long-lost relative. You have to earn your money through hard work and spend and save it wisely.

Photodisc/Getty Images

> **"The safest way to double your money is to fold it over and put it in your pocket."**
>
> Kin Hubbard, cartoonist, journalist, and philosopher

The Ins and Outs of Money Management

Early in your first term, if not before, build a realistic, working budget. Okay, creating a budget may sound like drudgery, but it is important. According to one study, only 44 percent of college students clearly understood the term *budget*.[5] In another study, 79 percent of college students—like Jessica—admitted that they never talked with their parents about a budget.[6] Many students never bother to create a budget—and plenty of those who do don't actually use it![7]

A budget is simply an itemized estimate of income and expenses that helps you develop a personal spending plan. When you break down your *money in* versus *money out*, you see reality in black and white, and you may be surprised by comparing the two totals. You may also realize that you need to put the skids on your unplanned spending. Complete Exercise 3.2 to help you develop a budget of your own.

Exercise 3.2 Your Monthly Budget

Part A: Monthly Income

Loans, grants, scholarships	$_____
Support from parents, other family members, spouse, etc.	$_____
Paycheck	$_____
Cash on hand	$_____
Other	$_____
Total	**$_____**

How much income do you expect to make per month? Make sure you figure in everything.

Next, begin recording your monthly expenditures. Start with fixed costs that remain the same from month to month, such as rent or a car payment. Do you pay tuition in installments, or is all your tuition due by a certain date? It may help to collect actual receipts or credit card bills and have them in front of you as you work. Once you begin recording, you may be surprised to find out exactly where your money goes.

(continued)

Part B: Monthly Expenses

Tuition	$_____
Room or rent/mortgage	$_____
Board or food (groceries)	$_____
Books, supplies for school	$_____
Transportation, car payment, etc.	$_____
Computer/electronics (printer cartridges, high-speed Internet hookup, etc.)	$_____
Travel (trips home, vacations, etc.)	$_____
Entertainment (movies, music CDs, DVDs, eating out)	$_____
Utilities (phone, electricity, heat, water, garbage removal, etc.)	$_____
Personal items (haircut/color, cosmetics, gym membership, etc.)	$_____
Credit card payments	$_____
Cash withdrawals	$_____
Other (child care, vet visits, etc.)	$_____
Total	$_____
Money IN from Part A	$_____
(Minus) Money OUT from Part B	$_____
Amount remaining to save or invest	$_____

Emotional Intelligence (EI) Research In the famous marshmallow challenge, students who could delay gratification of eating marshmallows placed in front of them as children were more successful later in life. Also, remember that EI can be developed—getting students to delay gratification of material things is often connected to self-control, which spills over into other parts of life.

Look over your expenses. Obviously, if your expenditure total is larger than your income, it's time to reevaluate and come up with a budget you can actually live with. If you've never kept a checkbook, used a credit card, or taken a financial management class, get the know-how you'll need to manage your money. Your school may offer a "managing your money" workshop through its learning center. Check out library materials or explore credible websites on this subject to learn all you can. After you get a handle on your current financial situation, it's even a good idea to start to save and invest whatever you can afford on a monthly basis. The future—which seems a long way off now—will arrive sooner than you think.

Exercise 3.3 Create a Spending Log

How much money do you spend on an average day? Take a look at this student's spending log, then complete one for yourself. Money has a way of slipping through our fingers. Choose one entire day that is representative of your spending, and use this chart to keep track of how you spend money. Write down *everything* from seemingly small, insignificant items to major purchases, and explain why you made that purchase. Your log may look something like this student's:

TIME	ITEM	LOCATION	AMOUNT	REASON
8:00 a.m.–9:00 a.m.	coffee and bagel	campus coffee cart	$ 3.50	overslept!
9:00 a.m.–10:00 a.m.	typing paper	bookstore	$ 2.50	history paper due
10:00 a.m.–11:00 a.m.	gas fill-up	convenience store	$35.00	running on fumes!
11:00 a.m.–12:00 p.m.	burger and fries	fast-food restaurant	$ 6.00	lunch on the run
12:00 p.m.–1:00 p.m.	toiletries, etc.	drugstore	$18.00	ran out
1:00 p.m.–2:00 p.m.	bottled water	bookstore	$ 2.50	forgot to bring
2:00 p.m.–3:00 p.m.	notebook, supplies	bookstore	$12.00	book bag stolen
3:00 p.m.–4:00 p.m.	STUDY TIME			
4:00 p.m.–5:00 p.m.	STUDY TIME			

5:00 p.m.–6:00 p.m.	pizza	nearby pizza place	$12.50	met friends
6:00 p.m.–7:00 p.m.	soft drink	bookstore	$ 1.50	bring to library
7:00 p.m.–8: 00 p.m.	candy bar	vending machine	$ 1.50	munchies!
8:00 p.m.–9:00 p.m.	laundry	campus laundromat	$ 5.00	out of clean clothes
9:00 p.m.–10:00 p.m.		STUDY TIME		
10:00 p.m.–11:00 p.m.		STUDY TIME		
11:00 p.m.–12:00 a.m.		weekend movie, online tickets, DVDs, CDs	$129.00	friends' recommendations
		cell phone upgrade	$20.00	need plan w/ more minutes

This student has spent $249 today without doing anything special! When you analyze his expenditures, you can find patterns. He seems to (1) spend money at the campus bookstore throughout the day, (2) spend relatively large amounts of money online, (3) be particularly vulnerable late at night, and (4) spend money grabbing food on the run. These are patterns he should be aware of if he wants to control his spending. He could pack food from home to save a significant amount of money, for example. Now create your own chart.

TIME	ITEM	LOCATION	AMOUNT	REASON
8:00 a.m.–9:00 a.m.				
9:00 a.m.–10:00 a.m.				
10:00 a.m.–11:00 a.m.				
11:00 a.m.–12:00 p.m.				
12:00 p.m.–1:00 p.m.				
1:00 p.m.–2:00 p.m.				
2:00 p.m.–3:00 p.m.				
3:00 p.m.–4:00 p.m.				
4:00 p.m.–5:00 p.m.				
5:00 p.m.–6:00 p.m.				
6:00 p.m.–7:00 p.m.				
7:00 p.m.–8: 00 p.m.				
8:00 p.m.–9:00 p.m.				
9:00 p.m.–10:00 p.m.				
10:00 p.m.–11:00 p.m.				

Activity Option Students might want to share how much they spend in a typical day. Group students by their spending from zero to $10, $10 to $50, and above $50. Have the groups identify some things that they could have done without and then share results with the class.

The Perils of Plastic

CHALLENGE ⟶ REACTION

Challenge: What are the pros and cons of using credit cards over cash?

Reaction: _____

College tuition is expensive, and so are housing, transportation, computers, cell phones, books, and food. College costs are spiraling upward, but not just because of tuition increases. Graduates often place the blame for their financial woes on the almighty credit card they signed up for that

> **"As a child, a library card takes you to exotic, faraway places. When you're grown up, a credit card does it."**
>
> **Sam Ewing, professional writer**

Emotional Intelligence (EI) Research Stress tolerance is an area of emotional intelligence that college students can relate to. There are a variety of stressors in college, but one can be controlled. While it may be easier for some students than others, impulse control, or the lack of it, is key for students in delaying gratification and thus sometimes avoiding unnecessary stress.

very first day of college. They stopped at a booth on campus, snapped up the credit card offer with zero percent interest (for the first month only, it turns out), and got a free T-shirt (that ended up costing a lot because of a hefty annual fee).

Credit cards make it easy for students to sink deeper and deeper into debt without even realizing it. And even though debt can become a real worry, many students still ask regularly, "Hey, where are we going for dinner tonight?" instead of eating food they've already paid for. In today's world of spontaneous pleasure-seeking and expensive toys, it's important to fully understand that, eventually, bills have to be paid.

Unlike previous generations of college students, credit cards have always been a part of your life. You spent your growing-up years watching adults whip out their credit cards faster than Wild Bill Hickok whipped out his pistol during Deadwood gunfights. It's the natural, ordinary thing to do, and it's much more convenient than paying with cash. However, recent research shows a modest decline in credit card abuse among college students, and that's good news. Perhaps students are beginning to understand the perils of plastic. Still, college students are offered an average of eight credit cards during the first week of school, and the average college student still carries four credit cards and has an average outstanding balance of $2,169.[8]

In fact, some students collect credit cards like your Grandmother collects pictures of you—and max them all out! Two-thirds of undergraduates make the minimum payment each month, and 11 percent say they can't even do that.[9] Everything bought on long-term credit costs more than it would if you paid cash. Eventually, monthly finance charges on credit cards can mount higher than the expenditures themselves. Just as for Jessica in the "FOCUS Challenge Case," spiraling out-of-control debt can creep up on you. In one study, university

Box 3.1 Financial Aid: Top-Ten FAQs

Most students need financial help of some kind to earn a college degree. Here is some information to help you navigate your way financially.[10]

1. **Who qualifies for financial aid?** You may not think you qualify for financial aid, but it's a good idea to apply anyway. You won't know until you try, and some types of aid are based on criteria other than need.

2. **What does FAFSA stand for? And where do I get a copy?** FAFSA stands for Free Application for Federal Student Aid, and you can get a copy from your campus Financial Aid office, a public library, by calling 1-800-4-FED-AID, or go to www.fafsa.ed.gov and fill out the FAFSA online.

3. **What types of financial aid exist?** You can receive financial aid in the form of scholarships, fellowships, loans, grants, or work-study awards. Generally, scholarships and fellowships are for students with special academic, artistic, or athletic abilities; students with interests in specialized fields; students from particular parts of the country; or students from underrepresented populations. Typically, you don't repay them. Loans and grants come in a variety of forms and from several possible sources, either government or private. Typically, loans must be repaid. In addition, if you qualify for a need-based work-study job on or off campus, you can earn an hourly wage to help pay for school.

4. **When should I apply?** You can apply for financial aid any time after January 1 of the year you intend to go to college (because tax information from the previous year is required), but you must be accepted and enrolled to receive funds.

5. **Do I have to reapply every year?** Yes. Your financial situation can change over time. Your brothers or sisters may start college while you're in school, for example, which can change your family's status.

6. **How can I keep my financial aid over my college years?** Assuming your financial situation remains fairly similar from year to year, you must demonstrate that you're making progress toward a degree in terms of credits and a minimum GPA.

7. **Who's responsible for paying back my loans?** You are. Others can help you, but ultimately the responsibility is yours and yours alone. If your parents forget to make a payment or don't pay a bill on time, you will be held responsible.

8. **If I leave school for a time, do I have to start repaying my loans right away?** Most loans have a grace period of six or nine months before you must begin repayment. You can request an extension if you "stop out," but you must do so before the grace period ends.

9. **If I get an outside scholarship, should I report it to the Financial Aid office on campus?** Yes. They'll adjust your financial aid package accordingly, but those are the rules.

10. **Where can I find out more?** Your best source of information is in the Office of Financial Aid right on your own campus. Or call the Federal Student Aid Information Center at 1-800-433-3243 and ask for a free copy of *The Student Guide: Financial Aid* from the U.S. Department of Education.

administrators stated that they lose more students to credit card debt than to academic failure.[11] Here are two interesting financial facts about plastic you may not know:

> **Graduating with an out-of-control credit card balance can make your life difficult for years to come.** Typically, a bad credit rating sticks with you for seven years. It may be difficult to get a loan or finance a big purchase until that time is over. If you're able to secure a loan, interest rates may be higher because of the black marks on your record. After you complete your college degree, you may want to get married, buy a car, or invest in a house. Look at these potentially shocking figures:

> The average cost of a wedding = $27,690[12]
> The average price of a new car = $28,000[13]
> The average price of a new house = $264,540[14]

Your ability to get a job or go to graduate school may be hurt by a bad credit rating. Employers, even medical schools, often run routine credit checks on applicants. Although the future may seem a long way off now,

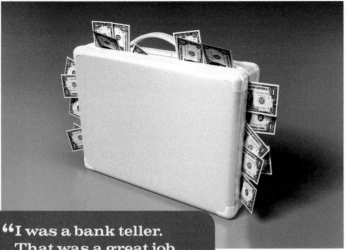

> **"I was a bank teller. That was a great job. I was bringing home $450,000 a week."**
>
> **Joel Lindley, comedian**

it's important to evaluate your short-term spending habits in terms of your long-term goals.

> **Graduating with a good credit rating helps.** Despite all the warnings you're reading in this chapter, you don't have to avoid paying by credit altogether. Establishing a good credit rating while you're in college can benefit you enormously, if you play your cards right. And you need to get a credit card in the first place to establish good credit. Eventually, if you build up your good credit by spending responsibly and paying your bills on time and in full, if possible, you'll be the beneficiary of your own financial wisdom when you do want to invest in a big-ticket item later.

INSIGHT ➔ ACTION

1. Look back at your spending log and identify your particular weaknesses. What are they? Why do you find buying these things so compelling?

2. Are there times of the day or people you're around that influence your spending? If so, describe them.

3. What actions can you take to prevent people and circumstances from adversely affecting your spending habits? Describe specific steps you plan to take.

Getting "Fiscally Fit": Ten Suggestions to Curb Your Credit Card Spending

Here are some financial recommendations worth serious consideration. While some of them may seem obvious, *knowing about* and *doing* are two different things. You'd be surprised at just how many students get stressed out by financial worries.

1. **Leave home without it.** Don't routinely take your credit card with you. Use cash and save your credit card for true emergencies. Do you really want to risk paying interest on today's ice cream cone years from now? Use your credit card for essential items only, like gas or groceries. We live in a world with unfathomable choices. When you put yourself in tempting situations, sometimes it's hard to resist.

2. **Don't spend money you don't have.** Only charge what you can pay for each month. Charging items feels different than paying cash for them. You think, optimistically, that you'll be able to pay when the time comes. Just because your credit card limit is $2,000 doesn't mean you need to spend that much each month. "Ca-ching! Ca-ching!" may be music to your ears now, but how about later when it's time to pay up? Remember that procrastination doesn't just apply to time; it applies to money, too. A spring break trip that costs $1,000 will take 12 years of minimal payments to pay off at an 18 percent interest rate. And that $1,000 trip will eventually cost you $2,115! You may assume that you'll pay off all your credit card bills when you graduate and

get a good job. But it's hard to get ahead when a quarter or more of your take-home salary is hijacked off the top to pay off your debt. When will you ever catch up?

3. **Distinguish between** *needs* **and** *wants*. Like Jessica, you may think you need particular items in order to be socially accepted (spending money just like everyone else), optimally satisfied (buying alternative food because residence hall food isn't to your liking), or physically attractive (forking over money for pricy manicures). Here's a rule of thumb: If charging something simply helps you move from "acceptable" to "amazing," it's not an emergency. Don't give in to short-term whims. Do you really need a mocha latté every day? A regular old cup of coffee a day sets you back $500 a year! Some enjoyable habits—like having pizza delivered regularly—really add up! Remember that sometimes spending fills an emotional void. Having a $65 new red hoodie is hardly a life-or-death matter. It may feel important at the time, but let it sit for a day, and see how you feel tomorrow.

4. **Understand how credit works.** It's important to know the basics. In one study, 71 percent of college students had no idea how much interest they were paying on their credit card bills.[15] Here are some terms you need to know:

> **Credit reports.** Your college or university keeps records about you even after you graduate—a transcript or history of your grades, for example. Just like your academic history, your financial history is maintained by a credit bureau, one of several credit-reporting agencies: Equifax, Experian, and TransUnion. Banks and stores submit your grades that together create your financial transcript. Your financial grades are based on factors like these: (1) how many credit cards you owe money on, (2) how much money you owe, and (3) how many late payments you make. Bad grades on your credit report can make your life difficult later.

> **Fees.** Credit card companies charge you in three ways: annual fees (a fee you must pay every year to use the card), finance charges (a charge for "loaning" you the money you can't pay back when your bill is due), and late fees (for missing a monthly payment deadline). Credit cards loan you money and charge you money to use it, and they sometimes use tricky rhetoric. Offers sound so good—how could anyone say no? For example, credit cards that advertise a zero percent interest are trying to entice you with an attractive offer that will soon switch to a normal interest rate. The fine print is worth reading. Student credit card interest rates and late fees can be substantially higher than those for working adults. Working adults may pay 14 percent to your 24 percent, for example. It may not be fair, but credit card companies aren't nice, friendly organizations that want you to have everything your heart desires. They're out to make money just like the stores, gas stations, and restaurants you buy from. If you expect to pay your bill in full each month, and you don't care about features such as frequent flyer miles or rebates, choose a card with no annual fee. If you can't pay the full bill each month, go for a lower

Emotional Intelligence (EI) Research Self-regard is an important emotional intelligence dimension that is strongly correlated with success in life. One way to enhance self-regard is to stop comparing one's self with others. Individuals who have to have the latest thing to look good or feel better for the moment may be compensating for low self-regard and esteem.

Teachable Moment Consider having students request a free online credit report. Check with your Financial Aid Office for suggestions. Similarly, ask if anyone in the class has had a credit report done and if they were surprised by what they found.

Sensitive Situation Remember that you may have students who are using credit cards for basic life necessities and not frivolous things. Often students who do not have financial help are using credit cards for books (or diapers if they are raising children) and not expensive whims.

interest rate. If you plan to get cash advances via your credit card, choose a card that charges lower fees for those. Look closely at how long the grace period is, what late fees you'll be charged (some as high as $50), and how much it'll cost you if you go over your charging limit. It's a matter of choosing wisely to match your needs. Shop around!

> **Credit card insurance.** Be aware that if someone steals your credit card or you lose it, you are only obligated to pay the first $50 of charges someone else racks up. (Keep a list of your credit card numbers and their customer service toll-free numbers in a safe place, and report your missing card to the credit card company right away, however.) According to the federal Truth in Lending Act, you *don't* need to buy credit card insurance to cover amounts over $50.[16]

> **The fine print.** How can you learn more? Read your credit card contract carefully. For example, with some cards, you start paying interest the moment you charge something. Under federal law, all credit card applications must disclose certain essential information, which is often on their website. Peruse the Federal Reserve website for vital, bottom line information.[17]

5. **Track your credit card expenses.** All kinds of tools—technology-based and other-wise—can help you discover where your money actually goes. If you get in the habit of recording every credit card purchase or entering it online, you'll come out ahead. Use a credit card with a low limit, or use a debit card to keep track of your spending. You must first establish a checking account at a bank, and then each time you use your debit card for a purchase, the amount you spend will be instantly deducted. Instead of waiting for your credit card statement to arrive to find out your financial state of affairs, you can keep track continually.

6. **Don't use your college grants or loans to pay off your credit card.** This is truly a losing proposition that can cause you to sink deeper and deeper into debt. If you rob Peter to pay Paul, as the saying goes, you'll never catch up. Normal daily consumer expenditures like groceries, meals out, and gas are viewed as bad debt if they get out of control. College tuition and mortgages—things that improve you in the long run, on the other hand, are considered good debt as long as you don't default on them. Don't mix the two pots.[18] Defaulting on (or discontinuing to pay back) a college loan has serious consequences. The Internal Revenue Service can withhold your U.S. personal income tax refund and apply it to the amount you owe, or your employer may be asked to deduct payments from your paycheck. If you return to school, you won't be entitled to additional federal student aid.[19] Typically, depending on the type of loan you have, if you're attending school at least half time, you have six to nine months after you graduate, leave school, or drop below half-time status before you must begin

"I've got all the money I'll ever need, if I die by four o'clock."

Henny Youngman, comedian

repaying your loan. Check with your funding agency or campus loan office for information that applies directly to you.[20]

7. **Don't juggle credit card balances.** One study found that some students had as many as twenty-two credit cards![21] Juggling money between credit cards shouldn't be perceived as an amazing, death-defying, acrobatic feat. You can become so preoccupied with managing your debt that you can't focus on anything else.

8. **Watch out for credit card identity theft scams.** Imagine this hypothetical situation: The week before school starts, you receive a call at home from (your college's name) with a credit card offer for new students. The person at the other end of the line not only offers you a free credit card, but also promises to send you a $200 gift certificate if you sign up. You'd just need to give the caller your Social Security number and your bank account information to get your new credit card into their system. Sound good? It isn't. Actually this situation isn't hypothetical. An investigation proved it was a clear case of identity theft.[22]

9. **If you're already in credit card trouble, ask for help.** Talk to your parents, an older brother or sister, an adult you trust, or someone who can help you figure

Teachable Moment Has anyone in the class had their identity stolen? Do they know of anyone that has? If so, would they be willing to share the experience with the class? Remind students that when they apply for credit, they are giving away their Social Security number, which is one of the main ways to steal another's identity.

YOUR TYPE IS ShOwing

What's the relationship between personality type and managing money? What would you predict? Here's what some experts say:

FINANCIAL PLANNERS. Picture an accountant in a prestigious Wall Street firm, sitting behind a desk, calculating your investment portfolio. There's a good chance he's an SJ (sensor and judger). Why? SJ's are detail-oriented, realistic, and organized. They work within clients' financial parameters and monitor saving and investing—just what you want in an accountant, right? In their personal lives, SJ's are often careful about spending money, too. They calculate, plan, spend, invest, and save. A student with a strong SJ preference might think twice about an exotic spring break vacation if she knew it would seriously blow her already-tight budget.

FUN-LOVING SPENDERS. Picture someone on a shopping spree, finding incredible bargains, and loving every minute of it. That's most likely an SP (sensor and perceiver). SP's are detail-oriented and practical just like SJ's, but they are also on a perpetual serendipity quest. They enjoy unplanned discoveries, and saving a dollar or two just makes it that much more fun. But they find everyday spending that must be done—like paying the rent—to be much less satisfying.

BIG-HEARTED PHILANTHROPISTS. Picture a generous, wealthy community leader who donates millions to a good cause. NF's (iNtuitive and feeler) are visionaries, people who don't just see things as they are, but who are able to envision how things *could* be. In particular, they build connections with others to help them accomplish their goals. An NF student might join with other campus leaders, solicit broad-based donations, and begin a scholarship fund for needy students.

GRAND SCHEMERS. Picture someone at the helm of a giant Fortune 500 corporation who has a big-picture view of the future. She's intuitive—she trusts her instincts—but she also thinks things through very carefully. On a personal level, NT's (iNtuitive and thinker) think about how they spend and save money, and they can work toward long-term financial goals. An NT student, for example, who might be planning to move to an off-campus apartment next year, might buy ahead—a bedspread on sale or a set of towels, for example.

Of course, personality type doesn't dictate your "fiscal fitness," but it can inform you about some of your possible spending tendencies. For example, extraverts often enjoy the social aspect of shopping with friends. And the more opportunities they allow themselves to do that, the more likely they may be to spend money.[23]

Activity Option As a class, develop some "fiscally fit" ideas. Ask the class to rank the top three practices that they believe are relatively easy to change and would help them stay "fiscally fit."

out what to do. Formulate a realistic plan to reduce your debt. Better yet, don't get yourself in financial trouble in the first place.

10. **Do more than simply read this chapter.** Put all this advice into action, and lower your stress level by setting credit card limits and enforcing them.

Activity Option For a "Your Type Is Showing" activity, divide students in the class based on perceivers and judgers (P's and J's). Give each group $100 of play money that they could use when they are off for a long weekend. What would each group do with the money and why? Tell students that they don't have to spend the money if they don't want to.

INSIGHT ⊖ ACTION

1. Do you ever find yourself using your credit card automatically without even thinking about whether or not you should be charging a particular item? Are you sometimes surprised by the size of your bills? Describe a time when this happened.

2. Describe a situation in which you spent more than you realized. What was it about the situation that may have contributed to your willingness to do that?

3. Of the ten suggestions to become more "fiscally fit" described in this section, which ones, specifically, will you act on? How will you accomplish your goals?

Technology Resources: Net Life

The Good Old Days. It used to be that college students went to class and listened to professors lecture. Of course, they still do. But today's classrooms are often much more creative. Look at these examples of how technology can enrich learning. Have you experienced any technology-enriched learning experiences like these in any of your classes?

> Instead of the large lecture course in physics, students at one university sit at round tables in groups of nine with three students sharing a laptop. Students follow the professor's PowerPoint presentation onscreen and even monitor results from real experiments done through sensors that feed into the computer.[24]

> American students in an intercultural communication class work with student counterparts in a college in Mexico City. Together they work online to negotiate a hypothetical joint venture between companies in the two countries.[25]

> Students take a freshman electrical engineering course in which they build robots. With a look only an engineer could love, robots are replete with wires, batteries, motors, and bumpers. Besides learning the electrical engineering theory behind what makes robots work, students must design robots that can pass the final exam by negotiating an obstacle course with 90-degree turns and nearly full-circle spins to the finish line.[26]

> Students in college classrooms across the country are learning one click at a time. Students are using handheld wireless remote controls— something like the one you use with your TV—to report in (for attendance purposes), answer quiz questions, vote on controversial issues, and give the professor feedback on their level of understanding.[27]

These classrooms provide fertile learning environments for diverse learning styles. Does that mean you can forget about those listening and note-taking skills you thought were important? Absolutely not! In fact, it may mean that in addition to those skills you need a highly cultivated array of *information literacy* tools—more about that later. Today, wikis, blogs, vlogs, IMs, YouTube, and Facebook are part of your active Net life on a busy campus in an information-rich world.

E-Learning versus C-Learning

CHALLENGE ⊝ REACTION

Challenge: List five potential disadvantages to e-learning and five potential solutions to deal with them.

Reaction: _____   _____
    _____   _____
    _____   _____
    _____   _____
    _____   _____

What do an American soldier in Afghanistan, a single mother of twin toddlers in California, and a victim of cerebral palsy in New York have in common? All three are taking the same online course in psychology. Instead of c-learning (traditionally, in the classroom), they're engaging in *distance education* or e-learning (electronically, online).

Of course, most of your college courses are hybrids: they each have an online component. You e-mail your professor, use software to track your progress, upload assignments, and download handouts, along with the classroom part of the course. But if you haven't already, chances are you'll be engaged in distance learning in a totally online environment for at least one of your college classes.

Teachable Moment Lead a discussion on personality type and learning electronically. What might work for extraverts (E's) or introverts (I's)? Can an E, for example, be disciplined enough to work independently online?

Chapter Crossover Refer students back to Chapter 2 and their personality and learning styles to help make even stronger connections to individual preferences.

What are the differences between e-learning and c-learning? E-learning is sometimes defined as structured learning that takes place without a teacher at the front of the room. If you're an independent, self-motivated learner, e-learning can be a great way to learn because you are in control.

> **You control *when* you learn.** Instead of that dreaded 8:00 a.m. class—the only section that's open when you register—you can schedule your e-learning when it's convenient for you. If you want to do your coursework at midnight in your pj's, who's to know?

> **You control *how* you learn.** If you are an introvert, e-learning may work well for you. You can work thoughtfully online and take all the time you need to reflect. If you are an extravert, however, you may become frustrated by the lack of warm bodies around. Jumping into threaded discussions and chatting online may satisfy some of those needs. If you're a kinesthetic learner, the keyboard action may suit you well. Since you're working independently, you can do whatever you need to do to accommodate your own learning style.

Stockbyte/Getty Images

> "It was not so very long ago that people thought that semiconductors were part-time orchestra leaders and microchips were very small snack foods."
>
> **Geraldine Ferraro, Democratic politician**

Comstock Images/Jupiter Images

> **You control how fast you learn.** You know for a fact that students learn at different rates. With e-learning, you don't have to feel you're slowing down the class if you continue a line of questioning or worry about getting left in the dust if everyone else is way ahead of you.

E-learning can be a very effective way to learn, but it does require some adjustments. Here are some suggestions for making the best of your e-learning opportunities.

1. **Work to obtain course material.** Instead of listening to your professor lecture at the front of the room, you will have to obtain information by downloading files or by reading lecture notes yourself. While this may sound like a deterrent to learning, some studies show that students work harder and longer online.

2. **Communicate your needs to your professor.** Your professor won't be able to see your quizzical looks when you don't understand something. Instead of wishing she'd somehow notice or hoping for the best, you'll need to take direct action by e-mailing her, for example.

3. **Stay in touch with other students in the course.** Use e-mail to communicate with your cyber-classmates to build an online learning community. They may be able to clarify an assignment or coach you through a tough spot.

4. **Take notes.** When you're sitting through a lecture, you handwrite notes to review later. If you're reading lecture notes online, open a word processing application and toggle back and forth for note-taking purposes.

5. **Keep your antivirus program up to date.** When you upload assignment files, you run the risk of infecting your professor's computer with whatever viruses your computer may have. Make sure your antivirus software is up to date to keep that embarrassing accident from happening (not only for online courses, but in general).

6. **Create a positive learning environment.** Since you'll most likely to do your e-learning at home or in your residence hall room, make sure the environment is conducive to learning. If your computer is next to the TV, it may take superhuman self-control to stay focused on your e-course. Do your work in a computer lab, or if you have a laptop, find a spot that's calm, well lit, and quiet.

7. **Use each login session as an opportunity to review.** It's natural—and preferable—to begin each online session by reviewing what you did or how much progress you made last time. Physically logging on can become a signal to take stock before moving forward with new course material.

8. **Call on your time management skills.** If your e-course is self-paced, you'll need to plan ahead, schedule due dates, and above all, discipline yourself to make continual progress. If you're sharing a computer with other family members, you'll need to negotiate a master schedule. Remember that you may need to be online at particular times to engage in class chats or discussions.[28]

"The illiterate of the 21st century will not be those who cannot read and write, but those who cannot learn, unlearn, and relearn."

Alvin Toffler, American writer and futurist

Sensitive Situation Keep in mind that there may be an electronic divide in the classroom. Even though computers are becoming as popular as television sets in households, not everyone has one. Or a computer at home may be outdated or shared by many. Remind students about on-campus labs, as well as free options, like hometown libraries, where they can access computers.

Teachable Moment What e-mail address do you use with your students? Is it campus e-mail or do you allow them to use a personal e-mail address? It is important to get students using their college e-mail accounts for all course-related work. By doing so, they check e-mail messages about school deadlines and announcements, as well as critical course updates. In some cases, faculty will not read e-mail from "redheadchick@aol.com," for example, as they are trying to avoid spam.

College Students and the Net:
The Good, the Bad, and the Ugly

CHALLENGE → REACTION

Challenge: What do you see as the best and worst aspects of using the Internet to help you learn in college?

Reaction: _____

The Good. You probably started using a computer sometime around your fourth or fifth birthday—maybe sooner. And now you can't imagine life without it. College students are the leading consumers of digital technology in the United States.[29] In one study, 79 percent of college students reported that the Internet has had a positive impact on their college academic experience.[30] For many of us, the Internet is how we get our news, our research, our entertainment, and our communication. When it comes to all the potential benefits of the Internet, think about advantages like these:

PhotoAlto/Getty Images

> **Currency.** While some of the information posted on the Internet is not particularly up to date, it is possible to access real-time information sources online. This is especially important when timing is everything—during a crisis or a national emergency, for example. Reports, articles, and studies that might take months to publish in conventional ways are available on the web as soon as they're written.

> **Availability.** The Internet never sleeps. If you can't sleep at 2:00 a.m., the Internet can keep you company. It can be a good friend to have. Unlike your real instructor who teaches other classes besides yours and attends marathon meetings, Professor Google is always in. For the most part, you can check your e-mail or log onto the Internet from wherever you are whenever you wish. The Internet is much more than one-stop shopping. It's one-stop everything. You can learn, work, listen, watch, shop, and communicate, all in one place.

> **Scope.** You can find out virtually anything you want to know on the Internet. You can get the recipe for multiple versions of the world's best chocolate chip cookie, find legal assistance if someone sideswipes your new set of wheels, and get medical advice on everything from <u>A</u>thlete's Foot to <u>Z</u>its. (Of course, real human beings are usually a better option for serious questions.)

> **Interactivity.** Unlike other media, the Internet lets you talk back—at least more quickly. You can write a letter to the editor of a newspaper and wait for a reply, or you can push buttons on your phone in response to an endless list of menu queries ("If you want directions in English, press 1 . . .") and finally get to a real-live human being. But the Internet lets you communicate instantaneously and incessantly. You can instant message to your heart's content, if you want to.

> **"For a list of all the ways technology has failed to improve the quality of life, please press three."**
>
> **Alice Kahn, technology author**

Activity Option Have students fill in the blank: My worst computer nightmare happened when _____. Have them share with the class. If no one offers an example, or you only get a few, hand out some index cards with situations like "lost my flash drive," "the power went off," "I ran out of paper," for example, and discuss ways to avoid these problems.

Emotional Intelligence (EI) Research Sometimes too much information is overwhelming, and sometimes too little information can be dangerous. While medical sites, like WebMD, are a great resource for students, they can also make students very stressed about minor medical issues. If they have just heard that their grandmother has cancer, they might go online to learn about it and be confronted suddenly with statistics that are frightening. From an EI perspective, students who have low impulse control, or weak reality testing, may jump to some very stressful, inaccurate conclusions.

> **Affordability.** As of January 2007, there were 11,093,529,692 Internet users worldwide; 210 million Americans are on the Net today.[31] For most of us, when it comes to the Internet, the price is right. After your initial investment in a computer, and your monthly access fee, you get a great deal for your money.

The Bad. Too much of a good thing—anything—can be bad. When anything becomes that central to our lives, it carries risks. Here are some Internet dangers worth contemplating:

> **Inaccuracy.** Often we take information presented to us at face value. The usual checks and balances to verify information on the Internet aren't always in place. Of course, online scholarly journals subject their published studies to peer review, and they only publish valid research online, but on many sites, the responsibility for verifying information rests with you—the information consumer. "Bob's Statistics Home Page" and the U.S. Census Bureau's website aren't equally valid.

> **Complacency.** It's easy to allow the convenience of the Internet to turn intellectual *curiosity* into intellectual *complacency*. Why bother doing hours of library research on the topic for your paper when others have already been there, done that, and published it on the Internet? If today's new definition of knowledge really has shifted, as experts say, from "being able to remember and repeat information to being able to find and use it," why not *find*

FOCUS ON CAREERS: JOHN M. HEARN JR., IT Systems Analyst

Q1: What did you major in, and where did you go to college? Why did you choose that particular school?

I received a bachelor's degree in Computer Engineering from the University of Michigan. I wanted a degree from a big engineering school with a first-rate reputation in my field. In my estimation, University of Michigan offered this, and I considered Ann Arbor to be one of the best college towns in the country, which just sealed the deal.

Q2: What do you do on a day-to-day basis in your job? What are your greatest challenges?

My department at Sanofi-Aventis Pharmaceuticals is responsible for engineering and maintaining the Common Desktop Solution for approximately 80,000 users. We analyze new technologies and evaluate whether and how they can benefit from that solution. But we are a pharmaceutical company, not a computer company, so we are supporting our employees as they do *their* jobs, primarily. On a day-to-day basis, my greatest challenges are not technical. Instead, they involve managing time and ideas and working with others as a team member.

Q3: As a career field, high-tech is sometimes described as a "hot" job market for college graduates. It seems to have its ups and downs, but maybe that's true for many different professions. Why did *you* decide on a high-tech career?

I have always been drawn to technology, and it has always come fairly easily to me. Because IT is my father's career field, my interest was always met with enthusiasm and encouragement, not only from him, but from everyone that I talked to. Problem solving and logic have always been strengths for me, and although I would have loved to have been a rock-star, I decided to go with a career for which success was more certain. If you decide on a career that's likely to lead to success, instead of one that may be a constant struggle, it's bound to provide you with more happiness. At the time I was entering college, the high-tech field was in the midst of the dot-com boom, and future job possibilities seemed to be limitless.

Q4: Is the job you have now your dream job? If not, what would your dream job be—and how would that job differ from the one you have now? Can students expect a dream job when they graduate—or does it take time to build a technical career?

I'm a fairly recent college graduate, so the honest answer to that question is no. Very few people land their dream jobs right out of college. By the time I graduated, the economic picture had changed somewhat. But fortunately, I could rely on connections I had made during an internship in college to find a job. Employers are always interested in experience in addition to classes and grades. Internships help you gain experience that's hard to get on your own. My advice is: Never lose sight of your dream job, but always remember that you have to "grow" into it.

Q5: What skills do college students need in order to be successful in high-tech jobs? Are math skills really all that essential?

Other than the obvious knowledge and aptitude, students really need to be able to adapt to an ever-changing job marketplace in order to be information on the Internet and *use* it? The ultimate use, some students think, is downloading someone else's paper.[32] What's wrong with that? Besides the issue of plagarism, however, remember that the *how* of learning is as important as the *what*. If all you ever did was cut, paste, and download, you wouldn't learn how to do research yourself. College helps you learn skills you will need later in life—critical thinking, research, and writing skills, for example. You may never have to give your boss a five-page paper on the poetry of Wordsworth, but you may need to give her a five-page summary of your progress on the Jones Project. Work-related assignments require critical thinking, research, and writing. No one's researched that particular topic before. You'll have to do it yourself, and your job *now* is to make sure you develop the skills to do your job *in the future.*

> **Reductionism.** Being able to find the answer to almost everything in a matter of seconds can give us the false impression that what we find so readily is enough. Using the Internet as your sole source of information can lure you into surface, rather than deep, learning. When information is reduced to screen shots, soundbites, and video clips, it's easy to become a "reductionist," someone who shrinks things into quick bytes. Many questions don't have quick answers, and many problems don't have simple solutions.[33]

Teachable Moment See if your institution uses a plagiarism checker, like www.Turnitin.com. Students submit their papers to this online site, and through some quick electronic checking on the Internet, the program can identify if the paper has been plagiarized and create a report to the instructor. It can catch as few as nine words in a string from a web page or news article that haven't been appropriately cited. Also, if some other students submitted the same paper to this site, or even just parts of it, you will be notified.

Chapter Crossover As students begin to think about careers, remind them that they will be exploring this topic more in Chapter 12.

successful. They also really need to love the industry. Depending on the specifics of your job, yes, math skills *are* very important to today's high-tech professional. Realistically, you won't be asked to perform long division on the job, but you must understand mathematical processes—how and why they work. It's not just about memorizing formulas or algorithms, it's about knowing how math works, so that you can—as the saying goes—just do it.

Q6: What do you wish you had learned or paid more attention to in college?
If I had a chance to start college all over again, I would get more involved on campus. I'd take advantage of co-curricular activities such as societies that create a product or develop a relationship with a real-world enterprise—anything that helps you *apply* what you're learning in classes.

Q7: Beyond a college degree in a technical field, what other personal or personality characteristics are required for success?
To thrive in this highly competitive job market, it's important to be *proactive*, rather than *reactive*. Don't *wait* for things to happen—*make* them happen! Here's an example of what I mean. Many students continue on to college because they believe it's natural, or necessary, or because someone else wants them to. They *react* to what's expected. But when they finish college, there is no natural next step. They must create their own next step. If you decide to enter the world of IT, develop your own career path. Be *proactive*. But make sure that your path is flexible enough to adapt to the volatile world of technology.

C CREATE a Career Outlook

COMPUTER SCIENTIST
Have you ever considered a high-tech career as a computer professional? Here are some facts about this career to consider and some questions about yourself to ponder.

Facts to Consider

Academic preparation required: a wide range, from an associate's to a doctoral degree; however, a bachelor's degree is required for most jobs

Future workforce demand: Rapid growth is expected, with over 450,000 new jobs projected between 2004 and 2014. The rapidly growing and changing world of technology has generated a variety of career paths—computer scientists, database administrators, network systems analysts, computer programmers, technology trainers, software engineers, e-commerce specialists, and so forth.

Work environment: Most workers in this career field work in quiet, clean offices; however, increasingly, employees telecommute at least part of the time. Many employees in technology-related careers work more than a standard forty-hour week.

Most common psychological type preferences: introverted, sensing, thinking, judging[34]

Essential skills: technical, logical thinking, focusing, communication, analytical, problem-solving, and teamwork skills

Questions to Ponder
1. Do you have (or could you acquire) the skills this career requires?
2. What would you find most satisfying about this type of career?
3. What would you find most challenging about this type of career?
4. Are you interested in a career like this? Why or why not?

For more information, see U.S. Department of Labor, Bureau of Labor Statistics, *Occupational Outlook Handbook, 2006–2007 Edition.*[35]

For more career activities online, go to http://www.academic.cengage.com/collegesuccess/staley to do the Team Career exercises.

The Ugly. The Internet can be used in perverse ways. Take a look at one student's social networking page in Figure 3.1 and see if you can see where things are headed.

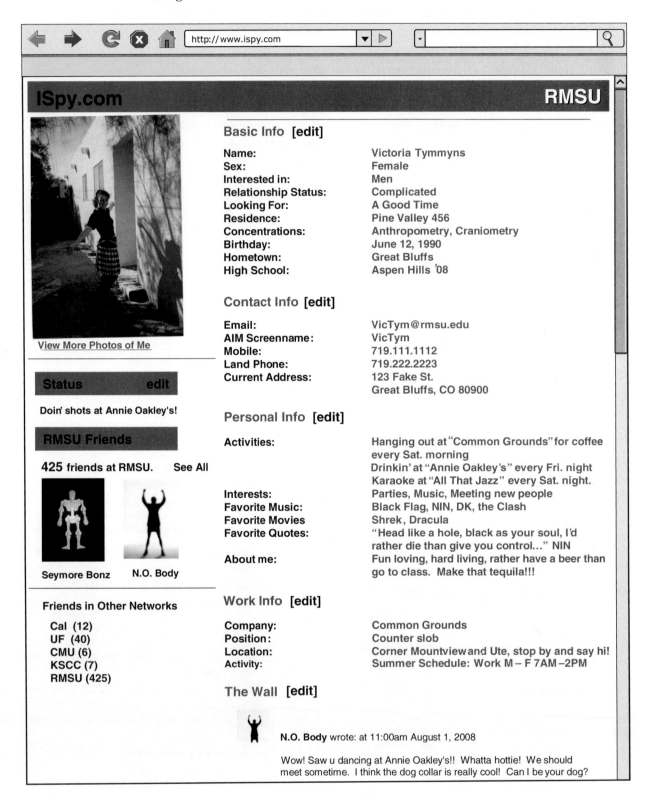

Figure 3.1

Fictional Ispy.com page

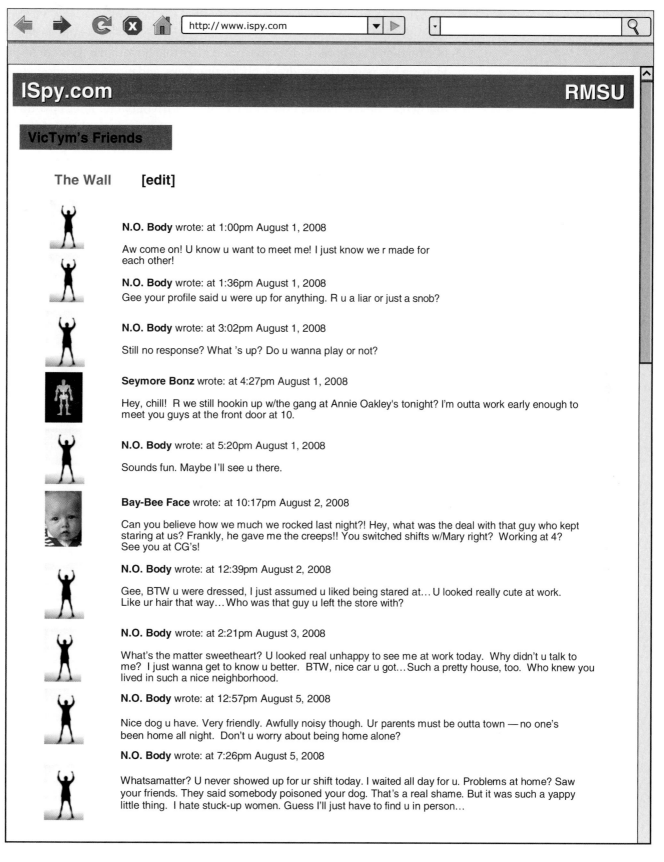

Figure 3.1

(continued)

Like the hypothetical Victoria Tymmyns (or her online name, VicTym) featured in Figure 3.1, some students publish inappropriate or confidential information on their Facebook and MySpace accounts that have dangerous consequences. Victoria has posted her address, phone numbers, and moment-by-moment whereabouts, and you can see that she's now being stalked by a predator. It's also true that what some students post in a moment of frivolity can later cost them a job opportunity. (Employers regularly check these sources for insider information on applicants.) News headlines sometimes report the dangers of Internet romances gone wrong. Researchers point out that almost half of U.S. children between ages 10 and 17 reported viewing pornography on the Internet over the past year; 80 percent say they stumbled on it accidentally by misspelling a word or while searching for unrelated content.[36] And some people are so addicted to the Net that they replace their uneventful real lives with seemingly exciting online ones.

What does all this have to do with you? Everything! It's important to remember that the Internet itself is neutral. It can be used constructively or destructively, based on the choices you make. It can be an exciting, invigorating, essential part of your college experience. Use it wisely!

Exercise 3.4 Technology Project: Group Ad

Working with two or three classmates and using PowerPoint, create a television ad (as professional-looking as possible) for the course for which you're using this book. Use text, images, and music. The advertisement shouldn't be long—two or three minutes, or the length of the song you use—but it should describe what the course is about and why other students should take it. Be as creative as you like! Once you've created your presentation, play your ad for the class. As an alternative, create a group ad for a campus resource—a campus support center, for example, or a student organization.

Library Resources and Your College Success

CHALLENGE ⊙ REACTION

Challenge: What does the term *information literacy* mean? By your definition, are you information literate?

Reaction: _____

You've heard it since you were a child: "The library is your friend." As a young child, it was exciting to go to the library, choose a book, check it out with your own library card, and bring it home to read. In college, the library is more than just a friend. It should become your best friend! Beyond Googling to find research for your assignments, learn your way around the actual, physical, non-cyber library on your campus. The library has many resources you won't find online, including real, honest-to-goodness librarians. Asking a reference librarian for help can save you hours of unproductive digging on your own.

Let's say, for example, that you are assigned a paper on a challenging subject in one of your courses, one you know absolutely nothing about right now. You might start by Googling your topic, but what can you find beyond the hits that come up immediately? Some of your instructors will insist you go beyond the Internet, avoid relying too much on encyclopedias and Wikipedia as you may have in your earlier schooling, and locate *primary* as opposed to *secondary* sources. Primary sources include authentic journals, historical letters, archaeological digs, or original art, for example. Secondary sources are once- (or more) removed—someone else reporting on or explaining primary sources. Primary sources are particularly important in some disciplines and in graduate work—writing a thesis, for example—after finishing an undergraduate degree.

After your initial exploration online, what's next? Here are three essential steps to making use of your campus's library:

1. Explore the catalog that lists all the books the library holds, most likely available electronically from the library's website.

2. Physically walk through the collections (books, periodicals—journals, magazines, and newspapers—audiovisual resources), and explore interlibrary loan possibilities. If you need a resource your library doesn't have, it's possible for your library to borrow it for you. (But be advised: Interlibrary loans take time, up to two weeks or longer. That's one of the reasons it's important to start your research projects early!)

3. Investigate *e-resources* (Internet and campus networks, databases, CDs, DVDs). On some campuses, the physical space for library books is shrinking. Space is being re-engineered by digitizing books and freeing up space for students to work individually or together on the changing assignments in college classes: designing websites and creating PowerPoint presentations, for example. There's a wealth of information at your fingertips, both online and in the stacks.[37]

Your campus library will be of help all the way through college. Start getting acquainted now!

❝I find that a great part of the information I have was acquired by looking up something and finding something else on the way.❞

Franklin P. Adams, American journalist and radio personality (1881–1960)

Teachable Moment Let students know that in addition to www.google.com, there is a more scholarly site called www.scholar.google.com, which searches scholarly works across many disciplines and includes books, abstracts, theses, and articles.

Exercise 3.5 The Campus Library: Drawing a Floor Plan

Make a date with a classmate to tour your campus's main library. One of you will be the "explorer," and the other the "recorder." As you walk through the building, the explorer will dictate what each section includes. The recorder will draw a floor plan, labeling each section. Remember to include every floor, and make your floor plan as accurate as possible, as if you were going to hand it out to new first-year students next year. As you work, answer these three questions:

1. Pinpoint the locations where you both expect to spend most of your actual time in the library, based on a major you may choose.

2. Where will you both feel most comfortable studying in the library: among the students working at long tables in the open, at a computer station of your own, or at a private desk away from other students?

3. What does your library have available that you couldn't find by doing Internet research exclusively?

Bring your floor plan to class to compare with the floor plans your classmates construct.

CHOOSE TO CHOOSE!

Have you ever thought about how many dozens, if not hundreds, of choices you make each day? From the second you wake up, you're making decisions, even about the simplest things, like whether to order a cappuccino or a latté; decaf, half-caf, or high-octane; nonfat, two-percent, or the real deal. Can you envision what it would be like to live in a "binary" culture, one in which the answer to many questions is simply "yes" or "no"? There is no infinitely long list of options to choose from. Believe it or not, such cultures exist.

We're lucky. Or are we? Psychologist and professor Barry Schwartz, in his book, *The Paradox of Choice: Why More Is Less* (2004), believes that our constant "forced choice" model of everyday life causes us to "invest time, energy, and no small amount of self-doubt, and dread." Choosing a new cell phone plan can take some people weeks while they research models of cell phones, minutes available, quotas of text messages, and Internet access, not to mention the fine print. Simply put: Being flooded with choices, while it feels luxurious, can be stressful and even unrewarding. Have you ever flipped through all two hundred channels available via your satellite dish, only to find there's nothing on worth watching? When each day is a nonstop stream of choice-making, it's enough to wear you down. Paralysis, anxiety, and stress rather than happiness, satisfaction, and perfection can be the result of too much "more."

Some of us, Schwartz says, are "maximizers"; we don't rest until we find the best. We spend inordinate amounts of time searching for some ideal, and when we finally settle on something, we regret choices we passed up. Others of us are "satisficers"; we're satisfied with what's good enough, based on our most important criteria. Of course, we all do some "maximizing" and some "satisficing," but generally, which are you?

Here are Schwartz's recommendations to lower our stress levels in a society where more can actually give us less, especially in terms of quality of life:

1. **Choose to choose.** Some decisions are worth lengthy deliberation; others aren't. Be conscious of the choices you make and whether they're worth the return on your investment. "Maximize" when it counts and "satisfice" when it doesn't. Don't let your time be sapped up with trivialities.

2. **Remember that there's always greener grass somewhere.** Someone will always have a better job than you do, a nicer apartment, or a more attractive romantic partner. Regret or envy can eat away at you, and second-guessing can bring unsettling dissatisfaction.

3. **Regret less and appreciate more.** While green grass does abound, so do sandpits and bumpy roads. That's an important realization, too! Value the good things you already have going for you.

4. **Build bridges, not walls.** Think about the ways in which the dozens of choices you've already made as a new college student give you your own unique profile or "choice-print": where you live, which classes you take, clubs you join, meal plan you select, campus events you attend, your small circle of friends, and on and on. Ironically, college is about becoming a community of learners, but we live in an age where individualism abounds. Remember that, and make conscious choices that will best help you succeed.[38]

> **"In a few hundred years, when the history of our time will be written from a long-term perspective, it is likely that the most important event historians will see is not technology, not the Internet, not e-commerce. It is an unprecedented change in the human condition. For the first time—literally—substantial and rapidly growing numbers of people have choices. For the first time, they will have to manage themselves. And society is totally unprepared for it."**
>
> Peter F. Drucker, management expert (1909–2005)

© Image 100/CORBIS

Information Literacy: Are You Literate?

Assume you are asked to write a five-page paper on *information literacy* for one of your classes. Where would you start? You know what literacy is, and you know what information is, but what is information literacy? Many experts would say it's *the* key to college success. If your reaction to this challenge was to go online, you're probably not alone. The first thing many students would do is Google the term. If you did that, you would get over fifty million hits. That's not much help—or rather it's too much help. What's next?

Let's say you scan the first ten hits, and you see the *Association of College and Research Libraries Institute for Information Literacy* site and the *National Forum for Information Literacy* home page, for example. You see that each of these pages lists links to dozens of other pages. You've begun your quest, and you're using your information literacy skills to research information literacy.

Information literacy is defined as knowing *when* you need information, *where* to find it, *what* it means, *whether* it's accurate, and *how* to use it. Information literacy includes six components, as seen in Figure 3.2. Think about them as a step-by-step process as you begin working on your next paper or presentation.[39]

Activity Option Have students list all of the Internet domains (for example, .com, .net, .org, and .edu) and brainstorm which might be the most reliable and credible. What features of a website might make someone suspicious?

Chapter Crossover Alert students that they will be exposed to more research techniques writing and speaking in Chapter 10. Remind them that research wil be a large part of their college courses, no matter which major they choose.

Emotional Intelligence (EI) Research The ability to manage stress is not only related to the type of stress but how we handle it. According to work done by Jerome Kagan, sensitive, quiet children are more prone to stress and panic disorders. But, keep in mind that quiet students may have much to say.

Emotional Intelligence (EI) Research Point out to students that comparing oneself to others is detrimental to developing strong emotional intelligence. Have students list their strengths, and if they're willing, discuss them.

Figure 3.2

Six Steps to Information Literacy

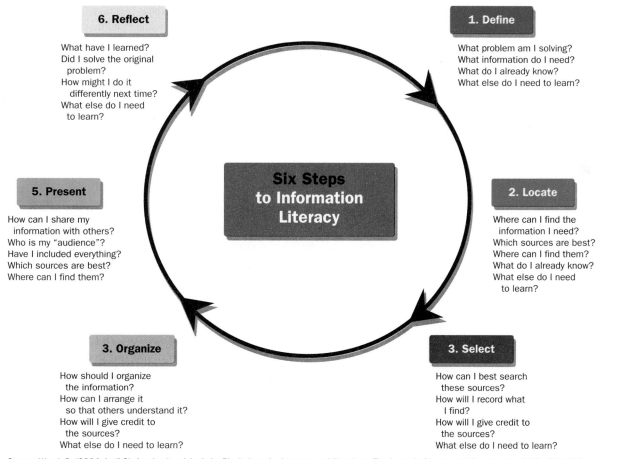

6. Reflect
What have I learned?
Did I solve the original
  problem?
How might I do it
  differently next time?
What else do I need
  to learn?

1. Define
What problem am I solving?
What information do I need?
What do I already know?
What else do I need to learn?

Six Steps to Information Literacy

5. Present
How can I share my
  information with others?
Who is my "audience"?
Have I included everything?
Which sources are best?
Where can I find them?

2. Locate
Where can I find the
  information I need?
Which sources are best?
Where can I find them?
What do I already know?
What else do I need
  to learn?

3. Organize
How should I organize
  the information?
How can I arrange it
  so that others understand it?
How will I give credit to
  the sources?
What else do I need to learn?

3. Select
How can I best search
  these sources?
How will I record what
  I find?
How will I give credit to
  the sources?
What else do I need to learn?

Source: Wood, G. (2004, April 9). Academic original sin: Plagiarism, the Internet, and librarians. *The Journal of Academic Librarianship, 30*(3), 237–242.

YOUR TOUGHEST CLASS

Identify a particular assignment in your most challenging class this term that will require you to use your information literacy skills. If your most challenging class does not include an assignment requiring you to use these particular skills, select another class in which a major project will challenge you to use them.

What is the specific assignment? For example, it could be "write a five-page paper in which you take a position on a controversial theme relating to our course topic." Now go through the six steps to information literacy as they relate to your assignment. What will you do to complete each step in order to do your best on your paper or presentation? Be as detailed as possible, answering the questions for each step.

1. DEFINE: _____
2. LOCATE: _____
   (a) Find three books on your topic, and list their titles, authors, publication dates, and publishers.
   (b) Find three articles from scholarly journals, and list their bibliographic information.
   (c) Work with one or more reference librarians, and list the librarian's name, and the day and time of your work session.
   (d) Find three relevant websites and list their URLs.
3. SELECT: _____
4. ORGANIZE: _____
5. PRESENT: _____
6. REFLECT: _____

Campus Resources:
HELP Is Not a Four-Letter Word

CHALLENGE ⊖ REACTION

Challenge: List five campus resources you already know about that first-year students should take advantage of. Identify the building and room number for each one.

Reaction: 1. _____
2. _____
3. _____
4. _____
5. _____

No student is an island; no student stands alone. It's not uncommon for new college students to feel isolated from time to time, even at a small school. Everything about your college experience is new, and you're adjusting gradually. That's why getting connected to other students, your instructors, and the campus itself is essential to your success in college. It's a simple but important notion, and not all students actually do it.

Some students, unfortunately, think that college should be like the drive-thru lane at the bank, which is designed to minimize time and effort. But think about it. How successful would you be at your eight-to-five job if you put in the minimum: arrived at eight on the dot every day, left at five o'clock sharp, maxed out your sick days when you weren't actually sick—and besides all those minimal investments, never got to know a soul, including your boss? In college, connections count.

Your college probably has an array of resources available to help you with almost anything that comes up. In the "FOCUS Challenge Case," Jessica struggles with an eating disorder. Perhaps you suffer from test anxiety, are terrorized by public speaking, freak out when your technology crashes, or wonder if you might have a learning disability. Whatever the problem, there's a place to go

Teachable Moment Share with students the fact that more women graduate from college than men. Also, women are more likely to ask for help than men. Get a discussion going on why this happens, and what can be done about ensuring men's success in college.

for help on campus. Even if your campus doesn't have the full array of support centers available on many huge campuses, student support professionals there can always direct you to services off campus.

Unfortunately, some students think that asking for help of any kind is a display of weakness or incompetence or somehow shameful. *I should be able to do this on my own!* they think, when actually, engaging in any new activity requires guidance. Here's an analogy: In 1979, Diana Nyad achieved the record for open-water swimming at 102.5 miles. But it took 51 other people to help her reach her goal (guides to check winds and currents, divers to look for sharks, and NASA nutrition experts to keep her from losing more than the 29 pounds she lost during that one swim).[40] Getting a college degree doesn't happen automatically or overnight. It takes a sustained academic investment, but you needn't go it alone. Your campus has all kinds of resources available for the taking, but you must take them. They won't come to you.

© William Whitehurst/CORBIS

> **"Information is not knowledge."**
>
> Albert Einstein, theoretical physicist
> (1879–1955)

First-Year Students' FAQs

Take a look at some of the FAQs students often voice during their first term in college.

Social Connections

> *How can I meet other students?* Does your campus have a Student Center, Student Union, or University Center? Whatever it's called, it's where students tend to go between classes. Take advantage of favorite gathering spots on campus. Not only can you meet people, but you can also scan the bulletin boards for the answers to many of the following questions. Want to find someone to carpool home with over winter break? Need to find a used laptop for sale? If you're finding it hard to meet people, could it be because you're not around? A newspaper advice column once featured a letter to "Dear Abby" from a forest ranger in a remote location who was lonely and just couldn't find women to date. To meet people, it helps to be where they are.

> *What student clubs and organizations are available?* If your campus has an active student government, it probably has an office somewhere on campus, most likely in the Student Center. The student newspaper and bulletin boards around campus are good sources of information about clubs, events, and activities. Some campuses have club booths set up at the beginning of the term so that it's easy to find the Young Democrats or Republicans, the Ski Club, or the chemistry honor society. Watch for an announcement about a Club Fair, or whatever your campus calls it. You may need to take the initiative yourself. Some student organizations reach out to new students, but others may not come to you. If your campus offers a Club Day, go and see what you can find out. Read bulletin board notices of upcoming meetings.

Sensitive Situation Remember that you have some shy, sensitive students in the class who may not check out a club on their own. Sometimes cultural issues dictate that students' first priority should be family over friends. But making connections is important to college success. Consider pairing up students to visit a club of interest together.

What are your interests? If you can't name any particular ones right away, it may be time to cultivate some to enrich your co-curricular experience.

> *What organizations are available to minority students?* If you're a member of an underrepresented population on campus, specific resources to connect you with other students may be available. Check with your Student Government Office to find out.

Academic Resources

> *How can I learn more about how I learn?* Check to see if your campus has a Learning Center, an office that helps with learning disabilities, or a place you can go to fill out a learning style instrument. You probably have a gut feeling about how you learn best, but you may want to verify your intuition or learn more about how to capitalize on it. Sometimes a modest fee is charged for diagnostic instruments, but the insights you gain may be well worth it. You can also find out for sure if you suspect you may have a learning disability. If you do, you can use the Learning Center to develop learning strategies to address your particular needs. See Box 3.2 for further information.

> *How can I become a better writer?* Is writing a strength for you or a challenge? Do you write easily with confidence or struggle with every word? Your campus probably has a Writing Center to help you think through your writing assignments. Tutors there won't help you fix grammatical errors or proofread, but they will help you formulate a strong thesis statement. You'll be asked what you're trying to communicate and then be given help putting your thoughts into words. The advice you get on one assignment will transfer to future assignments in other classes as well.

> *How can I become a better speaker?* If the thought of standing up in front of multiple pairs of peering eyes leaves you in a cold sweat, you may be a good candidate for your campus's Oral Communication Center. If your campus has one of these, consider asking to be videotaped and critiqued while you do a dry run. If you want to become a better public speaker, there's nothing quite as motivating as watching your distracting habits, like swaying from side to side or jingling the change in your pocket. This kind of support can help you develop good speaking habits and build confidence.

> *What if I need help with a challenging course?* Many campuses have discipline-based support centers: a Science Learning Center or a Math Learning Center, for example. Or particular courses may offer what's called Supplemental Instruction, extra help beyond class sessions with basic principles or homework assignments. Work with the course's Teaching Assistant, or hire your own tutor. Check out whatever options are available to you, and use them, rather than struggle on your own if you're not getting results.

> *I'm not sure which classes to take next. Who can help me?* Academic advisors are the experts on campus who can help you decide on a major, choose classes, and locate many other resources. Use their expertise, rather than guessing or listening to another student who's not sure either.

Sensitive Situation Sometimes students who have a documented learning disability do not disclose this in college. Their reasons may vary, but often they want a fresh start or don't want anyone to know. Also, college can be a time when students experiment with not taking medications or let them slide because Mom and Dad are not around to monitor. Share with students that both not disclosing and stopping medication are *not good ideas.* Remind the class where they can go if they need support in this area.

Chapter Crossover Chapters 6, 7, 8, 9, and 10 provide some specific strategies for students on how to study, read, write, take notes and tests, and present, and it may be helpful to alert students to these upcoming chapters.

> **"We are by nature observers and thereby learners. That is our permanent state."**
>
> **Ralph Waldo Emerson, American author (1803–1882)**

Box 3.2 Learning Disability? Five Ways to Help Yourself

Perhaps you were diagnosed with Attention-Deficit/Hyperactivity Disorder (ADHD) or dyslexia as a young child. If you're beginning your college career with a learning disability (LD), you're not alone. In a college or university with an enrollment of 25,000 students, for example, approximately 550 of those students have learning disabilities.[41] By some estimates, two-thirds of students with diagnosed LDs continue on to college after high school.[42]

Does a learning disability mean all the odds are against you? No, but there are some important steps you must take to help yourself. Successful college students with LDs recognize, understand, and accept them, and develop compensating strategies to offset them.

1. If you've been previously diagnosed with a learning disability, bring a copy of your evaluation or Individualized Education Plan (IEP) with you to campus. Some schools require documentation in order to use the institution's support services.

2. Locate the support services office on your campus and use it. These services are free and can make all the difference in your success.

3. Learn more about your specific LD. Read about it. Visit credible websites. Understanding the ins and outs of what you're up against is important.

4. If you need special accommodations such as taking exams somewhere other than the classroom, schedule an appointment with your professors early in the term to let them know. Having a learning disability doesn't mean you're required to do less work, but you'll get the support you need in order to do your best.

5. Remember that the advice in this book, which is helpful to all college students, can be even more useful to anyone with a learning disability. Time management strategies and study skills tailored to your specific LD are key. Don't let fear of failure immobilize you. Instead, keep your eye on the goal and take charge of your own learning.[43]

> *I'm thinking of dropping a class. How do I do it?* The Office of the Registrar or Office of Admissions and Records is where to go. They also help with things like transferring credits and obtaining transcripts. Think about the ramifications of dropping a class thoroughly, however. Will doing so change your financial aid status, for example?

Adjustment

> *What if I need a counselor?* College is a time of accelerated personal development and wonderful discoveries. But it may also be a time when you face challenging issues, such as leaving the comfort zone of your family; breaking up or beginning a new romance; or dealing with feelings of anxiety, isolation, or depression. Perhaps you're distracted by family problems or dealing with the loss of someone you care about. The Counseling Center on your campus can be a heartening resource to help you work through a variety of issues. Many students—more than ever, many colleges report—are taking advantage of what Counseling Centers have to offer. And if you find yourself in the middle of a real crisis, call the campus hotline for immediate help.

> *Where can I attend church, join a religious group, or speak with a pastor, rabbi, or priest?* Check your local phonebook, look for postings in your Student Union, or ask other students. Some campuses even have a church or chapel of their own.

Finances

> *Where can I find information about financial aid?* Your campus Financial Aid Office can help with loans, scholarships, and grants to pay for college.

Activity Option Create index cards with one campus resource on each card. Divide the class into two groups for an in-class pop quiz. Hold up a card, and the first group to buzz (they can use cell phones in class!) gets a chance to tell where it's located and what its purpose is. The team that wins gets a prize.

> *What if I run out of money?* If it's a real emergency—you lost the lease on an apartment, the residence halls are full, and you'll be living out of your car—help is available from the Red Cross or Salvation Army. If it's a matter of just blowing your budget, you can find advice, often free, from consumer credit agencies. Your campus may also offer free workshops on managing your money through a Learning Center or Student Success Center.

Logistics

> *How can I find my way around?* Some universities are like small cities. Often you can download a campus map from the college's website that will help. Even though you will look like a tourist, carry it around to lower your stress level when you need to find something for the first time.

> *Who can help me decide where to live next year?* Is residence hall life a good thing? If you're attending a college far from home, having everything close by is convenient, and thankfully someone else will do the cooking! If you happen to live in the same town where you're going to school, it's an expensive option. But there is evidence that living on campus helps students feel connected. Other students may prefer living on their own or perhaps sharing an apartment off campus. Consider factors such as the importance of social connections, your financial situation, and your ability to focus, despite distractions. Besides your family (and your pocketbook), your office of Residence Life or Student Housing can help with these decisions.

> *Can I work on campus?* Check with your Student Employment Office. Working on campus is not only convenient, but it can also help you become a more successful student. Travel time to work is cut down and you learn things about how your campus works.

Technology

> *What if I have a technology meltdown?* The new version of the old "my dog ate my homework" story relates to numerous variations on a theme: technology crashing. Your campus may not have round-the-clock advice from techies, but the Computer Help Desk can often solve what sounds like a complicated problem with simple advice. Also, use the campus computer labs. You can make good use of short blocks of time—or long ones—between classes.

Health

> *Are health services available to students?* Many campuses have a Student Health Center where you can find a range of free or inexpensive services—everything from flu shots to strep throat tests to birth control advice if you're sexually active.

> *What if I need more exercise?* It's easy to find out if your campus has a recreation center, or whether there are gyms you can frequent nearby. Or join an intramural team, coach a children's soccer team, or devote a chunk of time to power walking each day.

Majors and Careers

➤ *What do I want to be when I grow up?* Thinking ahead to a career when you graduate from college is sometimes difficult when so much is going on at the moment. What do you like to do? What people skills do you have? Do you like to work with your hands or in your head? These questions may be difficult to answer if you haven't had experience in a real career field. Sometimes a career is nothing like you imagined—or preparing for one entails much more than you'd predict. But college is a great time to explore your options. Become an intern to try out a career or visit your campus's Career Center. Experts there can give you diagnostic tests to help you discover a major and career for which you are well-suited. They may be able to set you up with an internship off campus, put you in touch with alumni who work in a career field of interest to you, or help you apply for a competitive fellowship.

Et cetera

➤ *Is child care available?* Many campuses, particularly those with returning adult students, have inexpensive child care available. Being able to drop off a child in the morning right on campus and pick him up after your classes are over can be a real enabler.

➤ *Where can I buy my books?* Textbooks are a significant investment these days, and it's important to buy the right editions for your classes. Should you support your campus bookstore or order online? Buying books online may save you money, although you'll have to wait for shipment. The bookstore is a much quicker option, and it's a good idea to find out where it is, no matter where you buy your books. You'll most likely need it for other school supplies.

➤ *Where can I find community service opportunities?* Volunteerism is often a part of high school requirements or church-related activities, and you may wish to continue your community service in college. Check to see if your campus has a Service Learning or Community Center, or look for specific classes that offer service learning opportunities.

➤ *What if I'm in need of Campus Security?* If you feel unsafe walking to your car late at night or you need information about parking permits on campus, check with the Campus Security or Public Safety Office. They're there for your protection.

What's the bottom line? Get to know your campus and its full range of offerings—and take advantage of everything that's in place to help you be as academically successful as possible.

Finances, technology, and campus support—three resources that can help you or hinder you in college. Learning to master money management, use technology productively, and make time to reap the benefits of all the support systems your campus has to offer will help you not only as a first-year student, but throughout your time in college.

Teachable Moment Have students do some investigating and report back to each other about online resources for buying books. Also, remind students that there may be a time lag for getting books, and if they are looking at used books, the condition can really vary—for example, some students hate to get books with too much highlighting.

Activity Option Have students develop a slogan on why students should use campus resources. For example, "when in debt . . . don't forget the Financial Aid Center located at _____."

Exercise 3.6 VARK Activity

Complete the recommended activity for your preferred VARK learning modality. If you are multimodal, select more than one activity. Your instructor may ask you to (a) give an oral report on your results in class, (b) send your results to him or her via e-mail, (c) post them online, or (d) contribute to a class chat.

 Visual: To help you understand how your campus works, draw an organizational chart that identifies the top levels of the campus hierarchy. Who is at the top of the institution, and who runs the various units?

 Aural: Make use of campus resources by attending a public lecture. Give a three-minute presentation to your classmates summarizing what you heard.

 Read/Write: List the main points for each of the three sections in this chapter. After your three lists are complete, prioritize the points in each section as they related to you, and identify actions you need to take to help you be more successful in college.

 Kinesthetic: Go on a short field trip with a classmate to learn the locations of all the campus support centers that are available to you. As you walk, sketch out a rough map that you can show your classmates and instructor in class.

For more practice online, go to http://www.academic.cengage.com/collegesuccess/staley to take the Challenge Yourself online quizzes.

NOW WHAT DO YOU THINK?

At the beginning of this chapter, Jessica Taylor, a frustrated student, faced a series of challenges as a new college student. Now after reading this chapter, would you respond differently to any of the questions you answered about the "FOCUS Challenge Case"?

REALITY CHECK

On a scale of 1 to 10, answer the following questions now that you've completed this chapter.

1 = not very/not much/very little/low   10 = very/a lot/very much/high

In hindsight, how much did you *really* know about this subject matter before reading the chapter?

1   2   3   4   5   6   7   8   9   1 0

How much do you think this information might affect your college success?

1   2   3   4   5   6   7   8   9   1 0

How much do you think this information might affect your career success after college?

1   2   3   4   5   6   7   8   9   1 0

How long did it actually take you to complete this chapter (both the reading and writing tasks)? _____ Hour(s) _____ Minutes

What score did you earn on the Challenge Yourself quiz at the end of the chapter? _____

Take a minute to compare these answers to your answers from the "Readiness Check" at the beginning of this chapter. What gaps exist between the similar questions? How might these gaps between what you thought before starting the chapter and what you now think after completing the chapter affect how you approach the next chapter in this book?

To download mp3 format audio summaries of this chapter, go to http://www .academic.cengage.com/collegesuccess/staley.

4 Managing Your Time and Energy

YOU'RE ABOUT TO DISCOVER...

> Why time management alone doesn't work

> How time management differs from energy management

> How to calculate your study hours

> How to schedule your way to success

> How common time-wasters creep in, and how to bust them

> How the P word can derail you

> How to realistically balance work, school, and personal life

Teachable Moment This chapter is about one of the "hottest" topics in student success courses. Students and instructors talk about managing time, but not much about managing oneself and one's energy. Let students know that there is no "one size fits all" approach in figuring out how to stay on top of things; they need to factor in their strengths and challenges when learning about managing time and energy and ultimately themselves!

"Today is the tomorrow we worried about yesterday."

Anonymous

Derek Johnson

As Derek Johnson walked out of his

World Civilizations class on Wednesday evening, he felt panicked. The professor had just assigned a twelve-page paper, due one month from today. *How could he?* Derek thought. *Doesn't he realize how busy most returning students are?* The syllabus had mentioned a paper, but twelve pages seemed downright excessive.

When Derek had decided to go back to college five years after he graduated from high school, he hadn't quite realized what a juggling act it would require. First, there was his family—his wife, Justine, his four-year-old daughter, Taura, and another baby due before winter break. Then there was his job, which was really quite demanding for an entry-level marketing position. He hoped that a degree in business would help him move into the management ranks, where the salaries were higher. Add to that singing in his church choir, coaching the youth soccer league, competing in cycling races, and working out every morning at the gym. Derek had been a high school athlete, and physical fitness was a priority for him.

His head began to swim as he thought about all his upcoming obligations: his mother's birthday next week, his dog's vet appointment, his brother who was coming to town for a visit, the training class he was required to attend for work. Something had to go, but he couldn't think of anything he was willing to sacrifice to make time for a twelve-page paper. Maybe he'd have to break down and buy one of those planners, but weren't most people who use those slightly, well … compulsive?

Still, the paper was to count as 25 percent of his final grade in the course. He decided he'd try and think of a topic for the paper on his way home. But then he remembered that his wife had asked him to stop at the store to pick up groceries. Somewhere on aisle 12, between the frozen pizza and the frozen yogurt, Derek's thoughts about his research paper vanished.

The following week, the professor asked the students in the class how their papers were coming along. Some students gave long soliloquies about their research progress, the wealth of sources they'd found, and the detailed outlines they'd put together. Derek didn't raise his hand.

A whole week has gone by, Derek thought on his way back to his car after class. *I have to get going!* Writing had never exactly

been Derek's strong suit. In fact, it was something he generally disliked doing. Through a great deal of hard work, he had managed to earn a 3.8 GPA in high school—a record he planned to continue. A course in World Civilizations—not even in his intended major—was *not* going to ruin things! The week had absolutely flown by, and there were plenty of good reasons why his paper was getting off to such a slow start.

It was true that Derek rarely wasted time, except for occasionally watching his favorite TV shows. But then again, with such a jam-packed schedule, he really felt the need to unwind once in a while. Regardless, he rarely missed his nightly study time from 11:00 p.m. to 1:00 a.m. Those two hours were reserved for homework, no matter what.

At the end of class two weeks later, Derek noticed that several students lined up to show the professor the first drafts of their papers. *That's it!* Derek thought to himself. *The paper is due next Wednesday. I'll spend Monday night, my only free night of the week, in the library. I can get there right after work and stay until 11:00 or so. That'll be five hours of concentrated time. I should be able to write it then.*

Despite his good intentions, Derek didn't arrive at the library until nearly 8:00 p.m., and his work session wasn't all that productive. As he sat in his library stall, he found himself obsessing about things that were bothering him at work. His boss was being difficult, and his team of coworkers couldn't come to an agreement on some important issues about their current project. Finally, when he glanced at his watch, he was shocked to see that it was already midnight! The library was closing, and he'd only written three pages. Where had the time gone?

On his way out to the car, his cell phone rang. It was Justine, wondering where he was. Taura was running a fever, and his boss had called about an emergency meeting at 7:00 a.m. *If one more thing goes wrong …* , Derek thought to himself. His twelve-page paper was due in two days.

WHAT DO **YOU** THINK?

Now that you've read about Derek Johnson, answer the following questions. You may not know all the answers yet, but you'll find out what you know and what you stand to gain by reading this chapter.

1. Describe Derek's time management strategies. Are they working? Is time management Derek's only problem?

2. How could calculating his study hours improve his productivity?

3. Describe the time-wasters that are a part of Derek's schedule. Do you think procrastination is an issue for Derek? What's behind his failure to make progress on his paper?

4. Identify three effective time management techniques Derek should begin to use.

5. Suggest three realistic ways for Derek to balance work, school, and personal life.

6. What aspects of Derek's situation can you relate to personally? What other time management issues are you experiencing in your life right now?

Before beginning to read this chapter, take two minutes to answer the following questions on a scale of 1 to 10. Your answers will help you assess how ready you are to focus.

1 = not very/not much/very little/low   10 = very/a lot/very much/high

Based on reading the "You're about to discover…" list and skimming this chapter, how much do you think you probably already know about the subject matter?

1   2   3   4   5   6   7   8   9   10

How much do you think this information might affect your college success?

1   2   3   4   5   6   7   8   9   10

How much do you think this information might affect your career success after college?

1   2   3   4   5   6   7   8   9   10

In general, how motivated are you to learn the material in this chapter?

1   2   3   4   5   6   7   8   9   10

This book describes four key factors related to intrinsic, or internal, motivation: curiosity, control, career outlook, and challenge. The next four questions relate to these **C-Factors:**

How *curious* are you about the content you expect to read in this chapter?

1   2   3   4   5   6   7   8   9   10

How much *control* do you expect to have over mastering the material in this chapter?

1   2   3   4   5   6   7   8   9   10

How much do you think this chapter might help you develop your *career outlook*?

1   2   3   4   5   6   7   8   9   10

How *challenging* do you think the material in this chapter will be for you?

1   2   3   4   5   6   7   8   9   10

Before beginning any task, including studying, it's important to check in with yourself to ensure that you're physically, intellectually, and emotionally ready to focus. How ready are you, physically, to focus on this chapter? (Are you rested, feeling well, and so on?)

1   2   3   4   5   6   7   8   9   10

How ready are you, intellectually, to focus on this chapter? (Are you thinking clearly, focused on this course, interested in this subject?)

1   2   3   4   5   6   7   8   9   10

How ready are you, emotionally, to focus on this chapter? (Are you calm, confident, composed?)

1   2   3   4   5   6   7   8   9   10

If your answer to any of the last three questions is below a 5 on the scale, you may need to address the issue you're facing prior to beginning this chapter. For example, if you're hungry, get a quick bite to eat. If you're feeling scattered, take a few moments to settle down and focus.

Finally, how long do you think it will take you to complete this chapter? _____ Hour(s) _____ Minutes

Teachable Moment Remember to refer back to the four C's that were introduced in Chapter 1 (curiosity, control, career outlook, and challenge). Zero in on control, and emphasize to students that they do have control over what they learn and do. Ask students to report on how long they think it will take them to complete the chapter. Ask if they were responding based on what they predicted and actually did in previous chapters.

Time Management Isn't Enough

CHALLENGE ⟶ REACTION

Challenge: What is *time management* and how does it work?

Reaction: _____

   _____

"In truth, people can generally make time for what they choose to do; it is not really the time but the will that is lacking."

Sir John Lubbock, British banker, politician, and archaeologist (1834–1913)

Years ago, the Rolling Stones first belted out these lyrics: "Time is on my side—yes, it is." The song was optimistic. It predicted that some fictitious woman would get tired of her new love and eventually come "runnin' back."

Today, many of us are pessimistic about time. We feel that time is working against us. Like Derek, we are overwhelmed—school, job, family, friends. The list goes on and on, specific to each of us, but lengthy for all of us. How can we get it all done?

In college and in your career, time management will be one of your greatest challenges. Why? The pace of life is accelerating. Today's world is about high-speed technology, rapid transit, information overload, and a frenetic lifestyle. Leisurely fine dining or family meals around the table have deteriorated into grabbing fast food on the run. Many of us try to cram more into our lives: one more activity, one more experience, one more obligation.

Sometimes we'd like to be able to just hit "insert" on the toolbar, and click on "hours." But if we had more time, would we *really* be more effective? Or would we just find new ways to devour it? According to British historian and satirist C. Northcote Parkinson, "work expands so as to fill the time available for its completion"—what's become known as Parkinson's Law. Have you ever experienced that phenomenon? If you have two hours to finish a project, it takes two hours. But if you have four, that's how long it takes. And interestingly, time *feels* flexible when it really isn't. Have you noticed that some of your classes seem short and others seem long, when they actually last the same amount of time? You may be highly engaged in one class by a dynamic instructor and bored in another by subject matter you find uninteresting. No one sped up or slowed down the clock in those two situations. The five hours Derek intended to spend at the library trying to finish his paper seemed like it would be enough time to him, but the time raced by, and he accomplished very little.

When it comes to real-time time management, we're all dealt the same hand. No matter who you are, you have the same 24 precious hours in a day, 168 jam-packed hours in a week as everyone else. We may not be able to change the natural laws of the universe, but we can learn more about making conscious, productive decisions, and—at the same time—finding the key to balance in our lives.

First, let's really understand what we mean by effective time management. There's no secret to it. It's simply planning, scheduling, and structuring your time to complete tasks you're responsible for efficiently and effectively. Perhaps you're a natural planner. You crave structure and welcome organizing strategies. Or you may be a person who despises the idea of restricting yourself to a schedule. But no matter which of these categories you fall into, you can improve your time management skills.

Digital Vision/Getty Images

"Don't confuse activity with accomplishment. 'Time = Success' is a myth."

Dr. Constance Staley, University of Colorado at Colorado Springs

Chapter Crossover Refer students back to what they learned about themselves in Chapter 2—their learning style preferences based on VARK and personality factors. See if you can get some students to volunteer to make some connections between their time and energy management skills and what they learned about themselves in Chapter 2. For example, since most teachers have read/write VARK preferences, read/write students may have less "translating" to do. Those who score as perceivers on MBTI-like instruments tend to start things late and then find themselves scrambling at the end. An activity comes later in this chapter, but it's good to get students thinking about this early on.

Emotional Intelligence (EI) Research Emotional intelligence is really an array of noncognitive abilities that strongly correlate with success in work and life. Even within the emotional intelligence realm, balance is important. For example, you could have tremendous skill in understanding yourself but still lack the ability to control your impulses. In this case, one might just think "Yup, I am really bad at delaying what I want." Remind students that it's the actual doing something about what you know about yourself that makes you successful.

Before delving into the details of time management skills, however, let's clarify one important point. There's a sense in which the phrase *time management* is misleading. Let's say you decide to spend an hour reading the assigned short story for your literature class. You may sit in the library with your book propped open in front of you from 3:00 to 4:00 o'clock on the dot. But you may not digest a single word you're reading. You may be going through the motions, reading on autopilot. Have you managed your time? Technically, yes. Your planner says, "Library, short story for Lit 101, 3:00–4:00 p.m." But did you get results? Time management expert Jeffrey Mayer asks provocatively in the title of his book: *If You Haven't Got the Time to Do It Right, When Will You Find the Time to Do It Over?* (1991). Now that's a good question!

It's not just about managing your time, it's about managing your attention. Attention management is the ability to focus your attention, not just your time, toward a designated activity so that you produce a desired result. Time management may get you through reading a chapter of your chemistry textbook, but attention management will ensure that you understand what you're reading. It's about *focus*. If you manage your attention during that hour, then you've managed your time productively. Without attention management, time management is pointless.

Succeeding in school, at work, and in life is not just about what you do. It's about what gets done. You can argue about the effort you put into an academic endeavor all you want, but it's doubtful your professor will say, "You know what? You're right. You deserve an A just for staying up late last night working on this paper." Activity and accomplishment aren't the same thing. Neither are quantity and quality. Results count. So don't confuse being busy with being successful. Staying busy isn't much of a challenge; being successful is.

The activity versus accomplishment distinction holds true in today's workplace as well. In terms of pay, there's been a shift of emphasis from *position* to *performance*, and from *status* to *contribution*. You don't simply make more money because of your title or your prestige within the organization. You're rewarded for results. Demands in today's fast-paced workplace make time management more important than ever.[1]

Here's a list of preliminary academic time-saving tips. However, remember that these suggestions won't give you a surefire recipe for academic success. To manage your time, you must also manage yourself: your energy, your behavior, your attention, your attitudes, *you*. Once you know how to manage all that, managing your time begins to work.

> Have a plan for your study session; include time allotments for each topic or task.

> Keep track of what derails you. If you come to understand your patterns, you may be better able to control them: *Oops, there I go again. I'm not going to give in to that temptation!*

> Turn off your phone or tell other people you live with that you don't want to be disturbed if a call comes in for you. Let them know what time they can tell callers to call you back.

Chapter Crossover Take a look ahead to Chapter 12 and think about how time management, or lack of it, impacts career choices.

Emotional Intelligence (EI) Research Students who have low impulse control and reality testing are really at risk for managing time effectively. These students might jump at the chance to run over to the student center with the intention of coming back in an hour and then beginning to study. They may have the best intentions, but the reality of the situation may be that they will bump into many friends, lose track of time, and before they know it hours have gone by.

> If you're working on your computer, work offline whenever possible. If you must be online to check sources frequently, don't give in to the temptation to check your social networking account or e-mail every ten minutes.

> Take two minutes to organize your workspace before beginning. Having the resources you need at your fingertips makes the session go much more smoothly, and you won't waste time searching for things you need.

> If you are in a study group, make sure everyone is clear about assigned tasks for the next session. Lack of clear communication about expectations is a big time-waster for study groups.

> Learn to say no. Saying no to someone, especially someone you care about, can feel awkward at first, but people close to you will understand that you can't do everything. Life is about choices, and choosing requires the use of the word *no*. Practice now: "No, thanks." "Sorry, can't do it this time." See? It's not that hard.

> Focus. You can't do anything if you try to do everything. Multitasking may work for simple matters, such as scheduling a doctor's appointment while heating up a snack in the microwave. But when it comes to tasks that require brainpower, such as studying or writing, you need a single-minded focus. If your attention is not given 100 percent to studying, you will most likely need to repeat your efforts. Why not do it right the first time?

> Slow down. As they say, "haste makes waste." Working at something a million miles a minute will most likely result in mistakes, superficial thinking, and poor decisions. Ironically, if you rush, you may run out of time and end up settling for less than your best.

> Don't make a habit of putting other people's priorities above your own. In other words, don't let their *lack* of planning affect your attempts to plan. Those who truly care for you will understand you need to stay focused on your priorities. At the same time, be prepared to shift your priorities as needed. In an emergency, you might need to help out a friend, a neighbor, or even possibly a stranger. Know the difference between legitimate interruptions and time-wasters, and then act accordingly.

INSIGHT ⊖ ACTION

1. How would you evaluate your time management skills right now? Would you give yourself an A, B, C, or below? Why?

2. Is attention management a challenge for you? When your mind wanders, where does it go?

3. What actions must you take to become a more effective time-attention manager?

Activity Option This is a great opportunity to get students to share with each other the letter grade they gave themselves and why. Pair up students, ask them to share with each other, and then give each other some tip that they think might help with a particular challenge. If time permits, let the entire class share. Students need to understand they are not alone in their challenges, but there are tips to get themselves refocused. You might bring up the topic of "flow." Once you get started and are on a roll, it can feel really good.

Energy, Our Most Precious Resource

"We live in a digital time. Our rhythms are rushed, rapid-fire and relentless, our days carved up into bits and bytes….We're wired up but we're melting down." So begins a bestselling book, *The Power of Full Engagement: Managing Energy, Not Time, Is the Key to High Performance and Personal Renewal* (2003). The authors, Jim Loehr and Tony Schwartz, have replaced the term *time management* with the term *energy management*. Their shift makes sense. Since most of us are operating in overdrive most of the time, energy is our most precious resource.

Energy management experts say you can't control time—everyone has a fixed amount—but you can manage your energy. And in fact, it's your responsibility to do so. Once a day is gone, it's gone. But your energy can be renewed. It's not just about managing your time or your attention, it's about having enough energy to do what you need to do.

Chapter Crossover Help students connect the concept of energy with wellness. Many of these same topics will be addressed in Chapter 13.

It's clear that some things are energy *drains*, zapping your drive: bad news, illness, interpersonal conflict, bureaucratic hassles, a heavy meal, rainy days.

Likewise, some things are energy *gains*, giving you a surge of fresh vitality: a new job, good friends, music, laughter, fruit, coffee. It's a good idea to recognize your own personal energy drains and gains so that you know how and when to replenish your supply.[2] Energy management experts say it's not just about *spending time*, it's about *expending energy*:

> *physical* energy

> *emotional* energy

> *mental* energy

> *spiritual* energy

Energy is multi-faceted. Winning a 100-mile cycling competition would leave you physically drained, but mentally sharp and emotionally charged, right?

Of the four dimensions of energy, let's take a closer look at the first two. To do your very best academically, it helps to be *physically* energized and *emotionally* connected. Physical energy is measured in terms of *quantity*. How much energy do you have—a lot or a little? Emotional energy, on the other hand, is measured by *quality*. What kind of energy do you have—positive or negative? If you

"Performance, health and happiness are grounded in the skillful management of energy."

Jim Loehr and Tony Schwartz,
from *The Power of Full Engagement*

put them together into a two-dimensional chart with *quantity* as the vertical axis and *quality* as the horizontal axis, you get something like Figure 4.1.

When you're operating in the upper right quadrant with high, positive energy, you're most productive, which makes sense. The question is: How do you get there? How do you make certain you're physically energized and emotionally connected so that you can do your best, academically?

Get Physically Energized

To make sure you're physically energized, try these suggestions.

1. **Go with the flow.** Have you noticed times of the day when it's easier to concentrate than others? Perhaps you regularly crash in the middle of the afternoon, for example. This is partly due to the patterns of electrical impulses in your brain, alpha rhythms that are unique to each individual. In other words, everyone has a biological clock. Paying attention to your body's natural rhythms is important. Plan to do activities that require you to be alert during your natural productivity peaks. That's better than plodding through a tough assignment when the energy just isn't there. Use low energy times to take care of mindless chores that require little to no brainpower.[3]

2. **Up and at 'em.** What about 8:00 a.m. classes? Don't use your body's natural rhythms as an excuse to sleep through class! ("I'm just not a morning person....") If you're truly not a morning person, don't sign up for early morning classes. Some freshmen get into the *social* habit of staying up late into the wee, small hours, and then they just can't get up in the morning. Sleeping through your obligations won't do much for your success—and you'll be playing a continual game of catch-up, which takes even more time.

Emotional Intelligence (EI) Research Individuals who lack optimism have difficulty being the best they can be (as well as difficulty maintaining relationships). One simple suggestion is to take a moment to think about *why* one might feel pessimistic about a situation and make a conscious decision to think more positively and do a little problem solving. For example, if a student lacks optimism and feels that he is going to fail Biology no matter what, what positive steps could he choose to take? He could seek out a tutor or find a study buddy, for example. If he has tried everything he can think of to succeed and still fails, what is the absolute worst that will happen? He'll probably just have to repeat the course.

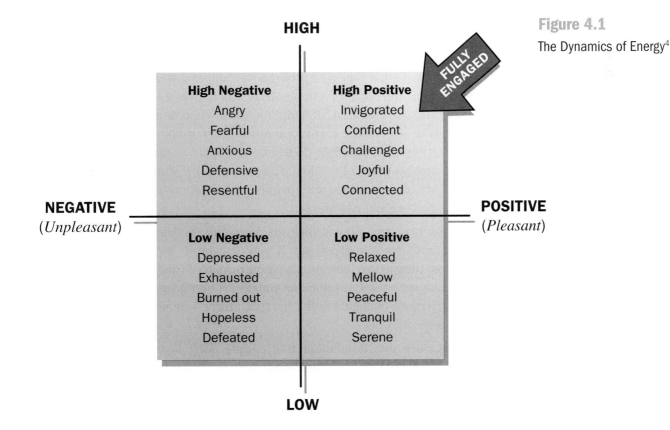

Figure 4.1

The Dynamics of Energy[4]

3. **Sleep at night, study during the day.** Burning the midnight oil and pulling all-nighters aren't the best ideas, either. It only takes one all-nighter to help you realize that a lack of sleep translates into a plunge in performance. Without proper sleep, your ability to understand and remember course material is impaired. Research shows that the average adult requires seven to eight hours of sleep each night. If you can't get that much for whatever reason, take a short afternoon nap. Did you know that the Three Mile Island nuclear meltdown in Pennsylvania in 1979 and the Chernobyl disaster in the Ukraine in 1986 took place at 4 a.m. and 1:23 a.m., respectively? Experts believe it's no coincidence that both these events took place when workers would normally be sleeping.[5]

4. **"Prime the pump."** You've heard it before: Food is the fuel that makes us run. The better the fuel, the smoother we run. It's that simple. A solid diet of carbs—pizza, chips, and cookies—jammed into the fuel tank of your car would certainly gum up the works! When the demands on your energy are high, such as exam week, use premium fuel. If you don't believe it, take a look at how many of your classmates get sick during midterms and finals. Watch what they're eating and note how much sleep they're getting, and you'll get some clues about why they're hacking and coughing their way through exams—or in bed missing them altogether.

Get Emotionally Connected

Physical needs count, to be sure, but emotional connections are part of the picture, too. See if you agree with these suggestions.

1. **Communicate like it matters.** Sometimes we save our best communicating for people we think we have to impress: teachers, bosses, or clients, for example. But what about the people we care about most in our lives? Sometimes these people get the leftovers after all the "important" communicating has been done for the day. Sometimes we're so comfortable with these people that we think we can let it all hang out, even when doing so is *not* a pretty sight. Vow to learn more about communicating at your best in valued personal relationships, and then do it. Communicate as if everything you said would actually come true—"Just drop dead," for instance—and watch the difference! Communicating with people we care about is one of our primary vehicles for personal renewal.

2. **Choose how you renew.** Finish this analogy: junk food is to physical energy as _____ is to emotional energy. If you answered "TV," you're absolutely right. Most people use television as their primary form of emotional renewal, but, like junk food, it's not that nutritious and it's easy to consume too much. Try more engaging activities that affirm you: singing or reading or playing a sport.[6]

3. **Let others renew you.** Remember that people don't just make demands on your time, they can provide emotional renewal. There's pure joy in a child's laugh, a friend's smile, a father's pat on the back. These small pleasures in life are priceless—prize them!

Manage Your Classroom Energy

Think of the implications of what you've been reading about—your energy management—on your in-class performance. When your attention meter is on empty and you can't concentrate on your instructor's presentation, energy management could be the problem—and the solution.

It's hard to manage your attention if you bring "High Negative" energy to class. Realistically, how easy is it to learn when you're feeling angry, fearful, anxious, defensive, or resentful? You may be terrified of the upcoming midterm exam or annoyed at the professor who lectures too quickly by simply reading Power-Point slides as they whiz by. In order to confront your "High Negative" energy and regain control of your attention, you may need to talk with your instructor. Explain how the course is overwhelming you and ask what you can to do ensure success. Make sure you keep up your end of the bargain, though, and do what you can to lower your "High Negative" energy yourself. If your anxiety is stemming from your own lack of preparation, that's an issue you can rectify on your own.

It's also hard to manage your attention if you bring "Low Negative" energy to class. Realistically, how easy is it to learn when you're feeling depressed, exhausted, burned out, hopeless, or defeated? In fact, these are times when some students simply don't come to class, period. But that begins a negative chain reaction. Once you get behind on course material, you become more depressed and hopeless about a positive outcome, and so begins a downward spiral. Even "Low Positive" energy can be counterproductive in class. Imagine yourself so relaxed, mellow, peaceful, tranquil, and serene that you zone out and nod off.

Is it possible to have too much "High Positive" energy? What if you're too invigorated, confident, challenged, joyful, and connected? What if you're so thrilled about some exciting news that you can't sit still? As you sit in your seat, some part of your anatomy is continuously moving because of stored-up nervous energy. Things seem to be moving too slowly, and you'd give anything to be able to get up and run around the room. Instead of running around the classroom, run to class or work out beforehand so that you use up some of your spare energy. If you're the kind of person who gets distracted easily, make sure you sit up front. Jump into the discussion by asking questions, and channel your energy into content-related, focused activities. If you find it difficult to manage your attention in a classroom full of friends, meet beforehand for coffee and compare notes on the reading assignment. Do whatever you must to manage your energy productively. It's your responsibility, and it's a vital part of the learning process.

Begin noticing your own energy patterns. Think about the requirements of each day, and the energy that you'll need as you progress from one activity to the next. Working out early in the morning may energize you for the rest of the day. Your most challenging class may temporarily deplete you, but after lunch or dinner, you're refreshed and ready to go again.

Teachable Moment Some students with high positive energy are successful and some are not. What is the difference? Get students talking about situations where they used their high energy to accomplish something positive related to school. Can they also give some not-so-positive examples?

> "Make the most of yourself, for that is all there is of you."
>
> **Ralph Waldo Emerson,**
> **American author (1803–1882)**

Activity Option Give students a chart with times for a full day (twenty-four hours). Have them quickly list their high-energy times. Come together as a group and compare. Are there common times among the group? You should see differences among the students. Now, ask students to volunteer to tell you when they typically study. Are they doing it during peak energy times?

Chapter Crossover It is really important to refer students back to Chapter 2 where they learned about their learning preferences in relation to personality type. Students should continually make connections about who they are and why they do what they do throughout this course.

Finally, although we've focused on physical and emotional energy here, remember that all four dimensions of energy—physical, emotional, mental, and spiritual—are interconnected. If you subtract one from the equation, you'll be firing on less than four cylinders. If you are fully engaged and living life to the fullest, all four dimensions of your energy equation will be in balance. Throughout this book, you'll read about all four dimensions of energy.

INSIGHT → ACTION

1. Do you feel that your energy fluctuates throughout an average day? Describe your biological clock.

2. What actions can you take to regulate your physical and emotional energy for the sake of your own productivity?

YOUR TYPE IS SHOWING

What does your psychological type say about your time management preferences? Fill in this quick assessment and see what your responses say about you.

4	3	2	1
Very much like me	Somewhat like me	Not much like me	Not at all like me

1. I am most motivated when I work on active tasks that let me move around or talk to people. (E) _____
2. I avoid tasks that don't fit my own personal value system. (F) _____
3. I don't get around to things I enjoy doing as often as I should. (T) _____
4. I often have to redo work, which takes time, because I've overlooked important details. (N) _____
5. I am reluctant to make a schedule; I prefer to be spontaneous. (P) _____
6. I sometimes get locked into a routine, even if it's not particularly productive. (S) _____
7. I have a fairly long attention span and don't mind reading or studying on my own. (I) _____
8. I am a natural at time management. I make schedules and stick to them. (J) _____
9. I work at what's most important first, even if I'd really rather work on something I like. (T) _____
10. I tend to avoid planning and jump right into things even if I make mistakes. (E) _____
11. I like to make things I do my own by adding my own touches. (N) _____
12. I prefer e-mail to face-to-face contact when scheduling events with other people. (I) _____
13. I sometimes organize my schedule based on who I'm interacting with. (F) _____
14. I often over-obligate myself with too many commitments. (P) _____
15. I sometimes resist changing my schedule when I should because I already have it well organized. (J) _____
16. I avoid schoolwork that seems too theoretical. (S) _____
17. I enjoy the social connections made in study groups. (E) _____
18. I usually work on the things I like first even if they're not the most urgent. (F) _____
19. I tend to be good at prioritizing and construct schedules that make sense. (T) _____
20. I dislike routines. (N) _____
21. I like to think about things for a while before I get started. (I) _____
22. If I were honest, I'd say I have quite a bit to learn about scheduling and prioritizing. (P) _____

23. I sometimes get bogged down in the details of a project. (S) _____

24. I make schedules and stick to them. (J) _____

Now total your scores for each of the MBTI scales. (There are three items related to each scale.)

Totals: _____ E _____ I _____ S _____ N _____ T _____ F _____ J _____ P _____

High Preference, 12–10	Medium Preference, 9–7	Low Preference, 6 or less

Does your score on this time management assessment reflect your SuccessType Learning Style Type Indicator? All aspects of psychological type can play a role in time management preferences.[7] But take a close look at your scores on the most important scale that relates to time management: Judging versus Perceiving. If you scored high on the Judging scale of the MBTI or SuccessTypes Learning Style Indicator, you've probably already bought a planner before reading this chapter and have all your upcoming commitments entered—and color-coded, no less.

If you scored high on the Perceiving scale, the words *schedule* and *prioritizing* may not be part of your vocabulary. Why would anyone submit to the slavery of a planner? You just do things when you need to do them, and most things get done. The key word in the last sentence is *most*. As you're responsible for more in an array of demanding college classes, what about all the things that will fall into the cracks? That could be a problem, couldn't it?

It's true that some people are natural planners and some aren't. If you're high on the Perceiving scale, you'll have to develop your own coping strategies. Many with your psychological type are very successful business-people, physicians, teachers, attorneys—you name it. A high score on the Perceiving scale is no excuse for not planning. Some P's who learn about their preferences make lists for everything. They realize that "Judging" is a requirement for success in most jobs, and they've learned coping mechanisms that serve them well. On the other hand, the spontaneity and curiosity that P's bring to the table can lead to success, too.[8] Take a look at some other possibilities for those for whom scheduling doesn't come naturally.

1. **Hire a personal assistant.** This advice is mostly facetious, but the principle is a good one. If something isn't a particular strength of yours, associate yourself with people for whom it is. A best friend who can call you and say, "Don't forget that our history paper is due Friday" can be a good thing. You don't want to over-rely on these people, but perhaps you can learn from them.

2. **Develop a routine that works.** Instead of managing time in increments by scheduling minutes and hours, think in terms of the flow of each day. Perhaps your days go something like this: Exercise (it won't get done otherwise) → Shower → Class → Lunch → Class → Library (quality quiet time to study and write) → Errands (saved for a relatively low energy time of day) → Dinner → Study. For some people who think in terms of linking events and the reasons for ordering events on a daily basis, this approach can work well. There's one caveat—you need to be able to estimate how long each event will take fairly accurately, so that the flow works.

3. **Identify one location you can always go to for reminders.** Some people use a well-located whiteboard, notes on the refrigerator, or messages taped to computer screens. Pick one place to go for reminders when you get off track. If you live with other people, you can share this space, and comment on other people's schedules, too.

"I'll Study in My Free Time" … and When Is That?

CHALLENGE ⮕ REACTION

Challenge: How do you spend your time?

Reaction: Self-Assessment—Where Did the Time Go?

Fill in the number of hours you spend doing each of the following, then multiply your answer by the number given (7 or 5 to figure weekly amounts) where appropriate.

(continued)

Number of hours per day

Sleeping: _____ × 7 = _____

Personal grooming (for example, showering, shaving, putting on makeup): _____ × 7 = _____

Eating (meals and snacks; include preparation or driving time): _____ × 7 = _____

Commuting during the week (to school and work): _____ × 5 = _____

Doing errands and chores: _____ × 7 = _____

Spending time with family (parents, children, or spouse): _____ × 7 = _____

Spending time with boyfriend or girlfriend _____ × 7 = _____

Number of hours per week

At work: _____

In classes: _____

At regularly scheduled functions (church, clubs, etc.): _____

Socializing, hanging out, watching TV, talking on the phone, etc.: _____

Now add up all the numbers in the far right column and subtract that amount from 168. This is the number of hours you have remaining in your week for that ever-important task of studying.

You may wish to revise how much time you spend on other activities of your life, based on your reaction.

Ask ten students when they study, and chances are at least eight will reply, "in my free time." The irony in this statement is that if you actually waited until you had free time to study, you probably never would. Truthfully, some students are amazed at how easily a day can race by without ever thinking about cracking a book. This is why you should actually *schedule* your study time, but to do that, you should first be aware of how you're currently spending those twenty-four hours of each day.

Notice that the "Challenge → Reaction" activity you just completed places studying at the bottom of the list, even though it's vital to your success in college. The exercise reflects a common attitude among college students, namely that studying is what takes place after everything else gets done. Where does schoolwork rank on *your* list of priorities?

If succeeding in college is a top priority for you, then make sure that you're devoting adequate time to schoolwork outside the classroom. Most instructors expect you to study two to three hours outside of class for every hour spent in class. If it's a particularly challenging class, you may need even more study time. You can use the following chart to calculate the total number of hours you ought to expect to study—effectively—each week:

Credit hours for less demanding classes: _____ × 2 hours = _____ hours

Credit hours for typical/average classes: _____ × 3 hours = _____ hours

Credit hours for more challenging classes: _____ × 4 hours = _____ hours

Expected total study time per week = _____ hours

Remember, just putting in the time won't guarantee that you'll truly *understand* what you're studying. You need to ensure that your study time is productive by focusing your attention and strategically selecting study techniques that work best for you.

Box 4.1 "It's Too Darn Nice Outside" (and Other Lame Excuses for Blowing Off Class)

Do you find yourself skipping class at times in order to do something else: getting an oil change for your car, soaking up the sun's rays, or socializing with some friends you ran into on the way to class? If so, ask yourself this: Would you walk into a gas station, put a $20 bill down on the counter to prepay for a tank of gas, and then put in a dollar's worth and drive off? Absolutely not, you say?

Would you buy a $10 movie ticket and then just toss it in the trash because you decided there was something else you'd rather do on the spur of the moment? No way!

Why, then, would you purchase much more expensive "tickets" to class—the average cost of an hour in class is roughly upwards of $100 per hour—and then toss them in the trash by not attending? Don't you value your money more than that? More importantly, don't you value *yourself* more than that?

The next time you're tempted to opt out of your scheduled classes, ask yourself if you really want to throw away money, in addition to the opportunity. Check your priorities, then put one foot in front of the other and walk into that classroom. In the long run, it's the best investment in your own future.

© Clayton J. Price/CORBIS

> **"What may be done at any time will be done at no time."**
>
> **Scottish Proverb**

ARE *YOU* CAUGHT IN THE NET?

It's noon. You decide to check your online life while you chow down a giant burrito. Three pokes and five new requests from potential friends. *Who are these people?* you wonder. You decide to start a new group called, the "Why do you want to be my friend when you don't even know me?" group. By 1:30 it has fifty-five members on campus. You ask yourself how you can get that interesting student who sits behind you in your biology class to poke you back. At 2:00, you decide on a whim to update your photo albums by uploading several shots from your weekend adventures. At 2:30 the response you've been waiting for finally pops up. The clock ticks away as you continue to poke around. You check your watch and are amazed to find that it's already 4:30. You realize that while you've made on-line contact with the object of your desire from your biology class, you've *missed* your real-life biology class. So has your new friend, apparently. Four and a half hours have just vanished from your day.

Does this scenario sound uncomfortably familiar? A few stolen moments start a chain reaction that stretches out for several hours. You hate to admit it, but you're caught in the Net: a social networking epidemic that's sweeping the college scene everywhere.

Just why is social networking so addicting? Is it due to the pure novelty of the medium? Is it the curiosity generated by the minute-by-minute changes posted? Is it the drive to amass an outrageous number of new friends to pump up your image? Is it simply to hook up with other people? The good news is that Facebook, MySpace, Xanga, Flickr, and similar sites help students connect, and connections are important to college success.

But experts also agree that social networking has the potential to become a time-consuming addiction that can take over your life, "by far the biggest procrastination tool amongst college students" today.[9] One addict confessed, "Sometimes I'll sign-off Facebook and just stare at the login screen like a cocaine addict looking at the edge of his coffee table, thinking to myself, 'Well, I've really got nothing better to do right now,' and then I sign right back on. That's when you know you're really addicted."[10]

© Rick Gomez/CORBIS

> **"The busier we are, the more important we seem to ourselves and, we imagine, to others."**
>
> Wayne Muller, from *Sabbath: Restoring the Sacred Rhythm of Rest*

Are *you* addicted? Ask yourself these questions: Do you obsess about your social life and get nervous if you haven't checked your account for a while? Do you make a run for any idle computer on campus to log on between classes? Do you spend hours searching for people you've met whose names you can't remember? Do you inflate your friends list with people you don't know? Do you feel frustrated when you find out someone you'd really like to meet doesn't have an account yet? Do you spend more time with your online friends than your real friends? Do you check your account when you first wake up in the morning and right before you go to bed at night to see what's changed? Do you interrupt yourself constantly to check your account while doing online academic research for your course projects? If the answers to multiple questions in this paragraph are yes, are you ready to face the possibility of a social networking addiction?[11]

Don't get caught in the Net. Instead of simply allowing yourself to drift off obsessively into cyberspace for hours on end, think about the impact of this obsession on your ability to manage your time and ensure your college success. Try these suggestions:

1. **Monitor your time online.** Estimate right now how much time you spend online per week. Then actually time yourself. Is your estimate accurate? Or are you way off base?

2. **Set limits.** Give yourself a hard-and-fast time limit, and stick to it.

3. **Shorten your social networking sessions.** Being online tends to distort time. You may think you've only been on for an hour when three hours have actually gone by. Set an old-fashioned timer, and when it goes off, get up and do something else.

4. **Separate work and play online.** It's easy to find yourself on a fun-seeking detour when you're supposed to be working on a research paper. When the two tasks are merged, it's easy to lose track of what's what. You end up wasting time because it feels as if you're doing something productive when you really aren't.

5. **Take a tech vacation.** Without getting freaked out, think about this option: Turn off your computer for a day, and then extend the time to a week or more. Use a computer lab on campus to complete your assignments, rather than tempting yourself to spend hours online in your room. Train yourself to withdraw, little by little.

6. **Get a life.** Take up yoga, chess, or swimming. Make some new friends, start a relationship, or join a club on campus. Occupy your time with real-time relationships and activities that are interesting and invigorating. Your real life might actually become more interesting if you open yourself up to other opportunities.

7. **Talk to people who care about you—a family member or a counselor on campus.** Recognizing the problem and admitting it are the first steps. Being one-sided isn't healthy, and secrecy and lies aren't a positive, productive way to live. There are experts and support groups available to help you overcome your addiction and make your real life more fulfilling.[12]

Schedule Your Way to Success

Sensitive Situation Keep in mind that there are still electronic and time divides. Some students may not have a computer at home, or not have the time to spend on electronic networking platforms because they're working three jobs to support themselves.

Activity Option Ask students to share with a partner how much time they spend online for things that are not school-related. How many times in the middle of working on the computer for some school-related activity do they respond to an IM or check their e-mail? Often? If this behavior is fairly typical, would they like to change? What could they do to improve their online habits? Give students about ten minutes and then have students report to the group. The goal will be to compare notes on how to improve online habits.

CHALLENGE → REACTION

Challenge: Can you remember how you spent all your time yesterday?

Reaction: Using the following Time Monitor, fill in as much as you can remember about how you spent your time yesterday from 7:00 a.m. to 10:00 p.m. Be as detailed as possible, right down to fifteen-minute segments.

7:00 _____	9:30 _____	12:00 _____	2:30 _____	5:00 _____	7:30 _____
7:15 _____	9:45 _____	12:15 _____	2:45 _____	5:15 _____	7:45 _____
7:30 _____	10:00 _____	12:30 _____	3:00 _____	5:30 _____	8:00 _____
7:45 _____	10:15 _____	12:45 _____	3:15 _____	5:45 _____	8:15 _____
8:00 _____	10:30 _____	1:00 _____	3:30 _____	6:00 _____	8:30 _____
8:15 _____	10:45 _____	1:15 _____	3:45 _____	6:15 _____	8:45 _____
8:30 _____	11:00 _____	1:30 _____	4:00 _____	6:30 _____	9:00 _____
8:45 _____	11:15 _____	1:45 _____	4:15 _____	6:45 _____	9:15 _____
9:00 _____	11:30 _____	2:00 _____	4:30 _____	7:00 _____	9:30 _____
9:15 _____	11:45 _____	2:15 _____	4:45 _____	7:15 _____	9:45 _____

(continued)

Now monitor how you use your time today (or tomorrow if you're reading this at night) on the following Time Monitor. Again, be very specific. You will refer back to this exercise later in this chapter.

7:00 _____	9:30 _____	12:00 _____	2:30 _____	5:00 _____	7:30 _____
7:15 _____	9:45 _____	12:15 _____	2:45 _____	5:15 _____	7:45 _____
7:30 _____	10:00 _____	12:30 _____	3:00 _____	5:30 _____	8:00 _____
7:45 _____	10:15 _____	12:45 _____	3:15 _____	5:45 _____	8:15 _____
8:00 _____	10:30 _____	1:00 _____	3:30 _____	6:00 _____	8:30 _____
8:15 _____	10:45 _____	1:15 _____	3:45 _____	6:15 _____	8:45 _____
8:30 _____	11:00 _____	1:30 _____	4:00 _____	6:30 _____	9:00 _____
8:45 _____	11:15 _____	1:45 _____	4:15 _____	6:45 _____	9:15 _____
9:00 _____	11:30 _____	2:00 _____	4:30 _____	7:00 _____	9:30 _____
9:15 _____	11:45 _____	2:15 _____	4:45 _____	7:15 _____	9:45 _____

There is no one right way to schedule your time, but if you experiment with the system presented in this book, you'll be on the right path. Eventually, you can tweak the system to make it uniquely your own. Try these eight steps, and schedule your way to success!

STEP 1: Fill Out a "Term on a Page" Calendar. Right up front, create a "Term on a Page" calendar that shows the entire school term on one page. (See Exercise 4.1.) This calendar allows you to see the big picture. You will need to have the syllabus from each of your classes and your school's course schedule to do this step properly. The following items should be transferred onto your "Term on a Page" calendar:

> Holidays when your school is closed

> Exam and quiz dates from your syllabi

> Project or paper deadlines from your syllabi

> Relevant administrative deadlines (*e.g.*, registration for the next term, drop dates)

> Birthdays and anniversaries to remember

> Important out-of-town travel

> Dates that pertain to other family members, such as days that your children's school is closed or that your spouse is out of town for a conference—anything that will impact your ability to attend classes or study

EXERCISE 4.1 Term on a Page

Take a few minutes right now to create your own Term on a Page using the charts in Figure 4.2.

Term _____ Year _____

Month:	Sunday	Monday	Tuesday	Wednesday	Thursday	Friday	Saturday

Month:	Sunday	Monday	Tuesday	Wednesday	Thursday	Friday	Saturday

Month:	Sunday	Monday	Tuesday	Wednesday	Thursday	Friday	Saturday

Month:	Sunday	Monday	Tuesday	Wednesday	Thursday	Friday	Saturday

Month:	Sunday	Monday	Tuesday	Wednesday	Thursday	Friday	Saturday

STEP 2: Invest in a Planner. While it's good to have the big picture, you must also develop an ongoing scheduling system that works for you. Using the "It's all right up here in my head" method is a surefire way to miss an important appointment, fly past the deadline for your term paper without a clue, or lose track of the time you have left to complete multiple projects. Oops!

Although your instructor will typically provide you with a class syllabus that lists test dates and assignment deadlines, trying to juggle multiple syllabi—not to mention your personal and work commitments—is enough to drive you crazy. You need *one* central clearinghouse for all of your important deadlines, appointments, and commitments. This central clearinghouse is a planner—a calendar book with space to write in each day. Derek Johnson in the "FOCUS Challenge Case" expressed his bias that planners are for nerds and neurotics. Not true! Most every successful person on the planet uses one.

When you go planner shopping, remember that you don't have to break the bank unless you want to. Of course if you want a PDA with bells and

Sensitive Situation It's important that we as instructors not tell students what we think is the best kind of planner. Some people do much better with a hard copy daily planner and others prefer the portability of a PDA. What is important is that students have a plan that works for them and that they stick to it.

FOCUS ON CAREERS: JUDITH CARA,
Community and Government Relations Manager, Intel Corporation

Courtesy of Judith Cara

Q1: What do you do in your job? What are the main responsibilities?

In my position at Intel, I have four major responsibilities: Media Relations, Government Affairs, Education Manager, and Community Relations Manager. For Media Relations, I'm responsible for managing Intel's external image in the state media and am basically the "face of Intel" in our local communities. Often, I proactively approach the local media if there is specific information that we'd like them to have about a grant that we've awarded to a local school, a new product that is being designed or manufactured locally, or a collaboration with a local non-profit organization. At other times, I have to react to a call from a print media reporter or handle an on-camera interview with a television station. For Government Affairs, I handle relationships with elected officials at the federal, state, county, and city levels, monitor legislation to see if there are any proposed bills that would negatively impact Intel, and introduce legislation that would be in the best interests of other high-tech or manufacturing companies. Although Public Affairs professionals are often seen as an overhead cost to a corporation—they don't contribute directly to the profit—government affairs is an area where we can negotiate significant savings for our employers. In particular, I have been able to negotiate tax incentives or compromise positions during tax audits that have saved the corporation millions of dollars. As Education Manager, I am responsible for implementing Intel's science, technology, engineering and math (STEM) programs in K-20 education in the state, as well as developing other STEM collaborations locally. I am asked to speak at national education conferences, have joined a couple of national education boards, and have even been on a panel with the

U.S. Secretary of Education. As part of Community Relations, this area covers a number of diverse activities including neighbor relations, the annual United Way campaign, our volunteerism programs—called Intel Involved—and philanthropic grants to local non-profit or education organizations. We also have quarterly meetings of our Community Advisory Panel (CAP), a group of local citizens who come to Intel to hear about what we're doing and to act as our eyes and ears in the community.

Q2: What are the three most important skills you need to do well in this career?

In my position, it is imperative to be able to keep all of the balls up in the air at the same time. This job is not for somebody who feels compelled to finish one task before moving on to the next one. When I leave home in the morning with a mental image of what needs to be done that day, I may not get any further than the end of my driveway before my cell phone rings and I find myself moving in a different direction in response to something that has arisen. I find this energizing, but I know some people who would be frustrated by this constant need to restructure each day's priorities. The field of public relations is all about relationships, so an outgoing personality, an ability to talk to strangers, and excellent networking skills are important. I often need to ask others for help, whether it's a city official who can assist me with a permitting issue or a newspaper reporter who has the ability to edit an article that may not be entirely favorable to the corporation. I don't want to give the impression that this is a one-way street. I also look for opportunities to assist these people with factory tours, an appointment to our Community Advisory Panel, or a silent auction item for a fundraising event.

whistles, you will have to invest a substantial amount of money. But if you know you're more likely to use an e-version than a paper-and-pencil version, and you've planned for one in your budget, go for it! Many new college students find that an ordinary paper-and-pencil daily calendar from an office supply store works best. Having a full page for each day means you can write your daily to-do list right in your planner (more on to-do lists later), and that can be a huge help.

STEP 3: Transfer Important Dates. The next step is to transfer important dates for the whole term from your "Term on a Page" overview to the appropriate days in your planner. This may seem repetitious, but there's a method to the madness. While it's important to be able to view all of your due dates together to create a big picture, it's equally important to have these dates recorded in your actual planner because you will use it more regularly—as the final authority on your schedule.

Teachable Moment Pose the following question to students: Is a public relations executive a good career choice for everyone? Why or why not?

Chapter Crossover Remind students that they will be exploring careers in Chapter 12 and to keep thinking about their own skills and strengths as they prepare for this chapter.

C CREATE a Career Outlook

PUBLIC RELATIONS/ COMMUNITY RELATIONS SPECIALIST

Have you ever considered a career in public relations? Here are some facts about this career to consider and some questions about yourself to ponder.

Facts to Consider

Academic preparation required: a college degree in public relations, communication, journalism, or some related field, along with an internship in public relations or similar work experience

Future workforce demand: Employment in this field is expected to grow at greater than average rates, but competition for entry-level jobs will be high.

Work environment: Public relations or communication specialists focus on building and maintaining an organization's relationship with the public. They work with the media, community members, interest groups, government, and investors, for example. They typically write press releases and speeches for top executives in the company and conduct the research for television special reports, newspaper stories, and magazine articles, often related to the environment, health, or energy. Public relations specialists often work forty-hour weeks, but they may occasionally need to work overtime or even around the clock during times of crisis.

Most common psychological type preferences: extraverted, intuitive, feeling, perceiving. Most common types are ENFP or ESTJ.[13]

Essential skills: creativity, initiative, communication, problem solving, and team working

Questions to Ponder

1. Do you have (or could you acquire) the skills this career requires?
2. What would you find most satisfying about this type of career?
3. What would you find most challenging about this type of career?
4. Are you interested in a career like this? Why or why not?

For more information, see U.S. Department of Labor, Bureau of Labor Statistics, *Occupational Outlook Handbook, 2006–2007 Edition*.[14]

For more career activities online, go to http://www.academic.cengage.com/collegesuccess/staley to do the Team Career exercises.

Q3: What is the most challenging time management issue in your job? How do you deal with it?
Public relations is definitely not a job for someone who wants to work 9 A.M. to 5 P.M. A school board meeting may require my presence until 11 P.M., or a telephone conference call with my counterparts in Asia can take place at 6 A.M. Of course, a 6 A.M. telephone call can be handled from my home and I still get a kick out of sitting at home in my pajamas, talking to my colleagues around the world, while my two dogs are sprawled across my feet!

Q4: How important is scheduling in your job?
Scheduling is an important component of my position, and Intel uses online meeting planning for calendar scheduling. At any given moment, my online calendar is up-to-date so that anyone can see times when I'm available for a meeting. Despite this, I sometimes get double or even triple booked, and then I need to prioritize which meeting is most important.

Q5: Is there a time when you didn't practice good time management skills and it hurt you from a career standpoint?
I can't think of a specific example in this category. I'm pretty obsessive about keeping things on schedule but I have learned that, if you miss a meeting, the other attendees assign all of the action items to you in your absence!

Q6: What advice would you give college students who are interested in exploring a career in public relations?
If you are interested in pursuing a public relations career, find a public relations professional in your community and ask that person to spend a little time with you. Job shadowing is a very effective way to see firsthand what is involved. Most of us are extraverts so we're happy to mentor others who have an interest in our field.

STEP 4: Set Intermediate Deadlines. After recording the important dates for the entire academic term, look at the individual due dates for major projects or papers that are assigned. Then set intermediate stepping-stone goals that will ultimately help you accomplish your final goals. Working backward from the due date, choose and record deadlines for completing certain chunks of the work. For example, if you have a research paper due, you could set an intermediate deadline for completing all of your initial research and other deadlines for the pre-writing, writing, and rewriting steps for the paper.

STEP 5: Schedule Fixed Activities for the Entire Term. Next you'll want to schedule in all fixed activities throughout the entire term: class meeting times and reading assignments, religious services you regularly attend, club meetings, and regular co-curricular activities such as athletics or choir. It's also a great idea to schedule brief review sessions for your classes. Of course, sometimes you'll be going directly into another class, but ten-minute segments of time before and after each class to review your notes helps prepare you for any surprise quizzes and dramatically improve your understanding and retention of the material.

STEP 6: Check for Schedule Conflicts. Now, take a final look at your planner. Do you notice any major scheduling conflicts, such as a planned business trip smack dab in the middle of midterm exam week? Look for these conflicts now, when there's plenty of time to adjust your plans and talk with your instructor to see what you can work out.

STEP 7: Schedule Flextime. In all the scheduling of important dates, checking and double-checking, don't forget one thing. You do need personal time for eating, sleeping, exercising, and other regular activities that don't have a set time frame. Despite your planner, life will happen. If you get a toothache, you'll need to see a dentist right away. Several times each week, you can count on something coming up that will offer you a chance (or force you) to revise your schedule. The decision of how high the item ranks on your priority list rests with you, but the point is to leave some wiggle room in your schedule.

STEP 8: Monitor Your Schedule Every Day. At this point, you've developed a working time management system. Now it's important to monitor your use of that system on a daily basis. Each night, take three minutes to review the day's activities. How well did you stick to your schedule? Did you accomplish the tasks you set out to do? Do you need to revise your schedule for the rest of the week based on something that happened—or didn't happen—today? This simple process will

Teachable Moment Some students may read the part about not skipping the review and revise part, and skip it anyway. Ask for some volunteers who are willing to share that they did step 8. Most likely, your J's and S's will volunteer. When students see that someone really did this, and it worked, it may motivate them to try. Another option: require students to send you an e-mail summarizing what they learned about their current time management practices and how they measure up.

Photodisc/Getty Images

"Nothing is so fatiguing as the eternal hanging on of an uncompleted task."

William James, American psychologist and philosopher (1842–1910)

help you better schedule your time in the future and give you a sense of accomplishment—or of the need for more discipline—for tasks completed, hours worked, and classes attended. Don't skip this step. It's the perfect way to bring closure to your day's work as a college student. When you're done reviewing your day's activities, take another five minutes to preview and adjust (if needed) tomorrow's schedule. Mentally playing out the day in advance will help you internalize what must be accomplished and help you create a pace for each day.

To Do or Not to Do? There *Is* No Question

Part of your personal time management system should be keeping an ongoing to-do list. While the concept of a to-do list sounds relatively simple, there are a few tricks of the trade.

Before the beginning of each school week, brainstorm all the things that you want or need to get done in the upcoming week. Using this random list of to-do items, assign a priority level next to each one. The A-B-C method is simple and easy to use:

A = must get this done; highest priority

B = very important, but not mandatory

C = would be nice to get done this week,
    but not necessary

The two factors to consider when assigning a priority level to a to-do item are *importance* and *urgency*, creating four time zones. Use Figure 4.3 as a guide.[15]

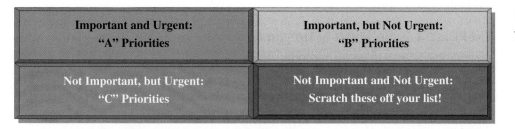

Figure 4.3
Time Zones

After you've assigned a time zone to each item, review your list of A and B priorities and ask yourself:

1. Do any of the items fit best with a particular day of the week? For example, donating blood may be a high priority task for you, yet you don't want to do it on a day when you have co-curricular sports planned. That might leave you with two available days in the upcoming week that you can donate blood.

2. Can any items be grouped together for easier execution? For example, you may have three errands to run downtown on your to-do list, so grouping them together will save you from making three separate trips.

3. Do any A and B priorities qualify as floating tasks that can be completed anytime, anywhere? For example, perhaps you were assigned an extra long reading assignment for one of your classes. It's both important and urgent, an A priority item. Bring your book to read while waiting at the dentist's office for your semi-annual teeth cleaning appointment, a B priority. Planning ahead can really help save time.

4. Do any priorities need to be shifted? As the days pass, some of your B priorities will become A priorities due to the urgency factor increasing. Or maybe an A priority will become a C priority because something changed about the task. This is normal.

As for those C priority to-do items, scratch them off the list right now. Life is too short to waste time on unimportant tasks. Give yourself permission to focus on what's important. Since time is a limited resource, one of the best ways to guarantee a successful college experience is to use it wisely. If you don't already use these tools on a regular basis, give them a shot. What do you have to lose except time?

Emotional Intelligence (EI) Research Daniel Goleman tells us that "emotions that simmer beneath the threshold of awareness can have a powerful impact on how we perceive and react....once the reaction is brought into awareness....he can reevaluate anew." Students need to understand *why* they prioritize things as important or not and the implications of their choices before they will make significant change.

INSIGHT ⊖ ACTION

Look back at the Time Monitors you completed in an earlier "Challenge → Reaction" activity when answering the following questions:

1. How could the use of a schedule have improved the way you used your time on those two days?

2. How could the use of a to-do list have improved the way you used your time on those two days?

Follow all the advice given in the chapter to this point for the upcoming week. Notice how much more efficient and effective you are with your precious and limited resource called time.

EXERCISE 4.2 So Much to Do—So Little Time

Assume this is your to-do list for today (Monday). Assign each item one of the four time zones described earlier: A, B, C (and strike through any items that are *not* urgent and *not* important). Finally, renumber the items to indicate which you would do first, which second, and so forth.

Start time: 9:00 a.m., Monday morning, during the second week of the fall term.

1. _____ Return Professor Jordan's call before class tomorrow. He left a message saying he wants to talk to you about some problems with your LIT 101 paper.

2. _____ Pick up your paycheck at McDonald's and get to the bank before it closes at 5:00 p.m. this afternoon.

3. _____ Call the new love interest in your life and ask about going to the party together this weekend before someone else does.

4. _____ Visit the Speech Center to get critiqued on your first speech due Friday. It's closed evenings.

5. _____ Call your favorite aunt. She lives overseas in a time zone seven hours ahead of yours. Today is her fortieth birthday.

6. _____ Stop by the Health Center to take advantage of free meningitis vaccinations today only.

7. _____ Listen to the new CD you bought yesterday.

8. _____ Leave a note asking your roommate to please stop leaving messes everywhere. It's really aggravating.

9. _____ Read the two chapters in your History textbook for the in-class quiz on Wednesday.

10. _____ Watch the first episode of the new reality TV show you've been waiting for at 9 p.m. tonight.

11. _____ Write a rough draft of the essay due in your composition class on Thursday.

12. _____ Check with your RA about inviting a high school friend to spend the weekend.

13. _____ Return the three library books that are a week overdue.

14. _____ Call your math Teaching Assistant and leave a message asking for an appointment during her office hours to get help with the homework due on Wednesday. Nearly everyone is confused about the assignment.

15. _____ Go to the campus Athletic Banquet tonight at 6 p.m. to receive your award.

Outline the criteria you used for making your decisions.

Activity Option Make two sets of index cards with the same tasks as listed in Exercise 4.2. Divide the class into two groups and have them decide as a group which time zones to put each task into. At the end of fifteen minutes, have one member of the team report the criteria used to place the cards in the zones to the class, what was eliminated, and what they observed about the different members in the groups. Then give each one of the fifteen cards to an individual student, and have them line up from left to right to indicate how they'd organize the day. They'll likely have to negotiate their positions.

How Time Flies!

CHALLENGE ⟶ REACTION

Challenge: What are the most common ways you waste time? What can be done about them?

Reaction: _____

_____

_____

Teachable Moment It is worth taking time to go around the room and have students name the ways they waste time, so students can see how others waste time, and discuss what they can do to stop. It helps when we realize we are not alone!

According to efficiency expert Michael Fortino, in a lifetime, the average American will spend:

➤ Seven years in the bathroom

➤ Six years eating

➤ Five years waiting in line

➤ Three years in meetings

➤ Two years playing telephone tag

➤ Eight months opening junk mail

➤ And six months waiting at red lights[16]

What a waste of time! We can't do much about some of these items, but what *can* we do about other time-wasters? Plan—schedule—organize! Think about the issue of control in time management, and write in examples for the following:

1. Things you think you can't control, and you can't: _____

2. Things you think you can't control, but you can: _____

3. Things you think you can control, but you can't: _____

4. Things you think you can control, but you don't: _____

5. Things you think you can control, and you can: _____

Perhaps you wrote in something like *medical emergencies* for (1). You could have written in *family or friends barging into your room* for (2). For (4), maybe you could control your *addiction to social networking*, but you don't. And for (5), perhaps you wrote in *your attention*. You're absolutely right. But what about (3)? Did anything fit there? Are there things you think you can control, but you can't? Try and think of something that would fit into (3), and then think of creative ways you really could control this situation if you tried.[17]

A recent ad for a well-known high-tech company asserts, "You can't control your boss, your workload, your weight, your backhand, your weeds, your dog, your life. At least now you can control your cursor."[18] Actually, you can control more than you think you can control—and if not control, at least manage. Your time, attention, and energy are three of these things. Time-wasters lurk in every corner waiting to steal your scheduled time from you. Watch out! Don't let them spend your time *for* you!

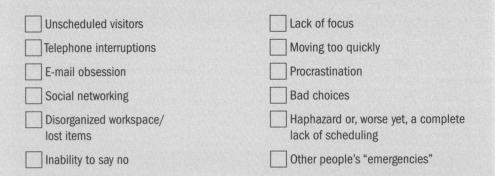

INSIGHT → ACTION

Here is a list of some of the most common ways students waste time. As you read through the list, check off those that occur in your life most frequently.

☐ Unscheduled visitors   ☐ Lack of focus

☐ Telephone interruptions   ☐ Moving too quickly

☐ E-mail obsession   ☐ Procrastination

☐ Social networking   ☐ Bad choices

☐ Disorganized workspace/   ☐ Haphazard or, worse yet, a complete
   lost items   lack of scheduling

☐ Inability to say no   ☐ Other people's "emergencies"

If you think time management is a limiting concept, but you checked three or more boxes, perhaps the notion of scheduling is sounding more useful. What actions can you take to deal with the issues you marked?

The P Word. Read This Section *Now*! ... or Maybe Tomorrow ... or the Next Day ... or ...

CHALLENGE ⊖ REACTION

Challenge: What are the most common reasons you procrastinate?

Reaction: _____

Picture this: You sit down to work on a challenging homework assignment. After a few minutes, you think, *Man, I'm thirsty*, so you get up and get a soda. Then you sit back down to continue your work. A few minutes later, you decide that some chips would go nicely with your soda and you head to the kitchen. Again, you sit down to face the task before you, as you concentrate more on eating than on working. Ten minutes go by and a nagging thought starts taking over: *Must do laundry*. Up you go again and throw a load of clothes in the washer. Before long you're wondering where all the time went. Since you only have an hour left before your next class, you think, *Why bother getting started now? Doing this project will take much more time than that, so I'll just start it tomorrow*. Despite good intentions at the beginning of your work session, you've just succeeded in accomplishing zip, nadda, nothing.

Congratulations! You—like thousands of other college students—have just successfully procrastinated! Researchers define procrastination as "needlessly delaying tasks to the point of experiencing subjective discomfort."[19] And according to researchers, 70 percent of college students admit to procrastinating on their assignments.[20]

You may be in the majority, but alas, in this case, there's no safety in numbers! We're all prone to procrastinate—to put things off until later—from time to time. In fact, in some instances, our society even rewards procrastination: storewide bargains for last-minute holiday shoppers and extended post office hours for income tax laggards on April 15, for example.

But academic procrastination is a major threat to your ability to succeed in college. And procrastination in the working world can actually bring your job, and ultimately your career, to a screeching halt. Plenty of people try to rationalize their procrastination by claiming that they work better under pressure. However, the challenge in college is that during some weeks of the term, every single class will have an assignment or test due, all at once, and if you procrastinate, you'll not only generate tremendous anxiety for yourself, but you'll lower your chances of succeeding on any of them.

Before you can control the procrastination monster in your life, it's important to understand *why* you procrastinate. Think about all the instances in which you don't procrastinate: meeting your friends for dinner, returning a phone call from a classmate, going to the store. Why are those things easy to do, but getting started on an assignment is difficult until you feel the jaws of a deadline closing down on you?[21] Procrastinators don't tend to be less

Emotional Intelligence (EI) Research Extraverted Perceivers focus on the moment, so they are easily taken away from a task. In addition, if one's EI impulse control, problem solving, and reality testing are not strong, it will be very difficult *not* to procrastinate. Students need to develop these EI skills to make the best use of the EP personality type.

Teachable Moment Remember that students need to understand the *why* of why they do things. This is an important "Challenge → Reaction" to debrief. It may be something that students want to share with you one-on-one. Use e-mail and respond to them and then come up with something that will help them "just do it!"

> **"Things which matter most should never be at the mercy of things which matter least."**
>
> Johann Wolfgang von Goethe, German writer and scholar (1749–1832)

smart or have a definitive psychological type. They do, however, tend to have lower self-confidence and get lost in their own thoughts.[22] The reasons for procrastinating vary from person to person, but once you know your own reasons for putting things off, you'll be in a better position to address the problem from its root cause.

The next time you find yourself procrastinating, ask yourself why. Procrastination is self-handicapping: "It's like running a full race with a knapsack full of bricks on your back. When you don't win, you can say it's not that you're not a good runner, it's just that you had this sack of bricks on your back."[23] In addition to understanding why you procrastinate, try these ten procrastination busters to help you kick the habit.

1. **Keep track (of your excuses).** Write them down consistently, and soon you'll be able to recognize them for what they are. Hold yourself accountable. Own your responsibilities—in school and in the rest of your life.

2. **Break down.** No, not psychologically, though sometimes it can feel like you're headed that way. Break your project into its smaller components. A term paper, for example, can be broken down into the following smaller parts: prospectus, thesis, research, outline, small chunks of writing, and bibliography. Completing smaller tasks along the way is much easier than facing a daunting monster of a project.

3. **Trick yourself.** When you feel like procrastinating, pick some aspect of the project that's easy and that you would have to do anyway. If the thought of an entire paper is overwhelming you, for example, work on the bibliography to start. Starting with something—*anything*—will get you into the rhythm of the work.

4. **Resolve issues.** If something's gnawing at you, making it difficult to concentrate, take care of it. Sometimes you must deal with a noisy roommate,

Emotional Intelligence (EI) Research Interpersonal skills are critical for success in college. Well-developed EI has to do with whether or not someone has empathy for others, has a good sense of social responsibility, and relates well with others. But, sometimes a strength can be overused. When a student misses a test because she was comforting her roommate who broke up with her boyfriend, we say that the student has too much empathy that resulted in a negative consequence.

your kids vying for your attention, or something equally intrusive. Then get down to work.

5. **Get real.** Set realistic goals for yourself. If you declare that you're going to finish a twelve-page paper in five hours as Derek did in the "Focus Challenge Case," you're already doomed. Procrastinators are characteristically optimistic. They underestimate how much time something will take. Make it a habit to keep track of how long assignments take you in all your courses so that you can be increasingly realistic over time.

6. **Think positively.** Our imaginations can work for or against us. Don't let yours go haywire with thoughts that you're not up to the task or that your professor will hate your paper, so why bother. It has been said that the average person has 65,000 to 75,000 thoughts a day, and that many of these are negative. Don't imagine what can go wrong with your project. Imagine what can go right by getting it done on time and doing it well. Assume the best and you'll find it easier to get started.

7. **Make a deal with yourself.** Even if it's only spending fifteen minutes on a task that day, do it so that you can see progress.

8. **Overcome fear.** Many of the reasons for procrastinating have to do with our personal fears. We may fear not doing something perfectly, or failing completely—or even the responsibility that comes with success to keep succeeding. But as Susan Jeffers, author and lecturer states, "Feel the fear, and do it anyway!"

9. **Get tough.** Sometimes projects simply require discipline. The best way to complete a daunting task is to simply dig in. Become your own taskmaster, crack the proverbial whip, and force yourself to focus on those things that are high priorities, but perhaps not your idea of fun. The thought of diving into that term paper is overwhelming to you, so you're waiting to be inspired. Bah! If you wait for inspiration, you may wait a long time.

10. **Acknowledge accomplishment.** We're not talking major shopping sprees at Neiman Marcus here. We're talking reasonable, meaningful rewards commensurate with the action completed. Go buy yourself a small treat, call your best friend in another state, take a relaxing soak in the bathtub, or do something to celebrate your accomplishments—big and small—along the way. Acknowledgment, from yourself or others, is a great motivator for tackling future projects.

YOUR TOUGHEST CLASS

Does procrastination enter into the picture when it comes to your most challenging course this term? What impact does procrastination have on your potential success in this course? On your life as a student?

Examine this list of common reasons people procrastinate. Which ones apply to you in your most challenging course? Put a checkmark next to all the reasons that help explain your tendency to procrastinate. For each item with a checkmark, list one thing you can do to control your learning in this course.

☐ Avoiding something you see as unpleasant

☐ Wanting to do something perfectly

☐ Feeling overwhelmed by all you have to do

☐ Being intimidated by the task itself

☐ Hoping to avoid responsibility

☐ Fearing failure

☐ Fearing success

☐ Fearing new or added responsibilities

☐ Not realizing how important the task is

☐ Reacting to your own internal conflict

☐ Protecting your self-esteem

☐ Waiting for a last-minute adrenaline rush

☐ Just plain not wanting to

Teachable Moment Keep driving home the point that we do have control of most everything and again, we do have total control of how we respond to something. When we fail, we either give up or pull ourselves up and figure out what to do about it.

Chapter Crossover Students should be making the connections between managing time and energy and wellness. Chapter 13 addresses wellness, but it is never too early get students thinking about the connections.

Beyond Juggling: *Realistically* Manage Work, School, and Personal Life

CHALLENGE ⟳ REACTION

Challenge: How do successful people juggle work, school, and personal life?

Reaction: _____

_____

Your personal time management needs depend on who you are and how many obligations you have. Today's college students are more diverse than ever. Like Derek Johnson, increasing numbers of college students are also parents, part-time employees, or full-time professionals, husbands or wives, community volunteers, soccer coaches, or Sunday school teachers. How on earth can you possibly juggle it all?

The answer? You can't. According to work-life balance expert Dawn Carlson, juggling is a knee-jerk coping mechanism—the default setting when time gets tight and it seems that nothing can be put on the back burner. If you, like millions of others, feel overworked, overcommitted, and exhausted at every turn, you may have already learned that you can't juggle your way to a balanced life. It's impossible.[24]

Think about it. A professional juggler—the kind you find at a carnival—focuses every bit of his attention to keep all the balls in the air. The minute he takes his eye off the ball for even a second, down it goes. It's no surprise that you constantly hear people say, "I dropped the ball" with this or that. Not even real jugglers can maintain their trick forever. In fact, the world-record holder in juggling, Anthony Gatto, was only able to keep seven clubs in the air (thrown at least twice without dropping) for a whopping 2 minutes 49 seconds.[25] That's it! So why do we even try to juggle our many responsibilities 24/7? Let's face it—it's a losing battle.

Now for the good news. Balance among work, school, and personal life is possible. All of us have three primary areas of our lives that should be in balance, ideally—meaningful work (including school), satisfying relationships, and a healthy lifestyle. In addition to work and relationships, we all need to take care of ourselves. See what you think of these five rebalancing strategies. The idea is you can't have it all, but you can have it better than you do now.

1. **Alternating.** If you use this strategy, your work-life balance comes in separate, concentrated doses. You may throw yourself into your career with abandon, and then cut back or quit work altogether and focus intensely on your family. You may give your job 110 percent during the week, but devote Saturdays to physical fitness or to your kids or running all the errands you've saved up during the week. Or you save Tuesdays and Thursdays for homework, and go to classes Mondays, Wednesdays, and Fridays. People who use this strategy alternate between important things, and it works for them. An alternator's motto is "I want to have it all, but just not all at once."

2. **Outsourcing.** An outsourcer's motto might be "I want to have it all, not do it all." This strategy helps you achieve work-life balance by giving someone else some of your responsibilities—usually in your personal life—to free up time for the tasks you care about most. If you have enough money, hire someone to clean the house or mow the lawn. If you don't, trade these jobs among family, friends, or neighbors who band together to help each other. Of course, there are ways this strategy could be misused by college students. Don't even think about outsourcing your research papers by having someone else write them or downloading them from the Internet with a charge card! Warning: This practice will definitely be hazardous to your academic health! In fact, your college career may be over!

3. **Bundling.** This strategy helps you rebalance your life by killing two birds with one stone. Examine your busy life and look for areas in which you can double dip, such as combining exercising with socializing. If your social life is suffering because of time constraints, take walks with a friend so that you can talk along the way. Do your laundry with your roommate so that you can chat about your classes. A bundler's motto is "I want

© Tetra Images/CORBIS

> **"The trouble with the rat race is that even if you win, you're still a rat."**
>
> Lily Tomlin, comedian

Emotional Intelligence (EI) Research Clearly, reality testing is very important to students' understanding of managing time, energy, and self. Often, students want to have and do it all, and if we can just get them to reflect, use their best intrapersonal intelligence, and understand themselves, they have a shot at being realistic.

> **"If we did all the things we were capable of doing, we would literally astound ourselves."**
>
> Thomas Edison, American inventor (1847–1931)

to get more mileage out of the things I do by combining activities." Bundling is efficient because it allows you to do two things at once.

4. **Techflexing.** Technology allows us to work from almost anywhere, anytime, using technology. If you telecommute from home several days a week for your job, you might get up early, spend some time on e-mail, go out for a run, have breakfast with your family, and then get back on your computer. In the office, you use instant messaging to stay connected to family members or a cell phone to call home while commuting to a business meeting. Chances are you can telecommute to your campus library and do research online, check in with your professor during online office hours, register for classes online, and pay all your bills online, including tuition. You can use technology, and the flexibility it gives you, to your advantage to merge important aspects of your life. A techflexer's motto is "I want to use technology to accomplish more, not be a slave to it."

5. **Simplifying.** People who use this strategy are ready to cry uncle. They've decided they don't want it all. They've reached a point where they make a permanent commitment to stop the craziness in their lives. The benefit of simplifying is greater freedom from details, stress, and the rat race. But there are trade-offs, of course. They may have to take a significant cut in pay in order to work fewer hours or at a less demanding job. But for them, it's worth it.[26]

These five strategies, used separately or in combination, have helped many people who are dealing with work, school, and family commitments at the same time. They all require certain trade-offs. None of these strategies is a magic solution.

But the alternative to rebalancing is more stress, more physical and emotional exhaustion, more frustration, and much less personal satisfaction. If you focus on rebalancing your life—making conscious choices and course corrections as you

Activity Option The five strategies listed here can help students use real-life techniques to balance multiple things. Write these five techniques on index cards, one per card, and make as many sets as you need so that each student in the class has at least three cards. Hand out the cards and ask students to work in pairs or small groups to come up with real-life examples and solutions for the technique on their card to present to the class.

Sensitive Situation You might briefly discuss with your students that it's okay to delegate or ask for help. It is not a sign of weakness.

go—small changes can have a big impact. Work-life balance isn't an all-or-nothing proposition. It's an ever-changing journey. So take it one step at a time.

For more practice online, go to http://www.academic.cengage.com/collegesuccess/staley to take the Challenge Yourself online quizzes.

INSIGHT → ACTION

If you feel the need to rebalance your life due to the pressures of managing work, school, family, and friends at the same time, take some time to work through the following Rebalancing Plan worksheet.[27]

Why do I need to rebalance? _____

What rebalancing strategies will I use? _____

How will I do it? _____

How will I let go of _____? _____

Tasks that I should completely eliminate: _____

Tasks that I can outsource or give to others: _____

Expectations of others that affect me: _____

Time-consuming possessions or relationships that bring little value to me: _____

_____

EXERCISE 4.3 VARK Activity

Complete the recommended activity for your preferred VARK learning modality. If you are multimodal, select more than one activity. Your instructor may ask you to (a) give an oral report on your results in class, (b) send your results to him or her via e-mail, (c) post them online, or (d) contribute to a class chat.

 Visual: Buy a set of adhesive colored dots from a local office supply store. Go through your planner, putting red dots by A priority items, yellow dots by B priority items, and green dots by C priority items.

 Aural: Go to the National Public Radio website at www.npr.org and listen to a program that will increase your understanding of time management, workplace skills, or a related subject.

 Read/Write: Find a helpful library book on time management skills and summarize three pointers that don't appear in this chapter in a paragraph of your own.

 Kinesthetic: Visit a place of work and interview employees about the value of time management skills and specific techniques they use to prioritize their daily activities. Bring your findings to class.

Activity Option Have students develop a five-slide PowerPoint presentation for the class describing the most important thing they learned in this chapter about managing time and energy. On the second slide they must include one challenge that they're facing and on the third, a specific activity they will do to help them manage the challenge. In the last slide they should describe a possible pitfall they may have to completing the activity and what benefit they will derive if they stick to their plan.

NOW WHAT DO YOU THINK?

At the beginning of this chapter, Derek Johnson, a frustrated and disgruntled student, faced a challenge. Now after reading this chapter, would you respond differently to any of the questions you answered about the "FOCUS Challenge Case"?

REALITY CHECK

On a scale of 1 to 10, answer the following questions now that you've completed this chapter.

1 = not very/not much/very little/low   10 = very/a lot/very much/high

In hindsight, how much did you *really* know about this subject matter before reading the chapter?

1   2   3   4   5   6   7   8   9   10

How much do you think this information might affect your college success?

1   2   3   4   5   6   7   8   9   10

How much do you think this information might affect your career success after college?

1   2   3   4   5   6   7   8   9   10

How long did it actually take you to complete this chapter (both the reading and writing tasks)? _____ Hour(s) _____ Minutes

Take a minute to compare these answers to your answers from the "Readiness Check" at the beginning of this chapter. What gaps exist between the similar questions? How might these gaps between what you thought before starting the chapter and what you now think after completing the chapter affect how you approach the next chapter in this book?

To download mp3 format audio summaries of this chapter, go to http://www.academic.cengage.com/collegesuccess/staley.

5 Thinking Critically and Creatively

YOU'RE ABOUT TO DISCOVER...

Teachable Moment Remind students that if they had graduated five years ago with a degree in computer science, for example—or even art—what they learned then would have changed or would be enriched by new knowledge now. Learning how to think allows individuals to be lifelong learners who can take new knowledge and figure out how to combine it with knowledge they already have.

> How focused thinking, critical thinking, and creative thinking are defined

> Why critical thinking is important

> How to use questions to think critically

> How a four-part model of critical thinking works

> Why reasoning is the foundation for critical thinking

> How to analyze arguments, assess assumptions, and consider claims

> How to avoid mistakes in reasoning

> What metacognition is and why it's important

> How you solve problems and make decisions

> How you think creatively

> How to become a more creative thinker

"Only when we know a little do we know anything; doubt grows with knowledge."

Johann Wolfgang von Goethe, German writer and scholar (1749–1832)

Annie Miller

Growing up in a big city was definitely a good

thing. So Annie Miller thought, anyway. Every day that went by, she missed L.A. more and more. She missed the fast pace, the diversity, the lifestyle. Why had she decided to go to a small college? She knew there had been reasons; it's just that she couldn't remember them from time to time. She guessed that it was probably because she wanted every aspect of her life at college to be different. She wanted to live on a different coast, have new friends, and study something exciting. Her huge high school had been amazing in its own way, but now she wanted a more personal education at a place where everyone knew everyone, like at the small liberal arts college she had chosen on the East Coast.

Her first semester of classes consisted of a college success course, an English composition class, Introduction to Poetry, and Philosophy 100. She was excited by the idea of learning in small classes with wise and learned professors. But Philosophy 100 had turned out to be a very challenging course. Professor Courtney had announced on the first day of class that he believed in the Socratic method of teaching. He taught by asking questions of students instead of lecturing. "Socrates, perhaps the greatest philosopher of all time," he announced the first day, "is the 'father' of critical thinking. In this class, you'll learn to think critically. *That* is what college is all about."

Professor Courtney began every class session with a hypothetical situation and always randomly chose a student to respond. His opening went something like this:

Assume it's Valentine's Day. A young man makes a trip to the biggest jewelry store in the mall to buy his fiancée a gift. He's saved up for a long time to afford 24 karat gold earrings and he's ready to choose the best money can buy. He finds the perfect pair and hands over his credit card. But when the salesclerk brings the receipt for him to sign, he notices that instead of $300, she has missed a digit, and the receipt reads $30. He now faces a dilemma: Does he sign and say nothing, or point out the error and pay the full amount? What should he do?

One student responded with, "He should sign his name and then take off quickly. This mistake was the clerk's, not his. If someone catches the mistake later, he can just claim he didn't notice. Maybe no one will ever figure it out, and he'll be $270 richer!"

Professor Courtney continued, "On what ethical principle do you base your response?" The student faltered, and the professor moved on to someone else, raising other points that hadn't been considered.

"But what if his fiancée decides to exchange the earrings for another pair? What if the clerk is fired for making a $270 mistake? What if the clerk were your sister or your best friend? What if the hero of a movie did what you're proposing? What if the clerk were you?" he continued. "What would Socrates say about what you should do? According to Socrates, no one errs intentionally. This means that whenever we do something wrong—including something *morally* wrong—it is out of ignorance rather than evil motives. If the young man decides to capitalize on the clerk's error, what are his motives—and are they evil? What would be the *right* thing to do?"

Professor Courtney continued putting students on the spot and raising questions posed by other philosophers they were studying. The questions seemed endless. Annie found herself listening more carefully than in her other classes so that she would be ready to jump in if called upon. And she silently thought through others' answers, too. Even though she had to admit that the learning environment was stimulating, speaking in front of other students made Annie nervous.

"There aren't always right answers," Professor Courtney told them. "What's important is thinking through the problem. The process of learning to think can be more important than the answer itself."

Frankly, that explanation didn't sit well with Annie. *If there aren't right answers, what am I doing in college? Things should be black and white, true or false, right or wrong. I'm paying tuition to hear what the professor thinks, not all the other students in class. He knows the right answers. Why doesn't he just tell us?*

Without fail, Annie always left Professor Courtney's class with a headache from thinking so hard. In fact, compared to Philosophy 100, all her other classes seemed effortless. She had to admit that she much preferred classes in which she could express herself creatively, like Introduction to Poetry.

WHAT DO **YOU** THINK?

Now that you've read about Annie Miller, answer the following questions. You may not know all the answers yet, but you'll find out what you know and what you stand to gain by reading this chapter.

1. How would the Socratic method of teaching used by Professor Courtney help first-year college students improve their critical thinking skills?

2. Do you agree with Professor Courtney's statement that "there aren't always right answers"? If that's true, why is getting a college education so important?

3. Even though Professor Courtney's teaching methods made her nervous, why did Annie find the learning environment in his class to be stimulating?

4. Annie says she prefers creative thinking to critical thinking. Are they two different things? Why or why not?

5. Identify three things Annie should do to get the most from Professor Courtney's class.

Before beginning to read this chapter, take two minutes to answer the following questions on a scale of 1 to 10. Your answers will help you assess how ready you are to focus.

1 = not very/not much/very little/low   10 = very/a lot/very much/high

Based on reading the "You're about to discover..." list and skimming this chapter, how much do you think you probably already know about the subject matter?

1 2 3 4 5 6 7 8 9 10

How much do you think this information might affect your college success?

1 2 3 4 5 6 7 8 9 10

How much do you think this information might affect your career success after college?

1 2 3 4 5 6 7 8 9 10

In general, how motivated are you to learn the material in this chapter?

1 2 3 4 5 6 7 8 9 10

This book describes four key factors related to intrinsic, or internal, motivation: curiosity, control, career outlook, and challenge. The next four questions relate to these **C-Factors**:

How *curious* are you about the content you expect to read in this chapter?

1 2 3 4 5 6 7 8 9 10

How much *control* do you expect to have over mastering the material in this chapter?

1 2 3 4 5 6 7 8 9 10

How much do you think this chapter might help you develop your *career outlook*?

1 2 3 4 5 6 7 8 9 10

How *challenging* do you think the material in this chapter will be for you?

1 2 3 4 5 6 7 8 9 10

Before beginning any task—including studying—it's important to check in with yourself to ensure that you're physically, intellectually, and emotionally ready to focus. How ready are you, physically, to focus on this chapter? (Are you rested, feeling well, and so on?)

1 2 3 4 5 6 7 8 9 10

How ready are you, intellectually, to focus on this chapter? (Are you thinking clearly, focused on this course, interested in this subject?)

1 2 3 4 5 6 7 8 9 10

How ready are you, emotionally, to focus on this chapter? (Are you calm, confident, composed?)

1 2 3 4 5 6 7 8 9 10

If your answer to any of the last three questions is below a 5 on the scale, you may need to address the issue you're facing prior to beginning this chapter. For example, if you're hungry, get a quick bite to eat. If you're feeling scattered, take a few moments to settle down and focus.

Finally, how long do you think it will take you to complete this chapter? _____ Hour(s) _____ Minutes

Rethinking Thinking

CHALLENGE ⟶ REACTION

Challenge: What's the difference between thinking and *critical* thinking?

Reaction: _____

Thinking is a natural, ongoing, everyday process we all engage in. In fact, we can't really turn it off, even if we try. We're always on. In the "FOCUS Challenge Case," Professor Courtney claims to help students learn how to think. But what does he mean? Everyone thinks all the time, right? It happens any time you talk to yourself, doesn't it? However, some experts say school teaches us how to regurgitate, not how to think. Perhaps Professor Courtney is onto something.

In many ways, thinking is like speaking. We all know how to speak; we've been doing it reasonably well since we were toddlers. But if you take a public speaking course, you're bound to be a better speaker by the end of it by knowing more about how to consciously direct your voice, gestures, and delivery.

In a similar way, you can become a better thinker by learning how to direct your brain. *Focused thinking*—thinking critically and creatively—is what this chapter is about.

Picture this: You're in the library. It's late, and you're tired. You're supposed to be studying for your political science test, but instead of thinking about foreign policy, your mind begins drifting toward the foreign vacation you took last summer, how tan you were when you returned, how much fun it was to be with your best friends, and where you'd like to visit next.

Would the mental process you're engaging in while sitting in the library be called *thinking*? For our purposes in this chapter, the answer is no. Here thinking is defined as a focused cognitive activity you engage in purposefully. You direct your thoughts toward a particular topic. You're the *active* thinker, not the *passive* daydreamer who is the victim of a wandering mind. Focused thinking involves zeroing in and managing your attention. It's deliberate and intentional, not haphazard or accidental. You choose to do it for a reason.

> **"'Knowledge is power.' Rather, knowledge is happiness. To have knowledge, deep broad knowledge, is to know truth from false and lofty things from low."**
>
> Helen Keller, American author, activist, and lecturer (1880–1968)

Did you know that developing your critical thinking skills goes hand in hand with developing your intellectual capacities as a college student? According to thinking experts like William Perry, who interviewed 400 males in academic difficulty at Harvard roughly fifty years ago, students develop intellectually along a continuum. Early on, most students view the world in terms of right or wrong, good or bad, black or white. They see teachers as having the right answers (as Annie Miller did), and students as the recipients of the right answers from teachers.

Later they come to understand that knowledge depends on context. They no longer wait for the "truth" to be handed down by instructors. Instead, they begin to value their own and others' opinions and perceive multiple points of view as valid. Toward the end of their college careers or in graduate school, students develop their own personal values, recognize that not all views are equal (some are better than others), and learn how to select the best alternative.

The point is that your critical thinking skills are developing as you go. Rarely does anyone have already fully developed critical thinking skills as a college freshman. But the same claim could also be true of a returning adult first-year student. At the beginning of any journey—like getting an education—there's always room to grow.

These are subtle patterns. You may not be aware of them. But for now, realize that you may not have mastered critical thinking yet, and that's to be expected. Learning to be a critical thinker is a process. If you continue to develop academically while you're in college, your thinking will become more sophisticated and you'll be better able to handle the complex material waiting for you in the advanced courses ahead. Ralph Waldo Emerson once said, "Stay at home in your mind. Don't recite other people's opinions. I hate quotations.

Chapter Crossover Focus is, of course, the title of the book and a reoccurring theme for success. Throughout this book, you will see "focusing" as fundamental to engaging in any activity. Remind students to look for this theme in all of the chapters.

Emotional Intelligence (EI) Research While we are able to continually develop our emotional intelligence skills, the beginning playing field is a bit different for males and females. All of the work done by Deborah Tannen on gender differences in communication patterns leads to the fact that males and females are raised differently, and that as a result, particularly in the emotional arena, men are more likely to talk about things, while women talk about emotions. Although women generally have more empathy than men, it can be developed. Having strong empathy, walking in another's shoes, or seeing the other side is critical to life success.

Emotional Intelligence (EI) Research Some researchers have taken the idea of a developmental continuum further by noting differences between males and females. As freshmen, females are more likely to take notes and study to do well. Males are more likely to interact more with their instructors. Later, females rely on others' opinions and collect ideas to construct their own knowledge. Males see the opinions of others as opportunities for debate or challenge. Finally, while females often have their own ideas, they also value the ideas of others. Males tend to process ideas more independently.

Tell me what you know." (Ironically, this famous quotation is about how much he hated quotations.) Learn to rely on your own thinking, not other people's.[1]

Focused thinking is like a two-sided coin. Sometimes when you think, you *produce* ideas. That's what this chapter calls *creative thinking*, and that's something we'll deal with later. The other side of thinking requires you to *evaluate* ideas—your own or someone else's. That's *critical thinking*. The word *critical* comes from the Greek word for *critic* (*kritikos*), meaning "to question or analyze." You focus on something, sort through the information, and decide which ideas are most sensible, logical, or useful. When you're thinking critically, you're asking questions, analyzing arguments, assessing assumptions, considering claims, avoiding mistakes in reasoning, problem solving, decision making, and all the while, thinking about your thinking. Which type of thinking is most important, not only to your college success but also to your career success in the future: critical or creative? The answer is both!

What Is Critical Thinking?

In 1910, John Dewey wrote a groundbreaking book about focused thinking, *How We Think*. In it, he said we need to examine, poke, prod, question, and think about what we are learning.[2]

Critical thinking is a particular kind of focused thinking. It is purposeful, reasoned, and goal-directed. It's thinking that aims to solve problems, calculate likelihood, weigh evidence, and make decisions.[3] In that sense, movie critics are critical thinkers because they look at a variety of standards (screenplay, acting, production quality, costumes, cinematography, and so forth) and then decide how a movie measures up. When you're thinking critically, you're not just fault-finding. You're being *discerning* of both faults and strengths. You're looking at how things measure up.[4]

Critical thinkers develop standards they can use to judge advertisements, political speeches, sales pitches, movies—you name it.[5] Critical thinking is not jumping to conclusions, buying arguments lock, stock, and barrel, accepting controversial ideas at face value, ignoring the facts, or disregarding the evidence.

Unfortunately, some people are noncritical thinkers. They may be biased or prejudiced or closed-minded. Other people are *selective* critical thinkers. When it comes to one particular subject, they shut down their minds. They can't explain their views, they're emotional about them, and they refuse to acknowledge any other position. Whether it's a supercharged issue such as animal rights, abortion, the death penalty, AIDS, religion, or politics, they believe what they believe, and that's all there is to it—or so they think. Their particular positions may be right or wrong in your view, but the important issue is whether they are thinking critically about them. Why do they believe these things? Only if they understand the *why*, can they explain their views to someone else or

> **"What we need is not the will to believe, but the will to find out."**
>
> Bertrand Russell, British philosopher, logician, and mathematician (1872–1970)

defend them under fire. The importance of *why* can't be overstated. Some people, of course, have already thought through their beliefs, and they understand their positions and the reasons for them very well. Arriving at that point is the goal of aspiring critical thinkers.

People have been thinking and writing about critical thinking for more than 2,000 years, since the time of Socrates. In the "FOCUS Challenge Case," Professor Courtney uses the Socratic method to teach students to think critically. He asks students to analyze particular situations, evaluate them, apply what they've learned in class, and communicate their recommendations. It's very likely that his students will be better critical thinkers after taking his course. Eventually, Annie may come to realize this and value the critical thinking skills she's developing.

Why Is Critical Thinking Important?

CHALLENGE ⮕ REACTION

Challenge: Why improve your critical thinking skills? In what specific ways will improved skills benefit you?

Reaction: _____

Activity Option Give students five minutes to write down this sentence: Thinking critically is "critical" to lifelong success because _____. Have students fill in the blank. Make a class list and come to some conclusions about why critical thinking is important—it's really connected to lifelong, self-directed (*I figured it out!*) learning.

Some experts are discouraged. They say that few college students graduate with refined critical thinking skills: "What a sad comment on modern educational systems that most learners neither value nor practice active, critical reflection. They are too busy studying to stop and think. Sadder still, many educators don't reflect either. They must be too busy 'teaching.'"[6] That's quite an indictment, but it's one that can be taken as a challenge! No matter what your college degree will be in, employers want graduates who can "communicate, analyze, and think critically."[7]

Why is critical thinking important? Every day millions of people are sold a bill of goods. They buy placebos to make them healthier. They take political promises at face value without scrutiny. Even in our advanced society, superstition is rampant. Rumors of widespread close encounters of many different kinds abound! You may be surprised to read that according to the National Science Foundation's surveys of Americans:

> **"It seems to me what is called for is an exquisite balance between two conflicting needs: the most skeptical scrutiny of all hypotheses that are served up to us and at the same time a great openness to new ideas.... If all ideas have equal validity then you are lost, because then it seems to me, no ideas have any validity at all."**
>
> **Carl Sagan, American astronomer (1934–1996)**

> 60 percent believe in ESP
> 40 percent believe astrology is scientific
> 32 percent believe in lucky numbers
> 70 percent think magnetic therapy is medically effective
> 30 percent believe that UFOs are space vehicles from other civilizations[8]

Can you believe that so many of us *don't* think critically?

Teachable Moment Using the examples here, ask students if they believe in any of these. If so, why do they? How did they come to trust these things? What evidence do they have? Suggest to students that these are some good topics for research papers, and how they might want to explore more. Don't assume that you, or they, really know the answers without fully researching and critically examining the arguments.

Exercise 5.1 And Just Why Is Critical Thinking Important?

Here is a list of reasons why it's important to improve your critical thinking skills. Beside each entry, mark the degree to which you'd like to concentrate your efforts as a college student, soon ready to enter a new career path. On a scale from 1 to 10 with 10 representing the highest degree, would you like to:

1. _____ **Become a more successful college student**? Most college courses require you to think critically (in answering essay questions, for example). In one study of over 1,100 college students, higher scores on critical thinking skills tests correlated highly with better grades.[9] There's even evidence that interaction with other students in co-curricular activities can help you develop as a critical thinker.[10] If you participate in a debate, serve as a panelist, organize a campus event, work on a campaign—all experiences outside the classroom—you can sharpen your ability to think critically, too.

2. _____ **Become a better citizen**? Critical thinking is the foundation of a strong democracy. Voters must think critically about candidates' messages and their likelihood of keeping campaign promises. It's easy to talk about balancing the budget, or lowering taxes, but the truth is these highly complex tasks are very challenging to carry out. The American public must sift through information and examine the soundness of politicians' arguments in order to keep our democracy strong.

3. _____ **Become a better employee**? A workforce of critical—and creative—thinkers helps the American economy thrive and individuals become more successful. The U.S. Department of Labor reports that today's jobs require employees who can deal with complexity, learn and perform multiple tasks, analyze and deal with a wide variety of options, identify problems, perceive alternative approaches, and select the best approach.[11] Employers are "practically begging" for employees who can "think, collaborate, communicate, coordinate, and create."[12]

4. _____ **Become a more savvy consumer**? In today's marketplace, everyone wants your dollars. If you acted on every ad you read in magazines or watch on television, you'd run out of money very quickly. You're told you need whitened teeth, colored hair, softened skin, strong mouthwash, and a host of other things in order to be attractive. Critical thinking will help you evaluate offers, avoid slick come-ons, and buy responsibly.

5. _____ **Build stronger relationships**? Critical thinking helps us understand our own and others' actions and become more responsible communicators. Whether with friends or romantic partners, relationships take work. Sometimes you have to figure out what your partner really means or listen between the lines for important clues. You have to persuade your partner that you're right about something or convince him or her to act on a request. Actually, critical thinking is at the heart of every relationship you care about.

6. _____ **Become a lifelong learner**? Your education doesn't end when you get your diploma. In many ways the real exams begin afterward when you put your classroom learning to the test. And in today's world you must continue to learn as you transition through jobs to give your life more meaning—personally and professionally. According to American humorist Sydney Joseph Perelman, "Learning is what most adults will do for a living in the 21st century." You'll need to keep expanding your skills, no matter what your career is. Innovation and change are the watchwords of today's workplace, and continual learning is the only way to survive and thrive.[13]

Teachable Moment Keep in mind that students may put 10's next to all of these because they sound like good ideas. Of course, they might really want to develop in all of them. But this exercise can be used to generate a good discussion of why they value some results of good critical thinking over others, especially at this particular point in their lives.

Chapter Crossover Remember that in Chapter 3 students explored managing resources. You might ask students "does anyone remember reading about this somewhere else?" when reading question 4 about being a savvy consumer.

In order to develop your critical thinking skills, you must pay attention to the processes and products of your own thoughts. You must become conscious of the way you think and develop a habit of examining the decisions you come to.[14] When your critical thinking skills are well developed, they actually play a role in everything you do. You exist in a state of "critical being."[15]

INSIGHT → ACTION

1. Identify a time, subject, or event in which you used your critical thinking skills for your own benefit. Perhaps you investigated the salary range for a new job or read editorials on a particular subject to gain new perspectives. Explain what you did, how you went about it, and why.

2. Find a controversial headline in the newspaper. How would you advise others to investigate its truth or falsehood?

Activity Option Play the "How Do I Know This Is True?" game. Bring in some headlines from the student or local newspaper. Put them on a PowerPoint slide or overhead, and show them to the class. Go around the room and have students fill in the following: I know this is true because _____. Any student can say "NOT" and then explain why it is not true. If it is true, and no one challenges, students just keep adding to why it's true.

Exercise 5.2 Critical Searching on the Internet

One place where critical thinking is extremely important today is on the Internet. The Information Age surrounds us with huge amounts of data made readily available through technology. How do we know what to believe? Whether or not it's true, we tend to think that if something is on television or in the newspaper or online, it must be important. But in any of these cases, we need to exercise our critical thinking skills. Just because information is online doesn't automatically give it credibility.

If you're like most students, you do some of your research for classes online; but some of what you see on screen may be bogus. You must cultivate your critical searching skills to weed out websites with inaccuracies and bias. Internet research is convenient, but it definitely has its pros and cons. Choose one of the following three assignments to complete. Each one will ask you to use your critical searching skills.

Assignment 1: Create a list of ten websites that pertain to your intended major. (If you're not sure of your major right now, choose one to explore anyway.) Evaluate the websites to see which ones seem most useful to you as a student.

Assignment 2: Compare websites with contradictory information. Choose a controversial subject such as abortion, the death penalty, cohabitation, religion, politics, holistic healing, euthanasia, or some other subject of interest. Find four websites on your topic and compare them on these characteristics: (1) currency, (2) accuracy, (3) authority, (4) objectivity, and (5) coverage. Which of the four websites gets the highest marks? Why?

Assignment 3: Compare the content of an informational website on a particular subject with a print resource on the same subject. List the pros and cons of each source.

Teachable Moment Get a discussion going about domains. What are the basic differences between a ".org" and a ".edu?" Between a ".com" and a ".gov"? Which would be more credible sources and why?

Activity Option For homework, ask students to find two websites on the same topic, one really credible website and one that is suspect. Students can choose their own topic or you can assign one. For example, if a student is interested in anorexia, she might find the National Institute of Mental Health has a good site, and someone with a personal homepage does not. The important part is that students have to defend their reasoning.

© John Lund/CORBIS

> **"Few people think more than two or three times a year. I have made an international reputation for myself by thinking once or twice a week."**
>
> **George Bernard Shaw, Irish literary critic, playwright, and essayist, 1925 Nobel Prize for Literature (1856–1950)**

Asking Questions: Inquiring Minds Want to Know

Here's something worth knowing: Good thinkers are good questioners. They're always asking, "who," "what," "why," and "how." "*Who* says so?" "*What* is he trying to convince me of?" "*Why* is he trying to influence me?" "*How* is he trying to do it?" Critical thinkers know how to uncover the truth by asking questions, and they realize that the kind of questions they ask is important. They move beyond the most basic, most obvious questions or the first questions that come to mind. Instead, they stretch their minds to maximize their learning.

The Question Pyramid is an interesting way of looking at focused thinking (see Figure 5.1). As you move up the pyramid, formulating and answering questions become increasingly difficult. Let's go back to the "FOCUS Challenge Case" with Annie Miller in her philosophy class for examples.

> ➤ Level 1 questions that Professor Courtney might ask are observable, obvious, and one-dimensional. They can be answered with a yes or no answer: "Do philosophers study ethics?" Not too challenging.

> ➤ Level 2 questions are slightly more challenging. They consist of the standard who and what questions, like, "Who is called the 'Father of Ethics'?" "What is ethics?" Level 2 questions are straightforward. They could be answered by memorizing a section of the textbook.

> "**The important thing is not to stop questioning.**"
>
> **Albert Einstein, theoretical physicist (1879–1955)**

Figure 5.1

The Question Pyramid

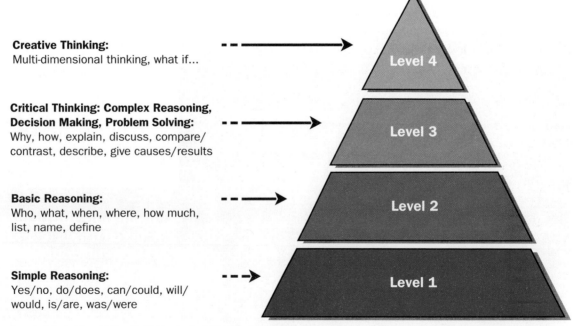

Creative Thinking:
Multi-dimensional thinking, what if...

Critical Thinking: Complex Reasoning, Decision Making, Problem Solving:
Why, how, explain, discuss, compare/contrast, describe, give causes/results

Basic Reasoning:
Who, what, when, where, how much, list, name, define

Simple Reasoning:
Yes/no, do/does, can/could, will/would, is/are, was/were

Level 4

Level 3

Level 2

Level 1

Source: Adapted from Hellyer, R., Robinson, C., & Sherwood, P. (1998). *Study skills for learning power.* New York: Houghton Mifflin, 18.

> Level 3 questions require actual critical thinking, "Why is the young man in Professor Courtney's story conflicted?" "Why is ethics studied by philosophers?" You'd need to develop your answer by thinking about possibilities, selecting a response, and backing it up with evidence.

> Level 4 questions require creative thinking, a subject for discussion later in this chapter, "What would a society entirely without ethics be like?" "How do you balance ethics and practicality?" Formulating answers to level 4 questions requires you to think for yourself and come up with your own unique, creative responses.

Teachable Moment Level 4 questions are directly connected to lifelong learning. Remember that this is a vital skill that employers want from their employees—the ability to think for yourself!

When you're asking questions instead of answering them, it's easy to get stuck at level 1 or 2, but with effort and a true understanding of how to ask questions, you can challenge yourself to learn more. In fact, most of your college courses will require this of you. So get a head start: After listening to a lecture, create a list of questions to see if you really understand the material. After reading an assigned chapter, create a list of questions to see how much you've digested. Understand the kind of questions you're asking, and move up the pyramid to improve your thinking skills.[16]

A Four-Part Model of Critical Thinking

CHALLENGE → REACTION

Challenge: Reasoning, problem solving, and decision making are all part of critical thinking. How are these three things related?

Reaction: _____

Like your writing or speaking skills, well-cultivated critical thinking skills can serve as the infrastructure for taking on all of your academic challenges. But now that we've defined critical thinking, let's ask an important related question: How do you do it? We'll look at the four primary components of critical thinking, and at the end of this chapter, we'll use a realistic news story, one that is relevant to many college campuses, to allow you to apply what you've learned and provide a memorable example.

Take a look at Figure 5.2 to preview the four-part model of critical thinking. You'll see right away that your reasoning skills underlie everything. They are the foundation upon which your problem-solving and decision-making skills rest, and your metacognitive skills, or thinking about your thinking, surround all the focused thinking you do.

"You cannot help but learn more as you take the world into your hands. Take it up reverently, for it is an old piece of clay, with millions of thumbprints on it."

John Updike, American writer

© Don Hammond/Design Pics/CORBIS

Figure 5.2
Critical Thinking Is Focused

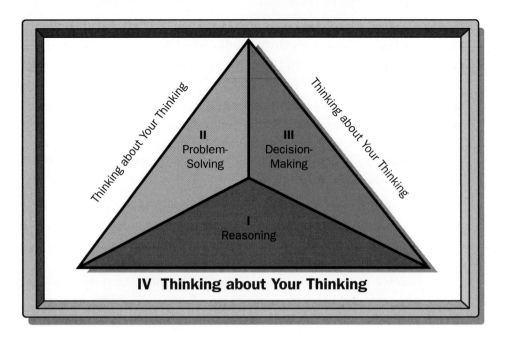

Triangle diagram with:
- II Problem-Solving
- III Decision-Making
- I Reasoning
- Thinking about Your Thinking (on both sides)
- **IV Thinking about Your Thinking** (at base)

I. Reasoning: The Foundation of Critical Thinking

Reasoning, the foundation of critical thinking, is the ability to infer a conclusion from one or more arguments. A strong argument is convincing because it offers evidence to back up its claim. If no one would disagree with what you're saying, it's not an argument. It's self-evident. "Grass is green" is not an argument. But "Cows that are grass-fed make the best meat" (if supporting evidence is provided) is. Do you see the difference? Because reasoning is the foundation for critical thinking, we'll concentrate much of our discussion there.

Think about your reasoning skills. How good are you at creating a sound argument? Let's say that you're trying to convince your roommate to stop inviting people into your room while you're studying for major exams. What evidence would you use to convince her? What's the likelihood of your success? How good are you at evaluating someone else's argument? For example, you're trying to decide whether an online discount is really a good deal. Would you take the advertiser's word for it or do some independent research to compare prices on your own?

Throughout the rest of this chapter, ask yourself: Are there ways I can improve my reasoning skills? As you critique your own skills, consider these reasoning nuts and bolts that are integral to creating and evaluating arguments.

Analyzing Arguments

Emotional Intelligence (EI) Research Many emotional intelligence skills are needed in order to be able to reason well. For college students, problem solving, reality testing, and flexibility are key. The black-and-white thinking of first-year college students can be an indication of these still developing skills.

> **"The aim of argument, or of discussion, should not be victory, but progress."**
>
> Joseph Joubert, French moralist
> (1754–1824)

CHALLENGE ⟳ REACTION

Challenge: What does the term *argument* have to do with critical thinking? How do you recognize a *sound* argument?

Reaction: _____

Have you ever seen the *Monty Python Flying Circus* "Argument Sketch"? In this bizarre skit a man comes to an "argument clinic" to buy an argument. The two arguers—"professional" and customer—engage in an interminably long, "yes, it is" "no, it isn't" squabble.

Critical thinking is about arguments. But when most of us think of an argument, that's the kind of bickering we think of. In the middle of the "Argument Clinic" sketch, however, the customer actually makes an important point. He protests that they're not really arguing; they're just contradicting each other. He continues, "An argument is a connected series of statements intended to establish a proposition." That's the kind of argument that's related to critical thinking.

Critical thinking is about an argument that *one* person puts forth. An op-ed piece in the newspaper contains an argument. (Op-ed stands for the page "opposite the editorial page" that features signed articles expressing personal viewpoints.) Both attorneys—prosecution and defense—put forth their closing arguments at the end of a trial. A politician puts forth an argument about where he stands on the issues. A professor puts forth an argument to persuade her class to learn important content in her discipline.

Arguments are said to be inductive or deductive. *Inductive* arguments go from specific observations to general conclusions. In criminal trials, the prosecution puts together individual pieces of evidence to prove that the defendant is guilty: eyewitnesses put him at the scene, the gun store salesman remembers selling him a pistol, and his fingerprints are on the weapon. Therefore, the prosecutor asserts that the defendant is guilty. Other arguments are said to be *deductive*, meaning they go from broad generalizations to specific conclusions. All serial killers have a particular psychological profile. The defendant has this psychological profile. Therefore the defendant is the killer.

What do arguments do? They propose a line of reasoning. They try to persuade. Arguments contain clear reasons to believe someone or something. Arguments say A plus B equals C. Once you understand what an argument is, you must also understand that arguments can be sound or unsound. If I tell you that two plus two equals four, chances are good that you'll believe me. If, on the other hand, I tell you two plus two equals five, you'll flatly deny it. If I say "Cats have fur." "Dogs have fur." "Therefore dogs are cats," you'll tell me I'm crazy—because it's an unsound argument.

The standard we use to test the soundness of arguments is logic, which is a fairly extensive topic. Let's just say for our purposes here that arguments are sound when the evidence to support the opinion they put forth is reasonable, more reasonable than the evidence supporting other opinions. The important point is that a sound argument provides at least one good reason to believe. Let's look at an example:

> *I don't see why all first-year students have to take Freshman Composition. It's a free country. Students shouldn't have to take courses they don't want to take.*

Based on our definition, is this example an argument? Why or why not? Is the statement "It's a free country" relevant? What does living in a free country have to do with the curricula in colleges and universities? Nothing. *Relevancy* is a condition needed for a sound argument.

Activity Option See if you can get your hands on a video of this *Monty Python* sketch for the class to watch or Google it and watch it online. After viewing it, divide the class into two groups to discuss the difference between an argument as defined in this chapter and a contradiction.

Sensitive Situation Students who are not very assertive may not like the word *argument* and see all arguments as confrontational. Help students see that it is really okay to persuade or challenge and that it is one of the hallmarks of good thinking.

Now look at this example:

I don't see why all first-year students have to take Freshman Composition. Many students have cultivated good writing skills in high school, and their Verbal SAT scores are 600 or higher.

Is this second example an argument? Why or why not? The first example doesn't give you a good reason to believe the argument; the second example does. A true argument must contain at least one reason for you to believe it.

Here's another warning. Not everything that sounds like an argument is one. Look at this example:

Everyone taking Calculus 100 failed the test last Friday. I took the test last Friday. Therefore, I will probably get an F in the course.

Is that a sound argument—or is something missing? Even though all three statements may be true, they don't constitute a sound argument. What grade has this student earned on earlier calculus tests? How many tests remain in the course? What other assignments figure into students' grades? The information present may not be adequate to predict an F in the course. *Adequacy* is another condition needed for a sound argument. This alternative, on the other hand, is a sound argument:

Everyone taking Calculus 100 failed the test last Friday. I took the test last Friday. Therefore, I earned an F on the test.

When you're assessing the soundness of an argument, you must look for two things: *relevance* and *adequacy*.[17]

Not all arguments are sound. Have you ever heard this tale? A scientist decided to embark on a new study to find out what intoxicates people. He devised an experiment to proceed in an orderly, methodical way. On Monday night, he drank three tall glasses of scotch and water, mixed in equal proportions. The next morning, he recorded his results: intoxication. On Tuesday night, he drank three tall glasses of whiskey and water. On Wednesday night, he drank three tall glasses of rum and water. On Thursday night, he drank three tall glasses of vodka and water. Each morning, his recorded results were identical. He had become highly intoxicated. His erroneous conclusion? Water makes people drunk.

Not only is it important to be able to construct sound arguments, but it's also important to be able to recognize them. As a consumer in today's information society, you must know when to buy into an argument, and when not to.

Assessing Assumptions

Posing as an addled social critic, Jonathan Swift wrote the words you see to the left centuries ago, even though they sound as if they could have been written now. Intellectual laziness among some people continues to be a problem even today.

When you're thinking critically, one of the most important kinds of questions you can ask is about the *assumptions* you or someone else is making, perhaps without even realizing it. Assumptions can limit our thinking. Consider these three well-known puzzles, and afterward, examine how the assumptions you brought with you interfered with solving them.

1. One day Kerry celebrated her birthday. Two days later her older twin brother, Harry, celebrated his birthday. How could that be?

2. A boy and his father are injured in a car accident. They're both rushed to the hospital, but the father dies. The boy needs surgery, so a physician is called in. The surgeon rushes into the operating room, takes one look at the boy, and gasps. "I can't operate on this boy," the surgeon says. "He's my son." How can this be?

3. A woman from New York married ten different men from that city, yet she did not break any laws. None of these men died, and she never divorced. How was this possible?

You may have solved these puzzles if you were willing to question the underlying assumptions that were holding you back. But you may have been baffled by several. For puzzle 2, for example, you may have assumed that surgeons are usually male, not female, and been temporarily stumped by the question. (Answers are upside down at the bottom of this page.)

People reveal their underlying assumptions in what they say. If you listen carefully, you can uncover them. "Go on for a graduate degree after I finish college? No way! I'm out of here in four years, no matter what!" This student's underlying assumption is that college itself isn't as important as what comes afterward (like making money). This student may just tolerate her classes without getting engaged in the subject matter, and she checks off requirements as quickly as she can. Too bad. Getting a college education can be a wonderfully exciting experience in and of itself!

Considering Claims

Evaluating claims is one of the most basic aspects of reasoning. A claim is a statement that can be true or false, but not both. This is different from a fact, which cannot be disputed. What's the difference between a *fact* and a *claim*? Facts can't be disputed; claims can be true or false, but they must be one or the other, not both.

FACT: Ronald Reagan, George H. Bush, and Bill Clinton have been presidents of the United States during the last thirty years.

CLAIM: Bill Clinton was the most popular American president in the last thirty years.

> "Great minds discuss ideas. Average minds discuss events. Small minds discuss people."
>
> **Eleanor Roosevelt, First Lady of the United States (1884–1962)**

Teachable Moment Students love challenging logic puzzles like these. Ask students if they have any to share. Offer extra credit to any student who brings in one for the next class.

Emotional Intelligence (EI) Research Students can also reveal their underlying assumptions and behaviors by how they act in class. Individuals with low independence are often unsure of their own ideas and much less likely to contribute and challenge arguments.

Sensitive Situation You can almost be certain that someone in your class, right now, is taking their parents' advice about a major and is struggling. Let students know that this is common and maybe it is just because their parents think that it is a good job market. Later in this course, in Chapter 12, they will learn more about careers and majors and can share this with their parents.

Box 5.1 Wanted: Liberal Arts Grads

Congratulations, college grads! Now begins your so-called real life. But here's a bummer: If you took your parents' well-meaning advice and majored in a seemingly useful discipline you really didn't care about, you may have made a mistake. According to research, most parents (75 percent) and college-age kids (85 percent) believe the point of college is to get a practical education to land a good job right out of school. But

CEOs queried in one survey were thinking more about long-term career development; only 37 percent of them said the purpose of a diploma is to acquire work skills. While the parents and kids took a dim view of liberal arts, business leaders called the humanities essential to developing critical-thinking (90 percent) and problem-solving (77 percent) skills. Develop the essential skills you need now for future success![18]

3. The woman is a justice of the peace.

2. The surgeon is the boy's mother.

1. Kerry and Harry are not twins. Harry and his brother are twins, and they are older than Kerry.

"Everyone is entitled to their own opinion, but not their own facts."

Senator Daniel Patrick Moynihan (1927–2003)

Activity Option This is another opportunity to take an article from the newspaper and look for arguments that support a fact (or not). Bring a short newspaper article to class (short and current is best, and something that will engage students). Follow the pyramid in Figure 5.3 to explore the reasoning. The class can work as a whole, or in small teams. This activity could also be used for homework.

The fact is obvious. The claim requires evidence to support it. As a critical thinker, it's important to use your reasoning skills to evaluate the accuracy and authenticity of evidence. Generally speaking, be wary of claims that

> are supported by unidentified sources ("Experts claim…").

> are made by interested parties who stand to gain ("Brought to you by the makers of…").

> are put forth by a lone individual claiming his experience as the norm ("I tried it and it worked for me!").

> use a bandwagon appeal ("Everybody's doing it.").

> lie with statistics ("over half" when it's really only 50.5 percent).

On the other hand, we must also keep an open mind and be flexible in our thinking. If you get good evidence to support a view that contradicts yours, be willing to modify your ideas. One way to evaluate the validity of claims is to use the Question Pyramid we discussed earlier. Consider claims by asking these four key questions: "who?" "what?" "why?" and "how?" Figure 5.3 shows how the questions progress from level 1 to 3.

Figure 5.3

The Question Pyramid

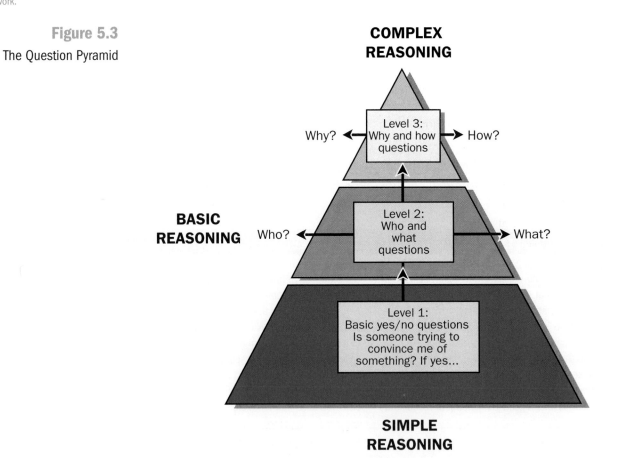

Source: Adapted from Hellyer, R., Robinson, C., & Sherwood, P. (1998). *Study skills for learning power.* New York: Houghton Mifflin, 18.

CHALLENGE → REACTION

Challenge: List as many reasoning mistakes as you can. Can you provide an example of one or two of them?

Reaction: _____

_____

> **"To treat your facts with imagination is one thing, but to imagine your facts is another."**
>
> **John Burroughs, writer on ecology (1837–1921)**

Although we can certainly improve our critical-thinking skills, it's impossible to be a perfect critical thinker 100 percent of the time. As thinkers, we make mistakes, and sometimes others try to trick us with defective arguments. It's important to cultivate both types of critical thinking skills: your *productive* skills, which you use as a speaker and writer, and your *receptive* skills, which you use as a reader and listener. As responsible communicators, we must understand what a sound argument is and know how to construct one ourselves. We must also understand what a defective argument is in order to avoid getting sucked in when we shouldn't.

Here is a top-ten list of logical fallacies, or false logic strategies, we can slip into—or others can use against us—if we're not careful. For each of the ten types, read through the example and then see if you can come up with one of your own.

1. **False cause and effect** (assuming one cause for something when other causes are possible, too)

   I moved into my new dorm room last month. I've failed every exam I've taken since. Living in the residence hall is blowing my GPA!

2. **Personal attack** (reacting to a challenge by attacking the challenger)

   How could anyone believe Professor Courtney's views on ethics? We all know he's a very poor teacher.

3. **Unwarranted assumption** (taking too much for granted without evidence)

   You say universities give women equal opportunities. I say they don't. Reply: It's true. I read it on a website.

4. **Emotional appeal** (appealing to someone's feelings in order to gain acceptance of an argument)

   If you care about the institution that made you what you are today, you'll dig deep into your pockets and send a financial contribution now.

5. **False authority** (attributing your argument to someone else in a supposed position of power to get you off the hook)

   I'd really like to be able to change your grade, but my Department Chair frowns upon that.

6. **Hasty conclusion** (jumping to a conclusion when other conclusions are possible)

   I'm sure my roommate stole my textbook. He's too cheap to buy his own.

7. **Straw man** (attempting to "prove" an argument by overstating, exaggerating, or oversimplifying the arguments of the opposing side)

   We should relax the entrance requirements to help attract more students. Reply: You actually want the quality of students here to take a nose dive? Oh, right, why don't we all just teach high school instead?

Emotional Intelligence (EI) Research Research by Bar-On (1997) found that the most important emotional and social skills involved in coping with job stress were self-regard, assertiveness, self-actualization, problem solving, stress tolerance, and optimism. It should be clear that all of these skills are key when dealing with others.

8. **Shifting the burden of proof** (shifting the responsibility of proving an assertion to someone else because you have no evidence for what you assert)

> *The zero-tolerance policy on alcohol in the residence halls is working.*
> *Reply: No, it's not. Reply back: Oh yeah? Prove it.*

9. **Oversimplification/overgeneralization** (reducing a complex issue to something very simple or stereotyping)

> *College professors have it made. They teach a couple classes a week*
> *for a few hours, and then they have free time the rest of the week.*
> *That's the kind of job I want!*

10. **Either/or thinking** (taking only an extreme position on an issue when other positions are possible)

> *Either we ban alcohol on campus or we'll go bankrupt from lawsuits.*

Exercise 5.3 Rocky Mountain State University Case Study and Simulation

Great Bluffs Herald

Saturday, September 20, 2008

Cheap Beer + Fraternities = Recipe for Death

Great Bluffs, Colorado It's that time of year again. The fall semester began last month at Rocky Mountain State University, and again this year, a student died of alcohol poisoning within the first three weeks of classes. Clark Cameron of Valdosta, Georgia, a Gamma Beta Gamma pledge, was found dead yesterday morning in the GBG fraternity house on campus. The body of the collapsed student was found in a third-floor bedroom. An anonymous call to 9-1-1 came in at 6:15 a.m.: "We've got a guy here. We can't wake him, and we know he drank way too much last night." Cameron was pronounced dead on arrival at Great Bluffs General Hospital.

The incident represented RMSU's third death from alcohol poisoning in as many years. Roland Bishop, the University's new president, is said to deeply mourn the loss of another RMSU freshman. "No student should die during his first few weeks of college—what should be one of the most exciting times of his life. It's insane and very, very sad."

The national Gamma Beta Gamma office has suspended the RMSU chapter until further notice and banned its 83 members from participating in any Greek events.

Bishop will convene a cross-university panel of faculty, staff, and students to investigate the Greek system on campus and drinking privileges at all campus social functions, including athletic events. Professor Juan Cordova,

Theology Department Chairperson, will head the new committee. A report with specific recommendations to President Bishop is expected by the end of the term.

Alcohol is to blame for the deaths of 1,400 college students per year, according to figures from the National Institute on Alcohol Abuse and Alcoholism. About 500,000 students between the ages of 18 and 24 are injured annually while under the influence of alcohol, more than 600,000 are assaulted by another student who has been drinking, and more than 70,000 students are victims of alcohol-related sexual assault or date rape.

Voted the number two party school in the nation, Rocky Mountain State University is known for its "party-hardy" social life. Away from home for the first time, many freshmen get swept up by the party scene. President Bishop's office indicates that moving "rush" further into the semester is one option under consideration. The president believes that students need more time to adjust to the transition from high school and get their academic careers underway. Being driven to drink, sometimes excessively, is often a "rite of passage" in sororities and fraternities, a spokesman for the President said in a telephone interview. The University will also explore creating several alcohol-free residence halls where students who want to buckle down academically can do so without fearing social pressure to party.

After this article appeared in the *Great Bluffs Herald*, many readers sent letters to the editor on September 21 and 22. Examine the following excerpts.

Trevor Ryan, RMSU Student, Denver, Colorado: "My first few weeks as a freshman at RMSU have been awesome. I knew I wanted to pledge GBG before I ever got here, and I have to say the "rush of rush" was totally cool—one of the highlights of my life so far. I'd do it all over again tomorrow. But I didn't want to join GBG just for the parties. It's an excellent organization with high academic standards. All the members say so."

Mitch Edgars, Father, Englewood, Colorado: "For me, college was a time of awakening. I had plenty of 'good times' and I want my son to do the same. You can't stop college kids from drinking. It's that simple. Sure, all college kids make mistakes. But if they're smart, they'll learn from them. I know my son pretty well, and he makes good decisions most of the time. I don't care what anybody says, experience is still the best teacher."

Carlos Cordova, RMSU Student, Brooklyn, New York: "This whole incident has been very hard on me. Clark was my roommate, and we were getting along great. I still can't believe this happened to him. Yeah, I was at the football game with him where he started drinking and then later at the frat party where he got totally wasted. But I lost him in the crowd, and I went back to the dorm around midnight. I wonder if I could have done something."

Evan Riley, RMSU Senior, Aspen, Colorado: "As president of the Interfraternity Council on campus, I feel fraternities and sororities across the country are being demonized by the press. We're not like that. We are service organizations and we participate in lots of community activities, like the Holiday Fundraiser in Great Bluffs. Last year GBG raised more money for the homeless than any other organization on campus. At a time like this, though, everybody forgets that. We become the bad guys. The University just wants someone to take the fall, and I know it's going to be us. It's unfortunate that a few irresponsible students ruin it for everyone. Ask anyone who's a member: overall, sororities and fraternities do much more good than bad. It's really not fair!"

Professor Ruby Pinnell, Biology Department, RMSU: "As a biologist, I see all the physiological damage today's college students are doing to themselves. The national study I spearheaded last year found that 31 percent of college students meet the clinical criteria for alcohol abuse, and 6 percent could be diagnosed as being alcohol-dependent. Young people don't realize that binge drinking could be risking serious damage to their brains now and actually cause increased memory loss later in adulthood. Many college males consume as many as 24 drinks in a row. These are very sad statistics."

Rufus Unser, Great Bluffs, Colorado, Citizen, Neighbor, and Voter: "I'm sick of my tax dollars going to fund institutions made up of immature college students who make bad decisions. A *Great Bluffs Herald* article published last year reported that neighbors living within one mile of college campuses are 135 percent more likely to suffer from public disturbances—also called "secondhand effects." My house is down the block from the GBG fraternity house, and sometimes the noise is so loud that I have to call the cops! Worse than that, I'm getting ready to sell my house and move into a retirement home next year. I'll bet my property values have dropped because of all the bad press! Higher education? That's a misnomer. 'Lower education' is more like it these days!"

Jim McArthur, Director, RMSU Residence Life: September is National Alcohol and Drug Addiction Recovery Month, and we're doing everything we can to help educate students about the risks of alcohol poisoning. The binge drinking problem at RMSU isn't unique, and it's not going to go away by itself. We offer weekly classes on drinking responsibly, but no one signs up for them. We put up posters about the dangers of alcohol all over campus, and we also train all of our RAs on alcohol abuse as part of their preparation for the job. They try to keep tabs on their freshmen, but to tell you the truth, I think some of the RAs drink a bit too much, too. This is society's problem, not just RMSU's."

Sergeant Rick Fuller, Great Bluffs Police Department: "I've worked in the Great Bluffs Police Department for 15 years now, and I've seen a dramatic rise in the number of arrests for alcohol

(continued)

possession by minors, arrests for selling alcohol to minors, and alcohol-related admissions to Great Bluffs General Hospital's ER. It's an epidemic, I'm afraid. I also know from my police work that alcohol abuse is a factor in 40 percent of violent crimes committed in the U.S."[19]

Now that you've read the story from the *Great Bluffs Herald* and the excerpts from letters to the editor, answer the following questions:

1. What are the facts relating to the alcohol problem at RMSU? How do you know they're *facts* and not *claims*?

2. Do you see logical fallacies in any of the eight letters to the editor of the *Great Bluffs Herald*? If so, which can you identify? What assumptions do the letter writers hold?

3. Identify an issue that has been generating debate on your campus, in your residence hall, or in a class. Make a list of the claims made on each side of the debate and consider each claim. Then, make a list of the arguments and evaluate each argument, looking at *relevancy* and *adequacy*. Next, list the assumptions that the arguments are based on. Finally, be creative and come up with a new approach to the issue. Is there another way to frame the debate? How can you look at the issue in an entirely different way?

Emotional Intelligence (EI) Research Impulse control, or lack of it, is often seen in college students as a significant predictor of success. Students should discuss how impulse control played a part in this tragedy.

Activity Option Alcohol on college campuses is a hot topic. Use this opportunity to talk about this issue and how it pertains to your campus. Brainstorm a list of questions that students would want to know about alcohol use and abuse on campus. Divide students into groups of two to three and give them a specific question from the list they just generated. Tell them to find the answer and bring it to class next week. Make sure that they tell you the source, and why they thought it was credible.

II. Problem Solving: The Basic How-To's

When you have to solve a problem, your critical thinking skills should move front and center. Perhaps you need to find a way to earn more money. You run short each month, and the last few days before payday are nerve-racking. What should you do? Use a gunshot approach and try many different strategies at once or devise a more precise way to get the best results? See if the following steps make sense to you and seem like something you might actually do.

STEP 1: Define the problem. What is the exact nature of the problem you face? Defining the exact nature of the problem is something you must do if you hope to solve it. For example:

> Is it that you don't meter your spending and run out of money long before the next paycheck?

> Is it that you don't have a budget and you spend money randomly?

STEP 2: Brainstorm possible options. List all of the possible solutions you can come up with. For example:

> Eat all your meals in the residence hall instead of hitting the fast-food joints so often.

> Stop ordering in pizza four nights a week when you get the munchies at midnight.

> Ask your parents for more money. They told you to let them know when you need more.

> Look for a job that pays more. Tips at the Pancake House where you work don't really amount to much.

> Capitalize on your particular skills to earn extra money. If you're a whiz at math, you could sign on as a tutor at the Math Learning Center on campus.

Emotional Intelligence (EI) Research Students who are flexible and are able to problem-solve (and see the steps to a problem) are much more likely to be successful in college. Take some time to look at a problem the class identifies and go step-by-step through the problem-solving process.

STEP 3: Devise criteria to evaluate each option. For example:

> *Distance* is important. Your car isn't very reliable, so it would be good to find a job you can walk or ride your bike to.

> *Good pay* is important. In the past, you've always had low-paying jobs. You need whatever solution you arrive at to be worth your while.

> *Time* is important. You're taking a challenging load of classes, and you need to keep up your grades to keep your scholarship.

STEP 4: Evaluate each option you've proposed. For example:

> Eat all your meals in the residence hall. (This is a good idea because you've already paid for those meals, regardless of which solution you choose.)

> Stop ordering in pizza four nights a week. (This is also a good option because impromptu expenses like this can mount exponentially.)

> Ask your parents for more money. (You'd really like to avoid this option. You know they're already making sacrifices to help you through school.)

> Get a job that pays more. (Unfortunately, your campus is half an hour from the center of town where all the posh restaurants are.)

> Capitalize on your particular skills to earn extra money. (Tutors are paid more than minimum wage, and the Math Learning Center is across from your residence hall.)

Chapter Crossover Remind students to look at Chapter 3 about managing one's money and Chapter 4 about managing one's time as important college survival skills.

STEP 5: Choose the best solution. In this case, it looks like the Math Learning Center fits the bill!

STEP 6: Plan how to achieve the best solution. When you call the Math Learning Center to find out how to apply, you discover that you need a letter of recommendation from a math professor. You e-mail your calculus professor and set up a meeting for later in the week. When the letter is ready, you call the Math Learning Center again to make an appointment to schedule an interview, and so forth.

STEP 7: Implement the solution and evaluate the results. A month or two after you take on the tutoring job, you evaluate if this solution is really the best one. You may need to request more hours or different days. Or you may find that this job leads to a better one as a Teaching Assistant for the math department. At any rate, you've used your critical thinking skills to solve a problem, systematically, logically, and effectively.

Chapter Crossover In Chapter 11 students will explore more about the components of emotional intelligence (EI). Let students know that EI and problem solving will be addressed. Encourage students to thumb through the book and look ahead.

III. Decision Making: What's Your Style?

Arguments lead to decisions, and it's important to make good ones! After you've evaluated the arguments put forth, you must often do something about them. Before you know it, you'll be deciding on a major if you haven't already, a career field, a place to live, a romantic partner—you name it.

When you have an important decision to make, your critical thinking skills should kick into action. The more important the decision, chances are the more thoughtful the process of deciding should be. But people make decisions in their own way. To some extent, decision making is individualistic. Take a look at the Decision Style Inventory in Exercise 5.4 to learn more about your decision-making style.

Exercise 5.4 Decision Style Inventory

Respond to each of the following twenty statements by marking your response according to the rules that follow. There are no right or wrong answers. Generally, the first impression that comes to mind is the best one to put down. Respond to each statement by assigning an 8 to the answer that is most appropriate (for you), a 4 next to the next most appropriate, then a 2, and finally a 1 for the least appropriate answer. In the following example, an individual prefers blue, brown, gray, and red in that order:

When picking clothes,

I prefer   Blue __8__   Red __1__   Brown __4__   Gray __2__

Each number may only be assigned once for each statement, and each of the four numbers must be used for each statement.

Decision Style Inventory

1. In my career, my prime objective will be to:
_____ (a) have a position with status.
_____ (b) be the best in my field.
_____ (c) achieve recognition for my work.
_____ (d) feel secure in my job.

2. I enjoy jobs that:
_____ (a) are technical and well defined.
_____ (b) have considerable variety.
_____ (c) allow independent action.
_____ (d) involve people.

3. If I were a boss, I'd expect people working for me to be:
_____ (a) productive and fast.
_____ (b) highly capable.
_____ (c) committed and responsive.
_____ (d) receptive to suggestions.

4. In my job, I'll look for:
_____ (a) practical results.
_____ (b) the best solutions.
_____ (c) new approaches or ideas.
_____ (d) good working environment.

5. I communicate best with others:
_____ (a) on a direct one-to-one basis.
_____ (b) in writing.
_____ (c) by having a discussion.
_____ (d) in a group meeting.

6. As I plan on the job, I'll emphasize:
_____ (a) current problems.
_____ (b) meeting objectives.
_____ (c) future goals.
_____ (d) developing the careers of people working for me.

7. When faced with solving a problem, I:
_____ (a) rely on proven approaches.
_____ (b) apply careful analysis.
_____ (c) look for creative approaches.
_____ (d) rely on my feelings.

8. When using information, I prefer:
_____ (a) specific facts.
_____ (b) accurate and complete information.
_____ (c) broad coverage of many options.
_____ (d) limited information that is easily understood.

9. When I am not sure about what to do, I:
_____ (a) rely on my intuition.
_____ (b) search for the facts.
_____ (c) look for a possible compromise.
_____ (d) wait before making a decision.

10. Whenever possible, I avoid:
_____ (a) long debates.
_____ (b) incomplete work.
_____ (c) using numbers or formulas.
_____ (d) conflict with others.

11. I am especially good at:
_____ (a) remembering dates and facts.
_____ (b) solving difficult problems.
_____ (c) seeing many possibilities.
_____ (d) interacting with others.

12. When time is important, I:
____ (a) decide and act quickly.
____ (b) follow plans and priorities.
____ (c) refuse to be pressured.
____ (d) seek guidance or support.

13. In social settings, I generally:
____ (a) speak with others.
____ (b) think about what is being said.
____ (c) observe what is going on.
____ (d) listen to the conversation.

14. I am good at remembering:
____ (a) people's names.
____ (b) places we met.
____ (c) people's faces.
____ (d) people's personalities.

15. The work I do will provide me:
____ (a) the power to influence others.
____ (b) challenging assignments.
____ (c) opportunities to achieve my personal goals.
____ (d) acceptance by the people I work with.

16. I work well with people who are:
____ (a) energetic and ambitious.
____ (b) self-confident.
____ (c) open-minded.
____ (d) positive and trusting.

17. When under stress, I:
____ (a) become anxious.
____ (b) concentrate on the problem.
____ (c) become frustrated.
____ (d) am forgetful.

18. Others consider me:
____ (a) aggressive.
____ (b) disciplined.
____ (c) imaginative.
____ (d) supportive.

19. My decisions typically are:
____ (a) realistic and direct.
____ (b) systematic and abstract.
____ (c) broad and flexible.
____ (d) sensitive to the needs of others.

20. I dislike:
____ (a) losing control.
____ (b) boring work.
____ (c) following rules.
____ (d) being rejected.

Totals: (a) _____ + (b) _____ + (c) _____ + (d) _____ = 300

(Note: The sum total for (a) + (b) + (c) + (d) should equal 300.)

Source: Adapted from Rowe, A. J., & Mason, R. O. (1987). *Managing with style: A guide to understanding, assessing, and improving decision making.* San Francisco: Jossey-Bass.

Chapter Crossover In order to reinforce students' thinking about their learning style preferences, remind them to look back at their SuccessTypes Learning Style Type Indicator and VARK scores. Tell them you will "quiz" them next class. By now, this information should be as easy to recall as telling you their names.

The results of this Decision Style Inventory have been collected from over 2,000 people and provide the basis for the book entitled *Managing with Style* by Alan J. Rowe and Richard O. Mason. After you complete your rankings, total your answers for each letter. Although the Decision Style Inventory is typically used with managers and you may not be one now, it is also a useful way to preview what your style may be when you do have a position of responsibility. The (a) answers represent a *directive* style, the (b) answers represent an *analytical* style, the (c) answers represent a *conceptual* style, and the (d) answers represent a *behavioral* style. Here's what the four styles mean:

> ➤ Directive. This decision-making style emphasizes the here and now. Directives prefer structure and using practical data to make decisions. They look for speed, efficiency, and results, and focus on short-term fixes. Directive decision makers base their decisions on experience, facts,

procedures, and rules, and they have energy and drive to get things done. On the down side, because they work quickly, they are sometimes satisfied with simplistic solutions.

> **Analytical.** This decision-making style emphasizes a logical approach. Analyticals search carefully for the best decision, and they sometimes get hung up with overanalyzing things and take too long to finally make a decision. They are sometimes considered to be impersonal because they may be more interested in the problem than in the people who have it. But they are good at working with data and doing careful analysis.

> **Conceptual.** This decision-making style emphasizes the big picture. Conceptuals are adaptable, insightful, and flexible, and they look for innovative solutions. They are sometimes too idealistic, but they take risks and are very creative.

> **Behavioral.** This decision-making style emphasizes people. Behaviorals enjoy people and the social aspects of work. They use their feelings to assess situations, communicate well, and are supportive of others. On the other hand, they are sometimes seen as wishy-washy or are criticized because they can't make hard decisions or can't say no.

Now look at your scores to see which of the four lettered answers has the highest score (generally representing your preferred decision-making style). Look for your second highest score (representing your backup style). If you hold a job outside of school, see if the descriptions sound like you in those settings. Whether you're in college to prepare for a career field or retool for a new one, eventually, you will have to make important decisions on a daily basis. It's useful to begin thinking about your decision-making style now.

Teachable Moment Remind students that even if they wear the "badge" of an organized personality type (J, for example) or a detailed person (an S), this alone does not make them a good decision maker. It's the big-picture portrait of a person—not only who they are, but what they do and how they do it! So the more they learn about themselves, and the more they reflect on what they do, the better they are able to succeed.

> **"Education is nothing more, nor less, than learning to think!"**
>
> Peter Facione, professor, administrator, author, consultant, and critical thinking expert

IV. Thinking about Your Thinking

One of the most important aspects of critical thinking is that it evaluates itself. As you're solving problems, for example, you're thinking about how you're thinking. You're assessing your progress as you go, analyzing the strengths and weaknesses in your thinking, and perhaps even coming up with better ways to do it. We call that metacognition, and that's one reason this book contains "Insight → Action" exercises—to give you opportunities to think about how you're thinking and make note of those thoughts.

Novice learners don't stop to evaluate their thinking and make revisions. Expert learners do. Actually, whenever you're faced with learning something new, metacognition involves three elements. Ultimately, these elements should become the foundation of all your learning experiences so that you improve your metacognitive skills as you go.

YOUR TYPE IS ShOwING

Researchers have found a relationship between the Decision Style Inventory and the Myers-Briggs Type Inventory style. Is that true for you? It makes sense that your personality and your decision-making style are related, doesn't it? Locate the two middle letters of your type in Figure 5.4 and see how your type correlates to a decision-making style. This is particularly helpful if you have completed the full MBTI.

Directive decision makers, for example, like well-defined goals, well-developed plans, and detailed calculations. People with those characteristics are typically ST's on the MBTI.

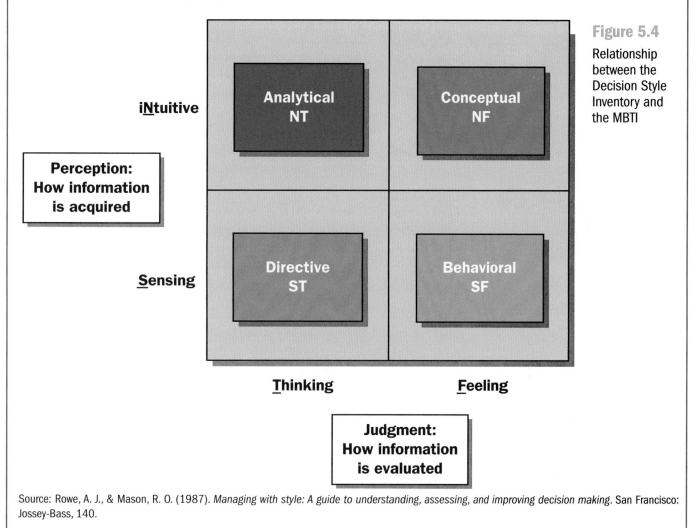

Figure 5.4

Relationship between the Decision Style Inventory and the MBTI

Source: Rowe, A. J., & Mason, R. O. (1987). *Managing with style: A guide to understanding, assessing, and improving decision making.* San Francisco: Jossey-Bass, 140.

> **Develop a plan of action.** Ask yourself what you already know that can help you learn something new. What direction do you want to go in your thinking? What should be your first task? How much time should you give yourself? Talk through your plan with someone else. It's even good to cultivate a thinking vocabulary so that you become more aware of your critical thinking skills and strengthen them.

> **Monitor your plan.** While you're working, ask yourself how you're doing. Are you staying on track? Are you moving in the right direction? Should you slow down or speed up? What should you do if you don't understand what you're doing? Keep track of what works for you and what doesn't. Assume responsibility for your own thinking and learning.

Activity Option Have the class fill in their names on a rough chart you draw on the board or create a PowerPoint slide or transparency of Figure 5.4 to indicate where they fit. You should do it first to model how you make decisions based on your personality type and decision-making style. Discuss your commonalities and differences as decision-makers and give some real examples to make the concepts more concrete to students.

Teachable Moment Have students reflect on what they do when faced with learning something new. Ask them why they go about things as they do, and if they had the chance to do it again, ask if they would do it differently. Get students to reflect whenever you can (in writing, in discussions, etc.).

PRNewsFoto/Jamster/NewsCom

> Evaluate the plan. How well did you do? Did you do better than expected or not as well as you expected? What could you have done differently? Can you apply what you just did here to future tasks? Give yourself some feedback.[20]

Becoming a Better Critical Thinker

Sharpening your critical thinking skills is vital because these skills underlie all the others in your academic repertoire. If you think well, you will be a better writer, a better presenter, a better listener, and a better reader. You will be more likely to engage more fully in your academic tasks because you will question, probe, analyze, and monitor yourself as you learn. Here are some suggestions for improving your skills. As you read them, think about how they pertain to you.

1. Admit when you don't know. If you don't know enough to think critically about something, admit it, and then find out more. With the volume of information available in today's world, we can't possibly know everything about anything. But the good news is that information is readily available. All you need to do is read, listen, point, and click to be well informed on many issues.

2. Realize you have buttons that can be pushed. We all have issues we're emotional about. That's normal. It's natural to feel strongly about some things, but it's also important to understand the reasons why so that you can articulate your views to someone else. And of course, realize that you're not the only one with buttons. Your teacher, roommate, significant other, boss, everyone else has them, too.

"And how is education supposed to make me feel smarter?"

Homer Simpson, television cartoon character, *The Simpsons*

Sensitive Situation We all have buttons that can be pushed, but some more so than others. Bring this to the attention of the class and give some examples such as derogatory words, generalizations (students from broken homes have "issues"), and so on. Remind students that most often, comments like these are simply born of the lack of knowledge, but they still can hurt.

FOCUS ON CAREERS: HAROLD "HALLIE" TYLER, Federal Judge

Q1: What do judges do on a day-to-day basis? What are the main responsibilities of the job?
In the United States, there are a large number of judges; what they do on a daily basis can be very different. Appellate judges, for example, listen to arguments and write opinions and judgments. Trial judges do the same, but they do other things such as empanel and instruct jurors; sentence persons found guilty of criminal misconduct; and swear in new citizens (if they are trial judges in the federal system). The main responsibilities of a judge are to uphold the law, strive for fairness, and possess courage to make painful decisions based upon the law and the facts.

Q2: What are three important skills a person needs in order to be a judge?
The three most important skills of judges are: (1) the ability to critically analyze facts that are usually conflicting; (2) to write clearly but simply, and (3) to be timely in deciding cases.

Q3: In the legal profession, how important is the art of asking questions? How do you know you're arriving at "the truth"—or not?
The art of asking questions clearly but completely is of crucial importance. This is so even if able lawyers are asking good questions. The search for truth is difficult as always, but close observation of witnesses and counsel can lead to good results. Seldom is one completely satisfied that truth is forthcoming, but surprisingly, the experience of trial judges enables them on occasion to discern truth from fiction because they see and hear the witnesses and the lawyers.

Q4: How do judges analyze arguments, assess assumptions, and consider claims? How important is your ability to do that in your career field?
Judges must be prepared to carefully analyze facts and law; this is a crucial skill; critical thinking and recollecting are necessary in all aspects of a judge's life, whether he or she be different kinds of judges, federal, state, or local. Particularly, federal judges have access to educated and intelligent clerks, but the last analysis has to be that of the judge.

3. **Learn more about the opposition.** Many times, it's more comfortable to avoid what we don't agree with and selectively validate what we already believe. But part of being a well-educated person means learning about the history, backgrounds, values, and techniques of people you disagree with so that you can anticipate and deal with their arguments more effectively.

4. **Trust and verify.** During the cold war, President Ronald Reagan liked to quote an old Russian saying to his Soviet counterpart, Mikhail Gorbachev: "Doveryay, no proveryay," or "Trust, but verify." Being a good critical thinker means achieving a balance between blind faith and healthy skepticism.

5. **Remember that critical thinking is the cornerstone of all academic achievement.** There's nothing more important than learning to think critically. In college and in life, the skills discussed in this chapter will make you a better college student, a better citizen, a better employee, a savvier consumer, a better relational partner, and a better lifelong learner.

Activity Option Ask students to respond to either one or both of the questions from this "Insight → Action" exercise. Consider using them as a homework assignment that can be e-mailed to you and one other class member. Before you respond to the student, have class members give each other feedback. Ask students to list the most significant things they learned from reading their classmate's reflection. Was their partner's response different from their own? Why or why not? Give examples. After you read the responses, give feedback to the students.

Teachable Moment Pose the following questions to your students: Is a judge a good career choice for everyone? Why or why not?

INSIGHT ⊖ ACTION

1. Provide real examples of critical thinking from any of your current classes. Are you being asked on exams to compare and contrast? To sort through evidence and make decisions? In class discussions are you encouraged to disagree with your instructor or classmates for the sake of a healthy, vigorous debate?

2. Can you describe your own intellectual progress as a critical thinker? Do you seem to fit the pattern that researchers have identified for those new to higher education? As this chapter suggests, do you think for yourself? Based on what you've read in this chapter, what can you do to strengthen your critical thinking skills?

C CREATE a Career Outlook

JUDGE

Have you ever considered a career as a judge, attorney, magistrate, or other legal professional? Here are some facts about this career to consider and some questions about yourself to ponder.

Facts to Consider

Academic preparation required: A bachelor's degree is required, but most workers in this career field have law degrees.

Future workforce demand: Prospects for new jobs will increase at an average rate in the future, although positions are competitive because of the status associated with serving on the bench.

Work environment: Judges apply the law in local, state, and federal courts, from minor traffic disputes to major corporate litigation. They work in law offices, law libraries, or courtrooms, directing juries on how to weigh the evidence, and then listening to their verdicts. Most judges work forty-hour weeks, but it is not uncommon to work longer hours.

Most common psychological type preferences: extraverted (and to a lesser extent introverted), sensing, thinking, judging[21]

Essential skills: reasoning, reading, writing, listening, researching, decision making

Questions to Ponder

1. Do you have (or could you acquire) the skills this career requires?
2. What would you find most satisfying about this type of career?
3. What would you find most challenging about this type of career?
4. Are you interested in a career like this? Why or why not?

For more information, see U.S. Department of Labor, Bureau of Labor Statistics, *Occupational Outlook Handbook, 2006-2007 Edition*.[22]

For more career activities online, go to http://www.academic.cengage.com/collegesuccess/staley to do the Team Career exercises.

Q5: Do law schools use the term *critical thinking*? Or do they use different terminology to describe reasoning, problem solving, and decision making, and reflecting and improving the thinking process as you go?
Law schools certainly use the term *critical thinking*. Since time immemorial, law teachers and judges in the United States and Great Britain constantly have used the term. They also write and talk about "the rule of reason." But this is another phrase to emphasize the need to rely upon critical thinking.

Q6: What advice would you give college students who are considering a legal career?
College students interested in a possible law career should be good readers, particularly of history; biographies of lawyers, judges, and statesmen; and the humanities. For my part, a course in the "dead languages," Latin and Greek, was helpful. A course in speed reading is of greater help than one can imagine.

Teachable Moment Remind students that a liberal education comes from the word *liberate*—to free. A liberal education is really about preparing students to free their minds to be critical thinkers and lifelong learners.

Unleash Your Creativity!

Whether you're eighteen or eighty-one, it's safe to say that your life has been changed by an unending stream of new inventions. Which of the following have come into existence during your lifetime? PDAs? Microsoft Windows? PlayStation? DVDs? Microwavable mac and cheese? Cell phones? IMAX movies? The artificial heart? High-speed Internet? Side-impact air bags? Singer Bob Dylan crooned memorable words in 1964: "The times, they are a-changin'." He was right then, and it's still true now.

Creativity affects us all. It's true that some of these items haven't made a big impact. But other inventions affect you every single day. In his bestselling book, *The Rise of the Creative Class*, Richard Florida discusses the accelerating role of creativity in our lives today: "We live in a time of great promise. We have evolved economic and social systems that tap human creativity and make use of it as never before. This in turn creates an unparalleled opportunity to raise our living standards, build a more humane and sustainable economy, and make our lives more complete."[23]

Florida notes that in 1900, less than 10 percent of American workers were doing creative work. Farms and factories were most people's work sites. Eighty years later, the figure had only risen to 20 percent. But today, a full third of our working population engages in employment that gets their creative juices flowing, whether they're artists, designers, writers, analysts, musicians, or entrepreneurs. The creative sector of our economy accounts for nearly half of all wage and salary income—$1.7 trillion per year. Today's "no collar" workplace is fueled by creativity. And Florida says, we've barely scratched the surface. Human creativity is virtually limitless.[24]

Diversity in our surroundings is one thing that increases the potential for creativity. Creativity comes in all sizes, ethnicities, preferences, and genders. If you're around other open-minded, flexible, tolerant, forward-looking, innovative people, you're more likely to live up to your own creative potential. And in case you're wondering, you don't have to be an artist to be creative. Creativity simply means finding new and better ways to do things. In many ways, it's a choice you make; you *decide* to be creative.[25]

What does all this have to do with you as an entering college student? Florida says that the rise of the creative sector has also changed the way people work and their expectations. No longer are many Americans' aspirations to make a million dollars and buy the house of their dreams. It's about having enough money to be comfortable while doing enjoyable, interesting, and creative work. The best people in any field aren't motivated solely by money. They are motivated by passion for what they do. Can it be true? Are our values changing?

College is a time to sort through your values and determine what you really want from this life of yours. It's about finding out who you are, what you want, why you want it, and how you can get it. Unleash your creativity now and begin building the future you'd like to live. Remember the warning of thinking expert Edward de Bono, "If you take no part in the design of your future, it will be designed for you by others."

Creativity: "Thinking Outside the ... Book"

CHALLENGE ⟶ REACTION

Challenge: What's the difference between *critical* thinking and *creative* thinking?

Reaction: _____

Do you believe this statement? *Everyone has creative potential.* It's true. Most of us deny it, however. "Me, creative? Nah!" We're often unaware of the untapped ability we have to think creatively. Try this experiment. Look at the following list of words, and divide the list into two (and only two) different categories, using any criteria you devise. Take a few moments and see what you come up with.

dog, salad, book, grasshopper, kettle, paper, garbage, candle

Whenever this experiment is tried, people always come up with very creative categories. They may divide the words into things that you buy at a store (dog, salad, kettle, paper, candle), things that move on their own (dog, grasshopper), things that have a distinct smell (dog, candle, garbage), words that have two consonants, and so forth. People never say it can't be done; they always *invent* categories. Interesting, isn't it? Our minds are hungry for the stimulation of a creative challenge.

Some people might assert that what the experiment demonstrates is intelligence, not creativity. People with average or above average IQs can come up with distinctive categories easily. Smart people, they'd say, are good at tasks like this, and people who come up with the best ideas must be geniuses.

The fact is that intelligence has more to do with coming up with the right answer, and creative thinking has more to do with coming up with multiple right answers. Often we get so focused on the *right* answer that we rush to find it instead of exploring all the possibilities. Creative thinking is thinking outside the box, or in terms of getting an education, perhaps we should call it thinking outside the book. Going beyond the obvious and exploring possibilities are important parts of becoming an educated person. Employers report that many college graduates today have specific skills, but that what they rarely see "is the ability to use the right-hand side of the brain—creativity, working in a team."[26] Here's one way to explain it. You see, there's a difference between thinking *reproductively* and thinking *productively*. *Reproductive* thinking asks: "What have I learned or experienced in the past that will help me solve this problem?" But when you're thinking *productively*, you generate as many alternative approaches as possible.

In Figure 5.1 we looked at the Question Pyramid. Creative thinking is at the top of the pyramid. It goes beyond critical thinking, is predictive, and multidimensional. It asks "What if ...?" questions. Here are some interesting ones: "What if everyone was allowed to tell one lie per day?" "What if no one could perceive colors?" "What if universities didn't exist?" "If you looked up a word like *squallizmotex* in the dictionary, what might it mean?"[27]

> "A mind that is stretched to a new idea never returns to its original dimensions."
>
> **Oliver Wendell Holmes, American poet (1809–1894)**

Emotional Intelligence (EI) Research It has been said that your IQ gets you the job, but your EQ (emotional quotient) helps you keep it and get promoted!

> "If you have an apple and I have an apple and we exchange these apples, then you and I will still each have one apple. But if you have an idea and I have an idea and we exchange these ideas, then each of us will have two ideas."
>
> **George Bernard Shaw, Irish literary critic, playwright, and essayist, 1925 Nobel Prize for Literature (1856–1950)**

Teachable Moment This is an important opportunity to get students to connect the Creative Potential Profile to their personality types. Quickly go around the room and have students tell you their type and what they think is their Creative Potential Profile.

Exercise 5.5 Creative Potential Profile

All of us have the potential to think creatively, but interestingly, we do so in different ways. Complete the Creative Potential Profile to explore your creative thinking potential by marking your responses on these twenty-five items. Place a 1 next to the item MOST like you, a 2 for the item MODERATELY like you, a 3 for the item that's a LITTLE like you, and a 4 for the item that's LEAST like you. Don't use a number more than once for an item, and use all four numbers each time.

Creative Potential Profile

1. I often wonder how to
____ (a) introduce change.
____ (b) discover new solutions.
____ (c) make ideas exciting.
____ (d) work best with people.

2. My strength is being
____ (a) decisive.
____ (b) thorough.
____ (c) imaginative.
____ (d) understanding.

3. Successful people are
____ (a) ambitious.
____ (b) disciplined.
____ (c) willing to take risks.
____ (d) self-confident.

4. I get my best results by
____ (a) focusing on current problems.
____ (b) applying careful analysis.
____ (c) trying new approaches.
____ (d) gaining the support of others.

5. I see the future as
____ (a) unknown.
____ (c) a challenge.
____ (b) providing many opportunities.
____ (d) facilitating change.

6. I appreciate teachers who
____ (a) explain ideas clearly.
____ (b) make learning interesting.
____ (c) recognize original ideas.
____ (d) involve others in learning.

7. People see me as
____ (a) energetic.
____ (b) persistent.
____ (c) a perfectionist.
____ (d) committed.

8. People who make things happen
____ (a) are highly motivated.
____ (b) enjoy experimenting.
____ (c) have the courage of their convictions.
____ (d) challenge the status quo.

9. Discoveries depend on
____ (a) being committed.
____ (b) being curious.
____ (c) being open-minded.
____ (d) having a broad perspective.

10. A good writer
____ (a) is convincing.
____ (b) presents new ideas.
____ (c) provides a unique perspective.
____ (d) has a compelling vision.

11. Breakthrough thinking
____ (a) makes progress possible.
____ (b) helps to solve difficult problems.
____ (c) explores new frontiers.
____ (d) encourages teamwork.

12. I dislike
____ (a) losing control.
____ (b) boring work.
____ (c) following rules.
____ (d) being rejected.

13. I communicate best by being
____ (a) direct.
____ (b) informative.
____ (c) interesting.
____ (d) open.

14. I am committed to
____ (a) achieving results.
____ (b) being the best at what I do.
____ (c) exploring new ideas.
____ (d) contributing to society.

15. Creative organizations
____ (a) look for good answers.
____ (b) encourage experimentation.
____ (c) allow freedom of expression.
____ (d) support new ideas.

16. Achieving results depends on being

____ (a) responsive.

____ (b) systematic.

____ (c) original.

____ (d) cooperative.

17. I prefer situations where I

____ (a) am in charge.

____ (b) have challenging assignments.

____ (c) can use my own ideas.

____ (d) can introduce change.

18. Change depends on

____ (a) gaining support.

____ (b) exploring options.

____ (c) independent thinking.

____ (d) inspiring others.

19. My goal is to

____ (a) accomplish my objectives.

____ (b) discover new approaches.

____ (c) have my ideas recognized.

____ (d) achieve progress.

20. Leaders

____ (a) assume responsibility.

____ (b) deal with complexity.

____ (c) visualize opportunities.

____ (d) empower others.

21. Ethical behavior

____ (a) is expected.

____ (b) requires honesty.

____ (c) emphasizes integrity.

____ (d) enhances society.

22. The arts

____ (a) help to improve designs.

____ (b) contribute new perspectives.

____ (c) broaden education.

____ (d) enrich people's lives.

23. Creative thinkers

____ (a) accomplish important goals.

____ (b) make significant discoveries.

____ (c) have leaps of imagination.

____ (d) turn their dreams into reality.

24. Breaking with tradition

____ (a) is seldom desirable.

____ (b) needs to be done carefully.

____ (b) provides new opportunities.

____ (d) helps to accomplish goals.

25. When under pressure, I

____ (a) trust my instincts.

____ (b) rely on known approaches.

____ (c) carefully explore my options.

____ (d) avoid conflict.

Totals: (a) _____ (b) _____ (c) _____ (d) _____

Source: Rowe, A. J. (2004). *Creative intelligence: Discovering the innovative potential in ourselves and others.* Upper Saddle River, NJ: Pearson Education, Inc.

According to creativity expert Alan Rowe, also an author of the Decision Style Inventory in Exercise 5.4, our creative intelligence demonstrates itself in four major styles. Look at your totals and see if the description for your lowest score (meaning your most preferred category) makes sense to you. Each of us has aspects of all four styles, but your raw scores may also tell you something about your creative potential.

> Intuitive (a). This creative style is best described as *resourceful*. If you are an Intuitive, you achieve goals, use common sense, and work to solve problems. You focus on results and rely on past experience to guide your actions. Managers, actors, and politicians are commonly Intuitives.

> Innovative (b). This creative style is best described as *curious*. Innovatives concentrate on problem solving, are systematic, and rely on data. They use original approaches, are willing to experiment, and focus on systematic inquiry. Scientists, engineers, and inventors typically demonstrate the Innovative creative style.

> **Imaginative (c).** This creative style is best described as *insightful.* Imaginatives are willing to take risks, have leaps of imagination, and are independent thinkers. They are able to visualize opportunities, are artistic, enjoy writing, and think outside the box. Artists, musicians, writers, and charismatic leaders are often Imaginatives.

> **Inspirational (d).** This creative style is best described as *visionary.* Inspirationals respond to societal needs, willingly give of themselves, and have the courage of their convictions. They focus on social change and the giving of themselves toward achieving it. They are often educators, motivational leaders, and writers.[28]

According to the Creative Potential Profile, which is your predominant style? Do your results seem accurate for you? Think about how you can make the best use of your natural style. How will your creativity affect the major or career you choose? Most people have more than one creative style. Remember that motivation, not general intelligence, is the key to creativity. You must be willing to tap your creative potential and challenge yourself to show it.[29]

Ten Ways to Become a More Creative Thinker

Becoming a more creative thinker may mean you need to accept your creativity and cultivate it. Consider these suggestions on how to think more creatively.

1. **Find new eyes.** Find a new perspective on old issues. Here's an interesting example. Years ago, a group of Japanese schoolchildren devised a new way to solve conflicts and build empathy for others' positions, called the Pillow Method. Figure 5.5 is an adaptation of it, based on the fact that a pillow has four sides and a middle, just like most problems.

   The middle or *mu* is the Zen expression for "it doesn't really matter." There is truth in all four positions. Try it: take a conflict you're having difficulty with at the moment, and write down all four sides and a middle.[30]

2. **Accept your creativity.** Many mindsets block creative thinking: "It can't be done!" "I'm just not the creative type." "I might look stupid!" Many people don't see themselves as creative. This perception can become a major stumbling block. If creativity isn't part of your self-image, you may need to revamp your image. Everyone has creative potential. You may just have to learn how to tap into yours.

3. **Make your thoughts visible.** For many of us, things become clear when we can see them, either in our mind's eye or displayed for us. Even Einstein, a scientist and mathematician, had a very visual mind. Sometimes if we write something down or sketch something out, we generate a new approach without really trying.

4. **Generate lots of ideas.** Thomas Edison held 1,093 patents, still the record. He gave himself idea quotients. The rule he set for himself was that he had to come up with a major invention every six months and a minor invention every ten days. Bach wrote a cantata every week, even if he was ill. According to two-time Nobel Prize winner Linus Pauling, "The best way to get a good idea is to get lots of ideas."

5. **Don't overcomplexify.** In hindsight, many of the most ingenious discoveries are embarrassingly simple. Biologist Thomas Huxley said, after reading

Activity Option Bring a pillow to class! Write some common first-year student statements on cards (roommate or family concerns are good ones) and ask students to come up in pairs and use the Pillow Method to address the problem.

Figure 5.5

The Pillow Method

Position 1—I'm right and you're wrong.
Position 2—You're right and I'm wrong.
Position 3—We're both right.
Position 4—We're both wrong.

Darwin's explanation of evolution: "How extremely stupid not to have thought of that!" It's common to bemoan our problems and allow anxiety to make them worse. But sometimes the most simple solution is the best one.[31]

6. **Capitalize on your mistakes.** Remember that Thomas Edison tried anything he could think of for a filament for the incandescent lamp, including a whisker from his best friend's beard. All in all, he tried about 1,800 things before finding the right one. Afterwards he said, "I've gained a lot of knowledge—I now know a thousand things that won't work."[32]

7. **Let it flow.** Mihaly Csikszentmihalyi, the author of *Flow: The Psychology of Optimal Experience* and many other books on creativity, discovered something interesting. For his doctoral thesis, he studied artists by taking pictures of them painting every three minutes. He was struck by how engaged they were in their work, so engaged that they seemed to forget everything around them. He began studying other "experts": rock climbers, chess players, dancers, musicians, surgeons. Regardless of the activity, these people forgot the time, themselves, and their problems. What did the activities have in common? Clear, high goals and immediate feedback. Athletes call it being in the zone. The zone is described as the ultimate human experience, where mind and body are united in purpose. Csikszentmihalyi's suggestions for achieving flow are these: Pick an enjoyable activity that is at or slightly above your ability level, screen out distractions, focus all your senses and emotions, and look for regular feedback on how you're doing.[33]

8. **Bounce ideas off others.** One good way to become more creative is to use your family or friends as sounding boards. Sometimes just verbalizing something helps you understand more about it. Each person who provides a critique will give you a new perspective, possibly worth considering.

9. **Stop searching for the "right" answer.** This advice doesn't pertain to your upcoming math exam. But it does to apply to situations in which there are many ways to solve a problem. There may be more than one acceptable solution. Fear of mistakes can be debilitating.

10. **Detach your self-concept.** For most of us, creativity is often linked to self-concept. An idea is your brainchild, and you want it to win approval. You've invested part of yourself in giving birth to it. But there's nothing like self-imposed judgment to shut down your creative juices. Your idea may not succeed on its own, but it may feed into someone else's idea and improve it. Or an idea you have about this problem may inform the next problem that challenges you. In the end, in addition to finding a workable solution, what's important is engaging in the creative process with others.

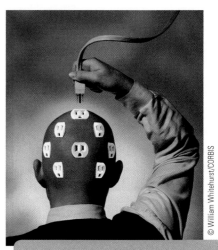

"A hunch is creativity trying to tell you something."

Frank Capra, Italian American film director (1897–1991)

Teachable Moment Remind students that there are not always right and wrong answers, that it's best to ask questions, and that we do learn from our mistakes. (Let's just hope the mistake isn't too costly!)

INSIGHT → ACTION

1. Do you see yourself as a creative person? Instead of thinking about whether you're creative or not, ask yourself this question, "*How* am I creative?"

2. Think of a problem you're facing right now. Use the Pillow Method described in Figure 5.5 to analyze the problem. Do you find this approach helpful?

3. Select two of the ten ways to become a more creative thinker suggested in this chapter, and write a statement about future actions based on these recommendations.

EXERCISE 5.6 VARK Activity

Complete the recommended activity for your preferred VARK learning modality. If you are multimodal, select more than one activity. Your instructor may ask you to (a) give an oral report on your results in class, (b) send your results to him or her via e-mail, (c) post them online, or (d) contribute to a class chat.

 Visual: Use the whitespace in this chapter or sticky notes to record insights about how the chapter applies to you. Note which section of the chapter contains the most personal applications for you.

 Aural: Talk through this chapter with a classmate or friend or read through your notes on this chapter aloud.

 Read/Write: Read a newspaper article on a current controversy perhaps involving college students, such as alcohol poisoning, and summarize the article's main points.

 Kinesthetic: Ask a friend to help you videotape interviews with other students on campus. Ask individual students if they see themselves as creative and why or why not. Show your production in class.

For more practice online, go to http://www.academic.cengage.com/collegesuccess/staley to take the Challenge Yourself online quizzes.

NOW WHAT DO YOU THINK?

At the beginning of this chapter, Annie Miller, a frustrated student, faced a challenge. Now after reading this chapter, would you respond differently to any of the questions you answered about the "FOCUS Challenge Case"?

REALITY CHECK

On a scale of 1 to 10, answer the following questions now that you've completed this chapter.

1 = not very/not much/very little/low   10 = very/a lot/very much/high

In hindsight, how much did you *really* know about this topic before reading the chapter?

1   2   3   4   5   6   7   8   9   10

How much do you think this information might affect your success in college?

1   2   3   4   5   6   7   8   9   10

How much do you think this information might affect your career success after college?

1   2   3   4   5   6   7   8   9   10

How long did it actually take you to complete this chapter? _____ Hour(s) _____ Minutes

Take a minute to compare these answers to your answers from the "Readiness Check" at the beginning of this chapter. What gaps exist between the similar questions? How might these gaps between what you thought before starting the chapter and what you now think after completing the chapter affect how you approach the next chapter in this book?

To download mp3 format audio summaries of this chapter, go to http://www.academic.cengage.com/collegesuccess/staley.

6 Engaging, Listening, and Note-Taking in Class

YOU'RE ABOUT TO DISCOVER...

Teachable Moment As you begin this chapter along with your students, again make sure they know that you are in this together. As they learn about themselves, you will, too, and sharing *your* learning is one way to engage your students in theirs. Who knows, you may even learn more about yourself!

> How to get engaged in class

> How to listen with focus

> How to vary your listening styles according to lecture styles

> How to ask questions in class

> How to take good notes

> How to use your notes to achieve the best results

"Every person in this life has something to teach me—and as soon as I accept that, I open myself to truly listening."

John Lahr, drama critic

Lindsey Collier

It was Lindsey Collier's first trip

home since classes started. Thanksgiving! In addition to the family's traditional feast, she was eager to see her eight-year-old sister, her brother who was a sophomore in high school, and her parents. After she left home, she began to appreciate her family more than ever. What great people they are, she kept thinking. Still, she wondered: Will they be glad to see me? Will I fit back into the family? Will Mom have converted my bedroom into a guest room? Will Dad still want to watch our favorite TV shows together? A million questions were running through her mind. Even though they talked on the phone and sent e-mails and text messages nearly every day, actually seeing her family for the first time in three months was going to seem strange. She imagined that Max, the family's golden retriever, would be the first one to greet her. She expected to miss him, but not this much!

She knew one thing for sure: Her parents would ask questions about how her classes were going. *Pretty well,* she thought. She'd gotten a B+ on her English paper, a B on her first math exam, an A on her College Success "Academic Autobiography," and an A− on her philosophy paper. But then there was her computer science course. That was a different story.

Her computer science instructor was a graduate teaching assistant. This was his first experience teaching a college course, he had announced on the first day of class, and English was his second language. His lectures were jam-packed with information that went right over Lindsey's head. Take last Wednesday's lecture, for example:

The real beginning of modern computers goes back to the seventeenth century and intellectual giants such as Descartes, Pascal, Leibnitz, and Napier. In mathematics, particularly, tremendous progress was made in revolutionizing how people saw the world, and their calculations became so laborious that they needed a more sophisticated computing machine.

The development of logarithms by the Scottish mathematician John Napier in 1614 stimulated the invention of the various devices that substituted the addition of logarithms for multiplication. Napier published his great work of logarithms in the book called *Rabdologia*. This was a remarkable invention since it enabled people to transform multiplication and division into simple addition and subtraction. His logarithm tables soon came into widespread use. Napier is often remembered more by another invention of his, nicknamed "Napier's Bones." This was a small instrument constructed of 10 rods, on which were engraved the multiplication tables. They are referred to as bones because the first set was made from ivory and resembled a set of bones. This simple device enabled people to carry out multiplication quickly if one of the numbers was only one digit (*i.e.*, $6 \times 6{,}742$).

The invention of logarithms led directly to the development of the slide rule. The first slide rule appeared in 1650 and was the result of the joint effort of two Englishmen, Edmund Gunter and the Reverend William Oughtred. The principle behind this device is one of two scales moving against each other. This invention was dormant until 1850 when a French Artillery officer, Amédée Mannheim, added the movable double-sided cursor, which gave it its appearance as we know it today. They gave it the name "astrolabe" because of its astronomical uses. The astrolabe was the true forerunner of the modern slide rule.[1]

Lindsey tried to pay attention to his words and copy down the writing scribbled all over the board, but no matter how hard she tried, her mind seemed to drift to the new guy she'd just met. Information seemed to fly out of her instructor's mouth at mach speed, and frankly, she used her instructor's accent as an excuse. Taking notes that quickly was just plain impossible. She tried giving him quizzical looks to communicate "Slow down, please," but he probably couldn't see her face in the back row.

Since nothing the professor said caught her interest, she knew that asking questions in class would only prove that she wasn't paying attention. Trying to read and take notes from the textbook chapters *before* class took more discipline than she could muster. Her usual strategy was to look like she was paying attention in class so that no one knew that her brain wasn't really there.

Lindsey had thought about trying to stop in during his office hours some morning, but she worked off-campus as a breakfast server at a local restaurant. She could try making an appointment with him, she thought, but was he really willing to meet with every single student who had a scheduling conflict? *That's why he has office hours*, she told herself. And after all, he was working hard at the same time to earn an advanced degree himself. Besides, did she really want to discuss how poorly she was doing? It was too late in the term to drop the class, and she needed the credits for financial aid. Still, she had to figure something out or computer science was going to blow her GPA and her parents' good opinion of her.

WHAT DO **YOU** THINK?

Now that you've read about Lindsey Collier, answer the following questions. You may not know all the answers yet, but you'll find out what you know and what you stand to gain by reading this chapter.

1. List five mistakes Lindsey is making.
2. Now list five things that Lindsey should do immediately to improve her computer science classroom experience.

Before beginning to read this chapter, take two minutes to answer the following questions on a scale of 1 to 10. Your answers will help you assess how ready you are to focus.

1 = not very/not much/very little/low   10 = very/a lot/very much/high

Based on reading the "You're about to discover..." list and skimming this chapter, how much do you think you probably already know about the subject matter?

1   2   3   4   5   6   7   8   9   10

How much do you think this information might affect your college success?

1   2   3   4   5   6   7   8   9   10

How much do you think this information might affect your career success after college?

1   2   3   4   5   6   7   8   9   10

In general, how motivated are you to learn the material in this chapter?

1   2   3   4   5   6   7   8   9   10

This book describes four key factors related to intrinsic, or internal, motivation: curiosity, control, career outlook, and challenge. The next four questions relate to these **C-Factors:**

How *curious* are you about the content you expect to read in this chapter?

1   2   3   4   5   6   7   8   9   10

How much *control* do you expect to have over mastering the material in this chapter?

1   2   3   4   5   6   7   8   9   10

How interested are you in this chapter in terms of developing your *career outlook*?

1   2   3   4   5   6   7   8   9   10

How *challenging* do you think the material in this chapter will be for you?

1   2   3   4   5   6   7   8   9   10

Before beginning any task—including studying—it's important to check in with yourself to ensure that you're physically, intellectually, and emotionally ready to focus. How ready are you, physically, to focus on this chapter? (Are you rested, feeling well, and so on?)

1   2   3   4   5   6   7   8   9   10

How ready are you, intellectually, to focus on this chapter? (Are you thinking clearly, focused on this course, interested in this subject?)

1   2   3   4   5   6   7   8   9   10

How ready are you, emotionally, to focus on this chapter? (Are you calm, confident, composed?)

1   2   3   4   5   6   7   8   9   10

If your answer to any of the last three questions is below a 5 on the scale, you may need to address the issue you're facing prior to beginning this chapter. For example, if you're hungry, get a quick bite to eat. If you're feeling scattered, take a few moments to settle down and focus.

Finally, how long do you think it will take you to complete this chapter? _____ Hour(s) _____ Minutes

---

Activity Option Use a "think-pair-share" approach to this activity. First, have students answer the "What Do *You* Think?" on their own, and then pair up with the student next to them. Pairs of students must agree on the top two mistakes that Lindsey is making, as well as the top two things that she must immediately do. Each pair of students reports to the class and a master list is made. Finally, ask students if there is something that they think is really critical that is not on the list. It is possible that one or two students may key in to some really important underlying issues that Lindsey needs to address.

Get Engaged in Class

CHALLENGE ⊜ REACTION

Challenge: What is *engagement*? Exactly what does it take to become engaged in class?

Reaction: _____

No, this chapter isn't about buying a ring and getting down on one knee. It's about your willingness to focus, listen, discuss, ask questions, take notes, and generally dive into your classes. It's about being a full participant in what you're learning, not just a spectator sitting on the sidelines. It's about not just memorizing information for exams and then forgetting it. You see, the secret to college success hinges on this one word: *engagement*.

Think about this analogy. How did you learn to swim? Did you read books about swimming? Did you Google the word and check out all the hits? Did you get advice from your friends about swimming? Did you sit on the edge of the pool and watch other people swim? No, you probably jumped in and got wet, right? The same thing is true with your college classes. The more willing you are to jump in and get wet, the more engaged you'll be in the learning process. It's your education, after all, so take the plunge!

Getting the most out of class means reading, listening, asking questions, participating, and taking good notes. Perhaps you think you've already learned all of these skills, but the truth is they are so important to your college success that it's worth the effort to find out for sure.

Dare to Prepare

If you want to get a head start on developing good academic habits in class, then start before you get there. Preparation separates students into two categories: those who excel at learning and those who don't. Although not all students see the value of preparation, do more than your classmates do—dare to prepare! Follow these suggestions and you'll find that it's easier to get engaged in class because you're ready.

> **"What actually correlates with success are not grades, but 'engagement'—genuine involvement in courses and campus activities. Engagement leads to 'deep learning,' or learning for understanding. That's very different from just memorizing stuff for an exam, then forgetting it."**
>
> **John Merrow, reporter, *USA Today***

1. **Look ahead.** By checking your course syllabus before class, you'll be prepared for the upcoming topic. You'll also avoid the "oops" factor of sitting down, looking around, and noticing that everyone else knows something you don't about what's supposed to happen today.

2. **Do the assigned reading.** If you have a reading assignment due for class, do it, and take notes as you read. Write in the margins of your textbook or on sticky notes. Question what you're reading and enter into a mental dialogue with the author. Having some background on the topic will do you a world of good in class. You will be able to listen more actively and participate more intelligently during any discussion: *Yes, I remember the chapter covering that topic*, you'll think when the instructor begins talking about something you recognize. Instead of hearing it for the first time, you'll *reinforce* what you've already read. According to one study, as few as one-third of your classmates will have done the assigned reading prior to class. That factoid isn't a reason to excuse yourself from reading; instead it gives you insider information on how *you* can shine in class by comparison.[2]

3. **Show up physically.** Not only is attending class important for your overall understanding of the material, but it may move your grade up a few notches. Even if attendance isn't required by your instructor, require it of yourself. Research says that missing classes is definitely related to your academic performance. And once you give yourself permission to skip one single, solitary class, it becomes easier to do it the next time,

Teachable Moment Ask students to think about a class they really enjoyed. What was it like? What did they do in the class? Did they ask questions? Work in groups? Was it only that the course material was interesting or did they or the instructor or other students do something to make it more interesting?

Chapter Crossover Remember that in Chapter 2 students learned about their learning styles. Some students are not naturally able to focus in on details. Students who are sensors will look at the syllabus step-by-step and be prepared. Those who are intuitives may not be tuned into details enough to prepare. Remind students to think about their types and compensate, if necessary, as they prepare to engage in their classes.

and the time after that, and so on. Studies indicate that on any given day, approximately one-third of your classmates will miss class, that most students think that several absences during a term is "the standard," and that among students who miss class often, only one-quarter do the reading to catch up.[3] Exercise good judgment, even if your classmates don't!

4. **Show up mentally.** Showing up means more than just occupying a seat in the classroom. It means assessing what you bring to the class as a learner on any particular day. Just as each chapter of this book asks you to do a "Readiness Check" before you begin reading, it's a good idea to do a mental "Readiness Check" when you arrive in class. Are you *physically, intellectually,* and *emotionally* ready to give it your best shot? If not, what can you do to rally for the cause?

5. **Choose your seat strategically.** Imagine paying $150 for a concert ticket, just like everyone else, and then electing to sit in the nosebleed section as high up and far away from the action as you could get. Sitting in the back means you're more likely to let your mind wander and less likely to hear clearly. Sitting in the front means you'll keep yourself accountable by being in full view of the instructor and the rest of the class. Studies show that there is a definite connection between students' academic performance and their seat location. What's the best spot for great concentration? Front and center, literally—the "T zone"! In one study, students who sat at the back of a large auditorium were six times more likely to fail the course, even though the instructor had assigned seats randomly![4] Not only will sitting in the T zone keep you alert throughout the class, but instructors tend to have higher opinions of the students who sit there.

6. **Bring your tools.** Bring a writing utensil and notebook with you to every class. Your instructor may also ask you to bring your textbook, calculator, a blue

Sensitive Situation There may be reasons why students don't want to sit in the T zone. Perhaps they want to be anonymous because they are afraid they will be called on. Remind students that if they have this kind of fear—to the point of almost panicking—it is good to talk with their advisor about what to do. Some individuals actually do have panic attacks when they have to present or are called upon. Think about raising the question about why someone might not want to sit in the T zone with your students and suggesting ways to cope or get help.

book for an exam, or other necessary items. If so, do it. Question: how seriously would you take a carpenter who showed up to work without a hammer, nails, and screwdriver? Get the point?

7. **Don't sit by your best friend.** Resist the temptation to sit next to your best buddy in order to catch up on all the latest campus news during class. Of course, it's important to have friends, but class is hardly the best time to devote yourself to helping your friendship blossom. You're there for a reason; now capitalize on it!

8. **Posture counts!** Your parents may have told you more than once as a kid: "Sit up straight!" Sitting up straight in class will help you develop a healthy mind. It's hard to focus when you're slouched into a position that screams, "I could really use a power nap about now!" When your body says, "I'm ready to learn," your mind follows suit.

9. **Maintain your health.** Being sick can wreak havoc on your ability to concentrate, listen well, and participate. Take the preventative approach by getting enough sleep, eating well, and exercising. Remember, *energy management* is key to your ability to focus. Depleted energy can lead to serious *dis*engagement.

10. **Focus.** After sitting down in class each day, take a moment to clear your head of all daydreams, to-do's, and worries. Take a deep breath and remind yourself of the opportunity to learn that lies ahead. Promise yourself you'll get the most from this class. Think of yourself as a reporter at a press conference, listening intently because you'll be writing a story about what's going on. You *will* be writing a "story"—often in response to an essay question on an exam!

Follow the Rules of Engagement

Just as is the case with most places you can think of, college classrooms have rules about how to behave. You don't find people yelling in church or staring at other people in elevators or telling jokes at funerals. There are rules about how to behave in a variety of contexts, and college classrooms are no exception. Here are a few rules of engagement that you should know about up front:

1. **Be aware that gab is not a gift.** Have you ever heard someone described as having the gift of gab? Usually a compliment, having the gift of gab means you're articulate. But in class, gabbing while others are speaking is inappropriate. And it's certainly not a gift—especially to your instructor. In fact, side conversations while your professor is lecturing or your classmates are contributing to the discussion is downright rude. If you're seated next to a gabber, don't get sucked in. Use body language to communicate that you're there to learn, not to gab. If that's not enough to set the gabber straight, politely say something like, "I really need to pay attention right now. Let's talk more later, okay?" If that doesn't work, move to a different seat next time. Eventually, you'll make your point. Don't let other students cheat you out of learning.

Emotional Intelligence (EI) Research There is such a thing as an overused strength. Some students have really strong interpersonal skills to the point where it can interfere with what they need to do. They place so much emphasis on friends that they can make bad choices (poor impulse control or even a lack of assertiveness) if they think they are doing something that interferes with a relationship.

Chapter Crossover Remind students that Chapter 13 focuses on wellness and that statistics show that students get sick around midterms and finals when they are cramming in too much with too little sleep.

> **"Politeness is the art of choosing among one's real thoughts."**
>
> **Adlai Stevenson II, U.S. Presidential candidate (1900–1965)**

Activity Option In addition to being cheated out of learning, the issue with interrupting class is really about a student's right to learn. When one student disrupts the class, they have robbed others of their right to learn and in a sense stolen their money. Sometimes students won't speak up about others who are unruly, but you can be sure that you have students in class who are upset if their learning is frequently disrupted. You might even ask students how they would feel if someone was constantly talking to their neighbor. To test this out, before class, ask two students to stage talking in class and then debrief. How did classmates feel about the disruption?

Teachable Moment Suggest students check with professors about what to do if they are late. There are times when something is unavoidable (*i.e.*, an accident). Also, keep in mind that if we expect students to be on time, then we, as instructors, have to adhere to the same rules.

2. **Control your hunger pangs.** If your class meets through a meal hour, get in the habit of eating before or after class. Crunching and munching in the classroom may get in the way of others' learning, not to mention the distraction caused by enticing smells. Instructors differ on their preferences here. Some find gum chewing annoying, and others will actually invite you to bring a snack to tide you over. It's a good idea to find out what your instructors' preferences are, and then abide by them.

3. **Turn off your cell phone, please!** There's a reason why people are asked to turn off their cell phones before concerts, athletic events, or movies. Imagine being in a jam-packed theater trying to follow the film's plot with cell phones going off every few seconds. Or while watching the movie, would you tune out to text your best friend every few minutes? You've paid good money to see a film. The same thing goes for your college classes.

4. **Better late than never?** Not to some instructors. Students arriving late and leaving early are annoying, not only to your instructor, but to your classmates. To them, it looks like you don't value the other students or the class content. How would you like dinner guests to arrive an hour late, after you'd slaved over a hot stove all day? Your instructors have prepared for class, and they feel the same way. Build in time to find a parking place, hike to the building where class is held, or stop for a coffee. Do everything you can to avoid coming late and leaving early. Preserve class time as a priority.

5. **Actively choose to engage, not disengage.** Engagement isn't something that just happens to you while you're not looking. You're sitting there, minding your own business, and zap—you suddenly realize that you've become engaged in learning. It's a choice you make, and sometimes it's a difficult choice because the material isn't naturally appealing to you, or the course is a required one you didn't choose, or you're just plain out of sorts. Choose to engage, anyway. Instead of actively choosing to *dis*engage in class by sleeping through lectures, surfing the Internet, or instant messaging friends, choose to engage by leaning forward, processing information, finding your own ways to connect to the material, and formulating questions to ask. Technology offers a particularly strong temptation to disengage. Besides possibly taking your attention away from course content, upright laptop screens block your view, making eye contact between your instructor and you difficult to maintain. Even though over half of college classrooms are now wireless, some instructors are banning laptops in large lecture classes or exerting control over what can be accessed, so that students aren't tempted to surf and check messages continuously during class. According to one study conducted in the business world, employees addicted to e-mail and text messages showed the equivalent of a ten-point drop in IQ! In some settings, multitasking just doesn't work well.[5]

If you're investing in a college education, then play by the rules of engagement. They're in place for your benefit.

INSIGHT → ACTION

1. Look over the ten Dare to Prepare suggestions at the beginning of this section. Which of the suggestions do you find most difficult to do? For which of your classes?

2. Which Rules of Engagement do you find students break most often in your classes? What advice would you give these students?

3. What can you do to increase your own engagement in the classroom?

Activity Option Divide the class into two groups. Ask students to discuss as a group the "Insight → Action" activity. Next, ask students to develop rules of engagement for the class. Compare lists and come up with a set of rules that the whole class can live by.

Box 6.1: Listening Tips If English Is Your Second Language

It's normal to feel overwhelmed in the classroom as a new student, but especially if your first language isn't English. The academic environment in higher education can be stressful and competitive. It's even more stressful if you're also dealing with a new and different culture. You will need to give yourself time to adapt to all of these changes. In the meantime, here are some suggestions for improving your ability to listen well in class:

- Talk to your instructor before the course begins. Let her know that English is not your native language, but that you're very interested in learning. Ask for any suggestions on how you can increase your chances of success in the class. Your instructor will most likely be willing to provide you with extra help, knowing you're willing to do your part to overcome the language barrier.

- Try to get the main points of your professor's lecture. You don't have to understand every word.

- Write down words to look up in the dictionary later. Keep a running list and check them all after class. Missing out on one important term can hurt your chances of understanding something else down the line.

- Don't be afraid to ask questions. If you're too uncomfortable to ask during class, make use of your professor's office hours or e-mail address to get your questions answered. Also, teaching assistants and peer tutors may be available to help you.

- Use all support materials available for the class. Find out if your instructor posts his notes on the course website or if they are available as handouts. Some professors offer guided notes or skeleton outlines for students to fill in throughout the lecture. Some large lectures are videotaped for viewing by students at a later time. Make full use of podcasts of lectures, if they're available, so that you can listen more than once to portions you found confusing in class. Use any tools available to help reinforce lecture content.

- Team up with a classmate whose native language is English. Clarify your notes and fill in gaps.

- Form a study group with other classmates. Meet on a regular basis so that you can help one another. Remember: just because your native language isn't English doesn't mean you don't have something to offer the other members of your study group.

- Be patient. It will take some time to adjust to the accents of your various instructors. After a few weeks of class, you'll find it easier to understand what is being said.

- Practice your English comprehension by listening to talk radio or watching television or movies. You'll hear a variety of regional accents, for example, and broaden your understanding of American culture.

- Take an "English as a Second Language" course if you think it would help. It's important to keep up with the academic demands of college, and further development of your English skills may improve your comprehension and boost your confidence.

- If you continue to feel overwhelmed and unable to cope after several weeks in school, find out if your campus has an International Students Office, and enlist support from people who are trained to help.[6]

Listening with Focus

Sensitive Situation Most likely your second-language speakers are going to be quiet and you may not even know that they are ESL students. Open the door for any student in the class to see you—or e-mail you—to let you know what they need and what you can provide. Give them some suggestions for how to retrieve the same kind of information from their other professors who may not have "opened the door."

CHALLENGE → REACTION

Challenge: What is *focused listening*? How can you achieve it?

Reaction: _____

Listening with focus is more than just physically hearing words as they stream by. It's actually a complicated process that's hard work.

"Easy Listening" Is for Elevators— Focused Listening Is for Classrooms

Stores, restaurants, and elevators are known for their programmed, background easy listening music. Chances are you hardly notice it's there. Listening in class, however, requires actual skill, and you'll be doing a great deal of it as a college student. Experts estimate that the average student spends 80 percent of class time listening to lectures.[7]

Many of us naively believe that listening is easy to do. If you happen to be around when there's something to listen to, you can't help but listen. Not so! Did you know that when you're listening at your best, your respiration rate, heartbeat, and body temperature all increase? Just as with aerobic exercise, your body works harder when you're engaging in focused listening. When all is said and done, listening is really about energy management. You can't listen well when your energy is zapped, when you've pulled the mother of all all-nighters, or when your stomach is growling with a vengeance. Focused listening means that you've cleared the deck for class, and you're focusing on engagement.

Here are some techniques for improving your listening skills in the classroom. Read through the list, then go back and check off the ones you're willing to try harder to do in class this week. As you'll see from practicing these techniques, it's not always easy to be a good listener. But the investment you make in improving your listening skills will pay off in countless ways.

- ☐ **Calm yourself.** Take a few deep breaths with your eyes closed to help you put all those nagging distractions on the back burner during class time.

- ☐ **Be open.** Like Lindsey in the "FOCUS Challenge Case," you may wonder how you'll ever use this information in your career. But keep an open mind and view your class as yet another opportunity to strengthen your intellect and learn something new. Wisdom comes from a broad understanding of many things, rather than from a consistently limited focus on practical information.

- ☐ **Don't make snap judgments.** Remember, you don't have to like your instructor's wardrobe to respect his knowledge. Focus on the content he's offering you. You may not even agree with what he's saying, but he may be leading up to a point you can't predict and turn the argument around. Don't jump to conclusions about content *or* style.

- ☐ **Assume responsibility.** Speak up! Ask questions! Even if you have a professor with an accent who's difficult to understand, the burden of clarification rests with you. You will interact with people with all sorts of accents, voices, and speech patterns throughout your life. It's up to you to improve the situation.

© Lucidio Studio Inc./CORBIS

> **"Listening looks easy, but it's not simple. Every head is a world."**
>
> **Cuban proverb**

- **Watch for gestures that communicate "Here comes something important!"** Some typical examples include raising an index finger, turning to face the class, leaning forward from behind the podium, walking up the aisle, or using specific facial expressions or gestures.

- **Listen for speech patterns that subtly communicate "Make sure you include this in your notes!"** For example, listen for changes in the rate, volume, or tone of speech, longer than usual pauses, or repeated information.

- **Uncover general themes or roadmaps for each lecture.** See if you can figure out where your instructor is taking you *while* he's taking you there. Always ask yourself, "Where's he going with this? What's he getting at? How does this relate to what was already said?" Or in Lindsey's case, "What do logarithms have to do with modern computers?"

- **Appreciate your instructor's prep time.** For every hour of lecture time, your teacher has worked for hours to prepare. Although she may make it look easy, her lecture has involved researching, organizing, creating a PowerPoint presentation, overheads, or a podcast, and preparing notes and handouts.

Activity Option Assign students to listen to the same lecture. You may have some on campus that you can download for the class in podcast format, or ask students to attend the same lecture. Have students watch for gestures and speech patterns to figure out what were the most important points. Have students return to class to report what they thought was most important. As an alternative, you can give a lecture or videotape someone to do this as an in-class activity.

Teachable Moment Ask students to identify the theme of the lecture in their last two classes. For students that get it right, ask them how they remembered. While they were in class, did they associate what was being discussed with something they knew or experienced (connected knowledge)? Were they prepared for class?

Listening Is More Than Hearing

Perhaps you've never thought about it, but, actually, listening and hearing aren't the same thing. Hearing—the physiological part—is only the first stage of a four-stage process. Listening is a much more complex process—especially *focused listening*, or listening at your best. The four stages of focused listening are as follows:

1. **Sensing:** receiving the sounds through your auditory system. As you sit in class, sound waves enter your ears and register in your brain.

2. **Interpreting:** understanding the message. Sounds themselves don't mean anything until you assign meaning to them. Instead of just random noise, the instructor's message must mean something to you.

3. **Evaluating:** weighing evidence. You decide if something is true or important by sorting fact from opinion. Both interpretation and evaluation in class may involve asking questions to clarify things.

4. **Responding:** providing feedback or taking action. You respond by participating in the discussion, asking significant questions, and taking down clear, meaningful notes to study later.[8]

Teachable Moment Have you ever come back from a meeting or conference where you took notes and then read them later only to find you weren't sure what they meant? Remind students that something as simple as writing legibly, having enough paper, and taking just a few minutes afterwards to clean up the notes helps you remember the important points.

As you're listening in class, you must cycle through all four of these stages. You must *sense* the sound waves coming from your instructor, a classmate, or a guest speaker, *interpret* them, *evaluate* them, and *respond* by jumping into the discussion yourself, asking questions, and taking the best notes you can. If you're not focused, it's possible to skip a step or "listen out of order." You may take notes without really *interpreting* what you're hearing. You're operating on autopilot—you skip the interpretation step completely, and write down things you don't really understand. (And consequently, you can't interpret your notes later.) Or you may try and write down every word you hear without *evaluating* its importance, getting bogged down in insignificant detail. If you want to get the most from your time spent in the classroom, it will help to pay attention to all four stages of focused listening.

Listen Hard!

It's estimated that college students spend ten hours per week listening to lectures.[9] Professors can speak 2,500–5,000 words during a fifty-minute lecture. That's a lot of words flying by at breakneck speed, so it's important to listen correctly. But what does *that* mean?

Generalize for a moment. Think about the various situations in which you find yourself listening. You often listen to empty chit-chat on your way to class. "Hey, how's it going?" when you spot your best friend in the hallway is an example, right? As you can imagine, listening in this type of situation doesn't require a lot of brainpower. Although you wouldn't want to spend too much time on chit-chat, if you refused to engage in any at all, you'd probably be seen by others as odd, withdrawn, shy, or arrogant.

You also listen in challenging situations, some that are emotionally charged; for example, a friend needs to vent, relieve stress, or verbalize her anxieties. Most people who are blowing off steam aren't looking for you to fix their problems. They just want to be heard and to hear something from you like "I understand" or "That's too bad."

Listening to chit-chat and listening in emotionally charged situations require what are called soft listening skills. You must be accepting, sensitive, and nonjudgmental. You don't have to assess, analyze, or conclude. You just have to be there for someone else.

But these two types of listening situations don't describe all the kinds of listening you do. Sometimes instead of soft listening skills, you need something altogether different. When you're listening to new information, as you do in your college classes, or when you're listening to someone trying to persuade you of something, you have to pay close attention, think critically, and ultimately make decisions about what you're hearing. Is something true or false? Right or wrong? How do you know? When you're listening to a person dispersing information or someone trying to persuade you, you need hard listening skills instead of soft ones. In situations like these you must be discerning, analytical, and decisive.

What's important about all of this? One mistake many students make in class is listening the wrong way. They should be using their hard listening skills, rather than sitting back and letting information waft over them. Soft listening skills don't help you in class. You must listen intently, think critically, and analyze carefully what you're hearing. It's important to note that neither listening mode is better than the other. They are each simply better suited to different situations. But soft listening won't get you the results you want in your classes. You don't need to be there for your instructor; you need to be there for yourself.[10]

Trick Yourself into Focused Listening

Some students are very good actors. They know how to look like they're listening. In class, they sit down, get out their notebooks, find a pen, assume

Emotional Intelligence (EI) Research Strong interpersonal skills are key to success in college and in life. Good empathy is an important sub-skill to build and maintain relationships. Really hearing another person means trying to understand his perspective and be able to mentally walk in his shoes.

Teachable Moment Have students visualize a sieve. If they were looking for treasure at the beach, they could use a sieve to sift through the sand. By putting sand through a sieve, large "important" objects would stay in the sieve, later to be assessed, while the unimportant sand would pass through. Tell students to use the same analogy when listening for main points in class. Sifting is a listening skill to be cultivated!

a listening posture, and then mentally go somewhere else. Lindsey in the "FOCUS Challenge Case" admitted to being one of these very good actors. While she's not doing herself any favors, it *is* possible to trick yourself into focused listening.

You may find many of your classes to be naturally fascinating learning experiences. But for others, you will need to be convinced. Even if you don't find Intro to Whatever to be the most engaging subject in the world, you may find yourself intrigued by your instructor. Most people are interested in other people. What makes him tick? Why was she drawn to this field? If you find it hard to get interested in the material, trick yourself by paying attention to the person delivering the message. Sometimes focusing on something about the speaker can help you focus on the subject matter, too. And you may just find out that you actually do find this class to be valuable. While tricking yourself isn't always a good idea, it *can* work if you know what you're doing and why.

Get Wired for Sound

Aural learners of the world unite! Increasingly professors are providing podcasts and videocasts of their lectures so that you can *preview* the lecture in advance or *review* it after class. Some textbooks (like this one) offer chapter summaries you can listen to on the subway, in the gym, at home during a blizzard, or in bed while recovering from the flu via your computer or digital-audio player. Log into the course website to download individual lectures or subscribe to a series of lectures your campus offers.

Regardless of your learning style, recorded lectures allow you to re-listen to difficult concepts as many times as needed. You can take part in the live action in class and take notes later while re-listening to the podcast. In one study, students who re-listened to a lecture one, two, or three times increased their lecture notes substantially each time.[11] And getting the same information via two sensory channels instead of just one can be a great aid to learning. (On the other hand, getting information about several *different* things at once—multitasking—can hurt comprehension and memory.)[12] Of course, recorded lectures aren't meant to excuse you from attending class, and in order to take advantage of them, you actually have to find time to listen to them. They're supplemental tools to *reinforce* learning for busy students on the go, which is virtually *everyone* these days.[13]

Identify Lecture Styles So You Can Modify Listening Styles

Regardless of how challenging it is to listen with focus, being successful in college will require you to do just that—focus—no matter what class or which professor. Sometimes your instructors are *facilitators*, who help you discover information on your own in new ways. Other times they are *orators*,

> **"The most basic and powerful way to connect to another person is to listen. Just listen. Perhaps the most important thing we ever give each other is our attention."**
>
> Rachel Naomi Remen, physician and author

Emotional Intelligence (EI) Research Although we can't control every situation, we can control how we respond. While it is easier for some than others, we do have control over our emotions, attitudes, and behaviors.

who lecture as their primary means of delivering information. If you're not an aural learner, listening with focus to lectures will be a challenge for you.

Chances are you won't be able to change your professors' lecturing styles. And even if you could, different students react differently to different lecture styles. But what you can do is expand your own skills as a listener—no matter what class or which instructor. Take a look at the lecture styles coming up and see if you recognize them.

C CULTIVATE Your Curiosity

QUIET YOUR MIND!

Have you ever noticed there's a play-by-play commentary going on inside your head, just like an NFL announcer during a big game: "On third down with no timeouts left. And here's the snap ... rookie Davis Jones busts off tackle for an eight-yard gain! It's close to a first down...." Compare that to your own play-by-play observations: "And here he comes ... Matt's walking straight toward me. He's getting closer. Maybe this is my big chance."

It's normal to comment internally about what's going on around you, and it's perfectly human to think that your own internal dialogue is the most important thing on the planet. Most of us do. The philosopher Descartes once said, "I think, therefore I am." The question isn't whether or not you're engaged in constant conversation with yourself; it's whether that conversation is productive and useful, and if not, how to make it so.

Sometimes this incessant, internal chatter makes it's hard to be fully present in class because of three P's: pressure, preoccupation, and priorities. While you're sitting there, you feel a rush of stress about your upcoming assignments; you worry about a sick relative you should attend to; and you obsess about whether you should tackle your calculus homework first tonight or start on your philosophy research paper. You feel overwhelmed. Productivity expert Kerry Gleeson believes, "This constant, unproductive preoccupation with all the things we have to do is the single largest consumer of time and energy."

Part of the problem you face trying to listen in class is fundamental to the listening process itself. People listen at a rate of 125–250 words per minute, but think at a rate of 1,000–3,000 words per minute. Where does your mind typically go during the extra time between listening and thinking? Do you use that time productively to *review* or *preview*—or do the three P's highjack your attention? It's true; we all have important things to worry about, but let's be honest: Excessive negativity, worry, and obsession can clutter your thinking so much that they shut you down. According to time management guru David Allen, "There is usually an inverse proportion between how much something is on your mind and how much it's getting done."[14]

> "Rule your mind or it will rule you."
>
> Horace (Roman poet, 65–8 B.C.)

In his book *Quiet Your Mind*, author John Selby reports that we can learn better control over our thoughts, and that the psychological and physiological benefits are well worth it. Being in a permanent state of flight or fight, the body's normal reaction to stress, is hazardous to your health.[15]

Here are some tips to coach yourself to quiet your mind:

- **Choose where to focus your attention.** Instead of allowing your mind to run *you*, make a conscious decision to run *it*. Horace may have lived many centuries ago, but he offers timeless advice in the quotation on this page.

- **Spend your free time; don't squander it.** Ask yourself whether you use leisure-time activities as an escape. For example, do you watch television, exercise, or surf the Net to *avoid* what you see as unpleasant but necessary tasks, rather than to *revitalize*? Consider whether your free time is about *something* or about *nothing*. Short bouts of nothing can be liberating, but long bouts of nothing can be opportunities for negative thoughts to move in and take over.

- **Worry less; do more.** Winston Churchill advised, "Let our advance worrying become advance thinking and planning." Worry is counterproductive; it drains us of the energy we need to get things done and keeps us from enjoying the present. Write down what's worrying you most, identify the worst that could possibly happen, and ask yourself if your fear is realistic. If it's not, let go of it and do something productive.

- **Forgive and forget.** Some people obsess over the past. They should have done X; if only Y had happened instead. Life is full of ups and downs, but it's important to keep moving. Actress and comedian Lily Tomlin once said, "Forgiveness means giving up all hope for a better past." Focus on the present tense.

- **Be present.** Remember grade school? Your teachers would call the roll every morning, and you'd answer "present" or "I'm here" when your name was called. Life coach Mark van Doren says, "There is one thing we can do, and the happiest people are those who can do it to the limit of their ability. We can be completely present. We can be all here. We can ... give all our attention to the opportunity before us."

> **The Rapid-Fire Lecturer:** You may have found yourself in a situation like Lindsey's with an instructor who lectures at breakneck speed. Listening and taking notes in a class like this are not easy. By the end of class your hand aches from gripping your pen and writing furiously. Since there'll be no time to relax, you'll need to make certain you're ready for this class by taking all the suggestions in this chapter to heart. Read ahead so that you recognize points the instructor makes. Also take advantage of whatever supplementary materials this teacher provides in the way of audio support, online lecture notes, or Power-Point handouts.

> **The Slow-Go Lecturer:** Instead of rushing, some lecturers move very slowly. They contemplate, ruminate, and chew on every word before uttering it. This lecturer proceeds so slowly that there are pauses—seconds long—between phrases, while he paces back and forth, pontificating. Your attention tends to drift because you become impatient. You may even tune out and stop listening. Instead, discipline yourself to use the extra time to your advantage by predicting what's coming next or by clarifying what's just been said in your own mind.

> **The All-Over-the-Map Lecturer:** Organization is not this lecturer's strong suit. While the lecture may be organized in the lecturer's mind, what comes out is difficult to follow. In this case, it will be up to you to organize the lecture content yourself.

> **The Content-Intensive Lecturer:** This lecturer is hardly aware that anyone else is in the room, intent on covering a certain amount of material in a particular amount of time. This teacher may use extensive discipline-specific jargon that you will need to learn rapidly to keep abreast. Prepare yourself for a potentially rich learning environment, but be sure to ask questions right away if you find yourself confused.

> **The Review-the-Text Lecturer:** This lecturer will follow the textbook closely, summarizing and highlighting important points. You may assume it's not important to attend class, but watch out for this trap! Receiving the same information in more than one format can be a great way to learn.

> **The Go-Beyond-the-Text Lecturer:** This lecturer will use class time to provide examples, tell stories, and bring in outside materials. Keeping up with reading in the text will be important so that you understand the additional information that you receive in class.

> **The Active-Learning Lecturer:** This lecturer may choose not to lecture at all or to intersperse short lectures with activities, role plays, or simulations. While you may find it easier to get engaged in class, and you'll most likely appreciate the teacher's creativity, remember that you are still responsible for connecting what happens in class to the course material itself. You will need to read, digest, and process the information on your own outside of class.

Emotional Intelligence (EI) Research Why is it that in the face of the same adverse situation some individuals feel hopeless while others are optimistic? It is how we choose to see the situation. Survivors of Hurricane Katrina who counted their blessings (their family was okay, a house is only a material thing that can be replaced), as opposed to those who felt hopeless, were more optimistic and better able to cope with the disaster.

Chapter Crossover Remind students to go back to Chapter 2 and review their learning types. It is really important that students make a connection with "who they are" and "what they need" when developing and modifying their listening skills.

Activity Option For homework, have students observe their other classes for a week and come to class briefly describing the type of lecturers they have. They must include one example that illustrates the type. As a class compare the types and strategize about how students can successfully adapt to the style.

YOUR TOUGHEST CLASS

Think about the courses you're taking this term. Use the following form to analyze your various professors' lecture styles. Be discrete as you listen and analyze their styles, of course, but after your chart is completed, decide what *you* can do as a listener to make adjustments in your toughest class. To get an idea of how to fill out the chart, look at what Lindsey's entries for her computer science class might have been. Filling out this chart for all your classes may give you some insights about why one particular class is your toughest and develop a set of actions that can help you become more successful.[16]

LECTURE STYLE ANALYSIS WORKSHEET					
COURSES	Example: *Computer Science 101*				
EMPHASIS Content, students, or both?	*Teacher emphasizes content, primarily. He lectures for the full class period with little student interaction.*				
ORGANIZATION Structured or unstructured	*Lectures seem unstructured with notes written all over the board.*				
PACE Fast, slow, or medium?	*Very fast*				
VISUAL AIDS Used? Useful?	*Board hard to see from the back of the room.*				
EXAMPLES Used? Useful?	*Few real examples are given that students can relate to.*				
LANGUAGE Terms defined? Vocabulary understandable?	*What is a logarithm, exactly? No, not defined.*				
DELIVERY Animated via body language?	*Although the teacher is trying to communicate, his delivery style isn't lively and interesting. Instructor doesn't seem to notice when students are lost.*				
QUESTIONS Encouraged?	*He rarely pauses to take questions.*				
Proposed adjustments in my toughest class:	*Make special arrangements to meet with the professor outside his office hours.*				

YOUR TYPE iS ShOwing

Just as instructors have lecturing styles, you and your classmates have listening preferences, based on your personality types. See if these research generalizations fit you.

- *Extraverts* prefer teachers who encourage lively discussion in class, while *introverts* prefer instructors who give clear lectures.
- *Sensors* care about teachers who give structured assignments, while *intuitives* want the freedom to think independently.
- *Thinkers* expect logical presentations from teachers; *feelers* want teachers who build rapport with their students.
- *Judgers* "demand" organization, while *perceivers* prefer to be entertained and inspired.[17]

When you find yourself in a classroom situation in which your listening preferences and your instructor's lecturing style are mismatched, it's up to you to find a pathway to bridge the two. Believe it or not, according to experts, the responsibility for effective communication lies with the listener, not the speaker!

Ask and You Shall Receive

CHALLENGE → REACTION

Challenge: What kinds of questions would you ask during Lindsey Collier's computer science lecture? Are there different kinds of questions to ask during lectures and in-class discussions? If so, what are they?

Reaction: _____

_____

Even if you listen carefully to every word your instructor utters, it's likely you won't understand them all. After all, your instructor is an expert in the subject you're studying, and you're a novice. At some point or other, you'll need clarification or elaboration, and the best way to get it will be to ask. Even though that makes sense, not all students ask questions in class. Why? See if you've excused yourself from asking questions for any of these reasons:

> I don't want to look stupid.

> I must be slow. Everyone else seems to be understanding.

> I'm too shy.

> I'll get the answer later from the textbook.

> I don't think my question is important enough.

> I don't want to derail the lecture. The instructor's on a roll.

> I don't want to draw attention to myself.

> I'm sure the instructor knows what he's talking about. He must be right.

"He who is ashamed of asking is ashamed of learning."

Danish Proverb

If any of these reasons for not asking questions in class applies to you, the good news is … you're in good company. Many students think this way. The bad news, of course, is that your question remains unasked, and therefore, unanswered.

The next time you find yourself in a situation where you don't understand something, consider these points.

1. **Remember that you're not in this alone.** Chances are you're probably not the only person in class who doesn't understand. Not only will you be doing yourself a favor by asking, but you'll also be helping someone else who's too shy to speak up. When it comes to the discipline at hand—whether it's philosophy, psychology, or chemistry—remember that you and your classmates are novices and the instructor is an expert. Asking questions is a natural part of that equation.

2. **Ask academically relevant questions when the time is right.** As opposed to "Why do we need to know this?" or "Why did you make the test so hard?" ask questions to clarify information. Don't ask questions designed to take your instructor off on a tangent (to delay the impending quiz, for example). If you're really interested in something that's not directly related to the material being covered, the best time to raise the question would be during your instructor's office hours. Otherwise, ask questions when the need to know is there.

3. **Save _personally_ relevant questions for later.** If your questions relate only to you (for example, you were ill and missed the last two classes), then don't ask in class. Set up an appointment with your instructor. You can also get answers by researching on your own, visiting or e-mailing your instructor, seeking out a teaching assistant or tutor, or working with a study group.

4. **Build on others' questions.** Listen to the questions other students ask. Use their questions to spark your own. Perhaps another student has a unique way of looking at the issue being discussed that will spark an idea for a follow-up question from you. Remember, to your instructor, good questions indicate _interest_, not _idiocy_.

5. **Consider that questions are a way to s-t-r-e-t-c-h your learning.** Of course, many of the questions you ask in class will be simple questions to clarify information. But be aware of this opportunity: You can ask questions that increasingly move you up the scale toward higher-order thinking. What does that mean? According to learning experts, thinking occurs on a progression of levels, from low (simple) to high (complex). Imaging yourself sitting in Lindsey's computer science course, and think of questions you could ask to move yourself up this progressive ladder:[18]

Knowledge: information and facts	_"Who developed logarithms in 1614?"_
Comprehension: understanding	_"Why were logarithms considered to be such a remarkable invention?"_
Application: using the information	_"How were logarithms used in those days? How are they used today?"_
Analysis: examine critically, separate into parts	_"How, exactly, did logarithms lead to the development of the slide rule?"_

Teachable Moment Have you ever heard "there is no such thing as a bad question" or "if you have the question, someone else may, too"? Structure this in class by using a variation of the Cross and Angelo One-Minute Paper: In the middle or at the end of a class, stop for one minute, and ask your students, "What is the most important thing you've learned?" and "What do you still have a question about?" Or ask, "What is the 'muddiest point' from class today?" Have them write their responses on index cards to turn in to you, so that you can address these items at the beginning of the next class.

Emotional Intelligence (EI) Research No matter how hard you try to encourage students, there will still be some who will not come to see you during office hours. Those with lower assertiveness skills are often shy, overcontrolled, and submissive. New college students may need some help with developing assertiveness. Low assertiveness is often connected with low independence—and developing both may take safe opportunities we create for students to practice. Consider requiring students to come see you in pairs to talk about an assignment. Or consider holding your office hours in the library, student cafeteria, or outside to make students feel more welcome.

Synthesis: combine into a whole

"What other influential historical developments in art or literature or philosophy were going on at the same time? What was the big picture?"

Evaluation: assess the relative value

"What was the most important invention leading to modern day computers?"

Remember, your college education is an expensive investment. You've paid to learn, and asking questions is a natural part of that learning experience. Don't be shy—put that hand in the air!

EXERCISE 6.1 One-Way versus Two-Way Listening

To demonstrate the value of asking questions, try this in-class exercise. A student volunteer, or class "lecturer," will briefly replace the instructor to describe to the rest of the class two different, simple figures she draws herself. Each figure should take up a full piece of paper. The rest of the class must then replicate the drawings as accurately as possible on their own paper as the class "lecturer" describes each figure during two rounds. The point of the exercise is to replicate the two figures the class "lecturer" has drawn as accurately as possible from her description alone.

Round 1: The volunteer should turn her back to the group (to eliminate nonverbal cues), hiding her paper from view, and give the class instructions for drawing Figure 1. No questions from the group are allowed. Note the exact amount of time it takes for the rest of the class to listen to the instructions and complete the drawing.

Round 2: Next, the volunteer should now turn around and face the class, giving instructions for drawing Figure 2. Students may ask questions of the "lecturer" to clarify and elaborate as much as is necessary to get the drawing right. Again, note the exact amount of time taken.

After both rounds of the exercise are done, the "lecturer" should ask class members whether they think their drawings closely resemble the two originals and count the number of students who think they drew Figure 1 correctly and the number of students who think they drew Figure 2 correctly. Then the "lecturer" should show the two original figures as drawn, and count the number of students who actually drew Figure 1 and Figure 2 correctly. Finally, as a group, discuss the two rounds and the value of asking questions in lecture classes. Even though questions take more time, the results are usually much better.

Elapsed Time	# *Think* Correct	# *Actually* Correct
Round 1		
Round 2		

Teachable Moment It's really important to drive home the point to students about asking for clarification. Ask students why they might not ask questions in a class, even if they know it will help. Some students rely on friends, which is not always an accurate way to get information.

How Do You Know What's Important?

So, information streams from your instructor's mouth at mach speed, right? What do you do about it? How do you decide what to write down and what to skip? You listen for key words, watch for nonverbal cues, and after a time, you begin to learn what your instructor, as a subject matter expert, values. At least that's the way it works for most students.

Unfortunately, professors don't speak in *italics*, or **bolded** font, or <u>underlined</u> script. While you can use cues such as these when you're recording notes as you read from a textbook, spoken language doesn't work that way. Try these suggestions:

1. **Listen for an organizing pattern.** Has the instructor been covering the history of modern computers by major chronological periods? Has she been listing contributors to the field by specific inventions? What's her *system*?

2. **Note whether a handout accompanies lecture materials.** If so, chances are that the information is considered to be important. If the instructor interrupts the lecture to give more detailed examples from a handout, he must consider doing so important enough to take up class time. Keep all handouts, and assume they'll be worth reviewing at exam time.

3. **Recognize verbal cues.** If portions of the lecture are highlighted verbally, these portions are probably important. Listen for signal words and phrases such as "There are three reasons..." "On the other hand..." "For example..." "In summary..." If your instructor begins, "In order to understand how the computer age came to be, we must take a look at how it began. Today we'll look at the role of two major inventions and their contributions to the history of modern computers," you've just received a clue about the importance of what's to come.

4. **When in doubt, write it down.** It may be that the instructor's point in including a particular section of material is based on background information you've not yet mastered. If you're not sure whether to write something down, use the motto, "Better safe than sorry." If you don't know a word she's using, leave a blank to show you omitted something, or sound it out as you're writing and come back to it later. Put the lecture in your own words for the most part, but write down formulas, definitions, charts, diagrams, and specific facts verbatim.

5. **Remember that note-taking is paradoxical.** The more you write, the less you're free to listen, take part, and become truly engaged. On the other hand, the more time you spend engaged in focused listening, the less you may be free to write down information. Find a happy medium for yourself for each of your classes, and use methods that work best for you to further enhance your learning.

EXERCISE 6.2 How Well Do You Listen?

Now that you've read about focused listening, see which of the following statements apply to you. Check the box that most applies to what you usually do in the classroom to assess your current level of listening skills. Use this self-assessment to develop a plan for improvement.

Listening Statements:	Always True of Me	Sometimes True of Me	Never True of Me
I stay awake during class.	☐	☐	☐
I maintain eye contact with the speaker.	☐	☐	☐
I don't *pretend* to be interested in the subject.	☐	☐	☐
I understand my instructor's questions.	☐	☐	☐
I try to summarize the information.	☐	☐	☐
I look for organizational patterns within material (*e.g.,* causes and effects, lists of items).	☐	☐	☐
I set a purpose for listening.	☐	☐	☐
I don't daydream during class.	☐	☐	☐
I try to predict what will come next.	☐	☐	☐
I take notes regularly.	☐	☐	☐
I ignore external distractions such as loud noises, late-arriving students, etc.	☐	☐	☐
I try to determine the speaker's purpose.	☐	☐	☐
I recognize that the speaker may be biased about the subject.	☐	☐	☐
I write down questions the instructor poses during class.	☐	☐	☐
I copy down items from the board or screen.	☐	☐	☐
Total check marks for each column:	☐	☐	☐

Add up the check marks in each column to learn the results of your analysis. Pay particular attention to the total in the "Always True of Me" column.

13–15 "Always True of Me": You're probably an excellent listener, both in the classroom and in other situations. Keep up the good work.

10–12 "Always True of Me": You are a good listener, but you need to fine-tune a few of your listening skills.

7–9 "Always True of Me": You need to change some behaviors so that you get more out of your classes.

8 or less "Always True of Me" or 7 or more "Never True of Me": You need to learn better listening skills if you want to achieve academic success in college.[19]

INSIGHT ⊛ ACTION

How well do you listen? Which behaviors will you target in order to become a better listener? Select three of the items in Exercise 6.2 to focus on. Start with any item that you marked as "Never True of Me" and practice doing that behavior in class for several days. Then practice with an additional behavior from that column, and so on. Put the insights you've gained about yourself from reading about listening into action in class.

Taking Lecture Notes: Different Strokes for Different Folks

CHALLENGE → REACTION

Challenge: Does taking notes help students learn? Why or why not?

Reaction: _____

Listening in class is one thing. Taking notes is quite another. You must be a good listener to take good notes, but being a good listener alone doesn't automatically make you a good note-taker. Taking notes in class is actually a very complicated process; there's much more to it than jotting down a grocery list so you won't forget something. Imagine yourself sitting next to Lindsey in her computer science class. What would you write down? How much of that lecture would you remember later if you hadn't taken notes? Note-taking is a crucial and complex skill, and doing well on tests isn't based on luck. It's based on combining preparation and opportunity, in other words, knowing how to take useful notes in class that work for you.

Actually, one reason that note-taking is so important in the learning process is that it uses all four VARK categories: *visual* (you see your professor and the screen, if overheads or PowerPoint slides are being used), *aural* (you listen to the lecture), *read/write* (you write what you see and hear so that you can read it later to review), and *kinesthetic* (the physical act of writing opens up a pathway to the brain). Have you ever thought about it that way before?

According to one study, 99 percent of college students take notes during lectures, and 94 percent of students believe that note-taking is important.[20] These are good signs, but are these students taking notes correctly, as a result of focused listening? If 99 percent of college students are taking notes, why isn't nearly everyone getting straight A's? Here are some reasons:

> Students typically only record less than 40 percent of the lecture's main content ideas in their notes.[21]

> Only 47 percent of students actually review their notes later to see what they've written.

> Only 29 percent edit their notes later by adding, deleting, or reorganizing material.

> A full 12 percent do nothing other than recopy them verbatim.

> Some students never do anything with their notes once they leave class![22]

Chapter Crossover Remind students about the discussion on using campus resources contained in Chapter 3. If their notes from class make no sense when it's time to study, perhaps they should take advantage of a note-taking workshop offered on campus. Searching out the help they need is playing it smart.

Riser/Getty Images

"Luck is what happens when preparation meets opportunity."

Darrell Royal, football coach

> In a recent study, students taking notes on laptops ended up with 5 percent lower GPAs than their counterparts using the old-fashioned paper-and-pencil method.[23] Why? Perhaps these results were due to techies' inability to stay focused on task, or the interference of the clicking sounds, or because the physical act of typing is quicker, giving note-takers less time to process information.

Does note-taking make a difference? Absolutely. During lectures, it serves two fundamental purposes: it helps you understand what you're learning at the time and it helps you preserve information to study later. In other words, both the *process* of note-taking (as you record information) and the *product* (your notes themselves) are important to learning. There is strong evidence that taking notes during a lecture leads to higher achievement than not taking notes, and working with your notes later increases your chances for academic achievement even more. The more notes you take (up to a point—it's possible to get too bogged down in trying to capture every detail), the higher still are your chances of succeeding, and vice versa. Studies show that if you take notes, you have a 50 percent chance of recalling that information at test time versus a 15 percent chance of remembering the same information if you didn't take notes.[24] In fact, for some students it adds up to the difference between passing and failing. Big difference!

But when it comes to note-taking, "different strokes for different folks" is literally true. Many different note-taking systems can work, and different systems work best for different learning styles. However, the more note-taking strategies you're aware of, the more options you'll have to choose from. On top of that, increasingly professors are providing online lecture notes, miniatures of PowerPoint lecture slides, lecture outlines as handouts, audio support, or some other form of note-taking assistance. But are these useful tools created by your instructors your long-awaited secret to success? There's no doubt they may help, but the most helpful tools are those you create yourself.

Whichever strategy you choose to use, an important question to ask is: What constitutes *good* notes? The answer is: Writing down an *accurate, complete, organized* account of what you hear in class (or read in your textbook, which is discussed elsewhere in this book). The last thing you want is a "What in the world did I mean by this?" reaction later. How will you know if your notes are good? Show them to your instructor and get input, or assess your strategy after you see your results on the first exam. Your note-taking skills should steadily improve as you evolve as a student.[25]

Chapter Crossover Note that two students in the same class, listening to the same lecture, can have very different notes. As described in Chapter 2, students who are detail-oriented sensors will have many pages and points. Intuitives will have brief notes, often scrawled on one page. Aural students may be so engrossed in listening to the lecture that they actually write very little and are at a loss when it comes time to study. Pointing out these tendencies based on learning style or personality-based preferences can provide students with self-insight.

The Cornell System

The Cornell format of note-taking, devised by educator Walter Pauk, suggests this. On each page of your notebook, draw a line from top to bottom about one and a half inches from the left edge of your paper. Take notes on the right side of the line. Leave the left side blank to fill in later with key words or questions you'd like answered. After class as you review your notes, put your hand over the right side and use the words or questions you've written on the left side as prompts.[26] By doing this to recall the lecture, you can get a good idea of how much of the information you've understood.

Figure 6.1

"The History of Modern Computers": Cornell System Example

Origins	Beginning of modern computers in 17th century. Descartes, Pascal, Leibnitz, and Napier revolutionized ancient view of world. Lots of progress made in math, and calculations difficult. More sophisticated computing machines needed.
Logarithms	Logarithms developed by the Scottish mathematician John Napier in 1614. Napier (clergyman, philosopher, and mathematician) played important role. Published his great work of logarithms in the book called _Rabdologia_. Enabled people to transform multiplication and division into simple addition and subtraction. Logarithm tables soon used by many people.
Napier's Bones	Napier is often remembered more by another invention of his, nicknamed "Napier's Bones." This was a small instrument constructed of 10 rods, on which were engraved the multiplication tables. They are referred to as bones because the first set was made from ivory and resembled a set of bones. This simple device enabled people to carry out multiplication in a fast manner provided one of the numbers was 1 digit only (i.e., 6 x 6,742).
Slide Rule	Invention of logarithms → development of slide rule. First slide rule in 1650 by two Englishmen, Edmund Gunter and the Reverend William Oughtred.
Astrolabe	Not used until 1850 when a French Artillery officer, Amédée Mannheim, added the movable double-sided cursor like today's. Called "astrolabe" because of astronomical uses. Forerunner of the modern slide rule.

Let's go back to Lindsey, sitting in her computer science course listening to this lecture, and see what her notes might look like in the Cornell format shown in Figure 6.1.

Lecture notes taken using the Cornell system are easy to follow, and they allow you to review information by key concepts at test time. Many students like and use the Cornell system. If you haven't tried it, do so and see what you think.

Mind Maps

An alternative to the Cornell system, or a way to expand on it, is to create mind maps. Mind maps use both sides of your brain: the logical, orderly left side and the visual, creative right side. Or think of the left side of your brain as the heavy-duty, brick-and-mortar content side and the right side as the artistic, designer side. What they're particularly good for is showing the relationship between ideas. Mind maps are a good note-taking method for visual learners, and just drawing one may help you remember the information, particularly if you're a kinesthetic learner. If you'd like to give mind mapping a try, here are some useful suggestions:

1. Use extra wide paper (11 × 17 or legal size, for example). You won't want to write vertically (which is hard to read) if you can help it.

2. Write the main concept of the lecture in the center of the page. Draw related concepts radiating out from the center.

3. Limit your labels to key words so that your mind map is visually clear.

4. Use colors, symbols, and images to make your mind map livelier and more memorable. Notice on the mind map in Figure 6.2 that names are in blue and terms are in red.

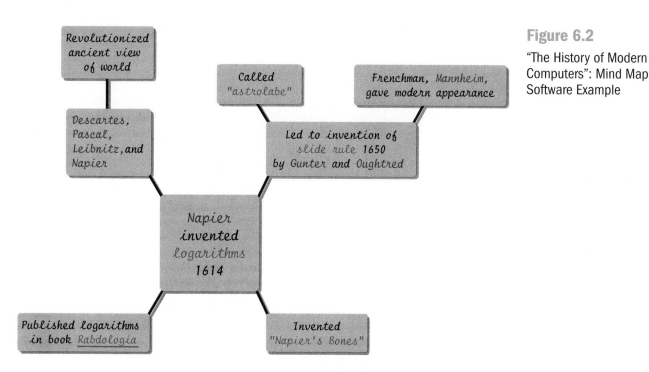

Figure 6.2

"The History of Modern Computers": Mind Map Software Example

5. Use software such as MindManager, MindManuals, MindPlugs, Mindmapper, or MindGenius, which are all powerful brainstorming and organizing tools. As you type, these programs will intuit relationships and help you draw a mind map on screen.

PowerPoint Miniatures

Some instructors provide full-text lecture notes online or copies of their PowerPoint slides (three or six miniatures on a page), either as handouts in class or as e-mail attachments (see Figure 6.3). Tools such as these assure you that you have all the main lecture points on paper, and although it's helpful to have them available as a tool, you still need to take notes on your own to help you process the information you're listening to in class.

Teachable Moment Ask students to share which technique, the Cornell system or mind maps, worked better in these examples and why. Does each method have pros and cons? Suggest to students that one system, used exactly as it has been presented, may not be the best for them. Encourage students to experiment with different parts of the Cornell system and mind mapping, and use parts of both. Maybe mind mapping can be used to summarize, after taking notes using the Cornell system.

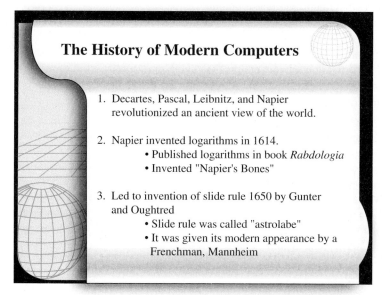

Figure 6.3

"The History of Modern Computers": PowerPoint Miniatures Example

> "I make progress by having people around me who are smarter than I am and listening to them. And I assume that everyone is smarter about something than I am."
>
> Henry J. Kaiser, American industrialist (1882–1967)

Parallel Note-Taking

Because many professors today provide e-support for lectures, either through web notes, hard copies of onscreen slides, lecture outlines, or a full transcript, new note-taking strategies may be particularly useful, if you go about them in the right way. One such strategy is called parallel note-taking.[27] Here's how it works, ideally.

If they're available, print out lecture notes *before* class and bring them with you, preferably in a ring binder. As your instructor lectures, use the back (blank) side of each page to record your own notes as the notes from the ongoing, real-time lecture face you. You can parallel what you're hearing from your instructor with your own on-the-spot, self-recorded notes, using a Cornell format on each blank page. It's the best of both worlds! You're reading, writing, and listening at the same time, fully immersing yourself in immediate and longer-lasting learning. Parallel note-taking can work after the lecture as well, or while you re-listen to a podcast version of the lecture. It reinforces the lecture; it doesn't substitute for going to class. Figure 6.4 illustrates parallel note-taking might look for Lindsey in her computer science class.

Figure 6.4

"The History of Modern Computers": Parallel Note-Taking Example

THE HISTORY OF MODERN COMPUTERS

Instructor's Lecture Notes

The real beginning of modern computers goes back to the 17th century. Having divorced themselves from all past speculations and authorities, such intellectual giants as Descartes, Pascal, Leibnitz, and Napier made a new beginning in philosophy, science, and mathematics, which was to revolutionize the ancient view of the world. In mathematics, particularly, such tremendous progress was made, and the attendant calculations became so laborious, that the need of more sophisticated computing machines became urgent. The development of logarithms by the Scottish mathematician John Napier (1550–1617) in 1614 stimulated the invention of various devices that substituted the addition of logarithms for multiplication. Napier played a key role in the history of computing.

THE HISTORY OF MODERN COMPUTERS

My In-Class Lecture Notes

Origins	*Beginning of modern computers in 17th century. Descartes, Pascal, Leibnitz, and Napier revolutionized ancient view of world. Lots of progress made in math, and calculations difficult. More sophisticated computing machines needed.*

INSIGHT → ACTION

What are your strengths and weaknesses as a note-taker? Are you a good listener? Can you write quickly and legibly? Do you ask questions easily? Use this opportunity to critique yourself and identify some areas for improvement.

Using Lecture Notes

Taking good notes is only part of the equation. To get the most value from your notes, you must actually *use* them. As soon as possible after class, take a few minutes to review your notes. If you find sections that are unclear, take time to fill in the gaps while things are still fresh in your mind. One professor found that students who filled in any missing points right after class were able to increase the amount of lecture points they recorded by as much as 50 percent. And students who worked with another student to reconstruct the lecture immediately after class were able to increase their number of noted lecture points even more![28]

This part of the note-taking process is often overlooked, yet it is one of the most helpful steps for learning and recall. If you don't review your notes within twenty-four hours, there's good evidence that you'll end up re*learning* rather than re*viewing*. Reviewing helps you go beyond just writing to actually making sure you understand what you wrote. These three techniques help you get the best use of your notes: manipulating, paraphrasing, and summarizing.

> **Manipulating** involves working with your notes by typing them out later, for example. Some research indicates that it's not writing down information that's most important. Manipulating information is what counts. Work with your notes. Fill in charts, draw diagrams, create a matrix, underline, highlight, organize. Cut a copy of the professor's lecture notes up into paragraphs, mix them up, and then put the lecture back together. Copy your notes onto flash cards. Manipulating information helps develop your reasoning skills, reduces your stress level, and can produce a more complete set of notes to study later.[29] And one other point worth noting: Research indicates that graphically organized notes may help you learn better than notes that are in a traditional linear form.[30]

> **Paraphrasing** is a process of putting your notes into your own words. Recopy your notes or your professor's prepared lecture notes, translating them into words you understand and examples that are meaningful to you. Paraphrasing is also a good way to self-test or to study with a classmate. If you can't find words of your own, perhaps you don't really understand the original notes. Sometimes students think they understand course material until the test proves otherwise, and then it's too late! Advance practice testing helps. Practice paraphrasing key concepts with a friend to see how well you both understand the material. Or ask yourself, if I had to explain this to someone who missed class, what words would I use?

> **Summarizing** is a process of writing a brief overview of all of your notes from one lecture. Imagine trying to take all your lecture notes from one class session and putting them on an index card. If you can do that, you've just written a summary. Why is it so important to rewrite your notes in this extremely condensed version? Research shows that

students who use the summarizing technique have far greater recall of the material than those who don't. In one study, students were given a multiple-choice quiz immediately following a lecture. One group in the study had written summaries; the other had not. There was no noticeable difference in the students' performance immediately following the lecture; however, when the same quiz was given twelve days later, the students who had used the summarizing technique did much better on the quiz than those who had not.[31]

Some students think that simply going over their notes is the best way to practice. Research shows that simply reading over your notes is a weak form of practice that does not transfer information into long-term memory.[32] You must actually *work with* the material, rearrange or reword it, or condense it to get the most academic bang for your buck. Active strategies always work better than more passive ones.

Manipulating, paraphrasing, and summarizing are more effective learning techniques. Even if your instructor provides you with verbatim notes online or hands you hard copies of her PowerPoint slides, you will still need to work with the information in order to learn it. Think of it this way. If you came to class with a friend you'd "hired" to take notes for you, who do you think would do better on the exam—him or you? Even if someone else hands

Teachable Moment Encourage a mental One-Minute Paper. As students are working with their notes, ask them to ask themselves, "What is the main point?" and "Is there anything else I need to know?"

FOCUS ON CAREERS: KAREN SPRINGEN, *Newsweek* Journalist

Courtesy of Karen Springen

Q1: What do you do in your job? What are your main responsibilities?

As a correspondent, I report stories for every section of the magazine. In the past eighteen years, I've covered serial killers, floods, hurricanes, AIDS, and the 1996 Olympics. In recent years, I've concentrated much of my reporting on health and family issues. It's my job to stay on the alert for good story ideas. It's also my job to make sense of all the conflicting data and to explain the story in a fair, compelling way. I need to quickly reach many people with different viewpoints on a topic. I often juggle many stories at once, reporting on a few pieces for the current week and several others for future weeks. Each of these stories requires talking to dozens of people. People often don't realize how many interviews we do because there isn't enough room in the finished article for quotes from most of the people we interview.

Q2: What are the three most important skills you need for doing your job well?

First—being thorough. You simply need to reach everyone. People buy *Newsweek* because they expect us to be fair and complete, which you can't be if you've only talked to one person. An old journalism professor advised us to "take that extra step and make that extra call." His advice still haunts me because it's true! Second—being fast. You simply can't ask for an "extension" when a story is this week's breaking news. You

can't have a blank page in *Newsweek*! I often stay up most of the night finishing my stories. It often feels like I'm still in college, finishing a term paper. But it's worth it. And third—keeping an open mind and being a good listener. Every day on this job, I interview someone who changes my mind about something. You're a better reporter if you ask "open-ended" questions, which allow people to talk and talk rather than just say "yes" or "no."

Q3: What is the most challenging aspect of your job?

Juggling so many stories and demands at once. If news breaks, we need to quickly change gears and switch to an entirely different story. The unpredictable nature of the world makes a reporter's life unpredictable, too.

Q4: How important are good listening skills in your job?

They're crucial. We simply ask questions. Then we just listen and write—or type—furiously. It's also important to listen closely so that you can ask good follow-up questions. I also always finish my interviews by asking whether there's anything else I should have asked and whether there's anyone else I should talk to.

Q5: How important is the ability to take good notes in your job?

Again, this ability is crucial. I am a crackerjack typist, which helps. If I'm doing a phone interview, I can essentially take a transcript of what someone is saying. It's harder if I'm out in the field with a notebook. I've you a set of notes, the truth is your ability to focus, listen, discuss, ask questions, take notes yourself, and get engaged in class are the things that help you learn best.

Teachable Moment Pose the following questions to your students: Is a journalist (reporter) a good career choice for everyone? Why or why not?

EXERCISE 6.3 Note-Taking 4-M

Practice your note-taking skills by doing this. Immediately after class, or during the lecture if your instructor allows, compare notes with a classmate by following these four steps:[33]

1. <u>M</u>atching—look for content areas where your notes match those of your classmate's.

2. <u>M</u>issing—look for content areas where one of you has missed something important and fill in the gaps.

3. <u>M</u>eaning—talk about what this lecture means. Why was it included in the course? Do you both understand the lecture's main points?

4. <u>M</u>easuring—quiz each other. Measure how much you learned from the lecture. Give each other some sample test questions to see if you understand important concepts.

C CREATE a Career Outlook

JOURNALIST

Have you ever considered a career as a reporter? Here are some facts about this career to consider and some questions about yourself to ponder.

Facts to Consider

Academic preparation required: a college degree in mass communication or journalism, with experience writing for school newspapers or broadcasting stations, summer jobs, or internships

Future workforce demand: Jobs within large metropolitan areas will be highly competitive with growth projected to be slow between now and 2014. Jobs working for smaller outlets, freelancing, or jobs requiring specialized skills in new technologies or specialized knowledge about particular subject matter may be on the rise, however.

Work environment: Reporters (journalists) often have hectic work schedules. They follow the news story, when it happens, where it happens. Travel may be required, and deadlines often dictate their schedules. Working hours vary, depending on their medium: newspaper, television or radio, or magazine.

Most common psychological type preferences: extraverted (or to a lesser extent, introverted), intuitive, feeling, and perceiving. Most common types are ENFP or INFP.[34]

Essential skills: writing, technology, interpretation, accuracy, flexibility, working quickly under pressure, and overall communication skills

Questions to Ponder

1. Do you have (or could you acquire) the skills this career requires?

2. What would you find most satisfying about this type of career?

3. What would you find most challenging about this type of career?

4. Are you interested in a career like this? Why or why not?

For more information, see U.S. Department of Labor, Bureau of Labor Statistics, *Occupational Outlook Handbook, 2006–2007 Edition.*[35]

For more career activities online, go to http://www.academic.cengage.com/collegesuccess/staley to do the Team Career exercises.

made up my own shorthand—a straight line for an "ing," for example. Most reporters do not rely on tape recorders. I've brought them along on occasion, but I still take notes in case the machine breaks or to capture details, such as whether someone is tapping their pencil, what someone looks like or what their office décor is like.

Q6: What advice do you have for college students who are thinking about pursuing a journalism career?

Write for your college newspaper. Get summer internships at newspapers or magazines. You need to have published "clips" to get a journalism job. And college papers are a great place to get them, along with invaluable on-the-job experience. Summer internships are also a wonderful way for you to see how a news operation works, and for the news operation to see how you work, too. Get reporting and writing tips from the pros at the places you land internships. Journalists are usually quite generous and remember what it was like being in your shoes. Many people at *Newsweek* were extremely kind to me when I first started. One busy editor took me to lunch and showed me how she carefully outlined her stories before she wrote them. Check your career counseling office and your college newspaper office for lists of alumni with jobs in journalism. Then you can e-mail those folks and ask them who you ought to contact about internships where they work. You can also ask them whether their publication ever uses "stringers"—that is, freelancers. Just try to get your foot in the door, and once it's there, don't let it out!

EXERCISE 6.4 VARK Activity

Complete the recommended activity for your preferred VARK learning modality. If you are multimodal, select more than one activity. Your instructor may ask you to (a) give an oral report on your results in class, (b) send your results to him or her via e-mail, (c) post them online, or (d) contribute to a class chat.

 Visual: Color-code a set of notes you've taken in one of your current classes to mark important themes (blue highlighter for main points, yellow highlighter for examples, etc.).

 Aural: Download a podcast from one of your most challenging classes this term. Re-listen to the lecture several times while filling in your notes from class, and compare the thoroughness and accuracy of your notes before and after your podcast experience. Alternatively, invite a classmate for coffee or a soft drink immediately after class to talk over the lecture you've just finished listening to. Make sure you actually talk about the lecture!

 Read/Write: Create a survey to hand out in one of your classes, asking students to identify their greatest note-taking challenges in one of their classes this term. Compile all the results and present them in the class for which you're using this textbook.

Kinesthetic: Conduct on-the-spot fake television news interviews on campus with a friend. Choose a spot on campus for "person on the street" interviews. Act like a reporter copying down information. Ask students for the number one reason they have trouble taking notes. Bring your results to class and role play giving the news report on TV.

For more practice online, go to http://www.academic.cengage.com/collegesuccess/staley to take the Challenge Yourself online quizzes.

 NOW WHAT DO YOU THINK?

At the beginning of this chapter, Lindsey Collier, a frustrated student, faced a challenge. Now after reading this chapter, would you respond differently to any of the questions you answered about the "FOCUS Challenge Case"?

REALITY CHECK

On a scale of 1 to 10, answer the following questions now that you've completed this chapter.

1 = not very/not much/very little/low   10 = very/a lot/very much/high

In hindsight, how much did you *really* know about this subject matter before reading the chapter?

1   2   3   4   5   6   7   8   9   10

How much do you think this information might affect your college success?

1   2   3   4   5   6   7   8   9   10

How much do you think this information might affect your career success after college?

1   2   3   4   5   6   7   8   9   10

How long did it actually take you to complete this chapter (both the reading and writing tasks)? _____ Hour(s) _____ Minutes

Take a minute to compare these answers to your answers from the "Readiness Check" at the beginning of this chapter. What gaps exist between the similar questions? How might these gaps between what you thought before starting the chapter and what you now think after completing the chapter affect how you approach the next chapter in this book?

To download mp3 format audio summaries of this chapter, go to http://www.academic.cengage.com/collegesuccess/staley.

7 Developing Your Memory

Chapter Crossover In Chapter 3 students were encouraged to make use of resources. When beginning this chapter, make sure *you* know all of the available resources on campus to help students so that you can provide their contact information. When the right moment comes up, if you can remind students where to get help, they will be more likely to use the service. Students can also look ahead to Chapter 8 to gets some tips on reading and studying.

Teachable Moment As you begin this chapter, get a feel for the number of students in the class who want to improve their ability to memorize information for exams. Most likely you will find just about everybody is interested. Have the class commit to each other that as a group, by the end of the chapter, they all will be better at knowing how to develop their memories. However, make sure you stress that memorization without understanding is short-lived and pointless. It is much easier to master what they comprehend.

YOU'RE ABOUT TO DISCOVER...

> Why memory is a process, not a thing

> How your memory works like a digital camera

> How to improve your memory using twenty different techniques

> How your memory can fail you

> How drugs affect your memory

"The true art of memory is the art of attention."

Samuel Johnson, British poet, essayist, and biographer (1709–1784)

Kevin Baxter

As he got ready for work one morning,

it finally hit him. He took a long, close look at himself in the mirror, and frankly, he didn't like what he saw. Kevin Baxter was a forty-year-old father of three who was dissatisfied with his life. Yes, he earned a decent income as a construction foreman, and yes, his job allowed him to work outdoors. To Kevin, being cooped up in an office from eight to five every day held little appeal. Being outdoors, where you could see the sky, feel the sunshine, and breathe fresh air, was what made him feel alive. The world outside was where he wanted to be, yet at the same time, he knew the world inside his head was withering away. Kevin realized he hadn't really learned much since high school. *I feel brain-dead; that's the best way to describe it*, he frequently thought. *I've run out of options, and I'm stuck.*

Clearly, dropping out of college his first semester twenty-two years ago had been the wrong decision for him. But at the time, he'd convinced himself that he wasn't college material. Besides, college had seemed so expensive, and he desperately wanted to be on his own and begin a life with Carol, his high school sweetheart. Unfortunately, that hadn't worked out well, either. Now he was a single dad whose children lived out of state. He very rarely saw them. Nothing had quite turned out as he had planned.

But in a way, his divorce had jolted him into the midlife crisis he needed to change things, and going back to college to earn a degree in architecture was the right decision for him now. He was sure of it. Working in construction, he frequently saw flaws in the architects' plans, and he'd often come up with better ideas. *This is a chance to start over again*, he thought to himself, *and I'm going to do it right this time.* So at forty, he quit his construction job and enrolled in his hometown college. His first-term courses consisted of Introduction to Architecture, Introduction to Philosophy, Introduction to Rhetoric and Writing, and Introduction to Art Design. For Kevin, college would be an introduction to many new things. Underneath it all, he had to admit that he was proud of himself. *Going back to college at forty takes guts*, he congratulated himself.

But halfway into the term, Kevin's confidence was shaken. Although he'd been a construction foreman on huge projects, after he got his first

midterm exam back, he wondered, *Am I too old to learn new things? I keep up with the reading, come to every class, do my assignments conscientiously, and study until I'm blue in the face! But things just don't seem to stick.* His exam didn't reflect the time he was investing, and frankly, he was embarrassed. Younger students without his years of experience were outperforming him. *That* bothered him. Kevin was getting discouraged about school and his academic capabilities.

Without a doubt, his most challenging class was philosophy. How could anyone memorize schools of philosophical thought and all those names and terms? What did Socrates, Plato, Aristotle, Galileo, and Descartes have in common, and what separated them? Philosophy was unlike anything he had ever tried to learn. He'd read a chapter four, five, or six times, and feel sure he knew it, but when he faced the exam, it seemed as if he'd never studied at all. Of course, it didn't help that while he was trying to focus, his kids would call to talk about their problems or a telephone solicitor would interrupt his reading. He'd even bought a set of colored highlighters after watching a young student next to him, madly yellowing everything in his textbook right before class started, but that didn't seem to help either. He never had problems at work remembering details, like ordering materials and managing multiple construction teams, but trying to distinguish Plato, Aristotle, and Socrates was hard for him, and many of the new terms he was learning didn't really seem to have any relevance to his life. More than once on the exam, he just couldn't come up with a term that was on the tip of his tongue.

Kevin hated to admit it, but doubts were beginning to creep in. Maybe being a construction foreman was as far as he could ever go in life, and he should have left well enough alone. Maybe college was the last place he should be. Maybe he should have been satisfied with what he'd already achieved, instead of putting everything on the line for more.

Emotional Intelligence (EI) Research Kevin is probably struggling with a number of issues that are related to his emotional intelligence. He is second-guessing many of his choices, he does not seem to be confident, his ability to problem-solve seems to be limited. Combining all these factors, he may be at risk for either dropping out or failing some classes.

Sensitive Situation Just as you did in other chapters, take advantage of this case study to discuss student behaviors and attitudes in a safe situation. Do students like Kevin feel insecure when they look around the classroom and see students that are twenty years younger than they are without the same kinds of responsibilities?

© Roy McMahon/CORBIS

WHAT DO **YOU** THINK?

Now that you've read about Kevin Baxter, answer the following questions. You may not know all the answers yet, but you'll find out what you know and what you stand to gain by reading this chapter.

1. Why is Kevin experiencing problems remembering course content in his philosophy class? List five reasons you identify from the case study.

2. Is Kevin too old to learn? Why or why not?

3. Identify three memory techniques that Kevin should use to help him memorize all the names and terms he needs to know.

4. If you were asked to explain how the memory process works and the scientific explanation behind his problems, what would you say?

> **"Vitality shows in not only the ability to persist, but in the ability to start over."**
>
> **F. Scott Fitzgerald, American author (1896–1940)**

Before beginning to read this chapter, take two minutes to answer the following questions on a scale of 1 to 10. Your answers will help you assess how ready you are to focus.

1 = not very/not much/very little/low   10 = very/a lot/very much/high

Based on reading the "You're about to discover..." list and skimming this chapter, how much do you think you probably already know about the subject matter?

1   2   3   4   5   6   7   8   9   10

How much do you think this information might affect your college success?

1   2   3   4   5   6   7   8   9   10

How much do you think this information might affect your career success after college?

1   2   3   4   5   6   7   8   9   10

In general, how motivated are you to learn the material in this chapter?

1   2   3   4   5   6   7   8   9   10

This book describes four key factors related to intrinsic, or internal, motivation: curiosity, control, career outlook, and challenge. The next four questions relate to these **C-Factors:**

How *curious* are you about the content you expect to read in this chapter?

1   2   3   4   5   6   7   8   9   10

How much *control* do you expect to have over mastering the material in this chapter?

1   2   3   4   5   6   7   8   9   10

How much do you think this chapter might help you develop your *career outlook*?

1   2   3   4   5   6   7   8   9   10

How *challenging* do you think the material in this chapter will be for you?

1   2   3   4   5   6   7   8   9   10

Before beginning any task—including studying—it's important to check in with yourself to ensure that you're physically, intellectually, and emotionally ready to focus. How ready are you, physically, to focus on this chapter? (Are you rested, feeling well, and so on?)

1   2   3   4   5   6   7   8   9   10

How ready are you, intellectually, to focus on this chapter? (Are you thinking clearly, focused on this course, interested in this subject?)

1   2   3   4   5   6   7   8   9   10

How ready are you, emotionally, to focus on this chapter? (Are you calm, confident, composed?)

1   2   3   4   5   6   7   8   9   10

If your answer to any of the last three questions is below a 5 on the scale, you may need to address the issue you're facing prior to beginning this chapter. For example, if you're hungry, get a quick bite to eat. If you're feeling scattered, take a few moments to settle down and focus.

Finally, how long do you think it will take you to complete this chapter?
_____ Hour(s) _____ Minutes

Activity Option Students should take a few minutes to share their responses to "What Do You Think" questions. Ask students to work in small groups and assign one or two questions to each group, then have them report to the class. If you have older, nontraditional students in the class, you might ask them to lead the groups.

Teachable Moment This is a great opportunity for community building. It is really fun to see what students remember and why. How old were they? See if you can get a few volunteers to recite something they remember from childhood memorization tasks. Why do they remember that particular item? Was the memory associated with a special moment or person?

"Memories Are Made of This"

CHALLENGE ➔ REACTION

Challenge: List something you memorized as a child: perhaps a poem, a song, or lines from a school play. Why do you remember this passage verbatim after all these years?

Reaction: _____

Your grandparents used to dance to a popular song called "Memories Are Made of This." Of what, exactly? What are your earliest memories and how old were you? Most of us have "childhood amnesia," as Sigmund Freud called it, until we're three and a half or so. You may remember playing in the sand on the beach during a family vacation, dressing up to attend your cousin's wedding, or riding on an airplane for the first time. Before that age, you may not remember things because you weren't paying attention, because you didn't have the language skills to encode the memories, or because you hadn't yet formed the web of interconnections in your brain that you have now.[1]

Whenever it was that those first memories became available to you, and no matter what they are, think about how chock full your memory is now with both significant and seemingly insignificant memories, going all the way back to that poem your teacher asked you to memorize in fourth grade, the one you still remember ten or more years later, oddly enough. Through the years, your memories will continue to accumulate, and interestingly, you'll never run out of room! It's a good thing, too. Imagine what life without memory would be like. We'd have the same conversations with the same people over and over again, and we'd need to relearn how to drive each time we got behind the wheel of a car. Fortunately, our memories do an amazing job of streamlining life for us.

But why is it that some old, seemingly useless entries are still there, like the poem or song you wrote down in the "Challenge → Reaction" activity, but new ones you're trying to "enter" for an exam don't seem to stick? Memory is a hot topic among scientists today, and research clusters around many of our attributes as human beings, including the following.

Culture. Our earliest memories—what they are and how old we were at the time—seem to be based partly on our culture. Children who are raised in cultures like ours that emphasize individuals' personal history and grow up with parents who talk with their children about such things, remember autobiographical events in their lives, and at an earlier age. On the other hand, Asian cultures value interdependence rather than individualism, and life events are not discussed to the extent they are in our culture. An American child's earliest memories tend to begin at around forty-two months; an Asian child's at fifty-seven months. Earliest memory age differences between cultures vary by up to two years, researchers say. In the U.S. culture, our personal histories are what define us. Our memories make us who we are, and we communicate these detailed stories to each other. The truth is, we remember what we must to get along in the culture we live in.[2]

Gender. Girls recall specific childhood experiences in more detail and at greater length than boys do.[3] They also remember more interpersonal experiences, using more references to emotion and relationships. Women are thought to have better recall of emotional childhood memories than men because they do more processing of those memories. Parents talk more to their daughters than they do their sons about interpersonal events, like how a movie might affect individual members of the family. More elaborate discussions produce more elaborate memories.[4]

Age. Scientists are working to understand the impact of aging on the brain. Do the young have better memories than the old? What conditions impair memory in both young children and older people? What preventive measures or remedies can be found? The memories of young children with ADHD, for example, are the focus of much scientific inquiry. Recent studies have investigated alternatives to medications for children with ADHD, such as computer games, and have found that training tasks in such games can be effective. First reports are that *RoboMemo*, software developed by a Swedish biotech firm, helps children with ADHD refine the ways their memories work.[5] At the other end of the age scale, namely the elderly, scientists are investigating the effects of Alzheimer's disease on memory. New studies suggest that the latest in brain-scanning technology may help monitor the effects of the disease and predict who may get it.[6]

"**Memory is the mother of all wisdom.**"

Aeschylus, ancient Greek dramatist and playwright, known as the founder of Greek tragedy (525–456 B.C.)

Sensitive Situation It is possible and even likely that you will have students from a variety of different cultures in your class. Keep in mind that while sharing information about different cultures is a very enriching experience, there may be students in the class who are hesitant to communicate for any number of reasons. Think about opening up the conversation by saying something like "It seems to me that we have a number of different cultures represented in this class. It would be great to learn about some cultural variations connected to memories. Would anyone like to contribute?" Don't put any one student on the spot.

Sensitive Situation In all likelihood you will have a student in one of your classes with ADHD or someone with a parent or grandparent with Alzheimer's. Treat this subject matter-of-factly, with a positive spin that includes a comment about how much research is being done in these areas with hopes for future positive approaches to managing both.

Memory: The *Long* and *Short* of It

CHALLENGE → REACTION

Challenge: How good is your memory? Fill out Parts A and B to begin applying the information in this chapter to your own memory.

Reaction: Subjective Memory Test

How would you rate your memory overall?

	Excellent					Poor
1	2	3	4	5	6	7

A. How often do the following *general* memory tasks present a problem for you?

	Never		Sometimes			Always	
1. Names	1	2	3	4	5	6	7
2. Where I've put things	1	2	3	4	5	6	7
3. Phone numbers I've just checked	1	2	3	4	5	6	7
4. Words	1	2	3	4	5	6	7
5. Knowing if I've already told someone something	1	2	3	4	5	6	7
6. Forgetting things people tell me	1	2	3	4	5	6	7
7. Faces	1	2	3	4	5	6	7
8. Directions	1	2	3	4	5	6	7
9. Forgetting what I started to do	1	2	3	4	5	6	7
10. Forgetting what I was saying	1	2	3	4	5	6	7
11. Remembering what I've done (lock the door, etc.)	1	2	3	4	5	6	7

B. How often do the following *academic* memory tasks present a problem for you?

	Never		Sometimes			Always	
12. What I've just been reading	1	2	3	4	5	6	7
13. What I read an hour ago	1	2	3	4	5	6	7
14. What I read last week	1	2	3	4	5	6	7
15. Assignment/Exam due dates	1	2	3	4	5	6	7
16. Appointments with instructors	1	2	3	4	5	6	7
17. Assignment details	1	2	3	4	5	6	7
18. Factual information for exams	1	2	3	4	5	6	7
19. Theoretical information for exams	1	2	3	4	5	6	7
20. Information from readings for exams	1	2	3	4	5	6	7
21. Information from in-class lectures for exams	1	2	3	4	5	6	7
22. Including everything I should study for exams	1	2	3	4	5	6	7

Activity Option This is a wonderful opportunity to get students in groups to disclose their different responses to Part A and Part B. In small groups, have them determine two to three reasons why they did better on one part (most likely it will be Part A). Have students stay in groups to look at Part B and decide which top three things they have trouble with. You can teach this chapter with the class working in teams to make sure that all students learn effective strategies for developing their memories.

These informal assessments may help you understand your own perceptions of how well your memory works. The lower your score on each portion, the better you perceive your memory to be. Do your scores for Part A and Part B differ? The general tasks in Part A are presented in the order of concern reported by older adults cited in one study (with the top items perceived as most problematic).[7] Are your priorities similar? Did your numbers drop as you went down the list?

In one recent study in which college students were asked which aspects of memory they most wanted to improve among general and academic tasks, the top three items were improving schoolwork or study skills, remembering what was read, and remembering specific facts and details.[8] Understandably, the academic aspects of memory were those most personally valued. Is that true for you, too? Are the items in Part B generally higher priorities for you now as a college student?

Most of us may not even realize just how important memory is. We talk about our memories as if they were something we own. We say we have good memories or bad memories, just like we have a crooked smile or nice one. But no one would ever say, "Hey, that's one nice-looking memory you've got there!" in the same way they'd say, "Wow, you have a really nice smile!" No brain surgeon could open up your head and evaluate your memory. Memory isn't a thing; it's a process. You can't see it or touch it or hold it. Even one specific memory has many different features: You can remember something by what you saw, smelled, heard, or felt. And even within one of these categories, individuals may differ in what they recall. You may be able to hum the movie's theme song, but your friend may remember conversations between the main characters almost verbatim.

Don't believe it when someone claims to have a one-size-fits-all, magic formula to help you unlock the secrets of your memory. It isn't that easy. Still, there are techniques which, when applied to the way you read your assignments or study for exams, can help you do your best, academically. We can only begin to grasp the rich complexities of memory by understanding it as a process. This chapter will examine how your memory works and suggest how you can best use it as a learning tool. However, it's important to recognize first that mastering memory depends on the answers to several questions like these:[9]

1. **Who is learning?** A calculus professor and a beginning calculus student would approach memorizing the main points of an article on math differently.

2. **What needs to be learned?** How you learn your lines for a play would differ from how you learn the Dutch masters' paintings for your art appreciation test.

3. **How will learning be tested?** Learning information to *recall* uses different memory techniques than learning information to *recognize*. Recognition requires that you select from several alternatives; recall requires that you come up with memorized information on your own.

4. **How long must the information be remembered?** Learning your multiplication tables as a child is something that must remain with you throughout your life. You use it on a daily basis to do routine things like figure how much it will cost you to fill up your gas tank. On the other hand, learning the date of the Battle of Hastings isn't quite as crucial to remember for the long haul.

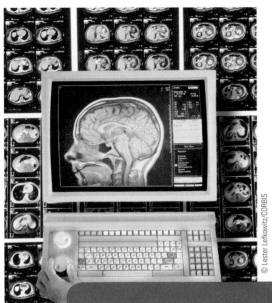

© Lester Lefkowitz/CORBIS

"The existence of forgetting has never been proved: We only know that some things don't come to mind when we want them."

Friedrich Nietzsche, German philosopher (1844–1900)

Teachable Moment This is an opportunity to remind students that mastering memory depends not only on the who, what, how, and how long but also on how they best learn. Ask students how they think their learning styles impact the way they can best memorize something.

EXERCISE 7.1 Test Your Memory

For a more objective assessment of your memory, try this test. Study the following list of words for up to one minute. Then cover them with your hand and see how many you can remember and list them in the right-hand column.

theory   _____

rehearsal   _____

student   _____

bone   _____

frostbite   _____

camera   _____

rose   _____

calculus   _____

lecture   _____

How many words were you able to remember? Which words did you forget? Unfamiliar words? Words that had no relevance to your life? What memory techniques did you use to help you remember?

INSIGHT ⭢ ACTION

1. From the list of items presented in Part B of the previous "Challenge → Reaction" activity, which ones do you find most challenging?

2. Why are these memory issues problematic for you? Do you know?

3. What, specifically, can you do to improve your memory in these areas?

The Three R's of Remembering: Record, Retain, Retrieve

CHALLENGE ⭢ REACTION

Challenge: Think of three ways in which using your memory is like taking pictures with a digital camera.

Reaction: 1. _____

                2. _____

                3. _____

Photodisc/Getty Images

> **"I have a photographic memory but once in a while I forget to take off the lens cap."**
>
> **Milton Berle, comedian (1908–2002)**

Improving your memory is easier if you understand how it works. Memory consists of three parts: your *sensory memory*, your *working memory* (called short-term memory by some psychologists), and your *long-term memory*. These three parts of the memorization process are connected to these three memory tasks: *recording*, *retaining*, and *retrieving* memories—the "Three R's of Remembering."[10]

Let's take a closer look at how all these things figure into your success in college. To do so, we'll compare the three R's of remembering to the process involved when taking pictures with a digital camera: record, retain, retrieve.

Your Sensory Memory: Focus

Consolidating memories in your brain is similar to taking pictures with a digital camera. Before we discuss the first R of remembering—namely, *Record*—we have to talk first about focus. Before you even push the button to snap a picture, you have to focus on your subject. Most digital cameras today focus on things automatically, and unlike older cameras, you don't have to turn the focus knob until the image is clear. But you do need to decide what to focus *on*. What do you want to take a picture of? Where will you point the camera? When it comes to your college classes and the role your memory plays in your success, remember that focus doesn't come automatically. It requires consciously deciding where to direct your attention.

Imagine this: You're on your way to class. You walk through a student demonstration and get brushed by members of the crowd. Then you cross a busy intersection a little too slowly and get honked at by a speeding car. Finally, you see a billboard you've never noticed before: "I love you, Whitney. Will you marry me? Carl." *How romantic*, you think to yourself.

You're engulfed in stimuli as you walk, but three major sensations just passed through your *sensory memory* in a few seconds, in this case, your *haptic* memory (touch, the crowd), your *echoic* memory (sounds, the car horn), and your *iconic* memory (sight, the billboard), all parts of your sensory memory. You have a different channel for each of these three senses. Most experts believe that your sensory memory retains an exact copy of what you've seen or heard—pure and unanalyzed—for less than a second.[11] Some of these images, or icons, will be transferred to your working memory, which we'll discuss next. This transfer depends on attention and focus.

To help you with attention management, consider the following suggestions:

1. **Slow down; you move too fast.** Imagine trying to take a photo of something on the way to class if you were running. Everything would be a blur; trying to take a picture would be futile. The busyness of everyday life is sometimes overwhelming. It's no wonder with so much going on—school, family, friends, romantic partners, work—that your attention gets splintered in many different directions. Focus requires your full attention aimed at one thing at a time. Turn down the music, turn off the television, shut down the six windows open on your browser, and focus. That's a challenge.

2. **Deal with it.** If something is driving you to distraction, maybe you need to take care of it first so that you *can* focus. Getting stuck won't help, but sometimes dealing with an urgent priority is an important first step toward managing your attention.

3. **Notice where you go.** Wandering thoughts are normal. In one study, college students were asked to identify what they were thinking about eight random times each day for one week. On average, they weren't thinking about what they were doing 30 percent of the time. Some students were "elsewhere" 80 to 90 percent of the time.[12] When *your* attention wanders off, where does

Emotional Intelligence Research A student's ability to manage stress is positively correlated with success in college. When individuals are stressed they can become impulsive and unable to focus on how to solve problems step-by-step. Remind students that these EI skills are often connected and impact each other.

it go? Is it often the same place? Knowing your mental tendencies is part of understanding what makes you tick. Then you can recognize the pattern when you notice it and work on changing it.

4. **Watch for signals.** As a college student, you'll probably take at least forty different courses from all sectors of your college and be exposed to literally thousands of facts. Not even a memory expert could master them all at once. You must be selective about focus. Interestingly, journalist David Shenk wrote in his book *Data Smog*, "Education is actually the limiting of information."[13] In a funny way, that's true, isn't it? Of all the things you could learn about a subject, you're most likely to learn the material presented by your instructor and through your course readings. Your textbooks will guide you as you read by using bold fonts, different colors, charts, tables, and headings. Think of them as animated .jpegs on the page, calling out, "Hey, look at me!" Then zoom in on those things. In class, watch the instructor's body language; listen to her inflection; notice what gets written on the board or which PowerPoint slides stay on the screen longer than others. Keep those handouts handy. Plenty of subtle signals exist, but you have to pay attention to them.

FOCUS ON CAREERS: DELANNA STUDI, Actress

Courtesy of DeLanna Studi

Q1: Tell us about your background. How did you decide on acting as a career, and what factors went into your decision?
I'm from a very small community in Oklahoma. Growing up, one of the ways we entertained ourselves was by telling stories. I am blessed with amazing parents who always told my sister and me that we could be and do anything we wanted. I started seriously thinking about acting as a career when I was a freshman in college. I remember sitting down with my parents and asking for their advice about my future. My father told me to "do what you can live with." He wanted me to look back on life and my decision without wondering "what if." My parents sent me to L.A. to get my start. They gave me five days to find an apartment and one month to complete five goals. If I succeeded, they said I could stay and pursue acting. That was eight years ago.

Q2: Memory is a key component of acting. The most common question actors report getting is, "How do you learn all those lines?" The amount of material you must learn for a film or play must be overwhelming! What's the first thing you do when you look at a new script?
I look at the script's title. It's amazing how many clues are in the title! Then I read it through once and try to visualize it. I try not to guess what character I might be playing or pass any judgment on any of the characters. I usually read a script three times in a row, the last time aloud.

Q3: Most people assume that actors learn their lines by rote, repeating them over and over. Is that what you do?
First, I learn the story. If I know the story I'm telling, the lines and dialogue come to me. True, the language may not be what I use in my daily life, but I focus on that later. I find that if I can tell the story in my own words, I can act it. Then I start memorizing the lines, and yes, sometimes it is by rote. There is a reason why the writer has chosen the words that are on the page. My job is to make those words mine.

Q4: Do you think of yourself as having a good memory? Do you simply learn your lines gradually, as if by magic, or do you work at it?
Generally, I have a horrible memory. For some reason, however—maybe just plain stubbornness—I don't have a lot of trouble memorizing lines. I'm a visual person, and I create an image for every word in every scene. I find that if I fully understand the story, it is like magic.

Q5: What special techniques do you use to learn a complicated script? Do you rehearse aloud? Do you practice with someone else playing the other part? Do you practice in front of a mirror to monitor your movements and expressions, too? Do you move through the stage directions to help you learn?
I do all of the above. I find that rehearsing aloud makes me hear the words. Reading to myself, I often unintentionally skip words or paraphrase; reading aloud makes me hit every word. It's amazing what you realize about the script as you hear it. When I rehearse with another actor, it's very liberating. All this time, I have been imagining what the other person is saying and in what tone. Hearing another living person say the words, I find myself listening carefully and hearing subtext. I also practice in front of my mirror because films deal with close-ups and theatre expects you to be theatrical. After I have rehearsed on set or stage, I practice the stage directions that are given to me. It is very important that I hit my mark, and it is even more important that the audience doesn't know that there is a mark!

Q6: How do you listen to your co-actors while you're acting, react to their lines, and still remember yours—all at the same time?
Acting is always about the other actor. If I remember that, the stage isn't frightening. If I know the story, I can react. If I have rehearsed, the words won't fail me.

Q7: In a play you have many more lines to remember, but you say the same lines every night. In a film, you have fewer lines to remember for the scene, but you only have a few opportunities to get it right, and many fewer rehearsals, if any. How do these differences affect how you approach learning a part?
I prepare for both in the same way, only with film, I have a shorter time frame within which to memorize. Usually with film, there aren't

5. **Get help if you need to.** If you have been diagnosed with ADHD, your brain is wired somewhat differently, affecting your memory and your ability to concentrate.[14] If you've not been diagnosed with a learning disability, but your attention appears to be extremely challenging to harness and you're not sure why, seek help from a counselor or learning specialist on campus. Challenges to your memory can be addressed by learning particular strategies.

Chapter Crossover There may be some wellness issues that underpin one's ability to focus. Sometimes simple stress with too much to do can be the culprit, but students can also be struggling with real depression. Chapter 13 addresses wellness and students may want to fast-forward and skim the chapter.

Your Working Memory: Record

After you've focused your camera on your subject, you're ready to take a picture, right? But with a digital camera, you don't just click and walk away. You actually click and then review the picture on the small viewing screen to decide whether you want to save it or delete it.

Similarly, *recording* sensory impressions involves an evaluation process that takes place in your short-term or *working memory*. Your working memory is like a review screen, where you review recently acquired sensory impressions, enhancing them with related information that you retrieve from your long-term

Teachable Moment DeLanna Studi says that acting is more about hard work than talent. Pose the following questions to your students: Is acting a good career choice for everyone? Why or why not?

as many monologues, so I focus on the story behind the dialogue. In most cases, film is shot out of sequence, so the trick is knowing where I just came from and the given circumstances. I do memorize every word, but I am not married to them because it isn't unusual in film to receive rewrites the morning of the shoot or during the shoot. Then I start memorizing and personalizing the text. I always do a fast-paced run-through before any performance though, just to test my memory.

Q8: How do you go from memory to meaning? How do you make sure you mean what you're saying? How do actors make each performance unique so that their lines don't sound memorized and flat?
I understand the story, I try to make the language my own, and I lay the foundation for meaning while I am memorizing. I think the key element is visualizing the play or movie during the first read. This sets the first layer of meaning; however, the images I used in the first read-through may not be the ones in my head for the final performance. I will have discovered in rehearsal if those images (personalizations) work, and I will have either scrapped them or enhanced them. The key to making each performance unique is listening. It reminds me of playing catch. I know my partner is going to throw the ball to me, I just don't know what size ball or how he will throw it. If I pay attention, I can catch whatever he throws.

Q9: What advice do you have for first-year college students about acting as a career?
Acting is 85 percent work and 15 percent talent. I believe if you commit fully and practice, you will become a better actor. My advice is hard work and patience. There are rarely overnight successes. You have to love the craft because it's not as glamorous as the media might lead you to believe! If this is what you really want to do as a career, it is a tough journey, but well worth the adventure.

C CREATE a Career Outlook

ACTOR
Have you ever considered a career as an actor? Here are some facts about this career to consider and some questions about yourself to ponder.

Facts to Consider

Academic preparation required: highly variable; actors come from many different academic backgrounds, including degrees in theatre and performing arts

Future workforce demand: Competition is fierce for prize roles, and actors may find themselves unemployed at times, supplementing their income in other ways.

Work environment: Actors work under pressure, typically for relatively short periods of time, ranging from one day to several months. They work long, irregular hours on television or movie sets or on the stage live, so they must be devoted to their craft and enjoy entertaining others.

Most common psychological type preferences: extraverted, intuitive, feeling, perceiving (or to a lesser extent, judging)[15]

Essential skills: creativity, memory, ability to follow direction, stress management; singing or dancing skills may also be helpful

Questions to Ponder

1. Do you have (or could you acquire) the skills this career requires?
2. What would you find most satisfying about this type of career?
3. What would you find most challenging about this type of career?
4. Are you interested in a career like this? Why or why not?

For more information, see U.S. Department of Labor, Bureau of Labor Statistics, *Occupational Outlook Handbook, 2006–2007 Edition.*[16]

For more career activities online, go to http://www.academic.cengage.com/collegesuccess/staley to do the Team Career exercises.

memory. In fact, your working memory is often involved in the focus process. You give selected, focused attention to some of what you see and hear because it has personal meaning for you or relates to something in your past experience. In our example of you walking to class, which of these three specific sensations you just experienced are you likely to remember: the crowd, the car, or the billboard? To stay true to the analogy, which one would you take a picture of? It depends, right? You may remember the billboard because you plan to show it to someone else later, or the demonstration because you disagree with its cause, or the car horn because it scared you.

The problem with working memory is that the length of time it can hold information is limited. You probably don't remember what you ate for dinner last Monday, do you? You'd have to reconstruct the memory based on other clues. Where was I? What was I doing? Who was I with?

The other problem with working memory is that it has limited capacity. It fills up quickly and then dumps what it doesn't need. If that weren't the case, our working memories would be cluttered with a chaotic array of useless information. Picture someone in the act of juggling with a number of balls in the air at once. Working memory helps us process the world as we encounter it, and it guides our actions, second by second. It's what you're using when you speak or listen (imagine if you forgot the beginning of a sentence by the time you got to the end), work math problems in your head, do a puzzle, follow directions, and read a book, for example.[17] If you look up a number in the campus directory, you can usually remember it long enough to walk over to the phone, right? A few minutes after you've dialed, however, the number is gone. Current estimates are that you can keep something in working memory for one to two minutes, giving your brain a chance to do a quick review, selecting what to save and what to delete.[18] Just how much information can your working memory hold? Look at these letters in the first example, and then close your eyes and try to repeat them back in order.

SAJANISMOELIHHEGNR

Can't do it? This task is virtually impossible because the string contains eighteen letters. Researchers believe that working memory can recall only seven pieces of information, plus or minus two.[19] (There's a reason why telephone numbers are prechunked for us.) Chunking these eighteen letters into five units helps considerably. Now look at the letters again in this second example and try to recall all eighteen.

SAJA NISM OELI HHEG NR

If we rearrange the letters into recognizable units as in the third example, it becomes even easier, right?

AN IS MAJOR ENGLISH HE

And if the words are rearranged to make perfect sense as in example four, the task becomes simple.

HE IS AN ENGLISH MAJOR

The principle of chunking is also used to move information from your working memory to your long-term memory bank, and it's used in memorization techniques that we will describe later in this chapter.

Activity Option For the next class, have students bring in a list of terms they need to memorize for another class. Often first-year students are taking biology or history, or even math formulas can work for this exercise. Have students present their challenges and, in small groups or as a whole class, brainstorm ways to chunk or categorize the information.

Your Long-Term Memory: Retain and Retrieve

Let's go back to our camera analogy. Once your camera's memory card gets full, you probably transfer the photos to your computer, or you print them out and put them in photo albums or picture frames. However, before you do that, you generally review the photos, decide how to arrange them, where to put them, whether to print them, and so forth. You may use the photos in different ways, printing some and putting them into photo albums, labeling and organizing them—maybe recreating an event through photos and captions. Or you may decide to put them into frames so you can see them all the time. In other words, you make the photos memorable by putting them into some kind of order or context.

Just as you must transfer photos from your camera's memory stick to a more permanent location with a larger capacity for storage, you must transfer information from short-term, or working, memory to long-term memory. You *retain* the information by transferring it, and this transfer is facilitated by reviewing and using it in a way that makes it memorable. It is this review process that we use when we study for a test. You transfer information to long-term memory by putting the information into a context that has meaning for you, linking new information to old information, creating stories or particular memory techniques, or organizing material so that it makes sense. You can link information, and you can also frame it by putting a mental border around it, just as you put pictures into frames. Sometimes you need to frame information to keep it distinct and separate from other information.

Your long-term memory is the computer in which you store new knowledge until you need to use it. However, while the memories that reside in long-term memory aren't easily disturbed, they can be challenging to retrieve.[20] Ideally, you'd like your memories to be readily available when you wish to retrieve them, just like the pictures or digital images that you have transferred to your

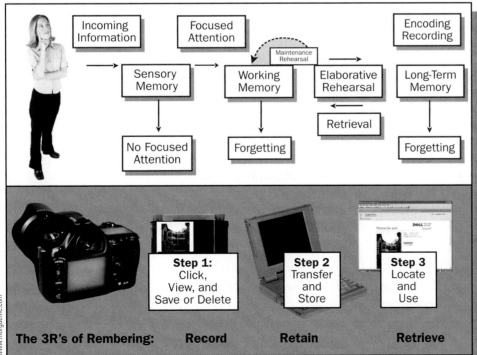

Figure 7.1

Your Memory as a Digital Camera

computer or put in a photo album. You can click on them to view them again, arrange them into a slideshow and publish them on the web, send them to your friends as e-mail attachments, or just review them yourself to recapture the earlier experience. If you just dump your photos onto your hard drive, or print them out and then put them into a box, with no organization or labeling system, how easy will it be to find a specific photo? Difficult, right? Retrieving information from your long-term memory can be equally challenging if you haven't organized your information, or created mental labels that will trigger data retrieval. Good recall often depends upon good storage techniques. The remainder of this chapter will be about steps 2 and 3, specifically how to *retain* information by transferring it from working memory into long-term memory and how to *retrieve* information when you need to.

Twenty Ways to Master Your Memory

CHALLENGE ⊖ REACTION

Challenge: If you were actually tasked with learning the random list of words presented in Exercise 7.1 to test your memory, how would you proceed? Identify the precise method you believe would work best for you.

Reaction: _____

Ladies and gentlemen! It's the final round of the International World Memory Championship. In this corner, representing the United Kingdom.... Wait—World Memory Championship? Is there such a thing? Yes, there is!

If you're thinking about entering, check over these details so you can start practicing your mental acrobatics now. The annual occasion consists of ten events over two days. Contestants memorize multiple packs of cards in an hour, random digits, a number spoken at a rate of two digits per second, a list of words, a poem, and names and faces in fifteen-minute segments, and they try to recall as much as they can from a fifteen-minute video. The World Memory Championship (also known as the Memoriad) was started in 1991 by memory expert Tony Buzan and British Chess Grand Master Raymond Keene. Here are some of their champion "mentathletes'" memorization records:

> 236 random numbers in 30 minutes

> the number pi to 20,013 places

> 2,000 foreign words in 18 hours

Still interested? Impossible, you say! How do they do it? They use strategies like the ones you're about to read in this chapter. They are physically fit so that oxygen flows to their brains and enhances their performance, and they're confident and positive. They practice their methods, finely honing them until they've reached the heights of mental discipline. And what's interesting is that they claim that with the right tools and strong determination, anyone can do it![21]

If that level of competition isn't quite what you had in mind, what can you do to sharpen your memory for the reading and test-taking you'll do in college? Try the following twenty techniques, grouped into five major categories (to help you remember them). These techniques are specifically designed to help you with the *retain* and *retrieve* parts of the memory process. As you consider each one, think about what you know about your own learning style. Particular strategies may work best for you based on your VARK or MBTI preferences.

Make It Stick

How do you actually move material from your working memory to your long-term memory? What will work best for you? Some techniques are more effective than others, but the following suggestions are a good start.[22]

Rehearse. Although it's not the most powerful memorization strategy available to you, especially by itself, repeating information helps. Nothing gets stored in your memory for long without practice. How did you learn those multiplication tables or that poem in fourth grade? Probably not by just reading it over once or twice.

Memory experts distinguish between *maintenance* (or shallow) rehearsal and *elaborative* rehearsal. Maintenance rehearsal helps you keep something in working memory for a short time. Repeating a phone number twenty times while you look for your cell phone might help you keep it there for several minutes, but will you remember it tomorrow when you need to call again? Probably not. Shallow rehearsal didn't work for Kevin in the "FOCUS Challenge Case," who just kept rereading course material. But when you repeat things, particularly over a long period of time, lasting neural connections are formed in your brain. You "hardwire" the learning. For many of us, repeating information out loud helps, too. Can you imagine an actor learning his lines by reading them over silently?

Elaborative rehearsal—actually working with the information—helps transfer information to long-term memory more effectively. Most of the techniques described in this chapter will focus on elaborative rehearsal techniques. Typically, we remember the elaborate over the simple.

photolibrary.com pty. ltd./Index Open

Figure 7.2

Which of these two pictures are you more likely to remember—the simple or the elaborate?

Overlearning helps you truly hardwire information, so that you can practically work in autopilot. When you think you've learned something, don't automatically assume it's time to move on. Keep working at it. The more you continue to work at it, the greater your degree of mastery.[23] Years ago, a researcher asked subjects to learn a list of nouns until they had memorized it. Then he asked some subjects to keep rehearsing it 50 percent or 100 percent as many times as it took them to learn it originally. As he measured how many nouns they remembered over the next twenty-eight days, recall increased with additional rehearsal time.[24] Keep on keeping on, as they say.

Space it out. Many studies show that studying for several hours at a time, as opposed to one long stretch, is much more effective. Clearing your entire day so that you can study calculus for six hours isn't the best idea. Your anxiety level would mount over that time, and fatigue would set in, keeping you from maximizing your memory. Yet many students think marathon study sessions prove diligence. "I just can't figure out why I didn't do well. I studied for six straight hours!" Instead, study in shorter spurts for several days leading up to the exam. Cramming may work in the short run, but your working memory will most likely dump what you think you've mastered right after the exam.

Separate it. Overcoming interference is a memory challenge. When you're tasked with learning similar, yet distinct, information, bleeding can occur. (No, it's not a health issue.) One body of knowledge can spill over into another. Imagine the confusion you'd experience if you tried to learn Spanish, French, Russian, and Chinese at the same time.

Kevin from the "FOCUS Challenge Case" had trouble differentiating between Plato, Aristotle, and Socrates. He would have benefited from deliberately working to separate the three philosophers as he studied by making his own compare-and-contrast chart, as in Figure 7.3, for example.

Interference presents a particular problem for college students because the subject matter in different courses often overlaps; one social science course may contain information that's similar to another's. Knowledge is interconnected; that's not the issue. It's the challenge of keeping knowledge bases separate for exams. If your sociology test is on Wednesday and your psychology test is on Friday, study sociology on Tuesday and psychology on Thursday. But if both tests are on Friday, separating the two bodies of information will be a challenge. Differentiate your study sessions as much as possible by studying for each test in a specific location or at a particular time of day, for example.[25]

Mind the middle. Perhaps you've heard of the serial-position effect. Research shows that we tend to remember what comes first because of the impression it makes on us, and what comes last because it's most recent. But what's in the middle sometimes tends to get lost.[26] That's an important principle for you to know. If you need to memorize a list of items, or a timeline, for example, pay particular attention to the middle. Use what we know from memory research to your advantage!

Make It Meaningful

Sometimes we make the mistake of creating artificial distinctions between thoughts and feelings, when in fact, emotions and personal connections play an important role in learning.

Chapter Crossover Spacing out studying makes perfect sense, but it is impossible to do if students aren't purposefully planning their time. Remind students that in Chapter 4 they learned how to manage time and energy. Even if they schedule themselves to study at 2 a.m., they won't have the energy to do what they planned.

Teachable Moment Brainstorm areas where students might get confused. Is it multiple formulas in chemistry and math? Is it a list of dates in history? Can you think back to a time when you were confused while studying something and share this with the students?

Figure 7.3

Philosophers' Compare-and-Contrast Chart

Category	Socrates	Plato	Aristotle
Life Dates	**469–399 B.C.**	**427–347 B.C.**	**384–322 B.C.**
Background	Son of a sculptor (Athenian)	Son of a wealthy aristocrat (Athenian)	Son of a court physician (Macedonian)
Founded (Schools)	None—walked on the streets of Athens talking to people	Academy	Lyceum
Taught as Students	Plato	Aristotle	Alexander the Great
Interesting Facts	Executed by hemlock for: 1. Disbelief in the traditional gods 2. Corrupting the youth	Left Athens after Socrates's execution: 1. Egypt 2. Italy 3. Studied with students of Pythagoras 4. Advised the ruling family of Syracuse	Created syllogistic logic: If a=b and b=c then a=c "If Socrates is a man, and men are mortal, then Socrates is mortal."
Major Writings	None. Scholars believe Plato's early dialogues reflect his thoughts.	• Early Dialogues (Socrates) • Middle Dialogues • Late Dialogues	• *Organon* • *Metaphysics* • *On the Soul* • *Poetics* • *Rhetoric* • *Eudemian Ethics* • *Nicomachean Ethics* • *Politics*
Summary of Philosophy	**Dialectic method:** Discovery of false beliefs and truth through asking questions. Started with a hypothesis, then argued for its opposite. Always resulted in a contradiction. Never came to a resolution.	Believed we forget all knowledge when we are born, but we can remember through **recollection:** belief that we can come to know fundamental truths through recalling our knowledge of the **forms**. **Forms** are eternal, abstract concepts that have an independent existence outside of the "sensible" world. They provide the foundation for all objects in the world, which are imperfect, temporary reproductions of the **forms**.	Rejected Plato's notion of the **form**. Believed the **substance** of all things was a combination of **matter** and **form**. Believed ultimate reality was **being *qua* being:** the idea that the structure of language and logic accurately mirrors reality. Analyzed language and logic to reveal the nature of reality.

Source: Nina Ellis, University of Colorado at Colorado Springs, 2007.

Emotional Intelligence (EI) Research On the other hand, Daniel Goleman tells us that "Circuits from the limbic brain to the prefrontal lobes mean that signals of strong emotion—anxiety, anger and the like—can create neural static, sabotaging the ability of the prefrontal lobe to maintain working memory. That is why when we are emotionally upset we say we 'just can't think straight'—and why continual emotional distress can create deficits in a child's intellectual abilities, crippling the capacity to learn."

Feel. Emotions and memories can team up in powerful ways. A piece of new information that makes you feel happy, angry, or sad lights up your amygdala, a small area of your brain that serves as your emotional center of operations. If a novel makes you cry or laugh or actually feel fear, you're likely to remember the story. If course content hooks into career goals you care about, you're likely to commit more of it to memory. Human beings care about other human beings and themselves, so the emotional side of new information (which you may have to create yourself) is a strong magnet for your memory.[27] All American adults remember where they were on September 11, 2001. Emotions enhance memory and recall.[28]

Connect. Create associations between what you're trying to commit to memory now and what you already know. That's why doing the reading assignment before class is so useful. During the lecture, you can think to yourself, *Oh, I remember that...and that...and that*. When you learn new information, it's almost as if you "file" it between other files already in place. If you know where to put it, instead of just stuffing it somewhere, that helps. Connecting it to previous knowledge also helps you retrieve the memory later.

Personalize. Find ways you can relate what you're memorizing to your own life. Okay, so you're thinking what do the plot and characters of *Pride and Prejudice*, a novel published by England's Jane Austin in 1813, possibly have to do with me now? Actually, there may be more similarities than you first think. Imagine the story taking place in your household. Do you have sisters? Does your mother worry about you marrying someone good enough for you? Do you have a close relationship with your father? Once you start actively searching for overlap, you may be surprised. This task is easier with some course content than others, but the very act of attempting to do this may be useful.

Make It Mnemonic

Some of the oldest ways to master your memory are through the use of mnemonic (pronounced *ne MON ik*) devices, verbal or visual memory aids, first used by Greek orators around 500 B.C. Imagine trying to remember a speech that goes on for hours; you'd need to devise specific ways to train your memory to keep working (without a teleprompter!). Although mnemonic devices can become complicated and aren't a solution to all memory challenges, for some students, these specialized elaborative rehearsal strategies can work well.

> **"Concentration is my motto—first honesty, then industry, then concentration."**
>
> **Andrew Carnegie, American businessman and philanthropist (1835–1919)**

ACT ON YOUR MEMORY!

Have you ever watched a movie, wondering how *do* actors learn all those lines? Do they have superhuman memory powers? The average movie-goer assumes that actors simply repeat their lines over and over until they learn them. However, actors themselves say that's not all there is to it.[29]

Actually, what actors are most concerned with is convincing you that they're not playing a role. British actor Michael Caine once commented, "You must be able to stand there *not* thinking of that line. You take it off the other actor's face. Otherwise, for your next line, you're not listening and not free to respond naturally, to act spontaneously."[30] But actors' contracts require them to be absolutely precise in conforming to the script, so how do they do it? Studying how actors learn their parts with precision has confirmed what learning experts know about memory.

Like DeLanna Studi from the "FOCUS on Careers" section, most actors aren't memory experts, but they do use the memory techniques described in this chapter. They manipulate the lines, elaborate on them to themselves, relate the lines to experiences or feelings of their own, or try writing or saying the lines themselves, rather than just reading them. Four of the techniques used by actors may also be useful to you as you try to commit course material to memory. Maybe you've even tried some of these techniques.

Chunking: Actors chunk their material into beats. For example, an actor might divide a half page of dialogue into three beats: to flirt, to sweet-talk, and to convince. In other words, the character would first flirt with the other actor, then sweet-talk him to lower his guard, and then convince him to do something he might not want to do. The results? Three chunks to remember instead of twelve lines of double-spaced text.

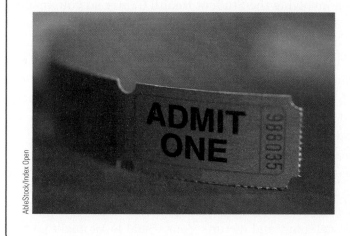

AbleStock/Index Open

Goal Setting: Notice that the chunks are based on goals, a strategy that also works well while you're studying. Actors ask themselves goal-oriented questions such as: "Should I be flirting with him here?" "Am I trying to sweet-talk him?" "Should I be trying to convince him to do something he doesn't really want to do?" In the same way, you can ask yourself, "Am I trying to learn the underlying formula so that I can work other problem sets?" or "Should I be coming up with my own reasons for why the play is considered to be Shakespeare's best comedy?" When you ask yourself goal-oriented questions while you study, you steer your actions, as actors do, toward learning. Eventually, actors know their lines; they're "off book" in acting jargon. Being off book is where you'll be during an exam, so asking goal-oriented questions while you study is a good idea.

Moving: Going through the motions while rehearsing their lines helps actors memorize them. Imagine the hypothetical actor whose goals were to flirt, to sweet-talk, and to convince, glancing toward the other actor from across the room, moving closer and smiling, and then touching his arm while making the persuasive case. The actor must know the meanings behind the movements to give meaning to the lines. (She could be glancing across the room to give a dirty look instead of to flirt, for example.) The meanings are tied to the movements, which are tied to the lines, and the lines become committed to memory. In one study, actors who were moving when they first spoke their lines had better recall than actors who didn't, even though they weren't moving during the test itself.[31] Likewise, when you study, moving around may help you learn. Even if you're not primarily a kinesthetic learner, pieces of information become tied to motions in ways that help you recall information. Some learning experts believe that mental actions—memory and understanding—are actually grounded in physical actions.[32]

Meaning: "Say what you mean" and "mean what you say" was Lewis Carroll's advice in *Alice's Adventures in Wonderland.* When actors like DeLanna Studi concentrate on truly meaning what they're saying, they learn their lines more easily than they do when they simply try to memorize them.[33] Researchers use the term *active experiencing* to refer to what actors do when they use all their physical, mental, and emotional channels to communicate the meaning of their lines to someone else, real or imagined. As you study course material, do the same thing. Imagine you need to communicate the information to someone you know who needs it. Put emotion into it: *warn* your friend, for example. Mean it! Use *all* your channels—physical, mental, and emotional—to communicate the meaning of what you're learning. In a sense, when you do this, *you* become an actor, and as a result, you "learn your lines."

Spell. Acrostics and acronyms are the simplest type of mnemonic device, words you create by putting together the first letters of what you want to memorize. Let's say, for example, that you want to learn the first five items in the list of random words in Exercise 7.1: theory, rehearsal, student, bone, and frostbite. You could create a bizarre acrostic such as Ten rabbits' soup bowls fell. If you had vowels to work with, you may also be able to create an acronym you can pronounce, such as RAM for Random Access Memory.

Activity Option Using the same list that students brought in to memorize for another class—or if they didn't do this before, have them bring in a list now—ask students to use a strategy from "Cultivate Your Curiosity" to learn the list. For example, if they choose goal setting and moving, they might set a goal such as learning all of the major battles of Civil War in American History while moving around the room to demonstrate the locations where the battles were fought.

Teachable Moment Mnemonic devices are a tried-and-true way of remembering things. You can probably recall one from your childhood. Tell your class. Do you remember how to spell *arithmetic*? (a rat in Tom's house might eat Tom's ice cream) Have students make up a mnemonic device for something they need to remember. You might even do this as a class with a few examples.

Locate. The Loci (pronounced *LO si*) mnemonic system was the original and only mnemonic system from the time of the Greeks around 500 B.C. until the middle of the seventeenth century. The Loci system is attributed to a story told by Cicero, an orator and statesman of ancient Rome. The story goes like this: While speaking at a banquet, a poet named Simonides was called outside to speak to someone. While he was outside, the roof of the banquet hall collapsed, and all the guests were crushed beyond recognition. He was able to identify them by remembering where each person was sitting. This gruesome task led him to devise a mnemonic device that cues memory by using locations, a device that was used by Greek and Roman orators to help them remember very long speeches by connecting particular points they wanted to make to real or imaginary locations in their minds.[34]

Using the Loci system requires two steps. First, think of a familiar path, setting, or route. Perhaps you decide on the path from your residence hall room to the classroom where your exam will be given. On your way, you always pass distinct markers: the fountain in the quad, a tunnel that takes you beneath a busy street, the recreation center's pool, the Student Health Center, and the Humanities Building parking lot. Perhaps you want to use these five locations to cue your memory to produce the first five items on our random list: theory, rehearsal, student, bone, and frostbite. You might picture saying hello to your science professor, a foundation of knowledge who always espouses *theory* in class, in the quad. Then you might imagine conducting a *rehearsal* of the student philharmonic orchestra in the tunnel, which would be a ridiculous sight. Then you envision *students* on the swim team thrashing about in the pool during a competition. You know about a recent financial scandal involving the Student Health Center so you imagine skeletons (*bones*) in the closet. And finally, you think of how terrible it would be to lose your room key and get a case of *frostbite* from spending the night in your car in the parking lot. Now without looking back, try it and see if it works for you. Of course, the optimal way the Loci system works is if the locations are familiar to *you*. Its main benefits are that it uses cues, incorporates associations, and orders information into a sequence, all of which aid in memory transfer and storage.[35]

Link or narrate. Instead of a Loci system, you can create a linking mnemonic to help you memorize a list. To do this, you must connect item A to item B, item B to item C, and so forth. Consider again the list of words you were challenged to remember and write down: theory, rehearsal, student, bone, frostbite, camera, rose, calculus, and lecture. Your visual links might go like this: (1) (theory + rehearsal) You imagine a *theoretician* at a *rehearsal* dinner. (2) (rehearsal + student) The rehearsal dinner is attended by student friends of the bride and groom. (3) (student + bone) One student is in a leg cast because of a broken bone, and so forth.

Another way to use this method is to create a story that links each cue: A geeky theoretician went to a rehearsal dinner, where he sat next to a student from one of his classes who had a broken leg (bone). The student injured his leg in a hiking accident in which he suffered a fall and got frostbite from exposure, and so forth. Each item is linked to the item before, except for the first one. You must find a cue to remember it independently to get the chain started.

Peg. The Peg system can be traced back to the mid-1600s, and it was extended to its modern method of using rhyming syllables by England's John Sambrook in 1879.[36] Remember the old nursery rhyme, "One, two, buckle my shoe"? The Peg system uses these rhyming pairs:

one—bun	six—sticks
two—shoe	seven—heaven
three—tree	eight—gate
four—door	nine—wine
five—hive	ten—hen

To use the Peg system, create *specific* images for yourself: a big, fat hamburger *bun*, a stiletto-heeled *shoe*, a weeping willow *tree*, and so forth, and hang the items you're trying to memorize on these mental "pegs" in order. To continue with our example, you'd picture a *theoretical* treatise stuffed between the hamburger *bun*, an image of a teenage girl's *rehearsal* of how to walk in her first pair of stiletto high-heeled *shoes*, a *student* sprawled out studying under a weeping willow *tree*, and so forth. Other types of Peg systems have been devised, but the rhyming system is the most common. But does it work with information other than lists, you might wonder? Try it for yourself to find out.

Activity Option Break the class into four groups and have them memorize all of the presidents of the United States or some other common list. (You might have to fill in the gaps for a few students.) Assign one group to use the spelling approach, another the locate, another the link or narrate, and the final group the peg system. Give groups about fifteen minutes to learn their lists, and then report back to the group the strategies they used and how successful they were.

Manipulate It

Although some of us tend to favor other modalities than kinesthetic learning, all of us can benefit from memory techniques with a kinesthetic basis. Actively doing something with information is a better way to commit it to memory than remaining passively disengaged. If you had three hours to study a textbook chapter that takes one hour to read, what should you do: read the chapter three times, or work with the material after reading it once? The second option is generally more effective. So what kinds of things should you *do*?

Mark it up. Be an active reader; interact with the text. People who are used to reading complex material—your instructors, for example—read slowly, chew on each word, and make copious notes in the margins, arguing, questioning, summarizing, or explaining. Take notes as you read, "talk" with the author, and write out your reactions. Highlighting can be somewhat helpful, but it's often not enough. It certainly wasn't for Kevin from the "FOCUS Challenge Case." Every time you reach for your highlighter, ask yourself why you want to highlight that passage. Why is it important? To commit information to memory, you must go beyond simply coloring.[37]

Mark it down. If you want to give yourself a break, don't bother committing something unimportant to memory. Just write it down. (Of course, you still have to remember where you put that piece of paper.) Writing something down is an obvious memory alternative; save your memory for more important tasks. If it's something you do want to remember, however, the physical act of writing itself can help. Unless the exam is open-book, however, actually bringing your notes with you at exam time could be hazardous to your academic health!

Organize. Arrange and rearrange the material you're trying to memorize. Outline it—putting concepts into hierarchical order can help you figure out important relationships. If you're trying to learn the responsibilities of the various branches of the government for your political science class, actually drawing a kind of written organizational chart is likely to help your essay answer flow better.

Picture. Drawings and mind maps can also be effective memory tools, particularly for visual learners. Think of drawing pictures to help you remember ridiculous visualizations or word associations. If you're trying to remember bones for your anatomy and physiology class, try Farsighted *Fibula*, Tempting *Tibia*, Party Girl *Patella*, Feathered *Femur*, and Pretty *Pelvis*. Any time you can engage in what's called dual coding, using more than one channel—verbal and visual—you'll likely reinforce what you're trying to memorize.[38]

Act. If you've always had a hankering to be a star on *The Bold and the Beautiful* or some other drama, consider putting motions to your memorizing. Act it out. If you're trying to memorize a famous speech like Martin Luther King, Jr.'s "I Have a Dream," deliver it in front of a mirror. Write a short script and ask your roommate to play opposite you, if it helps you remember who said what to whom for an exam in history, or obviously, theater.

Produce. There's good evidence that putting things in your own words is highly beneficial to remembering.[39] Redeliver the professor's lecture. Can you explain the concepts he explained, or do you stop after a few minutes and puzzle? Producing information requires you to dig deeper into your memory and reconstruct information, a process that engages you more actively and benefits you and your memory beyond simple recognition tasks. One of the very best ways to produce is to teach something to someone else. To do that successfully, you have to know it yourself, inside and out. Teaching adds another layer of responsibility for knowing something, yours *and* someone else's.

Test. Rather than assuming you remember something, test yourself. Create a multiple-choice, matching, or true-and-false test. Doing so requires you to ask: amidst this sea of information, what's important? Better yet, create essay questions that require you to organize and write what you know about a subject. Swap tests with a study mate, or create flashcards so that you can quiz yourself. Research shows that tests are "powerful memory enhancers." The simple act of taking a test helps you recall information, even if what you studied isn't on the test![40]

Make It Funny

Humor is an excellent memory-enhancing tool. Think about how easy it is to remember the plots of comedies you've seen at the movies or on television. For example, you may be able to remember conversations between *Friends*

Teachable Moment In a recent episode of *Grey's Anatomy*, one of the surgeons was famous for her flashcards that she had made when she was a resident studying for a big exam. All of the new residents wanted her cards. When students make flashcards—especially in classes like a foreign language—encourage them to hold onto them for the final exam and the next-level class, and be willing to share them with a friend.

or *The Simpsons* cast members in shows you've watched once or twice, almost verbatim, just because they tickled your funny bone.

Mock it. Experts on learning and the brain believe that the optimal condition for learning is *relaxed alertness*. Sounds like an oxymoron, doesn't it? How can you be relaxed and alert at the same time? Actually, it is possible when the challenge is high, but the threat is low.[41] What better way to create those conditions than through humor? And what better way to engage your memory than to be a stand-up (or sit-down) comic?

Think back to some of the funniest scenes you've ever seen from *Saturday Night Live* or *Monty Python's Flying Circus*. They're probably still vivid in your memory. Have you ever seen *Monty Python's* "Hell's Grannies" skit: a gang made up of the Monty Python men, dressed up as little old ladies, cigarettes hanging out of their mouths, beating up passers-by with their purses, and tearing through the streets on souped-up motorcycles? Even if you haven't, you can picture it. One way to generate humor is to put incongruous things together in a new context. Images like these are memorable, and you should ask yourself how you could apply your own humor to the material you're attempting to trigger your memory to learn. If you're having trouble separating Socrates and Plato, draw a picture of a crate full of socks next to Socrates' name and a can of PlayDoh® next to Plato's.

Create a David Letterman–like top-ten list of the reasons why Shakespeare's ten tragedies are tragic. Or rewrite a play—put Shakespeare's *Romeo and Juliet* into contemporary slang so that you can remember what "O Romeo, Romeo! Wherefore art thou Romeo?" really means. (Hint: it's not about his location.)[42] "Hey, Romeo. Why you gotta be a Montague, man?" Or if you can never remember which character is from the Montague family and which is a Capulet, write a silly limerick to help you remember:

> There once was a girl named Cap
>
> Who fell for a guy and was hap
>
> But her family and his
>
> Wouldn't stand for the biz
>
> So they both ended up playing taps.

Set it to music. Be imaginative. We tend to remember what's bizarre, funny, or even obscene![43]

INSIGHT ⊖ ACTION

1. Of the list of twenty ways to master your memory, which are your "regulars"? How well do they work for you, generally?

2. Which techniques have you never tried?

3. Choose a specific technique for an upcoming exam, do it with gusto, and note your results afterward.

4. Make a list of techniques that would work well for you, considering your psychological type and VARK preferences.

Chapter Crossover Chapter 2 focuses on the learning styles. Reinforce to students who are multimodal or students whose personality types are at midpoint on one or more of the four scales, rather than distinctly one type over another, that it's a good idea to study using a variety of tools.

YOUR TOUGHEST CLASS

Think about your most challenging class this semester. What kind of information in this class is difficult for you to commit to memory: complex readings, formulas, lecture material? Answer the following questions to help you realize the role sharpening your memory can play in your success.

- So far in this class, have you been engaging in maintenance rehearsal or elaborate rehearsal? Now that you have read the chapter, what evidence do you have that this is true?
- How have you studied for quizzes or exams? Provide examples for each of the five principles discussed in this chapter:

Make the material stick.

Make it meaningful.

Make use of mnemonic devices.

Manipulate the material to help learn it.

Make it funny.

- How successful have your memory strategies been? What will you do differently now?

Send your instructor in this class an e-mail, if appropriate, indicating your efforts and detailing your progress.

Activity Option Have students send you an e-mail summarizing this "Control Your Learning" activity. This reflective activity that will not only help students identify some major points that you want to stress, but it's an opportunity for you to give individuals suggestions for their toughest classes.

How Our Memories (uh...hmmm...) Fail Us

Imagine this: You meet someone at a school reception who says, "Hey, I know you! Remember? We met a year ago—it was September—at that fraternity party, and we even went out a few times. I've never forgotten you." You rack your brain. This person doesn't even look familiar. You wonder, *Am I being confused with someone else? Am I crazy? I have no recollection at all!* Later, you comb through your calendar to reconstruct that month. You weren't even attending your current school then. It couldn't have been you.

Digital cameras can malfunction, files we've saved can become corrupted, and sometimes our memories fail us, too. We forget things or alter them in our thinking. Think of how many times you have had to e-mail someone for a password because you've forgotten your original one. Think about the details of a past experience that would probably look a bit different now in instant replay mode. While our memories are one of the most complex tools we have, they're not perfect, and those imperfections fascinate scientists. In one famous experiment, researchers asked sixty-seven men in their late forties questions about their lives as high school freshmen—the same questions the researchers had asked them as actual students thirty-four years earlier. Interestingly, their memories of things were often a far cry from what they had indicated to be true so long ago.[44]

Here are seven ways our memories fail us from *The Seven Sins of Memory: How the Mind Forgets and Remembers*. See how many cause you to nod your head in recognition, and think about which ones particularly apply most to Kevin from the "FOCUS Challenge Case."

1. **Fading.** Memories are transient; they fade over time. You probably remember what you wore yesterday, but how about on October 5 a year ago? As time goes by, memories generally weaken.

2. **Absentmindedness.** Sometimes there's a disconnect between your focus and your memory. You were doing several things at one time—talking to the

girl next to you after class and checking your cell phone while stuffing your backpack—and now you have no idea what you did with your history textbook. It's not that the information is lost over time; it probably never registered in the first place because your attention was elsewhere. The famous musician Yo-Yo Ma once absentmindedly left his 2.5 million dollar cello in the trunk of a taxi. Fortunately, it was recovered by the police right away.

3. **Blocking.** It's right on the tip of your tongue, but you just can't quite retrieve it. You can see the face, but you can't conjure up the name. But later that day, without even trying, suddenly it comes to you. Psychologists call it TOT, the Tip of the Tongue phenomenon. You feel as if you're about to sneeze, but can't, and the word—whatever it is—just won't come to you.

4. **Misattribution.** You say to your friend, "Hey, that was an interesting story you told me about the new girl in our composition class." "What story?" your friend replies. Someone told you something, but you're wrong about who it was. Or you read a passage in one book, but think you've read it in another. Or you've dreamed about something for so long that the fantasy actually becomes real in your mind. Your memory deceives you by mistaking one source for another or tricks you by inventing a memory where none actually exists.

Teachable Moment You might ask students if they have ever thought someone said something that really someone else actually said. We can probably all remember doing this because of the strong association—embarrassment, maybe—attached to it.

5. **Suggestibility.** Sometimes you retain bits of information that you think are memories, but they really aren't. Here's an example: perhaps your mother has told you the cute anecdote about yourself as a two-year-old toddler so many times that you can now envision it, and you think you remember it. You were actually too young to remember anything, but the event has become real at someone else's suggestion.

6. **Bias.** Sometimes we knowingly, or more often unknowingly, rewrite history. We insist on some detail that, if we had the ability to go back in time to verify it, is actually wrong. But we remember it differently—and we're so sure! Perhaps someone has caught you in a trap in one of those instances by finding a piece of real evidence, and you've had to back down and admit that your memory is off a bit.

7. **Persistence.** Another way that memory plagues us is by nagging. You'd really like to forget something, but you just can't. You wake up in a cold sweat at 3 a.m., remembering the embarrassing thing you did at work or said in class. You'd like to be able to push the memory away, but it won't budge.

While these seven memory faults are aggravating and inconvenient at times, they also have value. Persistence may serve as a reminder to be more careful next time. Fading is the result of memory efficiency. Why waste time recalling outdated, insignificant details we no longer need? Chances are you can't recall something because you haven't needed to recently, and the memory connection has weakened. (This can happen if you don't keep up with your coursework. When it's exam time, and you haven't looked at your notes for weeks, the memory of what you'd studied long ago may have faded.) Generally, we remember what we need to remember in order to survive in the environment in which we live. We get the gist of things, and often the rest falls away. The point, however, is to take charge of the process of remembering![45]

Activity Option Have students quickly come up with a mnemonic sentence to remember the seven memory faults. Give them five minutes to do so, and then have a few students volunteer to read their sentences to the class.

Sensitive Situation Keep in mind that trouble with memory can be associated with some wellness and emotional intelligence issues. Remind students to send you an e-mail if they need some suggestions on how to address wellness or EI issues so you can get them headed in the right direction.

This Is Your Memory on Drugs

Recent discoveries of a class of memory-enhancing drugs may affect us in the future. Some day, getting your memory to kick into high gear may be as simple as popping a pill. On the other hand, hazardous chemicals such as alcohol and party drugs can adversely affect memory in ways you may not know about. This subject warrants careful consideration.

Memory-Enhancing Drugs

If you could walk down to the corner drugstore and buy a pill to sharpen your memory, would you do it? Many people would. Unfortunately, there is no such pill. But wait a minute; there is! The drug CX717 is what's called an ampakine, which works by boosting the chemical glutamate in your brain. Glutamate enhances your memory and makes learning easier. Really? If CX717 were widely available now, many people would be asking: Where does the line form? But are these memory-enhancing drugs really safe?

Invented by Dr. Gary Lynch at the University of California, CX717 may eventually be used to treat ADHD, Alzheimer's disease, and perhaps even jet-lagged travelers or big-time executives with high-stakes presentations on their agendas. Because of its short shelf life, there are no side effects, and the drug does not interfere with normal sleep patterns. Besides helping those with specific problems, memory-enhancing drugs like CX717 would be highly appealing to middle-aged adults who can never seem to remember where they parked their cars, or elderly people who forget to feed their cats. Scientists warn, however, that CX717 has not yet been approved by the FDA, and that the results of long-term "recreational" use are not known. A word of caution is in order.

Photos.com Select/Index Open

> "Memory is a complicated thing, a relative to truth, but not its twin."
>
> Barbara Kingsolver, American writer

A debate is brewing among scientists about the bioethics—or neuroethics in this case—of such brain-enhancing drugs. Will CX717 be available to everyone who wants it? What if some people can't afford it? What if all your peers are taking the drug; will you feel pressured to take it, too? What if your boss insists you need a pharmaceutical solution because your focus at work has fallen off? According to Arthur L. Caplan, the director of University of Pennsylvania's Bioethics Center, "The brain is the most personal organ we've got. Very few of us identify ourselves with our pancreas or our liver. But we do think of ourselves as being our brain. So if you change it, modify it, learn about it, you are looking at yourself."[46] The ethics debate over memory-enhancing drugs is likely to intensify.

If athletes aren't supposed to cheat by taking performance-enhancing drugs, would taking a memory-enhancing drug for better cognitive performance constitute "cheating," too? Some say yes. Mr. Caplan wrote in the September 2005 issue of *Scientific American*, "It is the essence of humanness to try to improve the world and oneself."[47] We take vitamins and drink coffee; what's the difference? But others object: Whatever happened to good, old-fashioned hard work? Do we really want our lives to be governed by pills to help us wake up, feel good, concentrate, and finally drop off to sleep at night? How do *you* feel about "better living through organic chemistry"?[48]

You may want to monitor where this debate goes in the future, but for now, cracking the books is still the best way to go!

Hazardous Chemicals

If you watched *Sesame Street* as a child, you probably remember the Muppet "dealer" who peddled letters of the alphabet. He'd open his raincoat, show you the goods, and say, "Pssst. Want to buy a letter S?" It was a silly but attention-getting way of helping children learn the alphabet.

On today's college campuses, there's another kind of peddling going on. Someone may offer to sell, swap, or give you a substance that promises great results, socially or academically. These aren't the kind of chemicals for which you need eye goggles and rubber gloves, but they are hazardous to you and your memory, and you need to know the risks.

Let's start with the most common drug of all, alcohol, one of the most powerful amnesic agents available. With even one or two drinks, alcohol can disrupt your ability to move information from short-term to long-term memory, and as the amount of alcohol increases, so does your memory impairment. High doses of alcohol can seriously affect your ability to learn something new and even lead to blackouts, such that you can't remember anything that happened while you were under the influence.[49] In one study, subjects' memories were even impaired when they *thought* they were drinking alcohol and weren't. Participants were asked to drink tonic water, but half were told they were drinking vodka and tonic, before participating in an eyewitness memory experiment. Subjects who believed they had drunk alcohol were more swayed by misleading information afterward, and although they were wrong about the accuracy of their views, interestingly, they were even more confident that they were right than the group of students who didn't think they'd drunk alcohol! The results suggest that even *thinking* you're under the influence can influence your memory![50]

Ecstasy, a popular club and party drug, is another chemical that's hazardous to your memory. According to the National Institute on Drug Abuse (NIDA), people who regularly use MDMA (3,4-methylenedioxymethamphetamine) are subjecting themselves to possible brain damage. In a brain imaging study using positron emission tomography (PET) scans, the brain images of regular users of ecstasy showed damage of serotonin nerve endings. Ecstasy users performed worse than control groups on tests measuring attention, memory, and learning, and the heavier the drug use, the more adverse the effects on memory.[51] One study that surveyed "X" users in Europe, the United States, and Australia, found that regular users were 23 percent more likely to report memory problems than nonusers.[52]

That's not all the sobering news. Besides alcohol and drugs, other substances you put in your mouth can affect your memory, too. All those double cheeseburgers and orders of fries wreak havoc on more than your waistline. Extensive studies with mice "provide direct evidence that fast food diets, particularly a diet high in saturated fats, can have an adverse effect on learning and memory."[53]

Emotional Intelligence (EI) Research According to Daniel Goleman, there are two emotional pathways to drug abuse. One occurs in those who use drugs (especially alcohol) to relieve stress. A second pathway occurs in individuals who are easily agitated, impulsive, or bored.

Your Type is Showing

What's the relationship between your psychological type and your memory? Practical research that would help you make the most of your memory is in short supply; however, you can extrapolate based on what you know about psychological type. What would you guess? Would you predict that Sensors are better at remembering facts, while iNtuitives recall big ideas? Would you envision that Judgers devise organized plans to memorize information, while Perceivers explore interesting tangents that could serve as retrieval cues? List your own predictions in the following chart and then discuss them with your classmates and instructor. Even though your predictions are based on your best guesses, you may realize some important generalizations as you discuss them.

Extravert	Introvert	Sensor	Intuitive	Thinker	Feeler	Judger	Perceiver

Deepen Your Memory

The point of this chapter is this: In a classic study conducted in the mid-1970s, two Swedish scholars decided to find out the difference between effective and ineffective learners. They gave students this task: read an essay, summarize it, and solve a problem. Then they interviewed the students to find out how they had approached the task.

The interviews revealed two types of learners. One group of students said things like, "I just tried to remember as much as I could" or "I just memorized what I read." Other students said, "I tried to look for the main idea" or "I looked for the point of the article." The professors who conducted the study then characterized the difference between *surface-level processing*, looking at words and numbers alone, and *deep-level processing*, searching for underlying meaning.[54] To become a truly focused learner, you must process information as you go. Dig deep!

There is no doubt that memory is at the heart of learning. In the days before digital cameras, film had to be developed or processed. However, it's still important to remember those terms as they relate to your memory.

EXERCISE 7.2 VARK ACTIVITY

Complete the recommended activity for your preferred VARK learning modality. If you are multimodal, select more than one activity. Your instructor may ask you to (a) give an oral report on your results in class, (b) send your results to him or her via e-mail, (c) post them online, or (d) contribute to a class chat.

Visual: Create a diagram that shows all of the steps a student should go through when committing challenging material to memory for an exam.

Aural: Re-listen to one of your professor's lectures via podcast and stop periodically to repeat the information to yourself.

Read/Write: Check out a library book on memory, and summarize a major section that's important to understanding memory as a process.

Kinesthetic: Demonstrate three memory techniques that work for you in front of your classmates, and let them guess what you're trying to portray..

For more practice online, go to http://www.academic.cengage.com/ collegesuccess/staley to take the Challenge Yourself online quizzes.

 **NOW WHAT DO YOU THINK?**

At the beginning of this chapter, Kevin Baxter, a frustrated and discouraged returning adult student, faced a challenge. Now after reading this chapter, would you respond differently to any of the questions you answered about the "FOCUS Challenge Case"?

On a scale of 1 to 10, answer the following questions now that you've completed this chapter.

1 = not very/not much/very little/low   10 = very/a lot/very much/high

In hindsight, how much did you *really* know about this topic before reading the chapter?

1   2   3   4   5   6   7   8   9   10

How much do you think this information might affect your success in college?

1   2   3   4   5   6   7   8   9   10

How much do you think this information might affect your career success after college?

1   2   3   4   5   6   7   8   9   10

How long did it actually take you to complete this chapter? _____ Hour(s) _____ Minutes

Take a minute to compare these answers to your answers from the "Readiness Check" at the beginning of this chapter. What gaps exist between the similar questions? How might these gaps between what you thought before starting the chapter and what you now think after completing the chapter affect how you approach the next chapter in this book?

Activity Option To conclude this chapter, students should communicate the most important memorization method they learned about in this chapter. Ask students to e-mail one classmate, or you, a short description of which strategy they selected and why. Put this all into one document and send it to the entire class as a list of best practices for students.

To download mp3 format audio summaries of this chapter, go to http://www .academic.cengage.com/collegesuccess/staley.

8 Reading and Studying

YOU'RE ABOUT TO DISCOVER...

Chapter Crossover In Chapter 3 students were encouraged to make use of resources. Does your campus have a learning center or a learning disability center, if students need help? What are their location and hours of operation? Make sure that *you* know all of the available resources on campus so that you will be able to direct your students who need extra coaching in studying and reading skills.

> Why reading is important

> How to engage in focused reading

> How to tackle reading assignments as an ESL student

> What metacognition is and how it can help you

> How to become in intentional learner

> Why learning is greater than the sum of its parts

"Reading is to the mind what exercise is to the body."
Joseph Addison, British politician and writer (1672–1719)

Katie Alexander

College would be a lot more fun it weren't

for all the reading and studying required. That was Katie Alexander's take on things. She wasn't much of a reader; she much preferred playing softball or volleyball with her friends to sitting in one spot with a book propped open in front of her. Reading for fun wasn't something she'd ever even consider doing. *Anyway, why read the book when you can just watch the movie?* she always asked. Katie was an energetic, active, outgoing person, and "doing" and "socializing" were her things. Reading and studying definitely weren't.

Actually, this was Katie's second attempt at college. She'd gone to a small liberal arts school right after high school, but the self-discipline required to read and study just wasn't there, so she dropped out. Working as a server for two years at a restaurant in her neighborhood helped her earn enough money to go back to school. "This time, *you* foot the bills," her parents had insisted. So now she was attending the local community college and determined to give it another go.

For Katie, reading and studying were hard work. She was smart enough to make it in college—she was sure of that—and this time around, she was more motivated. But reading was a labor-intensive activity that tried her patience, and after she'd read something, she was hard-pressed to summarize what it had been about. "In one eye and out the other" was the way she thought of her difficulties. Katie found it hard to focus, and things just didn't seem to stick. Before she knew it, she was off in some other world, thinking about her friends, or her schedule at work, or everything else she had to do.

Back in grade school, Katie had been labeled as a slow reader. She was never in the top reading group, and although she resented the label, she didn't quite know what do to about it. The last time reading had actually been a subject in school was sixth grade. Now, eight years later, she wondered if one of those speed-reading courses advertised online might be the answer.

Katie's roommate, Amanda, was an English major who loved to read. In fact, that's all she ever seemed to do. Her best friend, Brittney, however, had a different strategy. "There's so much required reading in all my classes that I don't even know where to start," Brittney admitted, "so I just don't do it. I go to class, listen to the lectures, and write down what the instructor has said on the essay tests. Learn to 'play the game'!"

But Brittney's strategy definitely wasn't going to work for Katie in Professor Harris-Black's Introduction to Ethnic Studies class. She'd assigned a shocking number of articles to read. The professor didn't even go over the readings in class, and her lectures were about all sorts of things, only some of which were related to the reading. Whenever she sat down to read an assignment, Katie found what to her were unfamiliar words and unnatural phrasing. The professor had suggested that students read with a dictionary at their sides, but who'd ever want to keep stopping to look up words? You'd never finish!

With a midterm exam coming up in her Ethnic Studies class next week, Katie was beginning to panic. She'd only read one of the nine articles assigned. In fact, she hadn't made it through the first article when she got discouraged and gave up. She knew the midterm essay test would be challenging. Winging it wouldn't work, and choosing to "watch the movie" instead of reading the book wasn't an option. Exactly what did Ethnic Studies have to do with anything, she puzzled, and why had her advisor suggested the course in the first place?

The night before the test, Katie decided to get serious. She sat down at her desk, armed with her yellow highlighter. As she began reading, however, she realized she didn't know exactly what to highlight since she didn't really understand what she was reading. Looking back at the page she had just finished, she saw that she had basically highlighted everything. Exasperated, Katie told herself that she couldn't go to bed until she'd finished reading everything, no matter when that was. She started with the second article, since she'd read the first one, and by morning, she'd be as ready as possible. Anyway, it wasn't up to her—it was up to Professor Harris-Black; she was the one making up the test.

Getting an A on her Introduction to Ethnic Studies midterm exam was probably out of the question, but if she could just manage to pass, Katie knew she would have to settle for that. On the other hand, she secretly hoped that maybe she'd just luck out.

WHAT DO **YOU** THINK?

Now that you've read about Katie Alexander, answer the following questions. You may not know all the answers yet, but you'll find out what you know and what you stand to gain by reading this chapter.

1. How would you characterize Katie as a student? Identify five specific problems described in this case study that could interfere with her college success.

2. Katie is probably an intelligent student, but she has decided that she dislikes reading and studying, so she avoids it. How important will these two skills be as she continues to pursue a college degree? Is she likely to succeed her second time around?

3. Is Katie like students you know? If so, in what ways, specifically?

4. Identify three specific things Katie should do to get her college career on track.

Emotional Intelligence (EI) Research There are at least two really important emotional intelligence skills that would help Katie: reality testing and problem solving. First, while it's good that she is optimistic and has hope, her beliefs are not grounded in reality. Also, her ability to problem-solve and figure out the steps she needs to take to tackle the reading is faulty.

Activity Option Take a few moments to discuss students' individual responses to the "What Do You Think" questions. You might ask students to work in small groups and come up with the three most important things a student like Katie should do and have each group report to the class.

Before beginning to read this chapter, take two minutes to answer the following questions on a scale of 1 to 10. Your answers will help you assess how ready you are to focus.

1 = not very/not much/very little/low   10 = very/a lot/very much/high

Based on reading the "You're about to discover…" list and skimming this chapter, how much do you think you probably already know about the subject matter?

    1   2   3   4   5   6   7   8   9   10

How much do you think this information might affect your college success?

    1   2   3   4   5   6   7   8   9   10

How much do you think this information might affect your career success after college?

    1   2   3   4   5   6   7   8   9   10

In general, how motivated are you to learn the material in this chapter?

    1   2   3   4   5   6   7   8   9   10

This book describes four key factors related to intrinsic, or internal, motivation: curiosity, control, career outlook, and challenge. The next four questions relate to these **C-Factors:**

How *curious* are you about the content you expect to read in this chapter?

    1   2   3   4   5   6   7   8   9   10

How much *control* do you expect to have over mastering the material in this chapter?

    1   2   3   4   5   6   7   8   9   10

How much do you think this chapter might help you develop your *career outlook*?

    1   2   3   4   5   6   7   8   9   10

How *challenging* do you think the material in this chapter will be for you?

    1   2   3   4   5   6   7   8   9   10

Before beginning any task, including studying, it's important to check in with yourself to ensure that you're physically, intellectually, and emotionally ready to focus. How ready are you, physically, to focus on this chapter? (Are you rested, feeling well, and so on?)

    1   2   3   4   5   6   7   8   9   10

How ready are you, intellectually, to focus on this chapter? (Are you thinking clearly, focused on this course, interested in this subject?)

    1   2   3   4   5   6   7   8   9   10

How ready are you, emotionally, to focus on this chapter? (Are you calm, confident, composed?)

    1   2   3   4   5   6   7   8   9   10

If your answer to any of the last three questions is below a 5 on the scale, you may need to address the issue you're facing prior to beginning this chapter. For example, if you're hungry, get a quick bite to eat. If you're feeling scattered, take a few moments to settle down and focus.

Finally, how long do you think it will take you to complete this chapter? _____ Hour(s) _____ Minutes

---

> **"Perhaps the most valuable result of all education is the ability to make yourself do the thing you have to do, when it ought to be done, whether you like it or not."**
>
> **Thomas Henry Huxley,**
> **British biologist (1825–1895)**

Teachable Moment Students will probably admit to not knowing as much as they should about this chapter's topic. Many students begin college with weak reading and study skills. Encourage them to really invest time and effort in this chapter. They are bound to learn some key skills and tips that they did not know before.

Who Needs to Read?

What's so important about reading? Teachers seem to think it's important, and parents consider it to be an admirable pastime, but times have changed, haven't they? Now you can just skim predigested information on websites, get a summary of the day's news from television, and watch movies for entertainment. Who needs to read? Look around the next time you're in a doctor or dentist's waiting room. You'll see some people staring at the TV screen mounted on the wall, others plugged into iPods, and still others working on their PDAs. A few may be skimming through magazines, but does anyone ever pick up a book to actually read it cover to cover anymore? Does it matter?

The answer, according to many experts, is a resounding yes, it does![1] Reading helped create civilization as we know it and taught us particular ways of thinking. "We are losing a sort of psychic habit, a logic, a sense of complexity, an ability to spot contradictions and even falsity," says Neil Postman, author of *Amusing Ourselves to Death*.[2] The losses will be felt, he predicts, in many aspects of our culture.

One fairly predictable result of doing anything less frequently is that eventually you may not do it as well. Practice keeps your skills from eroding. Even an Olympic athlete who doesn't stick with training gets rusty after a while. According to the 2003 National Survey of Adult Literacy, "The average American college graduate's literacy in English [has] declined significantly.... In 1992, 40 percent of the nation's college graduates scored at the proficient level ... on the 2003 test, only 31 percent of the graduates demonstrated those high-level skills." Why? "Literacy of college graduates had dropped because a rising number of young Americans in recent years had spent their free time watching television and surfing the Internet."[3]

Tom McCarthy/PhotoEdit

> **"You don't have to burn books to destroy a culture. Just get people to stop reading them."**
>
> **Ray Bradbury, science fiction writer**

As students read less, their reading skills deteriorate and they don't enjoy doing it. Conversely, the better you get at reading, the more you may enjoy it. Falling down every ten minutes the first time you get on skis isn't all that much fun, but once you can zip down the mountain like a pro, you begin to appreciate the sport.

According to experts, when we do read, we often do so while doing something else—quickly and with less focus. Some might say that reading was much more essential to previous generations because they didn't have all the choices we have today. Words like *lazy* and *bookworm* were used to describe Abraham Lincoln as a child because reading was all he ever wanted to do. Today, you'd be unlikely to hear those two particular insults combined. A hundred years ago, books took us places we could not easily go otherwise. Now there are much easier ways of getting there. Thomas Jefferson once told John Adams, "I cannot live without books." Evidently, today many people can.[4]

Like Katie from the "FOCUS Challenge Case," reading may not be your favorite pastime. You may feel about reading like many people do about eating cauliflower. You know it's good for you, but you'd prefer to avoid it. However, this chapter wouldn't be worth its weight in trees if it didn't try to convince you otherwise. One aspect of reading Katie particularly dislikes is that reading is not a social or physical activity. You can read with someone else in the room, of course, or talk about what you read afterward with friends, but basically, reading is something you do alone. It's a solitary activity that involves you, words on a page, an invisible author, and your brain. You need to do it with a minimum of physical movement. Reading while playing a game of volleyball would be tough to pull off.

If you enjoy reading, congratulations! When you settle in with an exciting novel, you can travel to the far corners of the Earth, turn back the clock to previous centuries, or fast-forward to a future that extends beyond your lifetime. You can inject yourself into the story and be someone else for a while.

Teachable Moment As convinced as we are about the value of reading, students may still not be convinced that watching a movie or getting information from the Internet is a less valuable way of learning to think. Point out the simple reality that in Katie's class, there is no movie, no *Spark* or *Cliffs Notes* to help her prepare for this exam. She needs to learn some strategies for reading.

Teachable Moment Ask students if they believe it is true that today you would not hear the words *lazy* and *bookworm* combined. What is the first word that comes into their heads when they know a student is doing all of the assigned readings for a class? They may not want to tell you!

Activity Option Consider meeting your students in the cafeteria for lunch every few weeks to discuss a book. If your campus has a Common Book program (where all entering students read the same book), you could dissect chapters together over lunch. Or, choose any book that students want to read and read it together. Think about something small—a book that might be appealing to "reluctant readers."

> **"It matters, if individuals are to retain any capacity to form their own judgments and opinions, that they continue to read for themselves."**
>
> **Harold Bloom, literary critic**

Novelist Scott Corbett once said: "I often feel sorry for people who don't read good books; they are missing a chance to lead an extra life." Whether or not you enjoy reading, it will be one of the primary skills you need to cultivate in college. According to one study, 85 percent of the learning you'll do in college requires careful reading.[5] First-year students often need to read and comprehend 150–200 pages per week in order to complete their academic assignments.[6]

What's more, reading skills go hand in hand with writing skills, which makes them even more important. The better you get at reading, the more you raise your probability of academic success. Katie's friend Brittney may be typical of some students you know who have chosen to skip the reading. But this is a dangerous, self-sabotaging strategy. Many of your classes will require intensive reading of complex material, including primary sources by original authors and scholarly research. If you complete reading assignments, and your classmates don't, think about how much ahead of the nonreaders *you* will be! Now is the time to begin enhancing these skills. But how do you become a better reader?

EXERCISE 8.1 What Is Your Reading Rate?

Before continuing, you'll need a stopwatch or a watch with a second hand. Keep track of how long it takes you to read the following article about getting a job. The object of the exercise isn't to race through; it's to read at your normal speed. After you read the article, you'll be asked to record your reading time and answer some questions to check your comprehension.

How Cool Is Your Job? Does It Even Matter?
By Adelle Waldman, Special to *The Wall Street Journal Online*

Dustin Goot has the kind of job that piques the interest of people he meets at parties, at least initially. The 27-year-old New Yorker is an associate editor of a glossy magazine aimed at young men, but his magazine—*Sync*—just launched last year, and many people haven't heard of it, which changes the dynamic.

"It seems like a cool job when you first say it," Mr. Goot says. But, "if you are at a magazine that not a lot of people have heard of, it's a bit of a letdown," he says. "People kind of shrug their shoulders." Mr. Goot may not be at a magazine with the name recognition of, say, *Sports Illustrated,* but in the complicated status hierarchy that emerges around the "coolness factor"—that is, how cool is your job?—Mr. Goot fares pretty well.

That's nothing to sneeze at. When we were in college, we all had the same job title—we were students. Sure, some schools are more prestigious than others, but at least among classmates at our own school, we were on pretty much equal ground. In a social setting, we might have bemoaned that we were judged on our appearances rather than our personalities, but it probably didn't occur to us that one day another basis for snap judgments would be added to the mix: the cachet of our jobs.

It's a biggie, and it's here to stay. For better or for worse, twentysomethings have to adjust to this new reality because for the rest of our lives, we can expect to be treated differently depending on the perceived prestige of our jobs.

So what happens if you love your job but it's not the kind of thing that commands instant respect at parties? Allison Predmore has been there. "When I tell people I am a social worker, they usually say something like, 'oh, that's nice, you must be a nice person,' and change the subject," says Ms. Predmore, who lives in Queens, N.Y., and turned 30 earlier this month.

Finding Your Own Niche

Her solution? She spends a lot of time with fellow social workers and others in the nonprofit sector—that is, people who tend to be on her same page, socially as well as financially. "I'm really not used to being with people who have a lot of disposable money to spend on a day to day basis," she says.

Besides, the fact that she really enjoys her work is more important to her than being treated like royalty at a party. That's something that many twentysomethings realize over the years, says Abby Wilner, co-author of "The Quarterlifer's Companion." We may be eternally judged by our jobs but that doesn't mean we'll always care quite so much if our title fails to bowl people over.

"When you are a senior in college or just a year or two out, a job is more conceptual or theoretical," Ms. Wilner says. That is, you don't have much else to gauge a job on other than how it sounds. But once the reality of working sets in—once you realize that work is not only a social signifier, but also the place where you'll spend about a third of your life—chances are, many other considerations, particularly how fulfilling the job is, tend to take precedence over the coolness factor, she says.

"After a couple years, you realize what's more important—the hours, who you are working with, what you are doing, possibilities for promotion," she says. "And you realize that while someone's job might sound cool, they might be miserable eight hours a day."

That doesn't mean that having a job that sounds glamorous isn't an added bonus, especially if it's an added bonus that comes on top of really liking the work, says Cathy Stocker, co-author with Ms. Wilner of "The Quarterlifer's Companion." "Glamour or coolness is just like another kind of compensation," Ms. Stocker says. Which is to say, it's one factor among many in evaluating a job, she says.

How Does Your Job Stack Up, Status-wise?

"In high school and college, there were set hoops to jump through," says Ms. Stocker. "You knew what the standards were and what being successful meant."

In the real world, it's not so clear. While investment bankers and management consultants rake in big bucks, money is far from the only factor in the complicated web of professional status. Some jobs are glamorous even if they're relatively low-paying—like, say, working in an entry-level position in fashion—while, to many people at least, doing things like the Peace Corps or Teach for America seem cool because they're considered exotic or admirable.

Hard to quantify as it is, you can measure your job status pretty easily. If you tell a stranger at a cocktail party what you do or where you work and, just like that, he or she seems to find you extremely smart and interesting and certainly worth talking to, then you have an impressive job. If that person instead reacts with a supercilious lack of interest and starts glancing around the room for other conversation partners, then your job is less glamorous (and the person you're talking to is unpardonably rude).

Some people seem to fare well in the brave new world of professional pecking orders, without ever breaking a sweat. It's just the nature of what they do.

Kevin Jasey didn't become an architect to impress people at parties, but he says it does the trick pretty well. Mr. Jasey, 29, is a project manager for a national architectural firm in Philadelphia. He has found that his chosen profession is creative and artsy enough to be interesting, but at the same time, it's seen as solid and professional. "It's pretty cool," he says. "It commands a certain type of respect."

And it counts even among people who make a lot more money, he says. Mr. Jasey's girlfriend is an investment banker, and he's often in crowds in which the majority of people are in a higher income bracket than he is.

But that doesn't mean they take him less seriously, he says. "They usually start asking my advice on their real estate holdings," he says. And more importantly, he really likes the work. "The profession is more important than the pay," he says.

(continued)

Sometimes a particularly harrowing experience can also help us to put concerns with status in a better perspective. Huong Do had such an experience. The 28-year-old research assistant works in public health in New York City. Ms. Do, who has a master's degree in statistics, really enjoys her work, but knows that to really rise in her field, she should return to school for a Ph.D. But she's not in a hurry.

Nor is she worried that many of her friends are medical students and residents who, a few years down the line, will be full-fledged doctors, earning a lot more money than she does and treated with all the respect that our society affords physicians. "I used to be the overachiever who wanted to go off in a blaze of glory and discover the cure for cancer," she says. But when she was 23, she herself was diagnosed with cancer.

"That shifted my whole perspective," says Ms. Do, who is in remission. "I saw people who didn't make it, and I learned that it is important to do what makes you happy."

It's a key life lesson. After all, we spend a lot more time at our desks than we do making small talk at parties.

From "How Cool Is Your Job? And Does It Even Matter? by Adelle Waldman, *Wall Street Journal* Online Edition, Oct. 24, 2005. Reprinted by permission.

Now let's see how you did.

Reading Speed: Stop! Look at your watch. Mark down how long it took you to read the article: _____ Minutes _____ Seconds. If you read this article in four to six minutes, your reading rate is average for a college student. (Note: Article contains 1,262 words. College students read 200–300 words per minute, on average.) If you read faster or slower than that, what does that mean? If it took longer than six minutes, but you answer the three questions in the "Reading Comprehension" that follows correctly, reading slowly may not be as much of a problem for you as you may think it is. Right about now, however, you may be thinking, *Hey, I don't have time to spare! I'm juggling several different courses, a job, family responsibilities—a dozen things.* That's the point! Read with focus so that you can record, retain, and retrieve information. If you don't understand what you read, it's difficult, if not impossible, to learn it. Reading without comprehension is just going through the motions.

Reading Comprehension: Answer the following questions without going back and rereading the article.

1. What was this article's main point? _____

2. What is the social worker's strategy to cope with how her job is perceived by others?
_____

3. What was the profession of the interviewee who believes that his job is seen as very prestigious even though he doesn't earn a high salary? _____

Now go back and check the accuracy of your answers. Are you "reading right"?

Read Right!

CHALLENGE ⟶ REACTION

Challenge: Are there *right* ways to read? What have you learned about reading in college thus far? Provide as many suggestions about reading right as you can.

Reaction: _____

_____

What do we know about reading? How *should* you tackle your many reading assignments in college? Consider these twelve essential points:[7]

1. **Understand what being a good reader is all about.** Reading isn't a race. Remember the old children's story about the tortoise and the hare? The turtle actually won the race because he plodded along, slowly and steadily, while the rabbit zipped all over the place and lost focus. The moral of that story applies to reading, too. Reading is a process; understanding is the goal. The point isn't simply to make it through the reading assignment by turning pages every few minutes so that you can finish the chapter in a certain amount of time. When your instructors read difficult material, which they do regularly in their profession, they don't rush. They chew on the tough parts, reread sections, and make notes to themselves in the margins. Reading requires you to back up occasionally, just like when you back up a DVD to catch something you missed: "What did he say to her? I didn't get that."

   Students sometimes mistakenly think that good readers are speed-readers.[8] Like Katie from the "FOCUS Challenge Case," they see the claims made by speed-reading courses, and they're tempted to sign on the dotted line. But reading has two components: speed and comprehension. Often, comprehension is sacrificed when speed is increased because most speed-readers actually just skim. You can't digest everything when your brain is trying to process information that quickly. Yes, you can improve your reading speed with focused effort, but more importantly, you can improve your comprehension skills by managing your attention. It's about focus. Science fiction writer Isaac Asimov once wrote, "I am not a speed reader. I am a speed understander."

2. **Take stock of your own reading challenges.** Which of the following are reading issues for you? Put a checkmark next to any that apply to you.[9]

___ boredom	___ vision	___ speed	___ comprehension	___ time
___ amount	___ interest	___ motivation	___ surroundings	___ fear
___ fluency	___ fatigue	___ level	___ retention	___ laziness

   Many people find reading challenging. You may have worked with an impatient teacher as a youngster, or you may have been taught using a method that didn't work well for you—factors that still cause you problems today. Reading involves visually recognizing symbols, transferring those visual cues to your brain, translating them into meaningful

Stockbyte/Getty Images

> **"I just got out of the hospital. I was in a speed-reading accident. I hit a bookmark."**
>
> **Steven Wright, comedian**

Chapter Crossover Generate a discussion with students about why people today often prefer other leisure time activities to reading. If the Internet surfaces as a common response, refer students back to the "Cultivate Your Curiosity" article in Chapter 4 called "Caught in the Net?"

signals—recording, retaining and retrieving information (here's where your memory kicks in)—and finally using these meanings to think, write, or speak. Reading challenges can be caused by *physical factors* (your vision, for example) and *psychological factors* (your attitude). If you want to become a better reader in the future, it's a good idea to assess honestly what's most challenging about the process for you right now.[10] If you simply don't like to read, try reframing the process in your own mind. Mark Twain once said, "Work and play are words used to describe the same thing under different circumstances." What circumstances can you create for yourself that would make reading more enjoyable?

3. **Adjust your reading style.** Reading requires versatility. Contrast these two situations: reading the menu on the wall at your local fast-food joint and poring over the menu at a fancy, high-end restaurant. You'd just scan the fast-food menu in a few seconds, wouldn't you? You wouldn't read word by word and ask: "Is the beef in that burger from grass-fed cattle?" "What, exactly, is in the 'special sauce'?" If you did, the exasperated attendant would probably blurt out, "Look, are you going to order something or not?" That kind of situation requires quick skimming. But you'd take some time to study the menu at a pricy restaurant you might go to with friends and family to celebrate your college graduation. It's an entirely different situation, and the information is more complicated. And if it's a fancy French restaurant, you might even need to ask the definitions of some terms like *canard* (duck) or *cassoulet* (a rich, hearty stew). That kind of situation requires slow, considered study, word by word. You're going to pay for what you choose, and you want the best results on your investment. That's true about college, too. You're investing in your college degree, so reading right is important!

You don't read a textbook or a novel in the same way you skip around when you read a magazine, only choosing articles that interest you: "How to Totally Redecorate Your Apartment on Fifty Bucks" or "Does Your Love Life Have a Pulse?" Books require starting at the beginning and reading straight through. The plot of most novels would be very different if readers just picked certain sections to read! The bottom line? Not everything should be read the same way. You'll face an enormous amount of reading in your combined college classes. The question is, what's fast food (to carry through with the analogy) and what's fine dining? According to research on reading, good readers know the difference and adjust their reading styles.[11]

Yes, some of the reading you'll do in college is fast food. You just need to skim to get the main points and then move on to the next homework item on your agenda. However, much of the reading you'll do in college is fine dining. That's why it's important to devote more time to reading and studying than you think you'll actually need. If you don't understand difficult material, go back and reread it, instead of assuming it will be explained by your instructor in class. Keep a dictionary at your side, and check unusual new terms. You'll be able to digest what you're reading much better.

READING WHEN ENGLISH IS YOUR SECOND LANGUAGE

Hints on Pronunciation for Foreigners

I take it you already know

Of laugh and bough and cough and dough?

Others may stumble but not you,

On hiccough, thorough, laugh and through.

Well done! And now you wish, perhaps,

To learn of less familiar traps?

Beware of heard, a dreadful word

That looks like beard and sounds like bird,

And dead: It's said like bed, not bead—

For goodness' sake don't call it "deed"!

Watch out for meat and great and threat

(They rhyme with suite and straight and debt.)

A moth is not a moth in mother

Nor both in bother, broth in brother

And here is not a match for there

Nor dear and fear for bear and pear,

And then there's dose and rose and lose—

Just look them up—and goose and choose,

And cork and work and card and ward,

And font and front and word and sword,

And do and go and thwart and cart—

Come, come, I've hardly made a start!

A dreadful language? Man alive.

I'd mastered it when I was five.

> —T.S.W. (only initials of writer known) or possibly written by
> George Bernard Shaw

Go ahead. Try reading the preceding poem aloud. Even if English is your first language, you probably had to pause and think about how to say a word occasionally. Most anyone would. English isn't exactly the easiest language in the world to learn, non-native English speakers say. It's filled with perplexing irregularities. Think about the raw courage it would take to pursue a college degree by reading and writing in a language other than your native tongue. If English is your first language, could *you* do it in German or Arabic or Hindi? That being acknowledged, what strategies can ESL (English as a Second Language) students use to help with challenging reading assignments?

1. Remember that spoken English differs from the written English you'll find in textbooks and academic articles. In casual conversation, you'll hear, "And she's . . . like, 'wow!' and I'm . . . like, 'really?'" If you read that in a book, you'd have no idea what the speakers were communicating about. But if you're standing next to the conversationalists in the hallway, you have a chance of figuring it out. Learning to speak informally in conversation is very different from learning to read scholarly discourse. When you read, there's no body language to rely on or real-live author around to whom you can address questions. Address these questions to your instructor or study-group mates instead.

2. Ask your English-speaking friends and instructors to coach you. For example, ESL speakers sometimes struggle with the hundreds of idioms found in English. Idioms are groups of words with a particular, nonliteral meaning. For example, "I have a frog in my throat" means your voice is hoarse, not that you literally have swallowed a green amphibian. Idioms must be learned as a set of words in order to communicate their intended meaning. If you change one word ("I have a *toad* in my throat"), the idiom doesn't work. Considering how many idioms English has and how freely English speakers use them without consciously thinking about it, non-native speakers may find learning them all to be a challenge. You'll more likely hear idioms spoken, rather than read them; however, you may come across them frequently in fiction or poetry assigned in a literature class. If you're an international student, ask about unique phrases that don't make sense to you.

3. Use the Internet or an online course to improve your language skills. According to one study, international students in an online course made significant gains in their language skills, compared with a control group of students who sat through the same course in a classroom. Online courses provide good exposure and practice in your reading and writing skills via e-mail, web searching, threaded discussions, and online postings.[12]

4. Try explaining what you're reading to someone else. Talking something through while you're reading, especially with a native English speaker, can help you clarify meanings on the spot—and may help the other student achieve better comprehension, too.

5. Mark up the textbook so that you can pursue difficult passages in greater detail later. Insert question marks in the margin. Read with your English–native tongue dictionary in front of you.

6. If you get completely stuck, find another book that may explain the concepts differently, or take a break and let your brain continue to decipher while you're doing something else.

4. **Converse with the author.** In every book you read, the author is trying to convince you of something. Take this book, for example. We have been engaged in a conversation all the way through. What do you know about me? What am I trying to persuade you to think about or do? Even though I'm not right in front of you in person on every page, you are forming impressions of me as you read, and I'm either convincing you to try the suggestions in this book or I'm not. As you read any book, argue with the author ("That's not how I see it!"), question her ("What makes you say that?"), agree with her ("Yes, right on!"), relate something she said earlier to something she's saying now ("But what about . . .?"). Instead of just coloring with your yellow highlighter, scribble comments in the margins, or keep a running commentary in a notebook. Make small ticks in the margins to mark words you'll look up in your dictionary at a good breaking point. Socrates once said "knowledge [does] not come from teaching but from questioning."[13] Reading is an active process, not a passive one in which the words just float by you. In fact, mark up this page right now! How do you decide what's really important? One thing you can do is ask your instructor in this course to show you his or her mark-ups in this book, and see if the two of you agree on what's important.

EXERCISE 8.2 A Press Conference with the Author

If you could interview the author of this text, what would you ask her? What would you like to know about her? What would you argue with her about? Play devil's advocate and come up with a list of challenging questions and the responses you think she'd provide. Then role-play this activity with one student playing the role of the author in a press conference on television and the rest of the class playing reporters from major newspapers and magazines of their choosing or as assigned by your instructor.

---

5. **Dissect the text.** Whether you did it virtually online or physically in a real lab, cutting up those little critters in your biology class helped you figure out what was what. The ability to dissect text is important in reading. As you read and make notes in the margins, write what and why statements. Try it: beside each paragraph on this page, write a one-sentence summary statement: a *what* statement. Put the author's words into your own words. Then write another sentence that focuses on *why* the paragraph is included. Does the paragraph contain *evidence* to make a point? Is it an *example* of something? Is it *counterevidence* the author will then refute? If you can tackle this recommendation, you'll do wonders for yourself when exam time rolls around. Think of an essay question on a test that asks, "Discuss three reasons why it's important to read right." You'd remember the why statements you've written in the margins of this section, and be ready with your answer!

EXERCISE 8.3 Marginal Notes

Go back through the section of this chapter on reading that you just completed. If you used a highlighter, make notes to yourself in the margins (or on another sheet of paper) about *why* you underlined a word, phrase, or section. Why did you consider that part to be important? Knowing the answers to these questions is more important than the act of "coloring."[14]

---

6. **Make detailed notes.** You'll be much more likely to actually master a challenging reading assignment if you keep a notebook beside you and take full-blown

notes as you read. Go back and forth, detailing main points and supporting evidence, so that you have a self-constructed outline by the time you've finished reading. If you're reading onscreen, open a new document and annotate there. The physical act of writing or typing can consolidate what you're reading and act as a form of rehearsal that helps you remember it later.

7. **Put things into context.** Reading requires a certain level of what's called cultural literacy, core knowledge that puts things into context and gives them meaning. Authors assume their readers have a common background. They refer to other books or current events, or historical milestones, and unless you know what they're referring to, what you're reading may not make sense to you. An example you might be familiar with is how the television show *Seinfeld* made real words that everyone now knows and uses out of fake ones: *yada yada yada*, for example. Those words are now part of our cultural literacy that have meaning for you and everyone you know, probably, but may not for people from another culture. They know the literacy of their own culture instead.

Imagine the "Far Side" cartoon in which a caveman and cavewoman (Mom and Dad) are reviewing the report card that Junior (who is slouched in the foreground) brought home to the cave. Dad says, "Oh look . . . this get better. 'F' in history! You even flunk something not happen yet." Getting the joke requires an amazing amount of cultural literacy:

> That American Moms and Dads typically review report cards with their children.

> That report cards are important to American parents.

> That students worry when their grades are poor.

> That cavemen and women spoke a rudimentary form of human language.

> That history is a subject taught in school.

> That history is a cumulative record of events over time.

These examples of cultural literacy are fairly easy to figure out, but what about this less familiar historical reference? You might think, for example, that Walt Whitman's 1888 poem "O Captain! My Captain!" is something a sailor wrote when his skipper died. Instead, it's a poem about Abraham Lincoln, who was assassinated as the Civil War drew to an end.

O captain! my captain! our fearful trip is done;
The ship has weathered every rack, the prize we sought is won;
The port is near, the bells I hear, the people all exulting,
While follow eyes the steady keel, the vessel grim and daring.

But O heart! heart! heart!
O the bleeding drops of red!
Where on the deck my captain lies,
Fallen cold and dead.

"Force yourself to reflect on what you read, paragraph by paragraph."

Samuel Taylor Colerifge, British poet (1772–1834)

Chapter Crossover Remind students that Chapter 6 contains good advice on taking notes, and that some of what is presented there on taking notes during lectures works for taking notes while reading, too.

Lincoln was the captain, the ship was the United States, the storm was the Civil War, and the prize was keeping the union together, surviving the war, and abolishing slavery. At the time, the poem held a highly prominent place in American cultural literacy. Whitman said he was asked to recite it so often that he was almost sorry he had ever written it.[15] Today, far fewer people in our culture know this once familiar reference. Did you? If you come across it in a book now, you are culturally literate and understand the reference. You're an insider, which is an important aspect of reading. Keep your eyes and ears open, read and listen, or buy a cultural literacy dictionary so that, as a reader, you're "in the know."[16]

8. **Don't avoid the tough stuff.** Much of the reading you'll do in college includes complicated sentences that are difficult to navigate. When you try reading complex passages aloud, you may stumble because you don't immediately recognize how the words are linked into phrases. But practicing reading aloud is one way you can become more conversant with difficult language. Many instructors teach their first-year students a common approach to reading and studying called SQ3R:

Survey—Skim to get the lay of the land quickly.

Question—Ask yourself what, why, and how questions. What is this article or chapter about? Why is it included? How might I use this information?

FOCUS ON CAREERS: BARBARA SWABY, Literacy Expert

Courtesy of Barbara Swaby

Q1: You're a national expert on reading. What attracted you to the field?
Literacy has always been a value in my family. Both my parents were educators and were vitally involved in literacy efforts. More critical to my decision, however, is the fact that I am a native of Jamaica in the West Indies. The illiteracy rates in my country of origin are high as are the poverty rates. I have long realized that the major weapon against poverty is education, which in my thinking is synonymous with literacy. These realities greatly formed my decision to work to develop literacy in young children.

Q2: What's the role of parents in helping children learn to read— and enjoy reading?
Way back in 1908, Edmund Huey said that the best place to learn to read is on a mother's lap or a father's knee. That statement is still true today. It is the parent that establishes the value for literacy in the home. It is the parent that should first provide emotionally powerful experiences with books, a daily time and predictable space for reading, and a love of the parents' personal favorites. The parent's role in developing literacy is significant and indispensable.

Q3: Is being a good reader about being a speed-reader? Or is there more to it?
It is true that speed is related to reading success; however, more related is the notion of fluency. Fluency not only relates to speed but also to achieving a balance between speed and expression, smoothness, pacing, and phrasing. Viewing speed as a major player in reading, especially without the balance of these other factors, is not only counterproductive

to reading, but detrimental to it as well. Fluency in reading is the result of the same factors required for fluency in any skill: Practice, Practice, Practice!

Q4: According to the National Assessment of Adult Literacy, reading for pleasure in America is in steep decline, especially among young adults. What are your theories about why this might be true?
The decline of reading for pleasure is not at all difficult to explain. One simply needs to look at the state of literacy among America's children. According to the National Assessment of Educational Progress (NAEP) in 2005, 69 percent of our eighth-grade students read at below proficient levels, so it is no surprise at all that these students grow up to be adults that are not avid or recreational readers. With so many options for entertainment, engaging in a somewhat difficult task such as reading may be overlooked as an option.

Q5: In your view, how important is reading to college success?
Reading *must* remain a mandatory and indispensable requirement of all college experiences. Inefficient reading skills probably account for the greatest failure in college courses, second only (in my opinion) to a failure to study enough or appropriately.

Q6: What are some of the main challenges college readers face? Do some students go about their reading assignments in the wrong way?
I believe that college students' literacy challenges begin with the sheer volume of reading they are expected to do (and rightly so) and the fact that they have not been exposed to these expectations in the past. Many

Read (1)—Go ahead now and read the entire assignment. Make notes in the margins or even create a study guide for yourself.

Recite (2)—Stop every now and then and talk to yourself. See if you can put what you're reading into your own words.

Review (3)—When you've finished, go back and summarize what you've learned.

One expert suggests, however, that for scholarly articles, original published research, and complicated academic prose, you may need to add a few R's to make a new formula, SQ6R:

Reflect (4)—You may need time to truly understand what you've read. Put it down and come back to it later—but definitely come back.

Rehash (5)—Communicate your views to your study partners. They may be having trouble deciphering the language, too, and multiple heads may be better than one. You may gain some insights from them, and vice versa.

Rethink (6)—Evaluate whether or not you understood the article on your own. Do you understand it better after rehashing it with other students? And finally, how will you use put the information you read to good use?[17]

students go about reading their required texts in unproductive ways. Many do not allocate sufficient time to study. Many confuse the acts of reading and studying. Many are not reading with enough personal engagement and not connecting themselves to what they're reading or connecting what they're reading to the world itself.

Q7: What's your best advice for first-year college students? How can they become better readers and therefore more successful in their college careers?
First, you should allocate enough time for reading texts and for study. Remember that all college texts are not equally difficult and that reading difficult texts successfully requires more than one reading. Second, separate the act of reading from that of studying. Although reading and studying have some things in common, *purpose* differentiates them. You can read with one of several purposes: to prepare for class discussion, for example, or simply to be entertained. When you study, however, you have a single, predetermined purpose. You will be accountable to someone else for what you read. You must know what you will be expected to learn, prioritize the information accordingly, and read closely, stopping to fix breaks in comprehension. Third, always reflect on what you read. Stop often and think about what you have read. If you are unable to remember or reflect on the material, then reread the material and try again. Taking notes on the text material may help, too. Finally, if you feel that you have a reading problem that you are unable to solve by yourself, by all means, seek assistance from your advisor or from the learning center on your campus. They are available precisely for that purpose.

C CREATE a Career Outlook

TEACHER
Have you ever considered a career as a teacher? Here are some facts about this career to consider and some questions about yourself to ponder.

Facts to Consider

Academic preparation required: Completion of a bachelor's degree, a teacher education program, and state licensure are required to teach in the U.S. public school system.

Future workforce demand: Because many current teachers are reaching retirement age, career opportunities are excellent although demand will vary somewhat by region, grade level, and subject matter.

Work environment: Many teachers work more than forty hours per week, including both classroom time and additional time required to prepare lesson plans and grade papers. They work ten months a year, typically, with two months off during the summer to travel, take college courses, or pursue outside interests. Teachers find their work rewarding although unruly students, accountability pressures (standardized testing of students), and imposed curricula can increase stress levels. Facilities can range from new, state-of-the-art to run-down and out-of-date.

Most common psychological type preferences: (for reading teachers, specifically) introverted (or to a lesser extent, extraverted), sensing, feeling, and judging[18]

Essential skills: reading; writing; communicating with students individually and as a class, and with parents, administrators, and other teachers; planning and evaluating assignments; managing a classroom; using technology; working with committees or team teaching; sensitivity to diversity

Questions to Ponder

1. Do you have (or could you acquire) the skills this career requires?
2. What would you find most satisfying about this type of career?
3. What would you find most challenging about this type of career?
4. Are you interested in a career like this? Why or why not?

For more information, see U.S. Department of Labor, Bureau of Labor Statistics, *Occupational Outlook Handbook, 2006–2007 Edition*.[19]

For more career activities online, go to http://www.academic.cengage.com/collegesuccess/staley to do the Team Career exercises.

Purestock/Jupiter Images

"Parents should play an inestimable role in children's learning to read and learning to love to read."

Barbara Swaby

Teachable Moment If any of the students guessed what the passage was about, ask them what hints they used to figure it out.

9. **Learn the language.** Every discipline has its own perspective and its own vocabulary. In many of the introductory classes you take, you'll spend a good deal of time and effort learning terms to be used in classes you'll take later. In order to study *advanced* biology, everyone has to learn the same language in *introductory* biology. You can't be calling things whatever you want to call them. You call it a respiratory system, but your classmate calls it a reproductive system. Imagine the medical problems that might bring on! Here's a fun challenge—read these three passages written by authors representing three different disciplines. All three authors (two of whom are my daughters) were asked to translate the same passage as a parody, using the language of their own discipline. See if you can guess what the original passage was and which disciplines these authors are representing.

Passage 1: Our human experience suggests that the light that radiates from a star actually shimmers, but we are forced to examine not only whether such a visual phenomenon is an accurate representation of reality, but also whether it truly constitutes empirical evidence of a star's fundamental existence. Such questioning could lead us to explore further the nature of the human condition and our very existence as inhabitants of the universe. —Shannon (Staley) Wood

Passage 2: The pinpoints of light we see in the night sky are the imprints left on our retinas by photons that have traveled hundreds of millions of light years across the near-vacuum of interstellar space. Experts theorize that stars are actually super-heated balls of hydrogen gas, so massive that the force of their own gravity triggers atomic fusion in their cores. This process produces electromagnetic energy, as well as subatomic particles and increasingly complex elements. By studying the stars, we gain valuable insights into the nature of matter, energy, and the space-time continuum. —Stephanie Staley

Passage 3: As we look out into the heavens late at night, we wonder what it all means. According to a recent survey, only 52 percent of Americans are "very happy" with their lives.[20] The pace and stress of modern-day life, the drive to succeed, the pressure to accumulate material wealth and have it all are evident in our society. Ironically, is happiness sacrificed in the pursuit? Can balance be achieved? What are the roles of spirituality, wellness, counseling, and drug therapies in coping with our complex lives? —Constance Staley

Can you guess the original passage? If you guessed "Twinkle, twinkle, twinkle little star; how I wonder what you are," you're right! These three authors were asked to parody their disciplines in a humorous way to make a point. The writer of Passage 1, a philosophy major, uses the poem to question the nature of reality. Passage 2's writer, an astrophysics major, translates it into a scientific treatise on stars. In Passage 3, your author, posing as a psychology major, is prompted to discuss personal adjustment and mental health. All three interpreted the original children's verse in different ways based on the "languages" spoken by their disciplines. In college you will learn about the humanities (philosophy, for example), the natural sciences (astrophysics, for example), and the social sciences (psychology, for example) as you take what are often called general education or core courses. It's important to get to know a discipline. Pay attention to its perspective, priorities, and practices as you read, study, and learn.

10. **Bring your reading to class.** Some of your instructors will infuse the outside course readings into their lectures. They may justify the readings in their course syllabus, preview the readings in class, talk about their importance, or create reading worksheets for use in small groups. If they don't, however, it's up to you to integrate them. Bring up the reading in class, ask questions about it, and find out how it relates to particular points in the lecture. Doing so is an important part of being responsible for your own learning.

Sensitive Situation Entering students learn quickly that some professors ask students to purchase and read books but don't address the readings in class or test students on them. Encourage students that if this is the case, it is their responsibility to ask how the readings and lectures should be integrated. Katie's friend Brittney learned not to "waste time" on the readings, but she is taking her chances, and at some point, her strategy won't work.

11. **Be inventive!** Students who are the best readers invent strategies that work for them. Perhaps you're an auditory learner. Reading assignments aloud might drive your roommate or another family member to distraction (so find a place where you can be alone), but it might be the perfect way for you to learn. If you're a kinesthetic learner, you might make copies of particular passages from your textbook and lecture notes, and build your own scrapbook for a course. Or cut up the professor's lecture notes into small chunks and reassemble them. Using what you know about yourself as a learner is a big part of college success, so don't just do what everyone else does or even follow your instructor's advice verbatim, if it doesn't work for you. Figure out what does, and then do it!

12. **Make friends with your dictionary.** Okay, so it's annoying to stop every few minutes to look up a word. It's absolutely necessary, however. From the preceding "Twinkle, Twinkle" examples, which terms would you need to look up? What does the term *empirical evidence* mean? What, exactly is the *space-time continuum*? Yes, sometimes it's important to break your stride, stop, and look up a word or phrase because what follows in the reading is based on that particular definition. Other times, these strategies might be appropriate:

Teachable Moment Students can also be encouraged to keep their own online course-specific glossaries. They can set up folders for separate classes by simply cutting and pasting from an online dictionary and refer back to it whenever they need to.

> Keep a stack of blank index cards next to you and write down the unknown word or phrase, the sentence it appears in, and the page number. Then when you have a sizable stack, or when you've scheduled a chunk of time, look up the whole stack.

> Try to guess the word's meaning from its context. Remember Lewis Carroll's "Jabberwocky" poem from *Through the Looking-Glass*? Even though the poem contains fabricated words, when you read it, you infer that something was moving around sometime, somewhere, right?

Brand X Pictures/Jupiter Images

> **"Outside of a dog, a book is man's best friend. Inside of a dog, it's too dark to read."**
>
> Groucho Marx, American comedian, actor, and singer (1890–1977)

'Twas brillig ← ['twas usually indicates a time, as in 'twas daybreak],

and the slithy toves ← [we don't know what *toves* are, but *slithy* sounds like a combination of slimy and slithering]

Did *gyre* and *gimble* in the *wabe* ← [the meaning of *wabe* is unclear, but *gyre* sounds like gyroscope, suggesting movement, and so forth]

Often you can infer a word's meaning from how it's used or from other words around it, but not always. Many of your courses will require you to learn precise meanings for new terms. If you can't detect the meaning from the context, use your dictionary—and see it as a friend, rather than an enemy.

INSIGHT ⟶ ACTION

1. How would you characterize your reading skills, based on all your years of schooling and feedback you have received from teachers? Are you an above average, average, or below average reader? Why?

2. What are your particular strengths as a reader? For example, do you enjoy reading, comprehend what you're reading fairly quickly, find it easy to focus, and so on? What are your particular weaknesses?

3. Considering how important reading will be to your college success, what can you do to improve? For example, would it be worthwhile to try reading for pleasure to see if you can become better at it? Can you set a timer to give yourself reading goals, or create practice quizzes to assess your comprehension?

C CONTROL Your Learning

YOUR TOUGHEST CLASS

Look back over the section of this chapter on reading and honestly assess the extent to which reading is part of what you find challenging about your toughest class.

1. Do you understand what being a good reader in this discipline is all about?

2. Do you understand, accept, and work to improve your reading skills in this course?

3. Do you adjust your reading style? If the reading required in this course is challenging, do you read more carefully and with more focus?

4. Do you converse with the author of the textbook for this course as you read?

5. Do you dissect the text, writing what and why statements in the margins of the textbook?

6. Do you make detailed notes?

7. Do you put things you read for this course into context? Is cultural literacy a part of the challenge you face?

8. Do you tackle the reading with gusto, even if it's tough stuff?

9. Are you learning the language of this discipline?

10. Do you bring up questions about the reading in class?

11. Do you invent your own reading strategies to help you?

12. Do you make regular use of your dictionary to help you understand what you're reading for this class?

Honestly assess the extent to which you do or don't practice these suggestions in your most challenging class this term. Make an action plan, citing which recommendations you'll put into effect immediately and how you'll do it. If it's appropriate, e-mail your plan to your instructor in this class.

Emotional Intelligence (EI) Research Individuals with low problem-solving skills see themselves stuck in situations without a way out. Reluctant readers often feel overwhelmed and don't have a step-by-step plan to improve their reading skills. Good problem-solvers figure out the problem, assess what they can do, set some goals, begin doing what they set out to do, and continually reassess.

Teachable Moment You may discover some students in your class who love to read. Ask them why they enjoy reading and to name some of their favorite books. Consider adopting a local elementary school and engage your students in a service learning project by reading to younger students or tutoring them in their reading skills.

Meta-what? Metacognition, Reading, and Studying

CHALLENGE ➔ REACTION

Challenge: What are your study habits like? To what extent do these ten statements apply to you? Write the number for each statement on the line preceeding it.

Never Sometimes Always

1 2 3 4 5 6 7

_____ 1. I understand myself as a learner.

_____ 2. When I'm studying something difficult, I realize when I'm stuck and ask for help.

_____ 3. I make a study plan and stick to it in order to master class material.

_____ 4. I do whatever I need to do in order to learn something.

_____ 5. I talk through my problems, understanding things while I study.

_____ 6. After I study something I think about how well it went.

_____ 7. I know *when* I learn best: morning, afternoon, or evening, for example.

_____ 8. I know *how* I study best: alone, with one other person, in a group, etc.

_____ 9. I know *where* I study best: at home, in a library study carrel, at my computer, etc.

_____ 10. I believe I'm in control of my own learning.

Reaction: Now tally your scores on this informal instrument. If you scored between 60 and 70 total points, you have excellent metacognitive skills. If you scored between 40 and 60 points, your skills are probably average. However, note any items you rated down in the 1 to 2 range, and then continue reading this section of the chapter carefully.

Talk about needing to use a dictionary! What does the word *metacognition* mean? Actually, scholars write long articles about the meaning of this term. *Meta* is an ancient Greek prefix that is often used to mean *about*. For example, metacommunication is communicating *about* the way you communicate. ("I feel humiliated when you tease me in front of other people. Can you *not* do that?" "When we both try to boss each other around, we end up fighting. Let's agree to talk through issues instead.")

Emotional Intelligence (EI) Research Metacognition requires some very well developed emotional intelligence skills. For example, one has to know oneself (intrapersonal capacity) and be able to accurately assess what one is doing. It also requires good problem solving, strong self-regard (an *I can do* attitude), self-actualization, impulse control, and accurate reality testing.

"**Being busy does not always mean real work. The object of all work is production or accomplishment and to either of these ends there must be forethought, system, planning, intelligence, and honest purpose, as well as perspiration. Seeming to do is not doing.**"

Thomas Edison, American inventor (1847–1931)

Since cognition means thinking and learning, metacognition is thinking about your thinking and learning about your learning. It's about identifying your learning goals, monitoring your progress, backing up or getting help when you're stuck, forging ahead when you're in the groove, and evaluating your results. Metacognition is about knowing yourself as a learner and about your ability (and motivation) to control your own learning. Some things are easy for you to learn; others are hard. You learn better at particular times in particular ways in particular surroundings. What do you know about yourself as a learner, and do you use that awareness *intentionally* to learn at your best?[21]

These questions may seem simple, but how do you know:

1. When you've finished a reading assignment?

2. When your paper is ready to turn in?

3. When you've finished studying for an exam?

When you're eating a meal, you know when you're full, right? But when it comes to academic work, how do you know when you're done? Like Katie, do you just run out of time, or do you know when you've learned what you need to learn and done all you need to do?[22] As a learner, *awareness*, *knowledge*, and *control* are three keys to your college success!

Metacognition is about having an "awareness of [your] own cognitive machinery and how the machinery works."[23] It's about knowing the limits of your own learning and memory capabilities, knowing how much you can accomplish within a certain amount of time, and knowing what learning strategies work for you.[24] Know your limits, but at the same time, stretch.

When it comes to reading and studying, you need a plan to help you focus. If you just sit down and start thinking about everything you have to do, it's easy to become overwhelmed. Which assignment should you start with? Which one is most important? Which one is most urgent? How much time should you devote to each one? Some students think they should somehow study everything at once, and since they can't actually do that, they give up before they even get started! Other students get derailed by the temptation to study what they like best or what's easiest, telling themselves that doing so will then motivate them to move on to more difficult challenges afterward. Beware of these rationalizations! Dale Carnegie once said, "Do the hard jobs first. The easy jobs will take care of themselves." He was right—focused learning requires making a master plan for studying, and you are the ideal person to create one that works for you. When it comes to learning, it's all about you—your motivation, your self-discipline, and your attention management!

Emotional Intelligence (EI) Research Daniel Goleman tells us that there is a readiness to learn as evidenced by children who were successful in Head Start programs. Included in some of the prerequisite skills are both intentionality (the wish and capacity to have an impact and act on it) and self-control (a sense of inner direction).

Complete the recommended activity for your preferred VARK learning modality. If you are multimodal, select more than one activity. Your instructor may ask you to (a) give an oral report on your results in class, (b) send your results to him or her via e-mail, (c) post them online, or (d) contribute to a class chat.

 Visual: Make bar graphs that depict how much time you spend per day reading assignments for each of your classes. Label the X axis with the days of the week and the Y axis with increments of hours/minutes.

 Aural: Reread what you consider to be the most useful part of this chapter aloud. As you read, stop and ask questions or make comments (aloud) to make sure you comprehend what you are reading.

 Read/Write: Reread what you consider to be the most important part of this chapter. As you read, insert what and why statements beside each paragraph throughout in the margins.

Kinesthetic: Make a copy of what you consider to be the most helpful part of this chapter. Also make copies of your notes from class or from your reading, and build a scrapbook to help you put everything together.

Becoming an Intentional Learner: Make a Master Study Plan

What's your favorite class this term? Or let's turn the question around: what's your least favorite class? Of course, it's easier to study a subject you find interesting, but T. S. Eliot is making an important point in the quote here: becoming an educated person may well require you to study things you wouldn't *choose* to study. Considering all you have to do, including your most and least favorite classes, what would making a master study plan look like? You've been there, done that all through your schooling, but do you *really* know how to study?

To begin, think about what you have to think about. What's your goal? Is it to finish your English essay by 10:00 P.M. so that you can start your algebra homework? Or is it to write the best essay you can possibly write? If you've allowed yourself one hour to read this chapter, but after an hour, you're still not finished, you have three choices: keep reading, finish later, or give up entirely. What's in your best interest, honestly? See if you find the following planning strategies helpful.

1. **Make sure you understand your assignments.** Understanding is critical to making a master plan. You can actually waste a great deal of time trying to read your instructor's mind after the fact: "Did she want us to *analyze* the play or *summarize* it?" "Were we supposed to do all the practice problems, or just the first set?" When you leave class, make sure you're clear on what's been assigned. If you're not, zap your professor an e-mail to find out.

> **"No one can become really educated without having pursued some study in which he took no interest."**
>
> **T. S. Eliot, American-born poet (1888–1965)**

2. **Schedule yourself to be three places at once.** Making a master plan requires you to think simultaneously about three different time zones:

   The past: Ask yourself what you already know. Is this a subject you've studied before? Have your study habits worked well for you in the past? How have you done your best work—in papers, on exams, on projects?

   The present: Ask yourself what you need to learn now. How interested are you in this material? How motivated are you to learn it? How much time will you devote to it?

   The future: Ask yourself how you'll go about learning it. Will you learn it using the strategies that work best for you? What learning factors will you control? Will you do what you can to change what's not working?[25]

3. **Talk through your learning challenges.** There's good evidence that talking to yourself while you're studying is a good thing. Rather than worrying about the stereotype that only crazy people do that, researchers find it helps you figure things out: *Okay, I understand the difference between a neurosis and a psychosis, but I'm not sure I can provide examples on the test.* Once you've heard yourself admit that, you know where to focus your efforts next.[26]

4. **Be a stickler.** Have you ever thought about how important accuracy is? For example, an accuracy rate of 99 instead of 100 percent would mean:

   > 40,900 babies born each year in the United States wouldn't be counted by the Census Bureau.[27] (Hopefully, one of them wouldn't be yours!)

   > 4,270 needed heart bypass operations a year wouldn't be done, most likely resulting in many premature deaths.[28]

   > 500 airplanes in U.S. skies each day wouldn't be directed by air traffic controllers.[29] Disastrous!

   As you read and study, remember these graphic examples. Be thorough. Read the entire assignment. Pay attention to details. Accuracy counts!

5. **Take study breaks.** The human attention span is limited, and according to some researchers, it's shrinking, rather than expanding.[30] Plan to take brief scheduled breaks to stretch, walk around, or grab a light snack every half hour during study sessions. Of course, it's important to sit down and get back to work again. Don't let a quick study break to get a snack multiply into several hours of television viewing that wasn't in the plan.

6. **Mix it up.** Put a little variety into your study sessions by switching from one subject to another, or from one mode of studying—for example, reading, self-quizzing, writing—to another. Variety helps you fight boredom and stay fresh. However, if you're on a roll, and finally understand the math problem you've been working on for an hour, ignore this suggestion.

7. **Review, review, review!** Review your course material often enough that you can retain and retrieve information at the level expected by your instructor. If you have to start fresh each time you come to class, trying to work from your memory of what was discussed during the last class, you'll always feel behind. To be even more focused, some students review *lecture* course material right after class (to help you remember it) and *discussion* course material right before class (so that you can participate in the discussion).

Chapter Crossover Tell students they may want to read ahead in Chapter 13. This chapter addresses wellness issues that might help students stay focused, and the chapter clearly outlines barriers to studying and student success.

8. **Find a study buddy.** Find a classmate who also values studying, and commit to keeping one another focused during study sessions. Go beyond just studying together. Create quizzes and hypothetical test questions for each another, and use your study partner to keep you on track.

9. **Estimate how long it will take.** Before starting an assignment, estimate the amount of time you will need to complete that assignment (just as you do at the start of each chapter of this book), and then compare that estimate to the actual amount of time the assignment took to complete. Getting into this habit helps you develop realistic schedules for future projects.

10. **Vary your study techniques by course content.** When you study math, it's important to do more than read. Working problem sets helps you actually develop the skills you need. When you study history, you study differently. You might draw a timeline of the events leading up to World War I, for example, or read various biographies of Elizabeth I of England to get a comprehensive view of how this queen ruled, compared to her father before her.[31]

11. **Study earlier, rather than later.** Whenever possible, study during the daytime rather than waiting until evening. Research shows that each hour used for study during the day is equal to one and a half hours at night. Another major study showed that students who study between 6:00 P.M. and midnight are twice as likely to earn A's as students who put off their studying until after midnight.[32]

12. **Create artificial deadlines for yourself.** Even though your professors will have set deadlines for various assignments, create your own deadlines that precede the ones they set. This will allow for any unforeseen emergencies, as well as give you time to give your assignment one last review before turning it in. "The dog ate my homework" story is so overused that it's lost its credibility, and it's well known that exam times bring great danger to students' relatives, especially fictitious ones! Remember that Murphy's Law is alive and well: "Whatever can go wrong will." Printer cartridges always run dry midway through printing your paper, and hard disks invariably crash while you're typing the last entry in your bibliography. Finish early, and you'll save yourself considerable trauma.

13. **Treat school as a job.** If you consider the amount of study time you need to budget for each hour of class time, and you're taking 12–15 credits, then essentially you're working a 36–45 hour/week job on campus. Arrive at "work" early and get your tasks done during "business hours" so you have more leisure time in the evenings.

14. **Show up.** Once you've decided to sit down to read or study, really commit yourself to showing up—being present emotionally and intellectually, not just physically. It's easy to look like you're "there" when you're really off somewhere in your head. If you're committed to getting a college education, then give it all you've got! Get help if you need it. If you have a diagnosed learning disability, or believe you might, find out where help is available on your campus. One of the best ways to compensate for a learning disability is by relying on metacognition. In other words, consciously controlling what isn't happening automatically is vital to your success.[33]

> **"He was always leaning forward, pushing something invisible ahead of him."**
>
> **James Thurber, American humorist, describing his energetic editor**

Emotional Intelligence (EI) Research Students often underestimate the time it will take to complete work. Dr. Richard Kadison in the December 10, 2004, issue of *The Chronicle of Higher Education* indicates that more than one-third of first-year students feel "frequently overwhelmed" with all they have to do. Low EI skills in both reality testing and impulse control can be a student's worst nightmare.

Sprinting to the Finish Line: When to Take Shortcuts

Let's be realistic. Planning is important, but there will be times when taking shortcuts will be the only way you can survive the onslaught of all you have to study. You may have many assignments that are all due in the same week or on the same day. You'll need to prioritize your time and make decisions about what to study. That's unavoidable. When you do need to find a way to accomplish more than is humanly possible, try the following suggestions.

1. **Triage.** With little time to spare, you must be efficient. Consider this analogy: If you're the physician on duty in the ER, and three patients come in at once, who will you take care of first: the fellow with strep throat, the woman with a sprained wrist, or the heart attack victim who needs CPR? It's called triage (see Figure 8.1). It sounds simple, but it's actually more complicated than you might think. (For example, what if the fellow who appears to have strep throat actually has a deadly, contagious virus that requires he be quarantined immediately?) Of all the material you need to study, ask what is most important, less important, and omittable. If you have several assignments due the same week, evaluate where you stand in each course and then determine where to place your emphasis. For example, if you are earning an A- in art history, a B + in world geography, and a C- in math, you know which course most needs your attention. Evaluate the material and ask yourself which topics have received the most attention in class and in the textbook. Then focus your study time on those topics, rather than trying to study everything. There won't be time for that, so make an informed "executive decision" and run with it.[34]

2. **Use every spare moment to study.** If flashcards work for you, take your flashcards with you everywhere, for example. If you have a few minutes to spare while

Figure 8.1

Triage

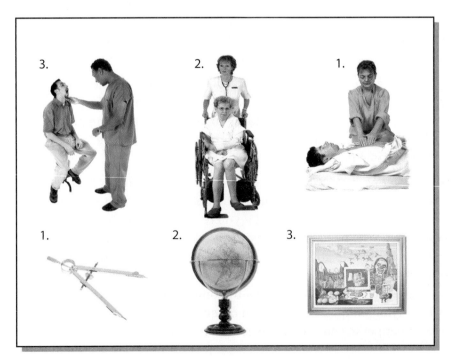

you're waiting in a line somewhere, whip them out and study. Organize your essay answer in your head while you're filling up at the pump. It's surprising: small amounts of focused time do add up.

3. **Give it the old one-two-three-four punch.** Immerse *all* your senses in the precious little amount of time you have to study: *read, write, listen,* and *speak* the material.

4. **Get a grip on your gaps.** Honesty is the best policy. Rather than glossing over what you don't know, assess your knowledge as accurately as possible, and fill in the gaps. This will do wonders for your confidence and your performance in all your classes.

5. **Cram, but only if it's warranted.** If you're ultra short on time due to a real emergency, and you have studying to do for several classes, focus on one class at a time. Despite all the warnings to the contrary, most college students find themselves cramming at some point. Be aware, however, that interference can be an obstacle to retrieving information. If you learn new information that is similar to something you already know, the old information can interfere. So if you're studying for a psychology test that contains some overlap with your sociology test, separate the study sessions by a day. Studies also show that cramming up to one hour before sleeping can help to minimize interference.[35] Nevertheless, continually remind yourself: What's my goal here? Is it to just get through twenty-five pages or is it to truly understand?

Box 8.1 When Optimism Can Actually Hurt You

Have you ever been in this situation? You have a big project to do for one of your classes, and you take comfort in the fact that the deadline is weeks away. *Thank goodness,* you think to yourself. *I have six weeks until this project is due—no sweat!*

In one study, researchers asked undergraduates to predict how long tasks would take them—from writing a thesis to fixing a bike. What they learned is that students habitually underestimate the time it takes to complete tasks—on average, by three weeks for larger projects, and several days for smaller ones. Psychologists call this phenomenon an "optimistic bias." Students tended to forget problems they may have faced when they completed similar projects in the past. Instead, they focused on how smoothly the project would go this time. Their optimism tricked them into a false sense of complacency. Be aware—and always build in extra time![36]

Emotional Intelligence (EI) Research There is a concept in EI that is called an overused strength. For example, a student with too much empathy can put the needs of others before himself. Thus, he might miss an exam to comfort a roommate who just broke up with a girlfriend. The overused strength of too much empathy can hurt a student if it's not grounded in reality.

Integrated Learning: Learning Is Greater Than the Sum of Its Parts

CHALLENGE ⊖ REACTION

Challenge: What is *integrated* learning? Can you define the term or predict what it means?

Reaction: _____

> "What do you consider to be the end purpose of education? Is it not to bring about an integrated individual?"
>
> Krishnamurti, Indian speaker and educator (1895–1986)

Activity Option Hand out topics on index cards to groups of students (3 to 4 in a group). Topics can be most anything, but examples might be things like stem cell research, global warming, or immigration. Give students five minutes to list all the disciplines they would have to study to fully understand the topic.

Integrated learning involves forming connections. It's easy to develop target fixation and think, "I'll put my psychology book away and study math now." In your mind, math and psychology are unrelated. Practically speaking, they're requirements that help you check off squares toward getting your college degree.

Although that's true—they *are* separate classes—they're interrelated in daily life. Most of the important problems you will face in your life won't have simple solutions. You won't be able to check off a square and be done with them. Turning to page 225 in your psychology book probably won't give you the answer in a flash. Even if a problem you face on the job requires a mathematical solution, you'll still need to integrate some psychology in order to convince your boss that your answer is right! Problems are multilayered and unscripted; they require you to come at them from different directions. Instead of just knowing X amount of math and Y amount of psychology, it's integrated learning that counts ultimately—the ability to make connections between classes and disciplines, between something you learned earlier and something you're trying to learn now, and between the classroom and your other experiences on campus, in the community, or on the job.[37] As you work to become a truly educated person, you begin to realize that knowledge intersects and overlaps. You may experience integrated learning as "aha moments":

> ➤ **Between disciplines** "My psychology professor was talking about dyscalculia, a mathematical learning disability, just yesterday in class."

> ➤ **Over time** "This psychological principle relates to what I studied in my history course last term."

> ➤ **Between contexts** "My service learning project is allowing me to experience first-hand what I'm learning in my psychology class."

That's precisely what you'll be doing in your career—applying what you're learning in class! The time to start forging connections is now at the beginning of your college career, and you can help make them happen. Here are some ways to begin.

1. **Take interdisciplinary courses.** Some classes intentionally demonstrate connections between disciplines. If you took a first-year seminar course called Street Beat, for example, you might learn about music, media, and culture from the perspectives of sociology, music, psychology, literature, and business. Courses such as these can be full of exciting and stimulating discoveries as a variety of disciplines focus on a particular topic.

2. **Forge connections yourself.** Many of your instructors will make connections for you. Your poetry instructor, for example, may also discuss the historical context during which a poem was written and how the poet was affected

by the art, literature, music, and philosophy of the day. But if those connections aren't made for you by your instructors, search for them yourself. Actively seek related information, and then find the connections.

3. **Look for links between classes.** Your instructors don't know what other classes you're taking, but you do. Find areas of commonality between them. Look for overlap. Most courses are "separated" by discipline, but there's no reason you can't connect them in your head. Your college experience may seem fragmented to you, but the sense of purpose you have as you work through courses can help you develop what playwrights call the "through line," the central idea or question the play pursues from start to finish. When it comes to getting a college education, keep the concept of a through line in your head. If you approach learning with a high level of self-awareness, you can bridge the breadth of your courses and deepen your learning.

4. **Join a learning community.** On many campuses, first-year students have an opportunity to be a part of a community of learners who take a particular set of classes—English, psychology, and physics, for example—together. When you do this, it's easy for dialogue to develop between you and your classmates about the integrated learning that's taking place. If no formal learning community program exists on your campus, start your own with classmates you notice who are taking several other classes with you. Talk about connections between classes with them.

5. **Examine a single skill across multiple courses.** Take your writing skills, for example: How does your writing compare in your composition class, your political science class, and your sociology class? Think outside the box of the "serial" classes you're taking, one after the other, and look at what you're doing concurrently in several.

6. **Connect contexts.** One of the main points of getting an education is being able to apply it. Connect what you're learning in the academic curriculum with your co-curricular experience. ("If I apply what I'm learning in my anatomy course, maybe I can improve my performance on the track team.") Connect what you're learning in class to what you do on the job. ("We just learned about the primacy-recency effect in my psychology class, and the chef asked us to push the specials tonight. That means I should welcome guests by first going over the list of specials, then let them talk for a while and bring their drinks, and then mention the specials again before I take their orders.")

7. **Build a learning portfolio.** While some institutions require their students to create a learning portfolio, electronically or on paper, every first-year student should begin this worthwhile undertaking. A learning portfolio is a rich, flexible file in which you reflect on your work, measure your progress, provide evidence of your accomplishments, and assess what you're learning *across* your courses. In many professions—art and architecture, for example—professionals build a portfolio to present the range and quality of their work to galleries or builders. A learning portfolio uses the same principles. In creating your own learning portfolio, you'll need to decide what to include and why, and in the process of building a portfolio you'll make some important discoveries about yourself as a learner. Think about

all the knowledge, skills, sensitivities, and values a graduate should be able to demonstrate. Here's a sample list:

Effective communication	Diversity
Information literacy	Ethics
Critical and creative thinking	An appreciation for the arts
Quantitative reasoning	Breadth of knowledge
Collaboration skills and teamwork	Depth of knowledge

A learning portfolio provides evidence of the quality of your work. It helps you recognize connections within and between classes, analyze your choices and patterns in relation to your areas of interest, and track your own learning curve. Select assignments to include that represent your strengths. Include papers from your classes, reflective essays, multimedia projects, an *academic* résumé that lists your courses and what you've learned from them, and a *co-curricular* résumé that lists all the activities and positions of leadership you've held in campus organizations. By the time you graduate, your learning portfolio will be an integrated summary of your entire college experience that you might even show to a potential employer or a graduate school interviewer.

Why is integrated learning so important? Making connections is the route to memory power and to learning itself. You learn best when you relate what you're learning to what you already know, to your life, and to the world around you. In other words, connections count.

The more we learn about the world, the more we realize it is an increasingly complex place. According to one scientist who studies air pollution, "What happens in Beijing will affect Boston, what happens in Boston will affect Paris, et cetera . . . this connectivity of the planet will come back at us time and time again."[38] Connectivity affects us all in ways we don't even realize. Becoming an integrated learner will help you build the skills you need to navigate the world in your chosen career and throughout your life.

Experts predict that "growing proportions of the nation's labor force are engaged in jobs that emphasize expert thinking or complex communication—tasks that computers cannot do." Expert thinking involves "effective pattern matching, based on detailed knowledge and metacognition, the set of skills used by the stumped expert to decide when to give up on one strategy, and what to try next." Complex communication is "the exchange of vast amounts of verbal and nonverbal information. The information flow is constantly adjusted as the communication evolves unpredictably."[39]

Integrated learning is a natural outgrowth of curiosity and passion. When you're truly fired up about what you're learning, you're more likely to pursue it and integrate on your own. Many of the academic habits you develop in your first year—good ones and not-so-good ones—will tend to stick with you throughout your time in college. If you can begin to think about integrated learning now, as a first-year student, imagine how much further ahead of your classmates you'll be by the time you graduate.

In your career, you'll need to be able to solve complex problems that require you to integrate your learning. Knowing isolated facts won't be enough. You will need to pull together what you've learned in many different courses to come up with a solution. The time to become an intentional, integrated learner is now!

> **"Non scholae sed vitae discrimus. (We do not learn for school, but for life.)"**
>
> **Lucius Annaeus Seneca, Roman philosopher and statesman (4 B.C.–A.D. 65)**

1. Choose two classes you're taking this semester. How are they connected? What overlap do you note in the content of both courses?

2. Whose responsibility is it to integrate learning? Is integrated learning something that teachers should do for you? Why or why not?

3. If you began building a learning portfolio this term, what would you include and why?

YOUR TYPE IS SHOWING

What does your psychological type have to do with your reading and studying skills? What would you predict? See if these descriptions apply to you.

Type, Reading, and Studying

Extravert (E)

Extraverts (like Katie) sometimes have difficulty concentrating on reading assignments for long periods of time. Reading aloud may help them to stay focused and benefit comprehension, too.

Introvert (I)

Introverts find it easier to concentrate for longer periods, but they sometimes wander off in their thoughts, either related to what they're reading or into something else entirely in a daydream.

Sensing (S)

As children, sensors sometimes find learning to read more challenging than intuitive children do. Sensors may learn to "break the code" of written language with the help of a teacher using experienced-based reading or phonics instruction.

Intuition (N)

Intuitives find it easier to understand and manipulate symbols, generally. However, they sometimes fall into the trap of neglecting the facts of a text and focusing more on the larger concepts or big picture.

Thinking (T)

Generally, thinkers are more tolerant of "dry" reading assignments than feelers are. They often focus more on the information content than they do on tone or style. They also tend to be more critical readers.

Feeling (F)

Feelers care about the tone and style of what they read, and they may choose to read something simply because they enjoy those qualities in an author. They also tend to be more eager about reading materials that have personal meaning for them.

Judging (J)

Judgers reach conclusions about what they're reading more quickly; however, they may rush to judgment on something they're reading, and then find when they reread it, that they've drawn the wrong conclusions.

Perceiving (P)

Perceivers sometimes enjoy reading because it helps them explore things they don't know much about. They tend to read more slowly or become so bogged down in their reading that they take too long to get to the related assignment.

When it comes to studying, the Sensing-iNtuition and Judging-Perceiving scales relate most to college success. For sensors studying means learning facts. That's something they're good at. But instructors often want to know more than that on exams: How do the facts connect? What do they mean? What's the bottom line? Intuitives, on the other hand, want to know what things mean right away. Where is this leading? What's the main point here? While the big picture is important, details count, too.

Judgers like to study with a plan. As soon as they receive an assignment, they often organize the steps involved and sketch out a timeline so that they feel they're making continual progress. Perceivers may prefer to look at all the angles first, and sometimes they spend so much time doing so that they are forced to make a snap decision at the last minute on exactly how to proceed.[40]

Do any of these descriptions fit you? What do they tell you about how to read and study to *your* best advantage?

A Final Word about Reading and Studying

Albert Einstein said this: "Never regard study as a duty, but as the enviable opportunity to learn to know the liberating influence of beauty in the realm of the spirit for your own personal joy and to the profit of the community to which your later work belongs." Reading and studying are what college is all about. Take his advice: consider the opportunities before you to become an expert thinker, an integrative and intentional learner, and a contributor to the community and world in which you live.

For more practice online, go to http://www.academic.cengage.com/collegesuccess/staley to take the Challenge Yourself online quizzes.

> **"'Tis not in mortals to command success, but we'll do more … we'll deserve it."**
>
> **Joseph Addison, English politician and writer (1672–1719)**

FOCUS CHALLENGE CASE

NOW WHAT DO YOU THINK?

At the beginning of this chapter, Katie Alexander, a frustrated and disgruntled student, faced a challenge. Now after reading this chapter, would you respond differently to any of the questions you answered about the "FOCUS Challenge Case"?

>>> >> > REALITY CHECK < << <<<

On a scale of 1 to 10, answer the following questions now that you've completed this chapter.

1 = not very/not much/very little/low   10 = very/a lot/very much/high

In hindsight, how much did you *really* know about this topic before reading the chapter?

1 2 3 4 5 6 7 8 9 10

How much do you think this information might affect your college success in college?

1 2 3 4 5 6 7 8 9 10

How much do you think this information might affect your career success after college?

1 2 3 4 5 6 7 8 9 10

How long did it actually take you to complete this chapter (both the reading and writing tasks)? _____ Hour(s) _____ Minutes

Take a minute to compare these answers to your answers from the "Readiness Check" at the beginning of this chapter. What gaps exist between the similar questions? How might these gaps between what you thought before starting the chapter and what you now think after completing the chapter affect how you approach the next chapter in this book?

Activity Option This is a good opportunity for reflection. Ask students to summarize their responses to the "Reality Check" and send it to you via e-mail. Tell students that they must also include references to both their VARK and MBTI types. Ask them to give at least two examples of when they were aware of how their types either helped or hindered their reading and studying.

To download mp3 format audio summaries of this chapter, go to http://www.academic.cengage.com/collegesuccess/staley.

9 Taking Tests

YOU'RE ABOUT TO DISCOVER...

Teachable Moment Obviously, test-taking is critical to college success. Remind students that they need to be thinking about how they learn and study best and how to get help for test anxiety, if that is an issue for them. Don't forget to share your experiences, too, particularly obstacles you've overcome.

> Why you should change your thinking about tests

> What to do before, during, and after a test

> Why cramming doesn't always work

> What test anxiety is and what to do about it

> How to take different kinds of tests differently

> How cheating can hurt your chances for success

"Focused mind power is one of the strongest forces on earth."
Mark Victor Hansen, motivational writer and speaker

Joe Cloud

"Joe College," that's me, Joe Cloud kept thinking to himself. His long-awaited opportunity to leave his small rural community on the reservation had finally arrived. He was at college in the big city, where life was vastly different. He would be different, too, he had convinced himself—somehow more outgoing, more athletic, more popular, more successful—more of everything.

Growing up in his town of 1,000, he had been the basketball king, the after-school grocery store shelf stocker, and the smartest guy in his high school of thirty-five. He was leaving a trail of victories behind him, and everyone in town appeared to have a stake in his future success in college. As the end of the summer approached, whenever people saw him in the grocery store, they'd yell out, "Hey, Joe, when are you leaving for college?"

Much to his parents' delight, Joe had even won a scholarship that would pay for all of his expenses. The condition, of course, was that he would be successful, graduate, and return to the reservation to give back to the community in some capacity. Joe hoped to teach English and coach basketball at his own high school. Secretly, he wondered how much more stressful his life would be at college, competing with students from all over the country for the best grades.

Now that classes were in full swing and midterms were approaching, Joe was beginning to feel the stress. Generally, things were going well, except for his killer calculus course. There were 350 students in the lecture course, and Professor Buchanan was very businesslike and aloof. Joe was building up a great deal of anxiety over the course. Never before had he failed at anything, and if he didn't keep his grades up, he'd lose his scholarship.

The first week had been a review of what he had learned in his high school calculus class. But things became more challenging quickly. The pace quickened to the point that Joe found himself frantically trying to keep up. Math had never been his best subject, but by applying himself and hitting the books, he'd always been able to squeak by.

However, as the midterm exam approached, Joe began experiencing a funny sensation when he entered class each week. As he approached the door, his breathing became shallow and rapid, his heart was pounding, and he felt light-headed when he sat in his seat. He finally had to get up and leave before passing out. Unfortunately, it was exam review day, too.

That evening at dinner, he talked over his experience with his friend, Chris. "I've been telling you to eat breakfast!" Chris said. "You have to start rolling out of bed earlier, man!" But deep within himself, Joe knew his problem was more than just skipping breakfast. His reaction to each class session had become progressively worse. *There's no way I'll pass this course,* he thought. *Not when my*

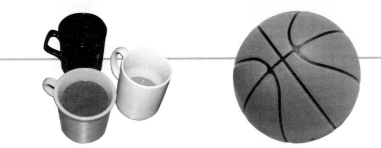

body is going to sabotage me like this. So much was riding on his success, and so many people were pulling for him. How could he disappoint them?

Although he hated to admit it, calculus had become so distasteful that Joe hadn't cracked the textbook since the day he had to get up and leave. He knew cramming was a bad idea, but he also knew that he had given himself no choice. The night before the midterm, Joe figured he'd study all night and forget about everything else that was due the next day. As the clock ticked into the wee hours of the morning, he was making trips to the coffee machine every forty-five minutes. Chris offered him some pills to help him stay awake, but Joe knew better. It was hard to focus, but the test was tomorrow, and he figured he had to pull an all-nighter if he wanted to pass at all. Dr. Buchanan had said the test would consist of calculus problems with the answers in multiple-choice format, so Joe got out his highlighter and started reading the textbook chapters.

The morning of the exam, Joe woke up suddenly with a feeling of dread weighing him down. When he glanced at his alarm clock, he saw that he had overslept. The exam would start across campus in fifteen minutes. His palms were sweaty, and his heart was racing again. He leaped out of bed, threw on some clothes, and ran out the door. When he got to class, he noticed that he'd forgotten his watch and his book bag with his calculator in it. As he sat down in a random empty seat, a student next to him leaned over and whispered, "I am totally freaked out about this test, aren't you?" That didn't help.

Joe finally worked up the nerve to look at the first question and realized he couldn't answer it. Frantically, he paged through the rest of the exam. It all looked unfamiliar. He was so tired that he was having trouble focusing. His seat gave him a perfect view of another student's answer sheet one row down and over. He struggled with the temptation. It was the longest fifty minutes of his life, and when Dr. Buchanan called "time," Joe put down his pencil and slumped back into his chair.

The next week when the exams were handed back, Joe expected the worst—and he got it. What he stared at was the worst grade he'd ever gotten on any test in his entire life. Disgusted, he threw his exam in the trash can at the front of the lecture hall on his way out. *Why is there so much emphasis on exams in college, anyway? I'll never have to take a test again when I get out of here,* he muttered to himself. He was only halfway through his first term, and his scholarship was already on the line.

Chapter Crossover Make sure students look ahead to Chapter 13. This chapter on wellness will help students learn particular strategies for managing stress.

WHAT DO **YOU** THINK?

Now that you've read about Joe Cloud, answer the following questions. You may not know all the answers yet, but you'll find out what you know and what you stand to gain by reading this chapter.

1. What should Joe have done differently *before*, *during*, and *after* the exam?
2. Does Joe have test anxiety? Why or why not?
3. What's the *right* way to study for a multiple-choice exam in a calculus course?
4. Does cramming work? Why or why not?
5. If you were Joe, would you have cheated to save your scholarship? Why or why not?

Activity Option Since students may not want to reveal their answers to number 5, you can use a variation of Angelo and Cross's One-Minute Paper to help debrief this case study. Ask students to take out a piece of paper (or you can provide index cards) and answer two questions anonymously: What is Joe's biggest challenge, and what is the one thing you would suggest that Joe do? Collect them, and report the results to the class.

Before beginning to read this chapter, take two minutes to answer the following questions on a scale of 1 to 10. Your answers will help you assess how ready you are to focus.

1 = not very/not much/very little/low   10 = very/a lot/very much/high

Based on reading the "You're about to discover..." list and skimming this chapter, how much do you think you probably already know about the subject matter?

1   2   3   4   5   6   7   8   9   10

How much do you think this information might affect your college success?

1   2   3   4   5   6   7   8   9   10

How much do you think this information might affect your career success after college?

1   2   3   4   5   6   7   8   9   10

In general, how motivated are you to learn the material in this chapter?

1   2   3   4   5   6   7   8   9   10

This book describes four key factors related to intrinsic, or internal, motivation: curiosity, control, career outlook, and challenge. The next four questions relate to these **C-Factors:**

How *curious* are you about the content you expect to read in this chapter?

1   2   3   4   5   6   7   8   9   10

How much *control* do you expect to have over mastering the material in this chapter?

1   2   3   4   5   6   7   8   9   10

How much do you think this chapter might help you develop your *career outlook*?

1   2   3   4   5   6   7   8   9   10

How *challenging* do you think the material in this chapter will be for you?

1   2   3   4   5   6   7   8   9   10

Before beginning any task, including studying, it's important to check in with yourself to ensure that you're physically, intellectually, and emotionally ready to focus. How ready are you, physically, to focus on this chapter? (Are you rested, feeling well, and so on?)

1   2   3   4   5   6   7   8   9   10

How ready are you, intellectually, to focus on this chapter? (Are you thinking clearly, focused on this course, interested in this subject?)

1   2   3   4   5   6   7   8   9   10

How ready are you, emotionally, to focus on this chapter? (Are you calm, confident, composed?)

1   2   3   4   5   6   7   8   9   10

If your answer to any of the last three questions is below a 5 on the scale, you may need to address the issue you're facing prior to beginning this chapter. For example, if you're hungry, get a quick bite to eat. If you're feeling scattered, take a few moments to settle down and focus.

Finally, how long do you think it will take you to complete this chapter? _____ Hour(s) _____ Minutes

---

Activity Option Generate a discussion with students about their level of interest in this chapter's material. Some students may believe that they are already good at taking tests. Some may have test anxiety and want to avoid the material. But if they don't care and are not good at test-taking, they are in big trouble. Ask students to jot down, anonymously, why they are or aren't interested in this chapter. Gather the responses and get a discussion going.

Emotional intelligence (EI) Research Daniel Goleman tells us that "people who are poor in this [managing emotions] are constantly battling feelings of distress, while those who excel in it can bounce back far more quickly from life's setbacks and upsets."

Testing 1, 2, 3 ... *Show* **What You** *Know*

Let's face it, life would be very different without grades in college, or time clocks on the job, or performance reviews throughout your career, wouldn't it? You wouldn't have to show up at work if you didn't feel like it, and you'd get a paycheck anyway. You wouldn't have to do a good job because no one would care. And you wouldn't have to write papers, or give presentations, or take tests in college. Not only would you benefit by having more free time, but your instructors wouldn't have to forge their way through stacks of papers assigning grades, either. What a wonderful world that would be—or would it? Realistically, it would probably bring total chaos.

Life's not like that. Results count. Accountability is the bottom line. Achievement is taken seriously. Like Joe in the "FOCUS Challenge Case," you may be thinking, "I'll never have to take another test once I get out of here," but exams are actually realistic representations of life's requirements. The experience of taking a test is similar to running a critical meeting or giving a high-stakes presentation on the job. You'll need to walk into the room, ready to show what you know, and answer unanticipated questions. The anxiety you feel before taking a test isn't much different from the anxiety you might feel in stressful situations in your career. Exams ask you to demonstrate your knowledge on the spot at a particular juncture in your learning. They help you compare your progress to that of other students and to your professor's set of expectations about what all students should know.[1] On the job, every day will be a test of your skills and abilities, and you'll get your "grade" when your supervisor gives you an accounting of your performance over the last six months or year. Tests are inevitable; so rather than bemoan them, perhaps we should change the way we think about them.

The first step of test-taking, of course, is to make sure you're prepared. All of the information in this chapter is worthless if you haven't gone to class or read the textbook or taken good notes during lectures. Miracles, by their very definition, are in very short supply. Nothing can substitute for being conscientious about your work. Think about preparing for an exam as you would for an athletic event. Imagine running the 26 mile, 385 yard Boston Marathon, billed as "the world's oldest and most prestigious road racing event." You'd have to work for months to develop the stamina you would need to finish successfully. You wouldn't want to just show up for kicks and wing it. If you did, at the very least, you'd probably pull a muscle. At the very worst, they'd carry you away on a stretcher.

> "Today the greatest single source of wealth is between your ears."
>
> **Brian Tracy, leadership and business speaker**

The same principle holds true for exams in college. In order to have the stamina required and avoid the "injury" of not doing well, tests require this same kind of step-by-step, long-term preparation. Tests in your courses will usually ask you to do one or more of the following:

> *Remember* or *recognize* specific facts

> *Compare, contrast, synthesize,* or *interpret* information

> *Apply* theories and principles to recognizable or new problems

> *Predict* the outcomes to a set of variables

> *Evaluate* the usefulness of ideas, theories, or methods for a particular situation

Look at all those italicized verbs, and you begin to see the span of what will be required of you in all your courses.

Think about taking tests as a three-stage project with a beginning, middle, and end. What do you do *before* the test to get ready? What do you do *during* the test to do your best? What do you do *after* the test to ensure a productive learning experience you can use for future exams? Taking a test can actually be a learning experience, and you can improve your performance incrementally as you learn to master the principles you'll read in this chapter.

Sensitive Situation Keep in mind that full-blown test anxiety or panic attacks are not all that uncommon. You may have students in your class who suffer from these problems. Take a minute to remind students where on campus they can get help for this.

Teachable Moment Ask students to think about how they prepare for tests. Are they a last-minute person? Do they always show up a little bit late? Do they cram too many things into a day? Do they prepare ahead of time for anything? Or do they just show up and take their chances in most areas of life? Get students to think about themselves and how they respond to tasks in general.

Before the Test: Calm Your Nerves by Preparing Carefully

CHALLENGE ⊝ REACTION

Challenge: List your five best specific ideas about how to prepare for tests. What works for you? Assume you are giving advice to a brand new student.

Reaction:
1. _____
2. _____
3. _____
4. _____
5. _____

As you read the upcoming sections about *before*, *during*, and *after* a test, evaluate how many of these suggestions would have helped Joe Cloud in our opening case study. Also think about how they apply to you. Put a plus sign (+) in front of each item you already do regularly and a (✓) in front of items you could start doing more regularly to improve your test-taking skills.

1. _____ **Begin preparing for an exam on the first day of class.** Nothing can replace consistent, regular study before and after each class. If you work along the way, then when it comes time for the exam, you will be much more ready and much less in need of heroic efforts. Keep up with the reading, even if there are things you'd rather be doing. Learning experts talk about the differences between *spaced* and *mass* learning. Spaced learning takes place over time; mass learning takes place all at once. For example, if you took piano lessons as a child, your teacher probably had you learn parts of a piece of music incrementally—a few bars at a time—until you learned the whole song. Imagine sitting at the piano as a six-year-old and trying to learn all of "Für Elise" in one sitting. While mass learning may work for some simple tasks, spaced learning is said to enhance retention by as much as 40 percent.[2]

2. _____ **Identify the days and times of all your exams for the whole term in your planner or PDA.** At the beginning of the term, write in the days and times of all the exams in all your courses—even finals, which will seem very far off. You'll thank yourself many times over for completing this essential task.

3. _____ **Find out exactly what the test will cover.** There's nothing more terrifying than having a classmate next to you say something like this before the exam begins, "I can't believe this test covers the entire first six chapters," when you thought it only covered the first four chapters. Clarify whether handouts will be included, previous quiz questions—anything you're not sure of. Phone or e-mail several other students, or better yet, ask your instructor questions like these: How long

Comstock Images/Jupiter Images

> **"If you would hit the mark, you must aim a little above it."**
>
> Henry Wadsworth Longfellow, American poet (1807–1882)

will the test be? What material will it cover? Which topics are most important? It's also a good idea to ask about criteria that will be used in grading. Do punctuation and grammar count? Will you be asked to turn in your notes or draft so that the instructor can see your work? Will there be an in-class review? All these questions are usually fair game.

4. _____ **Understand that specific types of preparation are required for specific types of tests.** As described in later sections in this chapter, objective and subjective tests should be approached differently. Online tests require that you know the answers to important questions up front. For example, will the test time out? Must you complete the exam once you start, or can you save your answers and come back to finish later? Should you compose essay answers elsewhere and paste them into the online exam so that you don't lose all your work in the case of a technology hiccup? Is the campus wireless system reliable enough for completing tests online?

5. _____ **Make a study schedule.** How many days are left to study? What will you accomplish each day? Don't decide you'll use whatever time is left over to study for your test. Usually there isn't any time left over. Time has a way of filling up all by itself. Remember—don't let what is "urgent" crowd out what is important.

6. _____ **Begin serious reviewing several days before the test.** The best strategy is "tending" the class material, just as you take care of other things you care about, like your car or your dog, consistently and regularly. After each lecture, work with your notes, revising, organizing, or summarizing them. Then several days before the exam, step up your effort. Divide up the work by days or study blocks. Begin consolidating your lecture notes and reading notes. Make flashcards, outlines, charts, summaries, tables, diagrams, whatever works for your learning style and fits the material.

7. _____ **Maximize your memory.** Research indicates that elaborate rehearsal is more effective than shallow rehearsal and specific techniques help transfer information from short-term to long-term memory. Remember to "Make It Stick" (rehearse, overlearn, space it out, separate it, and mind the middle), "Make It Meaningful" (feel, connect, and personalize), "Make It Mnemonic" (spell, locate, link or narrate, and peg), "Manipulate It" (mark it up, mark it down, organize, picture, act, produce, and test), and "Make It Funny" (mock it).

8. _____ **Get everything ready the night before.** To calm your nerves, lay out your clothes the night before the exam and pack your book bag with things you'll need: several pencils, erasers, scrap paper, your calculator, and a watch that works. Remove as much hassle as you can from test day. Joe Cloud would have been much better off if he had done this.

9. _____ **Manage your energy so that you're ready to focus and work quickly.** You've heard it before, but if you're exhausted or feverish, you're not as likely to "show what you know" as you will if you're healthy and rested. Exams tend to take their toll, energy-wise, so have reserves built up to sustain you. And don't resort to artificial stimulants, like drinking excessive amounts of coffee to stay awake. "All-nighters" are a college ritual. They may make you feel heroic, and people sometimes brag about having suffered through them, but they catch up with you, and they're a bad habit to get into. According

Teachable Moment Many students can and do make schedules for themselves; they just don't follow them. Share some tips on how you can stick to a schedule: be realistic, reward yourself, clear your work area, focus, and so on.

Chapter Crossover Remind students about Chapter 7 on developing your memory. There are many tips on memorizing; have students think about which memory tips were most helpful to them. Discuss how they used the memory chapter since reading it and how the techniques worked for them.

to one expert, "for every hour of sleep we lose, we drop one IQ point."[3] A series of all-nighters during midterms or final exams can seriously impair your intellectual performance.

Emotional Intelligence (EI) Research
Remember the concept of learned optimism. Optimism strongly connects with success and it can be learned.

10. _____ **Don't give in to a nonproductive, negative attitude.** Emotions are contagious. Stay away from other students who are freaked out or pessimistic about the exam. Think—and feel—for yourself. Make sure your self-coaching is productive ("I've studied this section for an hour; if it's on the exam, I'll nail it."), rather than punishing ("I'm so stupid. Why didn't I keep up with the reading?").

11. _____ **Study with other students.** Have you ever heard this quotation before: "To teach is to learn twice" (Joubert, French moralist, 1754–1824)? It's true. When you teach something to someone else, you must first learn it thoroughly yourself. Why not study with other students? You can take turns teaching one another, comparing class notes, and making practice exams for each other. For most of us, talking things through helps us figure them out as we go. Studying with other students is fun, and it can get you better results. But don't wait to be invited; take responsibility and start a study group yourself. And if you're concerned that a study group of several students may degenerate into a social club, study with just one other person—find a study buddy and commit to doing the work.

12. _____ **Remind yourself of your long-term goals.** Why are you going to college? All this sweat and toil is worth something or you wouldn't be doing it. Keep your sights on the finish line! Enjoy the feeling of accomplishing something now that contributes to your goal-oriented success later. Ask people who finish the Boston Marathon how they feel. The answers you'll get won't focus exclusively on the ordeal; they will celebrate the accomplishment—guaranteed!

13. _____ **Arrive at the classroom early, but not too early.** Get there early enough to get a seat where the lighting is good and you won't be distracted by other students, but don't arrive so early that you build up excessive anxiety during a long wait.

14. _____ **Don't pop pills to stay awake.** You may know students who use Ritalin, Adderall, Vicodin, and OxyContin as study aids. This is a bad idea. When these drugs are used for the wrong reasons, they can help you stay awake for hours and enter a dreamy state. The potential side effects include insomnia, nausea or vomiting, dizziness, palpitations, headaches, tremors and muscle twitching, even seizures. With such horrible potential health risks staring you in the face, not to mention possible legal sanctions if you obtain these drugs without a prescription, why not make things simple? Just study.[4]

15. _____ **Don't let open-book or take-home tests lull you into a false sense of security.** What could be easier than an

William B. Plowman/Getty Images

Christina Ripp wins the 2003 Boston Marathon Women's Wheelchair Division

open-book test? What could be better than taking a test in the comfort of your own home? Actually, these two types of tests require substantial preparation. Time is the issue here. If you're unfamiliar with the material, flipping through pages of notes or skipping around in the textbook won't help. Create a reference guide for yourself so that you can find various topics in your notes or textbook and use your time efficiently.

16. _____ **Don't mess with success.** If you're doing well and earning the grades you deserve, don't discard what is working for you. Honestly assess the efficiency and effectiveness of your current practices, and then decide what ideas from this chapter you should add to your test-taking preparation repertoire.

Activity Option Consider assigning pairs of students to one of the sixteen activities listed in this section and ask them to role-play the situation, either as described or if this suggestion isn't followed. One student could be assigned to act out going into the open-book test unprepared (number 15). The second student could become his "inner voice" and describe what is happening and what would happen if he followed this bullet's advice.

Cramming: Does "All or Nothing" Really Work?

CHALLENGE ⮕ REACTION

Challenge: Why is cramming for tests a bad idea? List as many reasons as you can.

Reaction: _____

_____

Activity Option Copy the A+ student tips and cut them into strips of paper. Hand one to each student in the class. Go around the class and ask each student to say why their tip would or would not work for them.

Box 9.1 Test Tips from A+ Students

- "I rewrite my notes immediately after each class, which helps me retain information. I schedule my classes at least an hour apart so I can do this."

- "When I rewrite my notes, I put them in test format. This helps enormously during the review process."

- "I find that flashcards are a great way to learn math formulas, definitions, or important concepts. For a foreign language class, I put the word on one side of the index card, and I draw a picture of the object on the other."

- "I go through the exam quickly and assign each question a level of difficulty: 1, 2, or 3, with 3 being the hardest. Then I answer all the 1's first and the 2's second. I know the 3's will take me some extra time."

- "I make flow charts to help me learn processes and relationships. As I create charts and tables, I 'play with' the information by labeling columns and rows, and that's how I learn it."

- "I rewrite my notes several times, and each time I do, I condense them into smaller and smaller amounts of information. Working with the same material over and over helps me learn."

- "I divide up the amount of material I have to study by the number of days before the test. That way I know exactly what I need to master each day."

- "If I have three tests scheduled for the same day, I study in three hour blocks and alternate among the three subjects. That keeps things interesting and energizes me."

- "In my experience, most of what is on tests comes from lectures. I think this is because teachers are most familiar with their own views."

- "In my experience, most of what is on tests comes from the textbook. I think this is because it saves teachers time to use the questions in the instructor's manual, rather than making them up from scratch."

- "I reread all my notes an hour before the test so that everything is fresh in my mind. I make sure I clear my schedule so that's possible."

- "When I finish studying for the night, I reward myself with a treat and then turn in."

- "I bring a candy bar to the exam. When I start feeling tired and my mind begins to wander, I refresh myself with a sugar high."

- "I always wear my 'lucky shirt' on exam day. It's worked for me so far!"[5]

Imagine yourself as the actor in the following scenarios. Compare these situations to cramming for tests.

> You don't eat for a week, and then at one sitting, you gorge for several hours on everything you can stuff into your mouth. Does that sound appealing to you? Probably not. It wouldn't work well either, would it? You can only hold so much.

> You haven't called your significant other since last year. Suddenly you appear at her door with candy, flowers, concert tickets, and dinner reservations at the most exclusive restaurant in town. You can't understand why she isn't happier to see you.

> You don't feed your dog for several months. When you finally bring him a plate loaded with ten T-bone steaks to make up for your neglect, you notice he's up and died on you. Oops!

Of course, these tongue-in-cheek, all-or-nothing situations are ridiculous, aren't they? How could anyone ever neglect such basic necessities of life? There's an important point to be made here. Many things in life require continuous tending: pets and people, for example. If you ignore them for a time, catching up is next to impossible. Your college courses should be added to the list.

Believe it or not, some students give themselves permission to follow this all-or-nothing principle in their academic work. They sail along without investing much time or energy in their studies, and then they try and make up for lost time right before an exam by cramming. The word *cram* provokes a distinct visual image, and rightly so. Picture yourself packing for spring break in a warm, sunny place and hardly being able to close your suitcase because it's crammed full. You can't decide what to bring so you bring everything you can think of.

The same holds for cramming for a test. You try to stuff your brain full of information, including things you won't need. Since you haven't taken the time to integrate the information and gather it into related chunks, you end up with random bits of unconnected data. Cramming is an attempt to overload information into your unreliable working memory. It's only available for a very short time. However, there are other reasons why cramming is a bad idea:

> Your anxiety level will surge.

> Your sleep will suffer.

> Your immune system may go haywire.

> You may oversleep and miss the exam altogether.

Despite the warnings here, most students cram at some time or other during their college careers, and doing so may even give them a temporary high and make them feel like they're suffering for a cause.[6] But generally, slow and steady wins the race.[7]

YoUR TypE iS ShOwing

How would you answer the following yes or no questions about your test-taking strategies as they may relate to your type?

1. I usually end up changing answers to some questions on exams, and usually lose points in the process. _____

2. Essay questions are much harder for me than true-false or multiple-choice questions. _____

3. If I had a choice, I'd take an exam in a room all by myself so that I could really concentrate. _____

4. I prefer open-ended questions that allow me to include everything I know. _____

5. Organizing my response to an essay question is difficult for me. I prefer to just start writing and see where the answer goes. _____

6. I sometimes read more into a question than is really there. _____

7. I usually end up making careless mistakes on exams. _____

8. I feel most comfortable answering questions that have a specific, concrete clue about the answer. _____

9. I take my time on tests, reading and rereading questions. _____

10. I understand my strengths and weaknesses as a test-taker, and I'm consciously working to improve. _____

Does personality type impact test-taking strategies? If so, how? You'd probably assume that an *introvert* would say yes to item 3, or that a *perceiver* would agree with item 4. Look at your responses and see how they relate to what you know about your type. According to one study, *judgers* are less likely than *perceivers* to change answers, and *introverts* who change their answers—as opposed to *extraverts*—are more likely to gain, rather than lose, points by doing so.[8]

Actually, the MBTI scale that shows the biggest differences on test-taking is the Sensing-iNuition scale. *Sensors* are less likely than *iNtuitives* to trust their hunches when answering text questions. They may read a question over and over, searching for some kind of concrete clue, so much so that they read into the question. They may miss the big picture, answer theoretical questions based on their own practical experience, and lose points by changing answers. People who are *iNtuitives* tend to jump to conclusions when they read test questions. They may fill in a missing word with their mind's eye, or make an inference upon which they base another inference until they are far afield from the answer the question is seeking.[9]

Do these research results apply to you?

Test-Taking: High Anxiety?

CHALLENGE ⮂ REACTION

Challenge: What is *test anxiety*? What are the symptoms? Do you have it?

Reaction: Fill out the following informal survey to determine whether or not you may have test anxiety. For each of the twelve statements, rate your degree of agreement or disagreement.

1	2	3	4	5
Disagree Completely	Disagree Somewhat	Unsure	Agree Somewhat	Agree Completely

1. I cringe when I suddenly realize on the day of an exam that a test is coming up. _____

2. I obsess about the possibility of failing an upcoming exam. _____

3. I often experience disappointment, anger, embarrassment, or some other emotional reaction during an exam. _____

4. I think that instructors secretly get enjoyment from watching students squirm over exams. _____

5. I experience physical symptoms such as an upset stomach, faintness, hyperventilation, or nausea before an exam. _____

6. I tend to zone out during exams; my mind goes blank. _____

7. I feel extreme pressure to please others by doing well on exams. _____

8. If I'm honest, I'd have to admit that I really don't know how to study for tests. _____

9. I'd much rather write a paper or give a presentation than take an exam. _____

10. I usually fear that my exam grade will be lower than that of other students. _____

11. After taking an exam, I obsess on my performance, going over and over questions that I think I may have missed. _____

12. I convince myself that I'm not good at taking exams even though I often do fairly well on them. _____

If your score equals 49–60, you are a likely candidate for test anxiety. For suggestions on how to manage your anxiety, read on.

If you scored between 37 and 48, you have some signs of anxiety and may need help in managing your stress level.

If you scored 36 or below, you most likely experience a normal amount of anxiety and have already developed coping skills to help you.

Sensitive Situation Make sure that you tell students who scored between 37 and 48 to think about how they are going to manage stress. Encourage them to use campus resources, and invite them to e-mail you if they are not exactly sure what to do. Stress can become debilitating for some students who get overwhelmed by events as the term continues.

> **"Positive thinking will let you do everything better than negative thinking will."**
>
> **Zig Ziglar, motivational speaker and author**

Test anxiety—what is it? And, more importantly, does it affect you? While most people think of text anxiety as a negative, the truth is, it's natural to be anxious before, during, and even after an exam. Most everyone is. In fact, some anxiety is useful. The adrenaline rush that accompanies anxiety can keep you alert and focused.

But for some students, like Joe Cloud, test anxiety takes over and sabotages their efforts. They may say, "I knew it all before the test, but when I saw the questions, everything I knew vanished before my very eyes." These students experience fainting spells or even gastric distress that requires them to leave the testing room periodically. Some of them may be reacting to prior bad experiences with exams. Others may put intense pressure on themselves because they're perfectionists. Clearly, there's evidence from medical science that too much anxiety can work against you. Corticosterone, a hormone released during times of extreme stress, can actually impair your ability to retrieve information from long-term memory.[10] Regardless of the reason, the first part of the solution is understanding exactly what test anxiety is. It has four different, but related, components:[11]

> ➤ cognitive aspects—nonproductive thoughts that run through your head before, during, and after an exam ("I have to get an A on this test. If I don't, I'll flunk out of school.")

- **emotional aspects**—negative feelings you experience related to the exam (disappointment, frustration, sadness, and so on)

- **behavioral aspects**—observable indications of stress (fidgeting, drumming your fingers on the desk, walking quickly, and so on)

- **physiological aspects**—counterproductive physiological reactions (dry mouth, butterflies in your stomach, palpitations, a tension headache, lightheadedness, and so on)

Since you can't expect the tests you take in college to change for your sake—to alleviate your anxiety—the possibility for change must come from within *you*. Consider these suggestions as they relate to the four indicators of test anxiety.

Teachable Moment Ask students how the cognitive, emotional, behavioral, and physiological aspects of stress are connected. Which might come first and impact the others?

Cognitive

- **Understand your testing strengths and challenges, based on your learning style.** Although research indicates that most students prefer multiple-choice tests over essay tests, you have your own strengths and preferences.[12] Your psychological type may provide insights into some of these.

- **Don't catastrophize!** Stop yourself from engaging in negative, unproductive self-talk. It's easy to imagine worst-case scenarios: "If I fail this exam, I'll lose my scholarship, and if I lose my scholarship, I won't be able to afford to go to college, and if I don't go to college, I'll probably end up as a homeless person, begging for change on the street." Negative thinking can easily spiral downward, and before you know it, you're thinking about major life catastrophes and the end of the world. Although some exams do have important outcomes, it's important to put things in perspective. Twenty years from now, who will know if you earned an 85 or an 88 on your philosophy test this week? Although this argument can be taken too far (so that you convince yourself that nothing matters much), if your test anxiety stems from perfectionism, this is an important point to remember.

Emotional

- **Monitor your moods.** Your emotions fluctuate based on many factors; they vary by type, intensity, and timing.[13] If you eat well and get enough sleep before an exam, your moods are more likely to be even-keeled than if you skip meals, ride the carbohydrate roller coaster, and pull all-nighters. An eight-hour sleep debt will cause your mood to take a nosedive.[14]

- **"Park" your problems if you can.** When you go into a store, you leave your car outside in the parking lot and come back to it when you're finished shopping. Think about how that analogy relates to taking a test. Everyone has problems. If we didn't we wouldn't be human. But obsessing on them during a test is counterproductive to say the least. Park them for a while. Focus on your work, and challenge yourself to do your best. Your worries won't go away, unfortunately;

Teachable Moment As a class, have students generate a list of things that they might park while studying for or taking a test. For example, they could park why their best friend seems a bit upset with them. They might park the fact that their money is running low and payday is not for a few more days. Parking thoughts that interfere with a task can help students focus.

they'll be around after you're done, when you're better able to take steps to deal with them.

Behavioral

> **Relieve some stress with physical activity.** Expend some of that extra, pent-up energy before the exam. Sprint to class or take a walk to clear your head in the hour before the test begins.

> **"Step out of your life" by spending time outdoors.** Being in the outdoors is liberating. There's a big world out there; it's easy to forget that when you're spending large amounts of time in classrooms or at work.

Physiological

> **Teach yourself how to relax.** Relaxation training can be used to overcome test anxiety. As simple as it sounds, that may involve learning how to breathe. Watch a new baby sleep, and you'll see instinctive, deep, even breathing in which only the baby's stomach moves up and down. As adults, when we're anxious, we breathe rapidly and shallowly, which doesn't sufficiently oxygenate our brains. Conversely, when we learn to breathe with our diaphragms by drawing in air through our nostrils, filling our entire lungs (not just the upper third), and exhaling completely and smoothly, as if trying to blow out a candle a foot in front of you, we begin the process of learning to relax.[15] Meditation, massage, and biofeedback can work, too.

> **Seek help from a professional.** An expert who works with anxiety-ridden college students can diagnose your problem and help you through it. While helping you learn to relax, a counselor or learning expert on or off campus may help you engage in "guided visualization." Guided visualization asks you to visualize yourself doing the things you need to do, leading up to your goal—in this case succeeding on your test. At each step of the way, you envision success, and then continue to rehearse those images in your mind.[16] Or a counselor might help you engage in "systematic desensitization," a technique in which you work to overcome your anxiety incrementally in very small steps.[17]

Chapter Crossover Ask students to look back at Chapter 5 on critical and creative thinking. What faulty assumptions about test-taking contribute to their test anxiety? What creative steps could they take to change their assumptions and thereby improve their test-taking strategies?

Activity Option Break up students into four groups and ask each group to focus on the cognitive, emotional, behavioral, or physiological aspect of test anxiety. Ask the groups to come up with five suggestions on how to deal with this area of anxiety.

INSIGHT ⊖ ACTION

1. Is test anxiety a problem for you? What are your reactions to taking tests in each of the four areas?

   • Cognitive   • Behavioral   • Emotional   • Physiological

2. Which of the suggestions in this section will you focus on in the future? How are these changes likely to affect your reaction to taking tests?

REDUCE MATH ANXIETY AND INCREASE YOUR TEST SCORES!

For some students, a particular kind of test anxiety can be debilitating. "I've always hated math, ever since I was grounded for not learning my multiplication tables as a kid." "I was humiliated. If I couldn't come up with the right answer at the board, everyone would laugh at me." "It started in ninth grade. Now when I'm handed a math test, I just stare at it and start hyperventilating. Numbers terrify me!"

Honestly, most people feel some twinge of anxiety about working a complex set of math problems on an exam. But if the preceding statements sound like ones you've uttered, and your level of anxiety interferes demonstrably with your test success, you may suffer from math anxiety. One expert estimates that roughly 20 to 25 percent of college students are in that category.[18] Some estimates are that as many as 85 percent of college students in introductory math classes experience some degree of math anxiety.[19]

According to one expert, "Math anxiety is an inability by an otherwise intelligent person to cope with quantification, and more generally mathematics."[20] If you're one of them, admitting the problem is the first step. Next, it's important to understand how math anxiety can work against you during exams so that you can do something about it. The most effective strategies to cope are direct and uncomplicated.[21]

Think back; perhaps you can speculate on the origin of your fear. It may have been a teacher or a class or a particular test. Perhaps your anxiety increased in junior high school, when social pressures

began to mount.[22] Experts believe math anxiety is *learned*, and that learning can result in *rationalization* ("Who wouldn't be terrified? No one could learn this!"), *suppression* ("I know I shouldn't feel this way, so I'm not going to!"), or *denial* ("I don't have math anxiety; I just don't like it!").[23]

Students with math anxiety take fewer math courses, are less successful in those courses, and therefore get less practice. Because they avoid math, they don't give themselves opportunities to perfect their skills. That can just make things worse. But that's not all there is to it.

Why and how does math anxiety affect people? Try this experiment: multiply 86×7. To arrive at the answer, you must first multiply 6×7, make note of the 2, and carry the 4. Then you must multiply 7×8 and add the 4 to arrive at 602. Notice the steps involved in such a simple calculation. You have to keep certain numbers in your head while you continue to work on other computations, which is often the case with math. Your working memory allows you to pull it off.

Working memory is your short-term, temporary-storage, limited-capacity memory. It's the memory you use to hold certain pieces of information—your brain's scratchpad—keeping them accessible for you to manipulate and update.[24] A task like multiplying 639×924 would exceed the capacity of most people's working memories, but some people have more capacity than others. Here's the kicker: Math anxiety actually decreases your working memory.

Why? Managing anxiety takes up working memory space that could be used to solve math problems. When anxiety is reduced, working memory space is freed up to use in more productive ways. Math anxiety also causes people to take longer to complete mathematical operations and make more errors.[25]

It's not the case that you get caught up in overthinking the math problem in front of you; you think and think and think about how to work the problem to arrive at the right answer. Instead, you focus too little on the problem at hand. Your working memory is hijacked by negative thoughts, causing you to choke.[26]

Here's an interesting twist: People with more working memory capacity can be most susceptible to choking. They come to rely on the extra capacity they normally use to achieve outstanding results. While you might think this group would be less affected (they have working memory to spare), researchers have found the opposite to be true.[27] In other words, the people with the highest probability for success can be the very people whose ability is most compromised when working under pressure.

The solution? Researchers suggest practicing for stressful exams under pressure. Set a timer, and tell yourself you must finish before it goes off. Make a game of it: for every question you miss on a practice exam, you must put a quarter in the kitty and pay off your roommate, spouse, or mom. In other words, practicing in an equally stressful environment (or nearly so) can improve your performance.[28] Since math anxiety is a learned fear, it can be unlearned. Researchers point out: That's the good news worth focusing on!

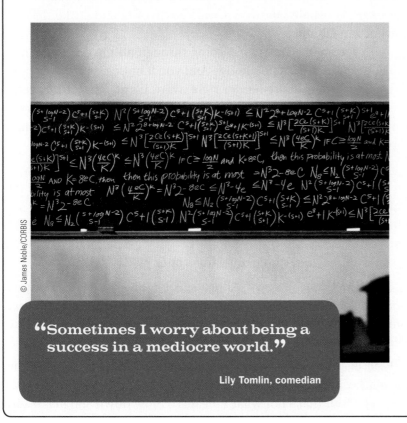

© James Noble/CORBIS

"Sometimes I worry about being a success in a mediocre world."

Lily Tomlin, comedian

During the Test: Focus and Work Hard

CHALLENGE ⟶ REACTION

Challenge: List five ways to focus and work hard during an exam that work for you. List one other technique you've never tried that you suspect would help you.

Reaction: 1. _____

2. _____

3. _____

4. _____

5. _____

_____

During an exam, the heat is on! Do you use these strategies? If not, which ones can you incorporate to improve your performance? Put a plus sign (+) in front of each item you already do regularly and a (✓) in front of items you could start doing more regularly to improve your test-taking skills.

1. _____ **Jot down what you don't want to forget right away.** When you first receive your exam, turn it over and jot down everything you want to make sure you remember—mnemonic devices, charts you've created, acronyms—assuming, of course, that writing on the test is allowed. Some students treat the exam itself as if it were a sacred document, but marking up your exam is usually allowed. Circle key words and strike through answers you eliminate.

2. _____ **Preview the exam.** Just going through all the questions may help you review terms you know. And you'll notice which questions are easier and which are harder right away. It's also likely that reading sample questions will trigger your memory and help you come up with information you need. After the first few minutes, you may relax a bit, and answers will come to you more easily.

3. _____ **Start with what you know.** Make sure you get credit for answers you know; don't waste time early on struggling with the more difficult questions. This strategy will also boost your confidence and help you relax. Studies show that running up against extremely difficult test questions at the beginning of a test can actually negatively impact accuracy on simpler questions later on.[29]

4. _____ **Weigh your answers.** Allocate your time based on the relative weight of the questions. Don't wrestle with one question for ten minutes when it's only worth one point. Go on to a more heavily weighted one.

5. _____ **Read directions thoroughly.** Misreading or skipping the directions altogether can be a lethal mistake. Remember that your instructor can't read your mind. ("But that's not what I meant!") Slow down and make sure you understand what you're being asked to do.

© William Whitehurst/CORBIS

"Ability will never catch up with the demand for it."

Malcolm S. Forbes, U.S. art collector, author, and publisher (1919–1990)

Box 9.2 Chew Your Way to an A, by Gum!

If you're an average American, you're chewing your life away—300 sticks of gum per year! Children in the United States spend about half a billion dollars on bubble gum every year.[30] For sure, Americans are loyal to their favorite pastime, chewing away the hours. But here's a provocative question out of the blue: Can chewing gum during an exam help you academically?

According to some researchers, chewing gum can actually improve your brain power. In a study conducted by British scientists, people who chewed gum scored 24 to 36 percent more on memory tests than those who didn't. Dr. Andrew Scholey, a researcher in human cognitive neuroscience at the University of Northumbria in Northern England, conducted an experiment in which three groups of 25 subjects took part. The first group chewed gum throughout, the second group had no gum, and the third group pretended to chew gum by making chewing motions.

Dr. Scholey speculates that the improved memory of gum-chewers may be due to the fact that chewing gum increases the heart rate, which then supplies more oxygen to the brain. Or the effect may have to do with the fact that chewing stimulates insulin production, which affects the part of the brain involved in memory.[31] Researchers say chewing gum doesn't improve your concentration, but it may improve your recall. Of course, some scientists are skeptical of Dr. Scholey's research. But chew it over yourself!

6. _____ Read questions carefully. Sometimes skipping over a word in the sentence (or filling one in where none exists) will cause you to jump to a false conclusion. Don't let your eyes (or your brain) play tricks on you!

7. _____ If the test has a mixed format, complete the multiple-choice questions first. Often instructors create exams using both *objective* (multiple-choice, true-false) questions and *subjective* questions (fill in the blank, essay). Generally, objective questions ask you to *recognize* answers from several alternatives, and subjective questions ask you to *recall* answers from memory. A multiple-choice question may remind you of something you want to include in an essay. Keep a pad of paper nearby during the exam. Jot down ideas as you answer multiple-choice questions. You'll feel more confident and do a better job if you keep a running list of ideas that occur to you as you go.

8. _____ Explain your answer to an ambiguous question in the margin of your test. You may point out a problem your instructor wasn't aware of or get partial credit.

9. _____ Change your answers if you're convinced you're wrong. Despite advice you've probably always received from teachers and classmates alike, changing answers when you're sure you've made a mistake is usually a good idea, not a bad one. In one study, less than 10 percent of students made changes that decreased their scores, while 74 percent made changes that increased their scores.[32]

10. _____ Ask your instructor for clarification. If the exam appears to have a typo or something seems askew, ask your instructor or proctor to clarify for you. Of course, if you ask for the definition of a word that is a clue, you probably won't get an answer,

Teachable Moment Ask your class: Are there any volunteers who would like to try chewing gum during exams and homework for a week? You might even bring gum to class to hand out. If any students take you up on the gum challenge, suggest that they come back to class to report their informal results. However, remind students that chewing gum is *not* a substitute for actual time on task!

"We all have ability. The difference is how we use it."

Stevie Wonder, singer and composer

but if you have a technical question or a question about the test-taking process, don't be afraid to ask.

11. _____ Pay attention to "aha" moments. Don't let your "aha" moments turn into "oh, no" moments. If you remember something you couldn't think of earlier, go back to that question and finish it right away.

12. _____ Don't give in to peer pressure. If, while you're working away, you look around and see that many students are leaving because they're already finished, don't panic. Take as much of the allotted time as you need. Everyone works at a different rate.

13. _____ Save time for review. When you're finished, go back over all your answers. Make sure you've circled the right letter or filled in the correct bubble. Be certain you've made all the points you intended to make in your

FOCUS ON CAREERS: BETH ROBINSON, The College Board

Courtesy of Beth Robinson

Q1: How did your career path lead you to your current position? What prepared you to work in an organization like The College Board?
I worked for fifteen years as an educator—eight of those years in a leadership role—first as a math teacher, then a school counselor, and then finally as a regional director of guidance. Over the years, I had a positive, ongoing relationship with the College Board, and when they had an opening, they invited me to join the organization and now I'm the Executive Director for the PSAT/NMSQT Program and College Planning Services.

Q2: Sometimes at the end of a course, students say, "I learned a great deal in that course, but my exam grades certainly don't show it!" or "I got an A on every test in that class, but I didn't learn a thing!" What do exams in college courses really accomplish?
College freshmen taking introductory courses are probably the students most likely to generate quotes like these because they are just beginning to take responsibility for their own learning. College courses require self-motivation. Therefore, students usually get out of their courses what they put into them. If students invest in their courses beyond the minimum expected, they will probably both learn and have their grades show it.

Q3: According to media reports, the public appears concerned about how much today's college students are really learning. Are tests a good way to find out?
By some accounts, today's college students only skim the surface of what needs to be learned, rather than working to become truly educated. Tests can indeed be a good means to assess learning as long as they assess thinking and not just the recall of facts. If you've truly learned something, you should understand it fully enough to transfer the learning to new situations.

Q4: What constitutes a good test?
I consulted my colleagues at ETS (Educational Testing Services), who are masters of test creation (the SAT, PSAT/NMSQT, and Advanced Placement tests for the College Board). A good test is one that fairly and consistently measures what it sets out to measure. A good test, therefore, always starts out with a clear sense of its intended purpose (to see if you know the rules of the road to obtain a driver's license, to see if you understand the main points covered in the chapter, and so forth.) After the purpose has been determined, a detailed set of specifications is agreed to. These specifications are the blueprint or recipe for the test. They say what material will be covered and in what proportion, the kinds of questions, and how hard the questions will be. Every test—standardized or not—should be constructed based on focus, content, difficulty level, and most importantly the "goal" of the test: what it is supposed to measure.

Q5: What are the qualities of a good test question? What differentiates a good test question from a bad one?
Most of the people who create our tests come from academia, either high school or college, and are powerful content specialists who understand what goes into the creation of a viable assessment. Writing good test questions is much harder than it looks. A good test question has all of the following characteristics (and bad ones lack these characteristics). It:

- Tests the right things. If the test is designed to see if you know how to drive, you wouldn't find on it a question about the authorship of *Moby Dick*. While this may seem obvious, it's important.
- Is clearly worded.
- Has a single best answer (if it's a multiple-choice question).
- Tests things worth testing, not trivial or tricky points.
- Isn't biased in favor of one particular group; the questions will not be easier for people with a certain kind of insider knowledge than for others.
- Is at an appropriate level of difficulty for the test-takers.
- Doesn't give away the right answer and includes wrong answers that are plausible.

Q6: In your view, why do some students choke on exams? Why do tests terrify them?
Sometimes students choke on exams because they simply aren't prepared. They hope they can fake it through whatever they don't

essay. Look at your work critically, as if you were the instructor. Careless errors can be costly!

14. _____ Be strategic about taking online tests. Often tests posted online are timed. If you're taking a distance education course or a classroom course with an online test component, watch for e-mail announcements that tests have been posted, and note particular instructions. When will the test expire and disappear? Can you reenter the test site and redo answers before you hit the submit button? Can you take tests collaboratively with other students? With online tests, of course, the other recommendations in this chapter for true-false or multiple-choice tests apply as well.

understand well. Preparing adequately, of course, is the cure. Other students may be obsessed with getting good grades. They have high self-expectations and usually high expectations imposed from home. They need to calm down, put tests and life in perspective, and develop a healthy level of support. Other students do all the right things to prepare for tests, but they never really analyze what they're studying, thus their depth of understanding may not hold up under the scrutiny of well-written tests. They have a history of poor test results that doesn't reflect their time investment, and that leads to fear at the mere mention of testing. These students could benefit by joining study groups and talking with teachers about what they've learned. Still other students are nervous and insecure, often for reasons unrelated to their actual abilities. They prefer homework, projects, classroom presentations, or any other means of showing their level of learning, understanding, and achievement. For these students, practicing is important. They should take multiple practice tests, review their results, and get very familiar with test directions, test question types, test expectations, and timing. The point is to make the testing environment familiar and comfortable well ahead of time, so that test day is just like any other day. Finally, some students are anxious because of learning disabilities or language issues. They need to take advantage of campus resources to get the help they need to improve.

Q7: Math anxiety appears to be a particularly serious issue among a fairly large segment of today's student population. Do you have a theory about why that may be true?
It's important for teachers and parents, even in children's early years, to emphasize the relevance of math and to exhibit contagious enthusiasm for it as a subject. Instead, some teachers and parents simply stress the monotonous aspects like memorizing multiplication tables. Sometimes teachers and parents even unwittingly pass on their own math anxiety. With the way math is taught today, alternative solutions to problems are encouraged; there is not just "one right way" to solve a problem. Students who think that they can't "do math" may just be thinking of solutions in a different way. If the teacher can evaluate the solution path the student has chosen, maybe the students can see that they really do know how to solve the problem. Once students see their own success in a subject, they usually come to like it.

C CREATE a Career Outlook

MANAGER, NONPROFIT ORGANIZATION

Have you ever considered a career in the nonprofit, as opposed to the for-profit, sector of the economy? Here are some facts about this career to consider and some questions about yourself to ponder.

Facts to Consider

Academic preparation required: Completion of a bachelor's degree is required and variable backgrounds are accepted, depending on the specific type of nonprofit organization and its mission.

Future workforce demand: Because of relatively low wages and high turnover, job prospects for the future are excellent.

Work environment: Those involved in advocacy, grant making, and civic organizations—nonprofits—affect many areas of our lives: politics, health, arts, religion, education, and social causes, for example. Typically, nonprofits are run by a small core of paid staff, and whatever fees they charge for services (if any) must not exceed expenses. Most nonprofit employees work in a team environment (working with volunteers, for example) and have variable schedules. They believe in the causes for which their organizations stand, are challenged by the need to raise funds, and find their work rewarding.

Most common psychological type preferences: A range of types may choose careers in the nonprofit sector. For example, sensing, thinking, and judging types may be attracted to executive director positions, while intuitive, feeling, and perceiving types are often motivated to work toward the causes nonprofit organizations promote.[33]

Essential skills: communicating, fund-raising, being sensitive to social issues

Questions to Ponder

1. Do you have (or could you acquire) the skills this career requires?
2. What would you find most satisfying about this type of career?
3. What would you find most challenging about this type of career?
4. Are you interested in a career like this? Why or why not?

For more information, see U.S. Department of Labor, Bureau of Labor Statistics, *Occupational Outlook Handbook, 2006–2007 Edition.*[34]

For more career activities online, go to http://www.academic.cengage.com/collegesuccess/staley to do the Team Career exercises.

Taking Objective Tests

CHALLENGE ⊖ REACTION

Challenge: Are there specific ways to take objective tests? Identify five suggestions that apply to true-false and multiple-choice tests.

Reaction: 1. _____

2. _____

3. _____

4. _____

5. _____

Many of the exams you'll take in college will be objective, rather than subjective, tests. Let's examine the best strategies for taking objective tests.

True-False: Truly a 50–50 Chance of Getting It Right?

Exam questions that test your recall are always more challenging than questions that test your recognition skills. T or F?

True-false tests may seem straightforward, but they can be tricky. You assume you have a 50–50 chance of answering correctly. But don't forget, you also have a 50–50 chance of answering incorrectly. Sometimes the wording of the statements makes the *process* of taking true-false tests more challenging than their *content*. Consider these helpful guidelines:

> **Watch for parts of statements that make the entire statement false.** The statement must be all true to be "true," and a few words may make an otherwise true statement "false." Here's an example:

Derek Bok, who was president of Harvard University for thirty years, once said, "If you think education is expensive, try ignorance." T or F

The main part of the statement is true; the quotation does belong to Derek Bok. Actually, however, Bok was president of Harvard from 1971 to 1991 (and returned to serve on an interim basis in 2006–2007), making the descriptive phrase about him, buried in the middle of the sentence, false. The entire statement, then, must be marked "false."

> **Assume statements are true until you can prove them false.** Statistically, exams usually contain more true answers than false ones. You have a better than 50 percent chance of being right if you guess "true." But teachers vary; yours may not follow the norm.

> **Watch for *absolutes;* they often make a statement false.** Words like *always, never,* and *entirely* often make otherwise true statements become false. "You can *always* get an A on an exam if you study for it." Unfortunately, no.

> **Look for *qualifiers;* they often make a statement true.** On the other hand, words like *sometimes, often,* and *ordinarily* often make statements true. "You can *sometimes* get an A on an exam if you study for it." Fortunately, yes.

Activity Option The answers to the seven interview questions are packed with good information about testing. Pair up students and give them ten minutes to identify the three most important points, in their opinion, that Beth Robinson makes and why. Student pairs can then report back to the class.

Teachable Moment Pose the following questions to students: "Is the manager of a nonprofit organization a good career choice for everyone? Why or why not?"

Sensitive Situation Multiple-choice and true-false statements can be really challenging for students with reading difficulties (who may or may not have undiagnosed learning disabilities). ESL students often struggle more with reading the questions than with knowing the answers. The qualifiers, negatives, and option to select more than one answer in multiple-choice questions can be especially difficult for challenged readers.

> Remember that negatives can be confusing. Is this statement true or false? "Students who don't lack motivation are likely to excel." "Don't lack" really means "have," right?

Multiple *Choice* or Multiple *Guess*?
Taking the Guess Work Out

Which of the following statements is (are) true?

a. Richard Greener, who became Harvard's first African American graduate in 1870, later became a lawyer, educator, and distinguished U.S. consul and diplomat.

b. Elizabeth Blackwell, who graduated from Geneva Medical College in New York, was the first woman in the United States to earn a medical degree.

c. Oberlin College was the first U.S. college to admit women and the last to admit African-American students on an equal footing with Caucasians.

d. a and b

e. a, b, and c

Are multiple-choice tests difficult for you? Often what's difficult about multiple-choice tests has more to do with the structure of the test than the content. Studying for these tests requires a particular approach, and if you master the approach, you'll find taking multiple-choice tests to be much easier. You can actually think of them as variants of true-false tests. [The correct answer to the question, by the way, is (d).]

> **Think of answers on your own before reading your choices.** You may get hung up on the wording of an answer. Answer it on your own so that you can recognize it, no matter how it's worded. You may want to do this by covering up the alternatives initially, and then proceeding after you know what you're looking for. Sometimes the alternatives will differ by only one or two words. It's easy to become confused.

> **Line up your test and answer sheet.** This sounds like a simple suggestion, but getting off a line can be very disruptive when you have to erase like crazy and start over!

> **Determine the TPI (time per item).** Divide the number of questions by the allotted time. If there are seventy-five questions to answer in an hour, you know that you'll need to work faster than one question per minute. Remember to save some time for review and revision at the end.

> **Don't decide answers based on the law of averages.** If you flip a coin three times, and it comes up "heads," most of us assume it's probably time for "tails" to come up next. Likewise, on exams, if you've answered (d) for three questions in a row, you may think it's time for an (a), (b), or (c). It may not be.

> **Using a process of elimination, guess if there's no penalty.** Some instructors subtract points for wrong answers, but if you do guess, guess wisely. And don't skip questions. Always mark something unless you're penalized for doing so. Take a look at this example:

Before you write an answer on an essay test, you should do all but the following:

a. Read all the questions.

b. Begin with the hardest question.

c. Look at what the questions are asking you to do, specifically.

d. Underline key words in the question.

You know that you should do (a). Reading all the questions before you start is a must. You know that option (d) makes sense, and so does (c). But you're not quite sure about option (b). You can eliminate (a), (c), and (d), so (b) must be the right answer based on a process of elimination. As you work, eliminate answers that you know are incorrect by marking through them ~~like this~~.

> **Look for highly similar pairs.** Sometimes two options will differ by a single word or the order of words. Often one of these is the right choice.

> **Look for contradictory answers.** If two statements are complete opposites, one of them is often the right choice.

> **Watch out for tricks intended to separate the prepared from the unprepared!** For example, avoid answers that are true in and of themselves, but not true when attached to the sentence stem or question being asked. For example, imagine this question option on a multiple-choice exam:

Global warming is considered to be a serious issue among some scientists because:

a. Former President Bill Clinton describes global warming as a greater threat to the world than terrorism.

While Clinton did espouse this view in a 2006 speech, it is not the reason for scientists' concern, so (a) isn't the correct answer.[35] Two other tips: generally, when numbers are in each alternative, choose numbers in the middle range. Choosing answers that are longer and more descriptive usually pays off, too.

> **Consider each answer as an individual true-false question.** Examine each option carefully, as if you had to decide if it were true or false, and use that analysis to make a decision about which option is correct.

> **Be wary of "all of the above" or "none of the above" options.** While instructors sometimes make these options the correct ones, it's also possible they resort to these options because making up enough plausible answers is challenging.

> **Watch for terminology that has been emphasized.** Look for key terms that appeared in your lecture notes and in chapters of the text. These words may provide links to the correct answer. Remember when taking multiple-choice tests that you are looking for the *best* answer, not simply the *right* one.[36]

Short-Answer, Fill in the Blank, and Matching Tests

Short-answer tests are like essay tests, which we'll discuss shortly, in many ways. You're required to come up with an organized, well-thought-through answer on your own. But instead of a long essay, you only need to write a paragraph or two. Is that easier? It may be, but

"**I am easily satisfied with the very best.**"

Winston Churchill, Prime Minister of England (1874–1965)

© Image Source/CORBIS

sometimes it's just as hard or harder to condense what you have to say about difficult concepts into fewer words. Generally, however, the suggestions for essay tests hold.

For fill in the blank tests, first think the statement through. What does it mean? Try inserting different words. Which one sounds best? Which one was used during lectures or appeared in the textbook? If one word looks awkward, try another one. Although it's not a completely reliable hint, look at the number of words, placement of spaces, and length of the space. If you don't know the exact terminology the question is looking for, insert descriptive words of your own. You may earn partial credit.

Matching tests require particular strategies, too. First of all, you must determine whether items should be used only once or if they can be reused. If it's not clear from the test directions, ask for clarification. Match the items you're certain about first and cross them out if once only is the rule. If you mismatch an item early on, all your subsequent choices will be wrong, too.

Teachable Moment Anytime you can bring in some real tests and go through the strategies, it will become more meaningful for students. Consider using the test bank provided for this book and use actual chapter examples.

INSIGHT ⊖ ACTION

Answer the following multiple-choice questions. Beneath each question, identify which of the principles of test-taking from this chapter you are using to identify the correct answer.

1. "I know of no more encouraging fact than the unquestionable ability of man to elevate his life by conscious endeavor." These words were said by:

   a. Bill Clinton

   b. Abraham Maslow

   c. Ronald Reagan

   d. Henry David Thoreau

   _____

2. Which of the following statements about the ACT test is not true?

   a. The ACT includes 215 multiple-choice questions.

   b. ACT results are accepted by virtually all U.S. colleges and universities.

   c. Students may take the ACT test as many times as they like.

   d. None of the above.

   _____

3. Which of the following suggestions about preparing for college is (are) true?

   a. Get involved in co-curricular activities in high school.

   b. Always take challenging courses that show your effort and ability.

   c. Involve your family in your decisions and preparation for college.

   d. Find a mentor, a teacher, or counselor who can give you good advice.

   e. All of the above.

   _____

[Answer key: (d), (d), (e)]

Taking Subjective Essay Tests

Essay Question: Please discuss the value of brain research in relation to our current knowledge of how learning takes place.

Sensitive Situation While some students have trouble with reading, just as many students have trouble with writing. Essay exams require students to be able to think, organize, and communicate thoughtfully and thoroughly. If your campus has a writing center, send students who need help there for coaching on how to construct essay exam answers.

Essay questions are difficult for some students because details are required. Rather than being able to *recognize* the correct answer, you must be able to *recall* it totally from your own memory. Here are some recommendations you should consider:

> **Save enough time for essays.** If the test has a mixed format, it's important to save enough time to write well-thought-through essays. Often objective questions such as multiple choice or true-false only count a point or two, whereas essay questions often count into the double digits.

> **Read all the questions before you start.** To sharpen your focus and avoid overlap, give yourself an overview of all the questions before you start writing.

> **Make brief notes.** Somewhere on the exam or on scratch paper, write a brief plan for your responses to essay questions. A few minutes of planning may be time well spent. As you plan your answer, keep basic questions in mind—*who, what, when, where,* and *why*—as an organizing framework.

> **State your thesis up front.** How will you handle this question? What's your plan of attack? Your first paragraph should include your basic argument in a thesis statement.

> **Provide support for your thesis.** Writing an answer to an essay question requires you to make assertions. However, it's not enough that you assert things; you must try to prove that they are true. If your thesis asserts that college students cheat more today than they did when your parents went to college, you must present evidence—statistics, examples, or expert testimony—to demonstrate that what you're asserting is true.

> **Zero in on the verb.** The heart of an essay question is its verb. Take a look at this list and think about how each verb dictates what is required:

> > **Analyze**—break into separate parts and examine or discuss each part

> > **Compare**—examine two or more things, find the similarities and differences (usually you emphasize the similarities)

> > **Contrast**—find the differences between two or more things

> > **Critique, criticize, or evaluate**—make a judgment, describe the worth of something

> > **Define**—provide the meaning (usually requires a short answer)

> > **Describe**—give a detailed account, list characteristics or qualities

> > **Discuss**—describe a cause/effect relationship, the significance of something, the pros and cons, or the role played by someone or something

> > **Enumerate**—list qualities, characteristics, events, and so on

> > **Explain**—similar to discuss

> > **Illustrate**—give concrete examples

> > **Interpret**—comment on, give examples, provide an explanation for, discuss

> > **Outline**—describe the plot, main ideas, or organization of something

Prove—support an argument with evidence from the text or class notes

Relate—show the relationship or connection between two things

State—explain in precise terms

Summarize—give a condensed account of key points, reduce to the essential components

Trace—describe a process or the development of something

> **Use terminology from the course.** Perhaps more than any other type of exam, an essay test allows you room to truly display your knowledge. Use the opportunity! Reflect new terms you have learned, and tie your answer directly to course content.

> **Rifle your answer, don't shotgun.** Here's an analogy: A shotgun fires many small metal pellets. A rifle fires a single bullet. When writing an essay answer, some students write down everything they know, hoping that something will be correct. You may actually lose points by doing this. It's better to target your answer and be precise.

> **Generalize if you're unsure of small, exact details.** You can't quite remember, was it 1884 or 1894? The best idea is to write, "Toward the end of the nineteenth century" instead of choosing one of the two and being wrong.

> **Follow all the rules.** When answering an essay question, it's important to be as concise yet thorough as possible. Enumerate your ideas ("There are *three* major…"). Avoid slang ("Wordsworth elaborated…" not "Wordsworth *jazzed up* the poem."). Refer to researchers or authors or noteworthy people by their last names ("Jung wrote…" not "Dr. Carl Jung wrote…").

> **Watch your grammar.** The reason why its important, to do this, is because many student's dont and there answers are marked wrong. They wish they would of done better afterwards. You get the point.

> **Write an answer that corresponds to how much the question is worth.** It's important to be concise, but generally, if one essay answer is worth 10 points and another is worth 25 points, your instructor will expect you to write more for the question that's worth more. A more detailed, thorough response is what is called for.

> **Put down what you do know.** If you see a question you didn't predict, don't panic. If you've studied, you know *something* that might help give you partial credit even if you don't know the answer in full.

> **Proofread and make sure your handwriting is legible.** While most instructors will count the number of points you covered and use specific standards, grading essays is a slightly subjective process. That means instructors must use their own judgment. A good essay answer is taken less seriously if it's littered with mistakes or a real mess to read. This is the real world; neatness counts. Anything you can do to create a positive impression may work in your favor.

> **If you run out of time, jot down any remaining points in the time that's left.** You may not get full credit, but partial credit is better than none.

> **Include a summary statement at the end.** Your essay answer should read like a real essay with an introduction, a body, and a conclusion. Don't just stop mid-sentence without wrapping things up.[37]

> "**Knowing is not enough; we must apply. Willing is not enough; we must do.**"
>
> **Johann Wolfgang von Goethe, German writer and scholar (1749–1832)**

YOUR TOUGHEST CLASS

Think about your most challenging class this term. Identify one key challenge you face in this class that relates to this chapter. Now develop a step-by-step action plan to deal with this one challenge. For example, Joe's calculus class was his most challenging. His action plan might look like this:

a. Reread the sections of the chapter on preparing for tests and test anxiety.

b. Meet with my professor to discuss my problems in her class.

c. Show her this action plan, and ask for her suggestions.

d. Keep a journal of my progress to note improvement and meet with her four more times this term.

Now do the same for *your* most challenging class.

1. _____
   _____

2. _____
   _____

3. _____
   _____

4. _____
   _____

Activity Option Have students make a four-slide PowerPoint presentation to share their step-by-step plan for their most challenging class. Make sure that students identify which class they are talking about and what makes it challenging.

Don't Cheat Yourself!

What if you were in one of these situations? How would you respond?

> You must get a good score on your anatomy and physiology test so that you don't lose your scholarship. A friend took the course last year and offers to give you a copy of the exam. The professor is known for using the same tests over and over again. He doesn't invest time in updating his exams, and students know it. If he doesn't care, why should you?

> Your parents are paying out-of-state tuition, and you can't afford to fail the midterm exam in your killer physics course. You decide to leave a file of notes and handouts behind the plumbing in the furthest stall of the restroom near the classroom where you'll take the test. All you have to do is ask to be excused from the exam to go to the restroom, and you can look up any answer that has you stumped.

> Many students in your communication major get through difficult exams by sharing answers via their cell phones. It's easy to dial your phone using one hand under the desk and text message answers to each other. "Hey, what did you put down for 2, 8, and 15?" "b, d, and c," your friend replies in an instant. The professors never notice, and the courses aren't all that interesting anyway.

> A friend of yours stores all the names and dates she'll need to know for her history exams on her pocket PC. With just one click she can call up whatever information she needs. "Try it," she says. "Everyone else does it, and you'll feel cheated if you don't cheat. If you don't do what other students do, you'll graduate with mediocre grades, and you'll never be able to compete for the jobs you've always wanted. Besides getting away with it here just helps prepare you for the business world where things are *really* cutthroat!"

> You hear about an entrepreneurial student on a nearby campus who operates an underground ghostwriting service. For $20 a page, he will guarantee you the grade you want (based on the grade you already have going in

> **"For nothing can seem foul to those that win."**
>
> **William Shakespeare, British poet and playwright (1564–1616)**

© Vera Berger/zefa/CORBIS

the course so that your paper won't raise the professor's suspicions), and he "doctors" each sentence so that the source can't be found on the Internet. You have four papers, a presentation, and an exam all due the same week, and one or two ghostwritten papers would only run you around $150 to $200. That's not all that much considering the tips you make as a server. Hmm....

How did you respond to these five scenarios? Are you aware of cheating schemes on your own campus? Could students you know be the ones these scenarios were written about? Notice that most of these students have practical-sounding reasons for what they are doing. If you want to cheat, it's not hard, and you can always blame someone else like your teachers or parents. What's the harm? You get better grades, your parents are pleased, your teachers feel gratified, your school brags about the fine academic record of its students, and you pat yourself on your back for skillfully managing a very busy, demanding life. Everyone wins, right? Wrong.

According to some studies, fifty years ago, one in five college students admitted to cheating. Today's figures range from 75 to 90 percent. Here's some straight talk about cheating:[38]

1. **Remember that cheating snowballs.** What started as secretly pocketing some kid's CD or glancing at your neighbor's reading test in grade school turns into writing a math formula between your fingers or hiding the names of the constellations under your shirt cuff in middle school. Then these juvenile violations turn into full-fledged, sophisticated infractions as students "download their workload" in high school and knowingly violate their school's Academic Integrity Policy in college. Where does it stop? With corporate scandal and newspaper headlines?

2. **Instead of saving time, cheating can take time.** Everyone is busy. Many students are working at jobs for pay in addition to taking classes. How can anyone get everything done that needs to get done? But instead of devising elaborate cheating schemes, which take time to coordinate, why not just use that time to study?

3. **If you cheat now, you'll pay later.** Sooner or later, cheating will catch up with you. You may get past your history professor or your calculus instructor this time, and you may even get good grades on others' work you turn in as your own. But someday your boss will ask you to write something, or do some research, or use a skill a student is expected to have mastered in college, and you won't know where to start.

4. **If you do get caught, cheating may do you in.** Some students cheat because they know other students have gotten away with it. Cheating for them is a thrill, and not getting caught is akin to winning or beating the system. Roll the dice and see what happens, they say. But you should know that professors are in the know these days. Academic hallways are abuzz with faculty talk about cheating. If you do get caught, your academic career may come to an abrupt halt.

5. **Cheating is just plain wrong.** You may or may not agree with this point, but it deserves some serious consideration. How would you like to be cheated out of money that's owed you or days off that are due you? The Golden Rule may sound old-fashioned, but the fact that it's been around for a long time with roots in a wide range of world cultures tells you something. "Intellectual Property" and "Academic Integrity" may not be as tangible as money you deserve or eight hours of free time, but they are commodities that are increasingly protected by every college and university.

What are your personal ethical standards? Are you willing to cut corners? Would you cheat to achieve top grades in college? What kind of "devil's bargain" would you be willing to strike?

If you're tempted, remember this. Sooner or later, cheating costs you—big time! Don't cheat yourself out of learning what you need to learn in college. Learning is not all about product—the exams, papers, grades, and diplomas themselves—it's about process, too. The process involves gaining skills that will prepare you for life after college. That's a goal worth working toward.

You can't go through life devising elaborate schemes, or hiring someone else to do your work for you, or rationalizing about finding a way to beat the system because you're too busy to do your own work. Cheating in your college classes now just makes it that much easier to risk cheating your employer—and yourself—later on the job. Look through newspapers or watch the evening news to see who's been caught lately. It's a competitive world out there, but more and more companies find that having a good reputation, which comes from valuing integrity, is good business. The bottom line is "Employees don't follow leaders they don't trust. Employers don't hire people or promote employees they don't trust. Clients don't buy from suppliers they don't trust."[39] Integrity starts now: *earn what you learn.*[40]

After the Test: Continue to Learn

CHALLENGE → REACTION

Challenge: What suggestions can you come up with for things to do after an exam—to help you remember the information, perhaps for a later exam or for another course, or do better next time?

Reaction: _____

After you finish an exam and get your results, you may be exhilarated or down-trodden. Regardless, exams can be excellent learning experiences if you take these steps. Put a plus sign (+) in front of each item you already do regularly and a (✓) in front of items you could start doing more regularly to improve your test-taking skills.

1. _____ Analyze your results. Conduct a thorough analysis of your test results. For example, an analysis like this one might tell you what kinds of questions are most problematic for you.

Type of Question	Points Earned/Right	Points Deducted/Wrong	Total
Multiple Choice	32	3	35
Fill in the Blank	15	2	17
True-False	20	8	28
Essay	10	10	20
Total	77	23	100

Or analyze your results by examining lecture questions versus textbook questions to find out where to concentrate your efforts on future tests. Or do an analysis by chapter content to tell you where to focus your time when studying for the final exam.

2. _____ **Read your instructor's comments and take them to heart.** In this chapter's "FOCUS Challenge Case," Joe Cloud threw his exam in the trash can at the front of the lecture hall after class. Instead, he should have used it to answer a series of important questions. After an exam, ask yourself: What was the instructor looking for? Was my writing ability critiqued? Does the test make more sense now than it did while I was taking it? Are there instructor's comments written on the test that I can learn from? What do the results of this exam teach me about preparing differently, perhaps, for the next test?

3. _____ **Explain your grade to yourself.** Where did you go wrong? Did you misread questions? Run out of time? Organize essay answers poorly? Does the grade reflect your effort? If not, why not? Did test anxiety get the better of you? On the other hand, if you studied hard and your grade reflects it, that's an explanation, too!

4. _____ **Be honest.** It's easy to get caught up in the blame game: "I would have gotten a better grade if the exam had been fairer, if the test had been shorter, if the material hadn't been so difficult, if I'd had more time to study...." Your instructors have heard every excuse in the book: "my dog ate my notes," "a relative died," "a family emergency made it impossible to study," "my hard drive crashed," "my roommate was sick"—you name it. Of course, sometimes crises do overtake events. But rather than pointing fingers elsewhere if you're disappointed with your results, be objective and look at what *you* can do differently next time.

5. _____ **Make a specific plan for the next test.** Most courses contain more than one exam. You'll probably have an opportunity to apply what you've learned and do better next time.

6. _____ **Approach your instructor politely if you believe your exam has been mismarked.** Sometimes teachers make mistakes. Sometimes they're interrupted while grading and forget to finish reading an essay answer, or the answer key is wrong, or they miscalculate. Even if the scoring is correct, it may be a good idea to approach your instructor for help about how to improve your next test score.

7. _____ **Reward yourself for good (study) behavior.** After you've worked hard to prepare and the exam is over, reward yourself—take in a movie, go out with friends, do something to celebrate your hard work.[41]

> **"A man's errors are his portals of discovery."**
>
> James Joyce, Irish novelist (1882–1941)

Emotional Intelligence (EI) Research A component of emotional intelligence is assertiveness. Students who are able to stand up for themselves are much more likely to be successful, whether it be standing up to their roommates, who make too much noise after midnight, or saying no to peer pressure to drink. Students with strong self-regard assert themselves, in positive ways. However, some students are simply shy. If so, encourage these students to leave a note or e-mail a professor if they have concerns about their exam scores in a course, if visiting a professor during office hours seems intimidating.

INSIGHT ⊖ ACTION

Reflect on your own situation and answer the following questions. As you assessed your own test-taking strategies earlier in this chapter, how many checkmarks did you make for the suggestions on *before*, *during*, and *after* tests, indicating potential areas for improvement? Which of the suggestions from all three sections will you try to focus on in the future? What test-taking problems have you had in the past, and how will this information help you?

EXERCISE 9.1 VARK Activity

Complete the recommended activity for your preferred VARK learning modality. If you are multimodal, select more than one activity. Your instructor may ask you to (a) give an oral report on your results in class, (b) send your results to him or her via e-mail, (c) post them online, or (d) contribute to a class chat.

 Visual: Make a flow chart to show how you will proceed *before*, *during*, and *after* the next test in one of your more challenging classes. Personalize the chart to show exactly what you will actually do.

 Aural: Talk to yourself as you study for an upcoming exam that will challenge your test-taking knowledge and skills. Ask yourself questions that you predict will appear on the exam and answer them aloud.

 Read/Write: Reduce the discussion of all the major topics that appear in this chapter into single-paragraph summaries.

 Kinesthetic: Construct a challenging practice test for an upcoming actual exam, and time yourself while taking it (to simulate the stress you'll face during the exam).

FOCUS CHALLENGE CASE

NOW WHAT DO YOU THINK?

At the beginning of this chapter, Joe Cloud, a frustrated and disgruntled student, faced a challenge. Now after reading this chapter, would you respond differently to any of the questions you answered about the "FOCUS Challenge Case"?

Activity Option For the final activity in the chapter, have students design a one-page tip sheet that contains suggestions for taking different types of tests that have personal relevance for them and e-mail it to you. Put all the tip sheets into one document and send it to the entire class.

For more practice online, go to http://www.academic.cengage.com/collegesuccess/staley to take the Challenge Yourself online quizzes.

>>> >> > REALITY CHECK ‹ ‹‹ ‹‹‹ ‹

On a scale of 1 to 10, answer the following questions now that you've completed this chapter.

1 = not very/not much/very little/low   10 = very/a lot/very much/high

In hindsight, how much did you *really* know about this topic before reading the chapter?

1   2   3   4   5   6   7   8   9   10

How much do you think this information might affect your success in college?

1   2   3   4   5   6   7   8   9   10

How much do you think this information might affect your career success after college?

1   2   3   4   5   6   7   8   9   10

How long did it actually take you to complete this chapter (both the reading and writing tasks)? _____Hour(s) _____Minutes

Take a minute to compare these answers to your answers from the "Readiness Check" at the beginning of this chapter. What gaps exist between the similar questions? How might these gaps between what you thought before starting the chapter and what you now think after completing the chapter affect how you approach the next chapter in this book?

To download mp3 format audio summaries of this chapter, go to http://www.academic.cengage.com/collegesuccess/staley.

10 Writing and Speaking

YOU'RE ABOUT TO DISCOVER...

Teachable Moment Without doubt, there's not a single course that students will take that doesn't require writing or speaking. These skills are typically designated as university-wide outcomes for success both in college and in the workplace.

> How writing works as a process: prewriting, writing, and rewriting

> How to avoid the three common writing traps of first-year students

> How to build a better paper via the seven C's

> How to avoid intentional and unintentional plagiarism

> Why your speaking skills are valuable

> How to overcome a fear of public speaking

> How to craft a winning presentation

> How to use PowerPoint as a visual aid

> How your personality traits relate to your speaking and writing preferences

"Work is either fun or drudgery. It depends on your attitude. I like fun."
Colleen C. Barrett, President and Corporate Secretary, Southwest Airlines

Darnell Williams

Quite honestly, Darnell Williams hadn't found high school all that challenging. Playing football his last two years had made it bearable. But at his school, if you showed up and had a pulse, you could count on passing your courses. There wasn't anything in particular he really wanted to do after high school, but he'd decided to go to the community college in his hometown anyway. Maybe something there would appeal to him.

But after two weeks, Darnell admitted that he didn't find his classes all that engaging. Although he was strong physically from working out for football, he knew he was out of shape academically. Homework was nonexistent for him in high school, but just how well would he do here? Now he wished he'd buckled down more in high school instead of blowing it off.

Since Darnell had no idea what classes to take, he figured he'd just get some required courses out of the way during his first term. He'd always heard people say, "College is about your communication skills, like writing and speaking. If your basic skills are good, and you're willing to work hard, you'll do fine." Based on that advice, he'd enrolled in two courses: Freshman Composition and Public Speaking.

Earlier that morning, Darnell had received an e-mail from his best friend, Curtis, at the large state university two hours from home. It read like this:

Man, I hope I can make it here! The competition is stiff, and I wish I'd taken more college prep courses. Remember how we had lots of tests in our high school classes—every couple of weeks? If we just memorized a few things, like math formulas, even if we didn't understand them, we could do well on tests. And since there were so many tests, one low grade didn't matter. Here, there's a midterm and a final exam. If I blow one of those, I'm in big trouble. How long B4 midterms 4 you? AFAIK, I'm already off to a rough start. I gotta just T+. GTG 8 :-) Curtis

Toward the end of the message, Darnell noticed that Curtis had slipped into the usual e-mail abbreviations like T+ for "think positively" and AFAIK for "as far as I know." *I wish I could write like that in my composition*

class, Darnell thought. *In e-mails and IMs, you can be informal, and no one worries about it. That's an easier way to write.* But he knew that kind of informality wouldn't fly with his teacher, Professor Compton.

But one particular aspect of the e-mail caught Darnell's attention. Even though they were at different schools, both he and Curtis noticed a big difference between high school and college. In his Freshman Composition class, there were no tests at all—just graded papers. And in his Public Speaking class, his whole grade would depend on four speeches he gave during the term.

Darnell wondered if he'd be more motivated in college if he could have signed up for some courses he'd actually been interested in, like Sports in Society or Modern American Cinema. Sports and movies were two of his favorite things, after all. How could studying topics like those *not* be interesting?

Maybe his public speaking course would be easier than his freshman composition course, he contemplated. Darnell was an extravert, and talking came naturally to him. But giving a formal speech in a room full of other students? That would be a new and unnerving experience.

As he sat down at his computer station, the tyranny of the blank screen stared him in the face. In high school, he hadn't been required to write anything longer than a few paragraphs. *I'm going to blame this aggravation on my senior year English teacher, Mr. Forester. This is his fault. He should have done a better job of preparing us for college*, he decided.

Just then, Professor Compton was reminding the students that they'd get back their first graded essays today. "I have to be honest with you, class," she'd admonished, "I expected more from you, and frankly, I'm disappointed in what you submitted. We have a lot of work to do this term!" *Ouch!* Darnell thought to himself. *I hope she's not talking about me!* He'd spent three hours writing his first paper and revised it four times.

Darnell held his breath as he looked at the paper she handed him, and then he saw it. At the top there was no grade at all—nothing but the teacher's note that said, "See me." *This college thing is going to be more challenging than I thought*, he said to himself. One thing was clear to him: He'd definitely have less time for movies and sports now that he was in college.

WHAT DO **YOU** THINK?

Now that you've read about Darnell Williams, answer the following questions. You may not know all the answers yet, but you'll find out what you know and what you stand to gain by reading this chapter.

1. Do you agree with Darnell that his high school English teacher is at fault because he should have done a better job of preparing his students for college?

2. Are the time and effort a student invests in doing an assignment a good predictor of the student's grade?

3. Is speaking anxiety or writing anxiety a problem for Darnell? Why or why not?

4. Identify three things Darnell should do to become more engaged in his speaking and writing classes.

Chapter Crossover Make sure students look ahead to Chapter 13. This chapter on wellness will help students learn particular strategies for managing stress.

Teachable Moment In many ways Darnell is lucky that his instructor wanted to see him. Most likely this professor is providing the opportunity for a one-on-one feedback session to help Darnell. Make sure you stress that the opportunity to get feedback from instructors early on in the class is important, as this will help students to be more successful. If their professors don't invite students to see them, encourage students to ask for a meeting or visit during office hours.

Activity Option Have students write a letter from Darnell to a younger sibling incorporating the four points listed in "What Do *You* Think?" This letter can be used in other activities in this chapter when writing skills are explored.

Before beginning to read this chapter, take two minutes to answer the following questions on a scale of 1 to 10. Your answers will help you assess how ready you are to focus.

1 = not very/not much/very little/low   10 = very/a lot/very much/high

Based on reading the "You're about to discover…" list and skimming this chapter, how much do you think you probably already know about the subject matter?

1   2   3   4   5   6   7   8   9   10

How much do you think this information might affect your college success?

1   2   3   4   5   6   7   8   9   10

How much do you think this information might affect your career success after college?

1   2   3   4   5   6   7   8   9   10

In general, how motivated are you to learn the material in this chapter?

1   2   3   4   5   6   7   8   9   10

This book describes four key factors related to intrinsic, or internal, motivation: curiosity, control, career outlook, and challenge. The next four questions relate to these **C-Factors:**

How *curious* are you about the content you expect to read in this chapter?

1   2   3   4   5   6   7   8   9   10

How much *control* do you expect to have over mastering the material in this chapter?

1   2   3   4   5   6   7   8   9   10

How much do you think this chapter might help you develop your *career outlook*?

1   2   3   4   5   6   7   8   9   10

How *challenging* do you think the material in this chapter will be for you?

1   2   3   4   5   6   7   8   9   10

Before beginning any task, including studying, it's important to check in with yourself to ensure that you're physically, intellectually, and emotionally ready to focus. How ready are you, physically, to focus on this chapter? (Are you rested, feeling well, and so on?)

1   2   3   4   5   6   7   8   9   10

How ready are you, intellectually, to focus on this chapter? (Are you thinking clearly, focused on this course, interested in this subject?)

1   2   3   4   5   6   7   8   9   10

How ready are you, emotionally, to focus on this chapter? (Are you calm, confident, composed?)

1   2   3   4   5   6   7   8   9   10

If your answer to any of the last three questions is below a 5 on the scale, you may need to address the issue you're facing prior to beginning this chapter. For example, if you're hungry, get a quick bite to eat. If you're feeling scattered, take a few moments to settle down and focus.

Finally, how long do you think it will take you to complete this chapter?
_____ Hour(s) _____ Minutes

Writing as a Process: Plan Your Work and Work Your Plan

Emotional Intelligence (EI) Research Students who have trouble with problem solving and impulse control may have difficulty with writing. For example, they may know that they must do a ten-page paper but not approach it using a step-by-step process, breaking down each part as they write. In addition, students who have below average impulse control may have difficulty delaying gratification, thus leaving difficult tasks until the last minute.

CHALLENGE ⟶ REACTION

Challenge: What are your views on writing?

Reaction: Answer the following ten true-false questions and then look for each item in the discussions that follow in this chapter.

1. Writing is a process that helps students learn to think critically. _____

2. Of the three components of the writing process (prewriting, writing, and rewriting), students should devote the most time to prewriting. _____

3. Most first-year students enter college with well-developed writing skills. _____

4. When students are having difficulty with a writing task, they should force themselves to sit down at their computers and just start typing anything related to the topic that comes to mind. _____

Think of this analogy: When you speak, you may not know exactly which words will come out, but you have some idea of what you want to say before you even open your mouth, right? Just as you prethink what you're going to say, you must prewrite what you're going to put down on paper. When you prewrite, you must ask yourself these questions:

1. **What is the assignment asking me to do?** Let's say that Assignment A asks you to summarize interviews with five of the best teachers on campus to find out what makes them so effective. Let's say another writing assignment, Assignment B, asks you to compare and contrast Shakespeare's *Romeo and Juliet* with *Hamlet* in terms of our ability as human beings to distinguish *appearance* from *reality*. You'd go about these two writing papers differently. Zero in on the verbs—*summarize* versus *compare* and *contrast*, in this case. That may help. The specifics of the assignment must be crystal clear to you, and if you're given a choice of topic, pick something that really interests you. That helps, too.

2. **Who is my audience, and what do I want them to know or do?** Who am I writing to? Assignment A is something you could write for several different audiences, for your composition class or for the school newspaper, for example. If you're writing for the school newspaper, you may aim for catchy phrasing, short sentences, and an intriguing title. Once you know who you're writing to or for, then you can ask: What do I want them to know? Am I trying to inform, persuade, or entertain them? What facts, opinions, and support will I need, and where will I find them?

3. **What background reading or research is required?** Assignment A would require you to find out which professors are known for their ability to engage students in learning and contact them to schedule interviews. Assignment B would require you to read both plays before you can write about them. Take careful notes, and as your research progresses, you'll find yourself forming an opinion, and you may also discover a useful way to organize what you're finding. For example, you may want to use a compare and contrast approach, a cause and effect approach, or a chronological approach in which you outline the steps, stages, or events that provide the framework for the paper.

4. **What is the problem to be solved?** In some cases, you can rephrase the assignment as a question or problem. For Assignment A, the underlying problem to be solved might be something like this: *How do the best professors teach? Or Why are some teachers better than others?* Formulating your topic as a problem or question might help to make it feel more concrete and therefore more workable.

© Marvy/CORBIS

finis origine pendet
(The end depends on the beginning.)

Manlius, first century Roman poet

Teachable Moment Point out to students that in the letter you had them write for Darnell earlier in the chapter, the audience was his sibling. Depending on who the audience is, the tone, style, and intent change.

5. **Compose a strong thesis statement.** Your paper's thesis statement should be the specific argument you're making, summarized into one sentence, ideally. Your thesis should be your paper in a nutshell, what you'd say if you could only say one thing. It should identify your position on the subject and outline how you plan to tackle it. For example, for Assignment A, your thesis may be something like: *"The best teachers know their disciplines inside and out, engage students in the classroom, and demonstrate caring for students and their learning."* Formulating a strong thesis is half the battle.

6. **Set in-between target dates for the three stages of writing, even if your instructor doesn't.** Some instructors will ask to see your work at each stage of the writing project. Others will simply list a final due date. Yes, that's your target date for completion, but don't assume that's the date you should be done. If you try to print your paper at 9:50 a.m. on October 5 for your 10 a.m. class, you can count on Murphy's Law rearing its ugly head. A printer cartridge will suddenly dry up, a paper jam will stop your printer dead in its tracks, or your hard drive will plummet to its death. To beat the odds, set in-between dates for prewriting, writing, and rewriting to keep the project moving along.

If you've taken any notes, or written out any questions or opinions or phrasings, you're helping yourself begin the writing process. Remember that your notes don't have to be grammatically correct or in any sense finished. Rather, they're raw material for later use.

> **"I must write it all out, at any cost. Writing is thinking. It is more than living, for it is being conscious of living."**
>
> **Anne Morrow Lindbergh, American writer and aviation pioneer (1906–2001)**

© Myron Jay Dorf/CORBIS

Writing

Have you ever experienced writer's block, sometimes called the tyranny of the blank page or nowadays, the blank screen? You sit down to write and suddenly go blank? Whatever you call it, you'll be relieved to know there are ways around it.

Some professional writers resort to strange, almost ritualistic strategies to get themselves going. Victor Hugo supposedly wrote in his study at the same time every day—naked! His valet was ordered to lock away all Hugo's clothes until he had finished each day's writing.[4] Apparently, the method worked—witness *Les Misérables.* But this technique may not be well received by your roommate or your family.

A simpler way of starting is to just write freely about whatever comes into your head, whether it's on target or not. Say, for example, your history professor wants a short essay by tomorrow on some aspect of the American Civil War. You've already prewritten this paper—you've done your assigned readings, you've taken notes in class, you've found some interesting books and useful websites, and you've discussed the war with classmates over the past week. Take a look at these techniques for starting the writing process.

1. **Begin by writing what's on your mind.**

   I'm having trouble starting this paper because there's so much to talk about in the Civil War. The question we always seem to come back to is "Why was the war fought?" Was it over slavery, states' rights, or the desire to retain the Union? Or was it a complicated merging of all these causes?

Now stop and look at what you've written. If you take away the first sentence and play with what's left, you'll discover a useful beginning for a first draft:

> In discussions on the American Civil War, the most important question seems to be this: "Why was the war fought?" Was it slavery, states' rights...?

2. **Begin with the words, "The purpose of this paper is...."** As in the previous example, you'll find yourself with plenty to say if you've already done your prewriting. And because you know you can later get rid of these starter words and change what follows, you're on your way to a useful first draft.

3. **Work with a tutor in your campus Writing Center.** Sometimes talking through the assignment with someone else can help, particularly if that person is a writing expert. Or talk it through with your roommate or a family member.

4. **Change the audience.** If it helps, assume you're writing your paper on the Civil War to someone who sharply disagrees with you or to a middle school student who just asked you a question. Sometimes thinking about your audience—instead of the topic in the abstract—helps you zero in on the writing task.

5. **Play a role.** Imagine yourself as Abraham Lincoln writing a speech for the American people or a network newscaster deciding what to include on the evening news in 1861. Separate yourself from the task, and see it from another perspective.

6. **Work from an outline, point by point.** Take the facts and ideas you collected during the prewriting stage and organize them in whatever way makes sense for now. It doesn't have to be perfect; in fact, you'll be better off if you expect your outline to change as you proceed. Put your thesis statement at the top of the outline and then build out summary sentences, which you can later turn into paragraphs for each point.

7. **Use an organizational pattern intentionally.** One obvious and critical question to consider during the writing stage is *how will I organize my paper?* Various organizational patterns are possible, and it's important to identify the one you'll use—and then use it.

> ➤ If you're describing something occurring along a timeline, stick to a *chronological* pattern. "The Civil War began in 1861, and over the course of the next four years it was to become the bloodiest war ever fought by Americans...."

> ➤ If you're posing a problem and then offering solutions, use a *problem-solution* pattern. "College students today face a quandary. Tuition has become so costly that they must work to pay for college, yet it is those hours on the job that may detract from their studies...."

> ➤ If you're identifying the similarities and differences between two things, use a *compare and contrast* format. "While Shakespeare's Hamlet and

Teachable Moment First-year seminar courses often include journal assignments. One purpose of assigning journals is to increase the amount and fluency of students' writing. Journals are a great way to accomplish this since they sometimes cover everyday things and events and issues that are on students' minds. Or "Insight → Action" boxes make great journal topics for self-reflection and change.

Activity Option Show your students some online examples of visual organizers for writing or provide handouts that explain visual techniques to help them become better writers. There are many visual organizing tools online or your writing center will have examples such as outlining, mapping, and brainstorming activities. Use one of the visual organizers to help students, as a class, structure an essay about why it's important to go to class.

Macbeth are both tragic figures, driven by self-delusion and confounded by madness, at the plays' ends, one has learned profound life lessons that remain for us today."

> Some natural or social science courses will ask you to write papers using a *cause and effect* pattern: "The lessening crime rate in the United States today is due to the increased presence of law enforcement in everyday life."

> You may instead use a *topical* pattern, describing the parts of a whole, a *spatial* pattern (that describes a visual idea or map), or a *journalistic* pattern (based on who, what, when, and where). Pick a pattern, and stick with it.[5]

YOUR TYPE iS ShOwing

Here are some provocative questions:

1. What do our MBTI personality traits tell about how we approach writing projects? Consider these findings:

   Extraverts tend to write from their own experience. They sometimes begin writing by talking through the topic. They jump into writing and make an outline later, and they feel a need to take breaks to refresh themselves with some external stimulation, like talking to someone else.

   Introverts tend to write from their own ideas, spend more time on prewriting, and write thoughtfully. They need quiet in order to concentrate on what they're writing.

   Sensors report more factual information. They tend to use writing habits that worked for them in the past, pay attention to mechanics and grammar, and write clearly and simply.

   Intuitives are likely to discuss concepts, use new approaches, pay attention to complexities, and write with subtlety.

   Thinkers tend to select writing topics that are impersonal, and they tend to write papers by following a particular structure, like working from an outline. They also focus more on the content of their papers than on the impact a paper may make on its reader.

   Feelers tend to write papers on topics they care about; they avoid topics that are dry and boring. They insert personal examples into their papers, and often begin with one sentence and then just follow their thoughts as they flow. They also anticipate a reader's reaction as they write.

   Judgers tend to choose a topic quickly, limit their research, and then set goals to complete the paper. The first drafts of their papers are likely to be underdeveloped, and their ideas are often stated emphatically, sometimes without adequate support.

   Perceivers often fall into the trap of choosing overly broad topics and then jumping into the research. They also tend to get stuck there, wanting to read one more book or add one more article. Sometimes their papers ramble on because they dislike excluding ideas and prefer to sharpen their focus as they work, not beforehand.[6]

2. Is communication apprehension (fear of public speaking) inborn or learned? In your estimation, on the four MBTI scales, who is more likely to be fearful of communicating?

_____ Introverts	or	_____ Extraverts	
_____ Sensors	or	_____ iNtuitives	
_____ Feelers	or	_____ Thinkers	
_____ Judgers	or	_____ Perceivers	

If you checked the boxes on the left, in particular the top three, you're correct. People who are introverts, sensors, and feelers tend to be more fearful of communicating publicly. Some experts believe that this research confirms that such fears are inborn, rather than learned. If basic personality components are observable at birth or early childhood, they say, perhaps communication apprehension is one of these traits. What do you think?[7]

Rewriting

In this last stage of the writing process, take a close look at what you've said and how you've said it. Make wording changes that provide your reader with the clearest, most powerful writing possible. Correct grammar, punctuation, spelling, and appearance. But besides these necessary technical fixes, you'll actually need to take a fresh look at what you've said.

Rewriting is often called "revision," and that's a powerful term. It means not merely changing, but literally re-seeing, re-en*vision*ing your work. Sometimes students think they're revising when they're actually just editing: tinkering with words and phrases, checking spelling, changing punctuation. But the word *revision* actually means more than that. It means making major organizational overhauls, if necessary. According to many writing experts, that's what you must be willing to do. You're on a search and destroy mission, if that's what it takes.[8] Try these suggestions for rewriting to see if they work for you:

> **"A C essay is an A essay turned in too soon."**
>
> **John C. Bean, Professor of English, Seattle University**

1. **Leave it alone.** To help you see your paper as others will see it, set it aside for a while. Go get a snack, wait until after your next class, but let some time elapse. Why? Because with new eyes, what you've written will look different. Of course, this suggestion isn't meant to serve as an excuse for a late paper ("I couldn't turn my paper in today because I need to wait before I rewrite."). That won't fly. But coming back later is usually illuminating. ("What? I wrote that? What was I thinking?") You might wonder how long to wait before returning to your writing. Horace, the Roman writer, advised his students to put their work aside for seven years before revising. For most of us, seven days, even seven <u>hours</u> may be too long! But if you can wait an hour, a day, or a weekend before revising, you'll have distanced yourself long enough to see your writing for what it is, and then improve it.

2. **Ask for feedback.** One way of discovering how your writing will affect others is simply to ask them. Share your writing before it becomes final.

3. **Edit ruthlessly!** Yes, there's a sense in which you are ego-involved in your writing. That's natural. Cutting a favorite phrase or section may feel like lopping off an arm or a leg. But sometimes it must be done. The goal here is to produce the best paper possible, even if it's painful!

4. **Proofread, proofread, proofread!** You may think you have just written an unbelievable essay, but if it's littered with errors, your instructor may pay more attention to those than to your paper's brilliant ideas. Sometimes it also helps to proofread out loud. Somehow hearing the words, especially if you're an aural learner, makes errors more apparent. Be positive there are no spelling errors, and be proud of the document's final appearance—paper

Chapter Crossover Remind students to go back to Chapter 2 and pay particular attention to their VARK and MBTI scores. They should easily be describing their type and learning style by now and should be able to tell you how this might impact their writing and speaking.

Sensitive Situation While it is a good idea to have students in class read each other's papers, keep in mind that you might have a student who is very embarrassed about his writing. Since you probably already are familiar with your students' work, if you have a student who is really struggling, you might want him to read a sample of your work, and you his, especially if this is an in-class activity.

clean, type dark and crisp, margins consistent, headings useful, names and references correct. And remember that Spellcheck, for all its convenience, can let you down. If the word you use is an actual one, but not the right on, it will give its approval, regardless. (Did you catch the spelling error in that last sentence? Spellcheck didn't.)

One more tip. Throughout these three stages be prepared to move fluidly from one to the other at the slightest provocation. If you're <u>rewriting</u> and you come across some <u>prewriting</u> information—new information that would prove useful—copy it down and fit it in. If in the <u>prewriting</u> stage you think of <u>writing</u> that strikes you as powerful—a good argument or a well-constructed phrase— write it down.[9]

INSIGHT ⊖ ACTION

1. Which of the three stages of the writing process is most challenging for you? Explain why. Are you eager to get going, so you skip prewriting? Do you have trouble getting your thoughts on paper as you write? Is time management an issue for you, so that there's no time left for rewriting?

2. Look over something you've written for a recent assignment, and recommend a strategy to overcome any unproductive tendencies.

Avoid These Three Writing Traps!

CHALLENGE ⊖ REACTION

Challenge: What are the most common weaknesses found in new college students' writing?

Reaction: Put a checkmark beside the ones you believe to be most common, and then put an asterisk beside the ones you see as the most difficult challenges to overcome in your own writing.

1. _____ Constructing sentences

2. _____ Varying sentences

3. _____ Punctuating sentences

4. _____ Organizing an essay

5. _____ Using language well

6. _____ Constructing a thesis statement

7. _____ Making sure of agreement (subject-verb, number, verb tense, etc.)

8. _____ Using the active/passive voice appropriately

9. _____ Writing for a particular audience

10. _____ Including the appropriate level of detail

11. _____ Constructing paragraphs

12. _____ Making sure of coherency between paragraphs

13. _____ Demonstrating good reasoning

14. _____ Integrating sources

15. _____ Documenting references

16. _____ Using correct grammar

Teachable Moment As a class, come up with the top five most common writing weaknesses from this list and the top five that are most difficult for class members themselves to overcome. It is good for students to see that they are not alone in the struggle to become an effective writer.

Take a look at the following assignments, which contain examples of three common first-year student writing traps: "and then" writing, "all about" writing, and "data dump" writing.[10] For each example, read the instructions for the assignment, then read the essay, identify the writer's thesis statement, and critique the writing. If you were offering advice to each writer, what would you say?

> Assignment 1: Describe a problem you have faced as a first-year student, one that other students could learn from, and identify a possible solution.

"And then" writing. Last summer, I worked for a bank in my hometown to earn money for college. I was told to show up for the interview at 8:30 a.m. I usually don't get up that early, so on Thursday night, I set my alarm clock, my cell phone alarm, and my clock radio to make sure I didn't miss it. Afterward, I thought that I had really hit it off with the interviewer. When I first got the job on a Friday, I was thrilled. Imagine me working for a bank! I thought that sounded like a prestigious job. That night, I e-mailed my sister, and she was really impressed. I decided to keep the news a secret to surprise my Mom and Dad a few days later. When I told them about the job over the weekend, they thought it sounded like a good idea, although my Dad said that he thought banks really shouldn't hire young people because they don't know the value of money. I would have been offended by that remark, but my Dad and I get along really well, so I didn't make an issue of it.

But after my first week at Citizen's National Bank, I found myself bored stiff. Counting bills and tallying numbers really aren't that interesting. I did meet this girl named Nicole, and she was kind of cool, but everyone else at the bank was a little standoffish, including my supervisor, Ned. I didn't want to have a strained relationship with my supervisor, so I was friendly with him and serious about getting my work done. But by the following Wednesday, I was ready to quit. I was able to hang on for two more weeks, but then I heard about an opening at the coffee shop close to my house that included free food. So that's where I ended up. The moral of this story is to only take a job if you are really interested in the work. And I've definitely decided not to major in accounting.

This essay is an example of "and then" writing, a writing trap that uses a chronological organizational pattern instead of a problem-solution organizational pattern as the assignment requested. The writer tells the story by recounting, "and then this happened," "and then that happened." What is the writer's thesis

PhotoObjects.Net/Jupiter Images

> **"We are not what we know but what we are willing to learn."**
>
> **Mary Catherine Bateson, writer and cultural anthropologist**

statement? Is it the next-to-the last sentence? *Only take a job if you are really interested in the work.* Instead of telling a story from start to finish, how would the essay change if the writer had asked a question like this: What mistakes do students make when looking for a job to help them pay for college? Then the writer could have organized the essay around the thesis statement (*Only take a job if you are really interested in the work.*) and found evidence, including her own experience, to back up the claim.

> Assignment 2: Write an essay on the American Civil War.

"All about" writing. The American Civil War was the greatest and only war ever fought on U.S. soil. More than three million soldiers fought, and 600,000 died. Many novels, movies, and documentaries have been created about it. Now that the Internet exists, we also have another way to study it.

On February 9, 1861, the Confederate States of America was formed with Jefferson Davis as president. The war actually began on April 12, when the Confederates, under General Pierre Beauregard, opened fire on Fort Sumter in Charleston, South Carolina. Soon thereafter, Virginia seceded from the Union, followed by Arkansas, Tennessee, and North Carolina, thus forming an eleven-state Confederacy.

One of the best known battles of the Civil War is the Battle of Gettysburg. There, General Robert E. Lee fought against Major General George G. Meade's Army of the Potomac. Confederate forces came from the west and north and drove Union defenders back through the streets of Cemetery Hill. After it was all over, General Lee began withdrawing his army toward Williamsport on the Potomac River. His train of wounded soldiers stretched more than fourteen miles.

One of the most interesting ways to learn about the Civil War is to read accounts in government documents and in the diaries and letters of soldiers. The Gettysburg Address, which begins, "Fourscore and seven years ago, our fathers brought forth on this continent, a new Nation...," delivered by President Lincoln on November 19, 1863, is perhaps the most famous piece of writing to come out of the war.[11]

This essay is an example of another writing trap, "all about" writing, in which the writer wants to say a little bit of everything about a topic. The essay reads as if it were an encyclopedia entry on the Civil War. You can even imagine what the headings (for each paragraph) might be: Beginnings of the War, Famous Battles, Writings from the War. But what question or problem is the writer exploring? What is the writer's thesis statement? Is there one?

Although much of the writing you did earlier in your academic career may have actually encouraged "all about" writing, it lacks the organizational structure required in college writing. Imagine how different the paper would be if the writer had begun with a thesis statement such as, "Why, hundreds of years later, is the Civil War still a fascinating subject?" Or "Why are many Americans today Civil War buffs?" Or consider how the paper would have read if the writer had organized the essay around a thesis statement such as "The Civil War remains a fascination for Americans today because of its location, impact, and personal meaning." The essay then could have elaborated on these three reasons: (1) historically, it was the only war ever fought on American soil, (2) it claimed more American lives than the combined total from all other wars in which Americans have fought, and (3) it figures into the family history of many Americans today. Do you see the difference?

> Assignment 3: Write a research paper on a subject that relates to our course content in Psychology 101.

"Data dump" writing. Often people are in relationships that are bad for them, but they don't know what to do about it. Of course, all relationships have their ups and downs, but addictive relationships involve continual frustration. You realize that the relationship has the potential to make you both happy, but it doesn't. "Bad relationships are chronically lacking in what one or both partners need. Such relationships can destroy self-esteem and prevent those involved from moving on in their careers or personal lives." Often addictive relationships are "fertile breeding grounds for loneliness, rage, and despair."

Remaining in an addictive relationship can be dangerous to your health! Physical abuse can play a role. According to some studies, 23 to 25 percent of college students have been victims of some type of abuse from their intimate dating partner. "Another study conducted at several college campuses showed that as many as one half of all college undergraduates have been faced with physical aggression from their partner." The stress of a bad relationship can also "drain energy and lower resistance to physical illness." You may choose to stay because you share finances or because it's just easier to stay rather than find a new partner.

How do you know if you are in an addictive relationship, and if you are, what do you do about it? First, examine your deep beliefs about love. Do you hear yourself saying things like this: "Love is forever" or "I'm not good enough for a better relationship"? Feelings like these can keep you stuck in a bad relationship even though you deserve better. In the book, Women Who Love Too Much, Robin Norwood describes a ten-step plan for getting out.[12]

This student has fallen into the trap of using "data dump" writing with no recognizable organizational pattern at all. She is overwhelmed with information and simply lists everything she has found out through her research. Typically, "data dump" writers string together quotations from their sources, partly because they have no confidence in their own ability to say things, giving their papers a patchwork format. What if the writer had begun with this thesis statement: "Bad relationships can be addicting because you don't know what a quality relationship is, you fear physical aggression, and you don't know how to end it."

Have you been an "and then," "all about," or "data dump" writer? As a new, less experienced college writer, it's easy to fall into these traps. But beyond avoiding these three traps, what should college writers do instead?

Teachable Moment Believe it or not, some students have not yet mastered the basic concepts of a thesis, topic sentence, and transitions. Perhaps they don't remember or were never taught these concepts. At this point in the chapter, they should have a clear understanding of a thesis, but see if anyone can explain the purpose of topic sentences and transitions.

INSIGHT → ACTION

1. Select a paper you've written in the past or one you've written this term. Analyze the paper to look for "and then," "all about," or "data dump" organizational patterns. Explain any evidence you find—pro or con.

2. As you become a more sophisticated writer in college, what specific steps will you take to avoid these three common writing problems?

RELIEVE STRESS THE "WRITE" WAY!

According to some experts, writing is the supreme human achievement. We can do it, and other species can't, right? How many A+ essays has your dog written? Have you ever shoved a pen and paper into your pet canary's cage to see what he comes up with? Yes, as humans, we write. But if we're honest, we'll admit that writing is both difficult and exhilarating. Sometimes it's hard to get going, but when it goes well, we're delighted with ourselves!

What makes prolific writers like Stephen King or Danielle Steel or John Updike not only able to write, but want to write, even *need* to write? That's a simple question with a complicated answer.

Neurologists have studied a specific area of the brain that controls the desire to write. In fact, an injury or abnormality in that part of the brain can lead to such an overwhelming desire to write that individuals will write on walls or toilet paper, using their own blood if they have no ink.

But here's something else you may not have considered. Did you know that writing can be therapeutic? Joyce Carol Oates, a famous contemporary author, once said, "I have forced myself to begin writing when I've been utterly exhausted, when I've felt my soul as thin as a playing card…and somehow the activity of writing changes everything." Ernest Hemingway put it in the vernacular, "When I don't write, I feel like s---." *Paradise Lost* author John Milton described feeling like a cow that needs to be milked.[13] Of course, you may be thinking, these people are or were professional writers. What about the rest of us?

It's well documented that writing about life experiences can benefit your physical and emotional health. Researchers at the University of Texas, Austin, conducted a study reported in the *Journal of Clinical Psychology* in which student subjects wrote about an assigned topic for fifteen minutes a day over four days. Later in the year, when these students were asked about their physical health, those who had written about emotional topics earlier in the experiment reported far fewer visits to the doctor.[14] In another study, patients suffering from asthma or rheumatoid arthritis who kept a daily journal reported lessened symptoms.[15] In a third study, students who wrote about personal trauma reported two-thirds fewer trips to the doctor than did students who wrote factual, impersonal essays. Even students in the study who wrote about fictional misfortunes that hadn't actually taken place experienced health benefits.[16] Amazing!

Think about these ten potential benefits as they relate to you. Writing can help you:

1. Organize your thoughts.
2. Gain control over debilitating emotions.
3. Work through personal problems.
4. Understand feelings that are general and vague.
5. Share your thoughts and feelings with others.
6. Record troubling feelings, releasing you from the hold they have over you.
7. Focus on things you should be thinking about, as opposed to obsessing on stressful situations you can't change.
8. Enter a state of "flow" in which you are optimally productive.
9. Benefit your autoimmune system.
10. Help you rally the strength you need to focus on your current priorities, like getting a college education.

Try writing about something that's troubling you. If you're interested, read more about this subject, or begin keeping a journal. You may be surprised at just how therapeutic the act of writing can be.[17]

Build a Better Paper: The Seven C's

CHALLENGE ⟶ REACTION

Challenge: Without looking ahead, can you identify seven traits of good writing (all beginning with the letter *C*) that college students should aim for?

Reaction:
1. _____   5. _____
2. _____   6. _____
3. _____   7. _____
4. _____

In many ways, writing is like building. But instead of using nails, planks, and sheetrock to construct our communication, we use words, sentences, and paragraphs. If one of your goals is to avoid the three common first-year writing traps, what should you do instead? Good question! Here are seven suggestions—all of which begin with *C* to help you remember them.[18] You can use these items as a checklist for papers you write, too, before you turn them in.

1. Be **C**lear. Unfortunately, the English language gives you endless opportunities to write something quite different from what you mean. The great storyteller and essayist E. B. White once gave this advice to writers: "When you say something, make sure you have said it. The chances of your having said it are only fair." His irony and wit are subtle, but effective. Of course, there are many ways to be unclear: You can flip through your thesaurus and use a word that sounds good, but isn't recognizable (as in *profundity*, below), or you can write a convoluted sentence that can't be understood. Compare the problems in these two sentences, both of which are unclear:

> **"Don't agonize. Organize."**
>
> **Florynce Kennedy, American lawyer and African American activist**

> ➤ *The profundity of the quotation overtook its author's intended meaning.*

> ➤ *The writing was profound, but on closer examination, not only was it devoid of content, but it was also characterized by a preponderance of flatulent words.*

"What was that again?" Yes, many of us will be able to figure out what these sentences mean, though perhaps we'll need to check the dictionary. Why would anyone write this way? Sometimes beginning college students decide they must write to *impress* rather than to *express*. They assume instructors like this kind of convoluted writing. They think it sounds more *academic*. Instructors see through that guise. Mean what you say, and say what you mean.

2. Be **C**omplete. Ask yourself what your reader needs to know. Sometimes we're so close to what we're writing that we leave out important information, or we fail to provide the background the reader needs to get our meaning. Put yourself in your reader's shoes. If you have trouble getting distance from your writing, ask someone else to read it, or take your paper to the Writing Center on campus.

3. Be **C**orrect. If your writing is littered with grammatical, spelling, and punctuation errors, you've already lost the battle. Unfortunately, including errors in your writing can lead readers to generalize that you also don't know what you're writing about. "If he didn't pay attention to technical details, perhaps his arguments are faulty, too. And maybe his sources are inaccurate, as well." If grammar, punctuation, and usage aren't your strong points, buy a grammar handbook or go to a credible website. Ask someone you know who's a crackerjack writer to look over your first draft.

But correctness doesn't stop with technical errors. It also includes using sexist language, for example, even without meaning to. Instead, catch yourself in the act. A good rule of thumb is to substitute <u>you</u> and <u>they</u> for he-his-him.

Instead of:	*The student must understand <u>his</u> assignment.*
Try:	*Students must understand <u>their</u> assignments.*
Or:	*As a student, <u>you</u> must understand <u>your</u> assignment.*

Or simply get rid of he-his-him by rephrasing:

Instead of:	*The successful executive makes up <u>his</u> mind quickly.*
Try:	*The successful executive decides quickly.*

Of course, what you don't want to do is make the fix so obvious that you send the wrong message: *The successful executive makes up his (her) mind quickly.* Without intending to, some readers may think you're implying that fewer corporate CEOs are women. While that might be true, factually, pointing it out through your writing might offend a reader. You might think we're past all that in this day and age, but you'd be surprised at the ways in which sexism still sneaks back in subtly when we're not careful!

4. **Be Concise.** Let's be honest. Back in high school, you may have been tempted once or twice to pad your writing, to stretch it out in order to meet a requirement, to go on and on about something because you had an assigned number of pages to fill. You may have used tricks like enlarging the font, increasing the margins, and repeating yourself by adding unnecessary paragraphs, for example. At the time, expanding may have seemed like a challenging task. But college students sometimes face the opposite problem: they find that writing *less* is more challenging than writing *more.* Mark Twain once wrote, "If I'd had more time, I would have written a shorter book." Writing with precision—saying exactly what you want to say with power and impact—is difficult. It's much easier to "run off at the fingers."

But think of this formula: A given idea expressed in many words has relatively little impact. But that same idea expressed in few well-chosen and well-combined words can be penetrating. You could say:

> *"Whether or not a penny, or any amount of money, is earned or saved, it has the same or at least a similar value, fiscally speaking, in the long run."*

Compare that weak, wordy blather with this concise expression of Ben Franklin's:

> *"A penny saved is a penny earned."*

5. **Be Compelling.** Your writing should be interesting, active, and vivid, so that people want to read what you have to say. Compare these two headlines about the Student Government Association in your campus newspaper. Which article would you want to read?

> ➤ *Protests against tuition increases have been led by student government.*

> ➤ *SGA leaders urge campus-wide protests over tuition hikes.*

The sentences create different images, don't they? The first sentence makes the situation sound like something that happens every day. Ho-hum. You probably wouldn't take a second look. The second sentence uses the active

> **"I am returning this otherwise good typing paper to you because someone has printed gibberish all over it and put your name at the top."**
>
> **English Professor, Ohio University**

voice (*leaders urge campus-wide protests*) instead of the passive voice (*protests have been led*), and the second sentence uses a more descriptive verb (*urge* versus *lead*) and noun (*hikes* versus *increases*). Of course, you can go too far (*SGA leaders spearhead crushing student fury over radical tuition upsurge*). But this principle is a good one to remember.

6. **Be Courteous.** Courtesy is important in any kind of writing. You don't want to make demands or insult your instructor. Courtesy is particularly important in e-mails you send. Take a look at this actual e-mail from a new first-year student:

Professor X,

I just looked at the online syllabus for University 101. Why didn't you tell us that our first e-mail journal is due on Monday? I couldn't get into student housing, so I will be very busy moving into an apartment downtown this weekend. Writing a journal for your class is the last thing I want to have to think about.

Matt

Inappropriate? You bet! If the student had let this e-mail sit for a while first, he might have calmed down enough to write a more courteous message, one that raised the concern without offending his instructor.

7. **Be Convincing.** You'll be a more successful writer if you support your views with solid evidence and credible testimonials. Give specific examples to illustrate your point—anecdotes, testimonials from experts, experiences, analogies, facts, statistics—and your writing will be more credible. And be clear about where you found your supporting evidence. As you take notes during the pre-writing stage, keep careful documentation. Forgetting to write down the name of a book, title of an article, or page number of a reference have resulted in many a late-night trip to the library or frantic searching through an online database.

Keep these seven C's in mind. The secret to learning to think in college is to become a better writer. And as you're learning critical thinking skills, you'll also become a more clear, complete, correct, concise, compelling, courteous, and convincing writer.

EXERCISE 10.1 Dearly Departed

This exercise may be carried out in one of two ways: speaking or writing. Either way, your goal is to research a famous historical figure. Instead of writing about a topic, write about a person. Choose someone you don't know much about, but someone who had something in common with you. If you are planning to major in math, you may wish to select a famous mathematician, who made extraordinary contributions to the field. Or, you may wish to research someone of your particular ethnicity.

Writing assignment: Research this person's background and accomplishments through library materials and online documents. Your task is to write an obituary about this person. Look at samples from *The New York Times*, where the obituaries for prominent people typically run a half to a full page (the equivalent of ten to fifteen pages, typed). Even though the subject is somber, you'll find the writing to be lively, artful, and sometimes even entertaining. Focus on the accomplishments of the person you chose and celebrate him or her.

Speaking assignment: Assume you have been asked to give a five- to ten-minute eulogy about your chosen person. Aim for a presentation that is respectful but lively, artful, and entertaining.[19]

Downloading Your Workload: The Easy Way Out?

One of the trickiest aspects of writing papers for your college courses can be expressed in these three words: *What is plagiarism?* To know the correct answer to this question, you may need to forget what you learned in high school. You should also understand the difference between *intentional* and *unintentional* plagiarism. *Intentional* plagiarism is deliberately downloading a paper from an online source or lifting text from a website or book, for example. However, you run the risk of committing *unintentional* plagiarism if you don't understand what plagiarism is or you forget the book in which you found the information so you don't attribute the words you've borrowed to someone else. Technology today makes plagiarism easy, but by the same token, detecting plagiarism has become easy for instructors, too. The bottom line? Follow the guidelines you get from your instructors. And if you don't understand the guidelines or your instructor assumes you already know them, ask questions. Both *intentional* and *unintentional* plagiarism can hurt you, academically. These FAQs will help.

Q1: If I list all the sources I used in writing a paper in the bibliography, won't that cover everything? List all your sources in the bibliography at the end of your paper, but also acknowledge the ideas of others

Teachable Moment Your institution may subscribe to an online plagiarism detector, such as *Turnitin*. Students submit their papers to this online platform and within minutes it is scanned for plagiarism. Specifically, the document is scanned for sentences (up to nine words in a row) that show up either on the Internet or in a paper that has already been submitted. If the student cites the information correctly, that is acceptable. Copies of the scanned papers are accessible to the faculty member with a report on possible plagiarism.

as you present them. Generally, it's a good idea to cite the original author soon after you present the quote or concept in your paper. Depending on the kind of paper you're writing—a research paper, for example—it's also useful to name the authors ("According to Staley, college success skills are critical in the first year of college.") Each discipline uses a particular format to cite references. These are called *stylesheets*, such as *MLA* (Modern Language Association), *APA* (American Psychological Association), or the *Chicago Manual of Style*. Check with your instructor if you're not certain which one to use.

Q2: Must I cite all my sources if I just put ideas into my own words? Yes, you must cite all your sources, even though you may think that doing so clutters up your paper. In academic writing, you must cite all the information you use, whether you paraphrase it, quote it, or summarize it. Some students are even taught bad habits in high school, for example, "It's not plagiarism if you change every fifth (or some number) word," so they write papers with a thesaurus close by. Unfortunately, that's not the way it works. Try reading what you'd like to paraphrase, and then cover the text with your hand and write what you remember. In this case, you'd still need to cite the reference, but since you're paraphrasing, you wouldn't use quotation marks.

Q3: But I didn't know anything at all about this subject before I started this assignment. Does that mean I should cite everything? Some ideas are common knowledge that need not be cited. For example, it's a well-known fact that the Civil War lasted from 1861 to 1865. If you cited this piece of common knowledge, who would you cite? Generally, however, your motto should be, "Better safe than sorry." As a general rule, you must cite *quotations*, *paraphrases*, or *summaries*. If you use the exact words of someone else, put quotation marks around them, or if they're longer than four lines, indent them. (And generally, only use long quotes if something has been said in a remarkable way.) Also cite specific facts you're using as support and distinctive ideas belonging to others, even if you don't agree with them.

Q4: I've been doing a lot of reading for this paper. Now I'm not really sure which ideas came from others, and which are my own. How do I avoid plagiarism? The best solution here is to take careful notes as you do your research and document where you found each piece of information. Avoid cutting and pasting text. That practice can backfire later when you can't remember what you've extracted, and what represents your own thoughts and wording. And remember this: plagiarism applies to speaking as well as writing![20]

Now look back at the example in the "Challenge → Reaction" box at the beginning of this section. If you indicated that this student could be accused of plagiarism, you're right. Go back over this section to make sure you understand why.

> **"Borrowed thoughts, like borrowed money, only show the poverty of the borrower."**
>
> Lady Marguerite Blessington, English socialite and writer (1789–1849)

Teachable Moment Share with students a great resource called Citation Machine. This online tool shows students how to create Works Cited and in-text citations in a variety of stylesheets.

> **"What's another word for 'Thesaurus'?"**
>
> Steven Wright, American comedian

INSIGHT ⊖ ACTION

1. Now that you know what plagiarism is, do you understand how to avoid it? Define plagiarism in your own words.

2. List three specific actions you will take to avoid plagiarism at all costs. For example, you may decide to begin taking notes on index cards and list a reference at the bottom of every card when you do research.

In a Manner of Speaking...

> **"The trouble with talking too fast is you may say something you haven't thought of yet."**
>
> **Ann Landers, syndicated advice columnist (1918–2002)**

Up until now, this chapter has focused on the importance of your writing skills to your success in college. What about your *speaking* skills? How important are those? You may be thinking something like this: *I'm not going to be a public speaker. I'm going to be a surgeon. I'll spend all my time hunched over an unconscious person lying on an operating table. All I'll need to know how to do is hold a scalpel with a steady hand.* But is that really true? What about the communicating you'll need to do with totally conscious hospital administrators, other physicians, and patients before and after surgery?

© Paul Cookin/Brand X/CORBIS

Most people think of public speaking as an episode, a one-time event. You stand up to give a speech, and when you're finished, you sit down. But actually, there's a sense in which all the speaking we do is public. If you find the idea of public speaking threatening, think of it more as a state of being than as an incident. By contrast, what would *private* speaking be? Thinking? On the job, you'll communicate with others every day. Unless you join a profession that requires you to take a vow of silence, you'll be speaking publicly all the time!

C CONTROL Your Learning

YOUR TOUGHEST CLASS

Think about the speaking and writing assignments in the most challenging course you're taking this term. If this course doesn't include a speaking or writing assignment—a math class, for example—think of a challenging writing or speaking assignment for another course.

What is the assignment? What will it require of you? Identify the aspects of the assignment that will be most challenging. Develop a step-by-step plan, based on the information you've read in this chapter, to help you do your best on the assignment. E-mail your plan to your professor in this course.

Scared Speechless?

CHALLENGE → REACTION

Challenge: Is speaking anxiety a problem for you?

Reaction: This instrument, the Personal Report of Public Speaking Anxiety (PRPSA), is composed of thirty-four statements concerning feelings about communicating with other people. Indicate the degree to which the statements apply to you by marking whether you (1) strongly agree, (2) agree, (3) are undecided, (4) disagree, or (5) strongly disagree with each statement. Work quickly; just record your first impression.[21]

1. _____ While preparing for giving a speech I feel tense and nervous.

2. _____ I feel tense when I see the words *speech* and *public speech* on a course outline when studying.

3. _____ My thoughts become confused and jumbled when I am giving a speech.

4. _____ Right after giving a speech I feel that I have had a pleasant experience.

5. _____ I get anxious when I think about a speech coming up.

6. _____ I have no fear of giving a speech.

7. _____ Although I am nervous just before starting a speech, I soon settle down after starting and feel calm and comfortable.

8. _____ I look forward to giving a speech.

9. _____ When the instructor announces a speaking assignment in class I can feel myself getting tense.

10. _____ My hands tremble when I am giving a speech.

11. _____ I feel relaxed while giving a speech.

12. _____ I enjoy preparing for a speech.

13. _____ I am in constant fear of forgetting what I prepared to say.

14. _____ I get anxious if someone asks me something about my topic that I do not know.

15. _____ I face the prospect of giving a speech with confidence.

16. _____ I feel that I am in complete possession of myself while giving a speech.

17. _____ My mind is clear when giving a speech.

18. _____ I do not dread giving a speech.

19. _____ I perspire just before starting a speech.

20. _____ My heart beats very fast just as I start a speech.

21. _____ I experience considerable anxiety while sitting in the room just before my speech starts.

22. _____ Certain parts of my body feel very tense and rigid while giving a speech.

23. _____ Realizing that only a little time remains in a speech makes me very tense and anxious.

24. _____ While giving a speech I know I can control my feelings of tension and stress.

Emotional Intelligence (EI) Research Students who do not have strong problem-solving abilities may not be able to identify the steps needed to help them with their assignments. They may be vague and general about what they plan to do. When students e-mail you their assignments, carefully look to see if they have broken down their plan into manageable and realistic steps.

25. _____ I breathe faster just before starting a speech.

26. _____ I feel comfortable and relaxed in the hour or so just before giving a speech.

27. _____ I do poorer on speeches because I am anxious.

28. _____ I feel anxious when the teacher announces the date of a speaking assignment.

29. _____ When I make a mistake while giving a speech, I find it hard to concentrate on the parts that follow.

30. _____ During an important speech I experience a feeling of helplessness building up inside me.

31. _____ I have trouble falling asleep the night before a speech.

32. _____ My heart beats very fast while I present a speech.

33. _____ I feel anxious while waiting to give my speech.

34. _____ While giving a speech I get so nervous I forget facts I really know.

To determine your score on the PRPSA, complete the following steps:

1. Add the scores for items 1, 2, 3, 5, 9, 10, 13, 14, 19, 20, 21, 22, 23, 25, 27, 28, 29, 30, 31, 32, 33, and 34.

2. Add the scores for items 4, 6, 7, 8, 11, 12, 15, 16, 17, 18, 24, and 26.

3. Complete the following formula: PRPSA = 132 − (total from step 1) + (total from step 2).

4. Your score on the PRPSA can range between 34 and 170. A score of:

   34–84 indicates a **very low** anxiety about public speaking.

   85–92 indicates a **moderately low** level of anxiety about public speaking.

   93–110 suggests **moderate** anxiety in most public speaking situations but not so severe that the individual cannot cope and be a successful speaker.

   111–119 suggests a **moderately high** anxiety about public speaking. People with such scores will tend to avoid public speaking.

   120–170 indicates a **very high** anxiety about public speaking. People with these scores will go to considerable lengths to avoid all types of public speaking situations.

Your score: _____

Used by permission of James C. McCroskey.

Sensitive Situation Most likely you will have at least one or two students who have very high anxiety about giving speeches in class. You may even have a student who stutters for whom the thought of having to stand up in front of class is unbearable. Make sure you tell students to let you know if they fall into the high anxiety category. Work with them outside or class, or bring them to the oral communication center, if one exists on your campus.

Are you, like Darnell in the "FOCUS Challenge Case," uneasy about giving speeches? Does the thought of speaking in front of a roomful of other students send you over the edge? If your score on the PRPSA is between 111 and 170, speech anxiety could be a problem for you in college. That's why it's important to address the subject now.

But remember this: you're not alone. By some estimates, over 41 percent of Americans suffer from speech anxiety. According to the original *Book of Lists*, public speaking is the number one fear in America. To get the full impact of this ranking, imagine possible runners-up: spiders crawling all over your body or balancing on a ledge fifty stories off the ground, for example. Even the chilling realization that we are all sentenced to die the day we are born—death itself—ranks number 7! But public speaking tops them all. If this is true, why has Hollywood bothered to produce horror movies about aliens or biological warfare or natural disasters? Imagine the Academy Award for best picture going to a *real* thriller called *Podium!*[22]

In a sense, a fear of public speaking makes sense. After all, when you give a speech, it's *you* up there. You feel vulnerable when all eyes are upon you. By contrast, when you write a paper, you and your paper are two separate entities. But having a few butterflies in your stomach when you give a presentation is actually good. It means you care about how well you do. On the other hand, philosophically speaking, it's also sad to realize that what people fear most is each other.

Just what is so terrifying about public speaking for some people? Is it that they visualize the worst happening? Going completely blank? Fumbling over words? Blathering like an idiot? Tripping on the way to the front of the room? Having a sudden attack of gastric distress that requires a quick exit? Research indicates that what speakers worry about most is that they'll tremble, shake, or show other visible signs of nervousness, more so than going blank, doing something embarrassing, being unable to continue talking, or saying foolish things that don't make sense.[23] But did you know that research also indicates that only 12 percent of everything you do while you're speaking tells your listeners that your nerves are getting the best of you?[24] That's not very much, is it?

Studies have also shown that your anxiety will fade quickly after you begin, peaking immediately before and during the first two minutes of your presentation. If you can make it that far, you're in for smooth sailing.[25]

Ten Ways to Oust Anxiety

"It takes one hour of preparation for each minute of presentation time."

Wayne Burgraff, eighteenth century American philosopher

CHALLENGE → REACTION

Challenge: Identify five techniques that help reduce speaking anxiety.

Reaction: 1. _____

2. _____

3. _____

4. _____

5. _____

Ask yourself this: What kinds of activities do you enjoy? Do you like to play tennis? Swim? Run? Listen to music? Watch a movie with friends? You look forward to doing the things you enjoy, right? If you can harness your anxiety and actually look forward to opportunities to speak, you'll build more confidence and get better at doing it. See if you think the items on this checklist of fear-suppressing suggestions might work for you.

Teachable Moment If individual students are really nervous about presenting, ask others in the class to encourage those who are fearful. Make sure everyone is supportive of one another. Tell them not to worry, and that it is okay if they make a mistake. Let students who are nervous go first, and when they are done be sure everyone in the class gives them a round of applause.

Activity Option Have students line up on a continuum with those who are nervous about presenting at one end and those who are not at the other. Have students trade perceptions of speech anxiety and what can be done to overcome it.

> **"All the great speakers were bad speakers at first."**
>
> Ralph Waldo Emerson, American essayist and poet (1803–1882)

Teachable Moment Remind students that this is a situation where their learning styles may help or interfere. Students who save things until the last minute may not leave enough time to practice. Students who are not strong in problem-solving or reality-testing skills may underestimate the steps and time needed to complete a task, leaving little time to rehearse.

1. **Ready, set, go.** Unfortunately some students deal with stage fright by avoiding it. Productive *preparation* is replaced by penalizing *procrastination*. But blowing off a speaking assignment is the absolute worst thing you can do. Being unprepared will cause your anxiety to skyrocket, and winging it won't help your presentation fly! The best antidote to anxiety is to *prepare, prepare, prepare*! Nothing will calm your nerves like preparation!

2. **Dress for success.** While you're busy giving a presentation, you don't want to be distracted with concerns about whether anyone will notice that your shirt is dirty or your jeans don't fit. Of course, what you say is more important than how you look. But confidence in your physical appearance can increase your confidence overall. It's a good idea to follow the one-upmanship rule and dress one notch above how your audience is likely to be dressed. In doing so, you communicate that you care enough to look your very best.

3. **Ease the tension with humor.** During a presentation, using humor doesn't necessarily mean telling a joke. Rather than telling a canned joke that may not go over, use your natural wit. Say something funny that occurs to you at the moment, rather than repeating a joke you read on the Internet. Humor can ease tensions, both for your audience and for you.

4. **Don't be a mannequin.** Looking stiff may make your presentation sound unnatural. Move around. Use gestures. Look at your audience. Talk as if you were conversing with each individual in the room alone. Don't act as if the bottoms of your shoes are covered with Super Glue™. Be real, be yourself, and you'll feel more confident.

5. **Practice in your presentation room.** If your presentation will be given in Main Hall, room 120, find a time when the room is empty and practice your presentation there. Doing so can help put you at ease during your actual speech. Things will look familiar to you, and you can use parts of the room as *prompts* to help you remember what to say next.

6. **Find some guinea pigs.** When you practice your presentation, do it in front of a live audience. Practice in front of your roommate, or your Mom—even your dog! Practicing in front of a mirror might work, too, but living beings naturally cause distractions, like coughing or sneezing (or panting, in your dog's case) that you may have to contend with during your actual speech.

7. **Channel your energy.** Think about how much energy it takes to be fearful. Before a speech, you may feel frightened, fretful, or restless. Harness your fear, and turn it into positive energy that increases your dynamism.

8. **Visualize success.** When you see yourself giving your presentation in your mind's eye, visualize success, not failure. Visualization is a kind of mental practice you do beforehand. Practicing success is much more productive than practicing failure.

9. **Remember that mistakes are made to be corrected.** If disaster strikes, remember that how you handle it is what's important. Perhaps you fear making a slip of the tongue or accidentally creating a "spoonerism." Spoonerisms are named after the Reverend Archibald William Spooner of Oxford University in the 1800s. He had a curious habit of swapping the first letters of the words in phrases accidentally, without even realizing it, often with humorous results. He would unintentionally say awkward things to the congregation, for example, while officiating at a wedding, "Son, it is now kisstomary to cuss the bride." He was so famous for this tendency that the term "spoonerism" was named after him. While such gaffs could be unnerving, a speaker could instead make the most of a few moments of lightheartedness![26]

10. **If you can't shake it, fake it.** If your nerves get the better of you, try this. Fake it. Pretend you're confident. Often role-playing a confident person works. You assume the role, and before you know it, your confidence begins to increase. Remember that generally speaking, people are interested in other people. Your classmates are rooting for you! After all, they'll be up front before long![27]

Craft a Winning Presentation: The Seven P's

CHALLENGE → REACTION

Challenge: Without looking further in this section, can you identify seven useful key points, all beginning with *P,* that relate to presentations?

Reaction:
1. _____   5. _____
2. _____   6. _____
3. _____   7. _____
4. _____

When you prepare for a presentation in one of your classes, what is your primary goal? To impress your instructor? To amaze your classmates? To do your absolute best? To get your presentation over with?

Many of the suggestions in this chapter so far apply to both writing and speaking. As both a writer and a speaker, you should be clear, complete, correct, concise, compelling, courteous, and convincing. You should choose an organizational pattern and use it to help your audience understand what you're saying. (Unlike reading a written paper, they only have one chance to hear your words go by.) You must have a strong thesis in a speech, just as you must in a paper. But let's examine some other advice that relates primarily to speaking. Use these suggestions to create winning presentations that set you apart in all your courses.[28]

1. **Purpose.** What is the purpose of your presentation? Often the purpose is given to you directly by your instructor: Prepare a five-minute speech *to inform....* But other assignments will allow you to select your own purpose: "The Trials and Tribulations of a Commuting Student" (to inform), "Sustainability in an Age of Materialism and Waste" (to persuade), "Five

Sure-Fire Ways to Flunk Out of College... Not!" (to entertain), "How Being President of the Student Body Can Change Your Life" (to inspire). Knowing exactly what you're trying to accomplish helps!

2. <u>P</u>eople. Who will be your listeners? Generally, you'll be speaking to an audience of students in your classes, right? But what are their specific characteristics as they relate to your purpose? For example, if you're addressing parents and friends at commencement, you might create a different speech than the one you'd present to your co-members of a student club on campus.

3. <u>P</u>lace. Where will you deliver your presentation? The location of your presentation may affect its tone and style. A presentation you might give to a group of tourists at a national park would allow for informality, and your visual aid would be the scenery around you. But if you gave the same presentation as a geography major to high school seniors visiting for the day, you'd undoubtedly be more formal and scholarly, using a PowerPoint presentation or pull-down maps in the classroom.

4. <u>P</u>reparation. How should you prepare your speech? Developing the content of a speech is often similar to writing a paper. You'll need to develop a thesis statement and find support for each point by researching examples, statistics, and expert testimonies. Depending on the assignment, you might develop a full written draft of your speech, or a detailed outline, or a set of PowerPoint slides with talking points. Then, after you know what you're

---

FOCUS ON CAREERS: LAUREN WARD LARSEN, Speaker, Johnson & Johnson

Courtesy of Lauren Ward Larsen

Q1: Describe the kinds of events at which you speak and the types of groups you work with. What is your purpose, typically, when you speak to an audience?

I speak at a variety of events all over the United States, designed to encourage people to donate blood. I became a National Blood Donation Advocate after receiving an enormous amount of donated blood during a near-fatal illness in 2000. I work for the Johnson & Johnson Corporation, through the American Red Cross, America's Blood Centers, and the American Association of Blood Banks. Blood center leaders invite me to their cities, and during an average trip, I typically speak at two to six events to audiences ranging from 20 to 1,200 people. I also give interviews on live radio and television to encourage people to donate their blood, time, or money. I do this by sharing a variety of personal stories—including my own—that illustrate the important role blood donation plays in saving lives. I want people to identify with the cause by putting a human face on it—a face that easily could have been their own.

Q2: Fear is a major factor for many speakers. But as someone who speaks professionally, do you still become nervous before presentations? If so, how do you manage your anxiety?

Absolutely! Although I've loved the adrenaline rush of public speaking since I was in high school, I still feel a bit of nervousness before going on stage. Now that I give roughly one hundred talks each year, my fear level has dropped quite a bit. I still get nervous, especially if something about the situation is particularly new or unusual, and I know it's tough to pay attention to the words being said when the speaker's armpits are

noticeably soggy and her face seems to be melting off! I handle my anxiety by taking a few minutes alone to calm myself beforehand. I remind myself that my words *will* touch the right people, those who are meant to be inspired by them. I ask myself to simply do the best that I am capable of doing that day—nothing more, nothing less.

Q3: What has been your worst nightmare as a speaker, and how did you triumph over it?

Someone once said something like this: We only realize the absolute, raw power of technology when it stops working. My worst nightmares occur when technology decides to do me in. Often, for example, my PowerPoint slides relate directly to the content of my speech. When the projector fails, for whatever reason, I've learned to rely on my natural wit. I make a joke about how fortunate the audience is to have missed what was coming up, or I find something funny about the situation to break the tension. I also check out every technology-related detail in advance, even down to the height of the microphone. At six feet one inch tall, the last thing I want to have to do is bend over to talk into it. Technology has its pros and cons, along with built-in prerequisites for glitch-free success.

Q4: This chapter identifies seven P's to keep in mind in order to craft a winning presentation: purpose, people, place, preparation, planning, personality, and performance. Which of these do you emphasize, personally, and why?

For me, the most important P is *people*. What I talk about is people helping other people. I once spoke to a group of fourth graders who were a very lively and fun group. At the end of my time with them, I asked them all to go home and ask their parents if they were blood donors. If their answer was "yes," they were to give their Mom or Dad a big hug and tell

going to say, you'll need to write an attention-grabbing introduction and a memorable conclusion.

5. Planning. What planning should you do? For example, are visual aids available, or do you need to bring your own? Is there a plug in the room, if you need one? Should you bring a backup of your presentation on a flash drive? Should you test the LCD projector to make any necessary adjustments? Planning is critical, and Murphy's Law has a reputation for a reason. Many a speaker has been unnerved at the last minute by some overlooked detail.

6. Personality. The question here is, How can you connect with the audience? How can you demonstrate your competence, charisma, and character to your listeners? Eye contact is important. Look at each person individually, if possible. Inspire trust by telling a story or relating your topic to some aspect of your own experience. Rather than playing a role, act natural and be yourself. People are typically interested in other people, and your audience wants you to succeed.

7. Performance. This last P relates to delivering your presentation. Rehearsal is important (although too much rehearsal can make your presentation sound singsongy and memorized). Beware of bringing a full

Teachable Moment Pose the following questions to your students: Is a career in marketing a good career choice for everyone? Why or why not?

C CREATE a Career Outlook

MARKETING

Lauren Ward Larsen moved from a career as a corporate marketing executive to a career as a professional speaker in which "marketing" the critical importance of donating blood is key. Have you ever considered a career in marketing? Here are some facts about this career to consider and some questions about yourself to ponder.

Facts to Consider

Academic preparation required: a college degree in marketing, public relations, communication, journalism, or some related field, along with an internship or similar work experience

Future workforce demand: Competition for entry-level jobs will be high.

Work environment: Most organizations are in business to make a profit by selling their products and services to the public. Marketing professionals research how best to represent these products and services by conducting research on potential buyers, advertising, competitors, purchasing trends, and pricing, for example, and developing ways to promote demand in the marketplace. Marketing firms can be large or small, and the pace within them is typically high-energy and brisk. Earnings are high, travel is often frequent, and the hours can be long and include weekends and evenings.

Most common psychological type preferences: extraverted, either sensing or intuitive, thinking, and judging or perceiving. The most common psychological types are ESTJ, ENTJ, or ENTP.[29]

Essential skills: creativity, initiative, technology, and communication skills

Questions to Ponder

1. Do you have (or could you acquire) the skills this career requires?
2. What would you find most satisfying about this type of career?
3. What would you find most challenging about this type of career?
4. Are you interested in a career like this? Why or why not?

For more information, see U.S. Department of Labor, Bureau of Labor Statistics, *Occupational Outlook Handbook, 2006–2007 Edition.*[30]

For more career activities online, go to http://www.academic.cengage.com/collegesuccess/staley to do the Team Career exercises.

them it was from me. I also asked them each to pinch the inside of their elbows as hard as they could. They did, laughing and yelping. Then I asked them if they would be willing to go through that again if it meant they could save the life of their best friend or one of their parents. They all yelled, "yes!" It will be eight years before those children will be old enough to donate blood, but some of them may just remember what the tall lady told them about the arm pinch that day when the time comes.

Q5: Many people couldn't do what you do. To what do you attribute your success as a speaker? In your opinion, what makes speakers dynamic?
I attribute my success as a speaker to knowing that I can make a difference. To me, a dynamic speaker is one who understands her audience enough to touch their hearts with her words. It's not enough to impress people's intellects with facts. In order to get your audience to take action, you must *inspire* them, not just *educate* them. And to inspire people you must create an authentic connection with them. You must look them in the eye and talk *with* them, not *at* them.

Q6: What advice would you give beginning college students about developing their speaking skills?
Don't stop at *studying* public speaking. Actually put yourself in front of others willingly and speak. Accept that you will be nervous because you will. Do what you must in order to calm your nerves, and enjoy your time in front of an audience. Then evaluate your presentation afterward, and listen to others' feedback. Eventually, with practice and gradual tweaking, your nervousness will subside and your skills will sharpen. You can become the speaker you'd like to be!

written draft to the podium. If you do, you may be tempted to read it, which is the last thing you want to do. Practice makes perfect, as the old saying goes, but make sure you're practicing *good* habits (as opposed to counter-productive ones). Aim for a dynamic delivery, both verbally and nonverbally, that helps keep your listeners listening.

EXERCISE 10.2 What Makes Speakers Dynamic? Pet Peeves!

This exercise is about dynamism, about making presentations come alive because you show that you are psychologically and physically invested in them. Speaking about something you feel strongly about is one way to increase your dynamism without even trying. What makes you really angry? What are your pet peeves? For this exercise, you and your classmates will volunteer to give a thirty second speech on a pet peeve: being tailgated, getting a ticket, running out of gas, or getting into the slow line at a store, for example. Your instructor will provide a rolled-up newspaper for the activity. As you speak, hit the side of the lectern or the desk at the front of the room with the newspaper from time to time for emphasis. (Although this activity is intended to generate strong emotions, be careful not to offend others with your language!) After all speakers have finished, as a class, generate a list of characteristics that make speakers appear more dynamic.[31]

PowerPoint or PowerPointless?
Five Ways to Make Your Presentations Stand Out

Have you ever heard the phrase "Death by PowerPoint"? It's real. It lurks everywhere from college classrooms to corporate conference rooms. Perhaps you've been at death's door yourself in one of your classes in which PowerPoint is used ineffectively. While PowerPoint has the potential to be a powerful visual aid, it can also be PowerPointless if some simple rules are ignored. Keep these five suggestions in mind to turn PowerPointless presentations into powerful ones.

1. **DO use your whole brain.** When it comes to designing PowerPoint presentations, the challenge is to combine useful information with compelling design. While you should never assume that content is less important than PowerPoint razzle-dazzle, it's possible to impress an audience with both content and creativity. Think of it as using both of your brain hemispheres at once—your logical, content-oriented left hemisphere and your creative, artistic-capable right hemisphere. For example, if you're giving a presentation on majoring in elementary education, you might want to use a font that looks like a child's printing on your title slide. (Just make sure it's legible, even from a distance. A good rule of thumb is to use 24 point font size or larger and keep your fonts simple unless you have a particular reason to change them.) You also might want to include a high-quality graphic like this one here:

Keith Levit Photography/Index Open

Much of the clip art that's available won't give your presentation a professional look, but many different graphics packages offer high-quality, realistic images. Ask yourself: "How can I create the best possible visual aid, one that gives me useful cues as a speaker and gives the audience worthwhile content as listeners?" Which of the following presentations would you rather listen to—Presentation 1 or Presentation 2?

Chapter Crossover In Chapter 3 students learned about campus resources. Is there a place on campus where students can get help with PowerPoint presentations? Often, technology units on campus have the resources and expertise to help, or an oral communication center that coaches in using PowerPoint as a visual aid. Ask students to find out what's available on your campus.

PowerPoint or PowerPointless?

Five Ways to Make Your Presentations Stand Out

Presentation 1

PowerPoint or PowerPointless?

Five Ways to Make Your Presentations Stand Out

Presentation 2

2. **DO** use color to *integrate* and *differentiate.* Use background colors to create a mood: soft colors for a subdued mood and bold colors for an energetic one. Here's one color-related technique. Choose an attractive color scheme and stick to it. That doesn't mean that every background on every slide must be the same. In fact, doing that may cause your listeners to OD from monotony. But if your title slide is blue, gold, and white, then use one, two, or all three of these colors in some hue or shade on every slide. Some speakers create PowerPoint presentations that seem fragmented and messy because the individual slides aren't connected visually. On a single slide, use contrasting colors to make particular points stand out.

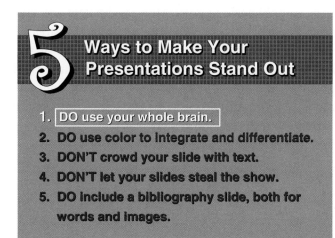

5 Ways to Make Your Presentations Stand Out

1. DO use your whole brain.
2. DO use color to integrate and differentiate.
3. DON'T crowd your slide with text.
4. DON'T let your slides steal the show.
5. DO include a bibliography slide, both for words and images.

3. **DON'T crowd your slides with text.** Your listeners won't pay attention to you if they're spending all their time reading. Be kind, and spare them the trouble by only displaying important words and phrases that make your points. Some of the most lethal PowerPoint presentations are those in which the speaker turns around, faces the screen, and flies through slide after slide, reading the text. The only way your listeners can live through that is if oxygen masks drop from the overhead compartments!

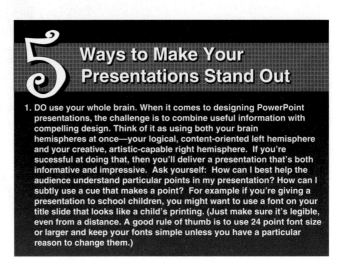

4. **DON'T let your slides steal the show.** Always remember that your slides themselves aren't your entire presentation. YOU are the speaker. Gun shots and screaming sirens shouldn't be used as sound effects unless, of course, the topic of your speech is gun control or ambulance response times. Anything used to excess—animations and transitions, for example—can do more harm than good. Use these effects sparingly and intentionally for emphasis, not randomly for their shock value. Remember, too, to use graphics that relate to your topic. An awesome picture that has nothing to do with your topic may leave your listeners wondering.

5. **DO include a bibliography slide, both for words and images.** Some students assume that plagiarism only pertains to writing papers. Not so! Always give credit where credit is due. List your references, either on individual slides (if you use a direct quote, for example) or at the end of your slideshow. If you pull a great graphic from a website, cite it. If you quote Benjamin Franklin ("A penny saved is a penny earned"), cite him. Not only are you doing the ethical thing, but you are letting your listeners know where they can find more information if they're interested.

If you follow these five basic rules, you can create winning PowerPoint presentations that stand out. Don't settle for MultiMediocrity! As famous football coach Vince Lombardi once said, "Excellence is achieved by the mastery of fundamentals."

INSIGHT ⊖ ACTION

1. Do you consider yourself to be a dynamic speaker? If so, identify the qualities that make you one. If not, what are you missing?

2. Of the seven P's, which will you most need to work on? Do you tend give one factor less attention than you should?

3. List three specific ways that you can improve your speaking skills in college.

Activity Option For the final in-class activity, students should develop a PowerPoint presentation on some aspect of writing and speaking. Assign students or groups of students to parts of this chapter such as "Avoid These Three Writing Traps," "Build a Better Paper: The Seven C's," "Ten Ways to Oust Anxiety," and so on. Use the five suggestions in the chapter about PowerPointless presentations as the criteria for assessing the presentation. Students can assess each other.

EXERCISE 10.3 VARK Activity

Complete the recommended activity for your preferred VARK learning modality. If you are multimodal, select more than one activity. Your instructor may ask you to (a) give an oral report on your results in class, (b) send your results to him or her via e-mail, (c) post them online, or (d) contribute to a class chat.

Visual: Storyboard (make rough sketches of each slide in sequence) an assigned PowerPoint presentation or create one for this chapter.

Aural: Deliberately talk through an assigned paper aloud as you write.

Read/Write: Write a paragraph summary of this chapter.

Kinesthetic: For a speech or paper you're preparing, write the major points, sub-points, and pieces of supporting evidence on index cards, one item per card. Then lay them all out on the floor and move them around until you are satisfied with the flow.

For more practice online, go to http://www.academic.cengage.com/collegesuccess/staley to take the Challenge Yourself online quizzes.

 # NOW WHAT DO YOU THINK?

At the beginning of this chapter, Darnell Williams faced a series of challenges as a new college student. Now after reading this chapter, would you respond differently to any of the questions you answered about the "FOCUS Challenge Case"?

On a scale of 1 to 10, answer the following questions now that you've completed this chapter.

1 = not very/not much/very little/low   10 = very/a lot/very much/high

In hindsight, how much did you *really* know about this subject matter before reading the chapter?

1   2   3   4   5   6   7   8   9   10

How much do you think this information might affect your college success?

1   2   3   4   5   6   7   8   9   10

How much do you think this information might affect your career success after college?

1   2   3   4   5   6   7   8   9   10

How long did it actually take you to complete this chapter (both the reading and writing tasks)? _____ Hour(s) _____ Minutes

Now take a minute to compare these answers to your answers from the "Readiness Check" at the beginning of this chapter. What gaps exist between the similar questions? How might these gaps between what you thought before starting the chapter and what you now think after completing the chapter affect how you approach the next chapter in this book?

To download mp3 format audio summaries of this chapter, go to http://www.academic.cengage.com/collegesuccess/staley.

11 Building Relationships, Valuing Diversity

YOU'RE ABOUT TO DISCOVER...

Teachable Moment Students who are most successful in college are those who make both academic progress and connect to you, other students, and the institution. Although students may not see the direct link initially, stress the fact that healthy relationships as well as understanding and appreciating diversity are critical to college success.

> What emotional intelligence is

> How EI relates to leadership

> Whether your EI can be improved

> How scientists define romantic love

> How communication is at the center of romantic relationships

> How to improve communication with people you care about

> How people manage conflict in five basic ways

> What constitutes a "danger signal" in a relationship

> Why diversity makes a difference

> Why service-learning is valuable

> Why global learning is important

"You must look into people, as well as at them."

Lord Chesterfield, British statesman (1694–1773)

Kia Washington

An emotional wreck. That's what Kia

Washington was. Since she first arrived on campus, it seemed that everything had gone wrong. Her best friend, Alicia, had decided to go to a different school at the last minute, she was closed out of what probably would have been her favorite class—Introduction to Literature—and she hadn't been able to get into campus housing because of a computer mix-up. If she lived off campus now, the Housing Office told her they'd guarantee her a room next term. To top it off, she was questioning her choice of classes and wondering why she couldn't decide on a major that would lead to a good job.

The apartment she'd managed to find close to campus was run down and barely affordable. She bought an inexpensive microwave, a mattress, and some towels, but she really didn't have the money to fix it up. Feeling completely alone and isolated, she found herself in tears more than once those first few weeks. Home, for all its faults, was looking better than it had when she lived there.

For most of her teenage years, Kia had lived with her Mom, who worked two jobs to support her and her brother, William. Although they got along well, her Mom was always too tired to do anything, it seemed, so they rarely spent much time together. And she never saw her father anymore. He'd remarried after the divorce and moved to another state. All through school, her family life had been rocky. Kia's parents, who probably cared for each other deep down, just couldn't get along. As a child, Kia sometimes retreated to her bedroom to wait out the arguments. Their decision to divorce five years ago had actually come as a relief.

Despite trouble at home, Kia had been a very good student in high school. Perhaps because home was a difficult place, she threw herself into her studies. She liked to read anything she could get her hands on, and doing homework had been a good escape. In fact, Kia kept to herself a good deal of the time. Meeting new people was one aspect of college she'd never really looked forward to. She preferred to just do her own thing, like listen to music by herself with her earplugs in between classes. Visiting the University Center to meet people and get connected wasn't something that interested her at all.

There really was only one other person that Kia cared about—Quentin. Throughout all of her high school years, Kia

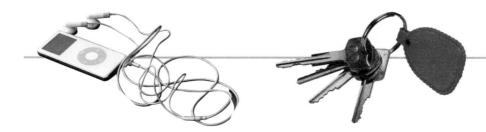

and Quentin had been inseparable. He'd chosen another college because her school didn't offer his major, but they spent most evenings on their cell phones, sometimes into the early morning hours. Quentin also happened to look like a movie star, and he was the funniest person Kia knew. No wonder every member of the female species was after him in high school. Luckily, he always told Kia that he wasn't in the market. But now that they were apart, she had to admit that she worried that he'd be in even greater demand in college. Holding onto him was her most important goal right now.

Most of the time, they got along really well, and fights were over quickly. Whenever a conflict came up, Kia exploded and Quentin just took it. He was the proverbial nice guy and she was—as her mother put it—moody. She often felt as if she was on an emotional roller coaster, and her temper got the best of her. Trying to communicate her way through a disagreement never seemed worth it to Kia. She'd spit out a few rude comments and then walk away or hang up. Fortunately, Quentin never seemed to hold a grudge.

But last Thursday, they'd had the worst fight ever on the phone over something silly; she couldn't even remember what. Suddenly she heard herself yelling into the phone, saying things she knew she'd regret. Quentin managed to get the words "control freak" out, and then this time *he* hung up. She hadn't heard from him since. He didn't return voicemails or e-mails, and his text messages abruptly stopped. She found herself obsessing about him, not able to sleep well or eat much over the weekend, and she couldn't face going to her classes on Monday or Tuesday. By Wednesday, she was so sick with worry that she couldn't drag herself out of bed.

Why does this have to be so hard? Kia kept asking herself. She'd decided to go to college to make a better *future* for herself. But right now the most important thing she had to do was get through the *present. My life is a soap opera*, she thought. And to anyone watching right now, she was right.

WHAT DO **YOU** THINK?

Now that you've read about Kia Washington, answer the following questions. You may not know all the answers yet, but you'll find out what you know and what you stand to gain by reading this chapter.

1. How would you characterize Kia's adjustment to college? Identify five specific problems described in this case study that could interfere with her college success.

2. To have done so well in school, Kia must be an intelligent person. But is her emotional quotient (EQ) different from her intelligence quotient (IQ)? Why or why not?

3. Kia's relationship with Quentin is the most important one in her life. What is she doing to contribute to the problems in the relationship? Will the relationship survive? If so, what would it take?

4. Describe Kia's conflict management style compared to Quentin's. What clues does the case study provide you?

5. Identify three things Kia should do to get her college success and her life on track.

Before beginning to read this chapter, take two minutes to answer the following questions on a scale of 1 to 10. Your answers will help you assess how ready you are to focus.

1 = not very/not much/very little/low   10 = very/a lot/very much/high

Based on reading the "You're about to discover..." list and skimming this chapter, how much do you think you probably already know about the subject matter?

1   2   3   4   5   6   7   8   9   10

How much do you think this information might affect your college success?

1   2   3   4   5   6   7   8   9   10

How much do you think this information might affect your career success after college?

1   2   3   4   5   6   7   8   9   10

In general, how motivated are you to learn the material in this chapter?

1   2   3   4   5   6   7   8   9   10

This book describes four key factors related to intrinsic, or internal, motivation: curiosity, control, career outlook, and challenge. The next four questions relate to these **C-Factors:**

How *curious* are you about the content you expect to read in this chapter?

1   2   3   4   5   6   7   8   9   10

How much *control* do you expect to have over mastering the material in this chapter?

1   2   3   4   5   6   7   8   9   10

How much do you think this chapter might help you develop your *career outlook*?

1   2   3   4   5   6   7   8   9   10

How *challenging* do you think the material in this chapter will be for you?

1   2   3   4   5   6   7   8   9   10

Before beginning any task, including studying, it's important to check in with yourself to ensure that you're physically, intellectually, and emotionally ready to focus. How ready are you, physically, to focus on this chapter? (Are you rested, feeling well, and so on?)

1   2   3   4   5   6   7   8   9   10

How ready are you, intellectually, to focus on this chapter? (Are you thinking clearly, focused on this course, interested in this subject?)

1   2   3   4   5   6   7   8   9   10

How ready are you, emotionally, to focus on this chapter? (Are you calm, confident, composed?)

1   2   3   4   5   6   7   8   9   10

If your answer to any of the last three questions is below a 5 on the scale, you may need to address the issue you're facing prior to beginning this chapter. For example, if you're hungry, get a quick bite to eat. If you're feeling scattered, take a few moments to settle down and focus.

Finally, how long do you think it will take you to complete this chapter? _____ Hour(s) _____ Minutes

---

Teachable Moment Take this opportunity to ask students to think about how they have responded to "Readiness Check" activities in other chapters. Have they become a mental habit, even in their other classes (which of course is one of the goals of this built-in feature)?

The Heart of College Success

CHALLENGE ⊖ REACTION

Challenge: How would you respond in the following situations?

Reaction: Read these five scenarios and identify your most likely reactions.[1]

1. You peer over a classmate's shoulder and notice she has copied your online response from a class chat and submitted it as her paper in the course, hoping the professor won't notice. What do you do?

   a. Tell the student off to set the record straight, right then and there.

   b. Tell the professor that someone has cheated.

   c. Ask the student where the research for the paper came from.

   d. Forget it. It's not worth the trouble. Cheaters lose in the end.

2. You're riding on a plane that hits a patch of extreme turbulence. What do you do?

   a. Grab hold of the person in the next seat and hold on for dear life.

   b. Close your eyes and wait it out.

Activity Option This is a great opportunity to use the "Visible Quiz" activity by Staley (2003). Make a set of four cards using a different color cardstock for each letter (a, b, c, d) for each student. Ask students to give their answers to the "Challenge → Reaction" questions by holding up their chosen card for each question. This activity provides you with immediate information on individual student's opinions and generates class discussion.

c. Read something or watch the movie to calm yourself until things improve.

d. Panic and lose your composure.

3. You receive a paper back in your toughest course and decide that your grade is unacceptable. What do you do?

a. Challenge the professor immediately after class to argue for a better grade.

b. Question whether or not you're really college material.

c. Reread the paper to honestly assess its quality and make a plan for improvement.

d. Deemphasize this course and focus on others in which you are more successful.

4. While kidding around with your friends, you hear one of them tell an offensive, blatantly racial joke. What do you do?

a. Decide to ignore the problem and thereby avoid being perceived as overly touchy.

b. Report the behavior to your residence hall advisor or an instructor.

c. Stop the group's conversation. Make the point that racial jokes can hurt and that it's important to be sensitive to others' reactions.

d. Tell your joke-telling friend later that racial jokes offend you.

5. You and your romantic partner are in the middle of a heated argument, and tempers are flaring. What do you do?

a. Stop, think about what you're trying to communicate, and say it as clearly and neutrally as possible.

b. Keep at it because if the issue generated that much emotion, it must be important to get to the bottom of it.

c. Take a twenty-minute time out and then continue your discussion.

d. Suggest that both of you apologize immediately and move on.

Every day, in many ways, you make choices about how you react to situations and other people. College is no exception. As a new college student, you're on your own, continually adapting to new situations, adjusting your past relationships with friends and family, and forming new ones rapidly.[2]

College is a time of transition; it can be an emotionally turbulent time. Even if you're a returning student who's been on your own for years, college will require you to make some major adjustments in your life. Trying to do so without the internal resources you need may be overwhelming, as it was for Kia Washington in the "FOCUS Challenge Case." When it looked as if the relationship that was most important to her was falling apart, so did she.

Here's a fundamental truth: College isn't just about your head. Yes, academics are the reason you're in college, but your heart plays a critical role in your success, too. From friends to romantic partners, how you handle relationships can make or break you academically. Emotional reactions to troubling circumstances have the raw potential to stop you dead in your tracks. As may be the case for Kia Washington, who most likely has the *academic* skills required for success, *nonacademic* issues can interfere. Of course, not everyone faces the string of misfortunes that she did, but how you manage your emotions and respond to stressful situations will impact your college success.

In college and in life, your EQ (emotional quotient), or *emotional intelligence*, can be just as important as your IQ (intelligence quotient). Studies show that first-year students often feel overwhelmed, lonely, homesick, or friendsick. Friendsickness can interfere with your adjustment to college.[3] In one study,

> **"Our emotions are the driving powers of our lives."**
>
> **Earl Riney, American clergyman (1885–1955)**

freshmen who felt the loneliest and most socially isolated had weaker immune systems than their counterparts who didn't report these feelings.[4] According to a former university administrator at a large, prestigious school, "More students leave college because of disillusionment, discouragement, or reduced motivation than because of lack of ability."[5] *That's* how important emotional intelligence is to college success! Begin now to refine the emotional skills you'll need to face whatever challenges come your way.

Perhaps you've found yourself in settings such as those described in the "Challenge → Reaction" situations you just read. You might need more actual details to make the best choice in these five scenarios, but according to some experts, choice (c) is the most emotionally intelligent one in each case. Do you agree? How do *you* make decisions such as these? What constitutes an emotionally intelligent response?

What Is Emotional Intelligence?

Many experts believe that intelligence is multifaceted. Rather than a narrow definition of intelligence, they believe in Multiple Intelligences: Linguistic, Logical-Mathematical, Spatial, Kinesthetic, Musical, Interpersonal, Intrapersonal, and Naturalistic.[6] Emotional intelligence may well be a combination, at least in part, of *intrapersonal* and *interpersonal* intelligences.

Emotional intelligence is a set of skills that determines how well you cope with the demands and pressures you face every day. How well do you understand yourself, empathize with others, draw on your inner resources, and encourage the same qualities in people you care about? Emotional intelligence involves having people skills, a positive outlook, and the capacity to adapt to change. You can see how Kia Washington's lack of emotional intelligence has the potential to derail her.

© William Whitehurst/CORBIS

"Managing your emotions is an inside job."

Doc Childre and Howard Martin, performance experts

Emotional intelligence can propel you through difficult situations. Take the case of the window washer during the September 11, 2001, World Trade Center terrorist attack. Six men—five of whom were executives—were trapped in an elevator after the first tower was hit. The sixth man, Jan Demezur, was a window washer who showed the others that the end of his squeegee could be used to pry open the elevator door. When the group finally forced the door open only to find the number 50 painted on the wall of the elevator shaft, they realized that their express elevator didn't stop at floor 50. There was no way out. Demezur began using the sharp edge of his squeegee to poke a hole in the wall. The six men took turns, scratching through three layers of drywall to safety. Under extreme pressure and the threat of imminent death, the window washer demonstrated ingenuity, confidence, optimism, teamwork, leadership, and emotional intelligence.[7]

In that elevator, the most effective individual wasn't the one who earned the most money, dressed the best, or had the highest status. It was the person who could rally others to extraordinary effort—the person who could connect with other people.

Research describes the powerful effects of emotional intelligence. For example, in a forty-year study of 450 boys who grew up in Somerville, Massachusetts, two-thirds came from poor families and one-third had below average IQs. Later in life, however, intelligence as traditionally defined had little to do with their success. What was more important was how well they handled frustration, controlled their emotions, and got along with others.[8] In another study looking back over the careers of scientists now in their seventies, social and emotional abilities were four times as important as IQ in determining professional success.[9] Of course, there's no doubt that IQ is important. You must be smart to become a scientist, or any type of professional, for that matter. But assuming you're qualified and prepared, how your career unfolds and how successful you actually are may have more to do with your EQ than it does your IQ.[10]

Research demonstrates that your emotions and your thought processes are closely connected.[11] There's also evidence that being in a happy mood can help you generate more creative solutions to problems.[12] The bottom line? New research links emotional intelligence to college success, and learning about the impact of EI in the first year of college helps students stay in school.[13]

As you read about the five scales of emotional intelligence (see Figure 11.1), begin assessing your own competence in these areas. We'll discuss how to gain a better understanding of your actual capabilities later in this chapter. As each scale is introduced, ask yourself whether you agree or disagree with the sample statement presented as it pertains to you.[14]

Intrapersonal Skills (Self-Awareness)

"It's hard for me to understand the way I feel." Agree or disagree?

To what extent are you in tune with your emotions? Do you fully realize when you're anxious, depressed, or elated? Or do you just generally feel up or down?

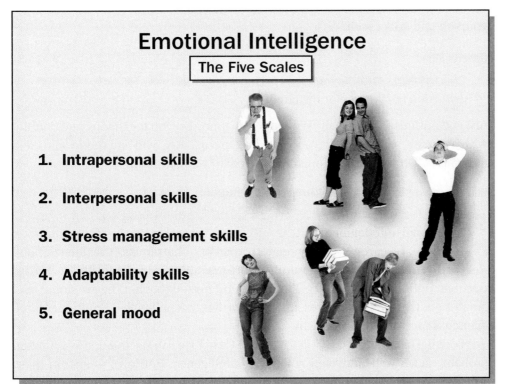

Emotional Intelligence

The Five Scales

1. **Intrapersonal skills**

2. **Interpersonal skills**

3. **Stress management skills**

4. **Adaptability skills**

5. **General mood**

Source: Bar-On (2005)

Teachable Moment Ask students to describe the characteristics of the best leaders they've known. Help them make connections between these characteristics and general scales of emotional intelligence, intrapersonal and interpersonal skills, stress management, adaptability, and general mood.

Emotional Intelligence (EI) Research Experts in emotional intelligence suggest that IQ may get you a job, but it's EQ that gets you promoted!

Chapter Crossover Students should be able to describe their VARK learning style and their personality type. Remind them to look back at Chapter 2 for this information. Also, remind students that knowing how they feel is not the same as knowing their learning and personality types.

Figure 11.1

The Five Scales of Emotional Intelligence

Are you aware of layers of emotions? Sometimes we show *anger*, for instance, when what we really feel is *fear*. (For example, Kia was in the habit of screaming angrily at her boyfriend, Quentin, when she actually desperately feared losing him.) Are you emotionally self-reliant, rather than emotionally dependent on others? Do you realize that no one else can truly make you happy, that you are responsible for creating your own emotional states? Do you set goals that relate to things *you* value and work toward achieving them? How well do you understand yourself and what makes you tick?

Interpersonal Skills (Relating to Others)

> *"I'm sensitive to the feelings of others."* Agree or disagree?

Are you aware of others' emotions and needs? Do you communicate with sensitivity and work to build positive relationships? Are you a good listener? Are you comfortable with others, and do you have confidence in your relationships with them?

Stress Management Skills

> *"I feel that it's hard for me to control my anxiety."* Agree or disagree?

Can you productively manage your emotions so that they work *for* you and not *against* you? Can you control destructive emotions? Can you work well under pressure? Are you in control, even when things get tense and difficult?

Adaptability Skills

> *"When trying to solve a problem, I look at each possibility and then decide on the best way."* Agree or disagree?

Are you flexible? Do you cope well when things *don't* go according to plan? Can you switch to a new plan when you need to? Do you manage change effectively? Can you anticipate problems and solve them as they come up? Do you rely on yourself and adapt well?

General Mood

> *"I generally expect things will turn out all right, despite setbacks from time to time."* Agree or disagree?

Are you optimistic and positive most of the time? Do you feel happy and content with yourself, others, and your life in general? Are you energetic and self-motivated? Do people tell you you're pleasant to be around?

From EQ-e: Post Secondary version. Reprinted by permission.

Emotional intelligence and its effects reverberate throughout our lives. For example, researchers study related concepts: "hardiness," "resilience," and "learned optimism."[15] Some people are more resistant to stress and illness. Hardy, resilient, optimistic people are confident, committed to what they're doing, feel greater control over their lives, and see hurdles as challenges. Emotional intelligence is part of the reason why.

Looking back at the "FOCUS Challenge Case," we can see that Kia Washington probably lacks well-cultivated emotional intelligence. Her level of skill in these five areas may help explain her difficulty controlling her moods, communicating with Quentin, managing stress, adjusting to college, and being positive and optimistic about working through her problems. Will she be academically successful? What do you think?

Emotional intelligence and its five scales are important in all aspects of life, including your future career.[16] When *Harvard Business Review* first published an article on the topic in 1998, it attracted more readers than any article in the journal's previous forty years. When the CEO of Johnson & Johnson read it, he ordered copies for the company's 400 top executives worldwide.[17]

Why? Emotional intelligence is a characteristic of true leaders. Immediately after the first shock of the September 11, 2001, tragedy, the world tuned in to a press conference with New York's Mayor Rudy Giuliani. He was asked to estimate the number of people who had lost their lives in the World Trade Center collapse that day, and his reply was this: "We don't know the exact number yet, but whatever the number, it will be more than we can bear." In that one sentence, Giuliani demonstrated one of the most important principles of true leadership. Leaders inspire by touching the feelings of others.[18]

Emotional Intelligence (EI) Research According to Goleman (1998), "IQ and technical skills are important, but emotional intelligence is the sine qua non of leadership. When I compared star performers with average ones in senior leadership positions, nearly 90% of the difference in their profiles was attributable to emotional intelligence factors rather than cognitive abilities."

Can Emotional Intelligence Be Improved?

Everyone wants well-developed emotional intelligence, but how do you get it? Can EI be learned? While researchers admit that genes definitely play a role, most experts believe that emotional intelligence can be increased. One of the most convincing pieces of evidence is from a study that followed a cohort of students over seven years. Students assessed their emotional intelligence, selected particular competencies to strengthen, and then each created an individual plan to develop them. Seven years later, their competencies remained high.[19]

Recent physiological research, indicating that the human brain's hippocampus is more "plastic" than originally thought, also endorses the notion that EI can be improved. New "mindfulness" training to help people regulate their own emotions actually alters parts of the brain. A group of scientists who received mindfulness training an hour a week for eight weeks had measurable changes in their brains and reported more positive emotions than their non-trained counterparts at the end of the eight weeks, and again four months later.[20] Researchers continue to study emotional intelligence to fully grasp its implications in many different areas of life, but its central role in college success is increasingly understood.

If you believe what this chapter says about the importance of emotional intelligence and college success, you're probably asking yourself what you can do about it. Are the skills related to emotional intelligence something *you* can work to improve?[21] And if so, how?

Seek honest input from others. It's hard to be objective about yourself. But it is possible to tap some of that

> **"What's going on in the inside shows on the outside."**
>
> **Earl Nightingale, success consultant**

© Robert Recker/zefa/CORBIS

Sensitive Situation Accepting honest feedback without becoming defensive isn't easy. However, emphasize that emotional intelligence can be developed with feedback and support.

necessary objectivity from those who interact with you regularly. How do they see you? Use other people as coaches to help you see which aspects of your emotional intelligence need strengthening.

Find an EI mentor. A mentor on the job is someone who's older and more experienced than you are and can help you navigate your way through tough problems and manage your career. Mentors help, and an EI mentor—someone with finely honed EI skills you admire—can provide you with invaluable advice about handling challenging emotional situations. Develop a personal relationship with someone whose wisdom you admire, be honest about your problems, and follow the guidance you get.

Complete an assessment tool. Other than just feeling up or down, or reflecting on how you handled problems when they came up, is there a way to know more about your own level of emotional intelligence? The oldest and most widely used instrument to measure emotional intelligence is the Emotional Quotient Inventory, the EQ-i, from which the sample statements for the five scales we have been discussing come. It was the first instrument of its kind to be published and the first to be validated by psychologists in the well-respected *Mental Measurement Yearbook* (1999).[22] The instrument asks you to respond to various statements by indicating that they are "very seldom true of me" to "very often true of me," and the results provide you with a self-assessment of your emotional intelligence on each of the five major scales and further subscales.

Teachable Moment If possible, have students take the EQ-i in class and refer back to it throughout the term. Students can look at their results and set goals to work on. It takes a minimum of about fifteen weeks (a semester) to see real changes in EQ-i.

As a part of the course for which you're using this textbook, you may have an opportunity to complete the EQ-i or an equivalent instrument. Check your campus's Counseling Center, too, to see if it offers EI assessment tools for students. You can also locate plenty of informal instruments online. They may not be valid, however, so be cautious about fully trusting their results.

Work with a counselor to learn more. Some areas of emotional intelligence may be too challenging to develop on your own. You may need some in-depth, one-on-one counseling to work on areas that need enrichment. Recognize that doing so isn't a stigma. Instead, you are taking advantage of the resources available on your campus and maximizing the potential for growth that can come during your college years.

Be patient with yourself. Learning to become more empathetic or more attuned to your partner's emotions in a close relationship aren't skills you can enhance overnight using cookbook techniques. Building emotional skills is a gradual process that involves awakening insights, acting on them, and noting the results over time.

Keep at it: Developing your emotional intelligence should be a long-term goal. It's safe to say that EI is something all of us can strengthen, if we're willing to work at it. Relationships that are important to us require the best of our emotional intelligence skills. In fact, studies show that the way in which we provide emotional support is strongly related to relationship satisfaction.[23]

Activity Option Each of the five scales of EI has subscales. Students can find these online [http://www.eiconsortium.org/measures/eqi.ht]. For example, stress management is comprised of two subscales: stress tolerance and impulse control. As a class, identify the two most challenging scales for students and identify the subscales that make up these scales. How do these connect with success in college?

INSIGHT ⊖ ACTION

1. Of the five EI scales, which do you experience as most challenging?

2. Have you attempted to improve your EI on one or more of the scales in the past? If so, what did you do and what were the results?

3. After reading this section of the chapter, what actions will you take to learn more about your EI and possibly work to improve it?

What Is This Thing Called Love?

Ah, romance.... Relationships—they're what make the world go 'round. Although 80 percent isn't a hard and fast number, Brian Tracy has a point. Relationships count, and for many of us, romantic ones count as much or more than others.

Some experts say people are attracted to people with similar characteristics: "Birds of a feather flock together." An alternative theory is that "opposites attract." Which characteristics do you find attractive? Most of us have strong ideas about what we want in someone else: good looks, intelligence, or honesty, for example. But here's a puzzler: what do *you* have to offer? If your parents, a friend, or a previous partner were to write up a classified ad for the personals or put your profile on a matchmaking website, what would they say about you? What qualities do you bring to a relationship—loyalty, humor, caring?

In *Why We Love* (2004), anthropologist Helen Fisher defines love in ways you may not have thought about before: the psychological and physiological characteristics of love. Fisher asked her 437 American subjects to agree or disagree with statements about their romantic partners such as "I have more energy when I am with _____." "My heart races when I hear _____'s voice." "When I'm in class/at work my mind wanders to _____." Interestingly, Fisher found that neither age, gender, sexual orientation, religion, nor ethnic group made a difference. Love is love, she found. Participants in the study shared characteristics such as these five.[24]

1. *Extreme energy.* When you're in love, your heart pounds, you are breathless, you feel as if you could "leap over tall buildings with a single bound." Your brain is "hopped up" on chemicals, and you have energy to spare.

2. *Imagined betterment.* Although most people in love can easily point out faults in their romantic partners, they tend to persuade themselves that these characteristics are unimportant, unique, or perhaps even charming.

3. *Interfering thoughts.* People in love spend inordinate amounts of time thinking about their partners. No matter how hard they try to think about other things, their thoughts return to him or her. In some studies, participants report that they spend more than 85 percent of their waking hours thinking about their romantic partners.[25]

4. *Mood swings.* Lovers soar with ecstasy and sink to the depths of despair, based on their romantic partners' responses. "She loves me; she loves me not" is a realistic obsession.

5. *Hypersensitivity.* People in love continuously watch and wait for clues about how their romantic partners feel about them. They hover by the phone or computer, and search endlessly for a meaningful sign, reinterpret a facial expression, or translate a word or phrase into relational terms. Often lovers can't eat or sleep because they are so hyperactive in their diligence.

"Eighty percent of life's satisfaction comes from meaningful relationships."

Brian Tracy, personal and career success author

Teachable Moment Individuals who can listen to themselves and understand how they are feeling are strong in intrapersonal emotional intelligence. Developing the habit of getting to the "why" of how one is feeling will enhance intrapersonal skills.

Activity Option In groups, ask students to develop the top five characteristics of an ideal partner and rank them in order of importance. Ask students to develop this same list for what they might be looking for when they're in their seventies. Are the two lists the same? Do rankings change? Is what they chose as top characteristics in their college years the same as what they predict they would choose later in life? Discuss this as a class.

BUILD RELATIONSHIPS, ONE DROP AT A TIME

After the Korean War, the U.S. Army's chief psychiatrist studied the psychological warfare used against 1,000 American prisoners of war who had been kept at a North Korean camp. He made a startling discovery: negativity kills.[26]

The prisoners had not been treated cruelly. They were given food, water, and shelter. They hadn't been tortured, yet many American soldiers died in the camp. They weren't surrounded by barbed wire and armed guards, yet no one ever tried to escape. Instead, many of them turned against each other, formed relationships with their North Korean guards, and when they were finally freed, many didn't even bother to call home when given the opportunity to let their loved ones know they were alive.

Many of these men died of extreme hopelessness caused by a total removal of emotional support. Soldiers were rewarded for informing on one another and required to stand up in groups of their peers and tell all the bad things they had ever done, as well as the good things they should have done. All positive letters from home were withheld, but negative ones telling of relatives passing away or wives divorcing their husbands were delivered right away. Even notices of overdue bills from collection agencies were passed along. Eventually, many of these American prisoners simply gave up. They died of "give up-itis," as they called it, raising the overall death rate in the camp to 38 percent—the highest American POW death rate in U.S. history.

The record of what happened raised this fundamental question, described in the *New York Times* and *Wall Street Journal* bestseller *How Full Is Your Bucket?* If negativity can have such a devastating impact, what can positivity do? That's where the analogy of buckets and dippers begins. Most of us will never endure the kind of psychological warfare these soldiers did, but all of us can examine the negativity we inflict on others, and by contrast, the positivity we can bring to others' lives.

How Full Is Your Bucket? by Tom Rath and Donald Clifton claims that each of us has an invisible bucket; we function at our best when our buckets are full. We each also have an invisible dipper. In every interaction, we use our dipper to fill others' buckets *or* to dip from them. The principle of the book is simple; following its advice, however, is challenging.

How Full Is Your Bucket? makes these five recommendations:

1. **Dip less.** Get in the habit of listening to yourself. Are your words cynical, insensitive, or critical? If so, push the pause button and rephrase what you're trying to communicate. Keep track by scoring your interactions as positive or negative, and set a goal of five positive exchanges for every negative one.

2. **Bring out the best.** By filling others' buckets, we set off a chain reaction that comes back to us. Imagine a scenario in which something really annoys you about your romantic partner, and you find yourself being critical much more often than you should be. If you make a conscious decision to focus instead on all the good things instead of the one bad thing, you'll have a positive impact on the relationship, and your partner will begin responding more positively to you. Watch and see!

3. **Make more than one best friend.** Who ever said people are only allowed one best friend? High-quality relationships improve the quality of your life. Bucket filling from the start is the way to begin a new best friendship, and regular bucket filling is how to keep it.

4. **Fill a drop at a time.** Giving a small unexpected gift is a great way to fill someone else's bucket. It needn't be much: a token, a trinket, a compliment, or a thank you. Put your positive comments in an e-mail or a note to make them last. Make a habit of giving "drops."

5. **Apply the Golden Rule backwards.** Rather than "Do unto others as you would have them do unto you," try this: "Do unto others as *they would have you do unto them.*"

How full is your bucket? In your interactions, are you filling or dipping? Building a relationship is a process that occurs one drop at a time.

We may assume that characteristics such as age or gender or sexual orientation differentiate the way people view their romantic partners. Not so; love is love, Fisher claims. But not quite.

Physiologically, love differs by type and stage. When you're newly infatuated with someone, your brain has elevated levels of dopamine and norepinephrine, chemicals that result in focused attention, exhilaration, hyperactivity, and goal-directed behaviors. Scientists also hypothesize that lovers have lower levels of serotonin in their brains. These three chemicals—higher levels of dopamine and norepinephrine and lower levels of serotonin—appear to be the physiological basis for passionate, exhilarating, romantic love.

However, later in life, after years of marriage, perhaps, these chemicals are overtaken by others. None of us could tolerate a continuous rush of stimulating chemicals and their intense effects forever! Unbridled passion and wild ecstasy are replaced by feelings of contentment and security. However, many couples remain "in love" for twenty, thirty, fifty, or more years. They may even describe themselves as more in love than when they first met. In one remarkable study, couples married more than twenty years rated themselves higher on romantic love than couples married only five years. Researchers noted that their results looked like those of high school seniors![27]

The chemistry of love points to a truth worth noting: Love is not just an emotion. Chemicals wax and wane; emotions come and go. Commitment goes beyond attraction, beyond emotion. It's a *decision* to invest—and continually *reinvest*—in a relationship. As Fisher writes, "Don't assume the relationship will last forever; build it one day at a time. And never give up."

Teachable Moment Ask students what is meant by "it's a decision to invest and continually reinvest in a relationship." Ask students to give examples.

Communicating in Intimate Relationships

CHALLENGE ⊖ REACTION

Challenge: Are you are involved in an intimate relationship right now? If so, which of these ten statements describe it? Put a checkmark in the "yes" or "no" column for each one.

Reaction: Put a checkmark in the "yes" or "no" column for each one.

	Yes	No
1. My partner is a very good listener.	____	____
2. My partner does not understand how I feel.	____	____
3. We have a good balance of leisure time spent together and separately.	____	____
4. We find it easy to think of things to do together.	____	____
5. I am very satisfied with how we talk to each other.	____	____
6. We are creative in how we handle our differences.	____	____
7. Making financial decisions is not difficult.	____	____
8. Our sexual relationship is satisfying and fulfilling.	____	____
9. We are both equally willing to make adjustments in the relationship.	____	____
10. I can share feelings and ideas with my partner during disagreements.	____	____

Now continue your reading to find out how other couples responded in a national study.

Sensitive Situation It's very possible that you have a few students in your class who have just broken up with a romantic partner. It could have been their choice or their partner's. Be sensitive to the fact that the wounds can be raw and deep, and conversations about love can be very emotionally upsetting to these students.

If you're in a romantic relationship right now, you may have wondered from time to time if it's truly a good one. In one study, 94 percent of college students reported having been in love, and over one-third reported three or more past love relationships.[28] Perhaps it was love at first sight, and you immediately announced to your friends or family that this was the one for you. Instead, perhaps right now you're with someone you've never really gotten to know very well; you're going through the motions. The relationship is convenient, fun for

Piglet sidled up to Pooh from behind. "Pooh!" he whispered." "Yes, Piglet?" "Nothing," said Piglet, taking Pooh's paw. "I just wanted to be sure of you."

A. A. Milne, British author (1882–1956)

the time being, but emotional intimacy isn't at the heart of it. If you're not in a romantic relationship at all right now, perhaps you're on the lookout for someone with potential.

It's not easy to know exactly what characterizes a healthy relationship. If you look around at others' relationships, you only see what those two people choose to display. It's easy to think: "I wish my relationship were as—fill in the blank—healthy, caring, or supportive" or "If only my romantic partner treated me as well as so-and-so's." But you have no way of knowing what goes on behind the scenes. Which issues have already been negotiated, and which remain to be tackled? Those things aren't obvious, unless someone deliberately chooses to disclose them to you. You can't always tell by watching. The problems between Kia and Quentin in the "FOCUS Challenge Case" were revealed to you as a reader, but they might not have been detectable to people around them.

What does it take? A study of 21,501 couples across the country compared the answers of the happiest couples to those of the unhappiest.[29] The areas of maximum difference between the two groups were found on responses like the following.

	Happy Couples	Unhappy Couples
1. My partner is a very good listener.	83%	18%
2. My partner does not understand how I feel.	13%	79%
3. We have a good balance of leisure time spent together and separately.	71%	17%
4. We find it easy to think of things to do together.	86%	28%
5. I am very satisfied with how we talk to each other.	90%	15%
6. We are creative in how we handle our differences.	78%	15%
7. Making financial decisions is not difficult.	80%	32%
8. Our sexual relationship is satisfying and fulfilling.	85%	29%
9. We are both equally willing to make adjustments in the relationship.	87%	46%
10. I can share feelings and ideas with my partner during disagreements.	85%	22%

[Note: numbers do not total 100 percent because of the study's design.]

Emotional Intelligence (EI) Research According to Daniel Goleman, "a new look at the causes of depression in the young pinpoints deficits in two areas of emotional competence: relationships skills, on the one hand, and a depression-promoting way of interpreting setbacks on the other."

Look at the highest percentages in the "Happy Couples" column. These results point to an all-important truth: Communication is at the heart of every quality relationship.

In relationships we sometimes communicate in ways that aren't productive. The work of communication specialist Deborah Tannen focuses on miscommunication between men and women. Remember the *Seinfeld* episode in which George's date asks him if he'd like to come up to her apartment for coffee when he takes her home? George completely misses the point and replies that he never drinks coffee late at night. She meant, "Would you like to continue our date?" but he took the question at face value. Later he kicked himself for being so slow-witted. Trying to "listen between the lines" in romantic relationships is a challenge. We say one thing and mean another, or we hope a partner can read our minds and then resent it when they do.

The classic work of psychiatrist Dr. George Bach and others can help relational partners communicate more openly and honestly and meet conflict head on. He described types of "crazymaking" that cause communication breakdowns and, at their worst, relationship failures. See if you recognize people you know—romantic partners or even friends—in these six types of crazymakers.[30]

> The TRAPPER: *Trappers* play an especially dirty trick by requesting a desired behavior from the other person and then attacking when the request is met.

> The BLAMER: *Blamers* are more interested in whose fault the problem is than they are in solving it.

> The MINDREADER: *Mindreaders* try to solve the problem by telling their partners what they're *really* thinking.

> The GUNNYSACKER: *Gunnysackers* save grudges. They fill up proverbial gunnysacks, and then dump all the contents on their partners at some "opportune" moment.

> The HIT AND RUN FIGHTER: *Hit and run fighters* attack and then leave the scene quickly without giving their partners a chance to explain or defend themselves.

> The "BENEDICT ARNOLD": *Benedict Arnolds* like to stir up trouble behind the scenes by playing "let's you and someone else fight."

Activity Option Divide the class into six groups and give each group a card with one of the examples: trapper, blamer, mindreader, gunnysacker, hit and run fighter, or Benedict Arnold. Groups should not show each other their card. Have two to three students from each group volunteer to role-play their example, while the other groups guess which "crazymaking" behavior they are portraying.

If you think you're a victim of crazymaking communication, what should you do about it? Try these five suggestions:

1. **Step back and try to figure out the situation.** Is the crazymaker making a request of you (to be more open, reliable, or responsible, for example)? If so, is the request reasonable, and are you willing?

2. **Become aware of the feelings behind the crazymaking.** Is your partner feeling powerless or vulnerable, for example?

3. **Try not to respond with anger, even though it's difficult.** Piling more wood on the fire certainly won't help to put it out.

4. **Check out your assumptions with the other person.** Ask, "Are you feeling frustrated? Is that what this is about? What would you like me to do?"

5. **Try and reach a mutually agreeable solution by changing communication patterns that aren't productive.**

Once you've identified any unproductive communication habits, you can work on improving your skills as well as your relationships. The following five suggestions are a place to start. Several of these recommendations work for any type of close relationship—friends or romantic partners.

Choose wisely. When it comes to selecting someone you may want to build a future with, don't settle. Seek someone who shares your values, whose background is compatible, but who is different enough to make life interesting. Choose someone who values productive communication as much as you do.

Let go of unrealistic expectations. Remember that although people live happily ever after in movies, in truth, all relationships have ups and downs. We're human; we make mistakes as communicators. Metaphorically speaking, one blip on the screen doesn't necessarily indicate that the whole program should be scrapped. Conversely, working on problems together strengthens your relationship.

Engage in preventative maintenance. You take your car in for a checkup every so many thousand miles to prevent major breakdowns; it's a good idea to do the same with relationships you care about. Keep the channels of communication open, and talk about small issues before they escalate into colossal ones. Make deposits into a positive "memory bank." Experts say that doing interesting new things together— going on a vacation, for example—can trigger renewed romantic love.[31]

Monitor your own communication. You can't change your partner, but you can change your own communication: "Although it takes two to have a relationship; it takes only one to change its quality."[32] Eliminate an annoying behavior or modify your conflict style. Be more tolerant of your partner's communication faults, too. Communicate your needs; relationships aren't guessing games. Check, don't assume. Remember that listening is one of the highest compliments you can pay someone. (You're important to me!) Instead of attacking, own your emotions by using the X-Y-Z formula: When you do X in situation Y, I feel Z. ("When you tease me [X] in front of other people [Y], I feel embarrassed and never know how to react [Z]" as opposed to "You always embarrass me! Stop it, will you?")[33] Working to increase your emotional intelligence doesn't mean denying all negative feelings; that would mean cutting off part of your psyche! How you choose to communicate those negative feelings is where the monitoring comes in.

Take the high road. Don't give in to momentary temptations that may lead to regret and possibly the end of a relationship with great potential. Without trust as the bedrock of your communication, little else matters. If you've promised yourself to someone, keep your promise.[34]

Teachable Moment Remind students that the only real thing they can change is how they respond. You can't always prevent things from happening (for example, natural disasters), but we can decide how we react to situations. How we respond to others influences how others respond to us.

EXERCISE 11.1 What's Your Conflict Style?

For each of the following statements, please rate your response on a scale of 1 to 5, with 1 representing "strongly agree" and 5 representing "strongly disagree."

1. _____ I usually end up compromising in conflict situations. (CO)

2. _____ Someone always loses in a conflict. (CP)

3. _____ I usually let other people "win" in conflicts because I often feel less strongly about the outcome than they do. (AC)

4. _____ When I really care about a relationship, I devote unusual amounts of time and energy into coming up with creative solutions so that each of us can get what we want. (CL)

5. _____ "Don't rock the boat" is a good philosophy. (AV)

6. _____ "Winning" in conflict situations gives me a real "high." (CP)

7. _____ Sacrificing what I want so that someone else can achieve a goal is often worth it. (AC)

8. _____ It's possible for both parties to "win" in conflict situations. (CL)

9. _____ Sometimes you have to settle for "part of the pie." (CO)

10. _____ I try to avoid conflict at all costs. It's not worth it. (AV)

From EQ-e: S Post Secondary version. Reprinted by permission.

Now find a partner in class and compare your responses. Circle the items on which the two of you differed most, for example, where one of you marked a "1" and the other a "5." See if you can explain your own choice and also come to understand your partner's thinking. On how many items did you differ? If the answer is "several" or "many," you might experience substantial conflict as roommates or romantic partners.

People often come at conflicts using differing styles. Not only do you disagree on the topic at hand—whatever it is—but you approach conflict itself differently. This quick quiz is based on a well-known, five-part model of conflict styles (see Figure 11.2). In our version of the model, the horizontal axis is labeled "Concern for Other" (or cooperativeness) and the vertical axis is labeled "Concern for Self" (or assertiveness).[35] See if you can identify the five styles as they're used by Kia, Quentin, yourself, and people you know.

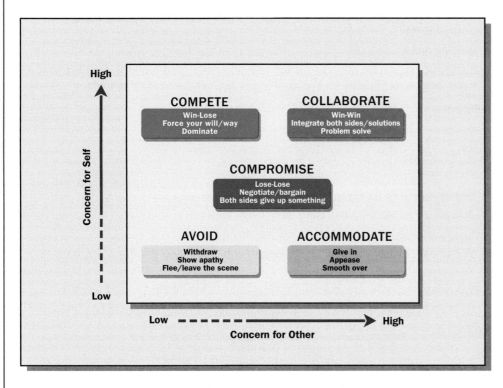

Figure 11.2

Conflict Management Styles

Where are your highest scores? Notice the letters at the end of the ten statements.

If you like to win and care most about your own goals, you **compete** (CP).

If you care more about the other person's goals, and give in, you **accommodate** (AC).

If you don't care about your goals or your partner's, you **avoid** (AV).

If you care somewhat about both and are willing to settle for "part of the pie," you **compromise** (CO). Strictly speaking, when you compromise, neither of you gets exactly what you want.

If you care about your own goals and your partner's, and you're willing to devote the time and energy required to reach a win-win solution, you **collaborate** (CL).

What's your style? Do you have a conflict style you're most comfortable with? Do you fall into the habit of using one style, even if it's not productive in particular situations? Flexibility is the key to managing conflicts productively, and if the relationship really counts, collaboration is the ideal.

Your Type is Showing

Which of the four type scales is best represented in each of the following sample dialogues between sets of romantic partners? Extravert or Introvert (E vs. I)? Sensing or iNtuition (S vs. N)? Thinking or Feeling (T vs. F)? Judging or Perceiving (J vs. P)? Conflict can emerge between partners when they differ on a scale or when they both display the same preference. For each scene, identify the psychological type you believe is being demonstrated by the two players and a rationale for the choice you've identified. Your instructor may ask for volunteers to play these roles in class, so that you can discuss them. Also, try reversing the roles, and see if the perceptions are different based on male-female stereotypes that exist in our society.

SCENE 1

She: Hey, I've been wondering about something.

He: Yes, what's that?

She: How come you don't like to go to parties with me?

He: What do you mean?

She: I mean, you always want to stay home and watch a movie or do something alone—just the two of us.

He: I hate parties; you know that. I'd rather just be with you. Why would I want to spend an evening with a bunch of people I don't even know?

She: Because it's fun! I love being around people!

He: Well, I don't. It's a drag. Besides all you do at parties is flirt with other men, and frankly I don't like that. If you like parties so much, maybe you'd better find yourself a new boyfriend who likes them, too!

She _____ vs. He _____ Rationale: _____

SCENE 2

He: Hey, I have a great plan for Saturday.

She: Yes, what's that?

He: We'll sleep in until 9, and then drive to the city to that new mall. Later we can have dinner at that restaurant I told you about, and get back home around 10 or so.

She: Why don't we just wait until Saturday and see what we feel like doing?

He: Because we have to plan ahead. I know you. You'll just sleep in until noon, and the day will already be half gone.

She: I don't like schedules; you know that. Why are you always trying to force me into following a "plan"?

He: Because somebody has to be in charge. And if it's not going to be you, it's going to have to be me!

She _____ vs. He _____ Rationale: _____

SCENE 3

She: Hey, I've come up with a great plan for Saturday.

He: Yes, so have I. What's yours?

She: We'll sleep in until 9, and then drive over to that new mall. Later we can have dinner at that restaurant I told you about, and get back home around 10 or so.

He: No, I was thinking about going out for a late breakfast, and then going to the matinee of that new movie we saw advertised. After that, we could stop and see my Mom. She owes me a check.

She: I don't really want to spend the afternoon cooped up in a theater. I'd rather get out of town for a change.

He: Well, if you'd rather see another movie, I guess we could. But I don't feel like driving very far. Besides, I have to work on my history paper on Sunday.

She: Why can't we ever agree on anything?

She _____ vs. He _____ Rationale: _____

SCENE 4

She: Hey, what do you want to do this weekend?

He: I don't know. What do you want to do?

She: Maybe we could go to a movie.

He: Maybe. Or we could hang out at the mall.

She: Maybe. What about hiking or cycling?

He: Yes, we could do that. Or maybe take a drive somewhere.

She: Yes, I guess. . . .

He: Let's just wait and see what comes up. . . .

She _____ vs. He _____ Rationale: _____

SCENE 5

She: We need to talk.

He: Why?

She: Because we need to reconnect. We've both been so busy. I feel like we need some time together this weekend.

He: Of course, we've been busy. I'm taking six courses, and they've increased my hours at work. You know I need the money for school.

She: I know all that, but I don't want all these other things to get in the way of "us."

He: What do you mean "get in the way of us"? We're still together, aren't we?

She: Yes, we're still together, but I want us to be really happy.

He: What do you mean "really happy"? I thought we were really happy. Don't we go out every weekend? Don't we eat dinner together every night? Don't we text message each other all day long?

She: Yes, we do, but I keep wondering how close we really are.

He: Oh, brother. You're not making any sense at all.

She _____ vs. He _____ Rationale: _____

Researchers who study relationships and psychological type have found the following:

- Between the two adages "birds of a feather flock together" and "opposites attract," when asked to identify the type of an ideal mate, most of us opt for similarity, particularly on the Sensing versus iNtuition scale.

- As a culture, we find extraversion more attractive than introversion.

- People have mixed feelings about Thinking versus Feeling, based on their own type, cultural stereotypes for men and women, and a natural preference for the feeling mode in a romantic partner.

- The highest potential for conflict is generated between an introverted man and an extraverted woman. Extraversion in women can be misinterpreted as flirting, which may generate jealousy in a partner.[36]

INSIGHT ⊖ ACTION

1. Do you agree with the suggestions for effective communication in this section? Which one do you think is most important? Why? Give an example of its importance from your own experience.

2. Choose one of the six crazymaking styles described, and create a script between two relational partners that illustrates the style.

3. Based on the informal activity Exercise 11.1 in this section, what is your preferred conflict style? Do you use it across the board or with particular individuals? How well does it work? Give several personal examples to prove your point.

4. Look back at the "Challenge → Reaction" activity at the beginning of this section. Are there particular items you could target to improve in your current relationship? What, specifically, might you choose to focus on, and how will you go about it?

Activity Option This is a great opportunity to divide the class into five groups and give each group a scene to play out while other groups guess the types. Discuss with the class what these couples could do to ease the conflict in their relationships.

Activity Option Ask students to respond to this "Insight → Action" activity by answering one or more of the questions using an essay format. Students should send their essay to you as an attachment to an e-mail message. It's an opportunity for you to make a personal connection with them.

Breaking Up Is Hard to Do

Research documents the far-reaching effects of bad relationships. They can hurt your job performance, your finances, your physical and mental health—even your life span.[37] Conflict with romantic partners, or with anyone you're in close proximity to—roommates, for example—can bring on major stress that affects your academic performance, not to mention your overall happiness.[38]

Unfortunately, movies and television often communicate—subtly or not so subtly—that conflict can be resolved by the end of the show. Just lighten up or settle down and you can resolve almost any problem. And if you can't, just swallow, take a deep breath, and move on. But life isn't like that, nor should it be. Managing the conflict in your life takes time, energy, and persistence. It requires understanding your natural tendencies, considering why you communicate as you do, and making productive choices as a communicator.

If you've ever monitored yourself during a particularly heated conflict, you may remember doing something like this: yelling in anger at someone at the top of your lungs, being interrupted by a phone call and suddenly communicating calmly and quietly to the caller, and then returning to the original shouting match after you hang up.

Why? We make *choices* as communicators. Sometimes our choices are productive ones, and sometimes they aren't. As a child, you may have heard the phrase: "Sticks and stones can break my bones, but words will never hurt me!" Actually, words *can* be used as weapons, and lethal ones at that! It's important to remember that we *do* choose what we say and how we behave. Our choices affect both the *process*—how things go during the conflict—and the *product*—how it turns out in the end. Negative choices produce destructive conflict that includes personal attacks, name calling, an unwillingness to listen, or the crazymaking strategies described earlier in this chapter. Positive choices are much more likely to bring productive conflict that helps us learn more about ourselves, our partners, and our relationships. Unfortunately, Kia Washington's choices led to a destructive conflict that may have ended her relationship with Quentin for good.

Just like healthy relationships, unhealthy ones have identifying characteristics, too. They may be unfulfilling, nonsupportive, or even abusive, for example. While every relationship can teach us something important about future ones, some red flags are worth our attention. Here are three to think about.[39] If you see these danger signals, it may be time to end the relationship, or if you and your partner both agree, to devote more time and energy toward improving it.

Danger signal 1: "All we ever do is fight!" This point seems obvious, but sometimes it's so obvious it's overlooked. All some couples talk about is how much they disagree or how wrong things are between them. As a general rule, if 50 percent

Chapter Crossover Remind students that they learned about campus resources in Chapter 3. Counseling might have helped Kia deal with some of the issues at the heart of her relationship with Quentin. Most college campuses have counseling resources for students. We all have times in life when we could use a little help.

> **"The difference between friendship and love is how much you can hurt each other."**
>
> Ashleigh Brilliant, author and cartoonist

or more of what you talk about is devoted to managing conflict, sit up and take notice. Fifty percent isn't a hard and fast number, of course. But when so much of your time is spent walking on eggshells to avoid conflict, airing your differences during conflict, or smoothing things over afterward, there's little time or energy left for other topics. Some couples fight fires continuously but never put them out. Eventually, running in place becomes tiring, and this relationship may have run its course. Assess the relationship and decide whether the investment is one you want to continue.

Danger signal 2: "Let's dig in deeper!" Can you imagine anyone saying something like this: "We've been going out for two years now, but we're just not getting along. I think if we got engaged, we'd both be more committed." Or consider a couple who is unhappily married, who say, "Maybe we should have a baby. That would bring us closer together." Whoa!

Statements such as these are danger signals. Relationships should escalate (or reach the next level of commitment) when we're satisfied with them, when we find them fulfilling, and when we are ready to take the next step together. Trying to force intimacy doesn't work. While this point makes sense intuitively, it's surprising how many couples fall into this trap. Sometimes it's one partner who becomes insecure and forces the issue. Forced escalation may even provide some short-term CPR; something new and interesting is happening. But if the effort isn't mutual and genuine, the brief revitalization won't last. People escalate relationships when they're happy with them, when they're afraid of losing them, or when they don't know what else to do. Only the first one of these reasons really works.

Figure 11.3 provides a visual example of a traditional pattern of relationship stages in our society. (Of course, the steps don't always occur in this order, nor are they even these particular steps.) At each step, the couple is making a decision about staying together. Ideally, relationships should escalate naturally

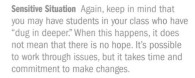

Sensitive Situation Again, keep in mind that you may have students in your class who have "dug in deeper." When this happens, it does not mean that there is no hope. It's possible to work through issues, but it takes time and commitment to make changes.

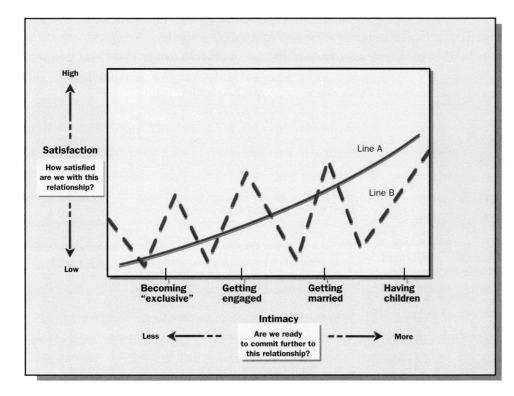

Figure 11.3
Moving to the Next Stage

along Line A; however, sometimes participants mistakenly force them to escalate unnaturally along Line B.

Danger signal 3: "This relationship just isn't worth it!" From two unique individuals, a third entity—a unique relationship—is born. The relationship you create with one person is unlike the one you'll create with anyone else. In a sense, you're a different person with Jack than you are with John or Mary. Not only are *you* different in many ways, but *your relationship* with each of these individuals is unique, too. Relationships, like individuals, have their own attitudes, values, and sensitivities. They can be liberating or smothering. That's why people talk about "taking part in" relationships, almost as if the relationship was separate from or beyond the two people themselves. Interestingly, relationships have a way of taking on a life of their own.

Being in a relationship comes with certain *costs* (giving up free time, not dating other people) and *rewards* (status, security, caring). Generally, people choose to stay in relationships they find rewarding, and they leave relationships they find too costly. But that's not always true; not all costs (or rewards) are equal. For the time being, you may decide that *security* (having *someone*) is a reward that outweighs the cost of putting up with the minor annoyances (costs) that come with a particular person, for example.

At some point, you may decide that a relationship just isn't worth it anymore. The costs outweigh the rewards. The relationship is suffocating or lifeless, and you find yourself thinking about having a relationship with someone else, or you're actually on the lookout for a new one. You may decide that greater rewards exist in a different relationship with someone else (even though that may be a false assumption). While subtle, a pervasive, persistent feeling that a relationship is no longer worth it, despite your best efforts, is worth your attention. It may be best to face this realization squarely and end the dissatisfying relationship honestly, rather than allowing another one to develop in secret.

When relationships end, the quality and quantity of communication between the two participants change. You may talk less frequently or less productively. It may happen over time as you drift apart or suddenly over a particular conflict. But as the golden oldie goes, "Breaking Up Is Hard to Do," and applying all the emotional intelligence you can muster will help you through it.

Emotional Intelligence (EI) Research Independence is a subscale of the intrapersonal scale of EQ. According to Stein and Book, independence "means taking charge of your own life, being your own person and seeking your own direction" (83). However, independence can also be an "overused strength" making it difficult for some individuals to commit to a relationship.

> "I'm very loyal in relationships. Even when I go out with my mom I don't look at other moms."
>
> **Garry Shandling, comedian**

C CONTROL Your Learning

YOUR TOUGHEST CLASS

Over the course of your college career, you'll take classes from excellent teachers, mediocre ones, and less preferable ones. What role does the relationship you have (or don't have) with your instructor play in your toughest class? Relationships with teachers have different power dynamics than other relationships in your life. Unlike your friends or romantic partners, instructors give grades (although students *earn* them) that can have long-term, high-stakes impact. Is the relationship you have with the instructor in your most challenging class as productive as it could be? Perhaps it is, but if not, try doing something about it.

Relationships of any kind have two participants. The only person you can control is yourself; however, your choices can affect the other person's actions. What can you do to make the relationship as productive as possible? Ask yourself these questions:

1. What behaviors or habits do I exhibit in this class that might be adversely affecting my relationship with my instructor?
2. What could I do instead to draw a more positive reaction?
3. If I were an instructor, what kinds of behaviors would I expect from students?
4. Can students help instructors become better teachers?
5. Can I make changes in my behavior that might improve my own learning?

Try a new set of behaviors in this class for a month, and then come back to this exercise and note the results you have observed.[40]

Diversity Makes a Difference

CHALLENGE → REACTION

Challenge: What are your views on diversity?

Reaction: Look at the following ten statements and indicate the extent to which you agree or disagree.

Strongly Agree	Agree	Not sure	Disagree	Strongly Disagree
1	2	3	4	5

1. Race is still a factor in hiring decisions today.

2. Multiculturalism implies that all cultures have equally valid viewpoints.

3. Workforce diversity improves the quality of work.

4. The number of male versus female corporate CEOs is nearing the halfway mark in the United States.

5. In some situations, sexual orientation is a justifiable basis for discrimination.

6. All cultures tend to see the rest of the world through their own cultural lens.

7. Feminism is a set of beliefs held by females.

8. A global perspective ensures objectivity.

9. Religious persecution is a thing of the past.

10. There is less racism in the United States today than there was ten years ago.

As you continue reading this section of the chapter, search for points relating to these topics. Also, your instructor may wish to use these ten items to begin a discussion in class.

These ten statements are intentionally provocative to stimulate your thinking. They relate to diversity: the differences between human beings based on gender, race, ethnicity, age, culture, physical features and abilities, mental capability, socioeconomic status, religion, politics, sexuality, gender identity, and points of view. Diversity is a fact of life. You've experienced it and learned about it throughout your schooling. Throughout your life, you've had relationships with all types of people. According to experts, if the entire population of schools, both elementary and secondary, in the United States were to shrink into one class of thirty students, ten students would come from minority groups. Of these, six would come from homes in which a language besides English is spoken, and one-third of the class would live in poverty.[41]

Although some of you may have grown up in a fairly homogeneous community with less racial, ethnic, or cultural diversity than others, no doubt you have experienced the multicultural nature of our society in many different ways, even in terms of food, music, and clothing, for example. The media have introduced you to aspects of diversity vicariously, and perhaps you've even traveled to other parts of the United States or the world yourself.

But here's the challenge: Has your experience with diversity and your learning about it in school truly made a difference in the way you think and act? Do you choose to diversify your awareness, your relationships, and yourself as a person? Do you think that the fact that we live in a multicultural society

Sensitive Situation Depending on the age, background, and maturity level of your students, it may or may not be a good idea to ask them to respond to the "Challenge → Reaction" questions in class. Some students, particularly those who are dualistic thinkers (black and white, right or wrong) or those who have not been exposed to diverse situations, have a less developed understanding of diversity. You might consider collecting individual class members' responses to first see where the class stands. This group report may illuminate you and keep you from generating an in-class discussion that takes you by surprise.

Teachable Moment Pose these questions to the class: Why might students think that tolerance and respect for people of other races, ethnicities, and lifestyles are among the least important goals for college learning?

in which we've all been taught to respect and appreciate diversity means that discrimination no longer exists?

Many college students today do believe that racial discrimination is no longer a problem. Been there; done that, they've concluded. According to a recent survey, "helping to promote racial understanding" was considered "essential" or "very important by only slightly more than one-third of incoming first-year students.[42] In another study, students were asked to identify the five most critical and two least critical outcomes of a college education from a list of sixteen possibilities. Tolerance and respect for people of other races, ethnicities, and lifestyles were identified as among the least important goals for college learning.[43] Why do you think they responded that way? Do they think they've already achieved these goals, or do they devalue them for other reasons?

If you conducted a survey on your campus to find out if discrimination exists, you might be surprised at the results. Research continues to show that minority students experience discrimination at higher rates than majority students. Many of us downplay the prejudice all human beings harbor to one extent or another. Our brains are "programmed" to group like entities and standardize our views about these groups, resulting in stereotypes. We feel safe around others like us and fear those unlike us.

Refraining from stereotyping groups of people and appreciating individuals for what they are could drastically alter the way we think and act. Perhaps you've always assumed that all nerds are A, all athletes are B, and all sorority women are C. What if you switched the labels around? Are the results ludicrous? When labels come to us easily, they are probably negative, and it's likely they apply to groups *other than* the ones *we* belong to. However, when you liberate yourself to think differently, you're not bogged down by tired, old labels. If you open up your thinking to new possibilities, all kinds of new options present themselves. Imagine a band made up of only trombones, a meal with nothing but potatoes, a song played on one note, or a world where everyone looks exactly like you. Diversity enriches our lives.

A University of Michigan study demonstrated that students who had more positive interactions with diverse peers, and in particular took a college course on diversity, were more likely to have more academic self-confidence, be more personally proactive, and be more disposed to developing better critical thinking skills.[44] Learning to deal effectively with diversity can actually change you as a college student!

Appreciate the American Mosaic

This November 18, 1993, *Time Magazine* cover featured a multiracial, computer-generated woman's face. The blended features were intended to show that increasingly Americans are a composite: the "New Face of America," the magazine called it. It's becoming more and more impossible to draw clear lines between what separates us physically. Tiger Woods tells people he's "Cablinasian," a term he created to reflect his Caucasian, Black, Indian, and Asian ancestry. Keanu Reeves is Hawaiian, Chinese, and Caucasian; Mariah Carey is Black, Venezuelan, and Caucasian; and Johnny Depp is Cherokee and Caucasian.[45] Most of us are a blend, but diversity is about more than physical appearance. Each of us is a unique human being.

Actually, college is a perfect time to immerse yourself in diversity—in the classroom and beyond it. Classrooms are becoming more diversely populated; it's true. By the standard definition, only 27 percent of today's college students are "traditional" (meaning a high school graduate who immediately goes on to college, depends on parents fully for financial support, and doesn't work or works only part-time). Most traditional students today don't fit the traditional definition of "traditional."[46] Adult nontraditional learners have varied backgrounds, interests, and approaches to getting an education. Often they try to work their way through systems that are designed around the needs of younger students.[47] Today, twice as many minority students are enrolled in college than were enrolled twenty years ago, and the number of Hispanic college students has tripled since 1980.[48] Diversity in higher education gives you an opportunity to expand your world view and develop empathy for others who have vastly different experiences.

Aside from meeting students of other races and ethnicities in college, taking advantage of diversity can help you become a more sophisticated thinker, one who can see problems from multiple perspectives, and a better-prepared employee, ready to hit the ground running in today's highly diverse workplace. Appreciating diversity also helps us become better citizens. Diversity is what our society is based on. In a democratic society such as ours, citizens must be able to recognize and endorse creative solutions to complex problems. A former Chief Justice of the U.S. Supreme Court, Charles Evans Hughes, once said, "When we lose the right to be different, we lose the privilege to be free."

Take a good look at this woman. She was created by a computer from a mix of several races. What you see is a remarkable preview of ...

THE NEW FACE OF AMERICA
How Immigrants Are Shaping the World's First Multicultural Society

Kin Wah Lam/Time Inc./Time & Life Picture/Getty Images

"We have become not a melting pot, but a beautiful mosaic. Different people, different beliefs, different yearnings, different hopes, different dreams."

Jimmy Carter, thirty-ninth president of the United States

Activity Option If you are comfortable with this activity, create a "Human Continuum" (Staley, 2003) as a way to launch a discussion about diversity in class. Create an imaginary line along the front of the room, for example, and label each opposite pole. You can use descriptors such as majority/minority, 100 percent American/foreign, and so on. Then ask students to place themselves along the line. You may be surprised at how students place themselves on this continuum. For example, students who are light-skinned may place themselves closer to a label for students of color than someone who has darker skin. Often, how we identify ourselves is by using internal, rather than external, indicators. Defining the meanings the two poles held for students can lead to a rich discussion.

EXERCISE 11.2 What's the Difference?

Find a partner to work with on this exercise. Individually, list all the various ways in which you differ: age, height, gender, eye color, hometown, and so on. When your instructor calls "time," read your lists aloud. The point of the exercise is to begin a discussion on the meaning of diversity, to explore its many different facets—beyond just external appearance—and to appreciate the fact that each individual is unique.[49]

One mistake many college students make is not taking advantage of what diversity offers them. Because like attracts like, they join groups of people just like themselves based on religion, sexual orientation, or majors, for example. You can choose to belong to the Young Republicans; the Gay, Lesbian, Bisexual, Transgender (GLBT) student group; or the Chemistry Honor Society. Joining a

Box 11.1 Service-Learning: Learning by Serving

Brand X Pictures/Getty Images

"We make a living by what we get, but we make a life by what we give."

Winston Churchill, Prime Minister of England (1874–1965)

One of the best ways to learn about diversity in college is by serving others. Instead of spending all your time in a classroom, imagine a class on aging in which you team up with an elder in your community and work together on a term project. You might help a senior write her memoirs, for example, or help an elderly man create a family tree for the next generation. You might be wondering, *How would that work? What could we possibly have in common—an 18-year-old teamed up with an 88-year-old?* You might be surprised.

What might you learn in a college reading course in which you tutor first graders at an inner-city elementary school, or a college success course in which you teach middle school students how to apply what you're learning right now about academic achievement? Centuries ago, a French philosopher wrote, "To teach is to learn twice." You need to know your stuff in order to teach it to someone else effectively, and you learn twice as much if you serve others who differ from you in important ways.

Campus Compact, a national organization with 950 member colleges, estimates that college student volunteering was worth $4.45 billion to the communities they served in 2004. They report that more than 30 percent of college students regularly do community service for approximately four hours per week.[50]

Beyond the dollars calculated, college students' community service provides invaluable support. Literally thousands of college students volunteered to help with Hurricane Katrina and Rita relief efforts in 2005, for example, to help displaced victims of one of the country's worst natural disasters ever.

However, here's an important point: *community service* and *service-learning* aren't quite the same thing.[51] Service-learning is specifically about the learning. It's a learning experience in which you connect what you're learning in the classroom for credit with what you're learning in the community. You're applying what you're learning, which in turn solidifies—and modifies—your perspective. "Service, combined with learning, adds value to each and transforms both."[52] While you're engaged in a service-learning experience, you'll also be engaged in critical reflection. Critical reflection is like critical thinking, recalling or looking back at the service experience and writing about what you're learning in a *continuous, connected, challenging,* and *contextualized* way.[53] That's not the same thing as donating your time for a good cause, as important as that is, in terms of you and your own personal development and the lives of the people you help.

Years ago, learning expert John Dewey wrote that the best learning experiences:

- Generate interest

- Are intrinsically worthwhile

- Present problems that evoke new curiosity and require new information

- Cover a considerable time span so that your learning evolves as you go[54]

Think about it: Might a service-learning project like helping an 88-year-old person, someone who's lived through nearly a century of triumphs and tragedies, record her life's story meet these four requirements?

The average number of college professors who include service-learning in their courses nearly tripled between 2000 and 2005. Search out these opportunities to enhance your own learning and your appreciation for diversity by serving other people.[55]

group of like students assures you a place where people accept you for who you are and you feel comfortable. Think about the groups you belong to and what they say about you.

Of course, being comfortable and feeling accepted are important. But instead, imagine choosing to join groups composed of very different types of people. Consider what philosopher and educator John Dewey once said, "Conflict…shocks us out of sheep-like passivity," or political philosopher Edmund Burke's words, "Our antagonist is our helper. He that wrestles with us strengthens our nerves, and sharpens our skill." A famous American lawyer, Louis Nizer, once put it like this: "Where there is no difference, there is only indifference." What about stretching ourselves to learn fully what diversity has the potential to teach us?[56]

Chapter Crossover Students learned about resources on campus in Chapter 3. Many colleges have a service-learning department or center on campus. Consider building service-learning into your class.

Teachable Moment You might want to ask the class if anyone would like to reveal a unique background. As an instructor do you have a "blend" in your background that you would be willing to tell them about?

EXERCISE 11.3 Circles of Awareness

Write your name in the center of the drawing, then label each of the surrounding circles with a word that represents a group with whom you identify. You may use categories such as age, gender, ethnicity, social, political, and so forth. After your drawing is labeled, your instructor will ask you to circulate around the room and find three classmates who have listed at least three of the same subgroups. Following that, you will be asked to find three students who listed at least three categories that you did not. In the second group you formed, based on differences, use the activity to discuss diversity, differences between individuals and groups, and how awareness can change behavior. Look over everyone's list, and to diversify your thinking, select one group on someone else's list, but not on yours. Find out more about that group, or decide to attend a group meeting to raise your awareness of differences between yourself and the group or between your preconceptions of what the group would be like, and what it's actually like.[57]

Teachable Moment It's a good idea to debrief Exercise 11.3. Ask students to indicate one or two things that they learned or were surprised about when doing this activity.

Your Name

Imagine you were engaged in a service-learning project for a class, working in your local soup kitchen. It's easy to look at a homeless person with a critical eye and think, "Why doesn't he just get a job?" But when you actually sit down and share a bowl of soup across the table, you might see things differently. You might hear stories of personal illness, family tragedy, unbelievable trauma—a string of coinciding misfortunes, the likes of which you've never contemplated. Rather than assigning all homeless people to a group with a negative label, learn more about the individuals that make up that group. You might change your views.

One professor says this: "I tell my students to keep in mind that everything they see is a snapshot. That guy drinking from a bottle in a paper bag, he's a photograph. How did he get to where he is? From there, we can share some of the rage at the inherent injustice that awaits so many of our poor children as they grow up. As we examine people, the snapshots become a motion picture that links the past, present, and future—what was, what is, what can be."[58]

Choose a stereotype you recognize, one you suspect you subscribe to if you're honest, and decide what you can do to test it. Ask yourself whether it affects your thinking and actions. For example, are you aware of these facts attesting to the persistence of stereotypes in our culture?

> **Sexism** is still an issue in corporate America. In 2002, 1 out of 13 executive vice presidents (or higher) in America's top 500 companies was a woman, up from 1 out of 40 in 1995. Then, only one of those companies had a female CEO; by 2003, seven did. Experts predict that by 2020, it could be 1 in 5; however, the numbers remain grossly lopsided.[59]

> **Racism** is still an issue in hiring decisions. A recent Gallup poll asked: "Do you feel that racial minorities in this country have job opportunities equal to whites, or not?" Among Caucasians, the answer was 55 percent yes and 43 percent no. (The rest were undecided.) Among

---

FOCUS ON CAREERS: LINDA HOLTZMAN,
Diversity Trainer

Q1: You're a corporate trainer. Are you an internal trainer, working within the Human Resources department of an organization, or are you an external trainer who works with a variety of companies as a consultant? What types of different companies have you worked with?
I am a university professor who teaches courses about diversity, and I conduct diversity training for corporations, nonprofit organizations, other colleges and universities, and school districts. Organizations hire me when they realize how important diversity is to their organization's goals, or when conflicts erupt and they believe diversity training will help.

Q2: How did you become interested in diversity training? What prepared you to do what you do?
I have a strong commitment to equity and social justice. I work to help individuals and institutions change. When that happens, people see and treat each other with greater respect, personally and professionally. I've studied diversity both formally and informally through my graduate degrees, my participation in national organizations, my

research and writing, and the way I choose to live my life. I immerse myself in diversity wherever I can, including where I live, where my children go to school, in what I read, in the arts, and in my friendships. I believe it's important to have an understanding of the deep culture of many diverse groups.

Q3: Describe a typical diversity training session. What types of skills do you teach employees? Does it work?
I have conducted training that is anywhere from three hours to six-day in-residence institutes. I approach diversity training in three different ways: from the *head*, from the *heart*, and with the *hand*. The *head* refers to the theories, concepts, and history. The *heart* refers to the emotional dimension of learning about diversity. My co-trainers and I spend a great deal of time in this realm since many of us have strong experiences, feelings, and fears about issues related to diversity. The *hand* refers to what participants can do to develop specific personal and organizational goals and strategies. My overall goal as a trainer is

African Americans, the answer was 17 percent yes and 81 percent no. You might also be shocked to read about an experiment conducted by University of Chicago and MIT economists in which fabricated applicants of one race were 50 percent more likely to be called for interviews than applicants of another race, based solely on racially based fictitious names! As one *Wall Street Journal* reporter noted, "Someday Americans will be able to speak of racial discrimination in hiring in the past tense. Not yet."[60]

> **Discrimination and stereotypes** persist. Students with disabilities report a "chilly classroom climate" for students with disabilities in higher education.[61] According to one college president, "With all [the change in racial demographics], diversity has become the largest issue behind unrest on campus, accounting for 39 percent of student protests."[62] A recent study of closeted and out gay and lesbian college students reported that these students perceived unfair treatment and a need to hide their identity from most other students. Both groups reported experiencing a similar amount of antigay attacks.[63] In 2005, 7,163 hate crimes were reported by 2,037 law enforcement agencies, according to the United States Department of Justice. Racially motivated crimes accounted for 56 percent, religious bias accounted for 15.7 percent, bias against sexual orientation for 14 percent, bias against disabilities by 0.6 percent, and bias against ethnicity or national origin accounted for 13.7 percent.[64] People still harm one another out of hatred for differences they may not understand.

Teachable Moment Some colleges have Common Reading Programs where all entering students read the same novel. If this is the case on your campus, ask students if they felt this book provided a springboard for conversation about diversity. If your campus does not have such a program, ask students what books they have recently read that provides diverse perspectives about groups or individuals,

Teachable Moment Pose the following questions to students: Is Human Resources a good career choice for everyone? Why or why not?

C CREATE a Career Outlook

HUMAN RESOURCES

Have you ever considered a career in Human Resources? Here are some facts about this career to consider and some questions about yourself to ponder.

Facts to Consider

Academic preparation required: a college degree in human resources, liberal arts, and often a business background or internship

Future workforce demand: Competition for entry-level jobs will be high.

Work environment: Human Resources departments, particularly in large organizations, fulfill many employee-oriented functions: training and development; recruiting, interviewing, and hiring; employee relations; and compensation and benefits (health insurance and pension plans). Increasingly, employers realize the value of training employees to improve their skills, build company loyalty, and increase business results through on-the-job training, classroom training, and e-learning.

Most common psychological type preferences: extraverted (or to a lesser extent, introverted), intuitive or sensing, thinking, perceiving (or judging). The most common reported types are ENTP, ESTJ, ENTJ, and INTJ.[65]

Essential skills: speaking, writing, teamwork, and problem solving

Questions to Ponder

1. Do you have (or could you acquire) the skills this career requires?
2. What would you find most satisfying about this type of career?
3. What would you find most challenging about this type of career?
4. Are you interested in a career like this? Why or why not?

For more information, see U.S. Department of Labor, Bureau of Labor Statistics, *Occupational Outlook Handbook, 2006–2007 Edition.*[66]

For more career activities online, go to http://www.academic.cengage.com/collegesuccess/staley to do the Team Career exercises.

to bring about change. When I see that beginning to happen, I know I'm doing something very important as a trainer.

Q4: In your experience, what types of skills do employees need to improve? What diversity challenges do today's employees face?
All of us have "learned" bias although it may be invisible to us. The first thing we must do is to actually "see" it. Once we see these blind spots within ourselves, we may be open to change if: (1) we have credible information, (2) we hear it from someone we trust, and (3) ironically, if we aren't forced to change. Many of us have been taught that it is better not to "notice" difference because that means we have risen above it. Many of the employees that I have worked with don't even want to talk about diversity because they are afraid they will say the wrong thing or that they will hurt someone, so I must provide a safe environment and call on all my facilitation skills. We can't resolve what we can't even talk about. But I'm a firm believer that diversity training can make a difference, and being a trainer is a great career if you want to help people change what they think, feel, and do.

Diversity makes a difference, and as educator Adela A. Allen once wrote, "We should acknowledge differences, we should greet differences, until difference makes no difference anymore." What can we do about it? Some campuses have launched programs in Sustained Dialogue, used in the past to deal with international tensions. This structured approach brings together students with different backgrounds for a year of deep conversation in small groups. Other colleges have developed similar programs to allow students to dialogue about deeply rooted prejudices—sometimes buried to an extent that they are not even realized—to discuss commonalities, and to recognize the potential for conflict—and change.[67] Raising awareness is a first step on the road to recognizing the reality and the richness of diversity.

Think Globally; Act Locally

The 1972 United Nations international conference on the human environment in Stockholm was the origin of the phrase "Think Globally, Act Locally." Perhaps you've heard it. Simply put, it originally meant "Do what you can to 'save the environment.'"

Today the phrase takes on added meaning. True, recycling is commonplace and *sustainability* is the watchword of modern corporations. Beyond environmental concerns, the world is characterized by networks of connections that span continents and distances. As citizens of the world, we are interdependent; small, seemingly insignificant actions can have monumental effects. Realize that we are all connected, if not geographically, then economically, militarily, socially, and technologically. The General Electric website allows users to select from forty

Cut and Deal Ltd/Index Open

different languages. Google offers an interface in over eighty languages.[68] By 2003, 66 percent of all e-commerce spending originated outside of the United States, and over 66 percent of all Internet users reside outside of North America.[69] A famous song title once made the claim: "We are the world."

Many universities now have Centers for the Study of Globalization, a major in Global Studies, or a general education requirement in Global Learning.[70] In today's world, a college education should enable you to

> Understand the world's peoples and problems

> Explore the historical roots of the dynamics and tensions in today's world

> Develop competencies across cultures so that you can navigate boundaries and see the world from multiple perspectives

> Investigate difficult, sometimes emotionally charged issues we face across and among cultures

> Engage in practical work with issues facing communities and societies

The education you get now must prepare you to solve the problems of the future. It will require you to look beyond the walls of your classrooms, refine your critical and creative thinking skills, and expand your worldview. The course for which you're using this textbook is a good place to start.

INSIGHT ⊖ ACTION

1. Do you think most college students value diversity? Why or why not?

2. Are there particular groups on campus you'd like to learn more about to develop and diversify your awareness? What might you learn by doing so?

3. Have you traveled outside the United States? If so, have those experiences broadened your worldview? How? If not, how might you do so even without the opportunity to travel and see differences firsthand?

Activity Option As was suggested early in this chapter, consider using this "Insight → Action" activity as a prompt for an essay. You can use all questions, or some, or even add a question to have students answer. Students can share the essay with each other for peer feedback, or hand it in or e-mail it to you.

EXERCISE 11.4 VARK Activity

Complete the recommended activity for your preferred VARK learning modality. If you are multimodal, select more than one activity. Your instructor may ask you to (a) give an oral report on your results in class, (b) send your results to him or her via e-mail, (c) post them online, or (d) contribute to a class chat.

 Visual: Make a chart of the five scales of emotional intelligence and select representative artwork or graphics for each scale to help you remember its meaning and importance.

 Aural: Ask a friend or classmate to describe a real, model relationship they know or have been a part of. Following their description, discuss the specific qualities that make this relationship work.

Read/Write: Write a case study about a real relationship using fictitious names that demonstrates some of the principles of conflict management described in this chapter.

Kinesthetic: Interview three international students on your campus about how college life differs between what they experience on your campus and what they might experience at colleges in their home country.

Activity Option The VARK activity is a great way for students to choose an aspect of the chapter that had meaning for them and present it to the class. Ask students to make four PowerPoint slides for their presentation. Students can also respond to both the "Now What Do You Think?" activity and the "Reality Check" by sending you an e-mail with their results, or by comparing their results in class with a partner.

 # NOW WHAT DO YOU THINK?

At the beginning of this chapter, Kia Washington faced a series of challenges as a new college student. Now after reading this chapter, would you respond differently to any of the questions you answered about the "FOCUS Challenge Case"?

For more practice online, go to http://www.academic.cengage.com/collegesuccess/staley to take the Challenge Yourself online quizzes.

REALITY CHECK

On a scale of 1 to 10, answer the following questions now that you've completed this chapter.

1 = not very/not much/very little/low   10 = very/a lot/very much/high

In hindsight, how much did you *really* know about this subject matter before reading the chapter?

1   2   3   4   5   6   7   8   9   10

How much do you think this information might affect your college success?

1   2   3   4   5   6   7   8   9   10

How much do you think this information might affect your career success after college?

1   2   3   4   5   6   7   8   9   10

How long did it actually take you to complete this chapter (both the reading and writing tasks)? _____ Hour(s) _____ Minutes

Now take a minute to compare these answers to your answers from the "Readiness Check" at the beginning of this chapter. What gaps exist between the similar questions? How might these gaps between what you thought before starting the chapter and what you now think after completing the chapter affect how you approach the next chapter in this book?

Activity Option For the final activity have students design a PowerPoint presentation (four slides) in groups on either the role of emotional intelligence, love, or conflict in the lives of college students and their success. Presentations should include a definition, describe possible challenges concerning the issue, its impact on college success, and suggestions on how to manage the challenge.

To download mp3 format audio summaries of this chapter, go to http://www .academic.cengage.com/collegesuccess/staley.

12 Choosing a College Major and Career

YOU'RE ABOUT TO DISCOVER...

Teachable Moment As you begin this chapter, remember that while choosing a major is critical to college success, the old thinking that students should enter college having already decided on their major isn't realistic. Students need to explore their options, learn about themselves, and ultimately choose a major that keeps them engaged and excited throughout college, one that will lead to productive and fulfilling life's work.

> Why "College in a Box" isn't an accurate view of coursework

> How the disciplines connect in the Circle of Learning

> How to build an Academic Map

> How to choose a major and a career

> How to focus your I's

> What a SWOT analysis is

> How to SCAN your skills

> Why majors and careers aren't the same thing

> How to consider your academic anatomy

> How to launch a career

> How internships, co-ops, and service-learning can give you experience

"Not all who wander are lost."

J. R. R. Tolkien, English author (1892–1973)

Ethan Cole

One thing was certain: Ethan Cole was unsure. Unsure of his abilities, unsure of which major to choose, unsure of what he wanted to do with his life, unsure of himself. Unsure of almost everything.

Ethan came from a good family, and his parents were actually his best friends. They had been very successful, and they wanted to share the wealth—literally— with their three children. They supported Ethan, no matter what. When he ended up in the principal's office time after time in grade school, they defended him. When he totaled his car in high school, they bought him another one. When he wanted to take a term off to travel and "find himself," they said yes without raising one, single eyebrow. And now that he was thinking of dropping out of college, they said he could move back home, so long as he agreed to a few ground rules and promised to take back his old chores, like mowing the yard. That seemed only fair to him.

The only thing Ethan was sure of was that skateboarding was his life right now. It's all he wanted to do and all he ever thought about. He'd look at a curve on a window frame or an arc in a picture and imagine what skating on it would feel like. All his friends were skateboarders, too, and he read skateboarder magazines and dreamed of the day he might even go pro. He realized not many people make a living at it, but a few really talented athletes did, and maybe—just maybe—he'd be one of them. Recently, he'd found out about the largest concrete skatepark on the globe, Black Pearl in the Grand Cayman Islands—62,000 square feet! He'd made a promise to himself to skate there someday. *Life couldn't get much better than that*, he thought.

But school...that was a different story. Schoolwork had never captured his attention. In primary school, his physician had diagnosed Attention Deficit Disorder (ADD), and in middle school, a learning specialist had discovered that Ethan was dyslexic. *No wonder I don't like school*, he remembered thinking then. But finally knowing why he couldn't focus didn't change his attitude. He still hated sitting in a classroom.

Despite these challenges, his parents had always told him he was smart. "You can do anything you want to do," they'd said. "Look at you: you're a good-looking

kid with plenty of talents. The world is your oyster!" *What a funny phrase*, he'd always thought when they said that. By the time he finally learned what it meant, he totally believed it. His life would become whatever he chose to make of it.

The problem was there were too many choices. How could anyone decide what he wanted to be when he was only nineteen? Ethan remembered liking geometry, he was good at creative writing, he played the drums like a real jazz musician, and he was an incredible artist. *But what do you do with* that *combination of skills?* he'd asked himself more than once. What possible college major and career would really fit him?

He'd managed to pull decent grades his first term—a B average—at the arts college close to home. He'd taken Freshman Composition, Introduction to Communication, Drawing 101, and Study Skills, and while he'd done well, none of the course material really sparked a genuine interest. His professors didn't take much of an interest in him, either. His Study Skills instructor was friendly and tried to interest him in the course, but Ethan had been hearing that information repeated in school for years now. He claimed he already had all those skills; he just wasn't motivated to apply them. Instead, he skateboarded every minute he could.

The more he thought about it, the more he thought it was a good idea to take a year off from college. He could get a job delivering pizzas, think about his life, and try to figure it all out. He'd have nobody to tell him what to do, nobody to hold him accountable, nobody to pressure him to study, nobody to force him into making decisions—and plenty of free time to skateboard.

WHAT DO **YOU** THINK?

Now that you've read about Ethan Cole, answer the following questions. You may not know all the answers yet, but you'll find out what you know and what you stand to gain by reading this chapter.

1. In your view, what will become of Ethan? What are his prospects for the future? Do you think he'll decide on a major and finish college? Why or why not?

2. Why is Ethan experiencing problems? Are these problems serious? Should they hold him back? List all the problems you can identify.

3. Which majors and careers might Ethan be well suited for? If you were an academic advisor, what advice would you give him?

4. Who would you send Ethan to on your campus for help? What are his options? What do you think he should do at this point?

Before beginning to read this chapter, take two minutes to answer the following questions on a scale of 1 to 10. Your answers will help you assess how ready you are to focus.

1 = not very/not much/very little/low   10 = very/a lot/very much/high

Based on reading the "You're about to discover..." list and skimming this chapter, how much do you think you probably already know about the subject matter?

1   2   3   4   5   6   7   8   9   10

How much do you think this information might affect your college success?

1   2   3   4   5   6   7   8   9   10

How much do you think this information might affect your career success after college?

1   2   3   4   5   6   7   8   9   10

In general, how motivated are you to learn the material in this chapter?

1   2   3   4   5   6   7   8   9   10

This book describes four key factors related to intrinsic, or internal, motivation: curiosity, control, career outlook, and challenge. The next four questions relate to these **C-Factors:**

How *curious* are you about the content you expect to read in this chapter?

1   2   3   4   5   6   7   8   9   10

How much *control* do you expect to have over mastering the material in this chapter?

1   2   3   4   5   6   7   8   9   10

How much do you think this chapter might help you develop your *career outlook?*

1   2   3   4   5   6   7   8   9   10

How *challenging* do you think the material in this chapter will be for you?

1   2   3   4   5   6   7   8   9   10

Before beginning any task, including studying, it's important to check in with yourself to ensure that you're physically, intellectually, and emotionally ready to focus. How ready are you, physically, to focus on this chapter? (Are you rested, feeling well, and so on?)

1   2   3   4   5   6   7   8   9   10

How ready are you, intellectually, to focus on this chapter? (Are you thinking clearly, focused on this course, interested in this subject?)

1   2   3   4   5   6   7   8   9   10

How ready are you, emotionally, to focus on this chapter? (Are you calm, confident, composed?)

1   2   3   4   5   6   7   8   9   10

If your answer to any of the last three questions is below a 5 on the scale, you may need to address the issue you're facing prior to beginning this chapter. For example, if you're hungry, get a quick bite to eat. If you're feeling scattered, take a few moments to settle down and focus.

Finally, how long do you think it will take you to complete this chapter?
_____ Hour(s) _____ Minutes

Sensitive Situation   It would not be at all surprising to have more than one student like Ethan in your class. It's possible that you will also have students who are very judgmental of Ethan. Make sure that you portray Ethan as a normal student who is struggling. How can he help himself, and if he were a member of our class, what could we do to support him?

What's the Connection?

CHALLENGE ⊖ REACTION

Challenge: Is there a connection between what you study in art, psychology, engineering, and chemistry? If so, how would you try to explain the relationships?

Reaction: _____

As a student, it's natural to try to be as efficient as possible. You're busy taking classes, working at a job, dealing with family issues, participating in co-curricular activities, developing relationships, and on and on. It's easy to get overwhelmed, and a common reaction we humans have to complexity is to try to simplify. So some students simplify by only studying what's on the test. Nothing more.

But college is not just a collection of random courses—a smattering of this and a smattering of that. And when you finally check off enough boxes, you get a degree in whatever you have the most credits in. That's not the way it's supposed to work.

College is about becoming an educated person, learning how to think, solve problems, and make decisions. College is much more than the "sum of its tests." It's about developing yourself as a person and becoming well-educated. What does it mean to be well-educated? Simply put: Being well-educated is about the pursuit of human excellence.[1]

Why do societies have colleges and universities? Why have they been around so long? Ancient Greece had Plato's Academy and Aristotle's Lyceum. The Sorbonne flourished in France in the Middle Ages. England's Cambridge and Oxford are two of the oldest English-language universities in the world. And Harvard, founded in 1636, was one of the first American institution of higher education.

Colleges and universities help societies *preserve the past* and *create the future*. Studying the history of the U.S. Constitution in a political science course as opposed to studying potential cures for cancer in a cell biology course are concrete examples. Colleges and universities help us look back (preserve the past) and look ahead (create the future).

> **"It takes courage to grow up and become who you really are."**
>
> e. e. cummings, American poet (1894–1962)

College in a Box?

Have you ever thought about the fact that college courses appear to exist in discrete "boxes"? Schools tend to place courses in academic departments, and your class schedule reflects these divisions. For example, your schedule this term might look something like the one in Figure 12.1.

This organizing system helps you keep things straight in your head, and it also helps your school organize a complex institution. The English department's budget is separate from the physics department's budget. Professors normally work in one department or another. And classes are categorized into particular academic disciplines.

Chapter Crossover Choosing a major involves many different things. In Chapter 1 students were asked to think about what drives them: their values, dreams, and goals. Also, in Chapter 2 students learned about themselves and the role personality and learning modalities play in choosing a career.

	M	T	W	Th	F
9–10	ENG			SOC	
10–11		PHY			
11–12			PSCI		PSCI

Figure 12.1

Most Schools Compartmentalize Learning

That's the bottom line. But something first-year students often wonder about is how to connect the dots. What's the big picture? Knowledge isn't quite as neat as departments and boxes; it's messy. It overlaps and converges. Despite the convenient institutional compartmentalization of knowledge on a college campus, you might be able to take a somewhat similar course in visual art from the art department, the computer science department, or the communication department. You've probably noticed that you sometimes hear something discussed in one of your classes that's also being discussed in another one. Knowledge is interconnected. College in a Box isn't an accurate way of looking at things.

Even though each discipline has its own history and identity and way of asking questions and finding answers, the disciplines aren't as distinct as your class schedule might lead you to believe. Let's explore how academic disciplines interrelate.

How Do the Disciplines Connect?

The Circle of Learning (see Figure 12.2) illustrates the interconnectedness of knowledge. Although this circle could be drawn in many different ways, using many different traditional academic disciplines, here is an example to get you thinking.[2]

It works like this. Let's start at the top of the circle with *math*, which is a basic "language" with rules and conventions, just like spoken language. You manipulate numbers and operations and functions, just as you manipulate sounds and words and sentences. Now, move clockwise around the circle.

Math is the fundamental language of *physics*, the study of atomic and subatomic particles. When atoms combine into elements, such as carbon and oxygen, the academic discipline is called *chemistry*. Chemicals combine to create living organisms studied in *biology* courses. Living organisms don't just exist, they think and behave, leading to the study of *psychology*. They also interact in groups, families, and organizations, which you study in *sociology*. You can also study units of living beings throughout time and across cultures in the discipline of *anthropology*. These units—people—who live and work together are typically governed or govern themselves, leading to *political science*. Let's keep going.

When an account of peoples and countries and their rulers is recorded, you study *history*. These written accounts, sometimes factual or sometimes fictional

Figure 12.2

The Circle of Learning

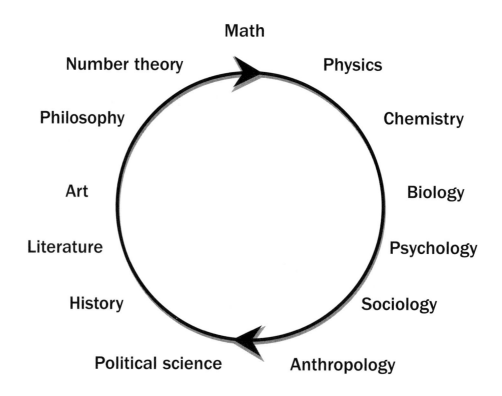

(for pleasure or intrigue) comprise the study of *literature*. Literature is one way to record impressions and provoke reactions—poetry is a good example—through the use of words. But images and symbols can do the same things—enter *art*. A particular question artists ask is "What is beauty?" otherwise known as *aesthetics*, which is also a particular topic of study in *philosophy*. Philosophy also includes another subspecialty called *number theory*, one of the earliest branches of pure mathematics. And now we're all the way around the Circle of Learning, arriving right back at *math*.

That's a quick rundown. Of course, many academic disciplines don't appear on this chart, but they could and should. A philosophy major might see her discipline at the center of the circle, or a geography major might say, "Hey, where's geography on this chart?" The circle, as it appears here, is representative. The point isn't which disciplines are represented. Instead, the Circle of Learning demonstrates that academic disciplines are interconnected because knowledge itself is interconnected. *Anthropology* (understanding people throughout time and across cultures) can provide an important foundation for *political science* (how people are governed or govern themselves), and *history* (a record of peoples and countries and rulers) can easily be the basis for *literature*. Capitalizing on what you're learning in one discipline can lead to deeper understanding in another.

In your career, you'll need to use knowledge without necessarily remembering in which course you learned it. You'll be thinking critically and creatively, solving problems, and calling upon all the skills you're cultivating in all the courses you're studying in college. The bottom line is that connections count. Recognize them, use them, and strengthen them to reinforce your learning.

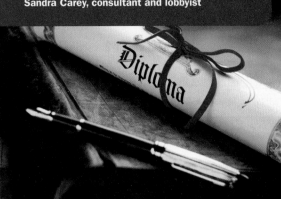

> **"Never mistake knowledge for wisdom. One helps you make a living; the other helps you make a life."**
>
> **Sandra Carey, consultant and lobbyist**

Photodisc/Getty Images

Activity Option In Figure 12.1 students saw a typical schedule. Have students list their own schedules in a similar format and then place their courses on the Circle of Learning. Can they describe connections between two or more of the classes they're taking this term?

Building an Academic Map

CHALLENGE → REACTION

Challenge: Considering all the different disciplines identified on the Circle of Learning, how would you answer these two broad questions: *What* do students study in college? Secondly, *why* do they study these things? Identify two broad areas of study and two reasons why, as humans, we want to know.

Reaction: _____

_____

_____

Here's a model you can use to help you make sense out of your college education. Your education starts when you're born and continues until right about now when you begin choosing an academic major—and then, of course, you'll continue learning throughout your life. See if the process of building an Academic Map helps you better understand what looks like a long checklist of requirements involved in earning a college degree.

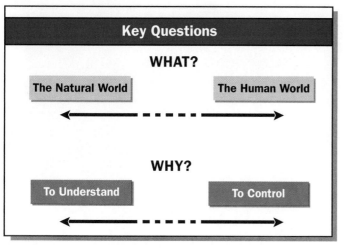

Figure 12.3

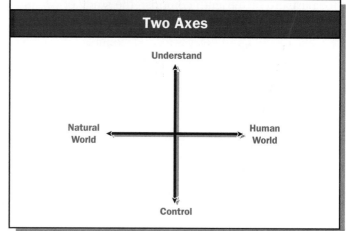

Figure 12.4

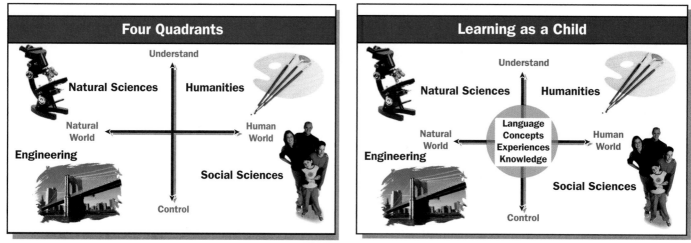

Figure 12.5

Figure 12.6

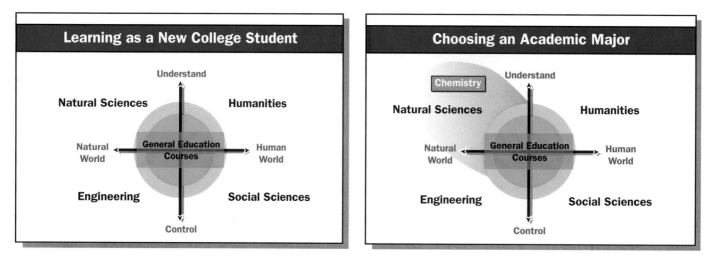

Figure 12.7

Figure 12.8

Key Questions

To start this discussion, here are the two most important questions we can ask (see Figure 12.3):

1. *What* do students study in college?
2. *Why* do they study these things?

Earlier we noted that some students try to simplify their lives by only studying what's on the test. Another way in which college students are tempted to simplify is by streamlining their choice of classes. If a course isn't directly related to their major or doesn't fulfill a requirement, they ask, "What does *this* course have to do with anything? I'll never use it for anything!"

But perhaps T. S. Eliot was right. Perhaps being a truly educated person means knowing something about many different things, even if they don't all grab your attention at first. Two fundamental questions about college may help explain why all this is so important.

> **"No one can become really educated without having pursued some study in which he took no interest."**
>
> **T. S. Eliot, American-born poet (1888–1965)**

> **WHAT?** *What* do you study in college? English, math, physics, psychology— you can generate a long list. In fact, if you take your answer far enough, you'll eventually say—everything under the sun! Notice that the word *university* has the same origin as the word *universe*. But a convenient and meaningful way of putting it is to say that you look at things in two opposite directions. In college, you look outward, into the *natural* world; and you look inward, into the *human* world. That's the simple answer to the question, "*What* do students study in college?"

> **WHY?** *Why* do college students study the natural world and the human world? At the most idealistic and theoretical end of the scale, human beings study *to understand* things. We're a naturally curious species, and we want to know how gravity works, why there is air, why the sky is blue, why parents are so hard to reason with (at times), how Congress works (or maybe why it sometimes doesn't). But at the most practical end of the scale, we study not just to understand things but also *to control* them—to make things and people do what we want them to do. We want to "control" concrete and steel to build better bridges, to make information flow faster through computers, to erect indestructible buildings, to write more award-winning novels—maybe even to develop better, stronger, faster, healthier, smarter people. And by the way, in this discussion, the word *control* is the correct scientific term to use. It doesn't mean *manipulate* in a negative way, but rather *do something with*, *use*, or *change* as opposed to merely *understand* intellectually.

So in terms of the two questions posed, we've now constructed two scales that look like what we see in Figure 12.3.

Two Axes

René Descartes, the seventeenth-century French mathematician and philosopher, taught that if you really want to understand how two things interact, put them on perpendicular axes. When you do that, look what happens in Figure 12.4.

Activity Option Have students break into groups to answer these two key questions. As each group writes its brief response to the two questions on the board, ask students to identify themes across groups' responses.

Four Quadrants

What we've now so neatly set up are the four quadrants that identify how many colleges and universities are organized. What do we call the academic departments that try to *understand*

> the natural world? The Natural Sciences (physics, chemistry, and biology, for example)

> the human world? The Humanities (history, literature, philosophy, et cetera)

And what do we call the disciplines that help us to *control*

> the natural world? The Engineering Sciences (mechanical, electrical, computer, et cetera)

> the human world? The Social Sciences (political science, economics, communication, et cetera)

What we now see in this matrix is a representation of many, if not most, institutions of higher education (see Figure 12.5). In fact, many schools are divided into Colleges or Divisions and have area requirements or core courses from these four quadrants. Now that we've set the stage, let's keep the discussion going.

Teachable Moment This is the perfect opportunity to get students to look at the courses they are required to take. Can students tell you why they think they are required to take these?

Learning as a Child

When does your education start? At birth, really—it starts right at the center of the matrix with language and basic knowledge (see Figure 12.6) and blows up like a balloon through grade school, middle school, and high school. Your education begins with things like this.

> Language—you learn how to transfer and work with information using *natural* languages (English, Spanish, and so on) and *artificial* languages (math, for example).

> Concepts—you learn that *big* and *little* are opposite sizes, that *before* precedes *after*; and that *birds* generally have feathers and fly, for example.

> Experiences—you learn what *hot* means when you touch the stove, sense being *wet* in the bathtub, and experience what *love* feels like from your family, for example.

> Knowledge—you learn common knowledge about our society and others', rules of behavior, right from wrong, and the history and culture of our country, for example.

Learning as a New College Student

Chapter Crossover Remind students to take a look at their personality types and VARK learning preferences (Chapter 2) when they respond to questions about controlling their learning in their toughest class. Can they make the connections?

Your college or university may require general education or core courses from all four quadrants as shown in Figure 12.7. At some institutions, the course for

C **CONTROL** Your Learning

YOUR TOUGHEST CLASS

Think about your most challenging class this semester. Is it a general education course or one required for your major? If it's a general education course, make a list of all the ways this course can help you either to further your career or to become a well-educated person.

If this course is one in your major, ask yourself why the challenge is so great. Do you understand the course content? Do you keep up with readings and assignments? Can you follow your professor's teaching style? Send your instructor in this class an e-mail indicating your specific efforts to do your best and detailing your progress.

which you're using this textbook is the central or introductory course for all of the general education requirements. General education courses are about fluid knowledge, being able to shift between quadrants when you need to, critical thinking, and problem solving. In today's information-rich world, focused knowledge is critical, but it often takes crossover skills to understand highly complex problems.

Here are some other key reasons why knowing things from all four quadrants is important. Even after you graduate with a degree in the major you've chosen, your future isn't cast in concrete. Things change.[3]

> In today's high-tech world, old jobs die and are reborn as new ones. Yesterday's film developer has been replaced by today's online photo sharing websites. Each year in the United States, 30 million jobs come to an end and 15 million jobs turn into vacancies to be filled by someone else. Those who can transfer their skills because they're broadly educated will fare best.

> Because salaries are lower, companies sometimes move jobs overseas—and as one expert says, "you never know whether it will be your job, or not."[4] The best way to ensure you're employed is to have broad-based skills you can use in more than one way.

> It's estimated that approximately 45 percent of the working population in the United States would change jobs if they could. While that may sound discouraging, look at it this way: There are no perfect jobs, and your goals and values may change over time. Be educationally primed and ready for change when you want to make a move.

> When the economy is healthy, 2.4 million new jobs are born in the United States each year. Being well-educated means you're better able to snap up an opportunity as soon as it knocks.

Activity Option Ask students to place their general education courses or core requirements in the four quadrants: Natural Science, Humanities, Engineering, and Social Sciences. Discuss students' rationales for their placement decisions.

Choosing an Academic Major

On top of these basic courses to broaden your knowledge, you'll also take a concentration of courses in your academic major—say, in chemistry (see Figure 12.8). Your personal Academic Map will continue to grow outward, but with a bulge in the direction of your major. It's skewed, but it still includes all four quadrants. Your Academic Map may not look exactly like someone else's, but it represents you and your college education, and the kinds of things you need to know in order to be a well-educated person.

EXERCISE 12.1 Think Tank

Working in groups of three to five students, imagine you graduated from college or university a few years ago, and you are now all rising young managers in a large corporation. Your boss calls one morning to tell you and your colleagues that she's naming all of you to a planning team to design a new product. You'll be part of a think tank, tasked with designing one of the following three items:

1. The next generation jumbo jet—the 797—which will be marketed worldwide in competition with European, Asian, Russian, and other American aircraft

2. A revolutionary new micro cell phone, which will have some features no other cell phone has ever had before

(continued)

3. A hot new magazine for college students, which will sell on newsstands on college campuses everywhere and be available through e-subscriptions as well

Within the group, decide which of the three tasks to brainstorm. Your team is to come up with a basic concept for this new product that will win a competition as the best overall design of its class in the world.

Sketch a basic design for your product and draw the Academic Map (two axes/four quadrants) just discussed in this chapter. What various academic disciplines will your team need to draw upon as you develop your plans? If you choose task 1, for example, you'll surely need to draw from the field of aeronautical engineering—that's obvious. But what other kinds of knowledge must your think tank members bring to the table?

When all teams are ready, your instructor will ask each team to list its suggestions on an Academic Map a team member draws on the board. Try as best you can to write the disciplines in their appropriate quadrants. The point of this team exercise is to demonstrate visually the integrated nature of a truly productive education at work in the world of work.[5]

INSIGHT ⊖ ACTION

1. What "boxes" are you studying this term? Do they seem distinct or connected? Why? How?

2. Plot the college courses you've taken this term on your own Academic Map. If you had to predict the quadrant you'll emphasize (major in), which one would it be? Why?

3. Looking over possible classes to take next term, what actions will you take to fill in your Academic Map?

photolibrary.com pty. ltd/Index Open

How to Choose a Major and a Career

Like many students, you probably put value in how well college prepares you for a profession.[6] Choosing a college major and directing yourself toward a prospective career can be stressful. Many students feel pressure to make the right decision—and make it right now! You might hear conflicting advice from family members that put a high priority on financial success above other important factors, and feel overwhelmed by the number of possibilities from which to choose.[7] You may know what you want to do with the rest of your life right now, but many of your classmates don't, and even if they *say* they do, they may well change their minds several times. Yes, these decisions are important. But where do you start? The decision-making process should involve these critical steps. If you're still deciding, or even if you think you already have, consider how they apply to you.

Step 1: Follow Your Bliss

In an ideal world, which major and career would you choose? Don't think about anything except the actual content you'd be studying. Don't consider career opportunities, requirements, difficulty, or anything else that might keep you from making these choices in an ideal world. What are you passionate about? If it's skateboarding, think about which majors might apply. Majoring in physics would help you understand skateboard ascent versus decent, trajectories, spin, and angles. Majoring in landscape architecture would allow you to design skateparks. You would spend time outdoors, build computer and 3-D models of parks, and perhaps even interview other skateboarders about desirable features. Majoring in journalism would put you in a good position to write for a skateboarding magazine.

Like Ethan Cole from the "FOCUS Challenge Case," you may be wondering what to do with your life. Perhaps the *idealist* in you has one potential career in mind and the *realist* in you has another. The $300,000 salary you'd earn as a surgeon may look very compelling until you consider the years of medical school required after college, the time invested in an internship and residency, and the still further years of necessary specialization. It takes long-term diligence, commitment, dedication, and resources—yours or borrowed ones—to make that dream come true. Do these factors lessen the appeal?

Perhaps there's conflict between your *idealism* and your family's *pragmatism*. Comedian Robin Williams once said, "When I told my father I was going to be an actor, he said, 'Fine, but study welding just in case.'"

And perhaps you just don't know yet. If that's the case, don't panic. Despite the increased pressure these days to choose the right major because of rising tuition and a changeable economy, Ethan Cole is right: it's hard to have it all figured out from the start.[8] Some college students rush into something that doesn't suit them, which just increases their stress level later. Other students delay making a decision for many different reasons; they are instead waiters, wonderers, wanderers, or watchers. Many college graduates are still tweaking their plans! While you don't want to leap before you look, there's also a sense in which declaring a major can help you gain focus as you work through all your courses. That's the positive side of choosing wisely.

One thing is certain: you'll be a happier, more productive person if you do what *you* want to do *and* pursue it vigorously. When it comes to success, ability (*Can* you do it?) and effort (Are you *willing* to invest what it takes?) go hand in hand. Research shows that most first-year college students choose a major based on interest first. However, women base their decisions on aptitude second, while men are more influenced by career advancement opportunities and salary.[9]

Whatever your motivation, remember this. It's unusual for people to become truly successful halfheartedly. There are undeniable emotional and psychological components involved in success. Look at what some successful people have had to say, and note their use of emotional words such as *passion*, *love*, and *heart*:

> ➤ *God gave me a special talent to play the game…maybe he didn't give me a talent, he gave me a __passion__.* (Wayne Gretzky, called the greatest player in the history of hockey)

© Bryan Allen/CORBIS

> **"Follow your bliss and be what you want to be. Don't climb the ladder of success only to find it's leaning against the wrong wall."**
>
> **Dr. Bernie Siegel, physician and writer**

Teachable Moment A great book by Mihaly Csikszentmihalyi, *The Evolving Self: The Psychology of Optimal Experience*, stresses the importance of doing what one enjoys to experience peak flow or a psychological high.

> *To waste time doing something you don't really <u>love</u> is, to me, the ultimate waste of time.* (Peter Jennings, ABC Nightly News, 1938–2005)

> *My father always told me, "Find a job you <u>love</u> and you'll never have to work a day in your life.* (Jim Fox, former player, LA Kings, NHL Hockey)

> *I am seeking, I am striving, I am in it with all my <u>heart</u>.* (Vincent van Gogh, Dutch painter, 1853–1890)

> *When <u>love</u> and skill work together, expect a masterpiece.* (John Ruskin, Oxford University scholar and writer, 1819–1900)

> *To <u>love</u> what you do and feel that it matters—how could anything be more fun?* (Katherine Graham, publisher, *Washington Post*, 1917–2001)

> *My <u>heart</u> is in the work.* (Andrew Carnegie, American industrialist, richest man in the world in 1901)

Emotional Intelligence (EI) Research According to Stein and Book, "reality testing is the capacity to see things objectively, the way they are, rather than the way we wish or fear them to be." While it is great to have dreams, they must be grounded in reality. Reality testing is also connected to problem solving. If you have a goal and the reality of the situation indicates it is not going to happen overnight, what steps can help you realize your goal?

Having said that, what if your "bliss" just isn't feasible? You'd give anything to play for the NBA, but you're five foot two and female. You dream of being a rock star, but you can't carry a tune. Then it may be time to set aside the idealism and resurrect the realism in you. Maybe then it's time to translate—or shift—your dreams into goals.

Why do students tend to choose particular majors and careers? Research says these factors about you tend to be some of the most important:

1. **Your salary motivation.** While salary is certainly something you should be interested in, too much emphasis can force you to choose a major you're not really suited for, which can then lead you to decide college isn't for you.[10]

2. **Your brain.** Research indicates that students who are left-brained (whose left hemispheres are dominant) most often choose majors such as business, engineering, and science. Students who are right-brained choose majors such as education, nursing, communication, and law.[11]

3. **Your Mom.** While past research has focused on the effect fathers or both parents have on helping their children choose a major, recent studies show that mothers are influential, most readily through emotional channels, for example.[12]

4. **A faculty role model.** You may be attracted to a particular major because a teacher—a female, or a minority—someone like you, serves as a role model.[13]

5. **Your personality.** We'll explore this topic later in the "Your Type Is Showing" feature.

Sensitive Situation Be alert to the fact that the mothers of some students in the room may no longer be around or were never a major influence in their lives. While this research is valid, you can elaborate that in addition to mothers, there are other individuals in our lives who can influence our career paths. Ask for volunteers to tell who else in their lives influenced their decision to come to college or the career path they will take. How about you?

Teachable Moment This is a good place to ask students about what kind of courses might have helped Tony Hawk with his sports franchise?

Can Ethan translate his dreams into goals and become a professional skateboarder? Perhaps. Skateboarding's biggest champ, Tony Hawk, is reputed to earn as much as $10 million a year as a one-man sports franchise. But even he admits that advancing age and potential injuries might cause him to shift gears in the near future.[14]

How many professional skateboarders are there—especially compared to other professionals such as teachers, architects, and physicians? When the statistics are against you, achieving success isn't impossible, but it might take more than expert skill. It might also take some luck. However, Barbara Bush once wisely said, "You just don't luck into things as much as you'd like to think you do. You build step by step, whether it's friendships or opportunities."

FOCUS YOUR I'S!

The huge printing presses of a major Chicago newspaper began malfunctioning on the Saturday before Christmas, putting all the revenue for advertising that was to appear in the Sunday paper in jeopardy. None of the technicians could track down the problem. Finally, a frantic call was made to the retired printer who had worked with these presses for over forty years. "We'll pay anything; just come in and fix them," he was told.

When he arrived, he walked around for a few minutes, surveying the presses; then he approached one of the control panels and opened it. He removed a dime from his pocket, turned a screw ¼ of a turn, and said, "The presses will now work correctly." After being profusely thanked, he was told to submit a bill for his work.

The bill arrived a few days later, for $10,000.00! Not wanting to pay such a huge amount for so little work, the printer was told to please itemize his charges, with the hope that he would reduce the amount once he had to identify his services. The revised bill arrived: $1.00 for turning the screw; $9,999.00 for knowing which screw to turn. (Anonymous)

So what does it take? After forty years on the job, the retired printer knew many things, including one elusive but critical piece of knowledge—which screw to turn. But perhaps you're just starting out, and experience is something you don't have yet. Or perhaps you're an adult returning to school to boost your career or shift to a new one. No matter where you are on your journey, how will you achieve life and career success?

Some experts on growing up in our society say it's difficult to transition into adulthood. For many college students today, childhood was where they were given an abundance of opportunities: baseball, tennis, soccer, art, music, dance, travel. Their parents—with whom they have close ties—are zealous in their desire to help their children become successful. Ethan's parents, for example, solved his problems *for him,* constantly bailing him out of trouble—all with good intentions. They may have been so eager to help that they tried to motivate him with "ladder talk": "If you do well at the local campus, then you can get admitted to the big university, and if you graduate with a high grade point average there, you can get into a really good law school, and if you do well there, you'll be offered a job with a prestigious firm, and if you prove yourself to your superiors there, eventually you'll make partner." See how it goes—up the ladder of success? This type of communication, which is intended to *encourage,* can actually *discourage* a student like Ethan. Such a long chain of challenging hurdles looks like an impossible dream.

Mel Levine, author of *Ready or Not, Here Life Comes,* says, "We are in the midst of an epidemic of work-life unreadiness because an alarming number of emerging adults are unable to find a good fit between their minds and their career directions....Because they are not finding their way, they may feel as if they are going nowhere and have nowhere to go."[15]

How can anyone have nowhere to go with more than 12,000 different occupations or careers to choose from with 8,000 alternative job titles—for a total of over 20,000 options?[16] Some students, like Ethan, start college and become overwhelmed. Sometime during the first year, or possibly later, they take a step back and announce in so many words, "There are too many choices. I refuse to choose at all."[17]

Here's another tough issue many college graduates face when entering the world of work. Many of them have already categorized

work as boring because their part-time jobs in high school and college *were* boring. They don't want to climb the ladder of success. They'd like to skip the bottom and start somewhere closer to the top rung.

But every job involves some element of grunt work, even those at the top. No job is round-the-clock fun, and in every new job, eventually the honeymoon is over, and the tough challenges begin. To adjust to the day-in-and-day-out world of work, a mindset shift is required. After college, you'll launch your *career,* which is more than just a series of *jobs.* Earl Nightingale, American radio announcer, author, and speaker, once said, "The driving force of a career must come from the individual. Remember: jobs are owned by the company; you own your career!"

The simple truth is this: building a career takes time, persistence, dedication, and focus. Seemingly overnight successes like J. K. Rowling of *Harry Potter* fame are rare; steady progress toward a goal is the norm.[18] NASCAR champion Dale Earnhardt said, "You win some, you lose some, you wreck some." His point was that in life you'll make some right turns, some wrong turns, and maybe even some U-turns. But fear or indecision shouldn't immobilize you. Keep driving!

So what does it take to launch your career successfully? You'll need to focus your I's on four things: **I**nner direction, **I**nterpretation, **I**nstrumentation, and **I**nteraction—the four I's of career-life readiness. Here's what they mean.[19]

Inner direction. You've lived with yourself for some time now, but how well do you know yourself? How accurate is your view of yourself? Can you honestly and accurately appraise your potential? Do you know where are you headed and why? Are you well suited for your major and career destinations? You must first understand the inner you before you can direct it toward a career that fits.

Interpretation. Memorization isn't the most important skill you'll need in most careers. But many students have memorized their way through countless classes, becoming very good at it, but often not fully understanding what they're learning. Somehow they get by, but they miss the *larger principles* beneath the *specific facts* they've memorized. On the job there's more required than repeating back what the boss has told you. You must interpret the information and apply it in your own way, which will demonstrate whether you do (or don't) understand what you're doing.

Instrumentation. In your career, you'll need a toolkit filled with an array of abilities—engaging in high-level thinking, brainstorming, problem solving, making decisions, tapping your creativity, and cultivating both hard (technical) and soft (interpersonal) skills. And not only must you know *how* to use each of these tools, but you'll need to know *when* and *why.*

Interaction. Lee Iacocca, former CEO of Chrysler, once said, "You can have brilliant ideas, but if you can't get them across, your brains won't get you anywhere." Business (or any profession) isn't just about facts and figures. It's about people, sensitivities, values, and relationships—not products, not machines, not words in a report. While these things are important, too, chances are that people will be what help you build your career. Without people to buy, sell, trade, consume, or produce, there is no business.

These four I's are keys to your future. The more you focus your I's, the better prepared you'll be for the challenges ahead. The German poet and dramatist Johann Wolfgang von Goethe (1749–1832) wrote these words—true then and true today: *Whatever you do or dream, you can begin it. Boldness has genius, power and magic in it. Begin it now.*

Teachable Moment What do students think about the printing press anecdote? Was the repair the retired printer made worth $10,000? Why or why not?

Activity Option Ask students to interview a person who is very successful in a career. What does the person do, what specific jobs has the person held previously, and for how long? Students can do this as an outside assignment and bring their findings to class. Were there many instant success stories? Probably not.

Emotional Intelligence (EI) Research Inner direction is closely connected to the EI skill of intrapersonal capacity. According to Bar-On and Handley, "this conceptual component of emotional, personal and social intelligence is associated with fenreal [sic] feelings of security, inner strength, self-assuredness, self-confidence, and feelings of self-adequacy." Without high regard for self, one can never achieve what is possible.

> **"The privilege of a lifetime is being who you are."**
>
> Joseph Campbell, American professor and writer (1904–1987)

Activity Option The ten questions here can be turned into a project. First, find out which majors most students are interested in. Group students together and have each group interview for one major. Make sure that all majors of interest in the class are covered. In the same groups, have students develop a fact sheet about the major to be presented in class and distributed to all students.

Step 2: Conduct Preliminary Research

Has it ever occurred to you that you may not have all the facts—accurate ones—about your ideal major? Do you know what it *really* takes? Have you gotten your information from qualified sources—or are you basing your opinion on your roommate's reaction to one course he took in the major or on the campus grapevine?

Try an experiment. Choose three majors you're considering, one of which is your ideal major, and send yourself on a fact-finding mission. To find out if you're on target, obtain the answers to the following ten questions for each of the three possibilities. Go to the physical location (department) where each major is housed, and interview a professor. The experiment requires legwork; don't just let your fingers do the clicking.

1. What is the major?
2. Who is the interviewee?
3. What is the name of the academic department where this major is housed? Where are the department offices physically located on campus?
4. Which introductory courses in this major would inform you about your interests and abilities?
5. Which upper-level courses in this major interest you? (List three.)
6. What are the department's entry requirements to become a major?
7. How many students major in this discipline on your campus?
8. Which required course in the major do students usually find most challenging? Which is most engaging? Which is most valued? Why?
9. How would the interviewee describe the reputation of this department on campus? What is it known for?
10. From the interviewee's perspective, why should a student major in this discipline?

After you complete your interviews, review the facts. Did you change any of your opinions, based on what you learned?[20]

Step 3: Take a Good Look at Yourself

CHALLENGE ➔ REACTION

Challenge: Take a good look at yourself and answer the following questions about how you prefer to work.

Reaction: Rank each item 1 or 2 based on your general preference. While many careers, if not most, require both, your task is to decide which of the two you prefer.

I prefer to work at a job:

1. Alone	_____	With other people	_____
2. Indoors	_____	Outdoors	_____
3. With people	_____	With equipment or materials	_____

4. Directing/leading others _____	Being directed/led by others _____	
5. Producing information _____	Managing information _____	
6. In an organized, step-by-step way _____	In a big-idea, holistic way _____	
7. Starting things _____	Completing things _____	
8. Involving a product _____	Involving a service _____	
9. Solving challenging problems _____	Generating creative ideas _____	
10. Finding information _____	Applying information _____	
11. Teaching/training others in groups _____	Advising/coaching others one-on-one _____	

Now look at your eleven first choices. Identify several career fields that come to mind that would allow you to achieve as many of them as possible.

Activity Option After students complete the "Challenge → Reaction" activity, ask them to fill in the blanks in the following sentence and bring it to the next class: *Based on what I discovered about myself in doing this activity, three career choices for me are _____, _____, and _____, because _____.*

Here's a bottom-line question: For you—as Dr. Bernie Siegel would say—what *is* the "right wall" to lean your ladder of success on? How do you know? Many first-year college students don't know. They don't have enough experience under their belts to plan for a lifetime. They're in college to *discover*. It all comes down to questions this book has been asking you all along: Who are you? And what do you want? If you're unsure of how to proceed in your decision making, follow these recommendations to see if they help you bring your future into focus.

Send in the SWOT Team!

A SWOT analysis is an excellent way to begin taking a good look at yourself in relation to your future. SWOT stands for Strengths, Weaknesses, Opportunities, and Threats. SWOT analyses are typically used in business, but creating one for yourself may be useful when it comes to deciding on a college major and a career.

Earlier this chapter asked you to build a personal Academic Map. Your SWOT analysis can borrow this format to help you create a potential career profile. Make a matrix with four quadrants, label each one, and fill them in as objectively as you can.

> **Strengths** are traits that give you a leg up. These are talents you can capitalize on and qualities you can develop.

> **Weaknesses** are traits that currently work against you. You can, however, work to reduce or eliminate them.

> **Opportunities** are conditions or circumstances that work in your favor, like a strong forecast for your prospective career's future.

> **Threats** are conditions that could have adverse effects. Some of these factors are beyond your control; however, sometimes you can successfully lessen their potential effects.

"Are you fit company for the person you wish to become?"

Anonymous

As you create the matrix, just as we did when building your Academic Map, begin with two basic questions:

What kinds of forces will impact your potential career?

Internal—forces inside you, such as motivation and skill

External—forces outside you that may affect your success: the job market or economy, for example

What kind of influence can these forces exert?

Positive—some forces will give you a boost toward your goals

Negative—other forces will work against you[21]

Let's complete a SWOT analysis for Ethan and his dream of becoming a professional skateboarder. Of course, you might say that, technically, he doesn't need an academic degree for that particular career. But if he wants to pursue related, more traditional careers—design a new skatepark or write for a skateboard magazine, for example—he would need an array of knowledge and enhanced skills from writing and design to finance and marketing. Besides, college isn't just about jobs, it's about living a fuller life as a well-educated person.

Look back at the "FOCUS Challenge Case," and see if you agree with the basic SWOT analysis shown in Figure 12.9.

Looking at his SWOT analysis, what would you conclude? Is professional skateboarding a good career option for him? In your view, do the opportunities outweigh the threats? For example, does the potential earning power of a professional skateboarder outweigh the risks associated with possible incapacitating injuries? Do his well-cultivated athletic skills compensate for his lack of discipline in other areas? If not, might he gravitate toward other potential careers, perhaps those that also involve skateboarding? "Ethan remembered liking geometry, he was good at creative writing, he played the drums like a real

Figure 12.9
SWOT Analysis

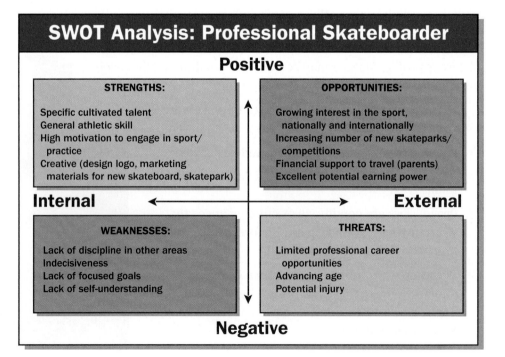

SWOT Analysis: Professional Skateboarder

Positive

STRENGTHS:

Specific cultivated talent
General athletic skill
High motivation to engage in sport/ practice
Creative (design logo, marketing materials for new skateboard, skatepark)

OPPORTUNITIES:

Growing interest in the sport, nationally and internationally
Increasing number of new skateparks/ competitions
Financial support to travel (parents)
Excellent potential earning power

Internal ←——————→ **External**

WEAKNESSES:

Lack of discipline in other areas
Indecisiveness
Lack of focused goals
Lack of self-understanding

THREATS:

Limited professional career opportunities
Advancing age
Potential injury

Negative

jazz musician, and he was an incredible artist." Do you see potential majors for him in college? Sports management? Kinesiology? Architecture? Journalism? Jazz studies? Creative writing? What should Ethan do?

Teachable Moment Get the class involved in a discussion about what Ethan should do. Is there anything else about Ethan they would like to know before they would make their recommendations? If so, what and why?

EXERCISE 12.2 Group Résumé

Your instructor will provide a sheet of newsprint and several markers per team of three to four students. Your job is to work on the floor, desktops, or somewhere with sufficient space to create a group résumé, highlighting the characteristics you bring with you that can help you succeed in college. Your collective qualifications may look like this:

Qualifications:

- · 16 combined years of high school success
- · average incoming GPA of 3.4
- · familiarity with Word, PowerPoint, Photoshop, and Excel
- · Internet savvy with specialization in academic resources
- · eager to learn
- · well-developed time management skills
- · interest in co-curricular activities

After each team has completed the task, hang the newsprint sheets on the walls to create a gallery and present your résumé to the rest of the class.[22]

> **"When I paint, the sea roars. The others splash about in the bath."**
>
> **Salvador Dalí, artist (1904–1989)**

Teachable Moment Encourage each student to go the campus career center to find out if there are any résumé writing workshops or samples résumés to compile. Also, encourage students to look online for résumé templates and bring at least one example to share with the class.

SCAN Your Skills

In 1990, the U.S. Secretary of Labor appointed a group called the Secretary's Commission on Achieving Necessary Skills (SCANS) to determine the skills young people need to succeed in the work world. The Commission worked long and hard to consider what highly skilled workers need in terms of reading, writing, thinking, computing, and interpersonal skills. Here's their list. As you look it over, assess your work-readiness in each area. In the blank that follows each item, decide whether you'd rate yourself as 1 (making good progress) or 2 (need further development).[23]

Basic Skills

➤ *Reading*—can find and understand written information in books, articles, reports, manuals, graphs, and schedules _____

➤ *Writing*—can communicate thoughts and ideas in writing in letters, directions, manuals, reports, graphs, and flow charts _____

➤ *Arithmetic*—can do basic math and decide on an appropriate tool from a variety of mathematical techniques _____

➤ *Listening*—can receive, understand, and respond to verbal messages _____

➤ *Speaking*—can communicate clearly in an organized fashion _____

Thinking Skills

➤ *Creative thinking*—can generate new ideas _____

➤ *Decision making*—can generate alternatives, consider risks, and choose the best solution _____

> *Problem solving*—can recognize problems, figure out solutions, and implement them _____

> *Visualizing*—can understand symbols, pictures, and graphs _____

> *Learning to learn*—can understand the learning process and how to learn in new situations _____

> *Reasoning*—can find a connection between two or more things and use it to solve a problem _____

Personal Qualities

> *Responsibility*—works diligently and pursues goals _____

> *Self-esteem*—believes in self-worth and has a healthy self-image _____

> *Sociability*—is friendly, adaptable, and tries to understand other's problems _____

> *Self-management*—uses self-control and self-discipline and sets personal goals _____

> *Integrity/honesty*—is honest and ethical in daily dealings with others _____

Resource Management

> *Time*—prioritizes, follows schedules, and manages time well _____

> *Money*—manages financial resources well _____

> *Material and facilities*—uses space and materials efficiently _____

> *Human resources*—works well with others in distributing work, evaluating others' performance, and giving feedback _____

Interpersonal

> *Participates as member of a team*—contributes to a team effort _____

> *Teaches others new skills*—can coach or train colleagues _____

> *Serves clients/customers*—works to meet customers' needs _____

> *Exercises leadership*—can align others and get them onboard _____

> *Negotiates*—helps others work through conflicts _____

> *Works with diversity*—works well with others from diverse backgrounds _____

Information

> *Acquires and evaluates information* _____

> *Organizes and maintains information* _____

> *Interprets and communicates information* _____

> *Uses computers to process information* _____

Systems

> *Understands systems*—works well within the people, structural, and technology systems within an organization _____

> *Monitors and corrects performance*—watches for trends *within* systems and works to correct any trends that are problems _____

> *Improves or designs systems*—thinks of ways to improve systems or develop new ones _____

Technology

> *Selects technology*—chooses the right tool for the right job _____

> *Applies technology to task*—understands what technology can do and how to make it work _____

> *Maintains and troubleshoots equipment*—tries to prevent equipment problems and solves problems when they occur _____

SCANS are broad and comprehensive. As a first-year college student, you wouldn't be expected to have them all mastered now. But notice that even though *FOCUS* isn't just about getting ready for the world of work, many of these skills are addressed throughout the book to help you get ready for your career—and hit the ground running. The skills you need for college and career success are more similar than you might imagine![24]

Chapter Crossover Assign pairs of students the categories listed (basic, thinking, personal, resource management, interpersonal, information, systems, and technology). Give them five minutes to find which chapters in this book address each topic.

Box 12.1 Five Ways to Open the Door (or Close It) during an Interview

By the time you graduate from college, you will have been interviewed many times to get a new job or to be admitted to graduate school, for example. And after you graduate, you'll go through a series of interviews on the path to the dream job you really want.

Often interviewers aren't particularly skilled at asking questions. They haven't been trained on how to interview prospective employees, so they just ask whatever questions come to them. And often, interviewees don't quite know what they're doing either.

Of course, you should always be honest, but there are various ways to communicate the same information. Telling an interviewer you "like to work alone" sounds antisocial. But if you say you "like to really focus on what you're doing without distractions," you've shown dedication to your work ethic. You also need to be aware of real pitfalls to avoid. See what you think of these suggestions.

1. **"You've got to ac-centuate the positive; e-liminate the negative."** To resurrect an old Bing Crosby song here, remember this piece of obvious advice. A trap question interviewers sometimes ask is, "What's your worst fault?" While you may be tempted to say the first thing that comes to mind, that could be a big mistake. "Umm…sleeping too much! I really like to sleep in. Sometimes I sleep half the day away." Not good. But some faults you could identify might actually be construed as strengths: "I have a little too much nervous energy. I'm always on the go. I like to stay busy."

2. **Stay focused.** "Tell me about yourself" is a common question interviewers ask. How much time do you have? Most of us like to talk about ourselves, but it's important to stay on track. Think possible questions

through in advance, and construct some hypothetical answers. When we're put on the spot, we can get tongue-tied. Keep your answers job-focused: what you liked about your last job, why you liked those aspects of it, what your long-term career goals are, and how this job can help you prepare. You don't need to go into your family background or your personal problems. And it's always a bad idea to bash a previous job or former boss. The interviewer may worry that you'll bring whatever didn't work there with you to this new job.

3. **Don't just give answers, get some.** A job interview is like a first date. Find out what you need to know. If the job is one you're interested in long-term, ask questions such as these three key ones:

   · **What does this company value?** Listen to the answer. Hard work? Achievement? Innovation? Communication skills? Doing things by the book? The answer will tell you about the personality of the company.

   · **What's a typical day like for *you*?** Ask the interviewer. An answer such as "I get up at 5:00 a.m., get here at 6:30 a.m., and go home around 7:00 p.m.— and then I do paperwork all evening" tells you something. This may—or may not—be the job or the company for you.

   · **What happened to the last person in this job?** If you find out he was promoted, that's one thing. But if you learn he was fired or quit, see if you can find out why. Maybe he had job performance problems, or maybe this is an impossible job that no one could do well.

(continued)

Remember, too, that interviews are conversations with give and take, not just one person doing all the giving and the other doing all the taking. Listen to the interviewer. She may be looking for an opportunity to tell you things she thinks are important, too.

4. **Watch for questions out of left field.** Some companies like to get creative with their interviewing. Microsoft, for example, is known for asking problem-solving questions, such as "If you could remove any of the fifty states, which would it be? Be prepared to give specific reasons why you chose the state you did." There is no right or wrong answer, although some answers are better than others. ("We should just nuke state X. I had a bad experience there once" would probably furrow some brows, and naming Washington state, where Microsoft is located, might be an inadvisable choice.) The interviewer just wants to hear how you think. Well-received answers "talk" an interviewer through underlying reasoning and present additional questions posed by the hypothetical situation.[25] Beware the interviewer with off-the-wall techniques: "I know most interviewers ask questions, but I don't. I consider the interview to be a time for *you* to ask *me* questions. What questions about this job or this company do you have?" "Uh ..." isn't an impressive answer. Read up on what to expect and good ways to respond before the big day. Remember: Today's interviewers are looking for more than technical skills; they're looking for critical thinking skills, problem-solving skills, and creativity.[26]

5. **Don't start off with salary questions.** Make sure the first question out of your mouth isn't, "So tell me about the salary, again? Any way to notch that up a bit?" The last thing you want to do is give the interviewer the idea you're just in it for the money. Of course, you are, but not just for that. More importantly, in every job you have, you'll gain experience and knowledge that will always better prepare you for the *next* job to come.

FOCUS ON CAREERS: TANYA SEXTON, Associate Partner, Lucas Group Consulting Firm

Courtesy of Tanya Sexton

Q1: What was your major in college? How does it relate to your current career field? How did you get from your college degree to where you are today?

I was an accounting major in college, and now I am a recruiter with a specialty in the accounting and finance fields, so it's a perfect fit. As a former accountant, I am able to earn credibility quickly with my hiring authorities and job candidates. I understand the responsibilities of the positions, structure of departments, and complexities of the profession. I started my career as a staff accountant for a local men's retailer in Chicago, became the Accounting Manager for a widely known Chicago-based service company, and eventually moved into a hybrid accounting/operations position that required me to travel. When I began traveling to where I work now, which was part of my territory, I knew that's where I belonged. And when I began a new job as a recruiter in 1999, I knew this was the career field for me. The rest is history.

Q2: What were the most important things you learned in college?

I think college provides critical broad-based skills. Learning about who I was as a person and what counts in life were important lessons. Time management was a very important piece. I worked at a job all through college, and managing a job along with my coursework is something that has benefited me to this day. I learned to be resourceful because I didn't have very much money, so I learned to budget. I met regularly with my professors and that prepared me to deal with authority figures. Of all the skills I gained, I think the interpersonal communication skills have been the most critical.

Q3: What do you and your colleagues do on a day-to-day basis?

Honestly, every day is different. We continually recruit talent and market the talent to hiring authorities. We spend lots of time on the telephone, screening candidates, matching them to the right jobs, presenting them to clients, briefing and debriefing them for interviews, and negotiating job offers.

Q4: What are employers looking for in the best college graduates today?

Employers look for a myriad of things. Internships add marketability to a college degree. Employers look at grade point averages overall and in graduates' majors. They look for strong verbal, written, and interpersonal communication skills. More and more, we hear that you can teach responsibilities of the job on the job, but the "soft skills," the "people skills," are not easily taught.

Q5: Outside of specific coursework, what should students be learning informally in college to help them succeed professionally?

Time management, conflict management, and stress management skills would be my top three. Students should remember, too, that they can

Test Your Strengths and Interests

If you're not sure which majors or careers might be good ones for you, consider using an assessment instrument to find out. Many such tools are available through your school's Counseling or Career Center, perhaps through your instructor for this course, or through particular career assessment workshops. These assessment tools don't focus on one specific job, but instead they give you general information about which types of work might fit you. And remember that's what you're looking for—general information, hints, suggestions, clues, something to go on. It's also a good idea to try more than one assessment tool. That way you can look for overlap—one test reinforcing the results of another. For the most part, standardized, published, paper-and-pencil assessments such as the Myers-Briggs Type Inventory and the Strong Interest Inventory are most reliable, but others, including popular online tests, can give you some helpful guidance as well. Here are several assessment tools that you may want to try that are available online. Some charge a fee to obtain your results; others are free.

> Livecareer's Free Career Test
> Career Planning Test
> The Career Key
> The Career Interests Game
> John Holland's Self-Directed Search
> The Princeton Review Career Quiz
> Analyze My Career

Activity Option Assign students a real or fictitious possible job opportunity (perhaps on campus or in the surrounding area) to research, and ask them to come to class prepared for a mock interview. Time permitting, let as many students participate in the mock interview as possible. The rest of the class should decide who they would hire and why.

Teachable Moment Find out ahead of time (or ask students to research) the tools available on your campus and whether there's an associated cost to use them.

Teachable Moment Pose the following questions to your students: Is a recruiter a good career choice for everyone? Why or why not?

C CREATE a Career Outlook

RECRUITER

Have you ever considered a career as a recruiter, placement, or employment specialist? Here are some facts about this career to consider and some questions about yourself to ponder.

Facts to Consider

Academic preparation required: A college degree in business, human resources, management, or communication would be good preparation.

Future workforce demand: Competition may be stiff because of plentiful numbers of qualified college graduates.

Work environment: Recruiters can either work inside a specific company's human resources department in its personnel office, or as a third-party agent, possibly within a consulting firm, that helps individual organizations find the best candidates for particular types of positions.

Most common psychological type preferences: extraverted (or to a lesser extent, introverted), intuitive or sensing, thinking, perceiving (or judging). The most common types are ENTP, ESTJ, ENJT and INTJ.[27]

Essential skills: interviewing, speaking, writing, decision-making, and technology skills (using the Internet for job searches, etc.)

Questions to Ponder

1. Do you have (or could you acquire) the skills this career requires?
2. What would you find most satisfying about this type of career?
3. What would you find most challenging about this type of career?
4. Are you interested in a career like this? Why or why not?

For more information, see U.S. Department of Labor, Bureau of Labor Statistics, *Occupational Outlook Handbook, 2006–2007 Edition.*[28]

For more career activities online, go to http://www.academic.cengage.com/collegesuccess/staley to do the Team Career exercises.

gain important skills from short-term, part-time jobs they hold while working their way through college. Being able to provide examples to a potential employer of how they were able to graduate with good grades while successfully holding down a job will go a long way. And recognition from past employers communicates a great deal to a potential new employer.

Q6: If employers were asked to identify which skills are in need of further development in today's college graduates, which skills would those be?
Work ethic. Employers say more recent graduates sometimes expect to automatically progress through the ranks without necessarily putting in the time to "earn their stripes."

Q7: You have devoted your career to helping employees find the right jobs and helping organizations find the right employees. Why do you consider these services to be so important?
Having the "right" team in place creates an environment in which employees are willing to give more of themselves to create a better organization, and they in turn are recognized and rewarded for what they do. Recruiters like me increase the chances that companies *will* have the right team in place. You might say I'm a "fitness expert"!

Step 4: Consider Your Major versus Your Career

CHALLENGE ⊖ REACTION

Challenge: What is the relationship between choosing a major and choosing a career?

Reaction: _____

Which comes first, the chicken or the egg? The major or the career? Silly question? The obvious answer, of course, is that you must first major in something in college before you can build a career on it. But the question isn't as straightforward as it seems.

Should you choose a major based on an intended career? Perhaps you know you want to be a science teacher, first and foremost. You don't know whether to major in one of the sciences or in education. You like all sciences, but teaching is your real interest. If you major in science, which one should it be (see Figure 12.10)?

Or instead, should you choose a major first, and then decide on a career? Say you made a firm decision to major in chemistry when your favorite science teacher did "mad scientist" experiments for the class in eighth grade. But at this point, you're not certain of the professional direction you'd like to pursue. Chemistry is your passion, but should you apply your chemistry degree as a forensic scientist, a physician, a researcher, or a teacher (see Figure 12.11)?

A few schools don't actually use the word *major*, preferring the term *concentration*, and some schools encourage *interdisciplinary studies*, a tailor-made system in which you create your own major with guidance from advisors and faculty. Other schools may even encourage double majors, which

Figure 12.10

Which Science Should a Science Teacher Major In?

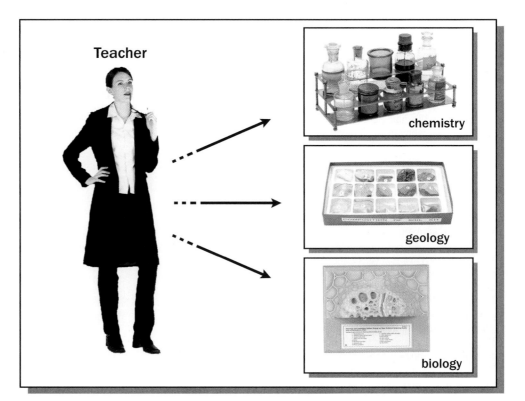

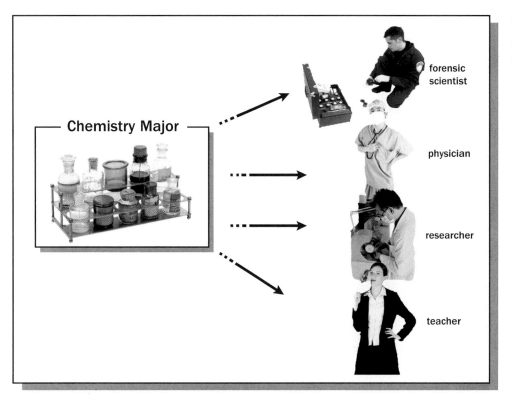

Figure 12.11

Which Career Should a Chemistry Major Choose?

Chemistry Major

forensic scientist

physician

researcher

teacher

can make sense, particularly some combinations (international business and Chinese language, for example). But by and large, the concept of having a major (and sometimes a minor) in college is the norm.

So which comes first—major or career? It depends.[29] The answer sounds ambivalent, and it's meant to. Although some professional degree programs put you into a particular track right away (nursing or engineering, for example), generally either direction can work well. Doors will open and close for you, and as you gain more knowledge and experience, you'll narrow your focus. As you learn more about your chosen major, you'll also learn about its specific career tracks. But it's important to remember that a major doesn't have to lock you into one specific career. And you can always narrow or refocus your area of emphasis in graduate school after you earn your undergraduate degree.[30]

What's Your Academic Anatomy?

Thinking about your academic anatomy is a simple way to begin to get a handle on what you find fulfilling. If you had to rank order the four parts of you listed in Figure 12.12, what would you put in first place? Second, third, and last? To get yourself thinking, ask these questions:

1. Do you find fulfillment by using your *head*? Do you enjoy solving complex problems or thinking through difficult situations? Do you like to reason things out, weigh evidence, and think critically? A philosophy major who continues on to a career in law might be what students with this preference choose, for example.

2. Do you find it satisfying to work with matters of the *heart*? Are you the kind of person others come to with problems because you listen and care? Does trying to make others happy make you happy? A psychology major who pursues a counseling career might be what students with this preference choose, for example.

Chapter Crossover Ask students to respond to Figure 12.12 by profiling their own academic anatomies. Then tie their responses back to their VARK and SuccessTypes. Is there a correlation? Are kinesthetic learners more likely to choose their hands or whole bodies? Are feelers more likely to choose their hearts, for example?

Figure 12.12

What's Your Academic Anatomy?

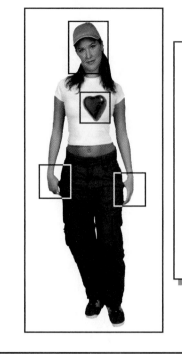

Another way of analyzing your preferences is by considering your "Academic Anatomy." What do you find most satisfying? Working with your

Head?
Heart?
Hands? or
Whole Body?

Sensitive Situation Sometimes people stereotypically think that jobs that use the hands (manual labor) are not as academic as others. You might point out that jobs that require this kind of labor, a plumber, for example, require high-level skills in other areas such as problem solving, interpersonal, and business skills, especially if plumbers are in business for themselves.

3. Do you like to create things with your *hands*? Do you enjoy making art? Doing hands-on projects? Building things out of other things? An architecture major who designs and builds models might be what students with this preference choose, for example.

4. Do you excel at physical activities that involve your *whole body*? Are you athletic? Do you like to stay active, no matter what you're doing? A physical therapy major who goes on to work in a rehabilitation facility helping stroke victims relearn to walk might be what students with this preference choose, for example.

Now look at your academic anatomy rankings. Of course, the truth is that "all of you" is involved in everything you do. And achieving balance is important. But what are your priorities? This type of simple analysis can be one way of informing you about who you are and where you should be headed.

However, no system for choosing a major is perfect. In fact, most are imperfect at best. Here are four things to consider.

1. Sometimes students who don't select a likely major based on their "anatomical preferences" can still be successful. A whole-body person (like Ethan Cole probably is) may decide to major in art (using his hands). But he'll have to find other ways to meet his whole-body needs unless he becomes a sculptor involved in creating large constructed projects.

2. You may intentionally choose an unlikely major. Perhaps art (using your hands) comes so naturally to you that you decide to major in astrophysics (using your head). You need the challenge to stay fully involved in getting your education. While it may sound unlikely, it's been known to happen.

3. You may choose an unlikely major because one particular course turns you on. You had no idea majoring in this subject was even possible, and you didn't know what it entailed. But you find studying it fascinating—so you shift gears to focus all your attention on it.

4. You may be equally engaged, no matter what. You love subjects that require using your head, hands, heart, and whole body. The anatomy of learning is less important to you than other factors—a teacher whose enthusiasm is contagious, for example.[31]

Ethan's rankings would probably go something like this: (1) whole body, (2) hands, (3) heart, and (4) head. And just because "head" is in last place for him doesn't mean he's doomed in college. A career as a financial analyst sitting behind a desk probably wouldn't be his cup of tea, for example. But it may well be yours. Whatever major and career he's thinking about—or you do—you may want to consider whether it's "anatomically correct."

INSIGHT ⟶ ACTION

1. Do a SWOT analysis on yourself. Describe your strengths, weaknesses, opportunities, and threats as they relate to a particular major you may be interested in. Describe the insights you gain from the process.

2. Assess your SCANS skills. Which areas are particular strengths of yours and which seem most challenging?

3. Have you taken a formal career strength or interest test? If not, locate one online, take it, and discuss the results.

4. Describe your academic anatomy. Is this something you've thought about before? What majors and careers might be "anatomically correct" for you?

Activity Option This is a great opportunity to have students first think about these questions, and then compare their responses with a partner's. Students can report back to the entire class on their answer to question 4.

EXERCISE 12.3 Get a Job!

Bring an employment ad from a newspaper or Internet website to class, perhaps for a job that's related to your prospective career. After carefully considering your individual ads in small groups of three or four, create an employment ad for the "job" of college student. For example, "_____ College/University seeks applicants with excellent skills in oral and written communication, problem solving, time management, and technology for positions as professional students preparing for a variety of future opportunities…." Your ad should list particular job requirements, benefits, information about your institution, and so on, and be as much like a real ad as possible. When your group is finished constructing its ad, present it to the entire class.[32]

How to Launch a Career

CHALLENGE ⟶ REACTION

Challenge: Assume you have $100,000 to spend on the following items. In a few minutes, your instructor will begin a real-live auction, putting one item at a time up for auction.

Reaction: Before the auction begins, budget your money in the first column. You may select as many items as you wish to bid on, but you may *not* place all your money on any single item. As the group auction proceeds, fill in the appropriate amounts that are actually spent by members of the class for each item.

(continued)

	BUDGETED AMOUNT	WINNING BID
1. Becoming the CEO of a leading Fortune 500 company	————	————
2. Being a top earner in your career field	————	————
3. Being the number one expert in your profession	————	————
4. Having good friends on the job	————	————
5. Being your own boss	————	————
6. Creating a good balance between productive work and a happy family life	————	————
7. Having opportunities for travel and adventure in your job	————	————
8. Doing work you find fully satisfying	————	————
9. Working in a beautiful setting	————	————
10. Being a lifelong learner so that your career can develop and change over time	————	————

Teachable Moment This is a great opportunity to generate a discussion about the "Challenge → Reaction" under "Step Three: Take a Good Look at Yourself." Did students' highest bids match their career preferences there? Are there differences between men and women? Do students vary based on their personality types or learning modalities?

Emotional Intelligence (EI) Research If the quality of one's relationship with his or her boss is the most important item connected to job satisfaction, then the ability to develop strong emotional intelligence for the workplace is critical. Bar-On and Handley report that the most important skills in coping with occupational stress are effective self-regard, assertiveness, self-actualization, problem solving, stress tolerance, and optimism.

After you graduate from college, it'll be time to launch your career, right? What do you really want from a career? What's important to you? Even though your views may change over time, it's important to start thinking about them now. Item 7, "Having opportunities for travel and adventure in your job," may be a top priority now, but item 6, "Creating a good balance between productive work and a happy family life," may be more appealing a few years down the road if you have several young children to parent.

Interestingly, according to research, the most important factor in job satisfaction isn't any of these ten items. The number one contributor to job satisfaction, statistically speaking, is the quality of your relationship with your boss.[33]

If all your jobs thus far have been just that—*jobs*—to help you pay the bills, how do you know what you want in a *career*? Your career is something you

© Jose Luis Pelaez, Inc./CORBIS

"You can be just like me. Don't just pussy foot around and sit on your assets. Unleash your ferocity upon an unsuspecting world."

Bette Midler, singer

haven't launched yet. Exactly how do you do that? You have to start somewhere, so perhaps you'd go online or open the want ads. You'd be likely to read this: *"Opening in…(anything). Experience required."* Isn't that the way it always goes? You have to *have* experience in order to get a job that will *give* you experience. So how do you launch a career?

This problem is one many college graduates face. Sure, they have experience. It's just not the right kind. They've bagged fries, mowed yards, bussed tables, and chauffeured pizzas to help pay for college expenses. If that's not the kind of experience the posted opening is looking for, how do you get the right kind? Try a job on for size.

> **Internships:** One way to gain experience is by trying things out. An internship, for example, is an opportunity for you to work alongside a professional in a career field of interest to you, and to learn from him or her. Your supervisor will mentor you, and you'll get a clearer picture of what the career field is like.

> **A Co-op Program:** Some schools have co-op programs that allow you to take classes and then apply what you've learned on the job, either alternatively or concurrently. You may take classes for a term and then work full-time for a term. A potential employer can get a sense of your potential, and you can gain practical experience.

> **Service-Learning:** An experience in which you volunteer your time, but not just as community "charity work," or classes with a service-learning component built right into the syllabus can give you valuable, practical experience. In these situations, your goal is to connect what you learn in your service work with what you're learning in class. The emphasis is on hands-on learning.

These experiences help you in two ways. First, they allow you to test a potential career field. The actual day-to-day work may be exactly what you expected, or not. They show you whether or not that particular career field is one you'd really be interested in. *I had no idea this field was so cutthroat, hectic, dull…exciting, stimulating, invigorating….* A thumbs-down can be just as informative as a thumbs-up. At least you can eliminate one option from your list. Second, internships, co-ops, and service-learning opportunities give you experience to list on your résumé. That's invaluable!

Sometimes internships are offered through your academic major department, or through a central office on campus, or sometimes you can pursue one on your own through the Internet or personal connections. If you want to major in journalism, for example, you might try contacting your local newspaper, a business magazine that focuses on your city, or some other published outlet to find out if they're willing to sponsor you. *I'm a journalism major at X university, and I'm looking for an internship opportunity. I'm particularly interested in working at the* Daily Planet, *especially on the Education Beat, because I'm trying to learn more about this city and its school system.* If you receive pay, it may be a modest amount. You're in a learning mode, and you don't have experience, after all. If you land the internship through your school, you may receive course credit instead of pay.

Teachable Moment Ask students if they know whether or not the major they are thinking of requires either an internship or service-learning that could help them gain helpful insights. If not, encourage students to consider doing this for real-life experience and application of their in-class learning.

Box 12.2 A Model Résumé

In today's competitive world, when literally hundreds of people may be applying for one choice position, how should a résumé be written? Can a résumé be appealing, but not flashy? Solid, but not stuffy? Professional, but still personal? Thorough, but brief? Take a look at Jennifer's and see what you think.

> This résumé uses a skills approach, rather than a chronological approach. A chronological approach works best if you have a career underway and can list various relevant positions that prepared you for this one.

JENNIFER DANIELS

> Center your name, and use a standard résumé format. Many companies now scan résumés so that they can be read conveniently from one source. Skip the neon pink paper. Go for a highly professional look.

Current Address
Evelyn Edwin Living-Learning Center
Rocky Mountain State University
Great Bluffs, CO 89898
(100) 555-6543 or jdaniels@rmsu.edu

Permanent Address:
1234 Aspen Way
Vail, CO 81657
(101) 555-9128

> Provide both your temporary address, if you're attending college away from home, and your actual home address. The employer may save your résumé and call you later, over the summer for example, if the current opening is filled by someone else.

CAREER OBJECTIVE

> Build your career objective according to the position's advertised needs. "One size fits all" doesn't work when it comes to résumés.

To obtain a position as a communications specialist in a large company, designing web pages, creating internal e-newsletters, and planning corporate events.

EDUCATION

> Provide numbers whenever you can. Text can be glossed over, but numbers stand out and make your accomplishments more quantifiable.

Rocky Mountain State University, Great Bluffs, CO
Bachelor of Arts, Communication Major, 2008 (Minor: Spanish)
GPA 3.6/4.0
Personally financed 80% of college tuition through employment and athletic scholarship

HONORS
Secretary, RMSU Freshman Honor Society
Vail "Invest in the Future" League Soccer Scholarship (4 years, chosen from 150 applicants)

SUMMARY OF BEST ACADEMIC COURSEWORK

> Select coursework that applies directly to the advertised position.

Organizational Communication   Advanced Composition
Business and Professional Communication   Emerging Technologies
Principles of Web Design   Event Planning

SKILLS
Technology
Part-time work, web-page design

> Technology is important in today's workplace. Don't underrate your competence. Many senior employees don't know as much as you do!

Proficient in Word, PowerPoint, Excel, Access, Macromedia Flash, Adobe Acrobat, and Photoshop
Event Planning
RMSU Freshman Honor Society, planned campus ceremonies for 1,000 guests (2 years)
Student Government, Campus Life Committee Chair (1 year)
Soccer Fundraising Events, Planning Committee Chair (3 years)
Writing
1st place winner, campus creative writing competition, 2007

EMPLOYMENT HISTORY

> If you're able, show that you have worked all throughout college to demonstrate your commitment to your goal.

Intern, Peak Industries, Human Resources Department, fall 2007
Student Assistant, Office of the Dean, Arts and Sciences, spring 2006
Residence Life, Floor Supervisor (2 years)
Hostess, Pancake Heaven, summers, 2006–2007

REFERENCES (available on request)

> Always obtain preapproval from your references, even if you don't list their names. You may be asked to provide them on a moment's notice.

The key to successful "trial" experiences such as internships is the relationship between you and your sponsor in the host organization. If you're not being given enough to do, or not allowed to test your competence in a particular area, speak up. The answer may be put in terms of "company policy," your "not quite ready for prime time" skills, or your supervisor's unwillingness to experiment in high-stakes areas. Nevertheless, the two of you must communicate about these kinds of important issues. No one can read your mind!

As you work your way toward launching your career, keep up with the latest information. Read up on interviewing (see Box 12.1), résumé writing (see Box 12.2), networking, hot career fields, and the latest employment trends. As you continue studying in your college courses, apply what you're learning—in your major and in your general education courses—to your future career. You'll be the winner!

Activity Option Find some examples of bad résumés. Check with your career center for examples. Give groups of students the same four or five résumés and ask them to rate the résumés on a scale of 1 to 10 with 10 representing best and to be prepared to justify their ratings.

INSIGHT ⟶ ACTION

1. What might keep you from choosing a major and career focus that you're actually interested in? Are these areas attractive enough for you to try to work out whatever might deter you?

2. What kinds of internship, co-op, or service-learning opportunities have you participated in? What did you learn from these experiences? If you've not participated, what opportunities are available on campus?

3. What specific actions can you take to help ensure that you choose a major and career wisely?

Your Type is Showing

What does your psychological type have to do with your college major and career choices? Actually, a great deal. It makes sense that your personality influences your choices in college. It's hard to imagine an extrovert, who derives energy from being around other people, enjoying a relatively solitary career as a forest ranger. Of course, some students choose a major for the wrong reasons: because all their friends have chosen it or because they hear it's easy. But your personality is the very core of who you are, so you need to know what possible effects it can have on your choices, statistically speaking. Which type are you?

· **"I want to decide and move on."** *EJ Types* (ESTJ, ESFJ, ENFJ, ENTJ) like to make a decision quickly and get it over with. They may talk over the process of deciding with friends or instructors since they're extraverted, and then just jump in with both feet early in their first term. They are organized students, keep track of credits, and work their way through a degree. If their intended major doesn't quite work out like they think it should, they'll jump ship quickly and try another. The wiser decision might be to slow down and learn more about other options.

· **"I want to major in everything!"** *EP Types* (ESTP, ESFP, ENFP, ENTP) want to take their time deciding. Closing off options by making a choice can be anxiety provoking for them, so they'd rather experiment for a while. And since they're extraverts, part of the process is talking through their options. They may try one major, and then another, and then another until they find a fit—or run out of time or money. They want to plunge into co-curricular activities, too—to experience it all! P students with J parents, however, can be at cross purposes. While the P student experiments, the J parent becomes frustrated. Sometimes P students can stall out, too. When presented with too many options, they may opt out entirely.

- "I want to be absolutely sure." *IJ Types* (ISTJ, ISFJ, INFJ, INTJ) research, think, and reflect before coming to any conclusion. They read books, consult websites, and consider all the information very carefully because they tend to stick with a decision once they've made it. And because they're introverts, they may spring their decisions on people (especially F's) who haven't been aware of what they're thinking. Their personalities work like computers: input, throughput, output!

- "I wish I knew what I was going be when I grow up!" *IP Types* (ISTP, ISFP, INFP, INTP) resist coming to a decision, so much so that they may miss important deadlines. ("You must sign up for academic advising by October 1!") Sometimes they need a nudge from someone, "Hey, did you know that you have to declare a major by your fifth semester?" IP's are wanderers. They'd rather believe that no decision is final so that they remain true to their inner values.[34]

Your Work Style

Each of the four dimensions of your type tells something about your likely work preferences. Here are some examples.

Extraverts (E)

Like activity and variety

Don't like red tape

Get impatient with long projects

Like to work with other people

Introverts (I)

Like to concentrate in quiet

Tend to be careful with details

Can focus on one project for a long time

Are content to work alone

Sensors (S)

Like order

Like to use skills they already have

Work steadily

Are rarely truly inspired

Are good at work that requires precision

Intuitives (N)

Dislike routine

Like learning new skills

Work in energy bursts

Act on their inspirations, good or bad

Dislike taking time to be precise

Thinkers (T)

Don't show emotion and don't know how to handle others' emotions

Like to work in an orderly setting

Can reprimand someone when needed

Are analytically oriented

Are firm with others

Feelers (F)

Are aware of others' feelings

Like to work in a harmonious setting

Dislike telling people unpleasant things

Are people-oriented

Are sympathetic with others

Judgers (J)

Like to work according to plan

Like to complete things

Dislike having the project they're working on interrupted

May not notice things that should get done

Want only what they need to know to get started

Perceivers (P)

Can adapt to changes

Like to leave things open to change

Sometimes start too many projects at once and have trouble finishing them all

May put off things they don't like doing

Want to know everything about a new project[35]

Your Career Choice

Finally, some studies show that the two middle letters (ST, SF, NT, or NF) of psychological type are relatively good predictors of what career fields people are attracted to. See if you find a career field you're considering in the four quadrants in Figure 12.13, and if what you're considering "fits" your type. But remember that research reports statistical regularities, not individual destinies.

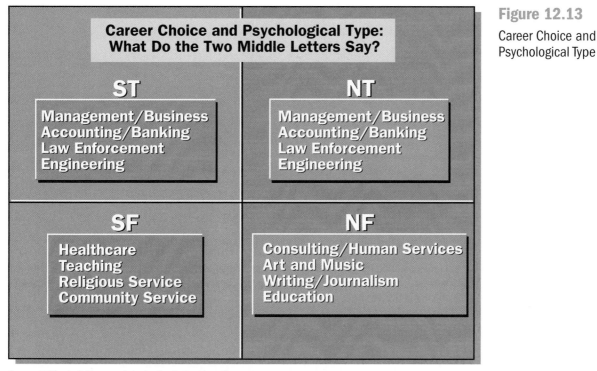

Figure 12.13
Career Choice and Psychological Type

Source: DiTiberio & Hammer, *Introduction to type in college.*

EXERCISE 12.4 VARK Activity

Complete the recommended activity for your preferred VARK learning modality. If you are multimodal, select more than one activity. Your instructor may ask you to (a) give an oral report on your results in class, (b) send your results to him or her via e-mail, (c) post them online, or (d) contribute to a class chat.

 Visual: Select a quotation from this chapter that was particularly memorable to you. Create a poster of the quote, using large font and graphics, to hang on a wall in your room.

 Aural: Talk through the Circle of Learning aloud to help you remember the connections between academic disciplines.

 Read/Write: Find a book that extends the ideas presented in this chapter. Select a passage that impresses you from the book to share with your classmates.

 Kinesthetic: Go on a "field trip" to the Career Center on your campus. Collect resources you find there and bring them to class.

Activity Option For the final activity in the chapter, ask students to design a five-slide PowerPoint presentation. Students must include a possible choice of major; a specific career within the major, including predictions about the availability of the job and salary information; and how this choice of major and career connects to information in the "Your Type Is Showing" box.

For more practice online, go to http://www.academic.cengage.com/ collegesuccess/staley to take the Challenge Yourself online quizzes.

FOCUS CHALLENGE CASE **NOW WHAT DO YOU THINK?**

At the beginning of this chapter, Ethan Cole, a confused and discouraged student, faced a challenge. Now after reading this chapter, would you respond differently to any of the questions you answered about the "FOCUS Challenge Case"?

REALITY CHECK

On a scale of 1 to 10, answer the following questions now that you've completed this chapter.

1 = not very/not much/very little/low   10 = very/a lot/very much/high

In hindsight, how much did you *really* know about this subject matter before reading the chapter?

1   2   3   4   5   6   7   8   9   10

How much do you think this information might affect your college success?

1   2   3   4   5   6   7   8   9   10

How much do you think this information might affect your career success after college?

1   2   3   4   5   6   7   8   9   10

How long did it actually take you to complete this chapter (both the reading and writing tasks)? _____ Hour(s) _____ Minutes

Take a minute to compare these answers to your answers from the "Readiness Check" at the beginning of this chapter. What gaps exist between the similar questions? How might these gaps between what you thought before starting the chapter and what you now think after completing the chapter affect how you approach the next chapter in this book?

Teachable Moment Students have probably had some eye-opening moments working through this chapter. Take a moment to go around the room and ask students to report on one key thing they learned. Students cannot repeat what someone else said. They can say "I learned that, too, but I also learned _____."

To download mp3 format audio summaries of this chapter, go to http://www .academic.cengage.com/collegesuccess/staley.

13 Working Toward Wellness

YOU'RE ABOUT TO DISCOVER...

Chapter Crossover As we come to the end of this book, it's important that students see that information does not stand in isolation. Much of the information in this chapter connects to other chapters. For example, issues of emotional well-being are discussed in Chapter 11 and are clearly connected to wellness.

> How wellness is defined

> Who is responsible for your wellness

> The importance of physical, mental, and spiritual health

> How to assess your own wellness choices by creating a Wellness Wheel

> How to deal with six aspects of wellness that affect first-year students: stress, nutrition, exercise, sleep, alcohol and drugs, and sex

> How to create a wellness plan for yourself that will impact your college success

"To keep the body in good health is a duty ... otherwise we shall not be able to keep our mind strong and clear."

Buddha (c. 563–483 B.C.)

Anthony Lopez

Anthony Lopez was average in nearly every

sense of the word. He wasn't a record-breaking athlete, nor was he the top student in his high school class. He was even sandwiched between two older brothers and two younger sisters. His brothers had excelled in college—one was an attorney and the other a computer engineer. Anthony knew that measuring up would be difficult for him. He wasn't exactly sure why he was in college or what career he might aim for, but he knew his parents expected him to be successful.

Now that he was here at the university, Anthony was going to make his mark. He was away from home for the first time ever, and he was having the time of his life! He'd already made loads of friends, and even the ladies, who regularly snubbed him in high school, thought he was worth getting to know here.

In the first weeks of school, Anthony did his part to help Huntington Hall live up to its reputation. Partying was especially heavy on Tuesday ("Boozeday") and Thursday ("Thirstday"), not to mention the weekends. Besides, drinking helped him forget his academic worries, which were beginning to mount, and bolstered his confidence with the opposite sex.

Weekends were supercharged with partying before and after football games and hitting all the bars within walking distance. Fake IDs weren't hard to get, and no one ever questioned him anyway. Most students got a buzz on before even leaving Huntington for a night of drinking so that they could keep their bar tabs down. The freedom he had in college was overwhelming. No one seemed to care if he cut class, turned in his assignments, or drank too much. From time to time he had thoughts about what he was going to do with his life, but fortunately, he could put questions like that out of his mind fairly easily.

After not calling home for a week, Anthony's Mom called him as he walked from his history class back to Huntington Hall for one of the regular Thursday night gatherings—this time in his room. He'd already decided to skip math because it was a huge lecture course, and he figured he was invisible among so many students anyway.

"Anthony, what's going on?" his Mom asked. "We haven't heard from you!" Suddenly Anthony realized she was right. "I've been really busy," he replied. "You know, college is hard work, Mom." He tried to sound convincing. "I'm sure you're working hard, Anthony, but I want to know about you. How are *you* doing?"

Then she started in with the usual list of parental questions: "Are you eating well?" "Sure, Mom," was his answer, although he knew his diet had changed radically since he left home—and not for the better. He hadn't gotten up in time for breakfast once, and his fast-food cravings were particularly hard to ignore. He'd been on the track team in high school, but even running had fallen by the wayside. "Are you getting enough rest?" "Yeah, Mom," he replied, although he and his buddies regularly played Texas Hold 'Em online late into the night. "Are you feeling okay? You sound like you have a cold." "It's nothing, Mom," he said, although his throat was awfully sore. "Are you making some friends?" "Am I ever!" he answered a little too enthusiastically. "How about girls? Have you met anyone worth mentioning?" "I'm a popular guy in college, Mom. You'd be surprised! I'm making my mark!" At the moment, he was juggling three different relationships, and although it was his least favorite of the three, one had recently become intimate, and without much warning, too.

When the questions came around to academics, Anthony's answers weren't so well rehearsed. "Have you had any exams in your math course yet? How did you do?" Anthony faltered, "Not too well, but I'll bring my grade up next time." Anthony didn't like the way the conversation was going. "Let me call you back later, Mom," he interrupted. Academics were down on his list of priorities, and his Mom's barrage of questions was making him very uncomfortable. What *was* foremost on his mind was the huge off-campus party coming up on Friday night.

However, Friday night was when Anthony's social life came to a screeching halt. The party was so big and noisy that neighbors called the campus police. Anthony and a few other students were issued an MIP, "Minor in Possession" ticket, a class C felony that came with a $500 fine and twelve hours of community service. According to state law, Anthony would lose his driver's license and insurance for thirty days, too. He'd had far too much to drink that night, and it showed.

Now what? An MIP was something that would definitely require a phone call home, and he'd have to face the consequences. He knew how disappointed his parents and older brothers would be. *I'm making my mark all right*, he thought to himself, *but this wasn't exactly what I had in mind.*

WHAT DO YOU THINK?

Now that you've read about Anthony Lopez, answer the following questions. You may not know all the answers yet, but you'll find out what you know and what you stand to gain by reading this chapter.

1. Is Anthony representative of students on your campus? In your opinion, why do these types of wellness problems arise among college students?

2. Do you predict that Anthony will be successful in college? Why or why not?

3. What would be required to reverse Anthony's rocky start to college?

4. List three specific areas for change after reviewing the case about Anthony.

Before beginning to read this chapter, take two minutes to answer the following questions on a scale of 1 to 10. Your answers will help you assess how ready you are to focus.

1 = not very/not much/very little/low   10 = very/a lot/very much/high

Based on reading the "You're about to discover..." list and skimming this chapter, how much do you think you probably already know about the subject matter?

1   2   3   4   5   6   7   8   9   10

How much do you think this information might affect your college success?

1   2   3   4   5   6   7   8   9   10

How much do you think this information might affect your career success after college?

1   2   3   4   5   6   7   8   9   10

In general, how motivated are you to learn the material in this chapter?

1   2   3   4   5   6   7   8   9   10

This book describes four key factors related to intrinsic, or internal, motivation: curiosity, control, career outlook, and challenge. The next four questions relate to these **C-Factors:**

How *curious* are you about the content you expect to read in this chapter?

1   2   3   4   5   6   7   8   9   10

How much *control* do you expect to have over mastering the material in this chapter?

1   2   3   4   5   6   7   8   9   10

How interested are you in this chapter in terms of developing your *career outlook*?

1   2   3   4   5   6   7   8   9   10

How *challenging* do you expect the material in this chapter to be for you?

1   2   3   4   5   6   7   8   9   10

Before beginning any task, including studying, it's important to check in with yourself to ensure that you're physically, intellectually, and emotionally ready to focus. How ready are you, physically, to focus on this chapter? (Are you rested, feeling well, and so on?)

1   2   3   4   5   6   7   8   9   10

How ready are you, intellectually, to focus on this chapter? (Are you thinking clearly, focused on this course, interested in this subject?)

1   2   3   4   5   6   7   8   9   10

How ready are you, emotionally, to focus on this chapter? (Are you calm, confident, composed?)

1   2   3   4   5   6   7   8   9   10

If your answer to any of the last three questions is below a 5 on the scale, you may need to address the issue you're facing prior to beginning this chapter. For example, if you're hungry, get a quick bite to eat. If you're feeling scattered, take a few moments to settle down and focus.

Finally, how long do you think it will take you to complete this chapter? _____ Hour(s) _____ Minutes

Teachable Moment Since this is the last chapter, ask students to take a minute to talk about the book. Is this the most interesting chapter? If not, which one is and why? Did their attitudes about the "Readiness Check" activity change over time? Why or why not? Did it become a productive habit that carried over into reading assignments for other courses?

EXERCISE 13.1 Wellness Survey

This chapter will focus on the relationship between wellness and college success. Six specific aspects of wellness are impacted by regular choices *you* make. Before you begin reading the chapter, complete this wellness survey. For each statement, mark one of the following responses:

Yes!	Yes	Not Sure	No	No!
5	4	3	2	1

1. STRESS

_____ 1. I control my stress level.

_____ 2. I find ways to relax and let off steam that are healthy and productive.

_____ 3. I'm aware of my limits and don't take on too much.

_____ 4. I make time for social activities that are reenergizing.

_____ 5. I learn from poor wellness choices I make and change my behavior.

_____ 6. I don't pattern my own wellness choices on those of my friends, particularly if they may cause problems for me.

_____ 7. I think before I act when it comes to choosing wellness.

_____ 8. I plan ahead to achieve a healthy lifestyle.

_____ 9. I understand the relationship between wellness and academic success and act accordingly.

_____ 10. I know that working toward wellness is key to the future I want for myself.

_____ **TOTAL SCORE for STRESS**

2. NUTRITION

_____ 1. I am knowledgeable about what constitutes a well-balanced, nutritious diet.

_____ 2. I eat frequently throughout the day to keep up my energy, as opposed to over-eating at mealtimes.

_____ 3. I eat at least five servings of fruits and vegetables per day.

_____ 4. I eat breakfast most or all mornings.

_____ 5. I use food for nourishment, rather than to comfort myself or relieve boredom.

_____ 6. I eat when I'm experiencing stomach hunger, rather than simply mouth hunger.

_____ 7. I avoid skipping meals to lose weight.

_____ 8. I avoid unhealthy foods, such as fast food or foods high in sugar, fat, or sodium.

_____ 9. I read food labels to learn the nutritional value of foods.

_____ 10. I pay attention to my body's signals about which foods make me feel fit and healthy.

_____ **TOTAL SCORE for NUTRITION**

3. EXERCISE

_____ 1. I recognize when I need to get some exercise.

_____ 2. I take advantage of natural opportunities to exercise, like climbing stairs instead of using elevators.

_____ 3. I am satisfied with the amount of exercise I get.

_____ 4. I enjoy exercising.

_____ 5. I try to get some exercise, even if in small amounts, every day.

_____ 6. I exercise moderately without overdoing it, which can be unhealthy.

_____ 7. I walk or ride my bike instead of driving whenever I can.

_____ 8. I have a regular exercise routine that I follow.

(continued)

_____ 9. I exercise to help elevate my mood when I feel anxious or depressed.

_____ 10. I use physical exercise to relieve stress.

_____ **TOTAL SCORE for EXERCISE**

4. SLEEP

_____ 1. I go to bed when I'm tired.

_____ 2. If I nap during the day, I make sure it's a short one in the early afternoon.

_____ 3. I get seven or more hours of sleep per night.

_____ 4. I don't vary the times I go to sleep and wake up by more than two hours during the week.

_____ 5. I don't study or read assignments in bed.

_____ 6. I am able to fall asleep on my own without resorting to pills.

_____ 7. I don't use alcohol to help me fall asleep.

_____ 8. I exercise regularly to help my sleeping habits.

_____ 9. I avoid caffeine late in the day.

_____ 10. I understand the importance of sleep to my academic success.

_____ **TOTAL SCORE for SLEEP**

5. ALCOHOL and DRUGS

_____ 1. I drink responsibly or not at all.

_____ 2. I don't need alcohol or drugs to have fun.

_____ 3. I don't drink with the intention of getting drunk.

_____ 4. I intervene when my friends are intoxicated or high and help them.

_____ 5. I limit my drinking episodes per week.

_____ 6. I associate with others who drink responsibly or not at all.

_____ 7. I think while I'm drinking and don't lose my good judgment.

_____ 8. I plan ahead when I'm out with friends and choose a designated driver beforehand.

_____ 9. I don't use alcohol or drugs to escape from my problems.

_____ 10. I don't let alcohol and parties affect my academic performance.

_____ **TOTAL SCORE for ALCOHOL**

6. SEX

_____ 1. I am sexually responsible and practice safe sex or abstain from sex.

_____ 2. I am considerate and appropriate in the ways I talk about sex.

_____ 3. I explore my own sexuality in ways that are both positive and pleasurable.

_____ 4. I feel good about my body.

_____ 5. I am comfortable with my sexual orientation.

_____ 6. I understand birth control options and exercise them, if appropriate.

_____ 7. I communicate clearly what I want or don't want from a partner, if appropriate.

_____ 8. I avoid unplanned sex.

_____ 9. I am content with the amount of sexual activity I engage in.

_____ 10. I allow others to express their sexual orientation, even if it is different from mine.

_____ **TOTAL SCORE for SEX**

You will use your scores on this survey later in the chapter to better understand yourself and your wellness choices and how they may be affecting you.

Sensitive Situation Having students discuss personal experiences with alcohol, drugs, and sex may not be a good idea. Rather, leave the door open if students want to contact you via e-mail or in some other private way. Do, however, look at group responses to stress, nutrition, exercise, and sleep. Divide the class into four and assign each group a topic. Ask students to come up with the items in their assigned topic that are most in need of improvement, collectively, and to report a brainstormed list of strategies for change to the rest of the class.

Health, Education, and Welfare

From 1953 to 1979, the United States government had a Department of Health, Education, and Welfare, and the secretary of HEW was a member of the president's cabinet. The history isn't important here, but the point that those three things—health, education, and welfare—are connected is. Although you may not have thought much about it, your health and well-being significantly impact your college success.

Without good health, education is at risk. Your physical, mental, and spiritual health affect your ability to learn. In a letter to John Garland Jefferson in 1790, Thomas Jefferson encouraged his studious young cousin to remember that "Exercise and recreation . . . are as necessary as reading. I will rather say more necessary because health is worth more than learning." What did Jefferson mean? Is his advice centuries ago still pertinent today?

Think about this: College is about learning and understanding, cultivating the "life of the mind," as it's sometimes called. However, the life of the mind is related to the state of the body. Your brain is obviously connected to the rest of you. Wellness—or a lack of it—can get in the way of an otherwise productive academic career. Wellness isn't merely the absence of illness. It's a process that moves you toward optimal health, based on smart choices. This chapter is about six specific areas of wellness that you can influence to improve your college success.

Physical health is only part of the picture. Mental health issues—depression or anxiety, for example—can also affect your efforts. Spiritual health that comes through searching and self-understanding provide the motivation to make the right wellness choices in the first place.

Emotional Intelligence (EI) Research Daniel Goleman reports that the medical evidence is clear: Individuals who are unable to effectively manage stress have higher levels and more severe cases of viruses, heart disease, cancer, and a host of other illnesses. "Broad relaxation techniques—which directly counter the physiological arousal of stress—are being used to ease the symptoms of a wide variety of chronic illnesses."

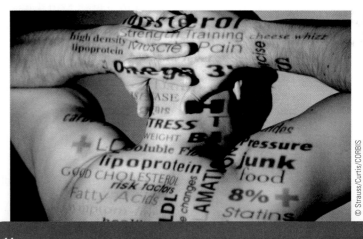

© Strauss/Curtis/CORBIS

"When health is absent, wisdom cannot reveal itself; Art cannot become manifest; Strength cannot be exerted; Wealth is useless; and Reason is powerless."

Herophilus, Greek physician, called the father of scientific anatomy

Here's a sobering wake-up call about wellness and first-year college students. First-year students represent 40 percent of undergraduate deaths from natural causes; 40 percent of all undergraduate suicides; 50 percent of all undergraduate deaths from falls from windows, balconies, and rooftops; and 47 percent of the undergraduates who die on campus.[1] Unfortunately, some first-year students seek thrills, ignore danger, or seriously overextend themselves and become one of these statistics. One reason is because the brains of young college students are still developing the circuitry that acts as an "early warning system" in the brains of older adults.[2]

These statistics are alarming, to be sure, but at the same time, knowing the risks and making wise choices can keep you safe. This chapter's intention isn't to alarm you, however; it's to equip you with the information you need to be at your best physically, psychologically, and academically. Unwise decisions may make adjusting to college more difficult than it needs to be; wise ones bolster your academic efforts.

Wellness is about making *informed* choices: knowing the range of choices you have, understanding why making productive choices is important, and then doing it. Wellness requires you to slow down, think, listen to your inner voice or your gut, and plan ahead.

It's easy to read the FOCUS Challenge Case about Anthony and pinpoint all the wellness mistakes he's making. As you read it, you may have been thinking, *That's not a good idea, Anthony!* or *You're going to regret doing that, Anthony!* It's not so easy, however, to be objective about your own wellness choices. What's easy is going with the flow and zipping right along without stopping to think. That's where this chapter comes in. Its goal is to change some *counterproductive* choices you may be making—and to validate *productive* ones. As you read, you will explore your physical, mental, and spiritual health; and you'll learn more about where to go if you need help. Later, you'll use the wellness survey you filled out in Exercise 13.1 to create your own Wellness Wheel to identify areas for improvement in the future.

Thomas Jefferson said that health is worth more than learning. Fortunately, you don't have to choose between the two in college. You can achieve both. But you do have to make choices—positive, productive ones—in order to achieve wellness. Much of the responsibility for a healthy lifestyle rests squarely on your own shoulders, and if insurmountable problems do surface, getting the help you need is vital. Find out the kinds of wellness resources available on your campus, where they're located, how to contact them, and what kind of help you can expect if you go.

In many ways, your degree of wellness is up to you. After all, who decides when you'll tuck yourself in at night, go back for seconds or thirds, or skip meals so that your jeans fit better? Who monitors your visits to the doctor, your stress levels, and your alcohol consumption? Who requires you to take the necessary precautions for safe sex or suggests you exercise to stay fit? Who does all these things? None other than you! Responsibility for wellness is the place to start this discussion. If you're not in agreement with this principle, you'll be in denial throughout much of the rest of the chapter.

Emotional Intelligence (EI) Research In a study by Parker et al. (2004), academically successful first-year students had higher levels of emotional intelligence in most of the EI components.

Chapter Crossover In Chapter 3 students learned about resources on campus. By now, they should know exactly where they can go to get whatever kind of help they need. You might ask the class if they have ever been to the student health center, if one is available on your campus. Ask them to tell the class where it is and what their experience was like. You may hear about something that didn't go quite right, but on the other hand, students may be surprised to find out about the array of services offered.

Emotional Intelligence (EI) Research In the same way that we take responsibility for our own wellness, we also take responsibility for our emotions. How we emotionally respond to stress can impact us physically. Learning how to respond effectively to stress and how to manage it is connected to physical and psychological well-being.

Physical Health: In Sickness and in Health

Of course, everyone loses at "germ warfare" from time to time. A virus may assault you, seemingly out of nowhere, or an infection may attack when you least expect it. What kinds of physical health problems do college students generally face?[3]

Acute Medical Problems. (Urgent—and important.) You need help fast! Appendicitis or toxic shock syndrome, for example, require immediate, life-or-death medical attention. Unfortunately, sometimes serious health problems occur among college students because they delay treatment by waiting for a convenient time between assignment due dates. Unfortunately, acute complications can set in.

Chronic Medical Problems. (Somewhat less urgent, but very important.) Approximately one-third of asthma sufferers and one-fourth of diabetics are diagnosed by the time they're in their thirties. While most college students are a relatively healthy group, cancer is the fifth leading cause of death among people between the ages of fifteen and twenty-four, following AIDS, accidents, homicide, and suicide.

Infectious Diseases. (An ounce of prevention ...) In many developing countries, infectious diseases such as mononucleosis (known to many as the kissing disease) occur in early childhood when they can be fought

"Take care of your body. It's the only place you have to live."

Jim Rohn, business philosopher and author

off fairly easily. In the United States, however, these infections are often contracted later, during your college years. Complications can sometimes occur, and illnesses in this category can be major reasons for medical withdrawals from college. Life-threatening infectious diseases, such as meningitis, have the capability to spread rapidly on a college campus where students are in close proximity. Or take another kind of infectious disease: sexually transmitted infections. Two-thirds of STIs occur in people under age twenty-five, and many of these diseases can have long-term consequences such as infertility or even cancer. Contagious illnesses are hard to avoid when you're surrounded by classmates or roommates who have them, so anything in this category is worth paying attention to.

You're likely to have your share of aches and pains, colds, and flu symptoms during your first year of college, but you should seek medical attention if you have any of these symptoms:

> Fever of 102.5 degrees or higher

> Headache accompanied by a stiff neck

Teachable Moment Pose the following questions to students: Is a physician a good career choice for everyone? Why or why not? Physicians tend to have high status, but there are pros and cons to the job. Lead a class discussion about why it's important to find careers that fit interests and personality types.

FOCUS ON CAREERS: JOHN TRAVIS, M.D., Wellness Pioneer

Q1: At what point in your life did you decide on medicine as a career? What personal and academic factors led you to that decision?

I decided on a medical career at about age 5. My father was a country doctor and surgeon, and the patients who came by the house after hours would often ask me if I wanted to be a doctor like my daddy when I grew up. It wasn't hard to figure out the right answer, but I know now that a deeper reason was that I longed for the respect and love from patients that I saw my father had, and that love was missing from my own childhood. The feelings of disconnection I had as a child eventually led to my work in infant wellness.

Q2: You have not only a medical degree, but also a master's degree in public health. Has your career taken twists and turns, and if so, how did those come about?

It became clear to me in medical school that writing prescriptions or cutting on people was not my calling. The Master's in Public Health was part of a residency in preventive medicine at Johns Hopkins and gave me a larger perspective on health. Most of what we were taught wasn't really prevention though, but early detection. It was during my last year of residency that I stumbled across a $2 book on the clearance table at the medical bookstore—*High Level Wellness* by Halbert Dunn, M.D. It put most of my eclectic interests into focus and gave me a model (and a name) for how to put together many preventive health components that I'd been exploring on my own. While I thought the word "wellness" was odd and would never catch on, I saw it as a way to frame my future work.

Q3: Much of your time is devoted to writing and lecturing about wellness issues. Do you now, or did you in the past, have a private practice?

I gave up the idea of a sick-care practice when I founded the Wellness Resource Center in 1975 in Mill Valley, California. There I saw "clients" (I think I was one of the first to make that distinction) with whom we were very careful to spell out that *they* were responsible for their well-being, not me as a doctor. Frequently they were simultaneously in treatment for a medical or psychological condition, which was fine, but to keep the distinctions clear, we had them sign a written contract to that effect. We helped them deal with stress, poor nutrition, lack of physical exercise, and many psychological issues. Four years of running the Center and speaking around the country gave me the experience to write the *Wellness Workbook*.

Q4: Many people think that wellness is the opposite of illness. Is that all there is to it? How do you define wellness?

Most people think wellness is the *absence* of illness. I realized there was a range of well-being probably as large as the range of symptoms and disease and postulated that the absence of illness is only a neutral point—no illness *or* wellness. To illustrate this idea I created the Illness/Wellness Continuum. Primarily it shows a range of wellness as well as illness. It also shows that wellness is approached by partnering with a "wellness coach," rather than a doctor telling you what to do. This fundamental difference in how wellness is approached is still not understood by most helping professionals.

The Illness / Wellness Continuum

PREMATURE DEATH ← | WELLNESS PARADIGM | → HIGH LEVEL WELLNESS

Disability · Symptoms · Signs · Awareness · Education · Growth

TREATMENT PARADIGM

NEUTRAL POINT
(NO DISCERNABLE ILLNESS OR WELLNESS)

- Unexplained, significant weight loss
- A mole that bleeds, itches, or changes shape, color, or size
- Sudden vomiting
- Difficulty swallowing
- Blood that is vomited or coughed up
- Alternating diarrhea and constipation
- Pain or blood with urination
- A lump or thickening in the breast
- Unusual discharge from your genitals
- Change in your menstrual cycle
- Pain in your abdomen that won't go away
- Persistent cough, chest pain, or trouble breathing
- *Any* symptom that doesn't seem to go away and worries you

Teachable Moment Ask students if they know all of the attendance policies of their instructors. Sometimes instructors won't count an absence as excused without a note from the health or wellness center. Others may have a policy that allows only X number of absences so that a student may need to save his absences for times when he really needs them.

C CREATE a Career Outlook

PHYSICIAN

Have you ever considered a career as a physician? Here are some facts about this career to consider and some questions about yourself to ponder.

Facts to Consider

Academic preparation required: four years of undergraduate school resulting in a college degree, four years of medical school, three to eight years of internship and residency, and medical board certification to obtain a state license to practice medicine

Future workforce demand: Job prospects are excellent, especially in low-income and rural locations.

Work environment: Physicians often work long, irregular hours. They diagnose illnesses, treat patients, perform medical procedures, and counsel patients on wellness. A Doctor of Medicine (M.D.) and Doctor of Osteopathic Medicine (D.O.) may perform similar services for patients; however, a D.O. often concentrates on patients' musculoskeletal systems and provides more holistic, preventative care. Physicians typically specialize in a particular area of medicine, such as psychiatry, surgery, cardiology, dermatology, gastroenterology, anesthesiology, family/general medicine, pediatrics, ophthalmology, or obstetrics and gynecology. Most physicians work in private or group practice offices, assisted by a staff of nurses and physicians' assistants (PAs), and in hospital settings.

Most common psychological type preferences: introverted, sensing, thinking (or to a lesser extent, feeling), and judging; most common type is ISTJ[4]

Essential skills: analytical skills, self-motivation, a willingness to serve others, an ability to work long hours and make decisions in stressful situations, and overall communication (bedside manner) skills

Questions to Ponder

1. Do you have (or could you acquire) the skills this career requires?
2. What would you find most satisfying about this type of career?
3. What would you find most challenging about this type of career?
4. Are you interested in a career like this? Why or why not?

For more information, see U.S. Department of Labor, Bureau of Labor Statistics, *Occupational Outlook Handbook, 2006–2007 Edition*.[5]

For more career activities online, go to http://www.academic.cengage.com/collegesuccess/staley to do the Team Career exercises.

Q5: In your view, why do people become ill? Why do we, as a country, see rising rates of cancer, heart attacks, and strokes, for example? What are we doing wrong?
I think most illnesses come about because we are leading lives of desperation—quiet or not. Most of us are profoundly disconnected—from ourselves, our families, and the earth. Now much of my work focuses on infants and children because of how we can impact their future wellness, more so than any wellness work we can do with adults. In 1999, I co-founded the Alliance for Transforming the Lives of Children with my wife and 11 other experts in birth and child development. This work continues to be my major wellness focus.

Q6: This chapter focuses on physical, mental, and spiritual health. Is one of these areas particularly important to achieving wellness in our lives?
Finding meaning through spirituality, self-exploration, or values clarification is fundamental. Without it, the other areas are meaningless (pun intended). There's little motivation to take responsibility for yourself without a sense of meaning—or to cope with the problems in the other areas, which I think are some of the symptoms that our lives are out of kilter in this area.

Q7: How does wellness impact college success?
Wellness impacts success in any area of life. It's hard to truly succeed (and I'm not talking just about accomplishments or praise) from a place of despair and hopelessness. Enhancing your own wellness through self-exploration and growth is right up there with academic pursuits.

Q8: What are the medical careers that you would recommend for someone interested in promoting wellness?
Honestly, I don't see medicine as the best path to a wellness career—perhaps it's even a hindrance. But regardless, my best advice is to find your passion and then pursue it relentlessly, despite any seeming limitations.

INSIGHT → ACTION

1. Do you have any physical symptoms of illness you're concerned about? If so, have you had them checked by a physician? If not, what's keeping you from doing that?

2. What do you do to avoid being around people who are ill and contagious? Do you take precautions against getting sick yourself?

3. How well do you know your own body? What are the usual signs of the onset of a cold, for example? Do you take steps to stop it early? If so, what do you do?

4. What steps can you take to improve your overall physical health? Will you commit to acting on your own advice?

Mental Health: Up or Down

CHALLENGE → REACTION

Challenge: Fill in the blanks for the following statement.

Reaction: I would seek the help of a counselor if I:

1. had negative feelings such as _____ , _____ , or _____ .

2. experienced changes in habits such as _____ .

3. had trouble doing academic tasks requiring _____ .

4. lost interest in _____ .

5. experienced _____ troublesome symptoms of depression for longer than _____ .

People who are mentally healthy have particular characteristics. They see things realistically, make and keep close relationships, do what's required of them, accept their own strengths and weaknesses, value themselves, and get fulfillment from life.[6] They may feel down on occasion, but they pop right back up again. According to the Centers for Disease Control and Prevention (CDC), the average American adult feels depressed or unhappy approximately three days per month. In their research, college-aged people (ages 18–24), smokers (a pack or more per day), and women reported more down days; people with good jobs and those who exercised regularly reported fewer days.[7]

College can be a particularly vulnerable time for ups and downs because of your new environment, new freedom, new pressures, and new temptations. One place to start examining your own ups and downs is to look at the wellness choices you're making. If you are engaging in excessive casual sex, running on no sleep, experimenting with drugs, or drinking too much alcohol too often, these unproductive choices could be contributing to feelings of unhappiness. But these behaviors can also be symptomatic of deeper problems, so it's important to pay attention.

Mental illness is "a diagnosable mental, behavioral or emotional disorder that interferes with one or more major activities in life, like dressing, eating or working."[8] Mental health problems include *anxiety* disorders (such as generalized anxiety disorder or obsessive-compulsive disorder), *mood* disorders (such as depression or bipolar disorder), and, more rarely, *psychotic* disorders (such as schizophrenia).

What causes mental illness? There's no germ we know of for depression or anxiety, and there's no easy answer to that question. However, several factors come into play. You can have a genetic predisposition to a particular mental illness, such as schizophrenia. Although rare in the general population, if you have a relative with schizophrenia, your odds of developing it go up.[9] However, startling new research reports that marijuana use has the potential to trigger schizophrenia.[10] Research also reveals that former chronic ecstasy users report higher levels of depression than their counterparts who don't use the drug.[11] Genetics are outside your control, but the choice to use drugs that may exacerbate an underlying predisposition is yours to make.

What types of mental health issues do college students sometimes face? Two key problems are worth examining in more detail.

Depression

Your psychological makeup may also be a key factor in developing some mental health problems. Some of us are highly sensitive, pessimistic, or have low self-esteem. These characteristics may make us more vulnerable to mental illness such as depression. Some students feel more down than up; for them, depression can become a serious health issue. They may feel isolated, even among so many hundreds of other students.

Clinical depression is a serous problem. It isn't a passing mood, and you can't simply pull yourself together and get over it. According to the National Institute of Mental Health (NIMH), approximately 9.5 percent of American adults, or 20.9 million people, suffer from some form of depression.[12] But depression can be treated, and 80 percent of those who ask for help get better.[13] Read the accounts from these college students to see if they sound like statements you've heard recently from anyone you know.

Catherine: "I haven't stopped crying since I got here weeks ago. I don't know what's wrong with me, but I feel empty and sad all the time, and no one seems to understand."

Alex: "I sleep all weekend, every weekend, and I'm still tired. I have trouble concentrating on my schoolwork, and nothing is as much fun as I thought it would be. Why can't I just buckle down and get on with it?"

John: "When I finally got to college, I wanted to 'come out' about being gay, but some of my buddies are always making jokes about homosexuals, so I've kept my mouth shut. Sometimes the stress is overwhelming, and I'm feeling pretty hopeless."

Are these students depressed? How would you know? The symptoms of major depression include:

> Sadness, anxiety, or feelings of emptiness

> Low energy and fatigue

> Loss of interest in enjoyable activities

> Changes in sleep patterns (insomnia, early waking, oversleeping)

> Appetite and weight changes (loss or gain)

> Feeling worthless or guilty or hopeless

"Every adversity, every failure, every heartache carries with it the seed of an equal or greater benefit."

Napoleon Hill, author, *Keys to Success: The 17 Principles of Personal Achievement* (1883–1970)

Emotional Intelligence (EI) Research According to Daniel Goleman, the likelihood of becoming depressed increases with age, and people born after 1955 are three times more likely to be depressed than their grandparents.

> Suicidal thoughts (or attempts)

> Trouble concentrating, remembering, or making decisions

> Excessive crying or irritability

> Aches and pains that come and go without explanation[14]

If five or more of these symptoms last for several weeks without letting up, and they interfere with your normal functioning, visit your campus counseling center to find out if depression is your problem. But depression is only one type of mood disorder. Bipolar disorder can be a confusing malady because periods of deep, dark depression alternate with periods of excitability, racing thoughts, and distractibility. Just when you decide depression may be your problem, you enter a period in which you can't sleep for days and are hyperactive.

If you suspect a mental health problem, and if you don't have the energy or courage to visit your campus counseling center alone, ask your best friend to go with you. Medication and counseling can help.[15] For example, drugs such as Zoloft, Paxil, or Lexapro help many people who suffer from depression, and lithium carbonate helps sufferers of bipolar disorder. Left untreated, depression can push people to the edge.

According to recent data, every year about 1,300 college students commit suicide and another 31,469 attempt to.[16] Always take suicidal thoughts, impulses, or attempts—your own or someone else's—seriously and get help right away. Tell your residence hall advisor, a teacher, a coach, a staff member—someone you know and trust—that you need professional help immediately. If you suspect a friend is contemplating hurting herself, ask her. Show your concern and persuade her to get help, rather than risking her decision to become a statistic. Call 911 or a suicide hotline. Experts say that talking about suicide to someone who is considering it doesn't push him over the edge. The most important factor is getting help, and you may play a role in saving his life.

The long list of public figures—historical and contemporary—who have suffered from depression might surprise you.[17] Abraham Lincoln (1809–1865), now considered one of the greatest American presidents, suffered from "melancholy" much of his life, and after he broke off his engagement to Mary Todd in 1841, his friends feared he would commit suicide and watched him around the clock. Eventually, he harnessed his depression by pouring all his energies into his political career. Sigmund Freud (1856–1939), the revolutionary psychoanalyst, was also a patient. He was fixated on his sex life and wrote 900 love letters to the woman he loved. He suffered from depression and despair and was, in fact, susceptible to many of the same problems he diagnosed in his patients. Marilyn Monroe (1926–1962), actress and "silver screen siren," couldn't beat depression and overdosed, it's believed, on barbiturates. She was under the constant care of a psychiatrist, even during the height of her career. Greg Louganis (b. 1960), winner of five Olympic medals and perhaps the best diver in history, had attempted suicide three times by the time he was eighteen. Louganis experienced severe inner turmoil about being gay, and he learned in 1987 that he was HIV-positive. He now speaks across the country about his life experiences as a role model for young people.

Today many modern-day celebrities are open about their battles with depression—Tipper Gore, Carrie Fisher, and Drew Barrymore, for example.[18] Historically, effective medications weren't available, and often people chose to suffer in silence. Today depression has come out of the closet. Public awareness is the goal, and getting help is the path to wellness.

Anxiety

For some students, anxiety skyrockets out of control, and some develop full-fledged anxiety disorders. Anxiety disorders are real, common, often linked to depression, and treatable. They include:

Generalized Anxiety Disorder (GAD): six months or more of extreme worry about things that aren't true immediate concerns, like health, loved ones, money, or jobs—or a generalized anxiety about everything

Obsessive-Compulsive Disorder (OCD): uncontrollable urges to perform repeated actions (like hand washing); making yourself follow specific, unrealistic rules (like forcing yourself to always do X before you do Y and Z) and becoming upset when you can't; and checking and rechecking something over and over even though you've already made sure

Panic Disorder: an attack in which your heart pounds, your chest hurts, you tremble, sweat, feel out of breath, and are overcome by dread; the attacks occur out of the blue, repeatedly, and without a recognizable physical cause

Phobias: deep fears that are irrational yet guide your behavior. Everyone has certain fears, but phobias are extreme. Some people have phobias related to heights (acrophobia) or confined spaces (claustrophobia), for example, and these fears are debilitating.

Help is available on your campus at the Counseling Center or Student Health Center. Check these online sources for further information, too:[19]

Mental Health America: www.nmha.org

Anxiety Disorders Association of America: www.adaa.org

Anxiety/Panic Attack Resource Site: www.anxietypanic.com

National Anxiety Foundation: http://lexington-on-line.com/naf.html

National Institute of Mental Health: www.nimh.nih.gov

Experts say about 10 percent of the student body on most campuses visits the campus counseling center each year, and many more could be helped by doing so.[20] The percentage of students seeking counseling increases from freshman to senior year.[21] But why wait? If you think you could be helped, take action now!

INSIGHT → ACTION

1. Are you in tune with how you feel emotionally? How do you know?

2. Are you generally optimistic about how your life is going? Why or why not?

3. From whom do you get support to help your outlook on life?

4. Which activities do you get involved in to help you stay positive about your college experience?

5. Would you recognize the symptoms of a mental health problem in yourself and seek help, if warranted?

Activity Option Is the glass half full or half empty? Go around the room and ask students to come up with one thing that is stressful to students in college (*i.e.,* failing a test, breaking up with a significant other, a pet dying, etc.). In this activity, have one student respond to the situation with a glass-half-empty response, while another gives a glass-half-full response. For example, "I failed the test, and I don't think I can pass the course" versus "I failed the test, and I am going to talk with the instructor to see what I can do to improve." The point is that often how we respond to life's setbacks directly impacts the result.

Spiritual Health: Department of the Interior

CHALLENGE → REACTION

Challenge: See if you can predict the findings of a recent large-scale national study on spirituality in first-year students.

Reaction: Roughly, what percentage of respondents indicated they:

1. search for meaning and purpose in life? _____%

2. are interested in spirituality? _____%

3. talk about meaning and purpose with friends? _____%

4. occasionally or frequently attend religious services? _____%

5. believe college should help them develop self-understanding? _____%

Continue reading for the answers to these questions.

Who are you? What do you want? For most students, college is a time of personal exploration and growth. Many students are searching for meaning in their lives. For some, it can be a time of struggle as they try to envision what appears to be a distant future. "What am I going to do with my life?" is a pervasive question. Nearly three-quarters of college freshmen report having discussions about the meaning and purpose of life with friends.[22]

According to a national study of 112,232 college students, four out of five first-year students are interested in spirituality, and nearly three-fourths report feeling a sense of connection with a higher power. Eighty-one percent say they attend religious services occasionally or frequently. Most college freshmen consider it "essential" or "very important" that college help increase their self-understanding (69 percent), help prepare them to be responsible citizens (67 percent), develop their personal values (67 percent), and assist in their emotional development (63 percent). Nearly half believe that college should help encourage their expression of spirituality.

Many college students are on a spiritual quest. Over half of first-year students report questioning their religious beliefs (57 percent) and nearly as many (52 percent) disagree with their families on religious matters. They also report a high level of religious tolerance and concern for others who are in difficulty.[23] Eighty-two percent report doing volunteer work while in high school. However, by the end of the first year of college, students report spending less time volunteering their time or attending religious services.[24]

Can college help you examine your values, find inner direction, and ponder the meaning of life? Think about the courses you're taking this term. Are questions that relate to spiritual health explored, directly or indirectly? A course in philosophy might be a natural place to begin thinking about them, or a course in psychology, or many others, actually. How about the course for which you're using this textbook? Are you being asked to explore your values and your aspirations? In the end, where any course takes you is determined partly by you, and many issues related to spirituality can be examined on your own while you're in college,

Teachable Moment It's important to point out that spirituality is not necessarily synonymous with religion. Also, students need to know that college is a good time to explore beliefs about spirituality in a thoughtful and meaningful way.

"It is not what we get but who we become, what we contribute...that gives meaning to our lives."

Anthony Robbins, motivational speaker and author

not necessarily during any particular class. There are also many ways to work on "your interior," such as yoga, meditation, prayer, or exercise. The point is to free up your mind and slow down long enough to search on your own. According to one recent study, college students who integrate spiritual components that help them make choices and assess risks into their lives report better health.[25]

If these values are important to you, make a conscious decision to pursue your personal search for meaning and purpose, despite the many conflicting demands of college life. Your college experience is as much about these vital questions as it is about preparing for a particular career.

INSIGHT ⊖ ACTION

1. Do you believe college will help you better understand yourself? How?

2. What will *your* role be in the pursuit of spiritual health?

3. What specific actions will you take in your search for meaning and purpose in life? Who might help you explore these questions? How will you get these individuals involved?

Sensitive Situation Responding to questions about spirituality may be a very private matter for some students, perhaps a better topic for journaling than for a full-class discussion. Don't put anyone on the spot.

You Take the Wheel!

We've already established that some aspects of wellness, like genetic predispositions, are outside your control. But other aspects are mostly or entirely up to you. The remainder of this chapter examines six areas of wellness that impact your college success. The bottom line? Your decisions in these six areas will greatly affect how quickly and how well you adjust to college.

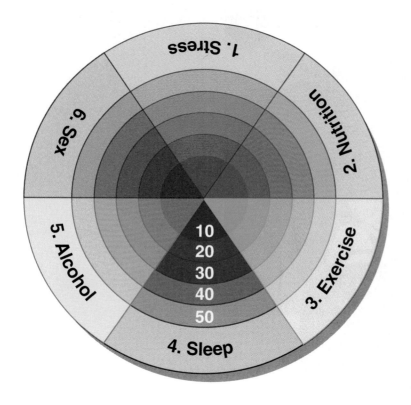

Figure 13.1

The Wellness Wheel

Now return to your completed wellness survey at the beginning of this chapter, and enter your scores for each of the six sectors on the Wellness Wheel in Figure 13.1 by placing a dot on or near the appropriate concentric circle (10, 20, 30, 40, or 50). Then connect the dots. While the survey isn't truly scientific, you will get a clear visual sense of where you are now and where to concentrate your future wellness efforts. For which of the six sectors did you score the lowest total? Were you surprised by your scores, or could you have predicted them?

How is your wheel shaped? Is it dented? Does the figure you get when you connect the dots fill up most of the wheel (representing healthy decisions), or is it smaller, closer to the hub (representing less healthy decisions)? Dots closer to the center represent areas for improvement.

Think back to the beginning of this chapter and the "FOCUS Challenge Case" character, Anthony Lopez. As a new first-year student, Anthony was making poor wellness choices in all six sectors affecting college success. If he had filled in the wellness survey honestly, his marks would have been close to the center all the way around the wheel. "Insight → Action" boxes throughout the rest of the chapter will ask you to develop a wellness action plan for yourself. Where do *you* need to focus?

EXERCISE 13.2 VARK Activity

Complete the recommended activity for your preferred VARK learning modality. If you are multimodal, select more than one activity. Your instructor may ask you to (a) give an oral report on your results in class, (b) send your results to him or her via e-mail, (c) post them online, or (d) contribute to a class chat.

 Visual: Redraw the Wellness Wheel in pie chart fashion by giving the six sectors different size slices, based on how important they are to you and your college success.

 Aural: Download an audio book or a National Public Radio podcast on one of the areas of wellness described in this chapter, and listen to it in your car or as you go about your daily routine.

 Read/Write: Read a book on some aspect of wellness you know nothing about. Choose a recent title or bestseller that has contributed to a national debate on this topic.

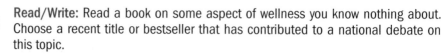 **Kinesthetic:** Take a field trip to your campus student health center. Find out as much as you can about the number of students seen each week and the types of illnesses treated. Then visit the campus counseling center to find out the same information.

Stress: Fast and Furious

CHALLENGE ⊖ REACTION

Challenge: Identify five sources of stress for first-year college students.

Reaction:
1. _____
2. _____
3. _____
4. _____
5. _____

Stress—isn't some stress good for you? Don't Olympic athletes, who train for years and perform on the world's stage, subject themselves to unbelievable stress, and isn't that stress part of what helps them achieve excellence? It's true that stress can produce results. Short-term stress—giving a speech or doing a tough math problem in your head—can actually bring out the best in you. However, long-term stress such as living through a natural disaster or caring for a disabled relative can take its toll. Stress can also come from distant trauma, such as child abuse in your past that continues to haunt you. Short-term stress "revs up" your immune system and protects you, but long-term or chronic stress tears it down, making you more vulnerable to illness.[26]

In some ways, stress is in the eye of the beholder. What's stressful to you may not be stressful to your best friend. There's a difference between stressors (the actual events or circumstances) and *perceived* stressors (how you react to them). Some experts say stress results from being both anxious and fatigued. Anxiety spikes your energy level, but if you're in a state of exhaustion at the same time, your body interprets the cross signals as stress.[27]

How do you know when you're reacting adversely to stress? Pay attention if you are depressed, irritable, anxious, fearful, lethargic, if you can't sleep (or sleep too much and still feel tired), wake up frequently, experience stomachaches, headaches, shakiness, excessive sweating, heartburn, nausea, rapid and shallow breathing, or frequent colds. Not coping well with stress can show up in your health, your relationships, your job, and your academic work.

So what's so stressful about college? Aside from the adjustment factor, basically, everything! Try these common factors on for size, and see if they produce stress in you, perhaps even in just reading about them.[28]

Goodbyes. For many students, homesickness and friendsickness generate stress. Perhaps you left an ill family member behind or a favorite pet that rarely left your side.

Hellos. Meeting so many new people, while exciting, can feel like pressure. Will you make friends quickly and easily? Will you be accepted for who you are? Nevertheless, forging connections helps provide you with the support system you need in a new situation.

UpperCut Images/Getty Images

"You are your choices."

Lucius Annaeus Seneca, Roman philosopher and statesman (4 B.C.–A.D. 65)

Emotional Intelligence (EI) Research The ability to be emotionally self-aware is fundamental to becoming emotionally intelligent. Being able to understand why you feel the way that you do and connect it to a source is the first step in making change.

> **"For fast-acting relief, try slowing down."**
>
> Lily Tomlin, Comedian

Teachable Moment Remind students that they do have control over many things in their lives maybe more than they know. If they truly have no control over a situation (for example, their parents' divorce), the thing they can control is how they respond to it.

Emotional Intelligence (EI) Research Consider having your students take the EQ-i assessment (Multi Health Systems). Check to see if anyone on your campus is certified to administer the instrument and provide feedback. The EQ-i is a valid tool that measures emotional intelligence in areas such as intrapersonal (including emotional self-awareness), interpersonal, stress management, and adaptability (which also includes problem solving) skills, and general mood.

Grades. Perhaps you're attending college on a scholarship, and keeping your grades up is a top priority for you, or test anxiety gets the better of you. If you're a perfectionist, you may put unrealistic expectations on yourself, too, and that can seriously augment stress.

Peaks and valleys. Terms in college—quarters or semesters—have a rhythm to them. Your energy requirements are continuous, but they spike for midterm and final exams. Peak times can bring stress that affects your immune system. Just listen to the hacking and coughing during exams; it's a fairly common soundtrack.

Academic load. College brings a relentless lineup of assignments. As soon as you turn in one assignment, another one is waiting right behind it. Each class by itself would require a substantial investment of time, let alone the aggregate.

Academic challenge. At the beginning of the term you may be reviewing material from high school in some of your courses, and your confidence may climb. You may even become overconfident. But soon your instructor will be moving into uncharted territory, and the learning curve will take off, perhaps bringing your stress level right along with it.

Finances. Are you working more hours than you should? Everyone has legitimate bills, but are lifestyle choices adding to your financial burden? If you can afford luxuries like tanning sessions or a gas-guzzling truck, that's one thing. But if you can't and they compound your stress, that's another.

Eating and sleeping habits. Now that you're in college, you may be running from one thing to the next, grabbing the wrong food (or no food at all) on the way, and not getting the sleep you need in order to cope. Stress begets stress, you could say, and the results can be unhealthy.

What can you do about stress that seems to be spiraling out of control in your life? Here are five suggestions that may help.

1. **Change the situation.** If you're living with an impossible roommate who stays up all night making a racket while you're trying to get some decent shut-eye, consider moving. Do what you can to take control of the situation that's generating the stress.

2. **Change your reaction.** If you can't change the situation, try to change the way you react to it. Rather than letting the anxiety continue to build up, bunk with a friend and get the sleep you need until the situation is resolved.

3. **Keep up.** Keep up with your academic work in all your classes. Letting assignments slip in even one class is a guaranteed stress inducer.

4. **Improve your problem-solving skills.** If you can figure out what to do about what's stressing you, and you have confidence in your problem-solving skills, you'll be better off.[29] Take a class in problem solving or read up on increasing your skills on your own.

5. **Work with an expert.** If none of these techniques helps, you may benefit from working with a physician or a counselor on campus. Stress has the potential to adversely affect your college experience. Research shows a relationship

between stress, low self-esteem, poor health habits, and reduced perceptions of health status.[30] You needn't continue to struggle with unmanageable stress when help is readily available close by. Take action to change things.

Sensitive Situation You may have a mix of students in your class with some having to work to support themselves or a family and others not. Regardless of their individual circumstances, however, most students have worked for pay at some point in the past and can respond to the issues above based on past, if not present, work status.

EXERCISE 13.3 Workplace Stress Survey

If you work for pay in addition to going to school, describe the organization for which you work. How many employees work there? What kind of work does the organization do? Describe your job. How long have you worked for this organization? What is your role?

Check the items that you consider to be workplace stressors in your current position. Each item includes several examples for clarification.

_____ 1. **Economic uncertainty:** the possibility of layoffs, mergers, acquisitions, closings

_____ 2. **Superiors:** a boss or bosses who are difficult to work for or who micro-manage

_____ 3. **Coworkers:** peers who don't pull their share, take credit for your work, or engage in destructive behavior

_____ 4. **Subordinates:** people you manage who are unmotivated or challenging to lead

_____ 5. **Workload:** too much work, too little work, not enough variety in the work

_____ 6. **Pace:** constant pressure, unrealistic deadlines

_____ 7. **Communication:** being kept in the dark about decisions, an overactive grape-vine, gossiping about other employees

_____ 8. **Role:** unclear expectations, conflicting job demands

_____ 9. **Physical environment:** noise, air quality, working conditions

_____ 10. **Safety:** threats, fears, harassment

Elaborate on your stress management techniques for one of the items you checked.

INSIGHT ⊖ ACTION

Keep a stress diary for a week. Record what causes you stress each day and how strongly you react. What symptoms appeared? How high was your stress level? What did you do about it? After a week, you'll have a substantial amount of data that not only tells you about your stress level but also your coping mechanisms. It's important to stay attuned to sensations and signals: "Hey, I must be really stressed out over this! My heart's racing and I feel panicky." It's also important to pay attention to what helps, like exercise, meditation, yoga, or prayer. Summarize your results, what you learned in doing this, and what actions you can take in the future to better manage the stress in your life.

Nutrition: Feast or Famine

CHALLENGE ⊖ REACTION

Challenge: What do you think the heading of this section refers to, specifically? Can you identify the two ends of the nutrition continuum as they refer to college students?

Reaction: _____

Nutrition Facts

Serving size 1 container, individual (64.0 g)

Amount Per Serving

Calories 296	Calories from Fat 127

% Daily Value*

Total Fat 14.1g	22 %
Saturated Fat 6.3g	31%
Cholesterol 0mg	0%
Sodium 1434mg	60%
Total Carbohydrates 36.8g	12%
Protein 5.6g	

Vitamin A 8%	•	Vitamin C 0%
Calcium 0%	•	Iron 12%

*Based on a 2000 calorie diet

http://www.calorie-count.com/calories/item/6582.html

Figure 13.2

Nutritional Label for Ramen Noodles

Chapter Crossover In Chapter 3 students learned about campus resources. Ask students what campus resources might help them to keep their weight under control. While it may be about what one eats, it's also about exercise. Encourage students to make good use of campus workout facilities or get involved in intramural athletics.

Many first-year students change their eating habits in college; specifically, they eat too much or too little. Some students pack on double-digit pounds, resulting in what is commonly known as the "freshman 15." If you're paying for a meal plan that includes all you can eat, you may unknowingly (or knowingly) max out your diet and your time to socialize with friends while you eat. Or perhaps you dislike the food at your school, or are trying to save money by eating tons of ramen noodles on your own. Did you know that ramen noodles are high in carbohydrates, low in vitamins and minerals, and high in sodium and fat (see Figure 13.2)?

In fact, many college favorites are loaded with calories. If you chow down on a cheeseburger and fries for lunch (600 + 600 = 1,200 calories) and four pieces of pizza with "the works" (2,400 calories), a side of garlic bread (400 calories), and a large soda (300 calories) for dinner, you've just weighed in with a grand total of 4,300 calories for the day, not including breakfast. (By the way, skipping breakfast in order to sleep in or cut down on calories is one of the biggest mistakes you can make. Breakfast *breaks* your overnight *fast*, replenishes the glucose in your body, and keeps your metabolism going all day.) To burn up 4,300 calories, you'd need to walk briskly for nearly six hours!

In one study, 764 college students (53 percent women, 47 percent men) had their height and weight measured and completed questionnaires about their exercise and dietary patterns. At the beginning of their first year, 29 percent reported that they didn't exercise, 70 percent didn't eat the recommended five servings of fruits and vegetables per day, and over 50 percent reported eating high-fat fast food at least three times during the previous week. Two hundred and ninety students were reassessed at the end of their second year, and 70 percent had gained weight.[31] Although researchers didn't find major changes in students' behaviors over that time, their incoming unhealthy behaviors may have caught up with them.

Does that mean you should totally avoid foods you love? In our culture, food is a social activity. We don't eat to live, some would say; we live to eat. However, if you begin to notice that your jeans are shrinking, and you just can't understand why, you may find the answer on the end of your fork! The United States has the highest obesity rate of any developed country, and obesity in America has become a leading national health concern with 66.3 percent of adults either overweight or obese today.[32] Grocery store shelves are stocked with a huge selection of tempting treats and prepackaged foods, and fast foods are readily available. Portion sizes have increased over time, too, and a less active lifestyle is part of the problem. Choosing taste and convenience over good nutrition has become far too common.

Think of yourself as an athlete in training. Eat sensibly—and pay attention to nutrition. Here are eleven key recommendations from the U.S. Department of Agriculture:

1. Consume a variety of foods and beverages, especially those packed with nutrients.

2. Limit less healthy foods. Saturated and trans fats, cholesterol, added sugars, and salt make food taste good, but they don't do your health any favors.

3. Balance the calories you take in with the energy you expend. If you're physically active, you need more fuel for your body. If you're not, eat moderately.

4. Keep your total fat intake to between 20 and 35 percent of the calories you eat and drink, with most fats limited to things like nuts, fish, and vegetable oils. The average American diet is fat-rich, but be aware! Many fat-free or low-fat food items contain more calories than their fat-laden counterparts. Become a faithful label reader, and pay particular attention to ingredients if you have food allergies.[33]

5. Eat roughly 2½ to 6½ cups of fruits and vegetables per day, and vary your selections. Grab an apple instead of a bag of chips.

6. Eat 3 or more ounces of whole-grain products each day (bread, cereal, and so on)

7. Drink (or eat) 3 cups of fat-free or low-fat milk or milk products (like cheese or yogurt) per day.

8. Choose lean meats or poultry—bake, broil, or grill it, and vary your selections with fish, beans, nuts, seeds, and peas.

9. Consume less than one teaspoon of salt (or sodium) per day.

10. Drink six to eight glasses of water per day to stay hydrated.

11. When in doubt, toss it out! Many foods spoil within two hours or less.[34]

"**Fear less, hope more, eat less, chew more, whine less, breathe more, talk less, say more, love more, and all good things will be yours.**"

Swedish proverb

While general guidelines are good, in the daily rush of campus life, it's even better to have a more specific plan for managing your weight. Many Body Mass Index (BMI) calculators are available online, which is a good place to start as you "weigh" these issues. Online BMI calculators give you an immediate assessment of whether you're underweight, normal, overweight, or obese by simply entering your height and weight.

EXERCISE 13.4 "How Do I Love Thee? Let Me Count the Ways"

What are your favorite foods? Are you a chocoholic? Do you crave salty snacks with a vengeance? Do you scarf down pizza like there's no tomorrow? Do you have any idea how many calories you devote to your food passions in one sitting? Next time you indulge, take note. Measure the volume of food (six slices of pizza, half a bag of chocolate kisses), and then tabulate the results via an online calorie calculator or by reading the label and doing the math. Fill in the number of calories here: _____. Are you surprised by the grand total? If the average adult needs roughly 2,000 calories per day, how much of your daily intake did you just consume? Remember, there's no need to abstain; just refrain from eating too much of your "love object" at one sitting.

Teachable Moment See if students can share with each other some healthy snacks that they enjoy. Sometimes stocking one's room with a few healthy snacks can cut down on trips to the vending machines.

CRAZY FOR FAST FOOD?

Does a double cheeseburger and a large order of fries sound good to you right about now? Does your mouth start to water even more when you think about adding a chocolate milkshake to your order? Now is the time to confess: Are you a fast-food junkie?

If you just whispered "yes" under your breath, you're not alone. According to Eric Schlosser's book, *Fast Food Nation,* "In 1970, Americans spent about $6 billion on fast food; in 2000, they spent more than $110 billion. Americans now spend more money on fast food than on higher education, personal computers, computer software, or new cars. They spend more on fast food than on movies, books, magazines, newspapers, videos, and recorded music—combined."[35]

Perhaps you're thinking: What's so bad about that? Who has time to cook these days? I'm in college, completing assignments for all my courses, holding down a job, and taking care of relationships. The drive-through lane saves my life!

But does it? In his 2004 Academy Award nominated documentary, *Super Size Me,* thirty-three-year-old producer Morgan Spurlock filmed an experiment. He traveled the country, eating only McDonald's fast food three times a day for a month, stopped exercising and adopted a sedentary lifestyle, and took a camera crew along to record his journey. Whenever he was asked if he wanted to supersize, his preset answer was yes. His other self-imposed rule was that he would try everything on the menu at least once.

The results were grim. Three physicians agreed to monitor Spurlock's health, and toward the end of the thirty-day experiment, they advised him to abandon it. His weight ballooned by nearly thirty pounds. He reported, "I got desperately ill. My face was splotchy and I had this huge gut, which I've never had in my life. … It was amazing and really frightening." He suffered from chest pains, depression, climbing blood pressure, sexual dysfunction, skyrocketing cholesterol, and liver damage.

What's the moral of this real-life story? To be sure, most fast food is loaded with calories, fat, and sodium, and McDonald's isn't the only culprit. Can you eat a healthy meal at a fast-food restaurant? Yes, it's possible, but you'll be healthier if you limit your high-calorie fast food, save it for a special treat, or just decide to fill up on portable fruits and veggies instead. You'll avoid the health risks of supersizing. Remember, it's been said, "You are what you eat." What does your diet say about *you*?[36]

Everett Collection

> **"Morgan Spurlock has crafted the ultimate contemporary horror story."**—*Jeanne Aufmuth, PALO ALTO WEEKLY*

> **"Will wipe the smile right off your Happy Meal."** —*Thomas Delapa, BOULDER WEEKLY*

> **"You'll never think the same way about those two all-beef patties."** —*Mark Caro, CHICAGO TRIBUNE*

Activity Option It is worth asking if anyone has seen the movie *Super Size Me*. If so, did it change the way they now look at fast food? Consider hosting a movie night (with healthy snacks) and tell students to come to the next class ready to discuss it.

For some students, college isn't one long feast, it's the origin of famine. The most common age for the onset of an eating disorder is eighteen, and a majority of American college women exhibit at least a few symptoms. In fact, over 90 percent of the 5 million Americans with eating disorders are female. One percent of adolescent girls develop anorexia and 2 to 3 percent develop bulimia.[37]

Anorexics see themselves as fat or flabby, even when others don't. They may literally starve themselves, induce vomiting, or exercise obsessively. Bulimics binge on food until they can't eat any more or are interrupted, and then induce vomiting or take large doses of laxatives and diuretics. Both anorexia and bulimia can have serious medical consequences.

In one study of college women attending a large pubic university, 17 percent of the 578 respondents were found to be struggling with a probable eating disorder. They indicated they would prefer to be helped by a friend.[38] "Friends don't let friends drive drunk" can be extended to many areas of wellness. Medication and therapy can be essential, too. Research indicates that body image and self-esteem are related, particularly for women.[39]

Sensitive Situation While friends can be a good resource for individuals struggling with an eating disorder, emphasize that very often professional intervention is needed. When eating disorders are addressed early, the chances of long-term consequences are diminished.

EXERCISE 13.5 Which Dinner Would You Order?

Consider these three dining options and decide which one would be the healthiest choice. Think in terms of fats, calories, and the various nutritional recommendations made in this chapter. Assume that you had cereal and a banana for breakfast and a slice of cheese pizza and a soda for lunch.

1. Vegetable Lasagna
   Caesar Salad
   Wheat roll with Butter
   Neapolitan Ice Cream

2. Roast Pork with Gravy
   Garlic Mashed Potatoes
   Corn on the Cob with Butter
   Chocolate Cake

3. Taco Salad
   Apple Pie a la Mode

Once you've made your choice, go to an online calorie and nutrient calculator to see how your selection measured up. Were you on target or surprised by the nutritional analysis you found online? The answers are upside down at the bottom of this page.

Activity Option Have students go online and calculate the number of calories they burned for the week. Students can use this website: http://www.caloriecontrol.org/exercalc.html.

Exercise: Don't Be a Couch Potato!

Research shows that just twenty minutes of exercise can help to calm you for as long as twenty-four hours. Vigorous exercise helps you get rid of excess adrenaline and pumps in endorphins that block pain and anxiety.[40] Research also shows that people who get regular exercise fall asleep more quickly and report fewer sleep difficulties. Pilots, who have bizarre sleep schedules due to long transoceanic flights, follow this advice. Morning walks are a good way to expose yourself to daylight and to get your exercise early in the day. In one study of college freshmen, students who increased their exercise during the first several months of school reported feeling more vigorous, less tired, and less stressed than those who exercised less than they had previously.[41]

Activity Option Get students up and out of their chairs by doing an exercise continuum. Ask students to place themselves on the imaginary continuum with one end representing "I have increased my exercise since I have come to college" and the other end representing those who have decreased their exercise. Ask students to report how changes in exercise make them feel. For those who are exercising, ask them to share their strategies with the class.

> **"If you eat 100 more food calories a day than you burn, you'll gain about one pound in a month. That's about 10 pounds in a year. The bottom line is that to lose weight, it's important to reduce calories and increase activity."**
>
> **Department of Health and Human Services; U.S. Department of Agriculture**

(Answers to Exercise 13.5: Meal 1: 1,059 cal, 67 g fat, 1,400 mg sodium; Meal 2: 770 cal, 29 g fat, 1,111 mg sodium; Meal 3: 1,993 cal, 95 g fat, 2,786 mg sodium. Note: Calorie count varies by portion size, preparation method, and restaurant/brand. Nutritional information sources: http://www.calorie-count.com/; http://www.benjerry.com/.)

"Lack of activity destroys the good condition of every human being, while movement and methodical physical exercise save it and preserve it."

Plato (c. 428–348 B.C.)

Activity Option Ask students to make the connection between their psychological type and the way they have approached exercise in the past. What is their type and what kind of exercise do they do, if any? If they don't exercise, can they figure out why based on their type? Ask students to send you a two-paragraph essay e-mail about their analysis.

Not only does exercise help you burn off cheeseburgers, recent brain-imaging and neurochemical studies indicate that "sweating makes you smart." Physical exercise helps reinforce existing connections between neurons and forge new ones via a protein called BDNF (brain-derived neurotrophic factor). A dense neural network helps you process and store information: "Learning is taking signals that come in from your senses and embedding them into brain anatomy," according to Dr. Vassilis Koliatsos, a psychiatrist at Johns Hopkins University. BDNF affects memory and mood; it literally helps rewire your brain.[42]

INSIGHT ⊖ ACTION

Keep an exercise log for a week. On a daily basis, record the type of physical activity, the length of time you do it, and the level of workout (mild, medium, or high exertion). Using an online exercise calculator, record the number of calories you burned.

	Sunday	Monday	Tuesday	Wednesday	Thursday	Friday	Saturday
Activity							
Time							
Exertion Level							
Calories Burned							

Your Type is Showing

Have you ever started a new exercise plan and then up and quit on yourself? If so, have you ever wondered why? Maybe you made a New Year's resolution to slim down or you decided to get buff to try out for the team. Over time you lost interest, however, and your new exercise plan died a slow death. One possible explanation might have been that the type of exercise you chose didn't fit your psychological type. Now there's a thought!

It makes sense that introverts would prefer activities they can pursue alone or with one close friend, like jogging or cycling. Extraverts might go for team sports or coordinated exercise, like volleyball or rowing. Sensors may like practical, results-oriented activities, like lifting weights, whereas iNtuitives may like creative activities such as aerobics set to music. Thinkers may prefer physical activities that require reasoning and logic, like timing your laps across the pool and figuring out ways to beat your own record. Feelers may prefer activities in which others can be part of an interconnected group effort, like team relay races. Judgers may prefer structured exercise routines, like yoga or aerobics. Perceivers, on the other hand, may enjoy spontaneity while they work out, like dancing or exploring new hiking paths, for example.

According to Canadian researcher Dr. James Gavin of Concordia University in Quebec, exercise regimens should "fit" people's personalities. Today, only one out of five North American adults participates in some type of regular exercise. But Dr. Gavin asks, "Does it fit with who the person is? Will it challenge long-standing habits? You might think of it this way: people have personalities … and so do sports and fitness activities. People generally feel better when they do activities within their comfort zones, i.e., that match their styles."

Of course, when it comes to exercise, body type, strength, and endurance count; but think, too, about your exercise preferences and your psychological type. Does your new fitness program fit you? If so, it may be much more likely to become part of your lifestyle.[43]

Sleep: Are You a Night Owl?

Does this describe you? You're running on no sleep—no sleep. You have bags under your eyes. You're dizzy, moody, irritable, anxious, or depressed. You can't keep your eyes from closing while reading your assignments, and you have to prop your head up to stay awake in class. You could be starring in a movie called *Sleepless in School*.

Unfortunately, this description fits thousands of first-year college students. When you're running on no sleep, being at your academic best is next to impossible. In fact, you can't really be at your best at anything. Sleep affects your academic performance and—believe it or not—may even adversely affect your decision to stay in college and succeed![44]

Many college students don't get enough sleep and don't get the right kind of sleep. Researchers believe the average college student needs eight to nine hours of sleep per night; some experts say as much as ten hours! But the actual number of hours college students are sleeping has been decreasing steadily for years.[45] Today, many college students average six hours or less per night, or go to bed at 4 a.m. and sleep until noon, upsetting the natural rhythm of their bodies based on nature's cycle of daylight and darkness. A once-in-a-while upset in your equilibrium isn't the end of the world, but if not getting enough sleep is your normal practice, you're incurring sleep debt. Think of sleep debt as a buildup of the cumulative amount of sleep you owe yourself to be at your best. If sleep debt were tracked like credit card debt, just how high would your bill be?

Sleep restores us physically and emotionally. It recharges our batteries. College students who don't get enough sleep—particularly REM (rapid eye movement) sleep that takes place most during the lasts few hours while dreaming occurs—may be hurting their chances at college success. Sleep deprivation causes problems like these:[46]

1. **Learning.** During REM sleep, your brain creates sleep spindles: one- to two-second bursts of brainwaves that help transfer information to long-term memory. Sleeping less than six hours may block the production of sleep spindles and result in less learning.[47] In tests comparing sleep-deprived students' learning with students who get eight hours of sleep, nonsleepers were less able to learn new information. Interestingly, many students rated their cognitive abilities as higher when they were sleep deprived, but all the evidence indicated the reverse was true.[48]

2. **Grade Point Average.** In one study that compared college students who were short sleepers (six hours or less), average sleepers (seven to eight hours), and long sleepers (nine or more hours), average GPAs reported for the three groups were 2.74, 3.01, and 3.24, respectively.[49]

3. **Relationship Strain.** Who wants to interact with a cranky, sleep-deprived person? Sleep deprivation may put your relationships at risk because of increased irritability and decreased interpersonal sensitivity. What's more, getting less sleep may start a chain reaction. In one study of college students' sleep troubles, worrying about relationships was the most often cited reason for not getting enough sleep.[50]

Image100/Jupiter Images

> **"Oh sleep! It is a gentle thing, Beloved from pole to pole."**
>
> Samuel Taylor Coleridge, English critic and poet (1772–1834)

Activity Option Ask everyone who went to bed before 10:00 p.m. more than half of the days of the week last week to stand. Have these students move to the front of the room on the left. Then ask in two-hour intervals for students to form groups around the room until everyone is out of their seats. Next ask groups to come up with a number between 1 and 10 that describes how rested and alert they feel. Compare group responses.

4. **Anxiety, Depression, and Illness.** Sleep deprivation triggers all sorts of emotional, psychological, and physical risks. Students who report getting less sleep appear to be less psychologically healthy and more prone to catching every bug that comes along.[51]

5. **Car Accidents.** According to the National Highway Traffic Safety Administration, fatigue accounts for approximately 1,550 deaths, 71,000 injuries, and more than 100,000 police-reported automobile crashes on our highways each year. Young drivers (ages 16–29) are particularly at risk.[52]

6. **Lowered Life Satisfaction.** In the grand scheme of things, getting less sleep seems to throw off everything. One study, for example, examined students' reported average length of sleep and their scores on a well-known life satisfaction scale. Getting less sleep was significantly related to being less satisfied with life in general.[53]

What should you do? Consider these simple, but important suggestions for avoiding sleep deprivation.[54]

> **Set a coffee deadline.** Just one cup of coffee within four to five hours of bedtime can cause you to have trouble falling asleep, reduce overall sleep time, make you waken more frequently, and produce lighter sleep.

> **Avoid using alcohol to help you sleep.** Alcohol may help you fall asleep more quickly, but it causes you to sleep in fragments, rather than continuously.[55]

> **Take an early afternoon nap or none at all.** A short nap after lunch can increase your ability to focus later in the day, but taking a long one too close to bedtime can reduce your overnight sleep quality.

> **Save your bed for sleeping.** Use your bed for sleeping exclusively, so that your mind associates being in that particular location with going to sleep, not reading, watching TV, or doing homework.

> **Stick to a routine.** Sleeping in on the weekends doesn't make up for lost sleep during the week. Try not to vary your sleep schedule by more than two hours in either direction. If you stay up late on Friday night, gradually move closer and closer to your normal bedtime over the weekend. Large variations in your sleep schedule can do almost as much damage as not getting enough sleep.

Thomas Edison, who believed sleep is a waste of time, invented the electric lightbulb in the late 1800s, hoping to reduce the human propensity to sleep. His invention worked, but he might be disturbed today to see the potential physical, psychological, and sometimes even academic, results.[56]

Teachable Moment Incompatible sleep schedules between roommates is a real challenge in college. Varying class schedules as well as different sleep habits and needs can cause extreme conflict. Ask students to identify a few common sleep-related roommate challenges they have experienced or heard about. Similar problems can be generated for commuting students when family members' sleep patterns conflict. Discuss ways to resolve these problems.

Teachable Moment Have any of your students had difficulty falling asleep? Sometimes when students stay up late studying or working on the computer, their minds are racing afterwards, and it's difficult to fall asleep. Last-minute cramming or cranking out a paper at midnight may lead to a very restless night's sleep.

INSIGHT ⊖ ACTION

Do you have any idea how much sleep you're actually getting? According to sleep experts, you should be getting seven or more hours per night, or a minimum of forty-nine hours per week. Keep a sleep log for a week. Every morning, write down the number of hours of sleep you've gotten.

Sunday	Monday	Tuesday	Wednesday	Thursday	Friday	Saturday
_____	_____	_____	_____	_____	_____	_____

Are you surprised to see the actual numbers? Is there much variation from night to night? From weekdays to weekends? Formulate a new strategy to become better rested.

Box 13.1 Some ZZZZZZZs Please

So not getting enough sleep is a bad idea, but what are college students doing instead of sleeping? Many stores and restaurants are open twenty-four hours a day, TV programming is continuous, and the Internet never rests. What *aren't* they doing?

Some students are Internet addicts, regularly choosing a computer over their pillows. For example, 26 percent of college men gamble in online card games like Texas Hold 'Em or Omaha High at least once a month, and 4 percent do so once a week or more. One student admitted playing 17,190 hands of online poker over three months, playing for 13 to 15 hours out of every 24.[57] Another student discovered he had logged 1,008 hours—42 full days—playing World of Warcraft online over 7 months. "He had what addicts call a 'moment of clarity,' and he decided to hang up his armor for good."[58] Still other students are MySpace.com or Facebook.com addicts, checking their accounts twenty or more times around the clock.

How do you know if you're addicted? Ask yourself these questions: Are you able to tolerate increasing amounts of leisure time online? Is your time online hurting your grades, your relationships, and your health? Are you losing sleep over it—literally?

Intentionally depriving prisoners of war of sleep is a controversial subject, considered by some to be a form of torture. There are reasons for that. If Internet addiction is keeping you up at night, do what you can to get some ZZZZZZs—please!

Alcohol and Drugs: The "Party Hardy" Syndrome

CHALLENGE ⟶ REACTION

Challenge: What is the common definition for *binge drinking*?

Reaction: _____

During the 1960s in the United States, many college students experimented with marijuana and hallucinogenic drugs like LSD. In recent studies, 30 percent of undergraduates say they have used marijuana in the last year. Ecstasy use has more than doubled on college campuses to 7.1 percent of students reporting they have used it in the last year. Opiates (other than heroin) were reportedly used by 7.3 percent, PCP by 4.8 percent, tranquilizers by 4.6 percent, and cocaine by 3.8 percent of college students in the last year.[59] Interestingly, students generally overestimate the number of other students who use drugs.[60]

Alcohol is today's drug of choice on most college campuses. Although 28 percent of college students smoke cigarettes, a habit that brings a well-known set of health risks, 85 percent report they have drunk alcohol in the last year.[61] Not all students drink as irresponsibly as Anthony from the "FOCUS Challenge Case," but there's no doubt that drinking is identified by many campuses as their top-ranking concern. Binge drinking, the leading cause of preventable death among college students, is typically described as four or more drinks in a row for a woman and five or more for a man.[62] High-risk drinking among college students has been linked to academic problems such as missed classes, lower grades, dropping out, failing, and other serious problems such as vandalism, unplanned sex, sexual assaults, fatalities, alcohol poisoning, and attempted suicides. Are you aware of these recent findings?

© Chuck Savage/CORBIS

"Drunkenness is simply voluntary insanity."

Lucius Annaeus Seneca, Roman philosopher and statesman (4 B.C.–A.D. 65)

> College students spend $5.5 billion on alcohol per year, more than they spend on coffee, tea, juice, soda, milk, and textbooks combined.[63]

> Adolescents may be more vulnerable to brain damage from excessive drinking than older adults.[64]

> Brief episodes of excessive drinking are damaging to the brain. "There is evidence that repeated, abrupt increases of alcohol levels in the brain, followed by abstinence, induces more damage than the same amount of alcohol taken uninterrupted in the same length of time."[65] Of course, the solution to this problem isn't to drink excessively all the time!

> College drinkers drink more, drink more often, and engage in more high-risk drinking than their counterparts the same age who aren't in college, and the beginning of the first year of college is when the most drinking occurs, period.[66]

> Approximately 1,700 college students between 18 and 24 years of age die each year from alcohol-related unintentional injuries.[67]

> Excessive drinking in college may put students at greater risk of alcohol dependence later in life.[68]

> Students tend to drink more if they believe their friends also drink excessively and do not disapprove.[69]

> In one study of community college students in which the average age was 26, 25 percent of the sample engaged in high-risk drinking.[70]

> College women who are preoccupied with alcohol are more likely to drink more.[71]

> College student drinking is lower in states with fewer high-risk adult drinkers and stricter alcohol control laws.[72]

> Heavier alcohol use in college may put both males and females at greater risk of heart disease later in life.[73]

If you and your friends do drink, remember this: The only thing that helps a drunken person sober up is time. Black coffee and cold showers are myths. Watch for symptoms of alcohol poisoning—a stupor or coma, vomiting, seizures, more than ten seconds between breaths, and a bluish skin color, indicating a very low body temperature. If you see these signs, call for help immediately. Putting someone to bed to sleep it off can be a lethal mistake.[74]

Know the facts, know the risks, and if you drink, drink responsibly. Pace yourself, keep track of how much alcohol you've had, or ask someone else to let you

Sensitive Situation There is a connection between any kind of substance abuse and anxiety or depression. Sometimes the reason for substance abuse is to numb the pain for something that is more deep-seated than partying. Students who self-medicate by abusing drugs or alcohol need to address the causes of their behavior.

C CONTROL Your Learning

YOUR TOUGHEST CLASS
Think about the most challenging course you're taking this term. Are wellness issues affecting your success? Think about these potential reactions from students:

1. Stress: "This class is so challenging academically that my stress level soars."
2. Nutrition: "I skip breakfast, right before this class. Hunger pangs distract me."
3. Exercise: "I feel lethargic and unable to jump into the discussion."
4. Sleep: "I stay up far too late, and sleep through this class."
5. Alcohol and drugs: "I make a habit of partying the night before this class and feel unwell."
6. Sex: "I'm so attracted to another classmate that I can't concentrate on the lecture!"

Contemplate the role wellness plays, and circle any of the six sectors of wellness that are impacting your success in this class. Develop a step-by-step plan, based on the information you've read in this chapter, to help you do your best. If it's appropriate, e-mail your plan to your professor in the course.

know when it's time to quit. Alternate alcoholic and nonalcoholic drinks, avoid drinking games—and remember: It *is* possible to have fun without alcohol!

INSIGHT ⊖ ACTION

Keep a record of your alcohol consumption over an average week. If you don't drink, skip this box. If you do, look at related factors, such as the cost in time, caloric intake, and money.

	Sunday	Monday	Tuesday	Wednesday	Thursday	Friday	Saturday	TOTAL
Number of Drinks in One Sitting								
Time Spent Drinking								
Calories Consumed								
Money Spent								

Are you surprised by what your record shows? Are your weekly totals in line with what you expected to see? What steps will you take to improve your wellness in this area, and how will you begin?

Sex: Better Safe Than Sorry

Intimacy, STIs, unplanned pregnancies, sexual orientation. Being sexual is part of being human, and for most college students, sex is a fact of life. In one national study, only 18 percent of women and 32 percent of men aged 18–24 reported never to have engaged in sex. The average number of partners students reported in the previous year was 1.2, and two-thirds of women and one-third of men said they were in committed relationships.[75] However, today increasing numbers of students are choosing abstinence or delaying sex until they find a partner they have first gotten to know in other ways.[76] Whatever choices you make are personal ones, and responsibility is key.

What do you need to know about sex in college? Here are twelve FAQs first-year students often ask.

1. *I'm a sexually active college woman. How do I know which type of contraception is best for me?* Consider these factors:

    Effectiveness. On the one hand, in order for a contraceptive to work, you must actually use it. "Just this once" can be one time too many. How conscientious are you? On the other hand, it's important to remember that no method of contraception is 100 percent reliable.

    Suitability. The pill has risks and side effects. It may not be appropriate for you if you only have sex on rare occasions. On the other hand, if you have multiple partners, you are at higher risk for STIs or HIV. Consider using a condom along with a cervical cap or diaphragm.

    Side effects. Discuss your personal health history with your physician, and make sure you understand what side effects may occur, so that you don't worry needlessly if they do.

    Cost. Pills, diaphragms, spermicidal foam or jelly, and condoms cost money. The most inexpensive contraceptive is abstinence!

Sensitive Situation Students probably won't want to share their results from this survey. Prior to having students fill in their personal data, you might make up a fictitious survey and share it with the class for discussion. Remind students that this activity is solely for their benefit. Students must assess their own behavior and decide what to do about it. Your job is to make them fully aware of the consequences.

Sensitive Situation Revealing how a very personal wellness issue is impacting their life may be a sensitive situation that students are not comfortable with. If you have a peer leader, this might be a place where, if appropriate, the peer leader can lead a discussion or respond to e-mails.

2. ***How would I know if I had an STI?*** Symptoms vary for men and women, but many STIs bring burning, itching, rash, sores, discharge, warts, blisters, and sometimes fever or flu-like symptoms. Some STIs have no symptoms whatsoever. If you have any concerns, visit your personal physician or Student Health Center for testing. It's also possible to contract more than one, and curing one does not necessarily cure another. More Americans are infected with STIs than at any other time in history, and the average American's chance of contracting an STI at some point is one in four.[77]

3. ***I'm a sexually active college man. Condoms destroy the pleasure. Do I have other options?*** Abstinence, "outercourse," and oral sex are always possibilities (although the last two options may not protect you from STIs). Withdrawal, the "rhythm method" (based on the woman's predicted ovulation), and female condoms are unreliable. A vasectomy is a radical decision with long-term consequences!

4. ***Whose responsibility is contraception, anyway? Isn't it usually up to the woman?*** For anatomical or societal reasons, or both, historically, contraception was seen more as a woman's responsibility than a man's. However, contraception is actually the responsibility of both partners. "The bottom line is that it takes two people to conceive a baby, and two people should be involved in deciding not to conceive a baby. In the process, they can also enhance their skills in communication, critical thinking, and negotiating."[78]

5. ***My partner insists on sex even when I say no. How can I be more convincing?*** Technically speaking, when one partner says no, and the other partner proceeds against her or his wishes, the situation could be labeled as rape. Women are more vulnerable than men, and various studies show that 25 to 60 percent of college men have coerced women into sex. Sometimes drugs like Rohypnol or GHB are involved: odorless and tasteless drugs that erase the memory of what happened. Assertive communication *at the beginning* of the relationship is critical. "When she says no, she really means yes" is a distorted view of reality that can have serious consequences for both partners.

6. ***I have decided to save sex for marriage, but my friends don't respect my decision. How can I explain my choice?*** Decisions about sex are highly personal. What's right for someone else may not be right for you, and reaching the right decision requires self-understanding. Abstinence is free, safe, and reliable. Don't be pushed into sex until you're ready, and be assertive and confident in your decision. Your friends may or may not understand, but they should respect your choice as the right one for you, even if they've decided differently for themselves.

7. ***I think (or already know) I'm gay, bisexual, or transgender. Should I "come out"?*** The decision to come out is a difficult one for many students. They worry about the reactions of family and friends. Some believe that homosexuality is immoral, based on upbringing and religious beliefs. Each individual is different. If you want to explore these issues, the counseling center on your campus can help. Studies show that most male and female homosexuals are happy and well adjusted, particularly those in long-term, committed relationships, and an estimated three to five million gay and lesbian couples have become parents through artificial insemination or adoption.[79]

8. ***I'm uncomfortable around gay people. What should I do?*** In a landmark national study conducted by the University of Chicago, 2.8 percent of men and 1.4 percent of women described themselves as homosexual.[80] If these statistics are representative (and they may be conservative for college campuses), of the approximately more than 15 million college students in the United States, that's 420,000 gay men and 210,000 lesbian women. College is about learning, and that includes exposing yourself to diverse viewpoints on a range of academic and nonacademic issues. If you close your mind, think about what you may be refusing to learn. Isolating yourself against others' sexual differences in college or later in the workplace is impossible, just as isolating yourself against people of other faiths, ethnicities, and races will be. College is the right place to embrace empathy and tolerance.

9. ***I want to be sexually responsible, but I don't like the idea of planning for sex because it makes me feel promiscuous and takes away the spontaneity. Should I really carry a condom around in my purse or wallet?*** "Be prepared": it's the Boy Scout motto. Many aspects of life require planning. If you were embarking on a long airplane flight without food service, you'd bring along a snack, wouldn't you? If you find preparing for a sexual encounter disruptive or unpleasant and you're female, use an alternative, longer-term form of contraception. The old saying "An ounce of prevention is worth a pound of cure" was never truer than it is here. Remember the ABC rule: Abstain, Be faithful, or use a Condom.[81]

10. ***My friend had a baby in high school; now I'm terrified that the same thing will happen to me. How can I get over my fear?*** Some amount of fear can lead you to make more responsible choices than your friend may have, but if the fear has become irrational and disrupts your life, a counselor may be able to help you work through it.

11. ***I'm particularly vulnerable to unplanned sex when I drink alcohol, but all my friends drink. I don't want to be ostracized; how can I say no?*** Although it may take courage, know yourself, and follow Shakespeare's advice: "to thine own self be true." Which types of situations are dangerous for you? Which friends tempt you to do things you regret? Drinking games, for example, chugging a drink whenever a certain word is spoken or song is played, are dangerous pastimes because it's hard to keep track of how much alcohol you've downed. If reckless friends are your problem, you might consider finding new ones!

12. ***It may sound strange, but I haven't met anyone at college I'd want to have sex with. Am I abnormal?*** No, you're not abnormal. Perhaps you've decided not to settle. You may well know what you're looking for in a romantic partner, and perhaps you've not yet met anyone who displays all these characteristics. Someone who shares your basic values but is different enough to make life interesting is worth searching for, and getting to know someone before jumping into a physical relationship is always smart. Be patient.

Lifesaver.

Condoms can protect you from AIDS and other sexually transmitted diseases.

They can be a lifesaver.

"**Contraceptives should be used on every conceivable occasion.**"

Spike Milligan, *The Last Goon Show of All*

Now that you've read about the six sectors of the Wellness Wheel, look at your profile once more. Are you satisfied with where you are now? Are you committed to "taking the wheel"? What can you do to maximize your wheel? If you follow through with the actions you've prescribed for yourself in this chapter, you'll most likely see the positive results of working toward wellness in all aspects of your life, including your college success.

> **"You can set yourself up to be sick, or you can choose to stay well."**
>
> **Wayne Dyer, self-help author and advocate**

INSIGHT ⟶ ACTION

Of the six sectors of the Wellness Wheel you've read about in this chapter, choose one on which to focus your improvement efforts. What will you do specifically to change your practices? Who can help you? What results do you predict? How are these changes likely to impact your college success?

For more practice online, go to http://www.academic.cengage.com/collegesuccess/staley to take the Challenge Yourself online quizzes.

NOW WHAT DO YOU THINK?

At the beginning of this chapter, Anthony Lopez, a frustrated student, faced a set of challenges. Now after reading this chapter, would you respond differently to any of the questions you answered about the "FOCUS Challenge Case"?

▸▸▸ ▸▸ ▸ REALITY CHECK ◂ ◂◂ ◂◂◂

On a scale of 1 to 10, answer the following questions now that you've completed this chapter.

1 = not very/not much/very little/low   10 = very/a lot/very much/high

In hindsight, how much did you *really* know about this subject matter before reading the chapter?

1　2　3　4　5　6　7　8　9　10

How much do you think this information might affect your college success?

1　2　3　4　5　6　7　8　9　10

How much do you think this information might affect your career success after college?

1　2　3　4　5　6　7　8　9　10

How long did it actually take you to complete this chapter (both the reading and writing tasks)? _____ Hour(s) _____ Minutes

Take a minute to compare these answers to your answers from the "Readiness Check" at the beginning of this chapter. What gaps exist between the similar questions? How might these gaps between what you thought before starting the chapter and what you now think after completing the chapter affect how you approach your next term of college?

To download mp3 format audio summaries of this chapter, go to http://www.academic.cengage.com/collegesuccess/staley.

FOCUS EXIT INTERVIEW

Although you have not quite completed your first term as a college student, we're interested in your reactions to college so far: how you have spent your time, what challenges you've experienced, and your general views about what college has been like. Please answer thoughtfully.

INFORMATION ABOUT YOU

Name _____

Student Number _____ Course/Section _____

Instructor _____

Gender _____ Age _____

INFORMATION ABOUT YOUR COLLEGE EXPERIENCE

1. **How did you find you learned best in college? (Check all that apply.)**

    ____ by looking at charts, maps, graphs

    ____ by looking at color-coded information

    ____ by looking at symbols and graphics

    ____ by listening to instructors' lectures

    ____ by listening to other students during an in-class discussion

    ____ by talking about course content with friends or roommates

    ____ by reading books

    ____ by writing papers

    ____ by taking notes

    ____ by going on field trips

    ____ by engaging in activities

    ____ by actually doing things

2. **For each of the following pairs of descriptors, which set sounds most like you based on what you've learned about yourself this term? (Please choose between the two options on each line and place a checkmark by your choice.)**

    ____ Extraverted and outgoing   or   ____ Introverted and quiet

    ____ Detail-oriented and practical   or   ____ Big-picture and future-oriented

    ____ Rational and truthful   or   ____ People-oriented and tactful

    ____ Organized and self-disciplined or   ____ Spontaneous and flexible

3. *FOCUS* **is about 13 different aspects of college life. Which did you find most interesting person-ally? Which contained information that you found to be most challenging to apply in your own life? (Check all that apply.)**

Most interested in	Most challenging to apply to myself		Most interested in	Most challenging to apply to myself	
____	____	Building dreams, setting goals	____	____	Developing your memory
____	____	Learning to learn	____	____	Reading and studying
____	____	Using resources: finances, technology, and campus support	____	____	Taking tests
____	____	Managing time and energy	____	____	Writing and speaking
____	____	Thinking critically and creatively	____	____	Building relationships, valuing diversity
____	____	Engaging, listening, and note-taking in class	____	____	Choosing a major and career
			____	____	Working toward wellness

4. **Which one of your classes was most challenging this term and why?**

    Which class? (course title *or* department and course number) _____

    Why?_____

    Did you succeed in this class? ____ yes ____ no

    Somewhat (please explain): _____

    _____

5. (18 on Entrance Interview) Were their initial expectations realistic? Some students have been told that college will be so intense that they should plan to study impossible amounts of time. Others are hoping to slide by with little investment. Realism is key to their continuing success.

6–8. (19–21 on Entrance Interview) Did their initial predictions hold? Were they engaged? Did they become integrated into the campus community? If so, how did they accomplish this? If not, why not? Did their motivation increase or decrease over the term? Were their initial concerns warranted? Did they end up working for pay for more hours than they anticipated, leaving few hours for academic work or co-curricular activities? The Exit Interview instrument provides an opportunity to discuss these issues further.

9–14. (22–27 on Entrance Interview) Are they now more certain or less certain about choosing a major, about continuing toward a degree, or about remaining at your institution? Why? What factors intervened?

5. **How many total hours per week did you spend outside of class studying for your college courses this term?**

____ 0–5   ____ 16–20   ____ 31–35

____ 6–10   ____ 21–25   ____ 36–40

____ 11–15 ____ 26–30   ____ 40+

6. **Which of the following on-campus resources did you use once or more this term? (Please check all that apply.)**

____ library

____ campus learning centers (whatever is available on your campus, such as a Writing Center, Math Learning Center, etc.)

____ computer labs

____ the Student Success Center or New Student Center, if one is available

____ the Counseling Center, if one is available

____ professors' office hours for individual meetings/conferences/help

____ student clubs or organizations

____ none

7. **For the following sets of opposite descriptive phrases, please put a checkmark on the line between the two that best represents your response.**

My first term of college:

challenged me academically	____ ____ ____ ____ ____	was easy
was very different from high school	____ ____ ____ ____ ____	was a lot like high school
was exciting	____ ____ ____ ____ ____	was dull
was interesting	____ ____ ____ ____ ____	was uninteresting
motivated me to continue	____ ____ ____ ____ ____	discouraged me
was fun	____ ____ ____ ____ ____	was boring
helped me feel a part of this campus	____ ____ ____ ____ ____	made me feel alienated

8. **Please mark your *top three areas of concern* relating to your first term of college by placing 1, 2, and 3 next to the items you choose.**

____ I did not fit in.

____ I did have difficulty making friends.

____ I was not academically successful.

____ My performance disappointed my family.

____ My personal life interfered with my studies.

____ My studies interfered with my personal life.

____ I had financial difficulties.

____ My job(s) interfered with my studies.

____ My studies interfered with my job.

____ My social life interfered with my studies.

____ My studies interfered with my social life.

____ My professors did not care about me as an individual.

____ I may not finish my degree.

____ I missed the company of my friends.

____ I missed the company of my family.

____ I did not manage my time well.

____ I was bored in my classes.

____ I felt intimidated by my professors.

____ I was overwhelmed by all I had to do.

____ other (please explain)

9. **Have you changed your thinking about selecting a major since entering college? Broadly speaking, now which area do you expect to major in?**

____ Arts & Sciences   ____ Nursing/Health Sciences

____ Education   ____ Business

____ Engineering   ____ other (please explain)

10. **How certain are you now of a chosen major (1 = totally sure, 5 = totally unsure)** ____

11. **How certain are you now that you will complete your degree? (1 = totally sure, 5 = totally unsure)** ____

12. **How certain are you now that you will complete your degree at this school? (1 = totally sure, 5 = totally unsure)** ____

13. **How certain are you now of your intended career choice? (1 = totally sure, 5 = totally unsure)** ____

14. **How certain are you now about whether you'll obtain an advanced degree after you finish college? (1 = totally sure, 5 = totally unsure)** ____

15. **What will your grade point average to be at the end of your first term of college?**

____ A+   ____ B+   ____ C+   ____ D or lower

____ A   ____ B   ____ C

____ A−   ____ B−   ____ C−

15. (28 on Entrance Interview) Was their initial prediction of their end-of-semester GPA accurate, lower than predicted, or higher?

16. **Which of the following sources of information about college turned out to be most accurate? (Mark your top three information sources with 1, 2, and 3.)**

____ TV and movies

____ friends/siblings who have already gone to college

____ discussions with teachers/counselors in high school

____ information I received from colleges in the mail

____ talks with my parents

____ talks with my friends who are also now freshmen

____ the Internet

____ other (please explain) _____

16. (29 on Entrance Interview) Which sources of information were most valid? Why? How much did their views change between the Entrance and Exit Interviews?

17. **How confident are you in yourself in each of the following areas now? (1 = very confident, 5 = not at all confident)**

____ overall academic ability   ____ technology skills

____ mathematical skills   ____ physical well being

____ leadership ability   ____ writing skills

____ reading skills   ____ social skills

____ public speaking skills   ____ emotional well being

____ study skills   ____ teamwork skills

17. (30 on Entrance Interview) If students were overconfident (or under-confident) when they began, they may have developed a more realistic perspective by now. Again, a conversation with you as they leave your course could be important in helping them develop a positive, but realistic, attitude toward future coursework.

31–33 appear on Entrance Interview only; these items do not key to Exit Interview.

18. **Why did you decide to go to college? Now that you've experienced your first term of college, how would you respond? (Check all that apply)**

____ because I want to build a better life for myself.

____ because I want to build a better life for my family.

____ because I want to be very well off financially in the future.

____ because I need a college education to achieve my dreams.

____ because my friends were going to college.

____ because my family encouraged me to go.

____ because it was expected of me.

____ because I was recruited for athletics.

____ because I want to continue learning.

____ because the career I am pursuing requires a degree.

____ because I was unsure of what I might do instead.

____ other (please explain) _____

18. (34 on Entrance Interview) Again, comparisons with their responses early in the term may show the growth critical to college success.

19. **Looking ahead, how satisfied do you expect to be with your decision to attend this school?**

____ very satisfied   ____ somewhat dissatisfied

____ satisfied   ____ very dissatisfied

____ not sure

19–21. (35–37 on Entrance Interview) The next few questions can help you gather important retention data and serve as a debriefing instrument for personal interviews.

20. **Which of the following statements best reflects your educational intention?**

____ I plan to stay at this school until I complete my degree.

____ I plan to transfer to another institution (please identify which one _____)

____ I plan to stop out of college for awhile (to work, for example) and then return to this school.

____ I plan to drop out of college.

21. **If you are thinking about transferring to another institution, why are you thinking of doing so?**

____ This school does not offer my intended major (which is _____).

____ This school is too small.

____ This school is too large.

____ This school is too expensive.

____ I don't feel I fit in.

____ I want to go to a school closer to home.

_____ I want to go to a school further from home.

_____ I want to be closer to my boy/girlfriend.

_____ I want to be closer to my friends.

_____ I will change job locations.

_____ I want to transfer from a two-year to a four-year institution.

_____ I want to transfer from a four-year to a two-year institution.

_____ other (please explain) _____

22. (38 on Entrance Interview) Did students meet their own hopes and expectations?

22. Did you achieve the outcomes you were hoping to achieve at the beginning of this term? Why or why not? _____
_____

23. This culminating question may produce very illuminating responses about the differences between students' *expectations* and *experience*.

23. What was the biggest difference between what you thought college would be like and what it was actually like for you? _____
_____

NOTES

CHAPTER 1

1. Multi-tasking adversely affects brain's learning, UCLA psychologists report. (2006, July 26). *ScienceDaily.* Available: http://www.sciencedaily.com/releases/2006/07/060726083302.htm.

2. Spielberg finally to graduate. (2002, May 15). BBC News. Available at http://news.bbc.co.uk/2/hi/entertainment/1988770.stm.

3. Cranton, P. (1994). *Understanding and promoting transformative learning: A guide for educators of adults.* San Francisco: Jossey-Bass.

4. Davis, J. R. (1993). *Better teaching, more learning.* Phoenix, AZ: Oryx Press.

5. French, B. F., & Oakes, W. (2003). Measuring academic intrinsic motivation in the first year of college: Reliability and validity evidence for a new instrument. *Journal of the First-Year Experience, 15*(1), 83–102; French, B. F. Executive summary of instruments utilized with systemwide first-year seminars. Policy Center on the First Year of College.; French, B. F., Immerkus, J. C., & Oakes, W. C. (2005). An examination of indicators of engineering students' success and persistence. *Journal of Engineering Education, 94*(4), 419–425.

6. Macdaid, G. P., McCaulley, M. H., & Kainz, R. I. (1986). *Atlas of type tables.* Gainesville, FL: Center for Applications of Psychological Type.

7. Also available at http://www.bls.gov/oco/ocos056.htm.

8. Based on Harrell, K. (2003). *Attitude is everything: 10 life-changing steps to turning attitude into action.* New York: HarperBusiness.

9. Dweck, C. S. (2000). *Self-theories: Their role in motivation, personality, and development.* New York: Psychology Press, p. 1.

10. Sax, L. J., Lindholm, J. A., Astin, A. W., Korn, W. S., & Mahoney, K. M. (2003). *The American freshman: National norms for fall 2002.* Los Angeles: Higher Education Research Institute, UCLA. Available: http://www.gseis.ucla.edu/heri/findings.html.

11. Berglas, S. & Jones, E. E. (1978). Drug choice as a self-handicapping strategy in response to noncontingent success. *Journal of Personality and Social Psychology, 36*, 405–417; Jones, E. E. & Berglas, S. (1978). Control of attributions about the self through self-handicapping strategies: The appeal of alcohol and the role of underachievement. *Personality and Social Psychology Bulletin, 4*, 200–206; Dweck, C. S. (2006). *Mindset: The new psychology of success.* New York: Random House.

12. Dweck, *Mindset,* 7.

13. Ibid., 7.

14. Dweck, C. S. (2000). *Self-theories: Their role in motivation, personality, and development.* New York: Psychology Press; Dweck, *Mindset.*

15. Robins, R. W., & Pals, J. (1998). *Implicit self-theories of ability in the academic domain: A test of Dweck's model.* Unpublished manuscript.

16. Mangels, J. A., Butterfield, B., Lamb, J., Good, C. D., & Dweck, C. S. (2006). Why do beliefs about intelligence influence learning success? A social cognitive neuroscience model. *Social Cognitive and Affective Neuroscience, 1*(2), 75–86.

17. Bauer, A. R., Grant, H., & Dweck, C. S. (2006). *Personal goals predict the level and impact of dysphoria.* Unpublished manuscript.

18. Association of American Colleges and Universities. (2002). *Greater Expectations: A New Vision of Learning as a Nation Goes to College.* Washington, DC:

19. Brooks, D. (2005, September 25). The education gap. *The New York Times,* pp. 4–11; Leonhardt, D. (2005, May 24). The college dropout boom. *The New York Times.* Available: http://www.nytimes.com/2005/05/24/national/class/EDUCATION-FINAL.html?pagewanted=print.

20. Hoover, E. (2006, February 24). Study finds school-college "disconnect" in curricula. *The Chronicle of Higher Education, 52*(25), A1.

21. Omara-Otunnu, E. (2006, July 24). Conference examines transition from high school to college. University of Connecticut *Advance.* Available at http://advance.uconn.edu/2006/060724/06072407.htm.

22. Data show value of college degree. (2005, April 8). *The Chronicle of Higher Education, 51*(31), A22.

23. Pascarella, E. T., & Terenzini, P. T. (2005). *How college affects students: A third decade of research.* San Francisco: Jossey-Bass, p. 403.

CHAPTER 2

1. Brookfield, S. (1995). *Becoming a critically reflective teacher.* San Francisco: Jossey-Bass, p. 62.

2. Leamnson, R. (1999). *Thinking about teaching and learning: Developing habits of learning with first year college and university students.* Sterling, VA: Stylus.

3. Livermore, B. (1992, September-October). Build a better brain. *Psychology Today.* Available at http://www.psychologytoday.com/articles/pto-19920901-000024.html.

4. Jozefowicz, C. (2004, May-June). Sweating makes you smart. *Psychology Today*. Available at http://psychology today.com/articles/pto-20040514-000004.html; Wu, A., Ying, Z., & Gomez-Pinilla, F. (2004). Dietary omega-3 fatty acids normalize BDNF levels, reduce oxidative damage, and counteract learning disability after traumatic brain injury in rats. *Journal of Neurotrauma, 21*, 1457–1467; PT Staff. (1998, March-April). Brain Boosters. *Psychology Today*; Alzheimer's Association. (2004). Think about your fu-ture. Maintain your brain. Available at http://www.alz.org/we_can_help_brain_health_maintain_your_brain.asp.

5. Associated Press. (2005, June 21). Brain exercise is key to healthy mind. Available at http://www.thirdage.com/news/articles/DAI/05/07/01/050701-01.html.

6. Springer, M. V., McIntosh, A. R., Winocur, G., & Grady, C. L. (2005). The relation between brain activity during memory tasks and years of education in young and older adults. *Neuropsychology, 19*(2), 181–192.

7. Caine, R. N., & Caine, G. (1994). *Making connections: Teaching and the human brain*. Menlo Park, CA: Addison Wesley.

8. Csikszentmihalyi, M. (2006). *Flow: The psychology of optimal experience*. New York: Academic Internet Publishers; Csikszentmihalyi, M. (1997). *Creativity: Flow and the psychology of discovery and invention*. New York: Harper Perennial; Gross, R. (1999). *Peak learning*. New York: Tarcher.

9. Caine & Caine, *Making connections*; Jensen, E. (2000). *Different brains, different learners*. San Diego: The Brain Store.

10. Brandt, R. (1998). *Powerful learning*. Alexandria, VA: Association for Supervision and Curriculum Development, p. 29.

11. Campbell, B. (1992). Multiple intelligences in action. *Childhood Education, 68*(4), 197–201; Gardner, H., & Hatch, T. (1989). Multiple intelligences go to school: Educational implications of the theory of multiple intelligences. *Educational Researcher, 18*(8), 4–9; Gardner, H. (1983). *Frames of Mind: The Theory of Multiple Intelligences*. New York: Basic Books.

12. Armstrong, T. (2000). *MI and cognitive skills*. Available at http://www.ascd.org/ed_topics/2000armstrong/chapter12.html.

13. Law of Supply and Demand. Wikipedia. Available at http://en.wikipedia.org/wiki/Supply_and_demand.

14. Armstrong, T. (1998–2000). *Multiple intelligences*. Available at http://www.thomasarmstrong.com/multiple_intelligences.htm.

15. Armstrong, T. (1994). *Multiple intelligences in the classroom*. Alexandria, VA: Association for Supervision and Curriculum Development; Gardner, *Frames of mind*; Gardner, H. (1993). *Multiple intelligences: The theory in practice*. New York: Basic Books; Checkley, K. (1997). The first seven . . . and the eighth: A conversation with Howard Gardner, *Educational Leadership, 55*(1), 8–13.

16. Davis, B. (1993). *Tools for teaching*. San Francisco: Jossey-Bass, p. 185.

17. Fleming, N. D. (1995). I'm different; not dumb: Modes of presentation (VARK) in the tertiary classroom. In A. Zeimer (Ed.), *Research and Development in Higher Education, Proceedings of the 1995 Annual Conference of the Higher Education and Research Development Society of Austral-asia (HERDSA), HERDSA, 18*, 308–313; Fleming, N. D., & Mills, C. (1992). Not another inventory, rather a catalyst for reflection. *To Improve the Academy, 11*, 137–149. Available at http://www.ntlf.com/html/lib/suppmat/74fleming.htm.

18. Fleming, I'm different; not dumb.

19. Neil Fleming, personal communication, November 14, 2006.

20. Fleming, N. D. (2005). *Teaching and learning styles: VARK strategies*. Christchurch, NZ: Microfilm Limited.

21. Macdaid, G. P., McCaulley, M. H., & Kainz, R. I. (1986). *Atlas of type tables*. Gainesville, FL: Center for Applications of Psychological Type.

22. Also available at http://www.bls.gov/oco/ocos066.htm.

23. Based on DiTiberio, J. K., & Hammer, A. L. (1993). *Introduction to type in college*. Palo Alto, CA: Consulting Psychologists Press.

24. Check Consulting Psychology Press at http://www.cpp.com/ or the Center for the Application of Psychological Type at http://www.capt.org/ for starters.

25. Pelley, J. W. (1997). *SuccessTypes for medical students: A program for improving academic performance*. Lubbock, TX: Texas Tech University, Extended Studies; Pelley, J. W. (2002). SuccessTypes Learning Style Indicator. Available at http://www.ttuhsc.edu/SOM/Success/LSTI.htm.

26. Based on DiTiberio & Hammer, *Introduction to type in college*.

27. Ibid.

Chapter 3

1. Leonhardt, D. (2005, May 24). The college dropout boom. *The New York Times*, p. A1, column 1.

2. Irvine, M. (22 January, 2007). Polls say wealth important to youth. Associated Press. Available: http://www.eons.com/love/feature/kids/polls-say-wealth-important-to-youth/12850

3. Farrell, E. F. (2005, February 4). More students plan to work to help pay for college. *The Chronicle of Higher Education, 51*(22), A1. Available online at http://chronicle.com/weekly/v51/i22/22a00101.htm.

4. Clark, K. (2005, 12 December). Econ 101: College is time to budget. *U.S. News & World Report, 139*(22), 62–63.

5. Kendrick, E. (1999). Give 'em credit: When is it right for students? *Austin Business Journal, 19*(25), 26.

6. Clark, Econ 101.

7. Joo, S. G., Grable, J. E., & Bagwell, D. C. (2003). Credit card attitudes and behaviors of college students. *College Student Journal, 37*(3), 405–420.

8. The Associated Press. (2005, May 24). College students carrying fewer credit cards. Available at http://www.msnbc.msn.com/id/7968677/.

9. Ibid.

10. Kantrowitz, M. (2007). FAQs about financial aid. FinAid: The Smart Student Guide to Financial Aid. Available at http://www.finaid.org/questions/faq.phtml.

11. Financial literacy statistics. Young Americans: Center for Financial Education. Available at http://www.yacenter.org/index.cfm?fuseAction=financialLiteracyStatistics.financialLiteracyStatistics.

12. See http://www.costofwedding.com/?gclid=CI-59NquhIoCFQLYYgodkjakRQ.

13. See http://www.motortrend.com/features/news/112_news030430_ave/.

14. See http://usgovinfo.about.com/od/consumerawareness/a/avghomeprice04.htm.

15. Norvilitis, J. M., & Santa Maria, P. (2002). Credit card debt on college campuses: Causes, consequences, and solutions. *College Student Journal, 36*(3), 356–364.

16. Fitzgerald, N. (2006). Getting fiscally fit. *Colleges & Careers, 24*(4). Available at http://content.careersandcolleges.com/article/articleview.do?articleId=2167&adcat=special.

17. Choosing a credit card. The Federal Reserve Board. Available at http://www.federalreserve.gov/pubs/shop/default.htm.

18. St. Amand, A. (2004). Being wise about personal finances. *The Northeastern News.* Available at http://media.www.nu-news.com/media/storage/paper600/news/2004/01/21/Style/Being.Wise.About.Personal.Finances-584276.shtml.

19. Kantrowitz, M. (2007). Defaulting on student loans. Fin Aid: The Smart Student Guide to Financial Aid. Available at http://www.finaid.org/loans/default.phtml.

20. Repaying student loans held by the U.S. Department of Education. Federal Student Aid. Available at http://www.ed.gov/offices/OSFAP/DCS/repaying.html.

21. Pinto, M. B., Mansfield, P. M., & Parente, D. H. (2004). Relationship of credit attitude and debt to self-esteem and locus of control in college age consumers. *Psychological Reports, 94*(3), 1405–1418.

22. College credit card offer is identity theft scam. (2005, 29 March). Available at http://www.nbc5.com/education/4330748/detail.html.

23. Trommelen, L. (2002). Money types. *MBTI Newsletter* from Association for Psychological Type, Canada, *1*(6).

24. Panek, R. (2005, January 16). 101 redefined. *The New York Times*, 4A, p. 32, column 1.

25. Kiernan, V. (2005, June 24). Use the smart classroom: A Spanish professor tries several tech tools. Teach in many locations at once: 5 professors connect using Internet video. *The Chronicle of Higher Education, 51*(42), B10.

26. Gose, B. (2005, June 24). Build robots: An engineering course that promotes hands-on skills. *The Chronicle of Higher Education, 51*(42), B4.

27. Zuckerman, E. (2005, May 16). College students click their way to better comprehension. *Detroit News.*; Dye, L. (2005, May 5). Students use clickers to help guide college lectures. ABC News. Available at http://abcnews.go.com/Technology/DyeHard/Story?id=727409&page=1; Carnevale, D. (2005, 24 June). Run a class like a game show: "Clickers" keep students involved. *The Chronicle of Higher Education, 51*(42), B3.

28. Bollet, R. M., & Fallon, S. (2002). Personalizing e-learning. *Educational Media International, 39*(1), 39–45; Thompson, G. (2001–2002). Overcoming your resistance to distance learning. *E-Learning Magazine*; Online student induction package. Available at http://www2.tafe.sa.edu.au/lsrsc/oes/induct/.

29. Roach, R. (2004). Survey unveils high-tech ownership profile of American college students. *Black Issues in Higher Education, 21*(16), 37.

30. Jones, S., & Madden, M. (2002). The Internet goes to college: How students are living in the future with today's technology. Pew Internet. Available at http://www.pewinternet.org/PPF/r/71/report_display.asp.

31. stats.com. Available at http://www.internetworldstats.com/stats.htm.

32. Simon, H. A. (1996). *Observations on the sciences of science learning.* Paper prepared for the Committee on Developments in the Science of Learning for the Sciences of Science Learning: An Interdisciplinary Discussion. Department of Psychology, Carnegie Mellon University.

33. Wood, G. (2004, 9 April). Academic original sin: Plagiarism, the Internet, and librarians. *The Journal of Academic Librarianship, 30*(3), 237–242.

34. Macdaid, G. P., McCaulley, M. H., & Kainz, R. I. (1986). *Atlas of type tables.* Gainesville, FL: Center for Applications of Psychological Type.

35. Available at http://www.bls.gov/oco/ocos042.htm and http://www.bls.gov/oco/cg/cgs033.htm.

36. Loppatto, E. (2007, 6 February). Porn viewed by almost half of kids, often mistakenly. *Bloomberg.com.* Available at http://www.bloomberg.com/apps/news?pid=20601103&sid=ap3R1lomUalk&refer=us.

37. Mangan, K. S. (2005, July 1). Packing up the books. *The Chronicle of Higher Education, 51*(43), A27; Carlson, S. (2005, October 7). The net generation goes to college. *Chronicle of Higher Education, 52*(7), A34.

38. Nathan, R. (2005). *My freshman year: What a professor learned by becoming a student.* Ithaca, NY: Cornell University Press.

39. Fitzgerald, M. A. (2004). Making the leap from high school to college. *Knowledge Quest, 32*(4), 19–24; Ehrmann, S. (2004). Beyond computer literacy: Implications of technology for the content of a college education. *Liberal Education.* Available at http://www.aacu.org/liberal education/le-fa04/le-fa04feature1.cfm.

40. Dweck, C. S. (2006). *Mindset: The new psychology of success.* New York: Random House. pp. 104–105.

41. Tessler, L. G. (1997). How college students with learning disabilities can advocate for themselves. LD OnLine. Available at http://www.ldonline.org/article/6136.

42. Mangrum, C. T., & Strichart, S. S. (Eds.) (1997). *Peterson's guide to colleges with programs for students with learning disabilities.* Princeton, NJ: Peterson's Guide.

43. Strichart, S. S., & Mangrum, C. T. II. (2002). *Teaching learning strategies and study skills to students with learning disabilities, attention deficit disorder, or special needs.* (3rd ed). Boston: Allyn and Bacon; Learning Disabilities Online. Available at http://ldonline.org; Sousa, D. A. (2001). *How the special needs brain learns.* Thousand Oaks, CA: Corwin Press.

CHAPTER 4

1. Cooper, R. K. (1991). *The performance edge.* Boston: Houghton Mifflin, p. 53.

2. Eade, D. M. (1998). Energy and success: Time management. *Clinician News*, July/August. Available at http://www.adv-leadership-grp.com/articles/energy.htm.

3. Bittel, L. R. (1991). *Right on time! The complete guide for time-pressured managers.* New York: McGraw-Hill, p. 16.

4. Loehr, J., & Schwartz, T. (2003). *The power of full engagement: Managing energy, not time, is the key to high performance and personal renewal.* New York: Free Press

5. Bittel, Right on time! p. 16.

6. Loehr, The power of full engagement.

7. Williams, R. L., Verble, J. S., Price, D. E., & Layne, B. H. (1995). Relationships between time-management practices and personality indices and types. *Journal of Psychological Type, 34,* 36–42.

8. Demarest, L. (2001). *Out of time: How the sixteen types manage their time and work.* Gainesville, FL: Center for Applications of Psychological Type.

9. Soumaré, F. (2006, February 24). The dangers of facebook addiction. *The Sophian.* Available at http://media.www.smithsophian.com/media/storage/paper587/news/2006/02/24/Opinions/The-Dangers.Of.Facebook.Addiction-1637444.shtml; Withall, R. (2005, November 18). Facing the facts about facebook. *The Villanovan.* Available at http://www.villanovan.com/media/paper581/news/2005/11/18/verge/facing.the.facts.about.facebook-1108785.shtml

10. Benner, J. (2005). Facebook more than a way of life. *The BG News.* Available at http://www.bgnews.com/media/storage/paper883/news/2005/11/15/NotNews/Facebook.More.Than.A.Way.Of.Life-1297340.shtml.

11. Greene, L. (2006, March 8). You might be a Facebook stalker if. . . . *Winonan.* Available at http://www.winona.edu/winonan/S2006/3-8-06/YoumightbeaFacebookstalkerif....htm; Hollister, L. (2005, October 5). Facebook addiction is needless, yet compelling. *The Volante Online.* Available at http://media.www.volanteonline.com/media/storage/paper468/news/2005/10/05/Opinion/Facebook.Addiction.Is.Needless.Yet.Compelling-1008873.shtml.

12. Greenfield, D. N. (1999). *Virtual addiction.* Oakland, CA: New Harbinger Publications; Yair, E., & Hamburger, A. (2005). *The social net.* Oxford: Oxford University Press; Young, K. S. (1998). *Caught in the net.* New York: John Wiley.

13. Macdaid, G. P., McCaulley, M. H., & Kainz, R. I. (1986). *Atlas of type tables.* Gainesville, FL: Center for Applications of Psychological Type.

14. Also available at http://www.bls.gov/oco/ocos086.htm.

15. Based on Covey, S. R., Merrill, A. R., & Merrill, R. R. (1996). *First things first: To live, to love, to learn, to leave a legacy.* New York: Free Press, 37.

16. Fortino, M. (2001). *E-mergency.* Groveland, CA: Omni Publishing.

17. Hobbs, C. R. (1987). *Time power.* New York: Harper & Row, pp. 9–10.

18. Can you really manage time? BusinessTown.com. Available at http://www.businesstown.com/time/time-can.asp.

19. Solomon, L. J., & Rothblum, E. D. (1984). Academic procrastination: Frequency and cognitive-behavioral correlates. *Journal of Counseling Psychology, 31,* 503–509.

20. Hoover, E. (2005, December 9). Tomorrow I love ya! *The Chronicle of Higher Education, 52*(16), A30–32.

21. Ferrari, J. R., McCown, W. G., & Johnson, J. (2002). *Procrastination and task avoidance: Theory, research, and treatment.* New York: Springer Publishing.

22. Schouwenburg, H. C., Lay, C. H., Pychyl, T. A., & Ferrari, J. R. (Eds.). (2004). *Counseling the procrastinator in academic settings.* Washington DC: American Psychological Association.

23. Hoover, Tomorrow I love ya!.

24. Sandholtz, K., Derr, B., Buckner, K., & Carlson, D. (2002). *Beyond juggling: Rebalancing your busy life.* San Francisco: Berrett-Koehler Publishers.

25. Juggling Club. Wikepedia. Available at http://en.wikipedia.org/wiki/Clubs_%28juggling%29.

26. Adapted from Sandholtz et al., *Beyond juggling.*

27. Ibid.

Chapter 5

1. Perry, W. (1970). *Forms of intellectual and ethical development in the college years.* New York: Holt, Rinehart & Winston; Perry, W. G. Jr. (1981). Cognitive and ethical growth: The making of meaning. In A. Chickering & Associates (Eds.), *The Modern American College: Responding to the New Realities of Diverse Students and a Changing Society.* San Francisco: Jossey-Bass; Erickson, B. L., Peters, C. B., & Strommer, D. W. (2006). Teaching first-year college students. San Francisco: Jossey-Bass; Belenky, M. F., Clinchy, B. M., Goldberger, N. R., & Tarule, J. M. (1986). *Women's ways of knowing.* New York: Basic Books; Pascarella, E. T., & Terenzini, P. T. (1991). *How college affects students.* San Francisco: Jossey-Bass; Magolda, M. B. (1988). *The impact of the freshman year on epistemological development: Gender differences.* Paper presented at the meeting of the American Educational Research Association, New Orleans; Magolda, M. B. B. (2006). Intellectual development in the college years. (2006, May/June). *Change, 38*(3), 50–54.

2. Dewey, J. (1910). *How we think.* Lexington, MA: Heath.

3. Halx, M. D., & Reybold, E. (2005). A pedagogy of force: Faculty perspective of critical thinking capacity in undergraduate students. *The Journal of General Education, 54*(4), 293–315.

4. Walkner, P., & Finney, N. (1999). Skill development and critical thinking in higher education. *Teaching in Higher Education, 4*(4), 531–548.

5. Diestler, S. (2001). *Becoming a critical thinker: A user friendly manual.* Upper Saddle River, NJ: Prentice Hall.

6. Hammond, M., & Collins, R. (1991). *Self-directed learning: Critical practice.* London: Kogan Page; Walkner & Finney, Skill development and critical thinking in higher education, 163.

7. Klein, A. (2007, January 17). Broader skills best for college grads. *Education Week, 26*(19), 14.

8. Schermer, M. (2002). Smart people believe weird things. *Skeptic.* ScientificAmerican.com. Available at http://www.sciam.com/article.cfm?id=smart-people-believe-weir.

9. Falcione, P. A. (1998). *Critical thinking: What it is and why it counts.* Millbrae, CA: California Academic Press.

10. Twale, D., & Sanders, C. S. (1999). Impact of nonclassroom experiences on critical thinking ability. *NASPA Journal, 36*(2), 133–146.

11. Thomas, C., & Smoot, G. (1994, February/March). Critical thinking: A vital work skill. *Trust for Educational Leadership, 23,* 34-38.

12. Kaplan-Leiserson, E. (2004). Workforce of tomorrow: How can we prepare *all* youth for future work success? *Training & Development, 58*(4), 12–14. 13. Based in part on Brookfield, S. D. (1987). *Developing critical thinkers: Challenging adults to explore alternative ways of thinking and acting.* San Francisco: Jossey-Bass.

13. Halpern, D. F. (1996). *Thought and knowledge: An introduction to critical thinking.* Mahwah, NJ: Lawrence Erlbaum.

14. Barnett, R. (1997). *Higher education: A critical business.* Buckingham: SRHE, and Open University Press.

15. Wade, C. (1995). Using writing to develop and assess critical thinking. *Teaching of Psychology, 22*(1), 24–28.

16. Van den Brink-Budgen, R. (2000). *Critical thinking for students.* (3rd ed.). Oxford: How to Books; Ruggiero, V. R. (2001). *Becoming a critical thinker.* (4th ed.). Boston: Houghton Mifflin.

17. Wanted: Liberal arts grads. *Fortune* (1997, May 12), 135(9), 151.

18. Although the case in this story is fictitious, it is representative of the drinking problems on many college campuses. Facts were taken from College binge drinking issues. About.com. Available at http://alcoholism.about.com/od/college/, and ideas were suggested by Students' initiation with booze. (2004, October 3). *Denver Post*, p. 2E.

19. Blakey, E., & Spence, S. (1990). Developing metacognition. ERIC Clearinghouse on Information Resources, Syracuse NY. Available at http://www.vtaide.com/png/ERIC/Metacognition.htm.

20. Macdaid, G. P., McCaulley, M. H., & Kainz, R. I. (1986). *Atlas of type tables*. Gainesville, FL: Center for Applications of Psychological Type.

21. Also available at http://www.bls.gov/oco/ocos272.htm.

22. Florida, R. (2002). The rise of the creative class: And how it's transforming work, leisure, community and everyday life. New York: Basic Books, xii.

23. Ibid.

24. Sternberg. R. J. (2004). Teaching college students that creativity is a decision. *Guidance & Counseling*, 19(4), 196–200.

25. Vance, E. (2007, February 2). College graduates lack key skills, report says. *The Chronicle of Higher Education*, 53(22), A30.

26. Kurtz, J. R. (1998). It's all in your mind! Creative thinking essential in times of change. *Outlook*, 66(3), 5.

28. Rowe, A. J. (2004). *Creative intelligences: discovering the innovative potential in ourselves and others*. Upper Saddle, NJ: Pearson Education, pp. 3–6, 34.

29. Michalko, M. (2001). *Cracking creativity: The secrets of creative genius*. Berkeley, CA: Ten Speed Press.

30. Adapted from Adler, R., & Towne, N. (1987). *Looking out/Looking in*. (5th ed.) New York: Holt, Rinehart, and Winston, pp. 99–100.

31. Douglas, J. H. (1977). The genius of everyman (2): Learning creativity. *Science News*, 111(8), 284–288.

32. Harris, R. (1998). Introduction to creative thinking. VirtualSalt. Available at http://www.virtualsalt.com/crebook1.htm.

33. Eby, D. Creativity and flow psychology. Talent Development Resources. Available at http://talentdevelop.com/articles/Page8.html.

CHAPTER 6

1. Based on http://www-sop.inria.fr/acacia/personnel/Fabien.Gandon/lecture/uk1999/history/.

2. Burchfield, C. M., & Sappington, J. (2000). Compliance with required reading assignments. *Teaching of Psychology*, 27(1), 58–60; Hobson, E. H. (2004). *Getting students to read: Fourteen tips*. IDEA Paper No. 40, Manhattan, KS: Kansas State University, Center for Faculty Evaluation and Development; Maleki, R. B., & Heerman, C. E. (1992). *Improving student reading*. IDEA Paper No. 26, Manhattan, KS: Kansas State University, Center for Faculty Evaluation and Development. Most Idea Center papers available at http://www.idea.ksu.edu/

3. Marburger, D. R. (2001). Absenteeism and undergraduate exam performance. *Journal of Economic Education*, 32, 99–109.

4. Perkins, K. K., & Wieman, C. E. (2005). The surprising impact of seat location on student performance. *The Physics Teacher*, 43(1), 30–33. Available: http://scitation.aip.org/journals/doc/PHTEAH-ft/vol_43/iss_1/30_1.html.

5. "Infomania" worse than marijuana. (2005, April 22). BBC News. Available http://news.bbc.co.uk/go/pr/fr/-/2/uk_news/4471607.stm; Bugeja, M. J. (2007, January 26). Distractions in the wireless classroom. *The Chronicle of Higher Education*, 53(21), C1. Available at http://chronicle.com/weekly/v53/i21/21c00101.htm; Young, J. R. (2006, June 2). The fight for classroom attention: Professor vs. laptop. *The Chronicle of Higher Education*, 52(39), A27. Available at http://chronicle.com/weekly/v52/i39/39a02701.htm.

6. Adapted from Mackie, V., & Bair, B. Tips for improving listening skills; International student and scholar services. University of Illinois at Urbana-Champaign. Available at http://www.ips.uiuc.edu/isss/pages/index.php?catID=2&pageID=75#listen.

7. Armbruster, B. B. (2000). Taking notes from lectures. In R. F. Flippo & D. C. Caverly (Eds.), *Handbook of college reading and study strategy research* (pp. 175–199). Mahwah, NJ: Erlbaum.

8. Staley, C. C., & Staley, R. S. (1992). *Communicating in business and the professions: The inside word*. Belmont, CA: Wadsworth, p. 223.

9. Hughes, C. A., & Suritsky, S. K. (1993). Notetaking skills and strategies for students with learning disabilities. *Preventing School Failure*, 38(1).

10. Staley & Staley, *Communicating in business and the professions*, pp. 229–236.

11. Kiewra, K. A., Mayer, R. E., Christensen, M., Kim, S., & Risch, N. (1991). Effects of repetition on recall and notetaking: Strategies for learning from lectures. *Journal of Educational Psychology*, 83, 120–123.

12. Mayer, R. E., & Moreno, R. (2003). Nine ways to reduce cognitive load in multimedia learning. *Educational Psychologist*, 38(1), 43–52.

13. Brock, R. (2005, October 28). Lectures on the go. *The Chronicle of Higher Education*, 52(10), A39–42; French, D. P. (2006). iPods: Informative or invasive? *Journal of College Science Teaching*, 36(1), 58–59; Hallett, V. (2005, October 17). Teaching with tech. *U.S. News & World Report*, 139(14), 54–58; *The Horizon Report*. (2006). Stanford, CA: The New Media Consortium.

14. Allen, D. (2001). *Getting things done: The art of stress-free productivity*. New York: Penguin Books, p. 21.

15. Selby, J. (2004). *Quiet your mind*. Makawao, Maui, HI: Inner Ocean Publishing.

16. Based on Staley, C. (2003). *50 ways to leave your lectern*. Belmont, CA: Wadsworth, pp. 80–81.

17. DiTiberio, J. K., & Hammer, A. L. (1993). *Introduction to type in college*. Palo Alto, CA: Consulting Psychologists Press.

18. Bloom, B. S. (Ed.). (1956). *A taxonomy of educational objectives (cognitive domain)*. New York: Longman.

19. Adapted from *Effective listening skills*. Elmhurst College Learning Center. Available at http://www.elmhurst.edu/library/learningcenter/Listening/listening_behaviors_survey.htm.

20. Palmatier, R. A., & Bennett, J. M. (1974). Note-taking habits of college students. *Journal of Reading*, 18, 215–218; Dunkel, P., & Davy, S. (1989). The heuristic of lecture notetaking: Perceptions of American and international students regarding the value and practices of notetaking. *English for Specific Purposes*, 8, 33–50.

21. Armbruster, *Handbook of college reading and study strategy research*.

22. Van Meter, P., Yokoi, L., & Pressley, M. (1994). College students' theory of note-taking derived from their perceptions of note-taking. *Journal of Educational Psychology*, 86, 323–338.

23. Read, B. (2007, February 1). Lecture-hall laptops hurt students' grades, study says. *The Chronicle of Higher Education.* Available at http://chronicle.com/wiredcampus/index.php?id=1847.

24. Davis, M., & Hult, R. (1997). Effects of writing summaries as a generative learning activity during note taking. *Teaching of Psychology 24*(1), 47–49; Boyle, J. R., & Weishaar, M. (2001). The effects of strategic notetaking on the recall and comprehension of lecture information for high school students with learning disabilities. *Learning Disabilities Research & Practice 16*(3); Kiewra, K. A. (2002). How classroom teachers can help students learn and teach them how to learn. *Theory into Practice 41*(2), 71–81; Kiewra, How classroom teachers can help students learn and teach them how to learn; Aiken, E. G., Thomas, G. S., & Shennum, W. A. (1975). Memory for a lecture: Effects of notes, lecture rate and informational density. *Journal of Educational Psychology, 67,* 439–444; Hughes, C. A., & Suritsky, S. K. (1994). Note-taking skills of university students with and without learning disabilities. *Journal of Learning Disabilities, 27,* 20–24.

25. Bonner, J. M., & Holliday, W. G. (2006). How college science students engage in note-taking strategies. *Journal of Research in Science Teaching, 43*(8), 786–818.

26. Pauk, W. (2000). *How to study in college.* Boston: Houghton Mifflin.

27. Pardini, E. A., Domizi, D. P., Forbes, D. A., & Pettis, G. V. (2005). Parallel note-taking: A strategy for effective use of Webnotes. *Journal of College Reading and Learning, 35*(2), 38–55. Available at http://www.biology.wustl.edu/pardini/TeachingMaterials/JCRL_spring2005_pardini.pdf.

28. Kiewra, How classroom teachers can help students learn and teach them how to learn.

29. Porte, L. K. (2001). Cut and paste 101. *Teaching Exceptional Children, 34*(2), 14–20.

30. Kiewra, K. A., DuBois, N. F., Christian, D., & McShane, A. (1988). Providing study notes: Comparison of three types of notes for review. *Journal of Educational Psychology, 80,* 595–597; Larkin, J. H., & Simon, J. A. (1987). Why a diagram is (sometimes) worth ten thousand words. *Cognitive Science, 11,* 65–99; Robinson, D. H., Katayama, A. D., DuBois, N. F., & DeVaney, T. (1998). Interactive effects of graphic organizers and delayed review in concept acquisition. *The Journal of Experimental Education, 67,* 17–31; Winn, W. (1991). Learning from maps and diagrams. *Educational Psychology Review, 3,* 211–247.

31. Kiewra, How classroom teachers can help students learn and teach them how to learn.

32. Craik, F. I. M., & Watkins, M. J. (1973). The role of rehearsal in short-term memory. *Journal of Verbal Learning and Verbal Behavior, 12,* 599–607.

33. Adapted from Staley, *50 Ways to Leave Your Lectern,* p. 116.

34. Macdaid, G. P., McCaulley, M. H., & Kainz, R. I. (1986). *Atlas of type tables.* Gainesville, FL: Center for Applications of Psychological Type.

CHAPTER 7

1. Gordon, B. (1995). *Memory: Remembering and forgetting in everyday life.* New York: Mastermedia Limited.

2. Winerman, L. (2005, September). The culture of memory. *Monitor on Psychology, 36*(8). Available at APA Online at http://www.apa.org/monitor/sep05/culture.html.

3. Buckner, J. P., & Fivush, R. (1998). Gender and self in children's autobiographical narratives. *Applied Cognitive Psychology, 12,* 407–429.

4. Buckner, J. P., & Fivush, R. (2002). Gendered themes in family reminiscing. *Memory, 8,* 401–412; Davis, P. (1999). Gender differences in autobiographical memory for childhood emotional experiences. *Journal of Personality and Social Psychology, 76,* 498–510; Pastorino, E., & Doyle-Portillo, S. (2006). *What is psychology?* Belmont, CA: Wadsworth.

5. Klingberg, T., Fernell, E., Olesen, P. J., Johnson, M., Gustafsson, P., Dahlstrom, K., Gillberg, C., Forssberg, H., & Westerberg, H. (2005). Computerized training of working memory in children with ADHD: A randomized, controlled trial. *Journal of the American Academy of Child & Adolescent Psychiatry, 44*(2), 177–186; Sinha, G. (2005, July 11). Training the brain. Scientific American.com. Available at http://www.sciam.com/article.cfm?chanID=sa006&colID=5&articleID=000560D5-7252-12B9-9A2C83414B7F0000.

6. Reinberg, S. (2005, November 15). Brain scan may spot Alzheimer's progression. Personal MD. Available at http://www.personalmd.com/news.jsp?nid=529119&l=E.

7. Bolla, K. I., Lindgren, K. N., Bonaccorsy, C., & Bleecker, M. L. (1991). Memory complaints in older adults: Fact or fiction? *Archives of Neurology, 48,* 61–64.

8. Higbee, K. L. (2004). What aspects of their memories do college students most want to improve? *College Student Journal, 38*(4), 552–556.

9. Higbee, K. L. (1988). *Your memory: How it works and how to improve it* (2nd ed.). New York: Prentice Hall.

10. Ibid.

11. Nairine, J. S. (2006). *Psychology: The adaptive mind.* Belmont, CA: Wadsworth/Thomson Learning.

12. Associated Press. (2007, March 20). Studies focus on wandering thoughts. Available at http://www.cbc.ca/technology/story/2007/03/20/tech-thoughts.html.

13. Shenk, D. (1997). *Data Smog: Surviving the information glut.* San Francisco: Harper San Francisco.

14. Klingberg et al., Computerized training of working memory in children with ADHD.

15. Macdaid, G. P., McCaulley, M. H., & Kainz, R. I. (1986). *Atlas of type tables.* Gainesville, FL: Center for Applications of Psychological Type.

16. Also available at http://www.bls.gov/oco/ocos093.htm.

17. Coon, D. (2006). *Psychology: A modular approach to mind and behavior.* Belmont, CA: Wadsworth/Thomson Learning; Nairine, *Psychology.*

18. Nairine, *Psychology.*

19. Miller, G. A. (1956). The magical number seven plus or minus two: Some limits on our capacity for processing information. *Psychological Review, 63,* 81–97.

20. The neurological scratchpad: what is working memory? (2004, July 7). Brain Connection.com. Available at http://www.brainconnection.com/topics/?main=fa/working-memory2; Kotbagi, H. (1997). Human memory. Human-Computer Interface. Available at http://www.cc.gatech.edu/classes/cs6751_97_winter/Topics/human-cap/memory.html; Memory. Dr. Brown's Psychology 1501 Home Page. Available at http://www.gpc.edu/~bbrown/psyc1501/memory/stm.htm; Clark, D. Memory: The three memory storage systems. Available at http://www.nwlink.com/~donclark/hrd/learning/memory.html; Kerry, S. (1999–2002). Memory and retention time. Education Reform.net. Available at http://www.education-reform.net/memory.htm; Goodhead, J. (1999). The difference between short-term and long-term memory [On-line].

21. World Memory Championships Homepage. Available at http://www.worldmemorychampionship.com/index.asp.

22. Rozakis, L. (2003). *Test-taking strategies and study skills for the utterly confused*. New York: McGraw Hill; Meyers, J. N. (2000). *The secrets of taking any test*. New York: Learning Express; Ehren, B. J. Mnemonic devices. Available at http://itc.gsu.edu/academymodules/a304/support/xpages/a304b0_20600.html; Lloyd, G. (1998–2004). Study skills: Memorize with mnemonics. Available at http://www.back2college.com/memorize.htm.

23. Willingham, D. T. (2004). Practice makes perfect—but only if you practice beyond the point of perfection. *American Educator*. Available at http://www.aft.org/pubs-reports/american_educator/spring2004/cogsci.html.

24. Krueger, W. C. F. (1929). The effect of overlearning on retention. *Journal of Experimental Psychology, 12,* 71–78.

25. Tigner, R. B. (1999). Putting memory research to good use: Hints from cognitive psychology. *College Teaching, 47*(4), 149–152.

26. Murdock, B. B., Jr. (1960). The distinctiveness of stimuli. *Psychological Reports, 67,* 16–31; Neath, I. (1993). Distinctiveness and serial position effects in recognition. *Memory & Cognition, 21,* 689–698.

27. Cahill, L. (2003). Similar neural mechanisms for emotion-induced memory impairment and enhancement. *Proceedings of the National Academy of Sciences, 100*(23), 13123–13124. Available at http://www.pnas.org/cgi/content/full/100/23/13123.

28. Dingfelder, S. F. (2005). Feelings' sway over memory. *Monitor on Psychology, 26*(8). Available at APA Online at http://www.apa.org/monitor/sep05/feelings.html.

29. Noice, H., & Noice, T. (2006). What studies of actors and acting can tell us about memory and cognitive functioning. *Current Directions in Psychological Science, 15*(1), 14–18.

30. Caine, M. (1990). *Acting in film: An actor's take on movie making*. New York: Applause Theatre Books.

31. Noice, T., Noice, H., & Kennedy, C. (2000). The contribution of movement on the recall of complex material. *Memory, 8,* 353–363.

32. Glenberg, A. M., & Kaschak, M. P. (2002). Grounding language in action. *Psychonomic Bulletin & Review, 9,* 558–565.

33. Noice & Noice, What studies of actors and acting can tell us about memory and cognitive functioning.

34. Higbee, *Your memory.*

35. Ibid.

36. Ibid.

37. Bean, J. (1996). *Engaging ideas*. San Francisco: Jossey-Bass.

38. Tigner, Putting memory research to good use.

39. Higbee, *Your memory.*

40. Chan, J. C. K., McDermott, K. B., & Roediger, H. L. III. (2007). Retrieval-induced facilitation: Initially nontested material can benefit from prior testing of related material. *Journal of Experimental Psychology, 135*(4), 552–571.

41. Caine, R. N., & Caine, G. (1997). *Education on the edge of possibility*. Alexandria, VA: Association for Supervision and Curriculum Development.

42. Jenkins, E. (2003, June). Somewhere, the bard weeps. *Columbia Journalism Review*. Available at http://www.cjr.org/issues/2003/3/lc.asp.

43. Berk, R. A. (2002). *Humor as an instructional defibrillator*. Sterling, VA: Stylus; Berk, R. A. (2003). *Professors are from Mars®, students are from Snickers®*. Sterling, VA: Stylus.

44. Offer, D., Kaiz, M., Howard, K. I., & Bennett, E. S. (2000). The altering of reporting experiences. *Journal of the American Academy of Child and Adolescent Psychiatry, 39,* 735–42.

45. Schacter, D. L. (2001). *The seven sins of memory: How the mind forgets and remembers*. Boston: Houghton Mifflin; Murray, B. (2003). The seven sins of memory. *Monitor on Psychology*. Available at APA Online at http://www.apa.org/monitor/oct03/sins.html.

46. Guterman, L. (2004, June 25). Gray matters. *The Chronicle of Higher Education, 50*(42), A22.

47. Ibid.

48. "Memory pill" for the forgetful. (2005, May 12). BBC News. Available at http://news.bbc.co.uk/2/hi/health/4539551.stm; Guterman, L. (2004, June 25). Gray matters. *The Chronicle of Higher Education, 50*(42), A22.

49. White, A. M., Signer, M. L., Kraus, C. L., & Swartzwelder, H. S. (2004). Experiential aspects of alcohol-induced blackouts among college students. *American Journal of Drug Alcohol Abuse, 30*(1), 205–224.

50. Assefi, S. L., & Garry, M. (2003). Absolut® memory distortions: Alcohol placebos influence the misinformation effect. *Psychological Science, 14*(1), 77–80.

51. Gouzoulis-Mayfrank, E., Daumann, J., Tuchtenhagen, F., Pelz, S., Becker, S., Kunert, H-J., Fimm, B., & Sass, H. (2000). Impaired cognitive performance in drug free users of recreational ecstasy. *Journal of Neurology, Neurosurgery, and Psychiatry, 68,* 719–725. Available at http://jnnp.bmj.com/cgi/content/abstract/68/6/719?ijkey=3f8bc1cc460f69242c7f2f360d1ec74a41611d00&keytype2=tf_ipsecsha.

52. Study links ecstasy, long-term memory loss. (2004, January 15). CNN.com. Available at http://www.cnn.com/2004/HEALTH/01/15/ecstasy.memory.reut/index.html.

53. High-fat diets hammer memory, more than a waistline worry. (2004, October 25). *Society for Neuroscience*. Available at http://www.sfn.org/index.cfm?pagename=news_102504c.

54. Tagg, J. (2004, March-April). Why learn? What we may really be teaching students. *About Campus,* 2–10; Marton, F., & Säljö, R. On qualitative differences in learning: I-Outcome and process. (1976). *British Journal of Educational Psychology, 46,* 4–11.

CHAPTER 8

1. Rogers, M. (2007, March-April). Is reading obsolete? *The Futurist,* 26–27; Waters, L. (2007, February 9). Time for reading. *The Chronicle of Higher Education, 53*(23), 1B6.

2. Postman, N. (1985). *Amusing ourselves to death*. New York: Penguin Books; Stephens, M. (1991, September 22). The death of reading. *Los Angeles Times Magazine*. Available at http://www.nyu.edu/classes/stephens/Death%20of%20Reading%20page.htm.

3. Dillon, S. (2005, December 16). Literacy falls for graduates from college, Testing Finds. *The New York Times*. Available at http://www.nytimes.com/2005/12/16/education/16literacy.html.

4. Stephens, The death of reading.

5. Caverly, D. C., Nicholson, S. A., & Radcliffe, R. (2004). The effectiveness of strategic reading instruction for college developmental readers. *Journal of College Reading and Learning, 35*(1), 25–49; Simpson, M. L., & Nist, S. L. (1997). Perspectives on learning history: A case study. *Journal of Literacy Research, 29*(3), 363–395.

6. Caverly, Nicholson, & Radcliffe, The effectiveness of strategic reading instruction for college developmental readers; Burrell, K. I., Tao, L., Simpson, M. L., & Mendez-Berrueta, H. (1997). How do we know what we are preparing students for? A reality check of one university's academic literacy demands. *Research & Teaching in Developmental Education, 13*, 15–70.

7. Bean, J. C. (1996). *Engaging ideas: The professor's guide to integrating writing, critical thinking, and active learning in the classroom.* San Francisco: Jossey-Bass; Wood, N. V. (1997). College reading instruction as reflected by current reading textbooks. *Journal of College Reading and Learning, 27*(3). 79–95.

8. Saumell, L., Hughes, M. T., & Lopate, K. (1999). Under-prepared college students' perceptions of reading: Are their perceptions different than other students? *Journal of College Reading and Learning, 29*(2), 123–125.

9. Buzan, T. (1983). *Use both sides of your brain.* New York: E. P. Dutton.

10. Ibid.

11. Sternberg, R. J. (1987). Teaching intelligence: The application of cognitive psychology to the improvement of intellectual skills. In J. B. Baron & R. J. Sternberg (Eds.), *Teaching thinking skills: Theory and practice.* New York: Freeman. pp. 182–218

12. Al-Jarf, R. S. (2002). Effect of online learning on struggling ESL college writers. San Antonio, TX: National Educational Computing Conference. Available at http://scholar.google.com/scholar?hl=en&lr=lang_en&q=cache:nUFnaTizpjgJ:dwc.hct.ac.ae/elearning/Research/SaudiResearchESL.pdf+ESL+college+success+recommendations.

13. Plato. (1956). *Protagoras and meno.* New York: Penguin.

14. Based on Bean, *Engaging ideas.*

15. See http://www.americaslibrary.gov/cgi-bin/page.cgi/jb/gilded/whitman_2.

16. Hirsch, Jr., E. D., Kett, J. F., & Trefil, J. (2002). *The new dictionary of cultural literacy: What every American needs to know.* New York: Houghton Mifflin.

17. Based partly on Williams, S. (2005). Guiding students through the jungle of research-based literature. *College Teaching, 53*(4), 137–139.

18. Macdaid, G. P., McCaulley, M. H., & Kainz, R. I. (1986). *Atlas of type tables.* Gainesville, FL: Center for Applications of Psychological Type.

19. Also available at http://www.bls.gov/oco/ocos069.htm.

20. Statistic Hargrove, T., & Stempel III, G. H. (2006, March 30). *Poll suggests path to happiness, if not mean-ing of life.* Newspolls.org.

21. Soldner, L. B. (1997). Self-assessment and the reflective reader. *Journal of College Reading and Learning, 28*(1), 5–11.

22. Van Blerkom, M. L., & Van Blerkom, D. L. (2004). Self-monitoring strategies used by developmental and non-developmental college students. *Journal of College Reading and Learning, 34*(2), 45–61.

23. Melchenbaum, D., Burland, S., Gruson, L., & Cameron, R. (1985). Metacognitive assessment. In S. Yussen (Ed.), *The growth of reflection in children.* Orlando, FL: Academic Press. p. 5

24. Hall, C. W. (2001). A measure of executive processing skills in college students. *College Student Journal, 35*(3), 442–450; Taylor, S. (1999). Better learning through better thinking: Developing students' metacognitive abilities. *Journal of College Reading and Learning, 30*(1), 34–45.

25. Learning to learn. Study Guides and Strategies. Available at http://www.studygs.net/metacognition.htm.

26. Simpson, M. L. (1994/1995). Talk throughs: A strategy for encouraging active learning across the content areas. *Journal of Reading, 38*(4), 296–304.

27. National Center for Health Statistics. Available at http://www.cdc.gov/nchs/fastats/births.htm.

28. American Heart Association. Available at http://www.americanheart.org/presenter.jhtml?identifier=4439.

29. How Air Traffic Control Works. Available at http://travel.howstuffworks.com/air-traffic-control.htm.

30. Elias, M. (2004, April 5). Frequent TV watching shortens kids' attention spans. *USA Today.* Available at http://www.usatoday.com/news/health/2004-04-05-tv-kids-attention-usat_x.htm.

31. Bol, L., Warkentin, R. W., Nunnery, J. A., & O'Connell, A. A. (1999). College students' study activities and their relationship to study context, reference course, and achievement. *College Student Journal, 33*(4). 608–622.

32. When students study makes a difference too. (2005, November). Recruitment & Retention. Available at http://www.magnapubs.com/pub/magnapubs_rr/19_11/news/598079-1.html.

33. Trainin, G., & Swanson, H. L. (2005). Cognition, meta-cognition, and achievement of college students with learning disabilities. *Learning Disability Quarterly, 28*, 261–272.

34. Cramming bites. Study Skills for College. Available at http://www.bmb.psu.edu/courses/psu16/troyan/study skills/cramming.htm; Final exams and cramming. Eastern Illinois University. Available at http://www.eiu.edu/~lrnasst/finals.htm.

35. Meyers, D. (2001). *Psychology* (6th ed.). New York: Worth Publishers.

36. Vergoth, K. (1995. July-August). Why you miss your deadlines . . . *Psychology Today.* Available at http://psychologytoday.com/articles/pto-19950701-000011.html.

37. Huber, M. T., & Hutchings, P. (2004). *Integrative learning: Mapping the terrain.* Washington, DC: The Association of American Colleges and Universities. Available at http://www.carnegiefoundation.org/dynamic/publications/mapping-terrain.pdf.

38. Moore, B. (2004). Interview by Betty Ann Boswer, *News Hour with Jim Lehrer,* PBS, September 9. In Huber, M. T., & Hutchings, P. (2004). *Integrative learning: Mapping the terrain.* Washington, DC: The Association of American Colleges and Universities. Available at http://www.carnegiefoundation.org/dynamic/publications/mapping-terrain.pdf.

39. Levy, F., & Mur-nane, R. J. (2005). *The new division of labor: How com-puters are creating the next job market.* Princeton, NJ: Princeton University Press; Dede, C. (2005, Fall). Teaching expert thinking. *Connections: New England's Journal of Higher Education.*

40. Jensen, G. H. (1986). Learning styles. In J. A. Provost & S. Anchors (Eds.). *Application of the Myers-Briggs type indicator in higher education.* Palo Alto, CA: Consulting Psychologists Press; DiTiberio, J. K., & Hammer, A. L. (1993). *Introduction to type in college.* Palo Alto, CA: Consulting Psychologists Press.

CHAPTER 9

1. Petress, K. (2004). What do college examinations accomplish? *College Student Journal, 38*(4), 521–522.

2. Thalheimer, W. (2002). *E-learning's unique—and seemingly unknown—capability.* Somerville, MA: Work-Learning Research.

3. Coren, S. (1996). *Sleep thieves.* New York: Free Press; Cox, K. (2004, October 14). The lights are on, but nobody's home. *The Oxford Student.* Available at http://www .oxfordstudent.com/mt2004wk1/Features/the_lights_ are_on,_but_nobody's_home.

4. Grant, K. B. (2003, September 4). Popping pills and taking tests. *The Ithacan Online.* Available at http://www.ithaca .edu/ithacan/articles/0309/04/news/2popping_pill.htm.

5. Based on Green, K. (2003). *Survey of 300 A+ students.* Berkeley, CA: Crème de la Crème Press.

6. Brinthaupt, T. M., & Shin, C. M. (2001). The relationship of academic cramming to flow experience. *College Student Journal, 35*(3), 457–472.

7. Tigner, R. B. (1999). Putting memory research to good use: Hints from cognitive psychology. *Journal of College Teaching, 47*(4), 149–152.

8. Frederickson, C. G. (1999). Multiple-choice answer changing: A type connection? *Journal of Psychological Type, 51,* 40–46.

9. Jensen, G. H. (1987). Learning styles. In J. A. Provost & S. Anchors (Eds.), *Applications of the Myers-Briggs type indicator in higher education.* p. 201. Palo Alto, CA: Consulting Psychologists Press.

10. Small, G. (2002). *The memory bible.* New York: Hyperion.

11. Counseling and Career Services. (2004). Do you have test anxiety? *Glendale Community College.* Available at http://www.gc.maricopa.edu/ccs/test.html.

12. Tozoglu, D., Tozoglu, M. D., Gurses, A., & Dogar, C. (2004). The students' perceptions: Essay versus multiple-choice type exams. *Journal of Baltic Science Education, 2*(6), 52–59.

13. Schutz, P. A., & Davis, H. A. (2000). Emotions and self-regulation during test taking. *Educational Psychologist, 35*(4), 243–256.

14. Coren, *Sleep thieves.*

15. Newman, E. (1996). *No more test anxiety.* Los Angeles, CA: Learning Skills Publications.

16. Ibid.

17. Kennedy, D. V., & Doepke, K. J. (1999). Multicomponent treatment of a test anxious college student. *Education & Treatment of Children, 22*(2), 203–217.

18. Perina, K. (2002). Sum of all fears. *Psychology Today.* Available at http://www.psychologytoday.com/articles/ pto-20021108-000001.html.

19. Perry, A. B. (2004). Decreasing math anxiety in college students. *College Student Journal, 38*(2), 321–324.

20. Krantz, S. G. (1999). *How to teach mathematics.* Providence, RI: American Mathematical Society.

21. Perry, Decreasing math anxiety in college students.

22. Perina, Sum of all fears.

23. Coping with math anxiety. (1997–2006). Platonic Realms MiniTexts. Available at http://www.mathacademy.com/ pr/minitext/anxiety/index.asp.

24. Jonides, J., Lacey, S. C., & Nee, D. E. (2005). Processes of working memory in mind and brain. *Current Directions in Psychological Science, 14*(1), 2–5.

25. Ashcraft, M. H., & Kirk, E. P. (2001). The relationships among working memory, math anxiety, and performance. *Journal of Experimental Psychology: General. 130*(2), 224–237.

26. Beilock, S. L., Kulp, C. A., Holt, L. E., & Carr, T. H. (2004). More on the fragility of performance: Choking under pressure in mathematical problem solving. *Journal of Experimental Psychology: General, 133*(4), 584–600.

27. Beilock, S. L., & Carr, T. H. (2005). When high-powered people fail: Working memory and "choking under pressure" in math. *Psychological Science. 16*(2), 101–105; Munger, D. (2005, May 18). Why some of us choke under pressure. Cognitive Daily. Available at http://science blogs.com/cognitivedaily/2005/05/why_some_of_us_ choke_under_pre.php; Mundell, E. J. (2005, March 9). Test pressure toughest on smartest. Lifespan. Available at http://www.lifespan.org/healthnews/2005/03/09/article 524405.html.

28. Mundell, Test pressure toughest on smartest.

29. Firmin, M., Hwang, C., Copella, M., & Clark, S. (2004). Learned helplessness: The effect of failure on test-taking. *Education, 124*(4), 688–693.

30. Sorokin, E. (2002, April 15). *Chewing gum expands the mind.* Memory-Improvement-Tips.com. Available at http://www.memory-improvement-tips.com/gum-and -memory.html; Young, E. (2002, 13 March). *Chewing gum improves memory.* NewScientist.com. Available at http://www.newscientist.com/article.ns?id=dn2039; Carter, H. (2002, March 14). *By gum, here's something for the memory to start chewing on.* Guardian Unlimited. Available at http://www.guardian.co.uk/Archive/Article/ 0,4273,4373825,00.html

31. Ibid.

32. Heidenberg, A. J., & Layne, B. H. (2000). Answer changing: A conditional argument. *College Student Journal, 34*(3), 440–451.

33. Hammer, A. L. (1993). *Introduction to type and careers.* Palo Alto, CA: Consulting Psychologists Press; Henderson-Loney, J. (1996). Steps and types: How the MBTI helped a treatment nonprofit develop an effective volunteer program. *Journal of Volunteer Administration, 15*(1), 29–34.

34. Also available at http://www.bls.gov/oco/cg/cgs054.htm.

35. See http://news.bbc.co.uk/2/hi/uk_news/scotland/glasgow _and_west/4755297.stm.

36. Preparing for multiple choice exams. (2006). York University. Available at http:www.yorku.ca/cdc/lsp/eponline/ exam4.htm.

37. Taking exams. Brockport High School. Available at http://www.frontiernet.net/~jlkeefer/takgexm.html. Adapted from Penn State University; On taking exams. University of New Mexico. Available at http://www.unm.edu/ ~quadl/college_learning/taking_exams.html; Lawrence, J. (2006). Tips for taking examinations. Lawrence Lab Homepage. Available at http://cobamide2.bio.pitt.edu/ testtips.htm; The multiple choice exam. (2003). Counselling Services, University of Victoria. Available at http://www.coun.uvic.ca/learning/exams/multiple-choice .html; General strategies for taking essay tests. GWired. Available at http://gwired.gwu.edu/counsel/asc/index .gw/Site_ID/46/Page_ID/14565/; Test taking tips: Guidelines for answering multiple-choice questions. Arizona State University. Available at http://neuer101.asu.edu/ additionaltestingtips.htm; Landsberger, J. (2007). True/ false tests. Study Guides and Strategies. Available at http://www.studygs.net/tsttak2.htm; Landsberger, J. (2007). Multiple choice tests. Study Guides and Strategies.

Available at http://www.studygs.net/tsttak3.htm; Landsberger, J. (2007). The essay exam. Study Guides and Strategies. Available at http://www.studygs.net/tsttak4.htm; Landsberger, J. (2007). Short answer tests. Study Guides and Strategies. Available at http://www.studygs.net/tsttak5.htm; Landsberger, J. (2007). Open book tests. Study Guides and Strategies. Available at http://www.studygs.net/tsttak7.htm; Rogers, T., & Kline, D. Test-taking advice: Especially for the multiple-choice challenged. University of Calgary. Available at http://www.psych.ucalgary.ca/undergraduate/current-students/student-support#tta; Rozakis, L. (2003). *Test-taking strategies and study skills for the utterly confused.* New York: McGraw-Hill; Meyers, J. N. (2000). *The secrets of taking any test.* New York: Learning Express; Robinson, A. (1993). *What smart students know.* New York: Crown Trade Paperbacks.

38. Plagiarism.org. Available at http://www.plagiarism.org/facts.html; A cheating crisis in America's schools. (2007, 17 April). ABC News. Available at http://abcnews.go.com/Primetime/print?id=132376.

39. Gostick, A., & Telford, D. (2003). *The integrity advantage.* Salt Lake City, UT: Gibbs Smith Publishers.

40. Caught cheating. (2004, April 29). *Primetime Live*, ABC News Transcript. Interview of college students by Charles Gibson; Zernike, K. (2002, November 2). With student cheating on the rise, more colleges are turning to honor codes. *The New York Times*, p. Q10, column 1, National Desk; Warren, R. (2003, October 20). Cheating: An easy way to cheat yourself. The Voyager via U-Wire. University Wire (www.uwire.com); Thomson, S. C. (2004, February 13). Amid wave of cheating, universities push "academic integrity." Knight Ridder/Tribune News Service. Available at http://www.highbeam.com/doc/1G1-113209265.html; Heyboer, K. (2003, August 23). Nearly half of college students say Internet plagiarism isn't cheating. *The Star-Ledger Newark, New Jersey*.; Kleiner, C., & Lord, M. (1999). The cheating game. *U.S. News & World Report.* Available at http://www.usnews.com/usnews/culture/articles/991122/archive_002427_8.htm.

41. Standardized tests. Mapping Your Future. Available at http://mapping-your-future.org/selecting/standard.htm; Grant, K. B. (2003). Popping pills and taking tests. The Ithacan Online. Available at http://www.ithaca.edu/ithacan/articles/0309/04/news/2popping_pill.htm; Survival strategies for taking tests. (2003). Indiana State University. Available at http://www.indstate.edu/isucceed/tests.htm; Cummins, C. (2004, May 14); Rogers & Kline, Test-taking advice; Rozakis, *Test-taking strategies and study skills for the utterly confused*; Meyers, *The secrets of taking any test*.

CHAPTER 10

1. 2002 Writing Assessment. U.S. Department of Education, Institute of Education Sciences, National Center for Education Statistics, National Assessment of Educational Progress (NAEP). Available at http://nces.ed.gov/nationsreportcard/writing/results2002/natachieve-schooltype-all.asp.

2. See http://www.askmen.com/men/entertainment/55c_stephen_king.html.

3. McCarroll, C. (2001). To learn to think in college, write—a lot. *Christian Science Monitor, 93*(177), 20. Available at http://www.wcu.edu/WritingCenter/isource.asp?page=learn_to_think.html.

4. De Vos, I. (1988, October). Getting started: How expert writers do it. *Training & Development Journal*, 18–19.

5. Elbow, P. (1998). *Writing with power: Techniques for mastering the writing process.* Oxford: Oxford

University Press; Mack, K. (1979). *Overcoming writing blocks.* New York: St. Martin's Press; Overcoming writer's block. Purdue University Online Writing Lab. Available at http://owl.english.purdue.edu/handouts/general/gl_block.html.

6. Jensen, G., & DiTiberio, J. K. (1984). Personality and individual writing processes. *College Composition and Communication, 35*(3), 285–300; DiTiberio, J. K., & Hammer, A. L. (1993). *Introduction to type in college.* Palo Alto, CA: Consulting Psychologists Press; Sampson, E. (2003). *Creative business presentations.* London: Kogan Page.

7. Opt, S. K., & Loffredo, D. A. (2000). Rethinking communication apprehension: A Myers-Briggs perspective. *Journal of Psychology, 134*(5), 556–570.

8. Bean, J. C. (1996). *Engaging ideas: The professor's guide to integrating writing, critical thinking and active learning in the classroom.* San Francisco: Jossey-Bass.

9. Portions of this section are based on Staley, C., & Staley, R. (1992). *Communicating in business and the professions: The inside word.* Belmont, CA: Wadsworth.

10. Bean, *Engaging ideas.*

11. Based on information taken from http://www.civilwar.com/.

12. Based on Self-help brochures. Counseling Center at the University of Illinois. Available at http://www.couns.uiuc.edu/Brochures/addict.htm.

13. Flaherty, A. W. (2003). Writing like crazy: A word on the brain. *The Chronicle of Higher Education, 50*(13), B6. Available at http://chronicle.com/weekly/v50/i13/13b00601.htm.

14. Pennebaker, J. W., & Seagal, J. D. (1999). Forming a story: The health benefits of narrative. *Journal of Clinical Psychology, 55*(10), 1243–1254; Perry, S. (2001, November-December). Right here, write now. *Psychology Today.* Available at http://cms.psychologytoday.com/articles/pto-20011101-000028.html.

15. Smyth, J. M., Stone, A. A., Hurewitz, A., & Kaell, A. (1999). Effects of writing about stressful experiences on symptom reduction in patients with asthma or rheumatoid arthritis: A randomized trial. *Journal of the American Medical Association, 281* (14), 1304–1309.

16. Can you write your way to good health? (1997, February). *Psychology Today.* Available at http://www.psychologytoday.com/articles/pto-19970201-000017.html.

17. Frisina, P. G., Borod, J. C., & Lepore, S. J. (2004, September). A meta-analysis of the effects of written emotional disclosure on the health outcomes of clinical populations. *Journal of Nervous & Mental Disease, 192*(9), 629–634. Available at http://www.jonmd.com/pt/re/jnmd/abstract.00005053-200409000-00008.htm;jsessionid=CQu2mD56gcX2VeykDB8Jql3Uhc3nLIOvPnDqU67H68tYCmThUcXN!-1860688455!-949856031!9001!-1; Solano, L., Donati, V., Pecci, F., Persichetti, S., & Colaci, A. (2003, May-June). Postoperative course after papilloma resection: Effects of written disclosure of the experience in subjects with different alexithymia levels. *Psychosomatic Medicine, 65*(3), 477–484. Available at http://www.jonmd.com/pt/re/jnmd/abstract.00006842-200305000-00021.htm;jsessionid=CQyQWNUWjoNF5a1BjWFnhZ6GJlgws2pqnAw0mfQlbfqlFvWXva0i!-1860688455!-949856031!9001!-1; Petrie, K. J., Booth, R. J., & Pennebaker, J. W. (1998). The immunological effects of thought suppression. *Journal of Personality and Social Psychology, 75*(5), 1264–1272; Lepore, S. J., & Smyth, J. M. (Eds.). (2002). The writing cure: How expressive writing promotes health and emotional well-being. Washington, DC: American Psychological Association; Pennebaker, J. W. (2004). *Writing to heal: A guided jour-*

nal for recovering from trauma and emotional upheaval. Oakland, CA: New Harbinger Publications.

18. Portions based on Staley & Staley, *Communicating in business and the professions.*

19. Idea taken from Foley, J. E. (2001). The freshman research paper: A near-death experience. *College Teaching 49*(3), 83–86.

20. Procter, M. (2006). *How not to plagiarize.* Office of Teaching Advancement, University of Toronto. Available at http://www.utoronto.ca/writing/plagsep.html; *Plagiarism: What it is and how to recognize and avoid it.* Indiana University. Available at http://www.indiana.edu/~wts/pamphlets/plagiarism.pdf.

21. McCroskey, J., & Richmond, V. P. (1992). *Communication: Apprehension, avoidance, and effectiveness* (3rd ed.). (Scottsdale, AZ: Gorsuch Scarisbrick, Publishers), pp. 127–128. Used with permission.

22. Staley & Staley, *Communicating in business and the professions.*

23. Public speaking. (1996, May-June). *Psychology Today.* Available at http://psychologytoday.com/articles/index.php?term=pto-19960501-000009.html.

24. Beaver, H. D. Got stage fright. Graduate School of Banking. Available at www.gsb.org/articles/Stage_Fright.htm.

25. Brownell, W. F., & Katula, R. A. (1984). The communication anxiety graph: A classroom tool for managing speech anxiety. *Communication Education 32*, 243–249.

26. Reverend Spooner's Tips of the Slung. (1995). *Reader's Digest Magazine.* Available at http://www.fun-with-words.com/spoon_history.html.

27. Staley & Staley, *Communicating in business and the professions*; Axtell, R. E. (1992). *Do's and taboos of public speaking: How to get those butterflies flying in formation.* New York: John Wiley & Sons.

28. Engleberg, I. N. (1994). *The principles of public presentation.* New York: HarperCollins; Daley, K., & Daley-Caravella, L. (2004). *Talk your way to the top.* New York: McGraw-Hill.

29. Hammer, A. L. (1993). *Introduction to type and careers.* Palo Alto, CA: Consulting Psychologists Press; Demarest, L. (1997). *Looking at type in the workplace.* Gainesville, FL: Center for Application of Psychological Type.

30. Also available at http://www.bls.gov/oco/print/ocos020.htm.

31. Staley, C. (2003). *50 ways to leave your lectern.* Belmont, CA: Wadsworth, pp. 138. Used with permission.

CHAPTER 11

1. Some situation topics suggested at Emotional Intelligence. Scottish Further Education Unit EI. http://www.sfeu.ac.uk/projects/emotional_intelligence.

2. Tinto, V. (1975). Dropout from higher education: A theoretical synthesis of recent research. *Review of Educational Research, 45,* 89–125; Tinto, V. (1993). *Leaving college: Rethinking the causes and cures of student attrition* (2nd ed.). Chicago: University of Chicago Press.

3. Paul, E. L., & Brier, S. (2001). Friendsickness in the transition to college: Precollege predictors and college adjustment correlates. *Journal of Counseling & Development, 79*(1), 77–89.

4. Pressman, S. D., Cohen, S., Miller, G. E., Barkin, A., Rabin, B. S., & Treanor, J. J. (2005). Loneliness, social network size, and immune response to influenza vaccination in college freshmen. *Health Psychology, 24*(3), 297–306;

Hitti, M. (2005, May 2). Researchers say lonely college freshmen show weaker immune response. WebMD Medical News. Available at http://www.webmd.com/balance/news/20050502/loneliness-may-hurt-your-health.

5. Clifton, D. O., & Anderson, E. (2001–2002). *Strengthsquest: Discover and develop your strengths in academics, career, and beyond.* Washington, DC: The Gallup Organization.

6. Gardner, H. (1993). *Multiple intelligences: The theory in practice.* New York: Basic Books; Checkley, K. (1997). The first seven . . . and the eighth: A conversation with Howard Gardner. Expanded Academic ASAP (online database). Original Publication: *Education,* 116.

7. Goleman, D. (2002, June 16). Could you be a leader? *Parade Magazine,* pp. 4–6.

8. Snarey, J. R., & Vaillant, G. E. (1985). How lower- and working-class youth become middle-class adults: The association between ego defense mechanisms and upward social mobility. *Child Development, 56*(4), 899–910.

9. Feist, G. J., & Barron, F. (1996, June). *Emotional intelligence and academic intelligence in career and life success.* Paper presented at the Annual Convention of the American Psychological Society, San Francisco, CA.

10. Emmerling, R. J., & Goleman, D. (2003). *Emotional intelligence issues and common misunderstandings.* The Consortium for Research on Emotional Intelligence in Organizations. Available at http://wwweiconsortium.org/research/EI_Issues_And_Common_Misunderstandings.pdf.

11. Grewal, D., & Salovey, P. (2005, July-August). Feeling smart: The science of emotional intelligence. *American Scientist, 93*(4), 330. Available at http://www.americanscientist.org/template/AssetDetail/assetid/44512.

12. Isen, A. M, Daubman, K. A., & Nowicki, G. P. (1987). Positive affect facilitates creative problem solving. *Journal of Personality and Social Psychology, 52*(6), 1122–1131.

13. Parker, J. D. A., Duffy, J. M., Wood, L. M., Bond, B. J., & Hogan, M. J. (2005). Academic achievement and emotional intelligence: Predicting the successful transition from high school to university. *Journal of the First Year Exper-ience & Students in Transition 17*(1), 67–78; Schutte, N. S., & Malouff, J. (2002). Incorporating emotional skills content in a college transition course enhances student retention. *Journal of the First Year Experience & Students in Transition 14*(1), 7–21.

14. EQ-i:S™ Post Secondary, Multi-Health Systems, Inc. North Tonawanda, NY. Available at http://www.mhs.com/index.htm. Used with permission.

15. Turning lemons into lemonade: Hardiness helps people turn stressful circumstances into opportunities. (2003, December 22). *Psychology Matters.* Available at APA Online at http://www.psychologymatters.org/hardiness.html; Marano, H. E. (2003). The art of resilience. *Psychology Today.* Available at http://www.psychologytoday.com/articles/pto-20030527-000009.html; Fischman, J. (1987). Getting tough: Can people learn to have disease-resistant personalities? *Psychology Today, 21,* 26–28; Friborg, O., Barlaug, D., Martinussen, M., Rosenvinge, J. H., & Hjemdal, O. (2005). Resilience in relation to personality and intelligence. *International Journal of Methods in Psychiatric Research, 14*(1), 29–42; Schulman, P. (1995). Explanatory style and achievement in school and work. In G. M. Buchanan & M. E. P. Seligman (Eds.), *Explanatory style* (pp. 159–171). Hillsdale, NJ: Lawrence Erlbaum; American Psychological Association. (1997). Learned optimism yields health benefits. *Discovery Health.* Available at http://health.discovery.com/centers/mental/articles/optimism/optimism.html.

16. Maher, K. (2004) Emotional intelligence is a factor in promotions. *CollegeJournal from the Wall Street Journal*. Available at http://www.collegejournal.com/columnists/thejungle/20040322-maher.html.

17. Cherniss, C. (2000). *Emotional Intelligence: What it is and why it matters*. Paper presented at the Annual Meeting of the Society for Industrial and Organizational Psychology, New Orleans, LA. Available at http://www.eiconsortium.org/research/what_is_emotional_intelligence.htm.

18. Goleman, Could you be a leader? p. 4.

19. Boyatzis, R. E., Cowan, S. S., & Kolb, D. A. (1995). *Innovations in professional education: Steps on a journey from teaching to learning*. San Francisco: Jossey-Bass.

20. Davidson, R. J., Kabat-Zinn, J., Schumacher, J., Rosenkranz, M., Muller, D., Santorelli, S. F., Urbanowski, F., Harrington, A., Bonus, K., & Sheridan, J. F. (2003). Alterations in brain and immune function produced by mindfulness meditation. *Psychosomatic Medicine*, *65*, 564–570. Available at http://psyphz.psych.wisc.edu/web/pubs/2003/alterations_by_mindfulness.pdf; Hughes, D. (2004). Interview with Daniel Goleman. Share Guide. Available at http://www.shareguide.com/Goleman.html.

21. Saxbe, D. (2004, November/December). The socially savvy. *Psychology Today*. Available at http://www.psychologytoday.com/articles/pto-3636.html.

22. Bar-On, R. (2006). The Bar-On model of emotional-social intelligence (ESI). *Psicothema*, *18* (Suppl.), 13–25. The Consortium for Research on Emotional Intelligence in Organizations. Available at http://www.eiconsortium.org/.

23. Cramer, D. (2004). Satisfaction with a romantic relationship, depression, support and conflict. *Psychology and Psychotherapy: Theory, Research and Practice*, *77*(4), 449–461.

24. Fisher, H. (2004). *Why we love*. New York: Henry Holt.

25. Beach, S. R. H., & Tesser, A. (1988). Love in marriage; a cognitive account. In R. J. Sternberg & M. L. Barnes (Eds.), *The Psychology of Love*. 330–355 New Haven, CT: Yale University Press; Hatfield, E., & Walster, G. W. (1978). *A new look at love*. Lanham, MD: University Press of America.

26. Rath, T., & Clifton, D. O. (2004). *How full is your bucket?* New York: Gallup Press.

27. Knox, D. H. (1970). Conceptions of love at three developmental levels. *The Family Coordinator*, *19*(2), 151–157; Fisher, *Why we love*.

28. Knox, D., Schacht, C., & Zusman, M. E. (1999, March). Love relationships among college students. *College Student Journal*, *33*(1), 149–154. Available at http://www.findarticles.com/p/articles/mi_m0FCR/is_1_33/ai_62894068.

29. Schwartz, P. (2003, May-June). Love is not all you need. *Psychology Today*. Available at http://www.psychologytoday.com/articles/pto-20030213-000002.html.

30. Bach, G. R., & Goldberg, H. (1974). *Creative aggression: The art of assertive living*. Garden City, NJ: Doubleday; Bach, G. R, & Wyden, P. (1972). *The intimate enemy: How to fight fair in love and marriage*. New York: Avon; Bach, G. R., Deutsch, R. M., (1985). *Stop! You're driving me crazy*. New York: Berkley Publishing Group; Tucker-Ladd, C. E. (1996–2006); *Driving each other crazy*. Psychological self-help. Available at http://psychologicalselfhelp.org/Chapter9/chap9_90.html.

31. Fisher, *Why we love*.

32. Fisher, R., & Brown, S. (1988). *Getting together: Building a relationship that gets to yes*. Boston: Houghton Mifflin, p. xi.

33. Hocker, J. L., & Wilmot, W. W. (2007). *Interpersonal conflict* (7th ed.). New York: McGraw-Hill. 34. Based in part on Marano, H. (2002). Relationship rules. *Psychology Today*. Available at http://www.psychologytoday.com/articles/pto-20041022-000003.html.

35. Thomas, K. (1977). Conflict and conflict management. In M. D. Dunnette (Ed.), *Handbook of industrial and organizational psychology*, 889-935 Chicago: Rand McNally; Kilmann, R., & Thomas, K. W. (1975). Interpersonal conflict-handling behavior as reflections of Jungian personality dimensions. *Psychological Reports*, *37*, 971–980; Rahim, M., & Magner, N. R. (1995). Confirmatory factor analysis of the styles of handling interpersonal conflict: First-order factor model and its invariance across groups. *Journal of Applied Psychology*, *80*, 122–132; Wilmot, W. W., & Hocker, J. L. (2001). *Interpersonal conflict* (6th ed.). New York: McGraw-Hill. Kilmann, R. H., and K. W. Thomas. (1977). Developing a Forced-Choice Measure of Conflict-Handling Behavior: The MODE Instrument," *Educational and psychological measurement*, *37*(2), 309–325.

36. Rytting, M., Ware, R., & Hopkins, P. (1992). Type and the ideal mate: Romantic attraction or type bias? *Journal of Psychological Type*, *24*, 3–12; Sherman, R. G. (1981). Typology and problems in intimate relationships. *Journal of Psychological Type*, *4*, 1–11.

37. (2006, March 3). Study: Bad relationships bad for heart. *CBS News*. Available at http://www.cbsnews.com/stories/2006/03/03/earlyshow/contributors/emilysenay/main1364889.shtml; (2005, December 5) Unhappy marriage: bad for your health. *WebMD*. Available at http://www.webmd.com/sex-relationships/news/20051205/unhappy-marriage-bad-for-your-health. Based on Keicolt-Glaser, J. (2005). *Archives of general psychiatry*, 62, 1377–1384.

38. Dusselier, L., Dunn, B., Wang, Y., Shelley, M. C., & Whalen, D. F. (2005). Personal, health, academic, and environmental predictors of stress for residence hall students. *Journal of American College Health*, *54*(1), 15–24; Hardigg, V., & Nobile, C. (1995). Living with a stranger. *U.S. News & World Report*, *119*(12), 90–91. Available at http://www.usnews.com/usnews/edu/articles/950925/archive_032964_print.htm; Nankin, J. (2005). Rules for roomies. *Careers & Colleges*, *25*(4), 29.

39. Miller, G. R., & Steinberg, M. (1975). *Between people: A new analysis of interpersonal communication*. Chicago: Science Research Associates.

40. Based on Walter, T. L. (2003). Turn a negative student-to-instructor relationship into a positive relationship. In C. Staley, *50 Ways to leave your lectern* (pp. 146–149). Belmont, CA: Wadsworth.

41. McLaughlin, B., & McLeod, B. (1996). *Educating all our students: Improving education for children from culturally and linguistically diverse backgrounds*. Final Report of the National Center for Research on Cultural Diversity and Second Language Learning. Available at http://www.ncela.gwu.edu/pubs/ncrcdsll/edall.htm.

42. Wyer, K. (2007). Today's college freshmen have family income 60% above national average, UCLA survey reveals. UCLA News. Available at http://www.gseis.ucla.edu/heri/PDFs/PR_TRENDS_40YR.pdf.

43. Humphrey, D., & Davenport, A. (2004, Summer/Fall). What really matters in college: How students view

and value liberal education. *Liberal Education*. Excerpt: Diversity and civic engagement outcomes ranked among least important. Available at http://www.diversityweb .org/Digest/vol9no1/vo9no1.pdf.

44. Laird, T. F. (2005). College students' experiences with diversity and their effects on academic self-confidence, social agency, and disposition toward critical thinking. *Research in Higher Education, 46*(4), 365–387.

45. Bucher, R. D. (2004). *Diversity consciousness: Opening our minds to people, cultures, and opportunities* (2nd ed.). Upper Saddle River, NJ: Pearson Education.

46. Moore, D. G. (2003, November 14). Toward a single definition of college. *The Chronicle of Higher Education, 50*(12), B7.

47. Pusser, B., Breneman, D. W., Gansneder, B. M., Kohl, K. J., Levin, J. S., Milam, J. H., & Turner, S. E. (2007). *Returning to learning: Adults' success in college is key to America's future.* Lumina Foundation. Available at http://www.luminafoundation.org/publications/Return tolearningApril2007.pdf.

48. Gomstyn, A. (2003, October 17). Minority enrollment in colleges more than doubled in past 20 years, study finds. *The Chronicle of Higher Education, 50*(8), A25; Schmidt, P. (2003, 28 November). Academe's Hispanic future. *The Chronicle of Higher Education, 50*(14), A8.

49. Staley, C. (2003). *50 ways to leave your lectern.* Belmont, CA: Wadsworth, p. 67. Based on Defining "Diversity." (1995). In B. Pike & C. Busse, *101 games for trainers* (p. 11). Minneapolis: Lakewood Books.

50. Farrell, E. F. (2005, August 5). Student volunteers are worth billions. *The Chronicle of Higher Education, 51*(48), A33.

51. Zlotkowski, E. (1999). Pedagogy and engagement. In R. G. Bringle, R. Games, & E. A. Malloy (Eds.). (1999). *Colleges and Universities as Citizens* (pp. 96–120). Needham Heights, MA: Allyn & Bacon.

52. Honnet, E. P., & Poulsen, S. J. (1989). *Principles of good practice for combining service and learning: A Wingspread special report.* Racine, WI: The Johnson Foundation. Available at http://www.servicelearning.org/ resources/online_documents/service-learning_standards/ principles_of_good_practice_for_combining_service_and_ learning_a_wingspread_special_report/index.php.

53. Eyler, J., Giles, Jr., D. E., & Schmiede, A. (1996). *A practitioner's guide to refection in service-learning: Student voices and reflections.* Nashville, TN: Vanderbilt University Press.

54. Dewey, J. (1933). *How we think.* Boston: Heath.

55. Farrell, Student volunteers are worth billions.

56. Carnes, M. C. (2005). Inciting speech. *Change, 37*(2), 6–11.

57. Based on Nilsen, L. B. (1998). The circles of _____. *Teaching at Its Best.* Bolton, MA: Anker Publishing.

58. Lyons, P. (2005, April 15). The truth about teaching about racism. *The Chronicle of Higher Education, 51*(32), B5.

59. Epstein, G. (2005, June 5) More women advance, but sexism persists. *College Journal from the Wall Street Journal.* Available at http://www.collegejournal.com/successwork/ workplacediversity/20030605-epstein.html.

60. Wessel, D. (2003, September 10). Race still a factor in hiring decisions. *CollegeJournal from the Wall Street Journal.* Available at http://www.collegejournal.com/forms/ printContent.asp?url=http://www.collegejournal.com/ successwork/workplacediversity/20030910-wessel.html.

61. Beilke, J. R., & Yssel, N. (1999). The chilly climate for students with disabilities in higher education. *College Student Journal, 33*(3), 364–372.

62. Parker, P. N. (2006, March-April). Sustained dialogue: How students are changing their own racial climate. *About Campus, 11*(1),17–23.

63. Gortmaker, V. J., & Brown, R. D. (2006). Out of the college closet: Differences in perceptions and experiences among out and closeted lesbian and gay students. *College Student Journal, 40*(3), 606–619.

64. Incidences and Statistics. (2005). Hate crime statistics 2005. Department of Justice, Uniform Crime Reporting Program. Available at http://www.fbi.gov/ucr/hc2005/ incidentsoffenses.htm.

65. Macdaid, G. P., McCaulley, M. H., & Kainz, R. I. (1986). *Atlas of type tables.* Gainesville, FL: Center for Applications of Psychological Type.

66. Also available at http://www.bls.gov/oco/print/ocos021.htm.

67. Parker, P. N. (2006, March-April). Sustained dialogue: How students are changing their own racial climate. *About Campus, 17–34.*

68. Bucher, R. D. (2004). *Diversity consciousness: Opening our minds to people, cultures, and opportunities* (2nd ed.). Upper Saddle River, NJ: Pearson Education.

69. Dwyer, T., & Flannigan, K. (2001). Web globalization: Write once, Deploy worldwide. Download PDF. Available amazon.com.

70. General Education for global learning. American Association of American Colleges & Universities. Available at http://www.aacu.org/SharedFutures/gened_global_ learning/index.cfm.

CHAPTER 12

1. Gregory, M. (2003, September 12). A liberal education is not a luxury. *The Chronicle of Higher Education, 50*(3), B16.

2. Staley, R. S., II. (2003). In C. Staley, *50 ways to leave your lectern* (pp. 70–74). Belmont, CA: Wadsworth.

3. Bolles, R. N. (2007). *What color is your parachute?* Berkeley, CA: Ten Speed Press; Bolles, R. N. (2005). *What color is your parachute?* Berkeley, CA: Ten Speed Press.

4. Bolles, R. N. (2005). p. xviii.

5. Staley, R. S., II, in Staley, *50 ways to leave your lectern.*

6. Farrell, E. F. (2006, December 12). Freshmen put high value on how well college prepares them for a profession, survey finds. *The Chronicle of Higher Education.* Available at http://chronicle.com/daily/2006/ 12/2006121202n.htm; Farrell, E. F. (2007, January 5). Report says freshmen put career prep first. *The Chronicle of Higher Education, 53*(18), A32.

7. Irvine, M. (2007, January 22). Polls say wealth important to youth. SFGate.com. Available at http://www.sfgate .com/cgi-bin/article.cgi?file=/n/a/2007/01/22/national/ a111238S28.DTL; Schwartz, B. (2004, January 23). The tyranny of choice. *The Chronicle of Higher Education, 50*(20), B6.

8. Koeppel, D. (2004, December 5). Choosing a college major: For love or for the money? *The New York Times,* section 10, p. 1, column 4. Available at http://www .nytimes.com/2004/12/05/jobs/05jmar.html?ex=12599 89200&en=51dcc14fa52a65e7&ei=5090&partner=rss userland; Dunham, K. J. (2004, March 2). No ivory tower: College students focus on career. *Wall Street Journal* (Eastern Edition), pp. B1, B8. Available at http://online .wsj.com/article/SB107818521697943524.html.

9. Malgwi, C. A., Howe, M. A., & Burnaby, P. A. (2005). Influences on students' choice of college major. *Journal of Education for Business, 80*(5), 275–282.

10. Leppel, K. (2005). College persistence and student attitudes toward financial success. *College Student Journal, 39*(2), 223–241.

11. Saleh, A. (2001). Brain hemisphericity and academic majors: A correlation study. *College Student Journal, 35*(2), 193–200.

12. Simpson, J. C. (2003). Mom matters: Maternal influence on the choice of academic major. *Sex Roles, 48*(9/10), 447–460.

13. Rask, K. N., & Bailey, E. M. (2002). Are faculty role models? Evidence from major choice in an undergraduate institution. *The Journal of Economic Education, 33*(2), 99–124.

14. Groom, N. (2005, June 6). Skateboard hero Hawk looks beyond the board. Ezilon Infobase. Available at http://www.ezilon.com/information/article_5382.shtml.

15. Levine, M. (2005). *Ready or not, here life comes.* New York: Simon & Schuster, p. 4; Levine, M. (2005, February 18). College graduates aren't ready for the real world. *The Chronicle of Higher Education, 51*(24), B11.

16. *Dictionary of occupational titles.* (1991). Washington, DC: Bureau of Labor Statistics. Or see O*Net Online (Occupational Information Network) at http://online.onetcenter.org/find/.

17. Based on Schwartz, The tyranny of choice.

18. See J. K. Rowling Biography at http://www.biography.com/search/article.jsp?aid=9465815&page=2&search=.

19. Levine, *Ready or not, here life comes.*

20. Based in part on Gordon, V. N., & Sears, S. J. (2004). *Selecting a college major: Exploration and decision making, 5th edition.* Upper Saddle River, NJ: Pearson Education.

21. Based on Hansen, R. S., & Hansen, K. *Using a SWOT analysis in your career planning.* Quintessential Careers. Available at http://www.quintcareers.com/SWOT_Analysis.html.

22. Staley, *50 ways to leave your lectern,* p. 33. Based on "Group Resume." (1995). In M. Silberman, *101 ways to make training active* (pp. 49–50). Johannesburg: Pfeiffer.

23. *What work requires of schools: A SCANS report for America 2000.* Academic Innovations. Available at http://www.academicinnovations.com/report.html; Secretary's commission on achieving necessary skills. (2006, March 9). U.S. Department of Labor. Available at http://wdr.doleta.gov/SCANS; SCANS skills: Foundation and competencies. (1996, July 10). EXTEND: SCANS Skills. Available at http://www.stolaf.edu/other/extend/Resources/scans.html.

24. Partenheimer, D. (2004, January 11). Abilities required for success in school don't differ greatly from those required in the real world. APA Online. Available at http://www.apa.org/releases/success.html.

25. *Job interviews get creative.* (2003, August 22). NPR. Available at http://www.npr.org/templates/story/story.php?storyId=1405340.

26. Vance, E. (2007, February 2). College graduates lack key skills, report says. *The Chronicle of Higher Education, 53*(22), A30.

27. Demarest, L. (1997). *Looking at type in the workplace.* Gainesville, FL: Center for Applications of Psychological Type.

28. Also available at http://www.bls.gov/oco/ocos021.htm; Recruiter. Wikipedia. Available at http://en.wikipedia.org/wiki/Recruiter.

29. Rowh, M. (2003, February-March). Choosing a major. *Career World, 31*(5), 21–23.

30. Ezarik, M. M. (2007, April-May). A major decision. *Career World, 35*(6), 20–22.

31. Rask & Bailey, Are faculty role models?

32. Based on Staley, *50 ways to leave your lectern,* p. 82.

33. Goldhaber, G. M. (1986). *Organizational communication* (4th ed.). Dubuque, IA: Wm. C. Brown, p. 236. In Staley, R. S., II, & Staley, C. C. (1992). *Communicating in business and the professions: The inside word.* Belmont, CA: Wadsworth.

34. DiTiberio, J. K., & Hammer, A. L. (1993). *Introduction to type in college.* Palo Alto, CA: Consulting Psychologists Press; Hammer, A. L. (1993). *Introduction to type and careers.* Palo Alto, CA: Consulting Psychologists Press.

35. Myers, I. B., & McCaulley, M. H. (1985). *Manual: A guide to the development and use of the Myers-Briggs type indicator.* Palo Alto, CA: Consulting Psychologists Press. In Golden, V. J., & Provost, J. A. (1987). *"The MBTI and career development;" Application of the Myers-Briggs type indicator in higher education.* Palo Alto, CA: Consulting Psychologists Press.

CHAPTER 13

1. Davis, R., & DeBarros, A. (2006, January 25). In college, first year is by far the riskiest. *USA Today.* Available at http://www.usatoday.com/news/nation/2006-01-24-campus-deaths-cover_x.htm.

2. Monastersky, R. (2007, January 12). Who's minding the teenage brain? *The Chronicle of Higher Education, 53*(19), A14.

3. Common health problems in college students. (2000). *Medem: Medical Library.* American Academy of Pediatrics. Available at http://www.medem.com/MedLB/article_detaillb.cfm?article_ID=ZZZG2JNPQ7C&sub_cat=18; Health problems of college students. *Journal of American College Health, 45*(6), 243–250.

4. Macdaid, G. P., McCaulley, M. H., & Kainz, R. I. (1986). *Atlas of type tables.* Gainesville, FL: Center for Applications of Psychological Type; Hammer, A. L. (1993). *Introduction to type and careers.* Palo Alto, CA: Consulting Psychologists Press.

5. Also available at http://www.bls.gov/oco/print/ocos074.htm.

6. Hales, D. (2006). *An invitation to health, brief.* Belmont, CA: Thomson Wadsworth, p. 32.

7. Kobau, R., Safran, M. A., Zack, M. M., Moriarty, D. G., & Chapman, D. (2004, July 30). Sad, blue, or depressed days, health behaviors and health-related quality of life, behavioral risk factor surveillance system, 1995–2000. *Health Quality of Life Outcomes, 2*(1).

8. Hilts, P. J. (1993, May 22). U.S. defines mental illness as standard for treatment. *The New York Times.* Available at http://query.nytimes.com/gst/fullpage.html?sec=health&res=9F0CE2D61F3FF931A15756C0A965958260.

9. Heredity and the Genetics of Schizophrenia. Schizophrenia.com. Available at http://www.schizophrenia.com/research/hereditygen.htm.

10. Scientists show how cannabis/marijuana may trigger schizophrenia. (2007, April 30). Schizophrenia.com. Schizophrenia Daily News Blog. Available at http://www.schizophrenia.com/sznews/archives/004987.html.

11. MacInnes, N., Handley, S. L., & Harding, G. F. (2001). Former chronic methylenedioxy methamphetamine (MDMA or ecstasy) users report mild depressive symptoms. *Journal of Psychopharmacology, 15*(3), 181–186.

12. Depression. (2000; updated 2006, September 13). National Institute of Mental Health. Available at http://www.nimh.nih.gov/publicat/depression.cfm.

13. National Institute of Mental Health. (1997; updated 2006, February 17). What do these students have in common? Bethesda, MD: National Institute of Mental Health, National Institutes of Health, U.S. Department of Health and Human Services (NIH Publication No. 00-4266). Available at http://www.nimh.nih.gov/publicat/students.cfm.

14. Ibid.

15. Ibid.

16. Farrell, E. F. (2005, December 16). Need therapy? Check your in box. *The Chronicle of Higher Education, 52*(17), A35.

17. Celebrity meltdown. (1999, November/December). *Psychology Today.* Available at http://www.psychologytoday.com/articles/pto-19991101-000035.html.

18. Ibid.

19. Anxiety disorders: What you need to know. (2007). Mental Health America. Available at http://www.mentalhealthamerica.net/go/information/get-info/anxiety-disorders/anxiety-disorders/anxiety-disorders-what-you-need-to-know.

20. Marano, H. E. (2004). Up against the ivy wall in 2004. *Psychology Today.* Available at http://www.psychologytoday.com/articles/pto-20040513-000004.html.

21. Benton, S. A., Robertson, J. M., Tseng, W., Newton, F. B., & Benton, S. L. (2003). Changes in counseling center client problems across 13 years. *Professional Psychology: Research and Practice, 34*(1), 66–72.

22. Astin, A. W., Astin, H. S., Lindholm, J. A., & Bryant, A. N. (2005). *The spiritual life of college students: A national study of college students' search for meaning and purpose.* Los Angeles: Higher Education Research Institute, UCLA.

23. Astin et al., *The spiritual life of college students;* Bartlett, T. (2005, April 22). Most freshmen say religion guides them. *The Chronicle of Higher Education, 51*(33), A1. Available at http://chronicle.com/weekly/v51/i33/33a00101.htm.

24. Saenz, V., & Wolf, D. (2006, February 16). Your First College Year Survey: Highlights from the 2005 YFCY. Available at http://www.sc.edu/fye/resources/assessment/essays/Saenz-2.16.06.html.

25. Nelms, L. W., Hutchins, E., Hutchins, D., & Pursley, R. J. (2007). Spirituality and the health of college students. *Journal of Religion and Health, 46*(2), 249–265.

26. Segerstrom, S. C., & Miller, G. E. (2004). Psychological stress and the human immune system: A meta-analytic study of 30 years of inquiry. *Psychological Bulletin, 130*(4), 601–630. Available at http://www.apa.org/journals/releases/bul1304601.pdf; (2004, July 4). Stress affects immunity in ways related to stress type and duration, as shown by nearly 300 studies. *APA Press Release.* Available at http://www.apa.org/releases/stress_immune.html.

27. Adelson, R. (2005, January 1). Hard-hitting hormones: The stress-depression link. *Monitor on Psychology, 36*(1). Available at APA Online at http://www.apa.org/monitor/jan05/hormones.html.

28. Ross, S. E., Niebling, B. C., & Heckert, T. M. (1999). Sources of stress among college students. *College Student Journal, 33*(2), 312–317.

29. Largo-Wight, E., Peterson, P. M., & Chen, W. W. (2005). Perceived problem solving, stress, and health among college students. *American Journal of Health Behavior, 29*(4), 360–370.

30. Hudd, S. S., Dumlao, J., Erdmann-Sager, D., Murray, D., Phan, E., Soukas, N., & Yokozuka, N. (2000). Stress at college: Effects on health habits, health status and self-esteem. *College Student Journal, 34*(2), 217–227.

31. Racette, S. B., Deusinger, S. S., Strube, M. J., Highstein, G. R., & Duesinger, R. H. (2005). Weight changes, exercise, and dietary patterns during freshman and sophomore years of college. *Journal of American College Health, 53*(6), 245–251.

32. Obesity still a problem. (2006, April 14). National Center for Health Statistics, Centers for Disease Control and Prevention. Available at http://www.cdc.gov/nchs/pressroom/06facts/obesity03_04.htm; Prevalence of overweight and obesity among adults: United States, 2003–2004. National Center for Health Statistics, Centers for Disease Control and Prevention. Available at http://www.cdc.gov/nchs/products/pubs/pubd/hestats/overweight/overwght_adult_03.htm.

33. Revised Dietary Guidelines to Help Americans Live Healthier Lives. (2005). U.S. Food and Drug Administration. Available at http://www.fda.gov/fdac/features/2005/205_diet.html.

34. USDA Dietary Guidelines for Americans, 2005. Available at http://www.health.gov/dietaryguidelines/dga2005/recommendations.htm.

35. Schlosser, E. (2002). *Fast food nation.* London: Harper Perennial.

36. Volpe, T. (2005). The fast food craze. Kagel Canyon, CA: Canyon Publishing.

37. College life and eating disorder. Healthyplace.com. Available at http://www.healthyplace.com/Communities/Eating_Disorders/women_3.asp.

38. Prouty, A. M., Protinsky, H. O., & Canady, D. (2002). College women: Eating behaviors and help-seeking preferences. *Adolescence, 37*(146), 353–363.

39. Lowery, S. E., Kurpius, S. E. R., Befort, C., Blanks, E. H., Sollenberger, S., Nicpon, M. F., & Huser, L. (2005). Body image, self-esteem, and health-related behaviors among male and female first year college students. *Journal of College Student Development, 46*(6), 612–623.

40. Shuster, W. G. (2001). Less stress? Yes! *Jewelers' Circular Keystone, 172*(2), 98.

41. Bray, S. R., & Born, H. A. (2004). Transition to university and vigorous physical activity: Implications for health and psychological well-being. *Journal of American College Health, 52*(4), 181–188.

42. Jozefowicz, C. (2004, June). Sweating makes you smart. *Psychology Today,* 56–58.

43. Huggins, C. E. (2005, January 17). Best fitness routine may depend on personality. MedlinePlus. From *The Physician and Sportsmedicine.* (2004, December). Available at http://web.archive.org/web/20050121121725/http://www.nlm.nih.gov/medlineplus/news/fullstory_22426.html.

44. Brown, F. C., & Buboltz, W. C., Jr. (2002). Applying sleep research to university students: Recommendations for developing a student sleep education program. *Journal of College Student Development, 43*(3), 411–416.

45. Jensen, D. R. (2003). Understanding sleep disorders in a college student population. *Journal of College Counseling, 6*(1), 25, 34.

46. Brown & Buboltz, Applying sleep research to university students.

47. Greer, M. (2004, July/August). Strengthen your brain by resting it. *Monitor on Psychology, 35*(7). Available at APA Online at http://www.apa.org/monitor/julaug04/strengthen.html.

48. Pilcher, J. J., & Walters, A. S. (1997). How sleep deprivation affects psychological variables related to college students' cognitive performance. *Journal of American College Health, 46,* 121–126.

49. Kelly, W. E., Kelly, K. E. & Clanton, R. C. (2001). The relationship between sleep length and grade-point average among college students. *College Student Journal, 35*(1), 84–86.

50. Kelly, W. E. (2003). Worry content associated with decreased sleep-length among college students: Sleep deprivation leads to increased worrying. *College Student Journal, 37,* 93–95.

51. Kelly, W. E. (2004). Sleep-length and life satisfaction in a college student sample. *College Student Journal, 38*(3), 428–430; Teli, P. (2002, September 25). College students' sleep habits harmful to health, study finds. *The Daily Orange.* Available at http://media.www.dailyorange.com/media/storage/paper522/news/2002/09/25/Feature/College.Students.Sleep.Habits.Harmful.To.Health.Study.Finds-280340.shtml.

52. Drowsy driving. National Sleep Foundation. Available at http://www.drowsydriving.org/site/c.lqLPIROCKtF/b.2708421/k.BD17/Home.htm.

53. Kelly, Sleep-length and life satisfaction in a college student sample.

54. Brown & Buboltz, Applying sleep research to university students.

55. Teli, College students' sleep habits harmful to health, study finds.

56. Coren, S. (1996). *Sleep thieves: An eye-opening exploration into the science and mysteries of sleep.* New York: Free Press.

57. Kerkstra, P. (2006, February 5). Online poker 101: A lesson in losing. *The Philadelphia Inquirer,* A01.

58. Farrell, E. (2005, September 2). Logging on, tuning out. *The Chronicle of Higher Education, 52*(2), A46.

59. Mohler-Kuo, M., Lee, J. E., & Wechsler, H. (2003). Trends in marijuana and other illicit drug use among college students: Results from 4 Harvard School of Public Health College Alcohol Study surveys: 1993–2001. *Journal of American College Health, 52*(1), 17–24; Hales, *An invitation to health,* p. 269.

60. Bon, S. R., Hittner, J. B., & Lawandales, J. P. (2001). Normative perceptions in relation to substance use and HIV-risky sexual behaviors of college students. *Journal of Psychology, 135*(2), 165.; Hales, *An invitation to health,* p. 269.

61. Hales, *An invitation to health,* p. 299.

62. College Alcohol Study. (2005). Harvard School of Public Health. Available at http://www.hsph.harvard.edu/cas/.

63. Nelson, T. F., Naimi, T. S., Brewer, R. D., & Wechsler H. (2005). The state sets the rate: The relationship of college binge drinking to state binge drinking rates and selected state alcohol control policies. *American Journal of Public Health, 95*(3), 441–446. Press release available at http://www.hsph.harvard.edu/cas/Documents/state/state_pr.html.

64. Ariniello, L. (2002, October). Young brains on alcohol. *Society for Neuroscience.* Available at http://www.sfn.org/index.cfm?pagename=brainBriefings_young BrainsOnAlcohol.

65. Townshend, J. M., & Duka, T. (2005). Binge drinking, cognitive performance and mood in a population of young social drinkers. *Alcoholism: Clinical & Experimental Research, 29*(3), 317–325; (2005). Binge Drinking Impairs Mood, Cognitive Performance. ACER News Release. About.com: Alcoholism and Substance Abuse. Available at http://alcoholism.about.com/od/dementia/a/blacer050315.htm.

66. Heavy drinking among college students can be predicted. (2004, March 25). Pacific Institute for Research and Evaluation. Available at http://resources.prev.org/HeavyDrinkingAmongCollegeStudentsMediaRelease.pdf.

67. Hingson, R. W. (2005). College alcohol problems exceed previous estimates. NIH News. National Institutes of Health. Available at http://www.nih.gov/news/pr/mar2005/niaaa-17.htm.

68. Jennison, K. M. (2004). The short-term effects and unintended long-term consequences of binge drinking in college: A 10-year follow-up study. *The American Journal of Drug and Alcohol Abuse, 30*(3), 659–684.

69. Strano, D. A., Cuomo, M. J., & Venable, R. H. (2004). Predictors of undergraduate student binge drinking. *Journal of College Counseling, 7,* 50–63.

70. Sheffield, F. D., Darkes, J., Del Boca, F. K., & Goldman, M. S. (2005). Binge drinking and alcohol-related problems among community college students: Implications for prevention policy. *Journal of American College Health, 54*(3), 137–141.

71. Marczinski, C. A., Bryant, R., Fillmore, M. T. (2005). The relationship between cognitive preoccupation with alcohol and alcohol use in male and female college students. *Addiction Research and Theory, 13*(4), 383–394.

72. Nelson et al., The state sets the rate.

73. Gupta, S., & Abedin, S. (2007, May 7). Keg parties and cardiacs. *Time, 169*(19), 76.

74. Facts about alcohol poisoning. (2005). College Drinking: Changing the Culture. Available at http://www.collegedrinkingprevention.gov/OtherAlcoholInformation/factsAboutAlcoholPoisoning.aspx.

75. Smarter Sex Survey. Available at http://SmarterSex.org.

76. Risky behaviors among high school students decreasing. (2004, August). *AORN Journal, 80*(2), 324.

77. Hales, *An invitation to health,* p. 216.

78. Ibid, p. 174.

79. Ibid, p. 163.

80. Laumann, E., Gagnon, J. H., Michael, R. T., and Michaels, S. (1994). *The social organization of sexuality: Sexual practices in the United States.* Chicago: University of Chicago Press.

81. Stammers, T. G. (2003, August). Abstinence under fire. *Postgraduate Medical Journal, 79,* 365–366.

TEXT CREDITS

Chapter 1. 8: Based on J. Bransford, et al. (2000). How People Learn: Brain, Mind, Experience, and School. Washington, DC: National Academy Press. **12:** French, B.F., & Oakes, W. (2003). Measuring academic intrinsic motivation in the first year of college: Reliability and validity evidence for a new instrument. Journal of the First Year Experience 15(1), 83–102.

Chapter 2. 52: N. Fleming. (2001–2007). VARK, a Guide to Learning Styles. Version 7.0. Available at http://www.vark-learn.com/english/page .asp?p=questionnaire. Used with permission from Neil Fleming. **60:** Adapted from Table 5.1 in SuccessTypes for Medical Students, J.W. Pelley and B.K. Dalley (Texas Tech Univ. Extended Learning, 1997). Used by permission of John W. Pelley.

Chapter 3. 88: Companion, M. (2006). Victoria Tymmyns Ispy.com. Used with permission.

Chapter 4. 132: Adapted from Sandholtz, K., Derr, B., Buckner, K., & Carlson, D. (2002). Beyond juggling: Rebalancing your busy life. San Francisco: Berrett-Koehler Publishing.

Chapter 8. 234: From "How Cool Is Your Job? And Does It Even Matter?" by Adelle Waldman, Wall Street Journal Online Edition, Oct. 24, 2005. Reprinted by permission.

Chapter 10. 311: Used by permission of James C. McCroskey.

Chapter 11. 329–330: From EQ-e:S Post Secondary version. Reprinted by permission.

PHOTO CREDITS

Ch. 8, p. 231: L to R: Photodisc/Getty; Photodisc/Getty; Ablestock/Index Open; Photodisc/Getty Images.

Ch. 9, p. 261: L to R: Cengage Learning; Eyewire/Getty; Eyewire/Getty; Photodisc/Getty

Ch. 10, p. 291: L to R: Cengage Learning; Eyewire/Getty; Comstock/Jupiter Images; Author; p. 319: Hemera Photo Objects

Ch. 11, p. 325: L to R: Cengage Learning; Comstock RF; Photodisc/Getty; Photodisc/Getty; p. 329: Hemera Photo Objects

Ch. 12, p. 357: L to R: Comstock RF/Jupiter Images; Eyewire/Getty; Artville/Getty; Photodisc/Getty

Ch. 13, p. 391: L to R: Cengage Lerning; VStock LLC/Index Open; www.morguefile.com; VStock LLC/Index Open

All other photo credits:

Chapter 1. 5: Left: FogStock LLC/Index Open 5: Right: PhotoObjects.net/Jupiter Images 6: Science Faction/Getty Images 17: ©Denis Scott/CORBIS 22: ©Patrick Giardino/CORBIS 24: Digital Vision/Getty Images 26: ©Grace/zefa/CORBIS 28: Photodisc/Getty Images 29: ©Mika/zefa/CORBIS 31: PhotoAlto/Jupiter Images

Chapter 2. 38: ©Darren Winter/CORBIS 39: ©Collin Anderson/Blend Images/CORBIS 44: PhotoAlto/Getty Images 51: ©Holger Winkler/zefa/CORBIS

Chapter 3. 71: Hot Ideas/Index Open 73: Photodisc/Getty Images 76: ©Susan Van Etten/Photo Edit 78: Brand X Pictures/Jupiter Images 80: ©Tom & Dee Ann McCarthy/CORBIS 83: Stockbyte/Getty Images 84: Comstock Images/Jupiter Images 85: PhotoAlto/Getty Images 92: ©Image100/CORBIS 95: ©William Whitehurst/CORBIS

Chapter 4. 105: Digital Vision/Getty Images 115: ©Clayton J. Price/CORBIS 116: ©Rick Gomez/CORBIS 122: Photodisc/Getty Images 128: Blend Images/Getty Images 131: ©Tetra Images/CORBIS 132: ©Image Source/CORBIS

Chapter 5. 143: ©John Lund/CORBIS 145: ©Don Hammond/Design Pics/CORBIS 149: Photos.com Select/Index Open 150: Photographer's Choice/Getty

Images 160: PRNewsFoto/Jamster/NewsCom 167: ©William Whitehurst/CORBIS

Chapter 6. 170: Photodisc/Getty Images 178: ©Lucidio Studio Inc./CORBIS 185: ©Tomas Rodriguez/Solus-Veer/CORBIS 190: Riser/Getty Images

Chapter 7. 201: ©Roy McMahon/CORBIS 205: ©Lester Lefkowitz/CORBIS 206: Photodisc/Getty Images 211: www.morguefile.com 213: photolibrary.com pty. ltd./Index Open 217: AbleStock/Index Open 224: Photos.com Select/Index Open

Chapter 8. 233: ©Tom McCarthy/PhotoEdit 237: Stockbyte/Getty Images 244: Purestock/JupiterImages 246: Brand X Pictures/Jupiter Images 248: Photodisc/Getty Images 254: ©Dale O'Dell/CORBIS 258: ©LWA-Dann Tardif/CORBIS

Chapter 9. 264: Comstock Images/Jupiter Images 266: William B. Plowman/Getty Images 270: Photodisc/Getty Images 273: ©James Noble/CORBIS 274: ©William Whitehurst/CORBIS 280: ©Image Source/CORBIS 284: ©Vera Berger/zefa/CORBIS

Chapter 10. 295: ©Marvyl/CORBIS 296: ©Myron Jay Dorf/CORBIS 299: Photodisc/Getty Images 301: PhotoObjects.Net/Jupiter Images 305: ©Hans Neleman/zefa/CORBIS 309: Torsten Silz/AFP/Getty Images 310: ©Paul Cooklin/Brand X/CORBIS 318: Keith Levit Photography/Index Open

Chapter 11. 328: ©William Whitehurst/CORBIS 331: ©Robert Recker/zefa/CORBIS 336: Everett Collection 347: Kin Wah Lam/Time Inc./Time & Life Picture/Getty Images 348: Brand X Pictures/Getty Images 352: Cut and Deal Ltd/Index Open

Chapter 12. 359: Brand X Pictures/Jupiter Images 361: Photodisc/Getty Images 366: photolibrary.com pty. ltd/Index Open 367: ©Bryan Allen/CORBIS 382: ©Jose Luis Pelaez, Inc./CORBIS

Chapter 13. 395: ©Strauss/Curtis/CORBIS 405: ©Eric Robert/CORBIS SYGMA 407: UpperCut Images/Getty Images 412: Everett Collection 414: ©Michael DeYoung/CORBIS 415: Image100/Jupiter Images 417: ©Chuck Savage/CORBIS 421: Reproduced with the permission of the South Australian Department of Health

INDEX

Intentional plagiarism, 308
Interaction, choosing major/career and, 369
Interactivity, Internet and, 85
Interdisciplinary studies, 378. *See also* Major
Interest rates, 79–80
Interests, choosing major/career and, 377
Interference, memory and, 214
Interfering thoughts, love and, 333
Intermediate deadlines, 122
Internal forces, defined, 372
Internal Revenue Service, 80
Internet
    college students and, 85–90
    critical searching on, 143
    reading and, 233
    as resource, 85–90
    social networking and, 116
Internships, 383, 385
Interpersonal intelligence, 45–50, 328, 329, 330
Interpersonal, SCANS and, 374
Interpersonal skills, listening and, 180
Interpret, defined, 282
Interpretation, choosing major/career and, 369
Interpreting, listening and, 179, 180
Interviews, choosing major/career and, 370,
    375–376, 385
"In the system," 7–9
Intimate relationships, communicating in, 335–341
Intrapersonal intelligence, 46, 48, 49, 328, 329–330
Intrinsic motivation, 12, 39
Introduction, on essay test, 283
Introverts
    exercise and, 414
    writing and, 298
Intuitives
    in creative potential profile, 165
    exercise and, 414
    writing and, 298
IQ. *See* Intelligence quotient (IQ)
IT systems analyst, as career, 86–87

J

James, William, 122
Jefferson, John Garland, 395
Jefferson, Thomas, 233, 395, 396
Jeffers, Susan, 129
Jennings, Peter, 368
Jobs. *See also* Career(s)
    choosing major/career and, 369
    launching career and, 382
John Holland's Self-Directed Search, 377
Johnson & Johnson, 316, 331
Johnson, Samuel, 199
Jordan, Michael, 16
Joubert, Joseph, 146, 266
Journalist, as career, 196–197

Journalistic pattern, 297
Journal of Clinical Psychology, 304
Judge, as career, 160–161
Judgers
    exercise and, 414
    lecture styles and, 185
    listening preferences of, 185
    writing and, 298
Jung, Carl, 59
Junk food, 110

K

Kahn, Alice, 85
Kaiser, Henry J., 194
Keene, Raymond, 212
Keller, Helen, 139
Kennedy, Florynce, 305
Kinesthetic intelligence, 328. *See also* Bodily-
    kinesthetic intelligence
Kingsolver, Barbara, 224
King, Stephen, 294, 304
Knowledge
    Academic Map and, 364
    asking questions and, 186
    Circle of Learning and, 361
    College in a Box and, 359–360
    learning and, 41
    in learning system, 8, 9
    metacognition and, 248
    tests and, 263
Koliatsos, Vassilis, 414
Korean War, psychological warfare in, 334
Krishnamurti, 254
Kruger, Justin, 25

L

Ladder talk, 369
Lahr, John, 169
Landers, Ann, 310
Language
    Academic Map and, 364
    attitude and, 15
    reading and, 244–245
Larsen, Lauren Ward, 316
Late fees, 79
LD. *See* Learning disabilities (LD)
Leadership
    EI and, 331
    SCANS and, 374
Learners
    college graduates and, 30
    effective, 226–227
    ineffective, 226–227
    intelligence and, 18, 19, 20
    intentional, 249–251

PCP, 417
PDA, 120, 264
Peaks, 408
Pearman, Roger, 64
Peer pressure, tests and, 276
Peg system, 219
Pelley, John, 59
Perceived stressors, defined, 407
Perceivers
    exercise and, 414
    writing and, 298
Performance
    ability/effort and, 19
    AIMS and, 25
    speaking and, 316, 317–318
    time management and, 106
Performance-based society, 19
Performers, intelligence and, 18, 19, 20
Perry, William, 139
Persistence, memory and, 223
Personal attack, as logical fallacy, 151
Personality
    choosing major/career and, 368
    learning and, 58–62
    speaking and, 316, 317
Personality type
    listening and, 185
    money management and, 81
    tests and, 269
    writing and, 298
Personal life, time management and, 130–133
Personal qualities, SCANS and, 374
Personal satisfaction, time management and, 133
Personal support system, graduating and, 27
Phobias, 403
Physical activity, tests and, 272
Physical appearance, speaking and, 314
Physical energy, 108–109, 110
Physical exhaustion, time management and, 132
Physical factors, in reading, 238
Physical health, 395, 397–400
Physical state, learning and, 40
Physician, as career, 399
Physiological aspects, of test anxiety, 271, 272
Picasso, Pablo, 50
Pillow Method, 166
Place, speaking and, 316
Plagiarism, 308–309, 320
Planner
    tests and, 264
    time management and, 120–121
Planning, speaking and, 316, 317
Planning ahead, 123–124
Plan of action, 159
Plato, 215, 414
Plato's Academy, 359
Pleasure, reading for, 242
Plotkin, Henry, 39

Polanyi, Michael, 41
Position, time management and, 106
Positive forces, defined, 374
Positivity, 334
Postman, Neil, 232
Powell, Colin, 7
PowerPoint, speaking and, 318–321
PowerPoint miniatures, for note-taking, 193
Practice, speaking and, 314
Pragmatism, 367
Preoccupation, listening and, 182
Preparation, 173–175, 314, 316–317
Presentations. *See* Speaking
Pressure, listening and, 182
Prewriting, 294–296
Primary sources, 91
Princeton Review Career Quiz, The, 377
Priorities
    choosing major/career and, 380
    free time and, 114, 115
    listening and, 182
    time management and, 107
    to-do list and, 123–124
Problem-solution pattern, 297
Problem solving
    choosing major/career and, 360, 382
    critical thinking and, 146, 149, 154–155
    reading and, 231
    SCANS and, 374
    writing and, 292
Process of elimination, on multiple-choice
        tests, 279
Procrastination, 127–129
Producing, memory and, 220
Productive skills, in critical thinking, 151
Productive thinking, 163
Professor
    attitude about, 17
    college, 56–57
Proofread
    on essay test, 283
    for writing, 299
Prove, defined, 283
Psychological factors, in reading, 238
Psychological type, 257, 271
    choosing major/career and, 385–387
    memory and, 226
    reading/studying and, 257
    relationships and, 340–341
    time management and, 112–113
    wellness and, 414
Psychological warfare, 334
Psychologist, as career, 14–15
Psychotic disorders, 401
Public relations/community relations specialist,
        as career, 121
Punctuation, writing and, 298
Purpose, speaking and, 315–316, 316